Jim Carmichel's
BOOK OF THE RIFLE

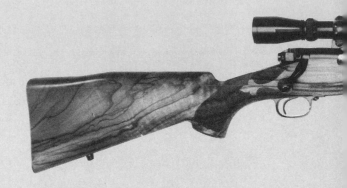

Jim Carmichel's

Published by

Outdoor Life Books, New York

BOOK OF THE RIFLE

PUBLISHED BY
    Outdoor Life Books
    Times Mirror Magazines, Inc.
    380 Madison Avenue
    New York, NY 10017

DISTRIBUTED TO THE TRADE BY
    Stackpole Books, Inc.
    Cameron and Kelker Streets
    Harrisburg, PA 17105

Library of Congress Cataloging-in-Publication Data
Carmichel, Jim.
Jim Carmichel's Book of the rifle.
Includes index.
1. Rifles. 2. Shooting. I. Title. II. Title:
Book of the rifle.
TS536.4.C36 1985   683.4'22   85-21603
ISBN 0-943822-55-6

EDITORIAL CONSULTANT: Robert Elman
DESIGN AND PRODUCTION CONSULTANT: Talisman Books, Inc.
BOOK DESIGN: Nancy Etheredge

Manufactured in the United States of America.

This book is dedicated
to
Dave Wolfe,
to whom I owe just about everything

CONTENTS

INTRODUCTION

When I began work on this book I promised that it would not only make experts of beginners but would even provide experts with fresh insights and new ways of understanding rifles and rifle performance. By giving the reader an in-depth understanding of firearms and showing him how to *think* about rifles and ammunition and their use, the book will enable him to answer his own questions.

The beginning premise was simple: to provide information that heretofore has not existed in shooting literature. Names, dates, model numbers, and ballistics tables are easy to find in any number of references. But the *"whys"* simply weren't available. When attempting to learn, for example, why a certain lot of ammunition may be more or less accurate than another lot of the same caliber by the same manufacturer, the reasons were not easily forthcoming. It was as if no one had asked the question before. The answers to this and hundreds of other such questions could only be learned firsthand by studies of manufacturing equipment, techniques, materials, and personnel.

Sometimes seemingly simple questions led to more questions, each of which had to be unraveled before a suitable explanation revealed itself. Often a simple telephone inquiry, which I expected to be answered in a moment, would lead to days or weeks of research by myself or a concerned and committed manufacturer. There were occasions when questions could be answered or theories tested only by designing and building specialized test equipment because none had existed before. A page of manuscript might go unfinished for months while experiments were conducted to provide information that might boil down to a single paragraph.

A source of constant perplexity was dealing with the "truisms" that infect the shooting world. More often than not, these truisms had never been proven by test and research. Scientific analysis was therefore required before they could be accepted or rejected. This would call for the building of even more test equipment or the designing of computer programs, while at the same time testing the patience of a publisher who longed to have the overdue manuscript on his desk.

Finally there was the challenge of sorting and deciphering an uncommonly large mass of facts and data. Information is worthless if not understood, and wasted if not wanted. The explanation of a problem that has perplexed firearms designers for years may be of no interest to the casual shooter, or an elegant equation that explains a ballistic phenomenon in stark clarity may be totally meaningless to the non-engineer.

Thus, in order to be useful, the data had to be presented in the lingo of the shooting range, using examples rather than arithmetic to illustrate and illuminate the remarkable things that happen when a trigger is pulled. But even when raw facts and data are refined to simple language, the taste remains bland until seasoned with experience and, in some guarded instances, opinion. This was the most enjoyable part.

Too many people have been involved in the writing of this book to list them separately, but they know who they are and they know they will always have my gratitude.

Jonesboro, Tennessee

Chapter 1

THOSE TWISTING GROOVES CALLED RIFLING

You don't need anyone to tell you that rifles are called rifles because of the twisting grooves cut or pressed into the inner surface of the barrel. Any firearms reference book will tell you that there are rifled barrels dating back to about the year 1500, perhaps a bit earlier. These early rifles were made in Germany and Austria, which is not surprising, considering the long history of gunmaking in these countries.

What is not so clear is how and why someone happened on the idea of cutting twisting grooves into a gun barrel so that the bullet would be made to spin. Nowadays, the logic of rifling is self-evident. We know that a spinning projectile goes straighter and farther than one that weaves and wobbles through the air without spin. If we don't learn it by shooting rifles, we are bound to discover it by watching quarterbacks throw those long *spiraling* passes, but how did the early gunsmiths figure it out? What clue told them they needed to rifle their barrels? Was there a deliberate attempt to improve firearms accuracy, or was it an accidental discovery? Whichever it was, we know that within a decade of Columbus's discovery of the New World, a German or an Austrian had also discovered rifling, and neither traveling or shooting has been the same since.

For many hundreds of years, mankind has been spinning tops. In parts of Malaya, the spinning of elaborate tops has been a popular competitive game longer than anyone can remember. The ancient Japanese and Chinese were great spinners of tops, so we can assume that the fascinating toys spread westward to post-Renaissance Europe by way of the silk routes. Students of top spinning tell me that by the 1500's, "top whipping" was a popular pastime in Europe, especially during the winter months when the exertion of top whipping helped peasants to warm themselves. This coincidence of dates is intriguing, isn't it? If the phenomenon of gyroscopic stability, in the form of a spinning top, was observed by a keen-witted gunmaker, it wouldn't have taken him long to apply the principle to a bullet.

But, perhaps, rifling arose in a different way. Some of the earliest "rifled" barrels were grooved, but the grooves were *straight* for the length of the barrel. What do you suppose the makers had in mind? Perhaps straight rifling was intended to stabilize the ball in the barrel, or perhaps it was an attempt to improve the gas seal by getting a "bite" on the ball. On the other hand, straight grooves may have been intended to accommodate black powder fouling. Once gunsmiths learned to cut straight rifling, however, you can be sure that spiraled rifling was only half a step away.

One more possibility is the spiraling motion imparted to some arrows by the slight angled pitch of the fletching (feathers). Did medieval archers know about this? If so, gunmakers may have borrowed the idea of a spinning projectile from arrow makers. If this was the case, why didn't they do it a lot earlier?

No matter how it came about, there is no doubt that the invention of the rifled barrel ranks as one of the world's greatest inventions. The effect it has had on the course of history should never be underestimated. Perhaps one of these days, a scholar will do an analysis of the social, political, and military impact of the rifled gun barrel. The revelations, I suspect, will be astonishing.

GYROSCOPIC EFFECT

The thrown football tells a lot about the motion of a spinning bullet because it is big and slow enough for us to see what is happening. The pointed ends of the ball are shaped more or less like a modern bullet, and when the quarterback tosses "the bomb," we can see that he gives the ball some spin so that it will fly point forward. But what if the projectile is round like a baseball instead of pointed like a football? Does it matter if it spins or not? Come to think of it, the bullets fired in early rifles were round, too.

It is right here, with round bullets, that we get our first solid grasp of the importance of rifling. If we watch a knuckleball artist at work, we quickly see that the essence of his throwing technique is to prevent the ball from spinning. As the non-rotating sphere travels toward the plate, it builds up uneven air pressure areas on its surface, which causes it to jump and jiggle in flight and thereby confuse the batter. If the ball is thrown so that it spins around its forward axis, potential atmospheric pressure points are dissipated before they can develop, and the baseball follows a straighter path.

If we apply this observation to a round bullet, we get some idea of how rifling imparts accuracy to its flight. The superb accuracy of a bullet fired from a rifle is the result of gyroscopic stability. The rapidly spinning bullet is a gyroscope, and in the manner of gyroscopes, it resists any force that tries to push it away from its intended direction. Did you have a toy gyroscope when you were a kid? If so, you will recall that when the wheel was spinning, the gyroscope would remain balanced on the tip of your finger or even on a piece of string. It seemed to defy gravity by not falling over even when it was tilted at an angle to the point of support. And you

A young athlete demonstrates gyroscopic stability by spinning a basketball on his fingertip. Because the basketball is round, it requires relatively low rotational speed in order to be stabilized.

A spinning gyroscope tends to remain balanced, or stabilized, its spin resisting any force that tries to push it off its direction or position. A bullet requires this kind of gyroscopic stability.

also noticed that when you tried to move the spinning gyroscope to the left or right, a mysterious force seemed to be resisting the change of position.

So it is with spinning bullets. In fact, the high rate of spin of a speeding bullet, be it round or pointed, causes it to be a very determined gyroscope. To give you an example, let's consider a 180-grain bullet fired from the muzzle of a .30/06 rifle at a velocity of 2,700 feet per second. The "pitch" of the rifling, otherwise known as the rate of twist, causes the bullet to make one complete revolution in every 10 inches of flight at the start of its travel. This figures out to some 3,240 revolutions per *second*. Times 60, this comes to an astounding 194,400 revolutions per minute. Even the little .22 Rimfire bullet averages over 50,000 RPM's and the plodding lead ball from a "Kentucky" rifle attains 20,000 RPM's or better. No wonder a bullet is such an efficient gyroscope.

When the bullet exits the muzzle, it slams into a wall of air which causes it to slow down. That .30/06 bullet, for example, has slowed down to 2,350 fps by the time it has gone just 100 yards. The speed of revolution, however, does not fall at nearly so high a rate. In fact, if you fired the .30/06 rifle straight up, the bullet would still be spinning at a terrific rate even when the forward motion stopped. And as the bullet falls to earth, the gyroscopic action still holds the bullet in a stable linear attitude.

To bear this out, artillerymen have often noted that when shells are fired upward at a very steep angle, they fall base down, demonstrating the gyroscopic stability that prevents the shell from turning over at the apex of its flight and falling point down.

Here we run into a seeming contradiction. When we watch our favorite quarterback in action, we see that the path of the football follows a curve, and that the angle of the ball to the horizontal changes so that it always flies point forward. In other words, the point of the ball, and its linear axis, is angled upward for the first part of the long throw and then tilts downward as the ball begins to fall. Conical bullets and artillery shells do the same thing, at least when they are fired at normal angles. How does this square with the gyroscope effect, which is supposed to keep the bullet's nose always pointed in one direction? The explanation is *gyroscopic precession,* a fancy phrase for a curious effect that air pressure has on the point of a speeding bullet. As the bullet starts to fall after reaching the highest point of its flight, a high-pressure area develops under the point and tries to push it up. The gyroscopic action says no to this and tries to counter the high-pressure area by pivoting the point of the bullet somewhat to the right or left (depending on the direction of spin). This puts the air pressure on the side of the bullet's point, so it ducks again, this time downward, then to the right or left again, and then upward, and then the precession is repeated. This constant wandering of the bullet's point around its axial direction of flight results in a *generally* point-forward flight. However, if the bullet is fired straight up (90°) or nearly straight up, the trajectory is so straight that the bullet doesn't "turn over" and remains pointed up while falling as well as while climbing.

We pick up many such fascinating tidbits from heavy artillery. Sporting bullets are so small and their flights are so short that experimental observation is almost impossible. Big artillery shells, on the other hand, are relatively easy to study. During World War I, when the Germans were shelling Paris with their legendary Paris Gun (sometimes incorrectly referred to as "Big Bertha"), the Parisians thought they were being bombed by high-flying aircraft. One day, a sharp-eyed observer happened to notice that there were angular holes in the walls of a "bombed out" building. By measuring the angle of the holes, he was able to prove that the bombs were really artillery shells and even calculated the approximate distance to the giant rifle.

RATE OF TWIST

The angle of pitch or rate of twist of rifling is expressed in inches per complete turn or revolution. The .30/06 rifle I mentioned earlier has a 10-inch twist. This means the bullet revolves one complete turn for each 10 inches of barrel length. Another common way of expressing this particular rate of twist is simply "one in 10."

If all rifles shot accurately with the same rate of twist, it would be very convenient, but the laws of nature grant us no such favor. Therefore rifles of different calibers and employing differing bullets require different rates of twist. This is because bullets of certain shapes and weights require a higher rate of spin to become gyroscopically stabilized than some others. As a general rule of thumb, bullets that are long and slender require a faster spin than do short fat ones. For example, the common .22 Rimfire bullet, which is rather short and squat in relation to its length, seems to be most accurate when fired from a barrel having a one-in-16-inch twist. The .458 Winchester Magnum slug, which is similarly plump, requires a one-in-14 twist. Muzzleloading rifles, which fire round lead balls, have the slowest twist of all, usually somewhere in the one-in-48- to one-in-66-inch range. On the other hand, long, pencil-like bullets such as those fired in, say, a 6.5mm Mannlicher require a twist as fast as one in 7½ inches.

In order to help clarify spin versus bullet shape, let's use a basketball. Anyone who has played or watched basketball has undoubtedly seen someone balancing a spinning ball on a fingertip. The spinning basketball is a great example of gyroscopic stability, and an equally good example of the relatively low rate of spin needed to stabilize a short, fat projectile, such as a round, muzzleloading bullet. But did you ever see anyone balance a spinning football on a fin-

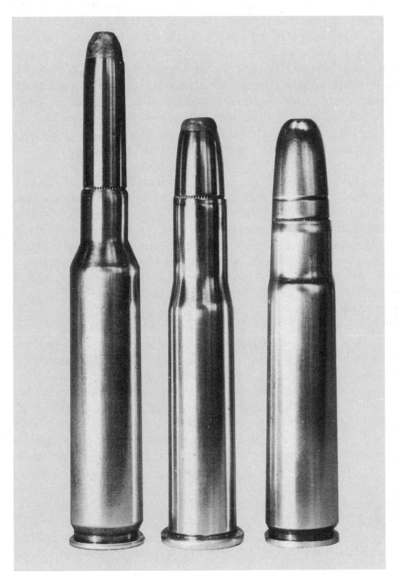

These three cartridges show wide variations in bullet shape —and stabilization requirements. From left: the 6.5mm cartridge has a long, slender bullet that requires a high rate of rotational spin for proper stabilization; the .30/30 has a more typical bullet that is stabilized by a moderate rate of spin; the short, fat bullet in the .35 Remington is stabilized by lower rotational speed.

gertip? That's unlikely because a football is relatively long in relation to its diameter and therefore requires a faster spin to become gyroscopically stabilized. You can, however, balance a spinning football vertically on a flat surface if you give it a fast-enough spin.

The need for a specific rate of spin to best stabilize a bullet of a given weight and diameter helps explain the relatively narrow range of bullet weights in a given caliber. Why not make, say, little 75-grain bullets for the .30/06, which might be used for varmint shooting, or perhaps 500-grain slugs, which could be used for elephants? As it is, the available .30/06 bullets range only from 110 to 220 grains, and this is the widest weight range available in any caliber and represents the workable extremes. The one-in-10 twist is almost but not quite too fast for the stubby 110-grain bullet, because it was originally intended for the longish 220-grain slug.

When a bullet is not spun fast enough, it is under-stabilized; if it spins too fast, it is over-stabilized. Either of these conditions results in, at best, loss of accuracy and sometimes something worse. Bullets without enough spin to be properly stabilized may wobble in flight, sometimes tilting or yawing widely in relation to the direction of flight, with the nose or base of the bullet, or both, following a spiral-like path in relation to the flight path. If the yaw becomes excessive, the air pressure on the side of the bullet may cause it to turn over and tumble end over end. When a bullet yaws, there is a notable loss of accuracy, and when it tumbles, accuracy goes completely to pot. Also, with the loss of point-on streamlining, the bullet loses velocity and energy at a much greater rate.

The familiar whine of a ricocheting bullet is typical of the sound made by a tumbling bullet. When a bullet strikes an object at a glancing angle, the spin (and therefore the gyroscopic stability) is lost and the projectile tumbles for the duration of its flight. During the Vietnam conflict, quite a fuss was made by an ill-informed press about the "buzz-saw effect" of the newly adopted 5.56mm service cartridge. According to some reports, the bullets tumbled end over end and cut through targets like buzz saws. This, of course, was utter nonsense. When fired in heavy cover, the little 55-grain 5.56 bullets (.22 caliber) did tend to tumble if they hit twigs, vines, and other vegetation. Despite the sinister buzzing sound, these tumbling bullets were far less deadly than the same bullets flying point-forward.

Occasionally, we see strange-looking, keyhole-shaped bullet holes in targets. These are made by yawing or tumbling bullets. These odd bullet holes are usually signs of an improper bullet-to-rifle match, a badly worn barrel, or a poorly constructed bullet. Whatever the cause, the result is an improperly stabilized bullet.

The disadvantages of an over-stabilized bullet are harder to explain. How can there be too much of a good thing? Some bullets simply can't stand too many RPM's and literally fly apart before they reach the target. This is most likely to happen when the bullet jacket is too thin to resist the centrifugal force. It's also true that applying a high rate of spin, say one in eight, is tougher on a bullet than firing it at the same velocity from a barrel with, for instance, a one-in-16 twist.

EXPANSION AND REVOLUTION

The rotational force of a spinning bullet is widely misunderstood. It is sometimes assumed, for instance, that the centrifugal force of the bullet's spin has a lot to do with how the bullet

Here are two kinds of yaw. At top, the bullet's nose spins around the axis. At bottom, the bullet's base spins around the axis. These conditions may be caused by a bullet defect, imperfect crowning, a worn-out barrel, or the wrong combination of bullet weight and rate of twist. Bullets routinely yaw slightly upon exiting the muzzle, then stabilize, or "go to sleep," after traveling several yards.

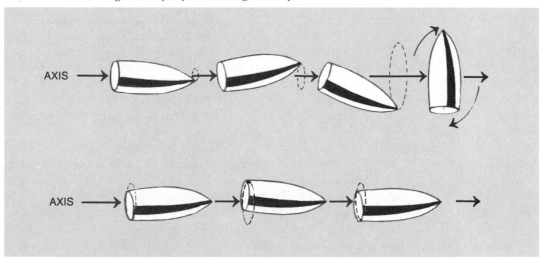

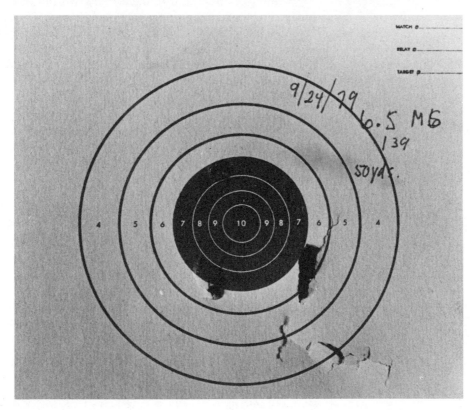

This target shows a "keyhole" print made by a tumbling or badly yawing bullet.

expands after it hits. This has often been "proven" by firing bullets into water and ballistic putty at different velocities and rotational speeds.

A few years ago, the research department of a large ammo maker wanted to determine the 300-yard expansion properties of a new bullet but didn't have a 300-yard range available. They figured they could solve the problem easily enough by handloading their test ammo to a reduced velocity that duplicated normal 300-yard velocity at only 25 yards. These tests showed that the new bullet would not expand well at 300-yard velocities. Jacket construction was therefore modified until they got what looked like ideal expansion at the reduced velocity. Later, when the new bullet was tested at a genuine 300 yards, the expansion properties were entirely different. Why?

After some head scratching, the engineers decided that the difference in the two tests was due to different rotational speeds. When muzzle velocity was reduced for the short-distance 300-yard simulation test, the rotational speed was reduced by about one-third. When fired at full velocity over an actual 300-yard range, the rotational speed was considerably higher. (As mentioned earlier in this chapter, a bullet's rate of spin is not lost nearly as fast as velocity.)

Does this tell us that bullet spin is important to performance on live game? Frankly, I am not convinced that it does. Expansion in living game tends to be totally different than it is in a test medium. I think ammo makers often kid themselves by designing bullets that give beautiful expansion in water or impact clay. Expansion in living animal tissue is something else.

A few years ago, I had an enlightening conversation with a bright mechanical engineer who specializes in ultra-precise metal-cutting techniques. He told me about air-driven drills that wind up to RPM's as high as the spin of modern pointed bullets. Despite the high rate of spin, the coasting drills have surprisingly little inertia and can be stopped, he told me, simply by pinching the smooth shank between the fingers. I'm not going to try this, but I am inclined to believe it.

In more practical terms, we can assume with a high degree of confidence that the spin of a bullet is arrested by the time it penetrates the tough hide of a big game animal. In fact, after examining hundreds of bullets removed from carcasses, I've never been able to find any conclusive evidence that the bullet was spinning as it expanded.

SPIN VS. ACCURACY

Several years ago I wrote a sentence which is still a source of endless pride: "No shooting subject is more likely to make one sound like an expert, and at the same time prove him a fool, than a discussion of rifling twist." I hope I am quoted on this; I may even make it my epitaph.

Though there are precise formulas for computing the correct rate of spin for any given bullet, the truth is that we often break the rules and get away with it. For example, the one-in-10-inch twist that we consider standard for the .30/06 was established for the U.S. .30/40 Krag and .30/03 cartridges, which were loaded with 220-grain bullets. Nowadays we shoot far more 150- and 180-grain bullets in the 06 than 220-grain bullets. Theoretically, the rate of twist should be slower. But why bother? We know the one in 10 works fine. When the 7.62 Nato round was adopted by the U.S. services, the traditional one-in-10 rate of twist was retained, but

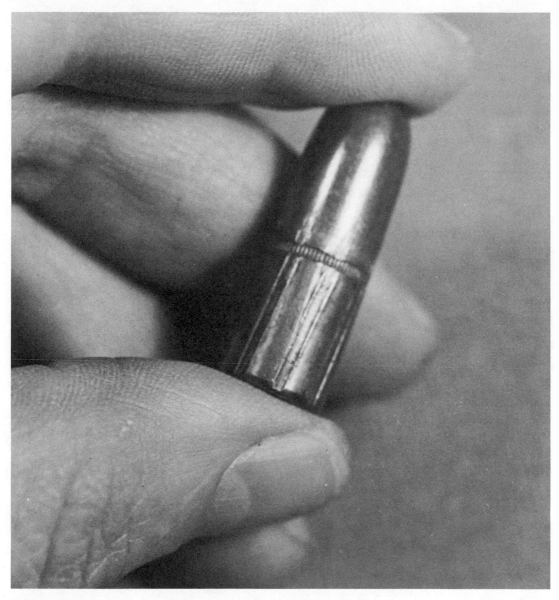

The rifling marks—or "engraving"—can be clearly seen on this bullet.

many sporting rifles in the civilian version (the .308 Winchester) are fitted with one-in-12 barrels.

I have a half-dozen or so heavy-barreled target rifles in .308 caliber. Some have one-in-10 barrels and some have one-in-12. All are wonderfully accurate, and I've never been able to prove that either twist gives better accuracy with any given bullet. In other words, there is some latitude within the extremes when determining rate of twist.

STANDARD RATES OF TWIST FOR DIFFERENT CALIBERS

Caliber	Rifle Maker	Inches Per One Revolution
.17 Remington	Most brands	9
.22 Short	Most brands	24
.22 Long Rifle	Most brands	16
.22 Hornet	Most brands	16
.218 Bee	Winchester	16
.219 Zipper	Winchester	14
.222 Remington	Most brands	14
.222 Remington Magnum	Most brands	14
.223 Remington	Remington	12
.223 Remington	Ruger Mini 14	10
.225 Winchester	Winchester	14
.22/250 Remington	Most brands	14
.22/250 Remington	Sako	12
.224 Weatherby	Weatherby	14
.220 Swift	Most brands	14
.243 Winchester	Winchester	10
.243 Winchester	Remington	9
.244 Remington	Most brands	12
6mm Remington	Most brands	9
.240 Weatherby Magnum	Weatherby	10
.250 Savage	Most brands	10
.257 Roberts	Most brands	10
.25/06	Most brands	10
.257 Weatherby Magnum	Weatherby	10
6.5mm Mannlicher Schoenauer	Mannlicher Schoenauer	8¼
6.5 × 55mm	Most brands	8
6.5mm Remington Magnum	Most brands	9
.264 Winchester Magnum	Most brands	9
.270 Winchester	Most brands	10
.270 Weatherby Magnum	Weatherby	10
7 × 57mm	Winchester	10
7 × 57mm	Ruger	9½
7 × 57mm	F.N.	8.7
7mm/08 Remington	Remington	9¼
7mm Express	Most brands	9
.284 Winchester	Most brands	10
7mm Remington Magnum	Remington	9
7mm Remington Magnum	Winchester & Ruger	9½
7mm Weatherby Magnum	Weatherby	10
.30 Cal. M-1 Carbine	Most brands	20
.30/30 W.C.F.	Most brands	12
.30 Remington	Most brands	12
.300 Savage	Most brands	12
.30/40 Krag	Most brands	10
.308 Winchester	Winchester	12
.308 Winchester	Remington	10

Caliber	Rifle Maker	Inches Per One Revolution
.30/06	Most brands	10
.300 H. & H. Magnum	Most brands	10
.308 Norma Magnum	Most brands	10
.300 Winchester Magnum	Most brands	10
.300 Weatherby Magnum	Weatherby	10
.32 Winchester Special	Most brands	16
8mm Mauser	Most brands	9½
8mm Remington Magnum	Most brands	10
.338 Winchester Magnum	Most brands	10
.340 Weatherby Magnum	Most brands	10
.348 Winchester	Most brands	12
.35 Remington	Most brands	16
.358 Winchester	Most brands	12
.358 Norma Magnum	Most brands	12
.375 H. & H. Magnum	Most brands	12
.378 Weatherby Magnum	Weatherby	12
.44 Magnum	Most brands	38
.444 Marlin	Most brands	38
.45/70	Most brands	20
.458 Winchester Magnum	Most brands	14
.460 Weatherby Magnum	Weatherby	16

RIFLING TYPES

Now that we have a pretty good idea of the importance of rifling, let's turn our attention to the rifling itself. When you look through a modern rifled barrel, you see four, five, six, seven, eight, or more spiraling grooves, or in the case of certain Springfield-pattern rifles made during World War II, you see only two grooves. Very likely, the rifling will be of the Enfield type, which is extremely popular these days because it is simple, relatively easy to manufacture, and extremely accurate.

Enfield rifling, which gets its name from the Government Arsenal at Enfield Lock, England, is relatively simple. Let's use it to describe how rifling works. As you see from the diagram on the next page the interior dimensions of a rifle barrel are the groove diameter and the bore diameter. The bore diameter represents the size of the hole originally bored in the barrel blank, hence its name. The grooves are cut or pressed after boring. In order to understand the fit of a rifle bullet in a barrel, let's consider the popular .30/06 caliber.

If you precisely measure the diameter of a .30/06 bullet with a micrometer, you will find that it measures .308-inch. And if you measure the *groove* diameter of a .30/06 barrel, you'll find that it also measures .308. Obviously, the bullet-to-barrel fit is perfect or, allowing for slight manufacturing tolerances, very nearly perfect. When the cartridge is fired, the rapidly expanding gasses pushing against the base of the bullet cause it to expand or "upset" slightly so that it fills and seals the bore tightly. As the bullet rushes down the barrel, the spiraling ridges between the grooves, called lands, press into the sides of the bullet. This gives the lands a tight grip on the bullet, thereby causing it to follow their rotational path. Once this rotation, or spin, is imparted to the bullet, the projectile continues to spin after leaving the muzzle. If you inspect

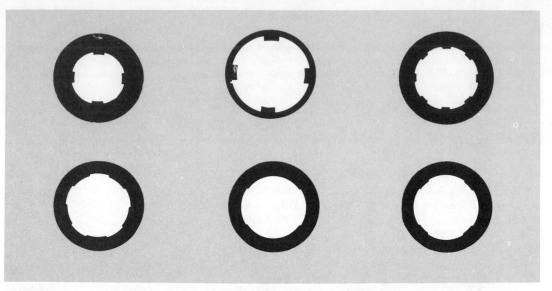

These diagrams all show versions of the fundamental Enfield type of rifling.

a recovered bullet you'll see that the grooves pressed, or "engraved," into the sides of the bullet by the lands are clearly evident.

You may ask how deeply do the lands bite into the bullet? The groove depth, or land height, whichever way you want to put it, of a .30/06 barrel is usually about four one-thousandths of an inch (.004). The land height of other calibers is proportionately less or greater, depending on the caliber. Arlie Gardner, president of the famous Douglas Barrel Company, and Ed Shilen, maker of the legendary target barrels, supply us with the groove depths of some representative calibers in thousandths, ten-thousandths, and hundred-thousandths of an inch:

Caliber	Bore Diameter	Groove Diameter	Groove Depth
.17	.168	.172	.002
.22 Rimfire	.217	.222	.0025
.22 Centerfire	.219	.224	.0025
.243 (6mm) (Shilen)	.236	.243	.0035
.243 (6mm) (Douglas)	.2375	.243	.00275
.25	.250	.257	.0035
6.5mm	.257	.264	.0035
.270	.270	.277	.0035
7mm	.276	.284	.004
.30	.300	.308	.004
8mm (Douglas)	.315	.323	.004
.338	.330	.338	.004
.35	.350	.358	.004
.375	.368	.375	.0035
.45	.450	.458	.004

The number of grooves and lands in a rifle barrel is largely a matter of manufacturer's preference. The famous 1903 Springfield, for instance, has four grooves, as does it successors, the M-1 Garand and M-14 .30-caliber service rifles. Likewise, Winchester Model 70 rifles in .30/06 caliber have four-groove barrels. This does not necessarily mean that four-groove barrels are best for the .30/06. The 1917 Enfield rifle has five grooves, while the .30-caliber barrels made by Douglas have six grooves, and Shilens have eight grooves. During the World War II armament production rush, some Model 1903A3 service rifles were made with two-groove barrels, and they shot quite well.

Some barrels, notably Marlin's Micro Groove, have a large number of extremely shallow grooves. The advantage of this rifling, aside from ease of production, is supposed to be minimal bullet deformation. However, for what it's worth, virtually all premium-grade, target-quality barrels have six or eight grooves. I must emphasize, though, that the accuracy of a barrel depends more on the quality of materials and the workmanship than on the number of grooves.

If you peer into a variety of modern rifle barrels, you will note that the grooves tend to be considerably wider than the lands. This was not always the case. In some older barrels, especially those of the last century, the grooves and lands were of equal width, or the lands were even wider.

DEVELOPMENT OF MODERN RIFLING

When you consider the apparent damage done to a bullet as it is forced through a rifle barrel, it is natural to wonder if its flight would be more accurate if it were not so badly damaged. This is a sound observation. As a matter of fact, a number of skilled inventors have wrestled with this question. Their efforts are worth discussing.

There is a fairly widespread belief that the reason the American Long Rifle of Revolutionary War fame was so deadly was because it was the first type of firearm to utilize the rifled barrel. This is hardly true since the principle of rifling had been applied to guns centuries earlier. In fact, among the European forces against whom the Colonials fought there were elite Jaeger units that were armed with rifled muskets. These beautifully made Jaeger (hunter) rifles were at least as accurate as the better "Kentucky" rifles, and the Jaeger sharpshooters were probably a match for the backwoods marksmen. There was, however, one big difference.

The European rifles were loaded by pounding a ball down the barrel so that the rifling bit into the lead projectile. Though this obviously gave the rifling a firm grip on the bullet, it was also a rather lengthy and noisy process. The Americans, on the other hand, loaded by enclosing the round bullet in a patch of greased buckskin or cloth. The patch engaged the rifling and transmitted the spin to the bullet. When loaded properly, the ball never touched the barrel. Loading a patched ball was almost silent and much faster than the Jaeger system.

If you were to examine a variety of American and European rifles dating from this period and before, you would be impressed by the seemingly endless forms of rifling. Virtually every gunmaker had an individual style of rifling, which was as representative as a trademark. Some patterns were so complex that their function was more ornamental than functional. By and large, the barrels intended to be loaded with a patched bullet are characterized by comparatively wide lands and narrow grooves. Since the patched ball rode on top of the lands, the extra width

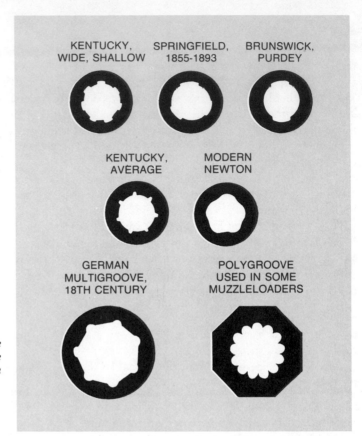

KENTUCKY,
WIDE, SHALLOW

SPRINGFIELD,
1855-1893

BRUNSWICK,
PURDEY

KENTUCKY,
AVERAGE

MODERN
NEWTON

GERMAN
MULTIGROOVE,
18TH CENTURY

POLYGROOVE
USED IN SOME
MUZZLELOADERS

These drawings show a wide variety of rifling types. Note the earlier versions used in muzzleloaders.

gave better support. A particularly interesting feature of many of these barrels, especially those made in America, is the use of seven lands and grooves. This odd number serves no advantage over, say, six or eight grooves. The odd number was apparently prompted by religious and social superstitions involving the number seven!

Barrels made for unpatched bullets tended to have sharp, narrow lands that cut into the ball with relatively little effort. So it was until the first part of the 1800's.

Clearly, neither of these situations was ideal. A more logical solution would have been to load the bullet from the breech end of the barrel so that it would be forced into the rifling when the gun was fired. Another would have been to use a bullet that, after being muzzleloaded in the usual way, would have expanded to engage the rifling. Nowadays, this problem seems simple enough to solve, but it kept inventors in a stew for half a century or so before workable solutions were discovered.

During the reign of Napoleon, French ordnance officers were encouraged to develop improved musketry, and considerable progress resulted from their experiments. A fellow by the name of Delvigne devised a system that featured a rimlike shoulder within the barrel just above the powder chamber. The shoulder stopped the muzzleloaded bullet and served as an anvil of sorts while the lead ball was pounded with an iron ramrod. The pounding caused the ball to expand laterally and fill the rifling. Delvigne's system worked, after a fashion, but a flattened ball proved to be a poor projectile.

A fellow Frenchman, Thouvenin, took the idea a step further by figuring out a means of expanding a pointed bullet on a postlike anvil in the center of the powder chamber. This worked better than Delvigne's system but still left a lot to be desired in the way of range, accuracy, and, especially, convenience in loading.

The problem was best solved by a dashing French captain of chasseurs, Claude-Etienne Minié, who reckoned that a conical bullet having a thin, hollow skirt would be sufficiently expanded to fill the rifling by the force of the powder gasses. He hit the nail on the head, and within a few years his system was widely used, not only by the European armies but in America as well. When the American States went to war with each other, the bullets favored by both the Blues and the Grays were of the type invented by Minié. Apparently no one told them the Frenchman's name was pronounced *me-nay*, so they just called 'em "minnie" balls!

While the French tinkered with the concept of expansion, their perennial rivals, the English, engaged themselves with a different concept. As the English saw it, a muzzleloaded bullet should fit the rifling from the onset. Rather than making the bullet fit the rifling by deforming it, they made rifling and bullets that matched each other in shape. One of the earliest workable attempts at this was the Brunswick bullet, which was essentially a round lead ball with a ring molded around its circumference. This ring fit into twin rifling grooves cut into the Brunswick barrel. The bullet was held fast by the rifling from the time it was loaded into the muzzle. The Brunswick system, which, by the way, was the brainchild of a Captain Berner in the service of the Duke of Brunswick, worked pretty well—except when the soldiers got excited and couldn't get the bullet ring aligned with the rifling grooves.

In these diagrams you see techniques that were used in the 19th century to make a bullet expand in order to engage the rifling.

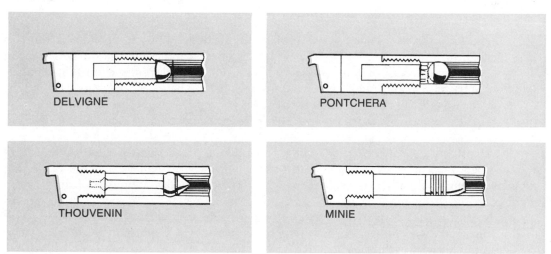

DELVIGNE

PONTCHERA

THOUVENIN

MINIE

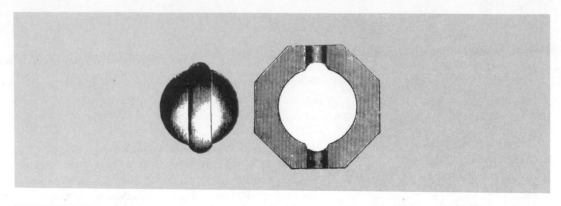

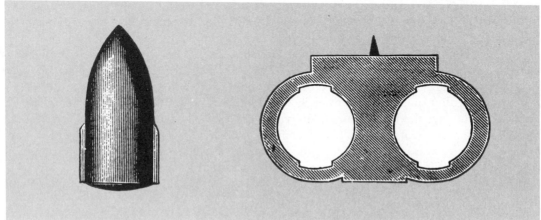

The Brunswick design was an early form of fitted bullet. The upper drawings show the bullet shape and rifling. Another approach was "Cape rifling," shown at bottom, in which the rifling grooves were engaged by fins molded on the sides of the bullet.

General John Jacobs followed a similar plan, but his bullet was conical and had four ribs that matched the four-groove rifling of the big Jacobs rifles. Another tack on the same general plan was to use bullets with an oval (Lancaster) or even an elliptical cross-section. These bullets were fired in barrels having a similarly shaped spiraling bore. There were no lands and grooves. The problem was difficulty of manufacture. British gunsmiths, the best in the world at that time, loved the challenge of cutting such peculiar bores and making matching bullet molds, but mass production was something else.

My favorite fitted-bullet concept is the famous Whitworth design. Imagine a pointed but straight-sided bullet with six flat sides (hexagonal). Now give the bullet a slight twist, so that the sides are angled slightly to the axis. That's the Whitworth bullet. Whitworth rifling, as you might guess, was simply a twisting, six-sided hole. Patented in 1854, Whitworth rifles proved remarkably accurate, and some were even used by snipers during the U.S. Civil War. Alas, it was an idea whose time was short. Eventually Joseph Whitworth was knighted by the Queen, but in recognition of his other achievements, such as Whitworth steel.

BREECHLOADING ARRIVES

The inventions of Whitworth, Minié, Jacobs, and all the others were made obsolete by the self-contained, breechloading cartridge. Once a workable means of loading a bullet from the breech end of a rifled barrel had been devised, it was a whole new ball game. Expansion on firing did the job, getting a bullet to take the rifling was no longer a problem. Now the problem that intrigued gunmakers was the configuration of the rifling. How many lands and grooves? What groove depth? How about the shape of the rifling? And the pitch? And so forth. What fun it was!

A British gentleman who contributed enormously to the sophistication of rifling was William Ellis Metford. Modern rifles still bear the fruits of Metford's late 19th-century work. One in particular is the characteristically shallow Metford groove depth. He also experimented with grooves of varying widths and received considerable recognition for his progressive, or gain-twist, rifling, which has an accelerating pitch that causes the bullet's rate of rotation to increase as it moves toward the muzzle. Metford also perfected a segmented rifling which featured shallow, round-bottomed grooves. The idea behind it was that if the corners of the grooves could be eliminated, there would be less of a powder-fouling problem. Interestingly, this is the rifling system used in the Arisaka rifles employed by Japanese forces during World War II.

The English and Americans loved to test the superiority of their rifling systems in various competitions and field trials. Some rifling methods did, indeed, seem to produce better accuracy than others, but usually for reasons not associated with the rifling itself. Probably the best example of this is the legendary Pope or Pope-Schalk system. Until his death in 1940, Harry Pope was recognized as the all-time master barrelmaker. His barrels were unmatched for accuracy, and anyone who was anyone just naturally used a Pope barrel. The shape of his rifling was distinguished by shallow, flat-bottomed grooves, and because Pope's barrels were so good,

Lancaster oval-bore rifling is shown at left. At center is a drawing of Whitworth rifling—a hexagonal design—with the bullet it accommodated. At right is an octagonal form of rifling manufactured by Shilen, a modern approach quite similar to the Whitworth.

These cross-sectional diagrams of a bore illustrate Metford segmented rifling.

These cross-sectional diagrams show the Pope type of rifling (right) and the Newton parabolic, or "ratchet" type.

This is Marlin Micro Groove rifling — essentially a form of Enfield rifling but with an unusually large number of lands and grooves.

This little implement is a carbide button—used to press the rifling into button-rifled barrels.

shooters figured that his rifling style must be the best. The real secret to the success of Pope's barrels, though, was the care he lavished on each stage of their manufacture. Any barrel bored that true and rifled with such exacting care had to be accurate. Today no one bothers to duplicate the exact shape of Pope rifling; it really wasn't all that good. And so it is with most other forms of rifling. Well-made rifled barrels are most always accurate.

Around the time of World War I, a ballistic genius by the name of Charles Newton began thinking about rifling and decided that since the bullet was guided by only one side of each land, only one side was needed. Accordingly, Newton rifles featured what has become known as parabolic, or "ratchet," rifling. Actually, Newton did not invent this type of rifling. It had been employed in England before, but he did prove it to be an excellent system. Again, though, it was no better than any other well-cut rifling. In any event, by the turn of the century or shortly after, further experimentation with rifling forms was mainly academic. The Enfield type had been adopted by most gunmakers, including the U.S. armories, and just about everyone was satisfied.

There are only two identifying features of Enfield rifling. The radius, or curve, of the groove bottom is consistent with the radius of the bullet diameter. To clarify: if the lands were peeled out of the bore, the remaining hole would be very nearly perfectly round. Also, the corners of the lands and the land tops are more or less square. Otherwise, Enfield rifling may have any number of grooves of any depth and width and any rate of twist.

HOW RIFLING IS CUT

Toward the end of the last century, gunmakers had pretty much decided that the "best" rifling was that type which was easiest to manufacture. The English armory at Enfield Lock had developed an efficient system of rifling. The barrel blank was bored; the hole was reamed to a smooth, uniform surface; then fine, evenly spaced grooves were cut into the walls in a simple, straightforward manner. The resulting rifling with its squarish lands certainly wasn't very fancy, but it seemed to work as well as any. Much of the machinery at the Enfield plant, you'll be interested to know, had been made in America.

The rifling was done with a single cutter attached to a rod. The cutter was drawn through

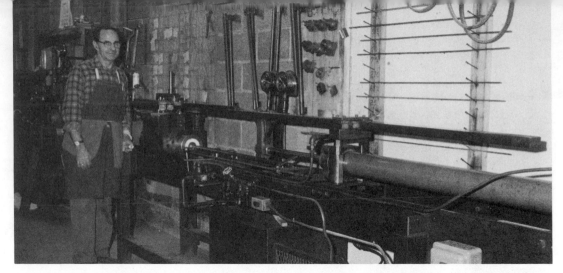

A hydraulic press pushes the carbide button through a bored and reamed barrel blank. The machine in this photo is at the Douglas Barrel plant.

the barrel, cutting a few ten-thousandths of an inch of steel from the bore. After making a single cut, the blade was moved a fifth of a revolution—a five-groove system—and another thin cut or scrape was made. When the cutter had made an equal cut in each groove, the cutting depth was increased, and the process was repeated, over and over, until the grooves were cut to full depth. As the cutter was drawn through the bore, it was also twisted so that spiraling grooves resulted. All this sounds rather complicated, but compared to some other techniques it was a piece of cake. It was so simple and efficient, in fact, that it was the standard barrelmaking procedure used by all U.S. makers up until World War II, and it is still used today in the production of some of our finest barrels.

Not long after the end of World War II, somebody got the idea of pushing a die, shaped like rifling in reverse, through a reamed barrel blank, and thereby ironing grooves into the barrel

This huge machine is a Winchester hammer forging mill. It literally hammers the shape of the rifling into a barrel blank.

walls. It worked like a charm and turned out to be so fast and easy that it is the most widely used system in the U.S. today. The little carbide die used to press the rifling into the barrel steel is called a button, and the system is known as button rifling.

More recently, a cold-swaging process, sometimes called hammer forging, has been employed in the production of rifled barrels. You can get a pretty good idea of how this works by squeezing modeling clay around a pencil and then withdrawing the pencil from the clay. The result is a perfectly formed negative, or reverse, image of the hexagonal pencil. Now let's machine a tough steel bar into a reverse image of the rifling. Stick this bar into a bored length of barrel steel and hammer the outside until the barrel is tightly squeezed around the rifled bar. Knock the bar out of the barrel, and inside the barrel is a perfect reverse copy of the rifled bar. In other words, it's a rifled barrel!

Of course, the process is more complicated than what I have described. The hammering is done on giant machines that literally knead the barrel steel around the forming mandrel like so much bread dough. The machinery is expensive, but the results are good. At present, this production method is used in the U.S. by Winchester, and it is widely employed in Europe, especially in Austria and Germany where the process originated.

Much if not most of the rifling formed by these incredible machines is of the traditional Enfield type. That is certainly true of the hammer-forged barrels made in America. However,

This high-temperature furnace is used by Douglas to anneal, or normalize, barrel stock before boring and rifling. Normalizing the steel removes potential stress points that might cause warping or bending during the manufacturing process.

since the hammer process can be used to form virtually any shape of rifling with equal ease, there has been a fair amount of experimentation with "new" shapes. Paradoxically, one of these new rifling forms is much like the old Lancaster oval bore. Another style, called polygon or polyform, is just the old Whitworth rifling all over again. Is anything ever really new? Among the claims being made for the "latest" rifling forms is increased barrel life. Considering that there are no lands to wear down, this is probably true, but accuracy is the real test, first, last, and always.

During the early 1970's, Ed Shilen, one of the world's best barrelmakers, began offering his own version of Whitworth rifling. The Shilen version was eight-sided (octagonal) whereas Sir Joseph's had six sides. Shilen claimed increased barrel life for his new rifling, and accuracy was equal to his Enfield-style barrels, but sales were slow so he gave it up after a few years.

Even as new rifling forms are being developed, similar advances are being made with the traditional Enfield style. As this is being written, the Shilen company is in the process of altering the design of their basic eight-groove Enfield rifling. For several years, the land-to-groove ratio in Shilen barrels was a uniform one to three, meaning that the grooves were three times as wide as the lands. Now Shilen finds that a good barrel can be made even better by using a one-to-two ratio. Barrel life is improved because the wider lands are more resistant to erosion. Of more importance, accuracy is improved, and the barrels tend to be less critical of ammo variations. Why? I don't know, and Ed Shilen doesn't either.

Obviously, there is still a lot to be learned about the rifled barrel.

Chapter 2

BUILDING TODAY'S SPORTING RIFLE

When word gets around that a major gunmaker is about to bring forth a new rifle, expectation sweeps across the land. According to the heralds, the newcomer possesses everything that could be wished of a royal heir to a great gunmaking dynasty, and such phrases as "old-time craftsmanship" and "new-world technology" ring across the shooting kingdom. With loving care, the proud parents unveil their offspring. The newborn is anointed by gun writers, those Guardians of the Faith, who raise their voices in a chorus of exaltation, which is especially loud if the loving parent sees fit to bestow paid advertisements.

With all this fanfare and whoopdeedo, shooters and hunters can barely contain themselves until that divine moment when the newcomer is finally set forth on that most worshipful of altars, the dealer's gunrack. There we touch, feel, prod, poke, caress, and stroke the newborn babe until at last our voices are united in that very familiar chant: "Why can't they make 'em like they used to?"

The reasons why they don't make 'em like they used to are so varied and complex that few shooters have more than a clue to the problems of modern gun manufacture. In fact, many individuals closely associated with the gun trade, including retailers, wholesalers, gunsmiths, advertising agents, and even manufacturer's representatives are frequently almost totally ignorant of the complications of mass gunmaking.

LO, THE VANISHING CRAFTSMAN

For example, we are often told that the age of great craftsmen has passed and that guns must necessarily be made with automated machines. This is by no means the case. Craftsmanship has and always will exist in direct quantitative and qualitative response to demand. Regardless of the skill required in any job, there will always be craftsmen of sufficient skill to perform the work *if* there is enough demand for that skill. This is a primary law of economics, and I'll give you an illustration of how it works.

In 1960, fewer than a dozen top-drawer custom rifle builders were making a living in the U.S. Speaking relatively, their work was expensive, and few shooters were willing to pay for their services. Two decades later, upwards of 50 highly talented riflemakers, especially custom stockmakers, were offering their talents to shooters and collectors of fine shooting ware. During the 1970's, new talent seemed to pop from under every rock, and this was not just an accident of the times; it was a direct response to demand. If, by chance, the demand for fine custom rifles were to slacken, there would be a corresponding drop in the number of skilled custom craftsmen.

With this in mind, let's step back in time to the late 1800's. At that time, one of the finest rifles ever produced in America, the Winchester Model 1886 lever gun, was being manufactured by what was considered to be mass-production methods. Gun lovers who have handled a Model 86 are unfailingly impressed by its beautifully fitted parts and "oiled-glass" functional smoothness. Every specimen that left Winchester's shipping dock was a masterpiece. Even though these rifles were made by what was then considered up-to-date mass production, a hell of a lot of highly skilled hand labor was involved. Who were those craftsmen, where did they get their skills, and why did their skills become obsolete?

These great craftsmen did not spring from any mythical fountain but were ordinary people who wanted steady work and modest comfort. Most of them learned their skills on the job, beginning as apprentices and working their way up year by year, skill by skill, to the better-paying job of master parts fitter or finisher.

So far as management was concerned, skill was a relative matter. They knew by several decades of early mass-production experience that whatever skills were necessary to the making of their guns could be developed and maintained within their organizations. They were correct in their realization that worker skill was an indefinitely renewable resource. What they could not have recognized was the approaching competition for workers possessing *any* degree of skill. How were the owners of a gun factory in Connecticut to know that within a few years a guy named Henry Ford in Michigan would be willing to pay hourly laborers as much for turning a crank or twisting a wrench as a master gunsmith earned in New Haven? How could they have known that the men of Jerome, Arizona, would soon receive the world's highest daily wages just for scratching and blasting copper ore out of the earth?

Even so, there was no mass exodus of skills from the great Eastern centers of gunmaking. Workers tend to be loyal to their trade and their employer, so the skilled gunmakers remained at their benches, passing along their legacy of craftsmanship.

However, as other industries grew, prospered, and hired more workers, the competition for skill increased, sending wages ever upward and causing management to seek substitutes for skill. This process might have been gradual, reaching well into the 20th century, had it not been for three major events. These were the First World War, the Great Depression, and World War II.

SCARCITY OF SKILLED WORKERS

The First World War created two adverse conditions. The first was a shortage of labor, and the second, a seeming paradox, was a superabundance of orders. Though mass production was a child of the arms industry (thanks to Whitney and Colt), and America was the cradle of mass production, it was not until the World War I arms buildup that gunmakers had a glimmering of what high-speed production really meant. It was no doubt a tempting vision, but gunmakers are traditionally a hidebound lot who prefer to proceed from one century into the next with utmost caution.

America's previous wars had always been followed by a return to the farms, factories, and workbenches. But World War I was different. The returning doughboys had seen Paris. They had also seen flying airplanes, ships that swam underwater, and many other surprising things. They wanted to see a lot more. Detroit, Chicago, California—those were the places to see them. To hell with the workbenches, files, sandpaper, and old-fashioned machinery of New England!

Even with the loss of workers and their potential skills, the gun-making business as it was known in 1890 would probably have continued unchanged for several decades after World War I. As a matter of fact, it appeared that it indeed would do so. During the adjustment period of the 1920's labor skills seemed to have achieved an ideal equilibrium with mass production. But then the Depression struck, and the demand for guns fell off so severely that a number of gun-making firms either closed their doors or were swallowed by other companies. Without a demand for guns, there was no demand for gunmaking skills. Why bother to learn a trade when no one wants the fruits of your skills?

This is not to say that all gunmaking skills languished. There was a large pool of skilled gunmakers right up to 1941, but as they retired, they were not replaced. They *could* have been replaced and very possibly *would* have been replaced as the world emerged from the Depression era. But again, the course of normal gunmaking was interrupted and overwhelmed by world war—a war that wrought such revolutions in life, industry, wealth, and society that there was no looking back.

World War II changed the sporting-arms industry so greatly because of three factors that crashed into each other with whirlwind intensity.

Uppermost in the minds of millions of returning American GI's was marrying the girl back home and buying the rifles and shotguns of their dreams. The demand for sporting arms was virtually without precedent. Normally, this would have presented no real problem. The gunmakers would simply have hired or trained more craftsmen in order to increase production. The real problem was that the pool of skilled gunmakers had declined during the Depression years and had dropped even lower as skilled hands were diverted to other jobs during the war.

Given enough time, say, five years, new craftsmen could have been trained, and things would have been much the same as they were in 1920. The problem was that all those ex-GI's didn't want to wait. They wanted the guns of their dreams *now!*

At the same time that gunmakers were wondering where and how long it would take to develop a fresh supply of skilled labor, they were also faced with competition from other job markets and increasing demands from militant labor unions. In other words, even if they did train a new labor force, they might not have been able to afford it. Clearly, guns built by hand at

1950 labor costs would have been prohibitively expensive. That's when another major force came into the picture: modern mass production.

AUTOMATED PRODUCTION

Not just mass-production machinery in terms of the 1880's or even the 1920's, but robot-like machinery capable of turning out a finished product with little or no help from human hands. World War II had given industry an opportunity to improve mass-production techniques for everything from shirts to ships, and the lessons had not been lost on gunmakers. If the gun industry was to meet post-war demands for sporting arms and to remain price-competitive, the only answer clearly lay in advanced mass-production engineering.

In the late 1940's, as today, most of America's consumer goods were mass produced. Though we seldom give it much thought, most of the durable goods we buy—cars, refrigerators, washing machines—are not only mass produced, they are *designed* to be mass produced. A manufacturer does not design a product and then figure out how it can be made in mass. Instead, from the very conception of a product idea, the maker builds in mass-producible features.

In this respect the sporting arms that existed in 1946 were impossible. Though almost all models were built on assembly lines, they required a lot of hand labor. What's more, most gun designs prevented any attempts at increased production speed. Obviously, if guns were to be truly mass produced, it was necessary to design them so that they could be produced with automated machinery.

The first major U.S. sporting arms maker to put the concept into operation was Remington. In the 1930's the most popular U.S. bolt-action rifle was Winchester's Model 70. To compete with the great Model 70, Remington introduced a beautiful bolt rifle called the Model 720 in 1941. The Model 720 Remington was an elegant and beautifully finished rifle that might very well have achieved popularity equal to that of Winchester's Model 70. In 1941, however, America got into the war, and production of the 720, along with all sporting arms, was set aside for emergency war production.

At war's end, Remington might have started making the beautiful Model 720 again, but by that time the writing was on the wall. What the company needed to meet post-war demands were guns that could be manufactured at high speed and sold at competitive prices. The answers were two revolutionary bolt-action rifles—the Models 721 and 722, which were the ancestors of today's Remington Model 700 bolt rifle. These were no-frills rifles, with no checkering on the stocks and with trigger guards made of simple bent steel. Compared to the great pre-war rifles, the 721 and the 722 were not very attractive, a shortcoming that was more than counterbalanced by the prices, which were $79.95 and $74.95, respectively. By comparison, a Model 70 Winchester that same year retailed for $106.00.

But being less expensive than the competition was not the whole reason for the success of Remington's rifles. What they really had going for them was tremendous strength and great accuracy. Even in today's ultra-accurate benchrest shooting, our most accurate rifles have not strayed far from the basic M-722 action design. The irony is inescapable. Despite great efforts to build beautifully hand-finished rifles, one of the most accurate guns was an inexpensive

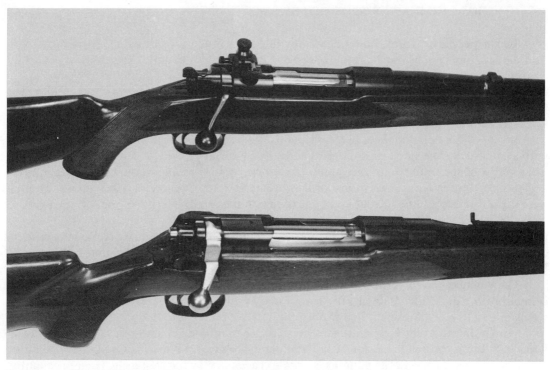

On the eve of World War II, Remington introduced the excellent Model 720 (bottom) to compete with the most popular bolt-action rifle of the 1930's, the Winchester Model 70.

mass-produced model requiring minimal laying on of hands during manufacture. The gunmaking industry could never be the same.

TWO TECHNOLOGICAL MONSTERS

Every technology engenders its own monsters, and high-speed gunmaking is no exception. A case in point is that many modern production engineers are so turned on to making everything with automated machinery that they fail to recognize that certain things can, in fact, be made by hand with greater precision, speed, and quality than by machine. In the same vein, some designers of high-speed machinery are so given to their quest for ever-higher production rates that they unnecessarily sacrifice both the quality and appearance of the product they wish to sell. I'll give you specific examples of both these monsters.

In the early 1960's, when gunmakers had almost totally sacrificed their souls on the altar of modern mass production, there was a widespread belief that hand checkering of stocks was a thing of the past. Hand checkering was a tedious job, combining high skill with a low rate of production. Accordingly, a new checkering system was developed which squeezed a design pattern into the wood with the aid of intense heat. This was the much-despised impressed checkering. Everyone agreed that it was ugly as sin, but gunmakers were in equal agreement that it was unavoidable if prices were to be kept in line.

But the people at Sturm, Ruger didn't buy the idea. As Bill Ruger saw it, checkering could be done economically by hand at a satisfactorily high rate. Accordingly, Lenard Brownell, a top custom stockmaker, was hired to teach a group of New England women to checker gunstocks using the same electric-powered hand-checkering tools used by most custom stockmakers. It was discovered that previously unskilled women could be trained to checker gunstocks with a speed that rivaled machine work while at the same time equaling the quality of the pre-war era.

Not long ago, a gunmaking firm called me in to help iron out problems they were having with a rifle stock. The stock was so ugly that the rifle was hard to sell, so the firm wanted me to improve the shape to make it more appealing. There was no problem about pointing out the stock's faults and making suggestions for improvements—any intelligent high-school kid could have suggested improvements. But every one of my suggestions was rebuffed by the engineering staff. They made the excuse that their new high-speed stock-shaping machine was incapable of rendering my recommended revisions. In exasperation, I finally asked to see the machine in operation and found out why their expensive new equipment couldn't make pretty rifle stocks. It was appalling!

The engineers were correct. The machine simply couldn't make anything approaching a delicate cut or gracefully formed line. It operated by means of a series of sanding belts that whisked away the wood like hay in a windstorm, but the machine could not make a concave cut smaller in radius than the large end-roller on which the sanding belts ran. There was no way in which this European-made machine could be adapted to make an attractive stock. Yet both the maker of the machine and the gunmaker were so caught up in their desire for fast production

Ideas for firearms improvements may come from a variety of sources. Here, the author (right) consults with designer Bill Ruger, founder of Sturm, Ruger, about the shaping of a small detail. Attention to such details can make the difference between a good gun and a great one.

that they overlooked the obvious necessity of producing good-looking stocks. What does it matter how fast a stock can be shaped if the result is so ugly that no one will buy it?

SO WHY DON'T *YOU* MAKE A RIFLE?

Just for the fun of it, let's say you love fine rifles and also happen to be fabulously rich. After years of lounging around the world's fanciest playgrounds pursued by beautiful women, you decide to make something of yourself and use your wealth to bring some style to hunting arms. After all, you shot grouse in Scotland, partridge in Spain, and elephant in Africa, always with the finest hand-wrought guns money could buy, and you figure it would be a nice gesture to bring fine guns to the average working guy.

The only problem with gunmaking, as you see it, is that gun manufacturers are too inbred and really don't understand what a good rifle should look like. The business needs a jolt of your refined good taste. You're going to make rifles the way they used to make 'em.

So you call in a few technicians, an accountant or two, plus a production squad, and outline what you have in mind. After some production studies, they present you with a rough outline of what it will cost to get into the business. Tooling-up figures don't matter because you've got plenty of money to finance your brainchild, but as a sporting proposition, you are determined to sell your rifle at a profit. The projections of what it would cost to make a rifle the way they used to gives you pause. According to your technicians and accountants, a skilled hand fitter can fit and polish the parts of a single rifle in two weeks. Of course, some of the work can be done by semi-skilled, lower-cost labor, but all and all, you'd better figure on an average wage of $10 an hour. For two weeks, this adds up to $800. To this is added $100 for raw materials and $50 for factory maintenance. And another $20 is added for insurance and liability.

Let's see now. That totals $960 for a base price, but we've got to add a slim profit margin of 15 percent, which rounds off at $1,100 dollars *wholesale* for each of your beautiful rifles. Of course, the retailer wants a profit too, so let's add 25 percent, which means that a rifle made the way they used to make 'em would cost only $1,466. Oh yes, there's the excise tax, so let's add another $100 or so.

Being a mega-millionaire and accustomed to spending thousands for custom guns, this sounds like a bargain, and you don't see how any sensible hunter could possibly resist one of your fine rifles. Your accountants, however, have a more realistic idea of what the average shooter is willing to pay for a rifle, which is about one-third the price of your dreamchild.

This is a stunning bit of news, because never before have you come face to face with a situation where quality had to be tempered by price. "Is it really true," you ask, still unbelieving, "that cost is always a factor in gun manufacture?" With few exceptions, you learn, price is the *first* consideration. The few exceptions are monied gun collectors who demand the very best in craftsmanship and are willing and able to pay for it. Their demands are catered to by the great gunmaking houses in England such as Holland and Holland or Purdey, and in the U.S. by Griffin & Howe, Wells, Champlin, the David Miller Company, and a few dozen one-man custom shops. For shooters who don't want to hock the farm but still want something distinctive, there are DuBiel and Weatherby, but if you want to sell a *lot* of rifles, you have to cater to the working man. Any way you look at it, that means you must be price-competitive.

"Okay," you say, still determined to bring style to the masses, "We're still going to make rifles. Let's figure out how to make the most beautiful, best-shooting, most dependable rifle we can at the least possible cost."

Your advisers, technicians, and accountants give you a rousing cheer. At last you're really going to be in the riflemaking business. With more than a little sadness, you realize that your dream of making rifles the way they used to is gone with the wind, defeated by shooters who endlessly yell for great craftsmanship but are unable to bear the cost. But possibly your dream of a great rifle has been replaced by an even nobler vision—a truly excellent and tasteful rifle that is at once both desirable *and* affordable. The challenge is irresistible, but the trail to success is rutted by more problems than you could imagine.

Your first bitter pill is the realization that even though the rifle will bear your name, will embody your basic design, and is to be financed by your dollars, it cannot incorporate some of your favorite features. For example, you've always liked a light trigger pull and feel that it is a definite aid to good shooting. Naturally you want your rifle to have a crisp pull of between two and three pounds, certainly not the seven- to 15-pound tug-of-war pulls of many modern rifles. You put this requirement on your list of specifications. The next day you get a memo from your legal staff that reads as follows:

"In response to your specification for a lightweight trigger pull, we must advise that from the legal standpoint such trigger mechanisms are not desirable. Given today's climate in regard to liability litigation, a trigger letoff weight of less than five pounds, as adjusted at the factory, may be blamed for accidental personal injury resulting from misuse. To protect the company from this sort of suit, we strongly advise that the trigger mechanism be adjusted to a substantial letoff weight, preferably not less than five pounds. Seven to 10 pounds is safer."

The obvious solution is to offer your rifle with an adjustable mechanism that can be set to "legally safe" limits at the factory but readjusted to a light pull by the buyer. The problem with this, you realize, is that when your customers first try the pull in a gunshop, it will feel sluggish and heavy. In fact, it will feel no better than the non-adjustable triggers on any number of other makes and models of rifles. With this realization also comes your first dim recognition of the problems riflemakers have faced for years.

But your motto is "never say never," so you push on to another goal—unrivaled accuracy. In this respect, you have some very definite ideas. Since the basic turnbolt mechanism is supposed to be the most accurate design, there is no doubt your rifle will be a bolt-action, but you have some ideas that will make the old war horse even more accurate. You've read, and heard experts say, that fast lock-time is a definite aid to accuracy. The reasoning is obvious. The faster the striker falls, the less time there will be for your aim to wander off target.

Traditionally, lock-time is improved in three ways: by shortening the distance the firing pin must travel; by making the striker and all other moving parts as light as possible so they will accelerate fast; and by using a powerful striker spring. These features sound reasonable, so you order your engineering staff to design the lightest firing pin ever made, the strongest firing-pin spring, and ultra-short firing-pin travel. What could be simpler?

Next day, you get a six-page engineer's report advising that while the basic goal of fast lock-time is indeed laudable, there are problems. The first is that a lightweight firing pin traveling only a short distance will not have sufficient momentum to deliver a reliably positive blow to a cartridge primer. In the event of hard primers, there might be misfires or, at best, irregular ignition that would result in poor accuracy.

The report goes on to say that the basic mechanical failings of a light firing pin and a short striker fall can be corrected to some extent by using an extremely stiff mainspring, but this leads to another problem. A stiff mainspring puts a heavy load on the trigger's sear surfaces. This calls for extensive sear-surface engagement, which in turn results in a loss of trigger-pull quality. If the sear engagement is not beefed up, there is a possibility of accidental discharge. Further, a stiff spring leads to difficult cocking, making the bolt hard to open and interfering with the overall smoothness of the rifle's operation.

The report concludes with the news that the possibility of accidental sear failure caused by an overly strong spring can be dealt with by designing a trigger mechanism featuring a series of levers that distribute the load. But this, of course, would require a trigger that is more expensive to make and more prone to malfunction.

Once again, even more forcibly this time, you realize that what you had innocently considered to be the faults of various commercially produced rifles were in fact unavoidable design traits dictated by necessity. Distasteful as these faults may be, you are no more able to sidestep them than any other manufacturer.

Crestfallen, you call the chief engineer into your office and ask him to explain the limits of lock-time. You learn that while your rifle can have significantly better lock-time than the old 98 Mausers and 03 Springfields, possibly even better than a Model 70 Winchester, the Remington Model 700 pretty much represents the state of the science for centerfire rifles manufactured for the mass market. In other words, the goal here is not to be "better than" but just to be "as good as."

You have promised yourself that your rifles will have wonderfully accurate barrels. To this end, you direct your materials buyer to take bids on top-quality barrels by the most famous makers. A good barrel is a work of art, and you want your barrels to be made by the greatest artists. Disappointment strikes again. Some of the small barrel shops don't bid because they are already back-ordered to their gills. Besides, they could never meet your quantity demands. Others, who do bid, ask so much for their barrels that your manufacturing costs would nearly double. If you are to be price-competitive, you must buy barrels from a mass manufacturer, which means that their accuracy will not be what you want, or you must make your own. The second option is appealing, but after a few inquiries you discover that while rifle barrels can be made most efficiently by the hammer-forging process, the machinery is terribly expensive, and paying for it would up the retail price by a large amount.

Though the choice is obvious, it is not the one you want to make. By using barrels mass manufactured by an outside vendor, you lose some of the quality and accuracy you'd hoped to offer. The great barrelmaking artists such as Hart, Shilen, Marquart, Douglas, Atkinson, McMillan, etc., make each barrel with loving care, but the large-scale commercial vendors, who are geared up to make thousands of barrels at the lowest possible price, cannot give each barrel the attention required for top accuracy. True, some of the mass-vendor barrels shoot with wonderful accuracy, but that's just the luck of the draw. Others out of the same batch may be dismally inaccurate.

This is the bitterest pill yet. By using mass-produced barrels from an outside vendor, you have less control over accuracy than, say, Remington or Winchester, who make their own barrels and thereby exercise total quality control. The bottom line is that your rifle may be *less* accurate than the competition.

One by one, your dreams of a great rifle are shattered. Problems completely out of your control are stripping away the grand features you had envisioned. Rather than racing ahead into the next century with your wonderful, but innocent, ideas, you may be forced to manufacture a gun technically inferior to the rifles already on the market. In any event, you have gained a lot of respect for the mass-made rifles that only weeks before were the objects of your scorn. More and more often, you find yourself asking: "How do they do it?"

One way you can beat them, though, is in the looks department. You have learned from your experience with fine custom guns that much of their beauty lies in distinctive styling seldom seen in mass-produced rifles. In fact, some rifles by famous American firms are definitely ugly, almost as if the makers had gone out of their way to eliminate every vestige of style and grace. This, as you see it, is one of their weakest points. Surely, you reason, all other factors being equal, a customer will select the best-looking rifle.

This time you hit the nail squarely on the head. Beauty, or lack thereof, is an important factor in the appeal of any firearm, but is frequently overlooked by manufacturers. "Overlooked" is really not the correct term, because any manufacturer likes to think his guns are attractive. Sometimes, though, they become so hidebound that they are unaware of what a stylish rifle is supposed to look like. Or, just as often, the engineer or marketing director who gives final approval to a particular stock design simply has no taste. Or, at other times, a company finds itself locked in on a particular stock shape without having given the matter ample thought.

One of the homeliest rifle stocks of recent times is to be found on the Remington Model 700. To be sure, the M-700 is one of the all-time best-selling centerfire rifles, and there is no denying the excellence of its mechanical design. But someone was asleep when the stock was designed. According to my inside sources, the stock never *was* really designed. It just happened. As I understand it, the engineering department made up a stock more or less to serve as a rough handle for the barreled action, and along the way, it became adopted as the official stock almost by accident. If someone had taken a few more days to think about the stock and had perhaps asked for some outside help, the Model 700 would certainly be an even greater rifle. That's why, during the mid-1970's, the folks at Remington attempted to produce a better-looking version of the 700 with the Model 700 Classic.

To support your desire to make a truly stylish rifle, there are success stories about some post-war classics. The first of these is the Ruger No. 1 Single-Shot rifle. From the end of World War II until 1965, virtually any gunmaker, wholesaler, retailer, or user of rifles would have told you that single-shot rifles were a thing of the past, totally out of step with today's gun-buying habits. Such opinions were held without reference to the possibility that a *good-looking* single-shot would sell. In 1966, Sturm, Ruger introduced the Model No. 1, and history was made. It had *appeal*. Without particularly caring that the new Ruger was capable of only one shot, and with little concern about its accuracy, lovers of rifles bought the No. 1 because they recognized it as a genuinely stylish rifle. In fact, early test reports of the Ruger Single-Shot indicated poor accuracy, but buyers seemed unconcerned.

Bill Ruger beat the system by going outside the confines of his company to hire Lenard Brownell, a stockmaker of international repute, to design his rifle stocks. In the arms industry,

Here are the Remington Model 700 BDL (top photograph) and the full-stocked International version of the Ruger No. 1 Single-Shot.

this was a radical idea. Traditionally, all stocks were designed "in house." Manufacturers took the view that they'd rather do it their way, even if it was the wrong way. In retrospect, we see that Ruger's revolutionary course of action was a very practical way to solve a problem that had plagued gunmakers for decades.

Building on the critical acclaim and consumer acceptance of the beautiful single-shot, Bill Ruger then offered his classically styled Model 77 repeating bolt rifle. Again, the stock design was by Brownell, and again, the rifle was an immediate hit. If you compare the Model 77 Ruger at the time of its introduction to America's two other premier bolt rifles, the Winchester M-70 and Remington's M-700, you will find that the M-77 wasn't all that much ahead of the game from the mechanical viewpoint. What made it outstanding was *looks!* The Ruger M-77 is beautifully stylish, and lovers of guns want to own it. Chalk up another success to good taste.

In 1980, Winchester's Model 70 was a pretty nice piece of equipment. It had been vastly upgraded in terms of stock shape and overall finish after the redesign disaster of the mid-60's, and was pretty well holding its own against the competition. Still, it wasn't anything you'd leave home for. In 1981 Winchester introduced a Featherweight Model 70 that captured the hearts of riflemen as had no other Winchester product in a generation. Why? Because of its stylish good looks and for no other reason whatever. It could be argued that the new M-70 Featherweight achieved instant success because it weighs somewhat less than the standard Model 70, but what about the earlier featherweights? Oldtimers recall that back in the 1950's, Winchester introduced a Featherweight Model 70 that was stocked almost identically to the standard weight version. The old Featherweight was moderately popular but not a runaway success, so we can't attribute the new Model 70 Featherweight's quick acceptance to the fact that it weighs a pound or two less than the standard version. No, the new Featherweight has better stock styling, and that is why it is so desirable.

Another modern success, largely based on styling appeal, is the trim little Kimber .22 Rimfire bolt-action rifle. It would seem that if there is anything the world doesn't need, it is another .22 rifle. But as the people at Kimber saw it, what the world *did* need was a handsomely styled .22. Originally, the designer had some good ideas for the mechanism, but the stock lacked style, so badly in fact that if the rifle had been marketed in the form I first saw, it would indeed have been only another .22. I pointed out this shortcoming and suggested that the stock should be designed by a top custom stockmaker. We got on the phone right then, and within minutes,

Blanks, or billets, of stock wood arrive at the factory as rough blocks, seen in the foreground. Behind them is an automatic shaping machine which will turn the stocks to nearly finished dimensions.

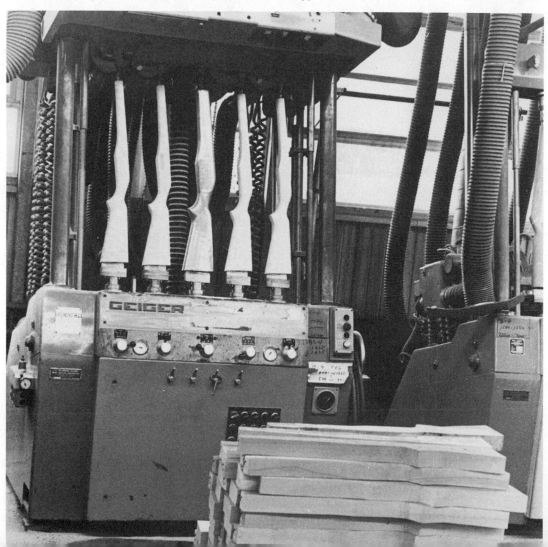

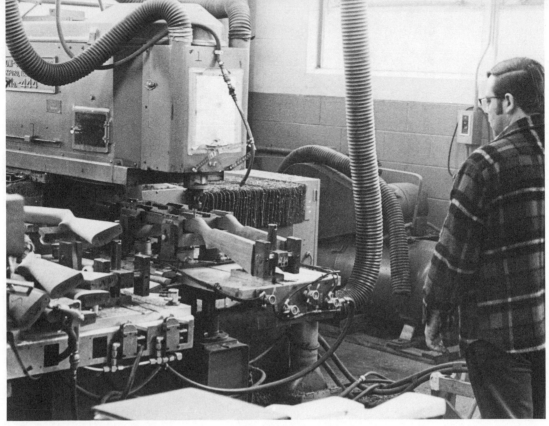

An electronically controlled machine makes the inletting cuts in the roughly shaped stocks. Each stock will then be rough-sanded manually.

After inletting and rough-sanding, a stock is fine-sanded. This operation is similar to what a home craftsman would do. Ordinary sandpaper on sanding blocks is used to obtain a perfectly smooth, well contoured finish.

The sanded stocks get a protective finish in a spraying chamber. Several coats may be applied to build up an even layer of finish—which may be varnish, lacquer, or any one of several plastics. The stocks will then be inspected again, and any blemishes will be rubbed out by hand.

Checkering can be done by several methods. At Ruger, it's done almost entirely by hand, and mostly by women like this skilled worker. Any home craftsman knows that hand checkering is difficult and tedious, yet these women become remarkably fast without sacrificing quality. Some manufacturers use this method, while others use automatic cutting machines to checker stocks, and some may even press the checkering in by mechanical means. Cut checkering looks and feels best, of course. Interestingly, the checkering tool seen here is the same type used by some of the top custom stockmakers to cut their checkering.

Finished and checkered, the stock must now be final-fitted to the metal. Generally, this requires more hand-work to obtain a perfect fit. Here, a Ruger craftsman makes a tiny cut on a No. 1 Single-Shot stock to get the desired wedding of wood to metal.

arrangements had been made for a genuinely classic stock. The new prototype stock cost many times more than the original in-house design, but it was money wisely spent. From the day of its introduction, the Kimber Model 82 has been a critical and commercial success despite a price tag well over $400. The reason is simple—people are willing to pay for a good-looking rifle.

Your new rifle will be well received if it possesses style and beauty, so hire the best professional stockmaker you can find and pay him what he demands. It will be the best bargain of your riflemaking career.

And don't present the stockmaker with a newly designed barreled action and say: "Here, make a pretty stock for this." Get him in on the act at the very beginning. The reason is that the engineering departments of various riflemaking firms all too often come up with a receiver that refuses to blend harmoniously with a wooden stock. Despite the best efforts of the stock-design department, they fight a losing battle from the beginning. If you've ever had a fine custom rifle built, or plan to do so, you are aware that the stockmaker doesn't start out by inletting your barreled action into a block of wood. First, he or a custom metalsmith must do a great deal of work to reshape the action so that the lines of the metal parts will flow gracefully into the stock's contours. Even great actions such as Mausers, Model 70's, Remingtons, and Springfields require considerable reshaping of metal if the total effect is to be genuinely graceful. Some actions, in fact, totally resist graceful stocking and can never be incorporated into a really good-looking rifle. It's also true that trigger guards are almost always so poorly shaped that considerable rebuilding or replacement is essential.

As a modern rifle manufacturer, you will be especially smart to call in a top stockmaker at the very beginning of your development program and get his thought on how the external metal surfaces should be shaped in order to achieve the best combined effect of wood and metal.

Finalize your stock design *before* you buy your stock-making machinery. That way, you can make sure you are getting equipment capable of making the stock the way you want it. All too often, gunmakers pay a ton of money for high-speed wood-forming machinery only to find that it is so limited in flexibility and capability that it can only produce clumsy stocks. This is one of the main reasons why there are so many unforgivably ugly stocks on today's guns.

METALWORK

You anticipated that your biggest problem in producing a stylish rifle would be the contouring of complex metal parts. It proves to be almost no problem at all. In fact, you find that you even have a choice of production techniques. In this respect, you are way ahead of riflemaking as it existed in 1950, because mass-production methods are now vastly more versatile than they were at that time. I'll give a specific example.

The Remington Models 721 and 722 (the 722 action is only a short version of the 721) are the best examples of early post-war mass-produced rifles. In case you're a newcomer to the shooting scene and have never examined the M-721 or M-722, the actions are identical to today's Model 700 Remington except for minor cosmetic changes. The receiver is round and could be described as a cylinder. There are no integral projections such as a recoil lug or magazine or trigger housings. This was done so that the receiver blank could be cut from round bar stock and then center-bored and the cuts made for bolt lugs, loading port, and magazine opening without a lot of fuss and bother. The bolt is a simple cylindrical affair. The bolt handle is made separately and attached later. Everything is round because that shape was most easily rendered by high-speed production tools of that era. A simple lathe cut virtually completed the external contouring of both the bolt and the receiver. Since almost no hand finishing was required and relatively few fixture changes were necessary, the mechanism was a marvel of design for high-speed production.

By comparision, the Winchester Model 70 action of the same era was a maze of complex forms, curves, and flats. Beginning as forgings, the bolt and receiver underwent an incredible number of machining operations, each one requiring complex fixtures and extensive "hands on" attention.

Naturally, the Model 721 action was considerably less expensive to manufacture, and this made Remington more competitive in the marketplace. This is why Winchester redesigned the Model 70 in 1964. They simplified the design in order to cut down on manufacturing costs.

In 1950's manufacturing terms, it appeared that rifle design was heading inexorably toward a monotonous roundness and sameness of shape. Apparently, the beautiful but complex action shapes of Mausers, pre-1964 Model 70's, 03 Springfields, and their kin would become a thing of the past just like the wonderful old 1886 Winchester lever rifle. The forecasters of this

Except for minor cosmetic changes, the action of today's Remington Model 700 (bottom) is virtually identical to that of the old Model 722.

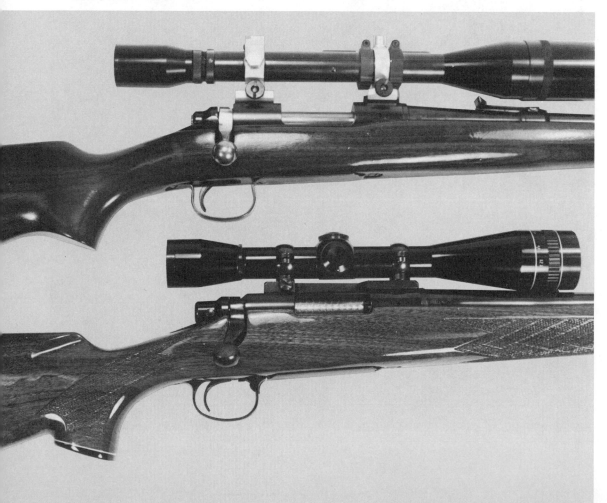

gloomy future had no way of knowing that revolutionary developments in automated, electronically controlled machinery lay just around the corner, or that an ancient metal-casting method would be applied to gunmaking in dramatic fashion.

INVESTMENT CASTING

Give a skilled machinist a bar of steel and he can turn, cut, grind, drill, and file it into any shape you desire, but the more complex the shape, the longer the process will take. Given the hourly wage of a union machinist or toolmaker plus the cost of the necessary tools and machinery, converting a hunk of steel into a particular shape is an expensive proposition. This problem has

In manufacturing a gun part by investment casting—the "lost-wax" process—the first step is to form a wax duplicate part in a wax injection mold. Here, an operator of an injection mold turns out hundreds of wax parts. The process takes only a few seconds in a high-production mold.

long plagued gun manufacturers because gun parts do tend to be exceedingly complex and multisurfaced.

Of course, there are any number of complex forms in our lives that are made of solid metal and yet are quite inexpensive. Most are made by casting. A very good example is an old-fashioned cornbread-stick mold made of cast iron. Another good example is an automobile carburetor housing, made by a die-casting process. The examples go on and on. Since casting

Here is a wax gun part—the receiver of a Ruger No. 1 Single-Shot rifle—as it comes from the mold. It's hard enough to be handled without damage. The square lumps on the moldings in the background are needed for the initial casting process but will be removed from the final product.

Assembling wax moldings into a "tree," as seen in this photo, requires considerable skill. The areas into which the steel will flow are called gates.

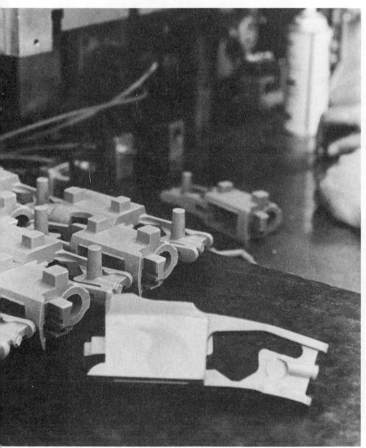

Each "tree" of wax moldings is dipped into a slurry that forms a ceramic coating. The coating is repeated and alternated with different materials until it becomes quite thick and heavy.

metal (pouring molten metal into a mold) is a simple and easy way to make complex parts, it would seem to be a natural way to make complicated gun parts. As a matter of fact, cannon barrels were once cast of iron, brass, or bronze, but traditional casting techniques proved unsatisfactory for small arms and were found to be woefully inadequate for modern breechloading firearms.

There are several problems associated with cast gun parts. Among the most significant drawbacks is the poor molecular structure of cast iron, which causes it to be brittle. Another is that ordinary casting procedures employ a mold of pressed sand that imparts a rough, grainy texture to the surface of the metal. Casting was considered to be a third-rate way of manufacturing third-rate implements, and there was considerable contempt for cast gun parts. Even when non-critical parts of guns, such as trigger guards, were made by casting it was a serious black mark against the gun. Good guns were not made with cast parts. This opinion held through World War II and was reinforced by reports that the Japanese had turned to casting the major parts of their rifles toward the war's end and had suffered a high failure rate due to blow-ups.

Now let's backtrack hundreds, perhaps thousands of years to the darkest interior of Africa. There a remarkably artistic Nigerian tribe produced (and still produces) a stunning variety of ceremonial masks, intricate tapestries, brilliant fabrics, and complexly molded metal artifacts.

How, it was asked, were they able to cast their ceremonial statuettes in so many delicate shapes? Through what casting process did they manage such minute detail?

The way they did it was simple, almost too simple to be believed. The idol was first sculpted in firm beeswax. The wax form was then coated, layer by layer, with fine, plasterlike mud. When dried, this coating formed a hard shell. The shell was then intensely heated until the beeswax melted and ran out through specially prepared holes. This left the hollow shell, which was a perfectly formed negative image of the original wax statuette. The next step was to melt brass, bronze, cooper, or gold and pour it into the mud mold. When the metal cooled and hardened, the mud shell was cracked and removed, leaving a perfect metal replica of the original wax sculpture. Since the wax model had melted away, the technique came to be known as the "lost-wax" process. The term is still used, but more often it is called *investment casting*.

Here is a close-up view of ceramic-coated molding "trees." At this point in the process the individual parts are scarcely recognizable.

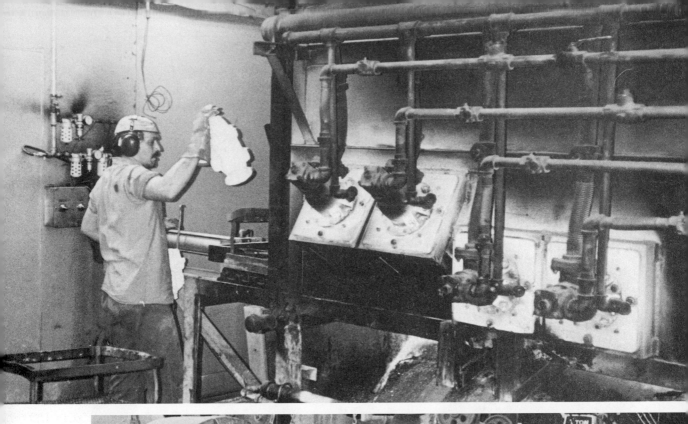

Left: The ceramic shell is heated in a furnace like this, which melts and burns out the wax. This leaves a hollow ceramic mold—a negative form of the gun part that is to be cast.

Bottom left: Before pouring alloyed steel or another specified metal, the ceramic molds are placed in an oven and heated to a temperature of several hundred degrees. Otherwise, the metals would cool too rapidly, would fail to fill the mold completely, and would form surface wrinkles. The large metal boxes at the lower right are shields designed to keep the molds hot.

Steel alloy, melted in an induction furnace, is poured into a crucible. The alloy is closely controlled and repeatedly checked to make certain it meets the manufacturer's specifications.

From the crucible, the molten alloy is carefully poured into the heated ceramic shells. This is the point at which the proper design of the molding "tree" becomes very important. It must be just right if the alloy is to fill each mold completely. After filling, the molds will be shielded again to assure gradual cooling.

Obviously, such a process has wonderful possibilities for the gun industry because intricate shapes can be cast almost as easily as simple ones. The only problems in the 1950's were almost universal prejudice against cast gun parts and certain metallurgical difficulties. For example, cast alloyed steel did not have a strong molecular structure.

The aircraft industry played a vital role in solving the metallurgical problems. In adapting the lost-wax process to the manufacture of complex parts for jet engines, sophisticated techniques for casting alloyed steel were developed so the cast steel rivaled the strength of machined steel. It could be heat-treated, tempered, softened, toughened, surface-hardened, or given any number of characteristics desirable in the manufacture of gun parts. In fact, the process was refined so greatly that tough springs could be made by investment casting. In the 1950's, the process was ready and waiting to be discovered by the gun industry. Who would be the first?

Actually, various gunmakers were beginning to take advantage of investment casting as a relatively inexpensive way of making certain complex parts. This was done very quietly because of the prejudice against cast gun parts.

One gunmaker—Sturm, Ruger—liked the idea of investment casting and wasn't afraid to say so. They had found that the process was an excellent way to manufacture the frame and grip straps of their revolvers, and in the early 1960's Ruger manufactured some major action compo-

After filling and cooling, the ceramic molds are stacked on racks and taken to a cleaning room such as this, where the ceramic will be removed from the steel.

To remove the casting, the "tree" is placed in an impact cabinet where the brittle ceramic coating is shattered. The steel parts in the foreground still bear clinging bits of ceramic which will be removed afterward.

What began as a "tree" of wax moldings is now a "tree" of steel rifle receivers. The connecting gates are still in place on the "trees" seen here, and ceramic fragments have not yet been cleaned away.

nents, including the receiver of the new No. 1 Single-Shot rifle, by the investment-casting technique. If you've ever marveled at the gracefully curved operating lever of the No. 1, you should know that the complex form is made by lost-wax casting. Not only did Ruger admit that they used investment casting, the company gloried in it and took pride in the advances they made with the ancient process. The Model 77 Ruger bolt rifle, their over/under shotgun, and the Mini-14 rifle, as well as their line of handguns, utilize investment castings for many major parts.

Since almost every firearm Ruger introduces is an unqualified success, there is no doubt that cast guns are now well accepted by the gun-loving public. In Europe the situation is much the same. Ruger guns are sought after, and a number of the great European gunmakers have adopted the lost-wax system. So if you decide on investment casting as the best, least expensive way of producing your new rifle, you'll be in good company.

THE COURSE OF MODERN TECHNOLOGY

Since World War II, the gun industry, spurred by ever intensifying competition at home and from abroad, has undergone a series of revolutionary changes in production methods. During

Amid a shower of sparks, a workman uses an abrasive wheel to saw apart each steel "tree."

Racks of gun parts await heat treatment in huge furnaces. This process will produce a molecular alignment necessary for maximum toughness, hardness, and wear-resistance.

An inspector tests a Ruger Model 77 receiver for dimensional uniformity. In the background are racks of these receivers. Gun parts are inspected repeatedly during all phases of manufacture.

the late 1940's, the trend was toward simple, round, easily machined shapes typified by the Remington M-721 and M-722. In the late 1950's and through the 1960's, investment casting became popular because it permitted the more traditional, gracefully complex gun forms to be produced at relatively low cost.

But then tape-controlled and computer-controlled machinery was developed, and we have come full circle. Once again, lathes and milling machines are carving blocks of steel into delicately graceful gun components just as they did in 1886. The difference is that the levers, wheels, and cranks are now controlled by electric impulses that guide the cutters to accuracy within thousandths of an inch. The machines do their work with such speed that machine work that took hours in 1936 is now accomplished in minutes or even seconds. In a pleasant little plant tucked away in a wooded Boston suburb, a series of alloy-steel blocks are clamped into an incredibly complicated machine, and a button is pushed. After a series of delicate, computer-controlled cuts, the blocks of steel are removed. They are now the finished receivers of Model 70 Winchester rifles. The parts were made so fast and with so little use of human hands that it cost only a few dollars to produce them. The machine itself is enormously expensive, however, and therein lies the chief expense of production. The key to ultimate economy, though, is that the machine can make thousands of receivers in a short time, and it doesn't care who pushes its start button. At last, skilled hands are truly replaced by wonderfully skilled machines at a competitive cost.

Thus, another new manufacturing possibility is open to you and your wonderful new rifle. Quality need not be compromised by cost, and beauty won't be sacrificed on the altar of necessity. You can have it all. You can build the most beautifully stylish rifle of all time. The techniques exist. There is only one thing that modern technology cannot do, and that is capture the hearts of gun buyers with a stylish, artistically graceful rifle. Great guns are the fruits of great designers. That is entirely up to you.

Like Longellow's "Organ of Guns," racks of Ruger Model 77 barreled actions, now blued and with bolts fitted, await the fitting of stocks.

Chapter 3

TODAY'S RIFLES—HOW GOOD?

Are modern rifles as good as their makers would have us believe? Do they reflect up-to-the-minute technology? Are they as accurate as they could be, and are they as safe as they should be? Are today's rifles produced in an engineering vacuum where output is more important than quality and profit more desirable than style? Have we really retrogressed since, say, the introduction of the 1898 Mauser, and has good taste in design been cast aside in favor of gaudy gimmicks? And does today's rifle buyer really care?

These are important questions that deserve careful answers, and some of them embody serious charges that demand explanations.

PRODUCT LIABILITY

From the viewpoint of nearly all American rifle makers, especially the big companies, the most important consideration is safety. Safety means sufficient mechanical strength to withstand the pressures of high-intensity cartridges, and also includes triggers, safety mechanisms, and related features that are intended to be proof against misuse. These concerns about misuse have resulted from an incredible series of legal actions taken against firearms manufacturers.

In Alaska a few years ago, a man managed to shoot himself in the leg while fooling around with his loaded revolver. Though the damage to his person was not permanent, and the accident was purely the result of the plaintiff's carelessness and in no way due to a mechanical malfunction, the jury awarded him millions of dollars. A young Texas hunter, who did not understand the function of his rifle and apparently had not even the vaguest knowledge of firearms safety, shot his father in the spine, causing paralysis, while attempting to unload a rifle *in a vehicle!* Again, a jury awarded a vast sum out of pity for the family and because they felt the gunmaker should pay. The list of such cases grows, and virtually all gunmakers have been involved. Of course, the insurance companies pay the damages, but with each claim and each courtroom case—won or lost—the cost of liability coverage creeps higher. Ultimately, it is the gun buyer who really pays the bill. At present, several dollars of the price of each new gun is earmarked for liability protection. Apparently, this trend will continue and can even become worse if judges and juries continue to award gigantic sums in cases where firearms misuse rather than mechanical failure is the culprit.

These court actions have forced gunmakers into a defensive position in design and development. I know of new and exciting firearms that will never make it out of research and development departments simply because of design features that improve performance and handling ease but might also be subject to human misuse.

My files are filled with letters from lovers of the old pre-1964 Model 70 Winchester action, bemoaning the fact that Winchester won't abandon the current design and go back to the earlier version. Even if the head men at Winchester (now U.S. Repeating Arms Company) wanted to do so, they couldn't because it could conceivably make the company vulnerable to a torrent of legal actions. The current Model 70 has a number of built-in features that make it at least theoretically safer than the Model 70's built before 1964. If the company went back to the older style it would be publicly abandoning certain *known* safety features. This is certainly not to say that the old Model 70 was unsafe. In fact, it was wonderfully rugged. It's just that every new or improved rifle must take advantage of state-of-the-art safety engineering or it will be attacked by those lawyers who are always looking for grounds on which to base multi-million-dollar liability suits.

LOCK-DOWN BOLTS

A very good example of the defensive posture of gunmakers will be evident over the coming years with regard to lock-down bolt handles.

As anyone who has ever messed with bolt-action centerfire rifles knows, when the safety catch is in the on position, the bolt handle is locked down. There are fairly good reasons for this feature from both the military and sporting viewpoints. Many sportsmen favor the locked bolt because brush could snag an unlocked bolt and open the action, which might dump a cartridge on the ground.

Most modern bolt rifles, I suspect, have bolt catches built into their safeties for no better reason than tradition. Tradition dies hard in the gun industry, even when the original purpose of a given design feature has been forgotten. Over the past several years, any number of gunmakers have asked me to explain the advantages of a safety-locking bolt handle and have been amazed to learn that the reasons aren't all that important.

A bolt catch linked to the safety mechanism has a weak point. For a moment between the time when the bolt closes and the safety is engaged, the rifle is loaded, cocked, and in the *fire* mode. When unloading, it's also true that the safety must be switched to the fire position before the bolt can be opened. Under almost any conceivable circumstances, all this is of no consequence whatever. Yet, at least one serious injury resulted from improper use of such a mechanism. In rational times, such incidents would be properly blamed on the person or persons who obviously acted unsafely, but these are not rational times. Guns, not the misusers of guns, are being unfairly blamed for accidents, causing the makers of guns to revolutionize their thinking in regard to accidental gun misuse. So, future bolt-action rifles will most likely feature safety mechanisms that do *not* lock the bolt handle closed. This very cautious engineering philosophy will dominate gun manufacture for years to come. It will make rifles safer but hopefully not at the expense of accuracy, convenience, and performance.

THE FOOLPROOF SAFETY

Speaking of safeties, I've often wondered if a truly foolproof safety can ever be designed. Most safety mechanisms are good, and some are marvels of design that have measured up to the test of time. The weak point is human. One of the most reliable safety mechanisms ever designed is the old Model 98 tab, or "wing," safety that blocks the striker. It is hard to imagine such a safety failing, yet I've seen it happen a couple of times. Actually, the mechanism didn't fail. The shooters, being excited or agitated at the time, flicked the wing to OFF when they were also pulling the trigger!

My thoughts about rifle safeties invariably lead me back to Lew Games, a professional African hunter. Lew habitually carries a bolt rifle with a round in the chamber with the striker down. Games, who has survived elephant stampedes and savage lion attacks, is fearful of rifle safeties and prefers to bypass them altogether. After loading his rifle and feeding a cartridge into the chamber, he grasps the bolt handle firmly, pulls the trigger, and gently lowers the bolt handle. With the sear released, the striker rides slowly down the cocking cam so that the firing pin comes to rest on the primer. The rifle is loaded and ready to fire, except that it is not cocked. Therefore, no amount of accidental trigger pulling or safety failure will allow it to fire.

As you might suspect, having the firing pin at rest on a live primer is not entirely safe either, but it is safer than it sounds because a sharp blow of the firing pin is required to activate a primer. Still, I feel that if the rifle were dropped at the right angle on a hard surface, it just might go off. Lew and I have argued this point repeatedly, but he steadfastly maintains that his system is safer than relying on a mechanical safety, especially in his case where the rifle is often handled by gun bearers. When he anticipates a shot, Lew simply flicks the bolt handle up and down. Quicker than the eye can follow, the sear catches the striker and he's ready to fire.

Though I don't agree with Games's method, which is also used by any number of African professionals, I do think he's got a good basic idea regarding rifle safeties. I've often considered carrying the idea a step further by designing a two-piece striker/firing-pin arrangement working on an inertia system. Thus, even with the rifle uncocked and the striker down, the firing pin would not be pressing on the primer. It's something to think about.

TRIGGERS

Many of today's rifles have truly wonderful triggers. They are safe and reliable and when properly adjusted, they permit excellent shot control. But what is "proper adjustment?" Ah, there's the rub, and an explanation is in order. America's early hunters and shooters, especially those of the early 1800's, were very much aware of the importance of a fine trigger pull to good marksmanship. Our first rifles, the Jaeger-style rifles built by German immigrants, frequently featured single- or double-set triggers that fired at the lightest twitch of a finger. During the first half of the last century, these hair triggers were so common that very few sporting rifles were made without them.

However, set triggers went out of style after the 1860's because they did not adapt especially well to the new breechloading repeaters. In Europe, especially Austria, Germany, and Switzerland, set triggers remained popular even after the development of repeating rifles, but American gunmakers gravitated to simple mechanisms that were reliable though difficult to pull. This trend was reinforced by the prevalence of American military-influenced target-shooting rules that specified rather heavy minimum poundage on the triggers of smallbore as well as big-bore target rifles. This was in direct contrast to European target rules which permitted, and thereby encouraged, light trigger pulls. Very little effort was made in U.S. to manufacture really good triggers until the 1950's. Even before the 1950's, however, the growth of varmint shooting as a sport and the development of varmint rifles as an industry began to

Set triggers were common on the better rifles made during the first half of the 19th century. This percussion rifle in the author's collection has a double set trigger.

create a demand for better triggers than those available on over-the-counter rifles. This fostered an accessory trigger industry, which flowered during the 1950's and '60's. These separate trigger mechanisms could be installed in almost any bolt rifle. What with all the World War II trophy rifles being converted to sporters, plus the Springfields, Enfields, and commercial rifles in need of better, lighter, crisper, more adjustable triggers, such names as Canjar, Mashburn, Jaeger, Timney, Dayton-Traister, etc., became household words.

Recognizing the demand for better triggers, especially mechanisms that could be easily adjusted to suit the desires of owners, more and more manufacturers offered post-World War II rifles with improved triggers. This is not to say that all triggers were changed. The mechanism of the Winchester Model 70 bolt gun was by any odds the best design of the pre-war era because it was reliable, consistent, and moderately adjustable. It was so good that the new Model 70 of 1964 and thereafter features a similar mechanism. But another post-war rifle, the Savage Model 110 bolt gun, wins all honors for the worst, hardest to pull, improvement-resistant trigger mechanism. It took its lead, no doubt, from the same company's Model 99 lever rifle, another tug of war.

By the 1970's, a good percentage of U.S.-made rifles did incorporate really good adjustable trigger mechanisms. Remington even offered a snappy two-ounce-pull model for the super-accurate Model 40-X rifles, a virtually unprecedented act among major American arms makers. All in all, the trigger picture was so good that American shooters became complacent and took adjustable triggers for granted. But then the legal ax fell and in obedience to orders from upstairs, the trigger pulls of American rifles and handguns started getting heavier. The trend continues. The better U.S.-made bolt-action rifles, rimfire as well as centerfire, still feature excellent trigger *designs,* but you'd scarcely know it by picking a new gun off a dealer's rack and snapping the trigger a couple of times. Most are set and sealed at the factory to a letoff weight of five pounds or more in an effort to avoid accidental misuse. If the owner wants a lighter pull, he has the option of adjusting the mechanism to an easier letoff, but this, as I see it, poses a dilemma for the manufacturer. Any trigger that can be adjusted or altered (they *all* can be in some way) can be improperly adjusted. The most frequent improper adjustment is to set the sear points with too little contact and thereby create a "slip-off" condition that might cause the gun to fire if the bolt is slammed hard. Thus, a trigger that was deliberately set to ultra-safe specifications at the factory becomes unsafe in the hands of a home tinkerer. Would it not be safer in the long run to adjust the trigger to a minimum but *safe* pull at the factory so that the owner will not be tempted to mess with it? (For more on triggers and how they work, see Chapter 6, *Triggering a Revolution.*)

EXTRACTION AND EJECTION

One of the most frequently criticized design features of today's rifles is the countersunk bolt face with enclosed extractor and ejector. No one objects to the idea of the countersunk bolt face itself because the safety advantages of surrounding the cartridge head with steel are self-apparent. The criticisms center around related case extraction and ejection mechanisms. They simply don't look very efficient or reliable.

The Winchester Model 70 trigger mechanism (top) had far and away the best design of the pre-World War II era, and it was retained in the new M-70 made in 1964 and thereafter. By the 1970's, Remington was offering a match-quality trigger (bottom) that could be adjusted to a two-ounce pull for the super-accurate Model 40-X rifles.

If you inspect the bolt of a Remington Model 700, for example, you'll see that the extractor is just a little flange-like hook made of bent steel. It's a tiny thing that doesn't appear to be capable of extracting a greased gumdrop from a baby's mouth, much less yanking a tightly wedged case from a rifle's chamber. The ejector is a small-diameter plunger housed in the bolt face and powered by a coil spring. When the bolt is closed on a round, the plunger is compressed and maintains steady forward pressure on the case. When the bolt is drawn rearward, the ejector plunger snaps the case out of the receiver port.

The reason the extractor *looks* inefficient is because it is so tiny in comparision to the oversize extractors we're accustomed to seeing on older bolt-action rifles. Most of us equate strength with size, and the little Remington extractor seems puny. But rather than compare extraction systems by size only, it's a lot wiser to compare them in terms of how they operate. Though it is seldom realized, the Remington Model 700 extractor is a lot like a Chinese finger prison in that the more pressure is exerted on it, the tighter it holds.

Here is a revealing comparison of bolt faces and extractors. At far left is a Mauser Model 98 bolt with the oversize extractor common to older bolt-actions. Next to it is an old Winchester Model 70 bolt; note the similarity of its extractor. Second from right is the currently produced M-70 bolt, which has an enclosed face, smaller extractor, and plunger-type ejector much like that of the Remington 700 seen at far right. The Remington has a tiny extractor in a totally enclosed face that has no cuts whatever—the famous Remington "ring-of-steel" bolt face. Supported by the strength of the bolt itself, the extractor needs no more strength and cannot spring away from the cartridge rim.

Let's look at extractors another way. When a traditional Mauser-type extractor lets go and fails to pull a stuck case out of the chamber, it's usually because it springs outward and slips over the case rim. Of course, this seldom happens, but I've experienced it several times with virtually every existing action type having an external leaf-type extractor. Fortunately, this never happened at a critical time. It always occurred when I had faulty ammo or when I was fooling around with some overly hot handloads at the test bench. By comparision, the Remington 700 extractor and similar systems can't easily override the cartridge rim. Being supported by the steel wall formed by the countersink, it can't spring away from the case. The Remington extractor doesn't need to be any stronger because it is supported by the tremendous strength of the bolt itself. Because the extractor can't back over the case rim, it has no choice but to hang on.

Tiring of all the amateur complaints they were getting about their miniature extractor, some engineers at Remington Arms concocted an empirical tug-of-war test between a standard Model 98 Mauser extractor and their Model 700. A steel rod was lathe-turned to cartridge diameter, with rims turned on each end. These rims were fitted into each bolt under the extractor in the way a cartridge rim fits. The bolts were fixtured into a giant laboratory instrument used to measure tensile strength. In a simple tug of war, the machine ran the pressure on each extractor up to hundreds and then thousands of pounds. Even the steel rod connecting the two extractor systems began to stretch, but then the Mauser extractor let go. The Remington extractor was victorious.

I didn't witness the test, but I did see movies of the event, and it was certainly impressive. While it left no doubt about the strength of the Remington system, the test may have been somewhat misleading. Had a brass rather than a steel rod connected the two bolts, the softer brass rim probably would have been torn away. Since the Remington extractor claw grasps less brass than the Mauser system, the rim in the Remington bolt might have failed first. In any event, there is no reason to doubt the strength of the Remington system. My own experience with Remington rifles bears this out because I've never had a failure. I have, however, had cases stuck so tight that I couldn't open the bolt; even after pounding on the bolt handle, the extractor did not let go.

The Remington-style plunger ejector is used on a number of modern bolt-action rifles. Like the tiny Remington extractor, it is subject to a number of criticisms. It looks too cheap, too easy to make, too easy to install. Even though cheap and easy is synonymous with good engineering, we shooters like our equipment to be composed of expensive parts, and if considerable labor is expended in their installation, all the better. Another complaint is that the plunger pushes the cartridge away from the bolt face until the bolt is pushed fully forward. The disadvantage here, it is claimed, is that the extractor therefore doesn't engage the rim until the bolt is completely closed. I'm not exactly sure why this qualifies as a serious complaint, but it comes up from time to time.

A more reasonable criticism of spring-loaded plunger ejectors, in my view, is that the plunger is applying hard pressure to the cartridge case as it is *withdrawn*. This pressure, pivoted at the extractor, causes the case to rub against the side of the chamber and then slap hard against the receiver when the case clears the chamber. This bothers me because sometimes a sharp corner inside the receiver snags the case and cuts a thin scratch in the brass. Most owners of such rifles haven't even noticed this, and very few care, except for a handful of painstaking handloaders who don't like scratched cases.

Another complaint lodged against plunger ejectors is the need for a hole in the bolt face in which to house the plungers. It is said this leaves a portion of the cartridge case head without support. What keeps this from being a valid criticism is that the small unsupported area of brass happens to be in the thickest and hardest part of the entire cartridge case. If indeed enough gas pressure were to be generated to blow out this small area of the case head, the rest of the case would have previously melted, disintegrated, or been blown to kingdom come along with most of the rifle.

As a matter of fact, I have completely removed the plunger ejectors from some of my special-purpose varmint and target rifles, leaving only an empty hole in the bolt face. I do this so the case won't be thrown out or scratched as described above. If I figured there was any danger whatever I wouldn't do it.

The most serious and valid charge against plunger ejectors as employed on modern rifles of various makes is that they can and do fail under certain circumstances. This usually happens in one of three ways. It happens when the cartridge rim is oversize and wedges tightly in the countersunk bolt recess. It can also happen if the bolt recess is packed with grit and debris that wedges itself around the rim. I've never had either of these two types of failures, but I have experienced a third type on several occasions. These failures happened when I was experimenting with extremely high-pressure handloads that were so hot that the primer pocket was blown open and the entire case head was considerably expanded. Under this excessive pressure, the case rim and head were so tightly kneaded into the bolt face that the ejector could not begin to function. The paradox here is that I fully expected violent case-head expansion, and the reason I elected to use an action of the Remington type was because of its superior strength.

Another paradox is the number of African trippers who say they would never use a rifle with a plunger ejector to hunt dangerous game. No hunter's so expert as one who has been to Africa once or twice. The amusing thing about such opinions is that the automatic ejectors on the vaunted double rifles, so often touted as the most reliable African rifles of all, are *spring-powered plungers!*

Ejectors of the Mauser type are indeed capable of exerting the most powerful and positive ejection force on a stubborn case. You can make the ejection as forceful or gentle as you wish simply by moderating or increasing the force with which you manipulate the bolt. If the case proves especially sticky, you can keep banging at it until you force it to pop out. Why then, you ask, don't all bolt rifles incorporate manual ejectors of Mauser persuasion?

The reason takes us to the very crux of today's design philosophy, especially in regard to action strength or "unit integrity." In order to get a clear idea of what this means, compare a Model 98 Mauser bolt, typical of the manual extraction system, to, say, a Remington Model 700 bolt, which is the archetype of the plunger system. If you've never noticed it before, the deep cut running through the left lug and continuing through the bolt face on the Mauser bolt will immediately catch your eye. The ejector passes through this cut. The lugs of the Model 700 have no such cut, and the bolt face forms an unbroken wall around the case head. If there were any Mauser-style cuts or openings in the Remington bolt, its design integrity would be lost. This is not to say that the strength of the Mauser is inadequate. It is adequate but it's just not in the same class with the more modern Remington design. It is pretty obvious that firearms designers really don't have much choice in this matter. Once a high level of integrity has been achieved, no one can back away from it.

There seem to be a few souls who don't understand the strength principles involved or don't care. A case in point is the industrious gunsmith — there may have been several — who advertised an "improvement" in the Remington M-700. For a fee, he would cut away part of the bolt-face wall and install an extractor from, as I recall, an M-16. Of course, he was playing on, and profiting from, rumors about the M-700's poor extractor. What he was really doing was critically reducing the integrity of the original design. He was also installing an extractor that is inferior to the original.

TODAY'S LOOK

Military historians say that the talents and tactics of General Robert E. Lee obsessed his wartime opponents. The same might be said of the way William Batterman Ruger dominates trends among designers of sporting arms. No one, not even among his most determined competitors, doubts the brilliance of his designs, yet he seems to succeed by doing the plainly obvious. How does a gunmaker find this plainly obvious path?

One way, or so it would seem, is simply to go forth across the land and ask shooters what kind of guns they want to buy. If a potential customer is given a voice in what his next gun will look like, surely he will be pleased with the results, won't he?

Several years ago, during a big trade show, a major arms maker gathered together a host of gun writers. After appropriate libations, they were shown a variety of stock design revisions that were being considered for a rifle of long-standing popularity. After mulling the matter over for a while, the gun writers were pretty much unanimous in their vote for one of the designs. Later, some top sporting-goods distributors were called in and asked to give their opinions of the proposed stock changes. The concerted opinion of the distributors differed greatly from that of the writers. Since distributors buy guns by the thousands, their opinion was taken to heart by the manufacturer, and the new stock was offered in their image. It was a total, unmitigated, and instant flop.

Quite possibly the stock design favored by the writers would have failed as well, but that's not the point. Where the manufacturer went wrong was in trying to design a gun by committee. The mechanical design of a firearm is applied engineering science, but the *shape* of a rifle is unquestionably an art form. Great rifles are great art, and great art is never achieved by committee. Goya, Picasso, El Greco, Dali, Michelangelo, Rembrandt, and Leonardo da Vinci were great artists, but if they could have pooled their talents on a single canvas the result would have been terrible.

Sometimes committee designs fail because the goal is not clearly established at the outset because the manufacturer doesn't know how to ask the right questions or can't interpret the answers. During the early 1970's, a major American gunmaker set out to design, once and for all, the great American autoloading shotgun. Nothing was to be spared in its design, development, and manufacture. To this end, teams of survey takers armed with reams of questionnaires met with sportsmen's groups across the country in an effort to discover what features were most desired.

The most universally desired features were then incorporated into the gun's configuration, and it was presented to the world in a blaze of publicity. Mechanically, it was one of the finest autoloaders ever manufactured. Stylistically it bombed, and production was discontinued after a few years. I attended the post-mortem and found the company heads in a state of disbelief. "How could it fail?" they wailed. "It had everything they asked for."

"Like what?" I asked.

"They said they wanted engraving, and we gave them engraving."

"The gun wasn't engraved," I observed. "It only had a tacky-looking design die-rolled on the side of the receiver. The question you *should* have asked is whether or not a gun buyer prefers cheap-looking rolled engraving or a plain, blued receiver."

"They wanted an oil-finished stock, and we gave them an oil-finished stock."

"What you gave them was a synthetic finish with a muddy color that only hid the natural beauty of the wood, " I remarked. "You mistook the request for a low-gloss finish to mean dull." And so the conversation went, on and on, the inevitable last rites of a committee-designed product.

When it comes to what features shooters want, I'm reminded of a computerized dating service. The applicant fills out a questionnaire, and a computer matches up couples according to their stated preferences. Yet computer match-ups are no more successful than blind luck. Shooters, like potential lovers, seldom know what they want until they see it. That's why the goal of a gunmaker is to capture the imaginations of rifle lovers and not be a slave to their stated wishes. Bill Ruger once summed it up perfectly: "A manufacturer who doesn't instinctively know what his guns should look like shouldn't be in the business."

Despite my critisism, I realize that the route to superior rifle design is fraught with blind curves and unexpected perils. In the course of design evolution, a manufacturer does not accomplish his objective in a single bound.

Some very interesting factors come to light when we compare today's rifles with those of the pre-World War II era. European rifles of that time were notably more attractive than those made in America. At the time when Germany's great Mauser sporters and Austria's exquisitely detailed Mannlichers were being built, rifle making in the U.S. was hallmarked by a general blandness. Now we have come full circle. The best American rifles in terms of engineering, performance, and appearance are vastly superior to Europe's finest efforts. This is largely because European rifle makers desperately want to sell their products in America and therefore cater to what they perceive as American tastes. Almost invariably, they only succeed in copying the worst features of American rifles. That's why today's European look in imports is a catchall of humpbacked combs, racy fore-end tips, flared gripcaps, white spacers, and glossy varnish. Shades of U.S.A., 1957!

While European riflemakers pursue the American dream, manufacturers here in the U.S. have lately made steady progress toward offering rifles that look almost as good as they shoot. The decade of the 1960's was for some manufacturers a series of stylistic blind alleys. Remington's M-700 is a good example of mediocre styling, and the 1964 Winchester exemplifies even worse stock design. But perhaps the fact that they were willing to experiment, to break

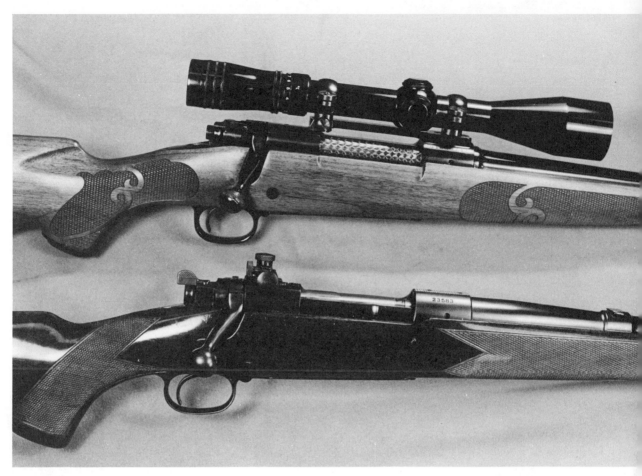

Here are an old and a new Model 70 Winchester. At top is the currently produced Featherweight version, and below it a pre-World War II M-70. Note the differences in action configuration as well as in the stocks.

away from the stylistic prison of the 1930's, was our first glimmering of hope. Given this desire to change, the only missing element was a clear conception of what good styling was all about. Take a look at the current Winchester Model 70 Featherweight, Remington's M-700 Classic, H&R's Model 340, Ruger's single-shot and bolt rifles. Obviously, the pieces are falling into the right places.

LOST IN THE CROWD

This discourse has dwelt mainly on bolt-action rifles. I confess to being an elitist about rifles. Most firearms authors are. Therefore, my thoughts naturally turn to bolt rifles during discus-

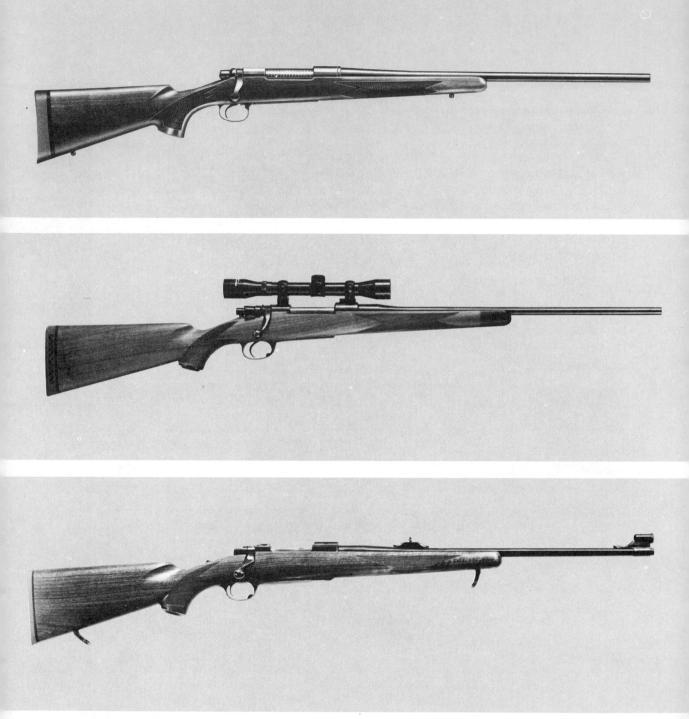

Like the Winchester Model 70 Featherweight, these three rifles are in production at the time of this writing and exemplify the stylistic improvements made in recent years. These bolt-action rifles, which look almost as good as they shoot, are (from top): the Remington Model 700 Classic, the Harrington & Richardson Model 340, and the Ruger Model 77.

sions of accuracy, performance, and beauty. But I'm not as much of a snob as some. A while back, I received a series of letters from some guy in Connecticut who insisted on letting me know that he is a perfect sportsman because he uses a single-shot rifle and that anyone who uses a lever, pump, or autoloading rifle is a low-life, a game violator, and shouldn't be allowed in the woods with decent sportsmen such as himself. To top off his tirade, he enclosed a photograph of himself with what is surely the smallest nubbin-horned pronghorn ever bagged in Wyoming. I wrote back, congratulating him on his fine marksmanship and pointing out that anyone who could hit a pronghorn that small could probably hit a gopher at the same yardage. I also suggested that if he has any sons, he should—please—let them hunt with someone else, preferably someone who uses a fast-firing repeater.

Another time I got a whole sack of mail following publication of a column in OUTDOOR LIFE in which I described a series of accuracy tests I had conducted with fast-firing repeaters.

In accuracy tests of two dozen fast-firing repeaters, the author punched tightly grouped bullet holes through the myth that only bolt-actions and single-shots are acceptably accurate and reliable. He fired 100 rounds in five-shot strings through each rifle at 100 yards. Not one rifle—lever, pump, or auto—malfunctioned. Average group size for all lever-actions was 3.53 inches, a very respectable average for big game rifles. Shown here are two of the traditional lever guns (from top): Winchester Model 94 and Marlin Model 336.

Some readers apparently refused to believe that any lever, pump, or autoloading rifle was capable of the accuracy I reported. One fellow in particular insisted that I "document" my report, but I never could figure out exactly what he meant. Clearly, though, he believed that only bolt-action rifles and perhaps a few single-shots are capable of respectable accuracy. He wasn't about to have his notions shaken by simple facts.

In truth, fast-shooters do indeed get a bum rap, and their cause has never been helped much by us gun writers. That's why I got involved in the abovementioned accuracy tests. Though I was concerned only with accuracy, the hundreds of rounds fired during the course of my tests also amounted to a critical appraisal of functional reliability. At the end of the test program, I realized that *not one rifle had malfunctioned a single time!*

I tested two dozen makes and models, including autoloaders, pumps, and lever-action rifles. My procedure was designed to test them the same way bolt-action target and varmint rifles are usually tested for accuracy. I used a benchrest with proper equipment, good ammo, high-magnification scopes, and benchrest-type targets. Each rifle was fired 100 rounds in five-shot strings, and all testing was done at the standard 100 yards. The shooting took a week, and the firing schedule was staggered so that each rifle was shot every day, and two consecutive five-shot groups were fired with each rifle, so the results would reflect the accuracy of the barrel while cold and while hot. A sidelight of the test was strong evidence that the fast repeaters, with their two-piece stock configuration, have relatively little tendency to change impact as the barrel heats.

The test results were amazing. The average group size for *all* lever rifles lumped together was 3.53 inches. Pumps did even better with an average of 3.20 inches, and autoloaders did best of all with a 2.57-inch average. A little Savage Model 170 pump in .30/30 caliber, which happened to be the least expensive rifle of the lot, stole the show by turning in two groups running

This is the pump-action Savage Model 170—least expensive of the fast-firing repeaters Carmichel tested for accuracy. This model in .30/30 stole the show with an average group size of less than two inches for 20 groups of five shots, fired with both a cold and hot barrel. Two groups measured less than an inch.

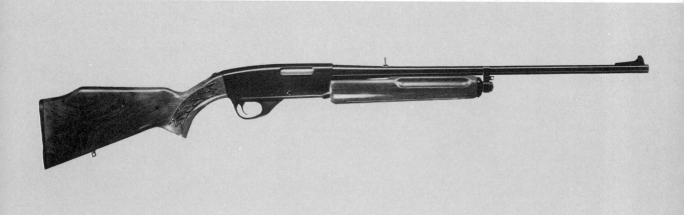

Among the most accurate fast repeaters tested was a .30/06 BAR. This Browning auto produced an average group size close to an inch in 20 strings of five shots. Autoloaders tended to be the best made of all repeaters tested.

under an inch and averaging under two inches for all 20 groups. How many bolt-action big game rifles have you tried that will do as well?

One reason the autoloaders did so well was that they tended to be the best made of all the rifles tested. One of the solid performers was a Browning BAR in .30/06 that was not only easy to shoot but averaged close to an inch in group size. One autoloader I did not include in the tests is my M-1A by Springfield Armory (not the old Government Arsenal). This .308 rifle, which is almost identical to the lately retired M-14 U.S. service rifle except there is no full-automatic selector switch, is a full-blown target rifle complete with heavy barrel capable of groups not much over half an inch. Though this rifle offers irrefutable testimony to the stunning accuracy of which autoloaders are capable, it is not a typical out-of-the-rack hunting rifle. Likewise, in the lever-rifle averages I did not include the performance of a Marlin M-336 in .219 Zipper chambering. Though it is easily capable of one-inch groups with handloads, it is no longer made, and in any event, doesn't qualify as a standard big game rifle.

I am of the opinion that today's fast-shooting repeaters are too often given short shrift by gun writers and similarly disposed self-appointed experts who simply dismiss anything but a bolt gun as a "satisfactory little brush gun for blue-collar deer hunters." This attitude is typified by the various "field reports" we see in shooting magazines. More often than not, an open-sighted rifle is taken right out of the box, fired a few rounds, and reported to be "reliable and accurate—the brush hunter's friend," or something equally inane. A while back, I read such a test report by a very well-known writer in a well-known periodical. A pump-action rifle was taken to task because of its tendency to "blow open" with each shot. Had the action really blown open just once, there would not have been any more shots. What really happened was a common occurrence when firing a centerfire pump-action rifle from a test bench. Upon firing, the shooter's shoulder is snapped back smartly by the rifle's recoil, but recovery is almost instantaneous. This rapid recovery motion shoves the rifle forward, dragging the *unlocked* forearm across the sandbags. In turn, this opens the action partially or totally and may even eject the spent case. The whole cycle of recoil and recovery happens so fast that the shooter doesn't realize what happened. He pulls the trigger and the rifle is lying there on the sandbags with the action open. This is all our revered gun writer was experiencing, but he reported that his test rifle blew open. His conclusion was that the caliber was "too powerful for the rifle's mechanism," and thus he badly misinformed thousands of readers. That's one of the problems facing today's quick-shooter. Too many gun writers simply don't bother to find out how, and how well, the rifles work, and why.

That's why the accuracy and mechanical excellence of many of today's fast repeaters, especially the autoloaders, remains largely unknown. This is particularly sad because much of today's very best firearms engineering is invested in the quick-shooters. But by the same token, it would appear that the makers of many, indeed most, lever-action, pump, and autoloading repeaters don't fully appreciate their own products.

Perhaps this problem is best typified by Browning's BAR autoloader. One has only to briefly handle and inspect the BAR to become aware that its designers were proud of what they were doing and wanted to provide the best-possible rifle. The wood is good, the checkering is well executed, and the stock configuration is comfortable and handsome. The feel and shooting characteristics of the BAR are much like those of a well-designed bolt rifle. But contrast the BAR's configuration with almost any other of today's quick repeaters and the differences in design philosophy, or rather lack of philosophy, are blatantly apparent. Some stocks are woefully out of date, and attempts to adapt them to modern tastes often make the situation worse. A case in point is today's Savage Model 99 lever-action rifle. As originally offered, the old 99 had one of the most graceful profiles ever created. The problem arose because the original stock had too much drop at comb and heel, even for open-sight shooting. Naturally, the old stock was all but impossible for efficient scope use. Over the years, Savage has attempted to compensate by reshaping the stock with modifications such as pistol grips and Monte Carlo combs. These alterations were attempts to heal the symptom without considering its real cause. What was and is needed is a complete redesign. This would be especially easy with the M-99 because the

Here the author tests Browning's excellent BAR, an autoloader with a handsome and comfortable stock configuration. Unlike some other repeaters, it has the feel and shooting characteristics of a good bolt-action.

action is closed with no protruding parts during the ejection cycle. Thus there are no limitations on the stock design possibilities.

Much the same can be said for Remington's post-war pump and autoloading centerfire rifles. Their problem, though, has been an endless quest to make what amounts to a shotgun stock look like a rifle stock. The forms this has taken range from the clumsy to the bizarre. Only halting progress has been made, even with the Model 4 and Model 6, Remington's latest. If the stock design is basically bad, no amount of "improvement" will make it significantly better. The only way is to start over and, if necessary, reshape the lines of the receiver in order not to be trapped into trying to correct its awkward shape. The deep curve of the Savage M-99 receiver, for example, precludes a graceful grip curve in today's context. All a designer really has to do is look at the Browning BAR stock to see how easily it can be done. If and when the stock configuration of today's fast-firing sporting rifles catches up to their mechanical excellence, the guns will be more appealing and more shootable, and they will achieve a new status among "elitist" shooters.

TODAY'S RIFLE BARRELS

A century ago, the accuracy of a rifle was considered to be almost entirely dependent on its barrel. The consensus was that if a rifle with a good barrel was loaded properly and aimed well, it just had to be accurate. Accordingly, if the rifle did not prove to be a good shooter, the blame fell entirely on the barrel. Mechanical wizards who could make accurate barrels became living legends. Even today, the names of some of the great ones—Pope, Schoyen, Scholck, Billinghurst, James, etc.—are still very much alive in shooting literature.

With the coming of the self-contained cartridge and repeating rifles, however, the emphasis switched to firepower. During the first half of the 20th century, rifle accuracy floundered. This is certainly not to say that there were no finely accurate rifles made during this period, for indeed there were, thousands upon thousands—greater numbers than ever before in history. But the rifles that did turn out to be accurate were largely an accident of large numbers. During this period, shooters and manufacturers were not fascinated by accuracy. Surprisingly, even the target games of that era placed relatively little emphasis on accuracy.

During the period following the Civil War and continuing to the outbreak of the World War I, a premium had been placed on rifle accuracy and individual marksmanship. Remember, this was the era of the great Creedmoor target matches and several other forms of target shooting that called for the best in shooting equipment. This was the era in which C.W. Rowland, using single-shot rifles, attained a level of accuracy that would not be surpassed until *after* World War II.

One of the reasons for the decline of accuracy was patriotic outrage against German-American shooting clubs during the Great War. These shooting groups had been the backbone of American target shooting and target-rifle building. When the clubs were forced to disband, many forms of target shooting disappeared. With few customers for fine target rifles, the craft more or less died away. To prove this point, consider the large number of great barrelmakers who plied their art *before* World War I, and the equally large number who earned wonderful reputations *after* World War II. How many great barrelmakers gained fame *between* the wars? There were only a few, notably Buhmiller, Sukalle, and Johnson.

Another reason for the decline of accuracy was the spread of military-type target shooting. These games were developed to demonstrate the flexibility and rapid-fire characteristics of the 1903 Springfield. Naturally, rapid-fire events became part of every tournament, as did shooting from a variety of positions. The rifles used in these new competitions were as accurate as practical considerations would allow, but they were not in the class with the wonderful single-shots

Between the two World Wars, the spread of military-style matches—involving rapid-fire events and shooting from a variety of positions—contributed little to the development of greater accuracy. The military match rifles used in these competitions, though reasonably accurate, were not in a class with the single-shots of the previous generation. Shown here is a military-style match in progress at Camp Perry.

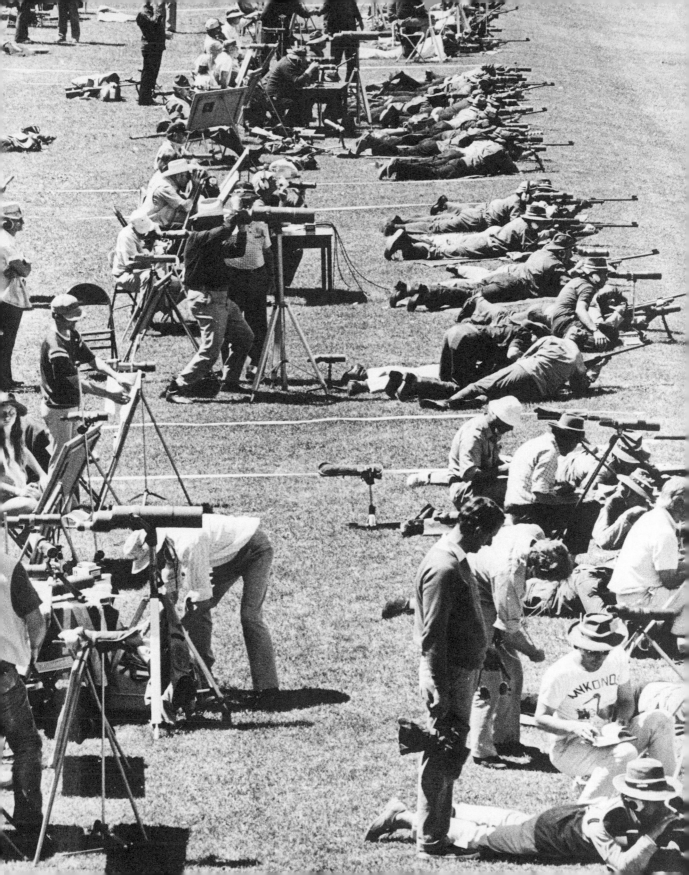

of the previous generation. If a Springfield match rifle happened to be accurate, that was fine, but if it wasn't, the shooter had to change barrels or rifles until he found one that was. Naturally, with the Springfield setting the pace, there was no need for commercial rifle makers to concern themselves much with improving the accuracy of their sporters. Most were considered good enough.

This situation might still be with us if it had not been for two separate but related developments just after World War II. One of these was the suddenly increased popularity of varmint shooting and the other was a resurgence of an old sport in modern dress—benchrest shooting.

Varmint shooting was and is important to the accuracy of today's rifles because it got shooters *thinking* about accuracy. Prior to World War II most varmint shooting was done by a handful of rifle fanatics. Though vocal, they had only a slight effect on the course of firearms manufacture. Most centerfire rifles made between the wars were sold to big game hunters who placed little premium on fine accuracy. Rifles capable of no better than mediocre or even poor accuracy were completely acceptable. Shooters didn't know what to expect in the way of accuracy and didn't think much about it as long as their rifles could hit a deer or bear at a reasonable distance.

With the post-war boom in varmint hunting, shooters—and riflemakers—developed well-established standards for accuracy. For a rifle to be capable of reliably hitting a crow or prairie dog at 300 yards, it had to be capable of shooting inside a one-inch circle at 100 yards. Thus, today's prevailing standard of 1 MOA (one minute of angle, or one inch at 100 yards) became the more or less official threshold of fine accuracy.

Further, shooters were no longer taking the word of the manufacturer that their rifles were accurate. Aided by telescopic sights of 10X or more, which permitted precise aiming, and super-accurate handloaded ammo, a shooter quickly found out if a given rifle was up to snuff. Rifles that didn't measure up were rejected and their makers suffered the blame.

Nearly all gunmakers resented this kind of investigation into the accuracy of their products and retreated to a defensive position that ultimately proved indefensible. Prior to 1940, riflemakers in the U.S. and elsewhere had grandly advertised the accuracy of their rifles without having a clearcut definition of accuracy. The better rifles were subjected to an accuracy test before shipping, but apparently the standard employed by each manufacturer was so generous that only the worst failed to pass. The manufacturer's accuracy standard was a well guarded secret. My first brush with the in-house accuracy bureaucracy occurred in the 1950's when I was testing a new Winchester Model 70 bull-barreled target rifle in .300 H&H caliber. I worked hard to save the money for this wonderful rifle and fully expected it to deliver the accuracy necessary to win the 1,000-yard target competitions of that era. But accuracy was downright pitiful. Some 100-yard groups ran as big as three inches or even more when fired from a benchrest. That rifle had no chance of grouping inside the 20-inch V-ring of the 1,000-yard targets used then. So I packed the rifle up and sent it back to Winchester along with a sampling of my test targets. I fully expected the rifle to be replaced, rebarreled, or serviced in whatever way needed to earn the title "Model 70 *Target* Rifle." To my surprise and annoyance, the rig was returned with a terse note stating that it fell "within the accuracy standards established by the company." They never told me what their accuracy standards were, but I'll bet a three-shot

Like the increased popularity of varmint shooting, the post-war resurgence of benchrest competition—an old sport in modern dress—spurred a new concentration on accuracy. Heavy bench rifles like that at top, in the unrestricted class, came close to eliminating human error (except in judgment of wind and mirage), thus placing great emphasis on the perfection of the mechanism itself and the ammunition.

group inside five inches would have passed muster. Judging by the tone of their letter, the brass at Winchester at that time didn't appreciate a hick from the hills of Tennessee implying that their premium match rifle was insufficiently accurate.

About then, the ivory tower that riflemakers had erected came tumbling down, torn asunder by hard-nosed varmint shooters who knew what they wanted in accuracy and wouldn't stand for anything less. The reason their demands were so effective was that there were so many of them, each one willing to spend money for a really accurate rifle. The manufacturers who had snubbed the complaints of a few thousand varmint shooters in the 1930's listened attentively to the demands of hundreds of thousands of varmint shooters in the 1950's.

One problem that could have been serious was the general lack of accuracy know-how in the shops of many major riflemakers. Their attitude toward accuracy was that which had prevailed for centuries. It held that accuracy was totally a function of the barrel and it was impossible to make consistently fine barrels.

That's where a new target game called benchrest became of overwhelming importance to the future of the world's rifles. The game started with a handful of shooters, and even today their total numbers wouldn't fill the lunchroom of a modest high school. Yet their influence has been revolutionary because of their systematic identification of the many factors affecting accuracy. Ask the head of a riflemaking concern what he thinks about benchrest shooters and he might tell you they're just a few guys running around with funny-looking rifles, but you can be damn sure his engineering staff has had plenty of sleepless nights trying to figure out why those funny-looking rifles are so wonderfully accurate and how they can capture some of the magic for their own factory rifles.

The bottom line has been production of increasingly accurate rifles and widespread acceptance among rifle manufacturers of the policy that rifle accuracy should meet standards acceptable to the consumer. In 1948, for example, a letter to a riflemaker complaining that one of their top-of-the-line bolt-action rifles would not shoot inside two inches would have met with a bluff response or no answer at all. The same letter today might not produce a helpful response, but you can be sure the person on the other end knows why you're complaining and is sympathetic to your problem.

When I became a firearms writer in the early 1960's, much of my reader mail came from happy shooters who told me about wonderful new-bought rifles capable of plunking five shots within a one-inch circle at 100 yards. Nowadays, only two decades later, I seldom get such joyous letters. Instead, readers tend to write me about accuracy only when a new rifle *won't* group inside an inch. How spoiled we've become!

Today's rifles are highly accurate, and on the average they are more accurate than anyone could have guessed back in 1950. Even so, rifle manufacturers have not yet achieved the holy grail of absolute uniformity in their products.

One might assume that all rifles of a given make, model, and caliber would deliver equal accuracy, but this is far from true. Rifles that appear to be identical often vary notably in accuracy. I've tested rifles out of the same manufacturing run that differed as much as three inches in average group size. This is usually explained by saying that the accuracy variation is due to differences in the respective barrels. Sometimes this is true, but just as often it isn't. Small variations in stock inletting affect accuracy and so does uneven locking-lug contact. I've stripped down some particularly poor performers and found such obvious defects as crossthreading of the barrel and receiver, a tapered barrel shank packed with putty, a warped receiver, action screws too long to tighten fully, and recoil lugs that contacted nothing.

I've found these faults in *expensive* rifles as well as cheap ones, so no manufacturer seems to be immune. Despite the obviousness of these problems, once the gun is taken apart it is difficult to criticize the manufacturer or even the inspectors because the assembly faults are often completely hidden. I suspect that the great majority of manufacturing and assembling errors that lead to poor performance go unnoticed and unreported simply because most rifles end up in the hands of casual, once-a-year deer hunters who aren't all that concerned about accuracy or don't know what to expect from their rifles.

On the other hand, individual rifle accuracy poses a dilemma for manufacturers. Riflemakers want their products to be safe, reliable, and accurate. Safety is built in and tested by firing proof loads before the gun leaves the factory. Functional reliablity is also tested at the factory, but an unreliable performer sometimes does find its way into the field. When a gun is returned to the factory with a complaint about unreliable function, it is thoroughly tested and any necessary corrections are gladly made in almost all cases. When a hunter complains that his rifle is not accurate, however, the problem becomes considerably more sticky, and the manufacturer, because of previous experience, knows he must assume a defensive position. Quite frankly, many complaints about poor accuracy are unjustified. Incorrectly mounted scopes, poor ammo, and most of all, poor shooting are frequent causes of poor accuracy. Though shooting from a solid benchrest may seem easy, some hunters never master the technique and cannot keep their shots inside a four-inch circle even with a very accurate rig.

With all these problems in mind, it is easy to understand why riflemakers don't like to get involved in dialogues with customers about accuracy. To do so would open a floodgate for complaints. Manufacturers find it wiser to keep quiet and alter only those rifles that prove to be wildly inaccurate.

I am certain that we gun writers contribute to consumer unrest and confusion about accuracy with our test reports on rifles. Reading over a batch of such reports, an innocent hunter might get the idea that all rifles are dazzlingly accurate — because few rifles tested fail to crash the magical 1 MOA barrier. I cannot speak for other writers, but for myself, I've almost given up publishing accuracy-test reports on new rifles. My reason is that testing one gun is not enough to provide a fair idea of *average* accuracy. In order to get a reasonable accounting of accuracy of a given make and model, it would be necessary to test at least five rifles, and 10 or more would be better. Most accuracy tests by gun writers involve only one sample rifle.

Even so, I doubt that rifles in the field would measure up to the accuracy reported in published test data. Again, I'm not speaking for other writers, but when I test a rifle for accuracy, I try to give it every possible advantage. Anything less would be unfair to the manufacturer. I use higher-magnification scopes than are normally used in the field. This makes aiming as precise as possible. I also use selected lots of ammunition, and my shooting is done from a benchrest under the best possible conditions. Added to this are years of benchrest-shooting experience. I tend to get the best out of every rifle.

Quite a bit of my mail comes from readers of OUTDOOR LIFE who are about to buy a new hunting rifle and want my opinion about which model is the most accurate. Frequently, I hedge a bit because the question is not easy to answer. If I knew for sure which model is most accurate, I'd happily come out with the facts, regardless of the consequences in advertising sales. The answer I have to give, however, is based on the *likelihood* of a particular model and caliber being accurate. For example, my testing of hunting rifles in .30/06 chambering has indicated that a certain model in this caliber tends to be more accurate on the average than other makes and models. But in another caliber, say 6mm Remington, another rifle tends to be more accurate. Even so, there is always the chance that a rifle buyer, acting on my advice, will go home with the rifle in a thousand that won't shoot inside a bucket.

Prior to World War II, virtually all rifle barrels were rifled by the age-old method of cutting grooves in the barrel wall. Done correctly and carefully, this results in superb rifling, and even today some of our most accurate match-grade barrels are made by custom barrelmakers who use the traditional cut system. But when used for mass manufacture, the old-fashioned cut system is subject to a number of problems, especially variations in dimensions. A rifling-machine operator who is merely putting in his time as an hourly wage earner or who has to keep track of a number of machines isn't likely to turn out a steady stream of perfect barrels with the

The inletting of a stock like this is crucial to performance. Having learned the importance of exact inletting, manufacturers of mass-produced rifles have adopted tape-controlled or electronically controlled cutting machinery that assures consistently precise inletting—hence, better accuracy.

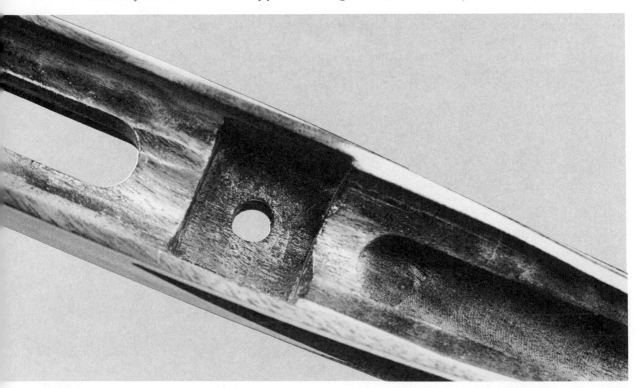

cut-rifling process. One might be two or three thousandths of an inch oversize while the next may be a thousandth or two tight. Naturally, these barrel-to-barrel variations cause variations in accuracy.

Today's barrels, especially those used on mass-produced guns, are usually made by the button or the hammer-forging process described in Chapter One. From the standpoint of accuracy, the advantage of these processes is that they are self-controlling in terms of dimensional uniformity and thereby tend to make up for any lack of interest on the part of the machine operator. This doesn't mean every barrel is flawless, but the barrels do tend to be very, very good, far better than mass-made cut barrels.

Because they are aware of the importance of exact inletting and its effect on accuracy, riflemakers have turned to tape-controlled or electronically controlled stock-inletting machinery. This results in faster production and more precise inletting cuts. Better inletting and better barrel-making techniques have been of overwhelming importance in improving the accuracy of today's rifles.

Today's riflemakers are beginning to put the pieces of the accuracy puzzle together, sometimes with astonishing results. A prime example is Remington's 40-X target rifle. Without question, the 40-X is the most accurate centerfire rifle ever offered by a major arms manufacturer. It is so accurate that it challenges the efforts of the best custom shops.

Such performance was only a dream prior to 1950. It was a happenstance of one lucky rifle in a hundred thousand. Today every rifle that leaves the 40-X shop is a dream come true.

All in all, the rifle of 1940 was a four on a scale of 10. Today, we're averaging close to a seven, and there are some eights already on dealers' shelves.

Chapter 4

. . . .

THE RIFLE STOCK—MORE THAN A HANDLE

. . . .

The single most visible—and recognizable—feature of a sporting rifle is its stock. At 50 paces, long before the details of a rifle's mechanism can be defined, the trained eye determines the make, model, and probably even the vintage of a rifle simply by the line, proportion, and finish of its stock. Lovers of sporting rifles wouldn't have it any other way.

Whereas military rifles tend to be stocked according to specifications set forth by blind men in military bureaucracies, and have all the style of an obese crutch (there *are* some notable exceptions), makers of sporting rifles have recognized for centuries that the soul of a rifle is its stock. It is the stock of a good rifle that first catches our eye. It is the stock that we want to touch, that makes us want to snap the rifle to our shoulder to get the "feel." If the rifle feels awkward and ill balanced, the problem is probably the stock. If it feels lithe and quick in the hand, with the sights true before the eye, the reason is the stock.

Shoulder-fired rifles were still new on the hunting scene when gunmakers singled out the stock as the prime object of their artistic expression. Accordingly, German princes went afield with wheellock rifles of such elaborate stock embellishment that today these firearms reside in the world's great art museums. Wood was carved with exquisite detail and often overlaid with tiles of ivory or bone which, in turn, were incised with delicate hunting scenes.

With the passage of centuries the rifle stock became more businesslike, more attuned to the needs of the marksman, but no less an expression of the maker's artistic urges. In Colonial America, where the wilderness began at the gunsmith's door and survival depended on the

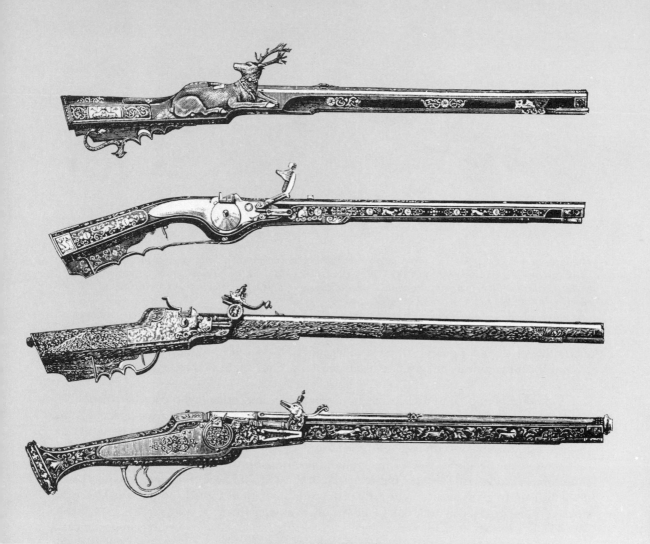

Wheellocks made for sporting use were often lavishly embellished works of art, their stocks intricately carved and inlaid with incised ivory or bone. These stocks tended to be very short, sometimes straight, sometimes dropping sharply. Either way, they were not designed for aiming in the modern sense. These examples are from W.W. Greener's 19th-century classic treatise, The Gun and Its Development.

trueness of a bullet's flight, gunsmiths created stocks of unique character and beauty to grace the deadly long rifle.

Sadly, the industrial age proved to be strangely incompatible with elegant or even good rifle stocks. It was not that good rifle stocks resist being fashioned on mass-production equipment, but because industrialized manufacture was the handmaiden of repeating firearms. The emphasis of rifle design was so intently concentrated on fast firing mechanisms that stocks were little more than an afterthought. Thus began an unfortunate habit that has persisted to the present day. This indifference to sensible stock design among many major riflemakers explains why

Manufacturers of early repeating arms, concentrating on mechanical improvements, failed to incorporate sensible stock design. This Winchester Model 1873 sporter in deluxe grade has an unusual feature, a pistol grip instead of the standard straight grip, and the wood is beautifully figured, but the stockmaker gave the comb and heel enough drop to impede aiming and exaggerate recoil.

such otherwise revolutionary rifles as the legendary Model 1873 Winchester bore stocks of miserable configuration and unshootable dimensions. The trait has yet to be bred out of the industry.

I've never been able to understand how gunmakers and others who consider themselves experts on shooting matters can be so concerned about proper shotgun fit while at the same time be totally oblivious to the necessity of good rifle stocking. To be sure, the dimensions of a shotgun's stock *are* more critical than those for a rifle, because the shotgun must be stocked so that it automatically points where the shooter looks. By contrast, the rifleman may consciously adapt himself to his rifle's stock. But why should the rifleman need to adapt? It would be no more difficult to manufacture a correctly fitting rifle stock than a good shotgun stock. Yet the stock continues to be the weak link in *almost all* commercially made rifles.

The fact is that the shape and dimensions of a rifle's stock are of enormous importance to the combined performances of the rifle and the man who shoots it. I've often felt that the ultimate *shooter's* rifle would be one that is conceived primarily from the standpoint of the stock, with the firing mechanism then designed to serve the stock. Traditionally, however, a rifle's mechanics are designed and developed first, a barrel screwed in place second and, finally, the stock added without much thought.

The paradox is that two of the more vital elements that determine a rifle's ultimate success, how it looks and how it feels, are left almost to chance. This is at odds with what most other manufacturers of consumer goods have come to recognize: the overwhelming importance of what's known as "industrial design." Fantastic salaries, far exceeding those paid to top engineers, are given the artistic geniuses who can integrate an engineering concept into a unit that looks good and feels good. If I were a gun manufacturer, I'd hire the best stockmaker I could find, give him a top salary, and put him in charge of coordinating design and manufacture.

Several years back a bold gunmaker by the name of Bill Ruger followed that course when he hired ace stockmaker Lenard Brownell to design the stocks for his rifles and to head up the company's stockmaking department. The stock Brownell designed for Ruger's Model 77 bolt-action rifle was far better looking than anything else being produced by a major American maker, and it spurred a trend toward "classic"-styled rifle stocks. But as good as it was and is—Ruger's M-77 stock missed the mark. Somewhere along the way someone lost his nerve and offered up a compromise where only steadfast boldness could win. The history of how this happened goes back beyond Ruger's efforts, and is, in fact, the story of commercial stock design, and why rifle stocks are what they are today.

HOW OUR STOCKS WENT WRONG

If I had to put a date on it, I'd say the year 1794 had a lot to do with today's stock design. That was the year the U.S. Congress authorized construction of two armories which were to manufacture small arms for the armies of the United States. One was at Harpers Ferry, West Virginia, the other at Springfield, Massachusetts. In 1795, at Springfield, came forth the "first" U.S. Musket. Of course, muskets had been made in America for years but mainly by "contract" firms and individuals. The significance of the 1795 Springfield musket, patterned after the French Charleville Model of 1763, is that it represented a more or less bureaucratic regulation of standards and dimensions. Once these dimensions were set in concrete, some of them weren't to be changed for generations—long after their purpose had been forgotten.

These early U.S. Musket stocks had an enormous amount of drop at the comb and heel. If you ever have a chance to handle one, bring it to your shoulder and try to sight it the way you would a modern rifle. You'll discover that when your cheek is on the comb you can't see over the barrel. And when you raise your head to see the target you lose a lot of facial contact with the stock. This means you lose some control. So how did those guys back then aim their muskets?

They probably aimed—or pointed—them well enough, because they used a significantly different shooting style. Remember, those muskets were flintlocks, and it's not much fun to get your eyes, hair, and other parts close to the lock when the things go off. That's why shooters of that era were inclined to assume an erect, head-back position when they pulled the trigger. You can get an idea of how they held their heads by studying old shooting prints. You'll note that their necks are straight, with only the jawline touching the stock. Needless to say, such a shooting stance calls for a stock with lots of drop. No wonder those old muskets and fowling pieces were as crooked as a cow's hock.

Decades passed and musket technology progressed through the percussion era, crept into the breechloading stage and, finally, entered the age of repeating rifles. But as mechanical technology progressed, no one thought to update stock design. Bureaucrats are reluctant to fiddle with the edicts of other bureaucrats so, as each new musket design was approved by the Ordnance Department, the stock dimensions of 1795 were stipulated. Of course, by the late 1800's no one remembered the reason for those old dimensions—or cared.

In the meantime the sights on U.S. Muskets were getting a lot better, and soldier-marksmen, no longer fearful of getting a shootin' eye full of sparks, were crawling forward on the stock's comb. But alas, the combs were so low that they had to hold their heads up at an awkward, unsupported angle.

The situation reached a minor crisis early in the 1920's when even the Ordnance Department had to admit, in rather obscure fashion, that the blessed 1903 Springfield was so poorly stocked that serious marksmanship was virtually ruled out. The crisis came to a head when they attempted to build what was to become known as the National Match Rifle for shooting competitions. Presumably, the brass at Springfield Armory called in a few competitive riflemen to make suggestions for improvement. I can imagine what was said. Target shooters are never shy about voicing their opinions, and to a man they must have condemned the stock dimensions of the M-1903 rifle. The upshot was a redesigned stock known as the Type-C which, in addition to having a pistol grip, had less drop at comb and heel. With this new stock it was at last possible for a marksman to plant his cheek on the comb and simultaneously see through the sights. Though relatively few National Match 1903 Springfields were made, they proved so shootable that the Type-C stock dimensions were adopted, with little change, for America's next — and greatest — military rifle, the M-1 Garand.

Now let's step back to the mid-1800's and look at the design and manufacture of commercial arms. Though dozens of inventors and gunmakers competed for the market (everyone wanted to build a gun to win the West) the most conspicuous name was Winchester. Improving on Henry's rifle, Oliver Winchester was obsessed with his lever-action rifle. He was not obsessed, however, with how well the stock fit the shooter. If you get your hands on an old Winchester 66 or 73, try snapping it to your shoulder and you'll find you're peering under the hammer rather than over the sights. I have a theory — and I emphasize that it's just a theory — that 19th-century gunmakers such as Oliver Winchester simply adopted the dimensions of U.S. Government small arms. That goes a long way toward explaining how stock shapes got into such a mess.

There's no documentary proof that commercial manufacturers accepted the antiquated government specifications and let it go at that, but something very much like proof is evident in any rifle manufactured prior to World War II — and *most* rifles made today. Probably the all-time worst offender from a major manufacturer is the Savage Model 99 lever-action rifle which, in its original form, was stocked to fit people with heads shaped like mules', and in recent years has been redesigned to accommodate persons with even more obscure skeletal deformities.

Traditionally, when gunmakers have sought to improve rifle stocks their efforts have been directed toward better wood, neater inletting, improved checkering, and brighter finishes, but not toward better dimensions. The classic example is the great Model 70 Winchester as it was conceived and executed in the 1930's. Improving on their Model 54 bolt-action rifle, the powers at Winchester elected to go all out and produce what honestly could be called the rifleman's rifle, one of the all-time greatest sporting firearms. They even consulted no less a stockmaking expert than Bob Owen to render the eye-pleasing forearm contour that has since become part and parcel of the Model 70 legend. But when it came to establishing the dimensions at the stock's comb and heel, they bowed to tradition and opted for the outdated, over-dropped style.

The late Lenard Brownell, Wyoming wizard of stockmaking, is shown at work. Brownell was both a free-thinking designer and meticulous craftsman. Bill Ruger hired him to design and supervise the making of his company's stocks, and Brownell left his unique mark on Ruger's line of rifles.

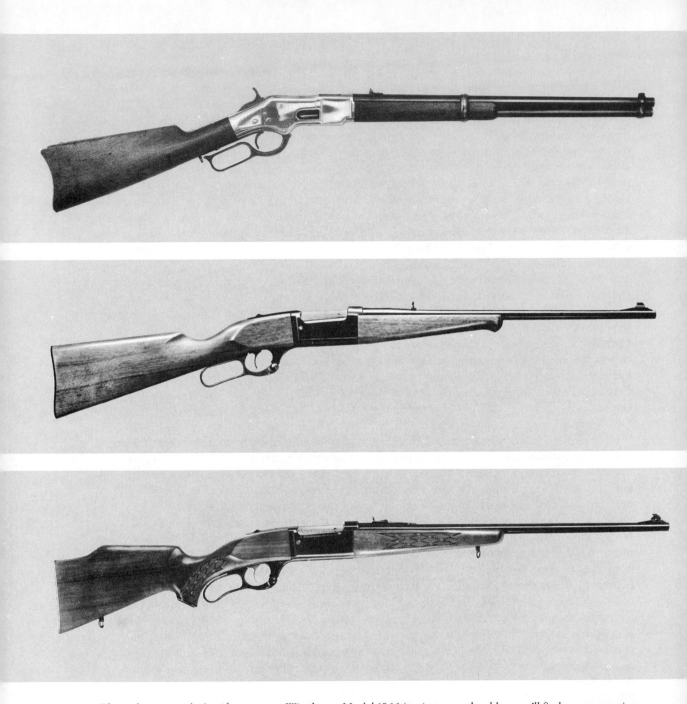

The author contends that if you snap a Winchester Model 1866 (top) to your shoulder, you'll find you are peering under the hammer rather than over the sights. He finds the Savage Model 99 factory stock equally awkward. It's shown in two of many versions—with straight grip and comb and with pistol grip and Monte Carlo comb.

EVILS OF TOO MUCH DROP

Occasionally I hear someone defend the old, crooked stocking by pointing out that those rifles were made before scopes became popular, so the dimensions were regulated for open sights. This defense fails when you snuggle the comb to your cheek and discover that rather than the sights, all you see is the tail end of the bolt or some similarly low-down region.

If you thumb through shooting books and manuals written during the 1930's, '40's, and even the 1950's, you'll discover that the rifle experts of that time allowed that the best magnifications for telescopic sights were 2.5X and 4X. Today's hunters commonly use considerably more powerful scopes. Why didn't the old-time writers recommend the same magnification as today's experts? There are, of course, several reasons but the most compelling involved the stock dimensions that prevailed during their time.

A low-magnification scope, in addition to having a wider field of view, has more latitude for lateral and axial eye-alignment error than a scope of higher magnification. When you look through a 2.5X or 4X scope you see a full field of view without having to align your eye as precisely as when you look through a higher-power scope. Thus, if you have a high-power scope mounted on a poorly stocked rifle, you have to weave and doddle your head trying to get your eye aligned. But if the rifle has proper dimensions at the heel and comb, the stock guides your eye to correct alignment with the scope so that you instantly see a full field with no "blacking out" at the edge of the field.

Aside from the problem of positioning the eye below the line of sight, a stock with too much drop at comb and heel unnecessarily punishes the shooter with added felt recoil. When you fire a big game rifle you feel recoil in two places: the first is on the shoulder and the other is on the jaw and face. The smack on the face is due to the rifle's violent upward jump, usually called "muzzle jump." This upward motion, which sometimes causes a bruised and swollen jaw, actually shouldn't happen at all and is the result of bad stock shape.

When a bullet is accelerated through a rifle's barrel, the "equal and opposite" reaction you feel as recoil should be coming *straight* back and not causing the rifle to rotate upward with painful force. The problem is caused by the direction of force (recoil) not being in line with the center of resistance (your shoulder). Since a rifle's buttplate is below the line of recoil, a pivotal motion is created which causes the rifle to pivot up and around the center of resistance. The more the center of resistance is displaced from the line of recoil, the greater the pivotal action. Therefore, the more drop at heel a gun has (in relation to the bore line), the greater is its tendency to fly up and whack you in the face. This is made worse when you have little or no face contact with the stock because the comb gets a flying start before landing a haymaker.

Conversely, stocks with relatively little drop at the heel have less tendency to pivot upward while recoiling. Also, when your face is in firm contact with the comb the punching effect is minimized. So as you see, a stock with too much drop at the heel and comb is an inherently evil thing. Yet shooters have been accepting miserable stock dimensions for longer than anyone can remember.

This Weatherby Mark V chambered for the .300 Weatherby Magnum shows the Monte Carlo comb, deep pistol grip, contrasts, and bright finish—that is, the generally radical stock design—that became a stylistic trademark of Roy Weatherby. If the configuration invited criticism, the use of beautiful Claro walnut invited admiration.

THE MONTE CARLO MADNESS

The form of factory-produced rifles changed dramatically following World War II—not necessarily for the better but certainly in interesting ways and for interesting reasons. The biggest single force in stock design was Roy Weatherby's Magnum rifles with their fancy inlays, Monte Carlo combs and bright finishes. Though Weatherby's radical stock designs have been condemned by critics who consider themselves pure of mind and spirit, the fact is that one of the main reasons the Weatherby look caught on so big was its refreshing change from the drabness of stocks made during that period. Any change would have been welcome. Moreover, Weatherby had a golden touch for publicity. Pictures of his glowing rifles constantly appeared in hunting and shooting publications, further whetting the public's appetite. The Monte Carlo comb had definitely arrived.

The humpbacked Monte Carlo comb on a rifle stock is mainly a stylistic feature, even though considerable claims have been made for its benefits. These benefits, such as they are, represent ways of dealing with the *symptoms* of a basic design problem without actually solving the problem itself: the stock design that prevailed for the century preceding World War II.

After spending four years at war, using all sorts of modern weapons, veterans were vastly more sophisticated in their thinking about rifles than hunters had been before the war. One thing they wanted for sure was telescopic sights, but, as mentioned, scopes and old-fashioned stocks don't go together. The Monte Carlo comb looked like the answer because it elevated the shooter's head so that his eye was better aligned with the scope. Though the Monte Carlo comb did indeed help in this respect, other claims have been made that are ludicrous.

One of my favorites is that the forward-sloping comb reduces recoil. If a rifle recoiled straight to the rear, a forward-sloping comb would indeed reduce the whack delivered to the face, but as we well know, rifles recoil upward, too, and this is what gives us a sore cheek and an occasional bloody nose. Part of the absurdity of the claim that a Monte Carlo stock reduces recoil is in the fact that the design principle of the Monte Carlo actually *increases* felt recoil. Remember, a Monte Carlo comb doesn't alter the stock's dimensions at the heel. In fact, for the Monte Carlo look to be most prominent, the out-of-date specifications for drop at heel had to be maintained and in some cases were even exaggerated.

Even though Weatherby was the motivating force behind the rush to the Monte Carlo look, he cannot be blamed for the result. The firms to be faulted — and few are exempt — are those that copied the Weatherby look without asking themselves if that was really the way a stock should be shaped. As usual, those who suffered, perhaps unknowingly, were the customers. A much wiser course would have been to straighten out existing stock designs by raising the drop at heel until it was equal, or nearly so, with the drop at the nose of comb.

This simple modification would have met three important criteria: First, it would have elevated the comb so that scopes could be used more efficiently; second, with the butt raised, the pivotal action of recoil would have been reduced, softening the upward punch; a third benefit would have been better-looking stocks. This is evident in the so-called classic-style stocks made by our top custom stockmakers and generally considered to be the most beautiful of all stock designs. A characteristic of the classic style is a high and straight comb line. If you lay a classic stock beside a typical Monte Carlo stock, you'll probably be surprised to discover that the comb of the classic is higher than the Monte Carlo, with the heel being a *lot* higher. This is why classic-style rifles are so easy to aim and comfortable to shoot.

The Monte Carlo look implies a lot more than a humpbacked comb. The stylistic package includes white plastic spacers and various other contrasting effects along with, of course, a glossy finish on wood and metal. By the 1960's the look had thoroughly infected the gun industry, both in America and abroad (Europeans are notorious for copying the worst features of American rifles), with such grand and conservative manufacturers as Remington and Winchester having soiled themselves with the Monte Carlo look and all the ugliness that can imply.

THE CLASSIC DESIGNS

The man who bucked the trend, to his everlasting credit and fortune, was Bill Ruger. Ruger was blessed with a sense of style and good taste to go along with his design genius and business acumen. When he set out to design and market a line of rifles, his sense of style dictated a more elegant approach to stock design and his delicate touch on the shooting public's pulse no doubt told him that we were ready for something other than the Monte Carlo look.

To put his plan into action he hired Lenard Brownell, one of the world's top custom stockmakers, not only to design the stocks for his rifles but to move to New Hampshire so he could oversee their production. It was a brillant idea and Ruger's rifles, the No. 1 Single-Shot and Model 77 bolt rifle, were smash hits in the marketplace and with the shooting press. Ruger stocks were so much better looking than anything else on the market that there wasn't even a second place. Even so, Ruger surrendered to tradition by ordaining that the drop dimensions follow traditional precepts. Had the butt been bent upward a few fractions of an inch, the stock would have been even better. Other features, however, especially the shape of the butt section and grip, were wonderful.

The success of Ruger's rifles got other gunmakers to scratching their heads. Clearly, he was taking a big chunk of the market, and it appeared that the trend was toward conservatively styled stocks. Early in the 1970's I was approached by Remington to design a classic-styled stock for the Model 700 bolt rifle. Though the Model 700 is one of the all-time great rifles, it has some features, such as the trigger guard assembly, that are as ugly as sin. Thus, designing a decent looking stock was something of an exercise in frustration, with the result being the Model 700 Classic. All in all, it didn't come out too badly—and looks a million times better than Remington's Monte Carlo stock, not to mention feeling better, too.

What gives me the most pleasure about Remington's "classic" rifle is that it forced other makers to come up with their own versions of a more or less classic stock. Winchester fell in line with the very well done Model 70 Featherweight.

The Ruger Model 77 (top) and Winchester Model 70 Featherweight typify the return of major riflemakers to the classic style of stock.

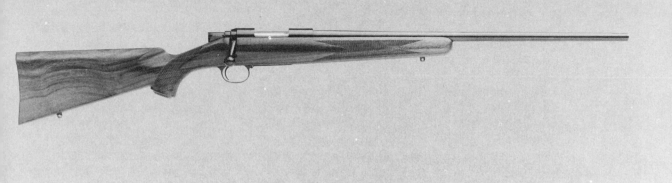

This is the Kimber Model 84 Classic, an aptly named rifle. When the company was contemplating production of the first Kimber, the author was asked to recommend a stock designer. He suggested Duane Wiebe, who created the classic-style stock that helped the Kimber to achieve unusually swift success.

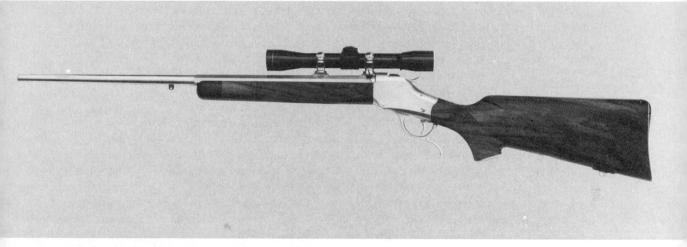

The genius of a fine stockmaker can smoothly wed a good old action to good new—that is, classic—concepts in wood configuration and style. This is a .30/30 Winchester High Wall restocked by Don Klein, whose work is noted for its grace and originality. The metalwork is by another top craftsman, Creighton Audette.

During the late '70's, while I was hunting with Jack Warne, a big shot at Omark Industries, he showed me a prototype of a rimfire bolt-action rifle he wanted to manufacture. Warne is a clever designer, and the rifle had great possibilities—except for the stock design. Warne knew the stock wasn't right and asked what should be done. I suggested that he consult a top stockmaker and have a stock designed in a truly classic style. My reckoning was that the market was ready for a stylish .22 in the mode of Winchester's discontinued Model 52 Sporter. Warne cogitated for a few months, and the next time we were together he asked me to recommend a stockmaker to design a stock for his new rifle. I suggested Duane Wiebe, and that very day gave him a call and laid out the whole plan. Wiebe liked the idea. The rest, as they say, is history. The result was the beautiful Kimber rifle, which was virtually an overnight success and is one of today's most desired rimfire rifles.

From my experience with the sporting firearms industry, I'd say that design fads run in about 20- to 25-year cycles. That means that the trend to the classic style in stock design will be in full bloom in the 1990's. As I write this, there reposes in my rifle rack a hush-hush prototype rifle that features the first truly classic-styled stock I've ever seen come out of a major gun factory. It has all the grace and beauty one could ever want in a rifle and is a dream to shoot. My guess is that it will create a revolution in the rifle industry and provide shooters, after only a century and a half of waiting, with a rifle stocked the way it should be. Sometimes the simplest things are the hardest to get.

THE MOST POPULAR WOOD

It's no big secret that the preferred wood for gunstocks is walnut. Even when a stock isn't walnut, the chances are that it has been stained to a walnut color. Some manufacturers are so determined to let their customers know that real walnut is used that they paste on a ridiculously worded sticker stating that the rifle or shotgun is stocked with "genuine *solid* walnut," as if to insure that some inferior material hadn't been overlaid with a thin layer of the real stuff.

In the United States, the wood most overwhelmingly used in commercial manufacture is the native black walnut *(Juglans nigra),* which grows over much of the country. I suppose the name comes from the color of the granite-shelled nuts, which are virtually black when dried, but it could come from the color of the wood itself, which can be as richly brown as a piece of Swiss chocolate. Black walnut can also be surprisingly pale, nearly as pale as ivory, and with an infinite variety of hues from the lightest to the darkest. Sometimes we find tremendous color variety within a single black-walnut stock, ranging from blond to near-black with streaks of purple and amber in between. This occurs when the block is sawed so that it includes both the light sapwood and darker heartwood. Many of today's commercial stocks of black walnut are of lighter-color and somewhat less desirable sapwood but stained to the more traditional dark color. Do-it-yourself gunstock refinishers are often startled to discover that, after a coat of finish remover and a brisk sanding, a stock cherished for its rich, "real walnut" color is as fair-skinned as a palomino mare.

In addition to its color extremes, black walnut occurs in a seemingly endless variety of texture, density, and grain structure. It is sometimes hard to believe that different samples could be of the same species. Even more unbelievably, a single tree can produce almost the full range of colors and yield stock blanks that vary tremendously in hardness and grain structure.

Occasionally, an abnormal growing condition will result in a wavy or uneven grain structure. When such wood is finished, it reflects light in beautiful rippling patterns. This is how we get the much-desired "fiddleback" and "feather" grain, aptly named for the feather-like pattern. This pattern usually occurs at the juncture or crotch of limbs or roots. Suppliers of stock blanks often dig up walnut stumps in the hope of discovering dense, richly figured wood that will fetch a premium price. Such prize blanks usually go to the custom gun departments of the major gunmakers where they are fitted to top-of-the-line models such as Winchester's Model 21 shotguns.

A wood supplier who tried to make a living by treasure-hunting for fancy grain probably would starve, so most concentrate on the plain, straight-grained blanks and planks that are the staple of the firearms and furniture industries. Fancy wood is considered a bonus.

Sadly perhaps, much of the really beautiful black walnut finds its way to the furniture market. A fancy log that might yield only a few stock blanks can be thinly sliced into hundreds of square feet of beautiful veneer. Thus veneer makers can afford to pay top prices for the best wood. As a result, top wood that has the good fortune to be fashioned into a beautiful rifle stock usually does so only because the supplier had a soft spot in his heart for fine guns.

In addition to its natural beauty and warmth of feel, black walnut machines freely, carves cleanly, has a good strength-to-weight ratio, is highly stable, finishes beautifully, and takes checkering well. So when it comes to making gunstocks, nothing fills the bill so well in so many respects, especially when you consider that black walnut is fairly abundant. Some custom gunmakers who dote on the more exotic and expensive species of walnut are fond of pointing out that the comparatively coarse grain structure of black walnut makes fine checkering impractical—the problem being that open spaces in the grain weaken the diamonds so that they chip off easily. With most stocks of black walnut this is true, but it's no real problem since the checkering on commercial stocks is almost never finer than 22 lines to the inch and more

Great stocks begin with great wood, and exceptional walnut is still available, despite inroads by the furniture industry. These two magnificent stock blanks were supplied by Bill Dowtin. A top-ranking stockmaker, Dowtin is also known as a supplier of high-quality blanks.

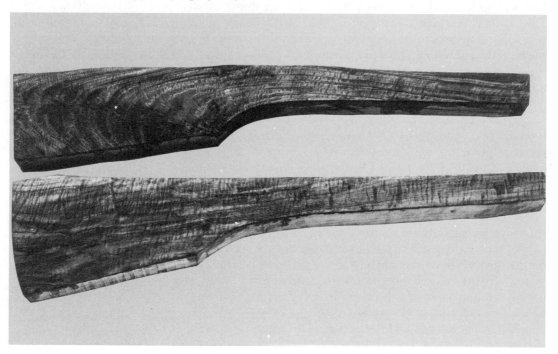

usually 18 lines. For the record, though, some black walnut blanks can be very tight-grained. I have a .35 Whelen rifle custom-stocked with a richly colored stock of black walnut that is one of the densest pieces of wood I've ever seen. A test panel was checkered 48 lines to the inch and each diamond felt like machined steel. But that stick is also one of the heaviest blanks I've ever hefted. It's great for the robust recoil of the big 250-grain bullets I fire in the Whelen, but is hardly the stuff flyweight rifles are stocked with.

Quite a bit has been written about figured wood being unstable and likely to warp, but I think such charges are mostly hearsay. I like beautifully figured stocks and have a number of rifles stocked with feathered and fiddlebacked wood. Ideally, according to knowledgeable stockmakers, stock blanks should be laid out and sawed so that the figure is in the butt section. The straight-grained part of the stock is less likely to warp and spoil accuracy by putting uneven pressure on the barrel and action. Stocks that have a "curly" or fiddleback pattern, however, are likely to be figured for their full length, and this is supposed to mean trouble.

I have a dozen or so rifles with this type of figure, and one of them does have a wandering forearm. It's a heavy-barreled varmint rifle with a beavertail forearm which, fortunately, has a margin of extra wood that permits enlargement of the barrel channel. Over the past decade or so, the forearm has warped nearly a quarter-inch, making it necessary to recut the channel three or four times in order for the barrel to remain free-floated. Obviously, a stock so determined to warp could bend a barrel enough to ruin accuracy or at least make it impossible to maintain any semblance of a working zero. And just as obviously, had this been my only experience with a fancy-grained stock I might have concluded that figured wood is the deadly enemy of accuracy.

But as it happens, I have other rifles that are blessed with beautifully figured wood from buttplate to fore-end tip. One is an out-of-the-box Ruger Model 77 bolt-action varmint rifle in .220 Swift chambering. The tight fiddleback pattern is especially prominent in the fore-end, which also happens to be inletted to a firm barrel contact. From the day this rifle came out of the box, it has been grouping five shots under a half-inch at 100 yards, and season after season the scope never needs to be adjusted. Once, on a lark, I shot this rifle in a benchrest tournament and damn near won the whole shootin' match.

In my adventures with rifle accuracy I've owned and tested straight-grained stocks that warped and changed the rifle's point of impact as often as a Tennessee coon hound scratches himself. Therefore, I'm not liable to make predictions about the stability of any stock blank, pretty or plain. Of vastly more importance to the stock's potential stability is how the blank is cured and finished. One thing I'll never do is reject a stock because it has too much figure in the fore-end section. It just might shoot as good as it looks.

One danger that does exist with highly figured wood is when the grain radically changes direction in the grip section. If the grain runs across the grip, it can easily snap in half. Though such a grain layout is always risky, the figure is often so breathtakingly beautiful that it's considered worth the gamble. Usually such blanks are used for shotguns or single-shot rifles that have a through-bolt which reinforces the grip, but even so they sometimes break early in life. When I visit the custom shops of the big gunmakers I occasionally dig through the scrap box, usually finding a few heartbreakingly beautiful stocks with such bad grain direction that they broke even before they were finished.

Naturally, using such a piece of wood for a bolt-action rifle, which has no reinforcement in

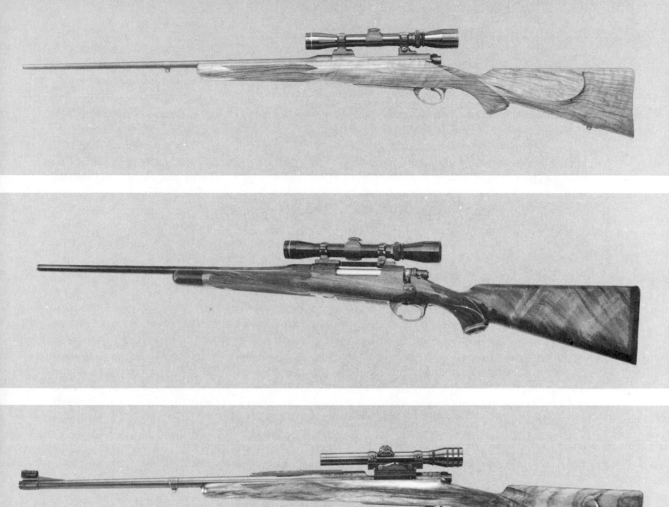

These rifles are all stocked in the classic mode, but each shows the personal flair of a different stockmaker. At top is a Winchester Model 70 stocked by a young Texan named Kevin Campbell, who also did some of the metalwork. The floorplate and trigger guard assembly are by Ted Blackburn. At center is a Remington Model 700 stocked and engraved by Winston Churchill, an acknowledged master of both arts. Again Ted Blackburn contributed the trigger guard unit. The rifle was built for Field & Stream *Executive Editor Dave Petzal, who christened it "The Immaculate Conception." At bottom is another Model 70, this one with a stock by Stanley Kevin and engraving by Pedini. Kevin's work is characterized by clean styling and faultless craftsmanship. Note that all three stocks have pronounced figuring, and two of the three are not at all straight-grained. The notion that figured wood spoils accuracy is mere myth.*

the grip area, is an invitation to disaster. Just such a rifle was once shipped to me and arrived with the stock neatly broken through at the grip. It was a gorgeous thing but, alas, too pretty to last.

The history of American black walnut as a cornerstone of the gunmaking industry goes back a lot further than is generally realized. The first guns made on this continent were not the graceful "Kentucky" long rifles of legend, but musket-like smoothbores and short-barreled rifles patterned after the *Jaeger* (hunting) rifles of Germany. When European gunsmiths brought their tools and talents to the New World, they naturally sought the wood most similar to the walnut of their native lands.

Two centuries later, when the American gun industry was getting cranked up in earnest, black walnut was again the wood of choice for everything from Colt's revolver grips to Henry repeating rifles to Springfield muskets. America's arsenals in particular loved black walnut and specified that only the straightest-grained heartwood was acceptable. And so it was right up through the World War II manufacture of the M-1 Garand rifle. Considering all those millions of heartwood blanks, one has to wonder how many carloads of sapwood were scrapped and how many thousands of tons of beautiful figured walnut were consigned to the factory furnaces.

One of the causes of the ever-rising prices of sporting firearms is the escalating price of black walnut. There's no shortage of trees for the moment, but there is intense competition for the lovely wood from the furniture industry—especially from foreign manufacturers, because the price of their native walnut is prohibitive. People tell me that if 20 black walnut trees are planted when a child is born, by the time he's of college age the trees will pay for his degree. And in the meantime they are nice to look at, producing cool shade and delicious nuts. A huge black walnut tree spreads its shading branches over the 200-yard benchrest at my rifle range, and many is the time I've pondered its crinkled skin, contemplating the rifle stocks that grow therein.

Black walnut is the standard by which other stock woods are compared.

THE OTHER WALNUTS

Among the most distinguishing and attractive features of the Weatherby rifles and shotguns, and other premium-grade guns, are stocks of brilliantly hued, highly contrasted walnut. And as if the distinctive coloration were not enough, the layers of color texture are frequently punctuated by dazzling swirls, ripples, and eddies of grain embellishment. This lavish-looking wood, which has come into its own as a stock material only since the 1950's, is a California product known as Claro walnut. Claro means light-colored, or clear.

For centuries this native of the arid California valleys served no particular purpose except to extend its shady arms over lazy Spanish casas, its roots spreading wide and deep in their quest for moisture. But when the California people-boom got rolling and the hazy vistas were carved into smoggy subdivisions, the spreading Claro trees were bulldozed from their place in the sun.

Until then, Claro walnut had never been seriously considered as a source of gunstocks. The beauty of its timber was well known, of course, having been used in the making of Spanish California's ornate furniture, but America's gunmaking centers were thousands of miles to the east and, in any event, the industry's traditions, which change very slowly when at all, were long since committed to black walnut.

By one of those peculiar twists of circumstance, a series of post-World War II events coincided to elevate Claro walnut to prominence in the gunstock hierarchy. The first was the sudden availability, or "discovery," of Claro walnut caused by the mass cutting of the trees. The second was an unpredicted interest in space-age rifle design. Stock configuration had changed little for generations, but the 1950's were watershed years in rifle thinking. The term "gun nut" was coined, and legions of gun nuts wanted racy-looking rifles with stocks of dazzling Claro walnut. Roy Weatherby, whose firm was located near the heart of Claro country, showed us how beautiful the wood could be. For a long while Claro walnut was the exclusive domain of the Weatherby Company plus some specialty shops, custom stockmakers, and makers of do-it-yourself semi-inletted stocks, but in recent times it has been used occasionally by the major gunmakers. The latter use is for higher-than-average grades of guns such as commemorative issues.

Despite its sometimes striking beauty, Claro walnut is not always the answer to an old maid's prayer. It does not take fine checkering well because of its open grain structure, and it tends to be rather brittle, which makes it want to split and splinter rather than cut cleanly. It also tends to be rather heavy and does not respond well to some finishes. When oil-type finishes are used on Claro walnut, it tends to darken and lose its fiery coloration. That's why it looks best with hard, clear-type finishes such as the glossy varnishes used by Weatherby. It is nowhere as expensive as good French or English walnut and therefore is a good choice for someone looking for the most figure and color for his money.

This elaborately engraved double rifle has a stock of Circassian walnut—that is, the Circassian variety of French walnut, which was not originally native to Circassia or France but may have been brought from Asia by Marco Polo. The wood is renowned for its rich coloring.

The nobility of stockmaking wood is French walnut. Even its schoolhouse name, *Juglans regia,* tells of its royal rank. Depending on where it grows, it may be known by different names such as Circassian or English walnut. According to legend, the French walnut nuts were brought from Persia by Marco Polo, who planted them in Italy, from whence they were planted across Europe, North Africa, and eventually in such far-flung places as New Zealand and America. The trees have long been harvested in France, and that's why the wood is most often called French walnut even though it is an export crop from Italy, Yugoslavia, Turkey, and India as well. Some especially beautiful *Juglans regia* grows in Russia's Circassian region. Noted for its rich coloration, the Circassian variety is perhaps the most desired gunstock wood of all, but it is hard to come by these days, as the Soviets want to keep it for themselves.

Periodically, representatives of the fancy London gunmaking houses, usually the managing directors themselves, make a pilgrimage to France where they select stock blanks for their fancy guns. The sorting, grading, and matching of the green blanks is a solemn responsibility, carried out with much hand-wringing and head-shaking.

French walnut has several great qualities, any one of which would make it the favorite of stockmakers. First of all, it cuts cleanly and easily. A stockmaker once compared cutting French

Here is the butt section of an English walnut stock gracing a Model 98 Mauser that was rebarreled to .257 Roberts caliber. This beautiful work is by master stockmaker Garnett Brawley of Prescott, Arizona. Note the spectacular grain—about one blank in 5,000 has such a perfect grip layout, and Brawley's finishing technique highlights the wood's natural beauty.

walnut to slicing firm cheese. Its dense grain allows it to take and hold fine checkering without chipping, and the small grain pores fill easily for a beautiful finish. The strength-to-weight ratio is the best of all walnuts. But most of all, it is the beauty of French walnut that makes it the all-time favorite stock wood. I would compare good French walnut to a sunset: the colors and textures are endless and no two are alike.

The demand for French walnut causes the price to be pretty steep, with a really fine blank costing upwards of $500 at the time of this writing, and the best samples going for over a grand! Naturally, such prices have created treasure hunts for sources of this fine wood, and it has been found in some unlikely places.

A few years back, when I was doing some bird shooting in the Northern India district of Kashmir, I took a day off to do a bit of shopping. In addition to the wonderfully soft Kashmir fabrics, the area is famous for handwoven carpets and exquisitely carved walnut furniture. According to legend, Marco Polo brought his seed walnuts from this area, so the abundance of walnut was not surprising. What did surprise me was the plainness of the wood in the otherwise beautiful furnishings. The richly carved walnut was as devoid of figure as a plastic cup. But when I pulled out the drawers on a few chests I discovered that the drawer bottoms and sides were made of some of the prettiest walnut I've ever seen. Obviously, the makers favor plain wood for their carving and consider the richly colored and figured wood scrap to be used for mundane fixtures. I figured that if I could find the source of the scrap wood, I would have some great stock wood for only a few dollars a blank. After all, a carved walnut chest in Kashmir at the time cost just $50 or so. I put out the word that I was interested in buying pieces of walnut big enough for gunstocks. In a couple of days merchants began to appear bearing neatly cut stock blanks, but without exception the wood was as stark and figureless as Aunt Martha's backside. "No, no," I'd tell them, "wood like this"— and I'd point to the fancy wood in the drawer bottoms. The merchants would just roll their eyes and stroke their heads at the suggestion. I never did get any good stock blanks, though I'm sure that somewhere in that mountainous region there's a treasure lode of great French walnut.

You already know what French walnuts taste like. You eat them at Christmas, only they aren't called French walnuts. They are those big wrinkle-shelled nuts we call English walnuts, and they mostly come from California. There the trees are called English walnuts, too, and so is the stock wood. It's the same stuff as French walnut, so don't be confused when you see a beautiful piece of stock called English walnut. The English walnut that comes from America's West Coast is as beautiful as any French walnut grown anywhere, and in the hands of America's top stockmakers has been fashioned into the most beautiful rifle stocks ever made.

MAPLE AND BIRCH

Back in the '50's and '60's, maple was a favorite wood with custom stockmakers as well as do-it-yourselfers, but by the late 1970's had gone almost entirely out of style. This is a shame because maple is one of America's traditional stock woods, being the stuff those glorious "Kentucky" long rifles were stocked with.

The wood itself is usually white, but it stains beautifully, especially maple having the wavy

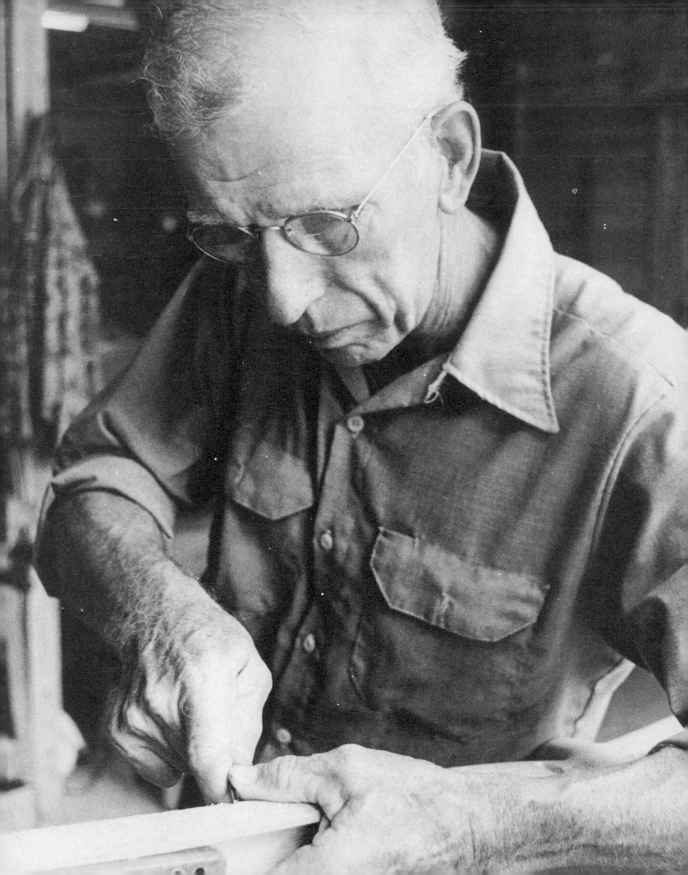

grain structure that produces the rippling "fiddleback" figure. Maple is an extremely strong wood, especially well suited to rifles with heavy recoil, and quite stable. In fact, maple has been used for target rifles with good success. I expect the reason maple has gone out of style with custom gun builders is that it is considered too gaudy for an era that favors conservative tones. One of these days it will be back in vogue, I expect. I hope so, because it is a great stock wood.

The "secret" wood in the gun industry is birch. Its weight, density, and working qualities are quite similar to those of walnut (even superior in some respects) but it doesn't have the natural beauty. Since it is less costly than walnut it is commonly used for inexpensive rimfire

Two of the author's target rifles. One has a conventional walnut stock. The other has a thumbhole stock of molded fiberglass, which has great advantages of strength, lightness, stability, and resistance to the elements.

A master at work — the late Hal Hartley of North Carolina. Hartley became famous for his richly figured stocks, which came from the mountain maples growing near his home.

rifles and bottom-of-the-line centerfire models. It can be stained to look very much like walnut, and most customers don't realize the difference. Since it is also a very stable wood, it is favored for target rifles. Some of Europe's most expensive target rifles are stocked with birch.

SYNTHETICS

In recent years, fiberglass stocks have made tremendous headway, and there is little doubt that this is the rifle-stock material of the future. The advantages of fiberglass and other synthetic materials are strength, lightness, stability, and resistance to the elements. Not counting the earlier uses of plastic and nylon for stocks, the current trend toward synthetics began with benchrest shooters who needed stocks that were both lighter and stronger than wood. Fiberglass-impregnated resins were already widely used for the "glass bedding" of rifles, so some bright fellows got the idea of making the whole stock of fiberglass. It worked so well that within a few years fiberglass stocks were a staple in the benchrest game and spilled over into other forms of target shooting. Even where lightness wasn't important, the stable, nonwarping properties of fiberglass stocks proved to be a measurable aid to accuracy.

Predictably, it was only a matter of time until hunters—especially sheep hunters, who spend most of their time going up and down mountains and thus cherish light rifles—caught on to the advantages of fiberglass. Not only are fiberglass stocks lighter by pounds but they are impervious to moisture, meaning that a mountain hunter's greatest fear—zero shifting because of weather—is virtually eliminated. At this writing, fiberglass stocks are mainly the product of custom suppliers and specialty rifle builders, but I am willing to bet a gold-plated pocket watch that by the 1990's all major rifle manufacturers will offer a rifle or two with a stock made of fiberglass or some other synthetic material. The more advanced guys are already using graphite, which is even lighter. Who knows what will follow? The innovations are an indication that the makers are beginning to pay some attention to stocks. Rifle manufacturers have been a long time learning this fundamental lesson, but at last they may be realizing that a stock is more than a handle.

Chapter 5

THE CUSTOM RIFLE STOCK

Nowhere does the genius of American gunmaking sparkle more brilliantly than in the stocks of custom rifles. Though the attention given to top stockmakers is a phenomenon of recent years, the tradition of great stockmaking goes back to Colonial times. The legendary "Kentucky" long rifle, for example, is a splendid example of custom stockmaking that is strikingly beautiful and uniquely American.

Following the Civil War, by which time most guns were the product of smoke-belching factories rather than walnut-scented one-man shops, fine custom gunmaking went into a near eclipse. This was mainly because of America's fascination with repeaters, a time of rifles with harsh mechanical lines that lent themselves not at all to elegant stockwork. During that time the best efforts of American stockmakers were concentrated on the exquisite target rifles used in the popular long-range and offhand Schuetzen-style competitions. For the most part, the names of those talented sculptors of gunstocks were never known beyond the doors of their workrooms, but the artistic wonders they worked with a piece of walnut are among the reasons collectors pay big money for those wonderful old single-shot target rifles.

The era of the great single-shot target rifles ended with the outbreak of the First World War and, had it not been for a peculiar twist of shooting fashion, fine American stockmaking could have sputtered to an end. The nail that saved the shoe that saved the horse was the timely mix of increased interest in big game hunting, especially in Alaska and Western Canada, wonderful new rimless cartridges such as the .30/06, and the availability of two sensational bolt-action rifles: the Model 1898 Mauser from Germany and America's Springfield Model of 1903.

The lever-action rifle, which had won the West and helped wipe out the buffalo herds, wasn't the rifle for an elegant hunter in exotic places. Elk required more bullet range, sheep needed better accuracy plus a flat trajectory, and it took more punch to down a bear than provided by most lever rifles. A bolt-action rifle and a hot new cartridge like the .30/06 offered everything in one neat, stylish package.

Ironically, in a nation of riflemen, America's armsmakers offered no classy bolt-action sporting rifles, and were not inclined to do so until much later. Thus a sporting chap who wanted to turn himself out with a stylish bolt rifle had to settle for one of the slick Mauser sporters made in Oberndorf, Germany, or a dainty, Austrian-made Mannlicher-Schoenauer. If he wanted to lay out bigger cash, there were elegant bolt rifles made by the fabled British firms and sold through posh shops in New York, Chicago and San Francisco. But then, gradually, a tantalizing alternative made itself known, the American-made custom-stocked bolt-action rifle.

EARLY BOLT-ACTION SPORTERS

To be technically correct we have to note that Springfield Armory did, in fact, produce a sporter version of the M-1903 service rifle which was sold commercially. Teddy Roosevelt used these Springfields on some of his hunts in Africa and other odd places, and had the highest praise for the rifle and .30/06 cartridge. But as nicely finished as Springfield Armory's sporters were, they were rather crude and clumsy when compared to the world's best bolt-action sporting rifles. The man who showed American sportsmen how beautiful a Springfield sporter could really be was master craftsman Louis Wundhammer who operated a gunshop in the sleepy little California town of Los Angeles. One of the features of a stock by this legendary craftsman was a convex curvature on the pistol grip which comfortably fitted the palm, a feature known in today's shooting lingo as a "Wundhammer Swell."

Wundhammer began "sporterizing" Springfields and Mausers before the new century was a decade old. His earlier stocks were styled along traditional German lines, which means they weren't all that great. But within a few years he developed a style all his own which could be called more American than European. A particularly interesting feature of Wundhammer's work, especially during his later period, was the use of elaborate checkering patterns as a medium of stock ornamentation. In many instances, Wundhammer's checkering could be called excessive, especially when the patterns adorned non-gripping parts of the stock (such as on each side of the action area), but there's no question that he was the father of the American school of custom stockmaking.

AN AMERICAN ART FORM

During the extravagant decade that followed the First World War, a number of stockmakers and houses of fine gunmaking became established in the U.S. In many ways these operations were similiar to the custom gunmaking firms in England and on the Continent, especially in terms of workmanship and overall quality. But whereas the established shops in England, Germany,

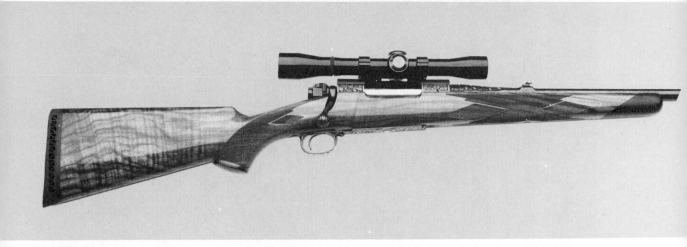

For a great many years, one of the best-known custom shops specializing in fine rifles has been Pachmayr Gun Works of Los Angeles. This masterpiece shows why. Pachmayr not only made the beautiful stock but did all of the metalwork and engraving. The same firm is also a supplier of magnificent walnut.

Austria, Belgium and France were dogmatic and unchanging in their approach to the making of fine rifles, the Americans were always willing to talk to the customer and try something new and different.

From 1910 until 1940 was a period of rapid evolution in American stockmaking thought, and from the late 1940's to the present has been a period of even faster change. During this time American custom-rifle stockmaking outdistanced the rest of the world by such a wide margin that it is fair to say great rifle stocks are almost exclusively a product of the United States. Stockmaking as an art form simply does not seem to exist anywhere else in the world. In Europe, for example, progress in stockmaking and design has been so slow and misdirected, by comparison, that European makers can't even comprehend the gap, much less compete.

The best-known of the custom shops specializing in fine rifles was Griffin & Howe, located in New York City, followed by Hoffman Arms of Ardmore, Oklahoma, and Pachmayr's of Los Angeles. Griffin & Howe, which served as the gunsmithing department of Abercrombie & Fitch for many years, developed a distinctive stock form that was—and is—highly recognizable for its stylish, functional lines. This feature, along with first-rate metalwork and superb engraving, put Griffin & Howe rifles on a par with the world's finest bolt-action rifles. And for the most part they were more shootable—meaning they were better hunting rifles—than just about anything else a stylish sportsman could buy.

While Griffin & Howe was turning out elegant custom rifles for the carriage trade, R. F. Sedgley, who operated a gunshop in Philadelphia, linked his name to the Springfield rifle for all time by virtue of a custom-stocked sporter that offered style and grace at an affordable price. Though the "Sedgley Springfields," as they came to be known, were not exactly characterized by magnificent stockwork, the work was more than competent and the lines were trim and functional and distinctly "American" in flavor. By re-heat treating inexpensive "low number" 1903

This is the distinctive Griffin & Howe cheekpiece. A connoisseur can always recognize the contours of a stock made by this famous New York shop. The rifle pictured is a .375 H&H Magnum Winchester Model 70 restocked with dark French walnut during the 1950's.

Springfield actions, Sedgley was able to offer the public a custom sporter, nicely stocked and complete with good checkering and Old World steel fittings, for only $65 in 1929. Or, for a hundred and a half, you got Circassian walnut and lots of engraving. Nowadays, collectors shell out a bushel of cash for one of these beautiful sporters.

THE RISE OF INDEPENDENT STOCKMAKERS

During this era another phenomenon presented itself: the independent stockmaker of national reputation. Until this time stockmakers had existed only within the confines of factories or all-purpose gunshops where they received little, if any, personal recognition. But as interest in custom rifles grew, with emphasis on fine stockmaking, the names of a few talented stockmakers became well known in shooting circles. With the passing of Louis Wundhammer, the best-known stockmakers of the 1920's and '30's were Bob Owen and Alvin Linden. Of these two, Owen is less remembered today but the effect he had on American stock design is probably greater than that of any other stockmaker before or since. For example, the Model 70 Winchester stock was styled by Owen, thus making his touch, if not his name, immortal, and the sumptuous lines and cross-section of the Owen forearm are widely copied by today's custom stockmakers.

Alvin Linden, who liked to be called "Old Scratch," had a knack for publicizing himself and, by virtue of his articles and books on stockmaking, not to mention some pretty good stockwork, became the first stockmaker to achieve widespread fame. He wrote articles on stocks and stockmaking in a salty, easy-to-read style and captivated his fans with descriptions of how he rough-shaped stocks with a hand ax.

Today's custom stockmakers owe a lot to Linden because he brought the craft out of the woodshed and gave it status at least equal to engraving. Since Linden's time, a top stockmaker is respected as an artist and enjoys all the celebrity to which that title is due. Linden's most lasting effects, for better or worse, were the result of a series of pamphlets on stockwork which included full-size drawings and detailed instructions on inletting and finishing. The drawings influenced a generation of stockmakers, inspiring them to achieve stocks of "classic" line and proportion, but some of his other instructions have proven less helpful. Linden's notions about how rifle accuracy is affected by the way the barrel and action are inletted into the stock were valid in concept but didn't work out so well in practice. Consequently, rifles stocked by him, and by legions of stockmakers following his precepts, tend to be as temperamental as

Here is a picture of "Old Scratch" himself—Alvin Linden of Wisconsin, putting the final touches on what appears to be a custom-stocked 20mm cannon. Linden had a sense of humor and a knack for publicizing himself (as this picture shows). He also made fine stocks, and his writings had a lasting influence on stockmaking.

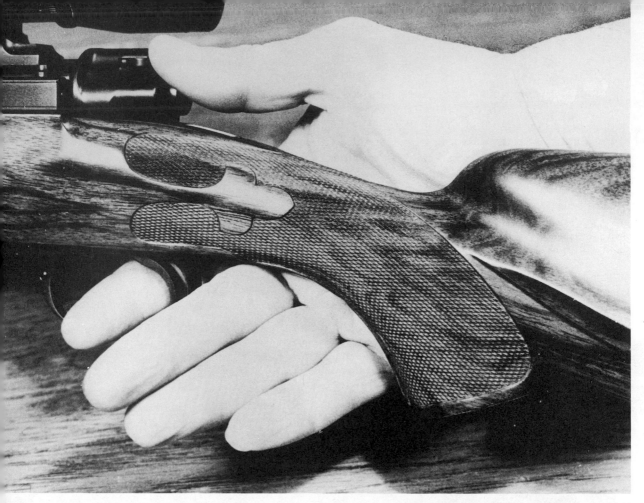

One key to good custom stock styling is the grip. This trim stock grip made by the famous Al Biesen fits the hand snugly and comfortably.

thoroughbred racehorses. Only recently have stockmakers begun to question the rules laid down by the great Linden and to look elsewhere for the secrets to *reliable* accuracy.

THE O'CONNOR INFLUENCE

During the decade of the 1950's, custom stockwork exploded on the shooting scene with unprecedented brilliance. This was a period of widespread interest in all phases of rifle design and performance, especially custom stocks. The man most responsible for this, other than a sudden crop of talented stockmakers, was Jack O'Connor, my predecessor at OUTDOOR LIFE. O'Connor was a man of refined taste who appreciated the elegant lines of a well-made custom stock and promoted the talents of up-and-coming craftsmen in the pages of OUTDOOR LIFE. This sort of exposure not only informed potential customers of who the best stockmakers were but created a craving for their work. Another writer and editor, John Amber, promoted custom riflemaking in the *Gun Digest,* further fueling the flaming interest in fine stockwork.

One particular debt owed to Jack O'Connor by gun lovers and gunmakers alike is for telling us what to look for in a good custom rifle stock. Until he took the subject in hand, a fine custom rifle, in the minds of most shooters, was a rather nebulous creation. But thanks to O'Connor's descriptive writing we gained a viable perspective of the good, the bad and the mediocre. Close inletting became not a relative commodity but an exactitude, and through his works we could sense the agonies of achieving perfect, borderless checkering. I was a teen-ager when O'Connor unveiled to the shooting world the talents of an unknown young stockmaker by the name of Al Biesen, and I, like thousands of other readers, pledged myself to one day own one of his wonderful rifles.

One understandable and very forgivable error O'Connor made in his assessment of the custom rifle scene was that great stockmakers occur only at rare intervals. After all, he probably knew no more than a dozen stockmakers throughout his career, of whom only four or five were top-drawer craftsmen. So naturally, O'Connor shared the common belief that fine stockmaking was a dying art and would someday disappear completely. How could he have predicted that he and OUTDOOR LIFE were creating an appreciation of custom rifles that would, by the simple arithmetic of supply and demand, not only spawn talented stockmakers in unprecedented numbers but inspire the stockmaker's craft to new levels of achievement? No art or craft has ever died away because of a shortage of artists or craftsmen. When and if the necessary talents seem to be on the wane it is simply because of reduced public demand. This was the situation that existed during the first half of this century. While there were few stockmakers around to keep the craft alive, there were precisely enough to supply the demand.

MODERN TRENDS

When I became OUTDOOR LIFE's Shooting Editor, one of the promises I made to myself was to continue the magazine's tradition of promoting the custom gunmaking crafts and encouraging beginning stockmakers. To this end I kept a list of both established and budding stockmakers and became acquainted with most of them. In 1970 there were, at most, no more than 12 to 15 American stockmakers whom I would consider top-rate. Then, year by year, more and more names trickled onto the list, becoming in the 1980's a comparative torrent of fresh new names. With so many craftsmen joining the ranks of stockmakers, it's almost impossible to keep my list up to date—but there are probably over 50 really terrific talents at work today. One of the most amazing things about today's bumper crop of new stockmakers is that they aren't guys trying to master the skills of the bench but, rather, by the time they present themselves to us, are already better than the "old masters" of a generation ago; and not just a little bit better, but a hell of a lot better. How has such a phenomenon come to pass?

A while back, when I was discussing the high level of today's custom stockwork with a group of top stockmakers, someone pointed out that the jet airliner has had a tremendous influence on the quality of today's work. The fast airplane has made it possible for stockmakers to travel widely and see the work of other craftsmen, usually at such places as the annual convention of the NRA, where our best gun work is on display.

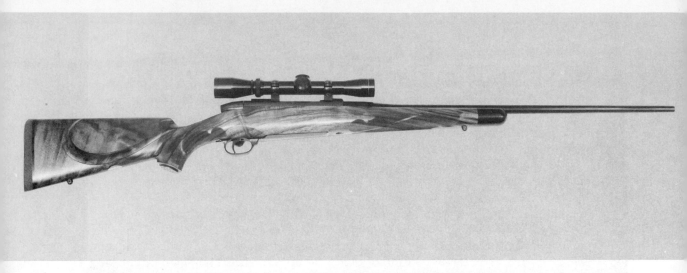

Note the exquisite checkering and the beautifully cut shadow line around the graceful cheekpiece of this left-handed Weatherby Mark V, stocked by Vermonter Winston Churchill. One of the world's finest engravers, Churchill is also among our greatest stockmakers. His detailing and finishing are flawless.

Back in Alvin Linden's time an American stockmaker worked in what can be described as a cultural and inspirational vacuum. Since a craftsman seldom saw the work of others except in books and magazines, he had little basis on which to judge his own work. Thus his work was inclined to resemble that of his teacher, with few if any changes inaugurated throughout his career. But when stockmakers began traveling around and seeing the work of others, they quickly realized not only that they would have to try harder to stay abreast of their craft, but in order to gain recognition they would have to break new ground. A nicely done bit of borderless checkering would no longer wow the critics. Now the checkering had to be presented in increasingly elaborate patterns, complete with narrow ribbons of uncheckered wood, entwined in mind-boggling, talent-challenging designs.

In recent years the custom rifle exhibits have become challenge matches of "one-upsmanship" between stockmakers. If a craftsman presents a stock featuring a more complex way of cutting a "bead" or shadow line around a cheekpiece, at the following show a half-dozen stockmakers will be proudly exhibiting even more elaborate variations on the theme.

This trend chiefly manifests itself in increasingly elaborate checkering patterns, but in recent times has spilled over into finely wrought embellishments. Known in the trade as "detail work," these extra-special features can be added to just about any part of the stock, but mainly occur as delicate moldings under the bolt stop (on Mauser stocks), around the bold-handle slot, or as flourishes to the cheekpiece line. Detail work may also take the form of fancy gripcaps, buttplates, triggerguards, and as combinations of woodwork and metalwork—an example of the latter being specially machined sling-swivel escutcheons framed by carved moldings.

Though these exquisite details are beautiful to behold, they are part of a trend that may have unfortunate consequences. First of all, they are so time-consuming to execute that the finished product is becoming increasingly expensive. A rifle lover of modest means who saves

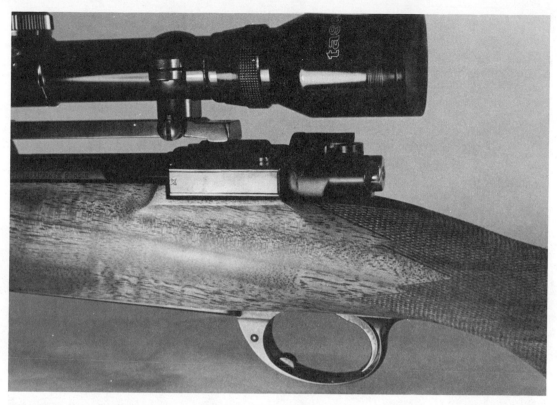

Here is an example of impressive molding under a Mauser bolt stop, executed by Texas stockmaker Sam Marino. Marino's work is in the classic style and shows English influences in the shaping and grip design.

This is a detail of a sumptuously grained stock on a Ruger No. 1. A sample of the work done by Joe Balickie of North Carolina, it exemplifies masterful detailing. Note the delicate molding around the sling-swivel escutcheon, the skeletal gripcap, and the delicately edged checkering pattern.

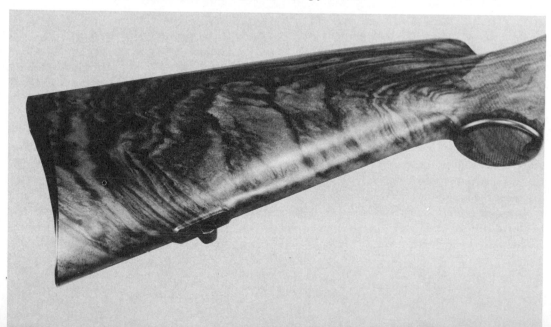

On this stock by Bob Emmons of Ohio, you see classic styling enhanced by originality. An unusual twist on the concept of the skeletal gripcap, it has a ring of ebony rather than steel. Using ebony made the job more difficult—and it also made the rifle more beautiful. Emmons is known for such touches.

his hard-earned pesos for the rifle of his dreams is finding that dream further and further out of reach. And the delicacy of the more elaborate moldings makes them particularly vulnerable to the knocks and scrapes to which a hunting rifle is inevitably heir. These factors are making some custom rifles mere showpieces rather than desirable examples of hunting equipment. This is a sad thing, because when the craft of stockmaking is directed away from the primary goal of achieving a superb sporting arm, then it becomes meaningless. Stockmaking immortality is earned by craftsmen such as Al Biesen and Dale Goens, who have perfected the hunting rifle as a unit of beauty *and* efficiency. When decoration becomes superfluous, and then a hindrance, the art declines.

So what is good stockmaking? What does the discerning connoisseur demand? We often read that the hallmarks of fine stockwork are close inletting and borderless checkering with no runovers at the edge of the pattern, and that the finish should be old-fashioned linseed oil, hand-rubbed to a dull luster. In truth, fine stockwork is far more than close inletting, borderless checkering, and a lustrous finish. In fact, when you compliment a top stockmaker on his air-tight inletting or razor-edged checkering borders, you're being more insulting than complimentary. These are only *basic* skills, something a budding craftsman learns long before he masters the subtleties of line and proportion. I've seen flawlessly inletted and checkered stocks that had to be ranked as amateurish because of other failings.

THE FACTS ABOUT GOOD INLETTING

Since the first step in making a custom stock is inletting, let's start there. In the relaxed days of yore, a custom stock was invariably begun from scratch, with the craftsman inletting the barreled action into a flat-sided, flat-topped block of wood. Quite a few of our leading stockmakers still do it that way, and all *can* do so if they wish. But in recent years many, if not most, custom rifle builders begin with a piece of wood that has 80 percent or more of the inletting and outside shaping done by a stock-turning machine. Initially this practice was condemned by some stockmakers and customers who insisted that if a stock were truly custom it should be hand-made from beginning to end. I'm told, however, that I eased the tension somewhat in my book, *The Modern Rifle,* published in the mid-1970's. My comments were simply that a customer shouldn't be concerned with how excess wood is removed from a blank; what the customer wants is a stock that features the styling *traits* of the craftsman, along with his characteristic inletting, finishing, checkering, and detailing. None of these can be diminished in any way by using a machine-shaped stock.

Don Allen makes a stock-carving machine used by many custom stockmakers for the initial rough shaping and inletting of a stock. Allen is also a top stockmaker himself. To produce this magnificent little Mauser in .250 Savage, he teamed with a fellow Minnesota craftsman, master metalsmith Ron Lampert. Allen used a very unusual stock blank that came from English walnut grafted to Claro. Lampert cut the action in half, removed an inch, then welded everything back together so flawlessly that the joining is invisible. He also did all the other metalwork, including the wing-type safety and trigger-bow floorplate release.

I think some critics do not understand what a machine-carved stock really is, believing it to be a fully finished product requiring no additional work, save a coat or two of finish, and thus equate such stocks with those on mass-produced rifles. Such is hardly the case.

Many of today's custom stockmakers own a stock-carving machine, usually one made by Don Allen, himself a top stockmaker and talented innovator. These rather expensive machines resemble a lathe somewhat and operate by duplicating a "master" stock. The carving is accomplished by a high-speed cutter that shaves the wood away like a router bit. Though large, commercial stockmaking firms use multiple-spindle machines; the machines used by custom stockmakers usually carve only one or two blanks at a time. If the operator is careful, the machine duplication of a stock requires several hours. The stock, as it comes from the machine, is rather roughly cut, undersize in the inletting and somewhat oversize on the outside. With a machine-carved stock in hand, the craftsman is still days or even weeks away from the finished product. From there on, it's *all* hand work.

Where a machine-carved stock made by a custom stockmaker mainly differs from a machine-carved stock by a mass supplier to the trade, such as Reinhart Fajen, is that the custom craftsman's stock is shaped to his exclusive pattern. Thus the end product retains the unique features that make us want to own a stock by that particular craftsman. In contrast, a semi-finished stock by a mass supplier is identical in shape to thousands of others.

When a stockmaker starts to work with a solid block of wood, he is faced with a considerable amount of lay-out and "figgerin' out" in order to get the metal parts started in the right direction. This is followed by a good bit of rough excavation to get excess wood out. When a machined-carved stock is used, most of this excess wood has already been cut away, leaving the stock ready for final inletting and bedding. (Inletting is fitting the metal into the wood, whereas bedding is fitting metal to wood *so that the rifle shoots accurately.* A rifle that appears to be inletted beautifully may, in fact, be bedded poorly.)

The final inletting and bedding of a semi-finished stock is no different from that of a plain blank. The craftsman "spots in" the metal, shaving and scraping away the smudges left by the inletting indicator, until metal and wood form a perfect fit. I've heard good inletting described as being so close that a cigarette paper couldn't be fitted between wood and metal. Though this might be a fair description of good factory-produced stockwork, it hardly does justice to the work of an accomplished stockmaker. It may not even be fair to say that the metal fits into the wood as if it grew there, because I don't think things in nature always grow that close. Proper inletting is so close that no space between wood and metal exists; it's as simple as that.

The entire inletting should be as beautiful to behold as the stock's external surfaces. And sometimes it is, indeed. I always make a point of taking the action out of a new custom rifle, especially one made by an up-and-coming craftsman, because the quality of the inletting says a lot about where that craftsman's heart is.

Once I ordered a stock from an unknown young stockmaker by the name of Duane Wiebe and was delighted to find the inletting to be a perfectly molded negative image of the action, barrel and trigger guard it encased. There was not even a chisel or scraper mark to mar the clean surfaces—it was absolutely beautiful. Today Wiebe is one of our best known and most respected stockmakers. Obviously, anyone who loves to inlet like that is bound to become a great stockmaker.

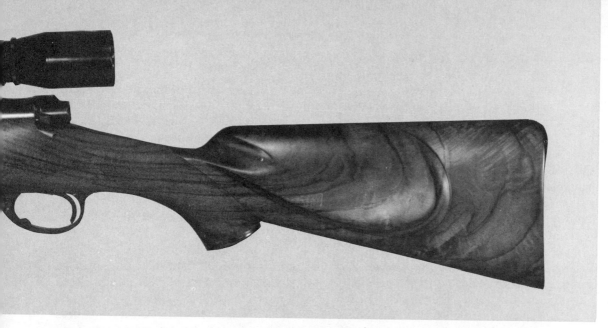

Here you see fine detail work on a 7mm Magnum Winchester Model 70 restocked for the author by Californi-an Duane Wiebe. The distinctive shaping of the cheekpiece includes a slight beveling of the edge to achieve a softening effect. Like all of Carmichel's custom guns, this is a working rifle, and the beveling is practical as well as handsome since it is less likely to be damaged than a sharply edged cheekpiece.

It would be hard to imagine a more difficult checkering pattern than the one Duane Wiebe used for the author's 7mm Remington Magnum — and the execution is magnificent.

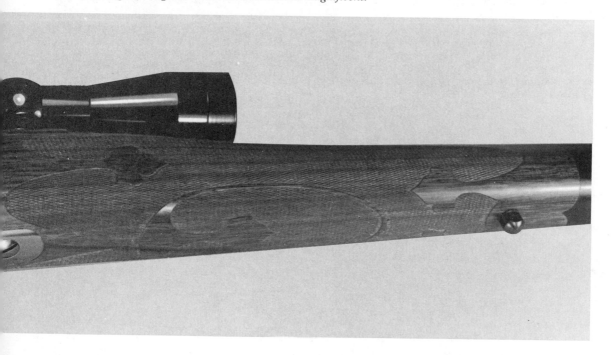

Another thing to remember about good inletting is that close does not mean tight. Occasionally a stockmaker will try to achieve the appearance of a close fit by hammering or pressing the metal into undersize inletting. This crushes the wood cells and can cause considerable weakening of the wood at the delicate edges of the inletting. The error of this practice manifests itself when you take the metal out and the wood splits or chips at the edges. Really good inletting is close but doesn't squeeze the metal. Once when I was admiring an example of magnificent inletting by Monty Kennedy, one of our all-time greatest stockmakers, I was amazed to find that the trigger guard would fall out of the wood simply by its own weight.

WHERE GLASS BEDDING BELONGS

Back in the 1950's, I think it was, when so-called "fiberglass bedding" appeared on the scene, some stockmakers got in a flap about its use being a "betrayal" to the craft of stockmaking. Since then, stockmakers have reached an accord with fiberglass or epoxy bedding techniques, and there is a more or less unspoken set of rules governing what is and what isn't acceptable. I have my own set of guidelines which are as fair as any:

Though glass bedding is the only way to go for target shooting, it is not very pleasing esthetically. When you order a custom stock you are hiring the stockmaker's skills, one of which is his talent for inletting. So naturally you want a display of these talents rather than a thick layer of epoxy that could be dumped in by any amateur. But I'm not saying that fiberglass has no place in a custom stock. If a stockmaker wants to put some around the recoil lug of a heavy-caliber rifle, I won't quibble. Also, since today's epoxy compounds are wonderfully waterproof, I'm not at all depressed when a coat of epoxy is used to seal the inletting. Basically, then, my

One of the most meticulous—and stylish—of today's stockmakers is Earl Milliron. This sleek, lightweight Mauser shows how Milliron creates somewhat racy styling without sacrificing classic contours.

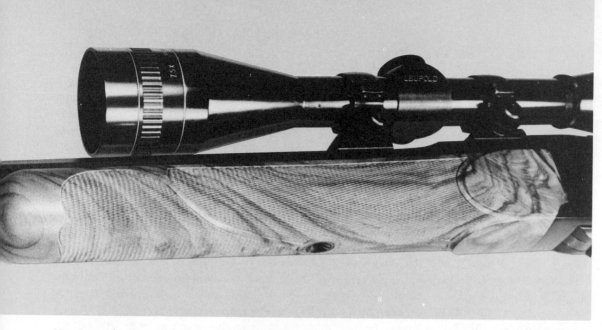

Here is another view of the Ruger No. 1 Single-Shot restocked for the author by Joe Balickie. Note the delicately ribboned checkering pattern and the molding where the stock flows from the receiver.

rules are simple. Fiberglass shouldn't be used to cover up sloppy work. And by all means it should be completely out of sight, not a filler for gaps between wood and metal. When used as a sealer, epoxy should not be colored but clear only, so the beauty of the inletting is brightly showcased.

STYLING AND CONTOURS

Though it is relatively easy to state what is good or bad inletting, judging the exterior of a custom stock is quite another matter. Whether we like the form and line of a particular stock is an almost wholly subjective judgment. Tastes in styling run the gamut from racy thumbhole jobs to starkly conservative classic shapes, and only a fool condemns the preferences of others. But without getting into that gray area of stock styling, there are a few guidelines for judging basic workmaship. Look for symmetry, flatness of surface, or evenness of curve. Also look for the boldness of contour that indicates that a stock stylist knows what he wants to do and how to do it. Sometimes we see the hint of a stylistic feature on a stock that doesn't seem to be quite completed, or is blurred at the edges so that we aren't sure what the stockmaker had in mind. This is usually the result of his not being sure of what he wanted to do, or an indication that he wanted to be different for the sake of being different, or had a bold idea and lost his nerve. The late Lenard Brownell, one of America's great stockmakers and the designer of the classic Ruger rifle stocks, once told me that a good stock sculptor is never afraid to be bold with stylistic features. Taking his advice, I look for fully developed details and stylistic flourishes.

A mastery of stock shaping shows in the way a stockmaker handles basic carpentry. Are the lines straight? Sight along (or place a straight edge along) the butt section from the buttplate to the grip area. The surface should be straight, not bowed or concave or rippled in and out. Do the flutes at the nose of the comb match or complement each other? Do they complement the curve of the pistol grip? Are they cleanly cut? Do the flats along either side of the barrel match in width and shape? And does one line flow into another logically and gracefully?

The sculpted detail work on some of today's custom stocks is truly amazing, but in order to be good it has to be perfect. What a stockmaker is saying when he adds a fancy piece of detail work, be it a double bead around the cheekpiece or delicate swivel moldings, is "Look at what I can do." If it isn't perfect, then obviously he can't do it and is reaching too far. So don't give extra points just because a stockmaker *attempts* something difficult, but only if he succeeds.

An up-and-coming stockmaker once asked what he could do to make his stocks really different. "Just be good," I told him. "That will be different enough."

According to most of what we hear and read about custom stocks, if the stockmaker doesn't work in the "classic" style he simply isn't worthy of our notice. Or could it be that classic-styled stocks are so great simply because our top craftsmen happen to favor that particular style? What if a great craftsman such as Al Biesen or Dale Goens just happened to prefer making stocks with rollover cheekpieces and thumbhole grips? Do you suppose that if such were the case these much-condemned features might be more readily accepted by devotees of the classical style?

In my opinion, the dean of today's stockmakers is Monty Kennedy. Though his name isn't as well-known as some of today's much publicized stockmakers, he is mentioned with reverence by other craftsmen. It was his great book *The Checkering and Carving of Gunstocks* that showed the World War II generation of stockmakers what good checkering, inletting and finishing should look like and provided a standard of excellence for all to pursue. Most of today's collections do not include a Kennedy rifle, and many aficionados of fine stockmaking have not even seen an example of his work. At this writing, Kennedy's output is limited but during his active years his clientele included princes, magnates and moguls. That's why his work is so seldom seen.

Kennedy was (and is) a master of the classic style, but that was only one of several styles in which he was fluent. When he executed a stock with a rollover cheekpiece and teardrop pistol grip complete with gripcap and fore-end tip of some gaudy wood, it was as much a masterpiece as his more conservative creations. A hunting pal of mine has a lightweight .280 stocked by Monty Kennedy that he has used with great joy and success on several of the big game hunts we've made together. Made of Yama wood, a lightweight, light-colored wood that was mildly in vogue a generation ago, the stock has a rollover cheekpiece and flared pistol grip that would, on sight, make a classical purist break out with a case of the hives. And for the record *I would absolutely love to own it*. In typical Kennedy fashion, everything about the stock is flawlessly executed and it is one of the sweetest-feeling rifles I've ever put to shoulder. The eye doesn't have to hunt for the sight and the finger doesn't grope for the trigger; everything about the stock does what it is supposed to do in the most efficient way imaginable.

The reason the stock feels so good—it's certainly as shootable as any classic-style stock I've ever fired—is because Kennedy is a great master of shaping a stock. The reason so many— most—stocks with rollover cheekpieces, hawknosed grip contours and other stylistic oddities feel uncomfortable and clumsy to shoot is simply that their makers don't know how a stock should be shaped. If these same individuals attempted a stock in the classic mode it, too, would

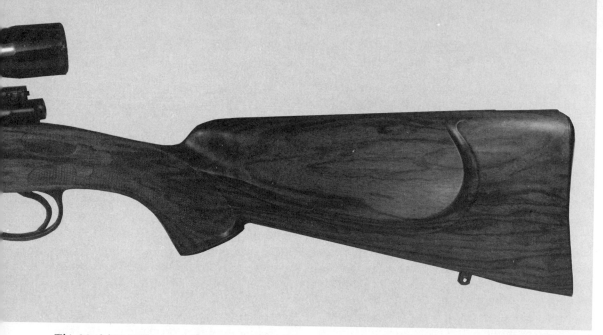

This Model 98 Mauser action was rebarreled and restocked by one of the all-time masters of custom riflemaking, Al Biesen of Spokane, Washington.

The distinctive fleur-de-lis checkering pattern on this stock is well known to the many fans of Al Biesen's rifles. Note the framed, three-dimensional appearance of this checkering. The effect is achieved by relieving the checkering area—that is, shaving away a thin layer of wood before cutting the diamonds. The technique is called inset checkering.

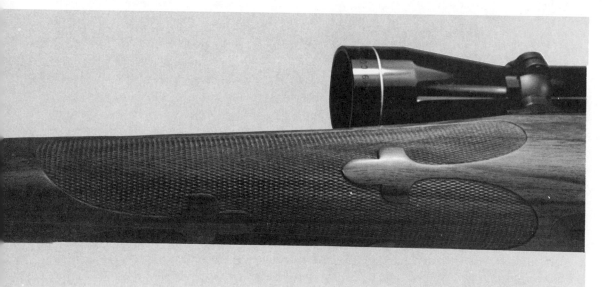

look and feel awkward. I've tried some so-called classic stocks that were as uncomfortable as the embrace of an iron maiden. The conclusion we have to reach is that the reason the best classic-style stocks look and feel so good is because they are the product of our best craftsmen.

I once had a conversation with a fellow who considered himself a stockmaker of sorts and was of the opinion that there wasn't anything all that great about the classic-style stock. "It's the easiest of all stocks to make," he insisted. "After all, there's nothing fancy about it. You can even leave off the cheekpiece and get away with it." Like many casual, and some not so casual, observers of stock design, the fellow had decided that any stock that didn't have a rollover cheekpiece, Monte Carlo comb, thumbhole grip and whiteline spacers must be a "classic" stock. This is hardly the case. A truly classic-style stock is one of the most difficult of all stock forms to master because of its subtle blend of curves and lines. It is certainly not a simple shape, and most stockmakers would probably agree it is the most complex to make. Indeed, some stockmakers have spent their careers producing what they consider to be "classic" stocks without even coming close.

Sometimes the stock of the Winchester Model 70 bolt rifle manufactured before 1964 is used as an example of a classic stock. I do not agree that it qualifies; it is too chubby in the butt section and has an awkward grip contour, along with some other stylistic aberrations. When asked to describe the real essence of the classic form my best answer is, "If you have to ask, you'll never understand."

One thing is certain, though—the classic style is not a strict form; there is considerable latitude for variation. Proof is the obvious fact that the individual styling of various stockmakers is easily recognized while the basic form remains unmistakably classic. The lines of a Dale Goens stock are vastly different from those of a stock made by Al Biesen, but no one would deny that both are classic. Bieson can even get away with a Monte Carlo comb when he wants to.

CHECKERING

One of the most distinctive features of today's best custom stocks is the fantastic checkering. Checkering as a form of ornamentation is an almost exclusively American art form. Our top craftsmen are so far ahead of the rest of the world that there is no point in making comparisons, and the gulf is getting wider. Much has been said about such features as "borderless checkering" and "runovers" without much clarification of what the terms mean or why they are important. Let's look into all of this.

The original purpose of checkering, of course, was to provide a nonslip gripping surface for the shooter's hands. It also had the pleasing effect of breaking up the expanses of plain wood, so checkering assumed a decorative role early in gunmaking history. Checkering is nothing more than crisscrossed rows of V-shaped cuts that form a bunch of tiny pyramid-shaped spires, usually called "diamonds." The rows of cuts that form these diamonds in a hand-cut checkering job are usually, but not always, cut one row at a time with a narrow file-like hand-powered tool or a wee electric-driven circular saw. If a hand-powered checkering tool is used, the craftsman deepens each row a bit at a time, and when the job is finished he may have traced each line three or four times, meaning he has made hundreds of individual cuts. Even when an electric tool is used, the final touching up is done with a hand tool.

One of the problems is keeping all the lines within the outlines of the pattern. When a stockmaker works close to the edge of the pattern with a rapid back-and-forth cutting motion, there is an ever-present danger that the tool will slip or jump across the pattern's edge and cause an ugly runover. Since every line of checkering has a boundary at each end, and there are hundreds of lines in a full pattern, the craftsman has many hundreds of opportunities to get his share of runovers.

One of the easier ways to hide runovers is to cut a contoured border around the pattern after the checkering is completed. Unless the runovers are really bad, a narrow border will nicely hide little slips of the checkering tool and may even add an attractive framing effect to the pattern. However, as checkering became more and more an artistic skill unto itself, the best checkerers sought to demonstrate their mastery of the checkering tool by leaving off the border, thus proclaiming to the world: "Look, I'm omitting the border so you can see for yourself that I don't make runovers."

So it came to pass that "borderless checkering" became the big thing, and most self-respecting stockmakers would rather be caught in a house of ill repute than with a bordering tool in their hand. For the most part, this was just fine because good borderless checkering is beautiful to behold. But just because a pattern doesn't have a border doesn't necessarily mean the checkering is good. Some borderless checkering we see is very, very bad. The edges of the pattern may be bumped and nicked rather than clean and smooth, or the lines may not be cut to

The grip area of this rifle typifies the restrained, elegant—quintessentially classic—stocks made by Griffin & Howe, one of the world's great gunsmithing firms. Note how the checkering saddles the pistol grip. Although the visible portion is bordered, portions of the traditional point pattern are borderless.

full depth because the checkerer lost his nerve as his tool approached the edge. If the V-cuts aren't cut to full depth the tops of the diamonds will be flat and shiny with stock finish. So when you see a borderless pattern, take a hard look at the diamonds around the edge.

Another problem with borderless checkering is that some patterns really do need a border to take away some of the plainness. That the borderless mania has gotten out of hand is evident in some of today's factory-produced stocks. The current issue of Remington's Model 700 rifle, for example, has some precise machine-cut checkering in a traditional point pattern. Yielding to what they perceived to be public demand, the people at Remington designed and programmed their fancy automatic checkering machines to cut a borderless pattern. The problem is that their simple point pattern would look a hell of a lot better if it *did* have a border.

The stylish Griffin & Howe custom stocks are about as classic as stocks get but they have long used a partial border to dress up their traditional point patterns. The border is quite delicate and would scarcely serve to cover up runovers if there were any. In such cases, the addition of a border not only increases the difficulty of the job, but also adds to the beauty of the checkering. Not much way they can be faulted for that. One of the best examples of a well-applied border is on a stock made for me by ace craftsman Bob Winter. Bob made the stock when he was first starting and he was under considerable pressure to demonstrate his ability to execute such refinements as borderless checkering. Yet, the point pattern I asked for begged for a border. So, allowing good taste to win out, he added a border to the points that achieved the perfect effect. In addition to my tremendous esteem for Winter's talents, I also hold great respect for his willingness to fly in the face of a popular fad and add a border where it was needed. If you can't judge a book by its cover then it's also true that you can't judge a checkering job by its borders—or lack thereof.

The relative size of all those little diamonds in a checkering pattern is expressed in lines to the inch, or just LPI's. This is simply the number of parallel V-cuts in an inch. The average number of LPI's in a factory stock is about 18. Coarser checkering, say 16 LPI, has an excellent gripping quality but doesn't look so good. Checkering of, say, 22 LPI or finer doesn't grip as well but looks better, so naturally custom stockmakers prefer fine-line checkering, sometimes as close as 32 LPI or even finer. Of course, not all wood can be checkered with such small diamonds because they tend to chip and fall off. As the checkering gets finer it not only becomes more difficult, but errors and mistakes become more glaringly obvious. Super fine-line checkering can be awesome to behold if done perfectly but can look terrible otherwise. Most custom stockmakers like to cut 26- or 28-LPI checkering.

Today's stockmakers are executing checkering patterns that were unimagined a generation ago. It might even be reasonable to say that in terms of both elaborateness and degree of difficulty, the quality of checkering is running ahead of the rest of the stock. Perhaps this is because stockmakers have gone about as far with stock design as they can and therefore must concentrate on the design and execution of their checkering in order to attract customers and to impress their peers.

A particularly notable feature of today's trend in checkering layouts is the inclusion of bands or "ribbons" in the pattern. These narrow strips of uncheckered wood add grace and delicacy to the pattern but greatly increase the degree of difficulty and time required to execute the job. Running a single ribbon through a forearm pattern doubles the degree of difficulty

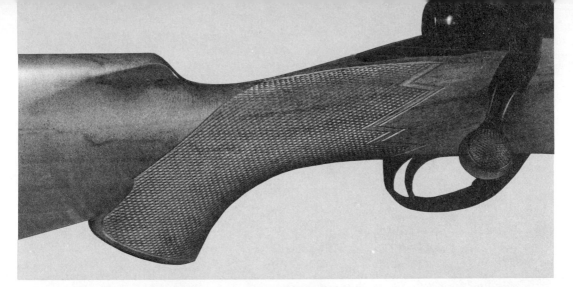

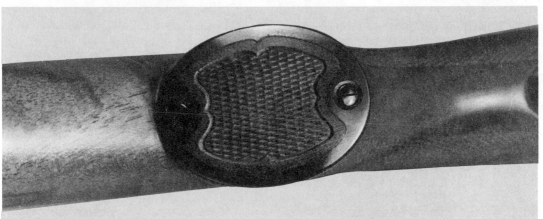

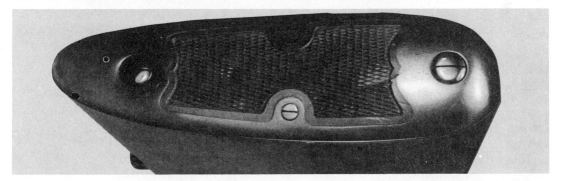

These are close-up views of the author's pre-1964 Winchester Model 70 rebarreled to .25/06 caliber. They show superlative detailing by South Dakota craftsman Bob Winter. The checkering on the pistol grip has handsome bordering at the front end and is borderless at the rear. The bottom of the grip is a baroque treatment combining checkering with a curvilinear skeleton cap. The checkered butt and skeleton buttplate carries out a variation of the theme. The dents and scratches were added by Carmichel—a risk that must be taken with skeleton buttplates on hunting rifles.

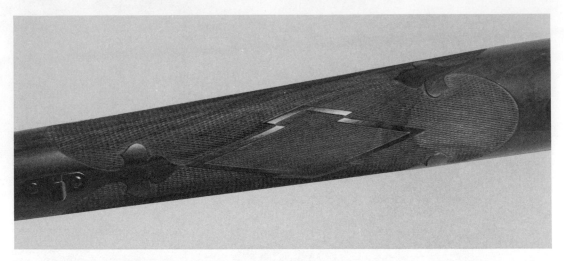

Maurice Ottmar, a Washington State stockmaker, created this magnificently checkered forearm pattern, whose combination of diamond ribbons and fleur-de-lis sets a standard for other carvers in design and execution. The area enclosed by the ribbon-edged banner is checkered in finer diamonds than the outer portion.

because the amount of edge area is doubled. When two or more interweaving ribbons are worked into the pattern you can imagine how much more difficult the stockmaker's task becomes. Needless to say, the price of such work has to be high because of the time involved.

METALSMITHING

The motivation that spurs stockmakers to achieve ever more complex and difficult checkering designs also manifests itself in elaborate embellishments such as skeleton buttplates and gripcaps and delicate detail work. Back in the '50's, when custom stockmaking began to get widespread attention, skeleton buttplates and gripcaps were scarcely heard of. These days they are not only commonplace but, like other areas of stockmaking, have become increasingly complex and challenging.

Until fairly recent times, a custom rifle was almost entirely a stockmaking project. A barrel might be recontoured or replaced, but the action, be it a Mauser, Springfield or whatever, was changed little if at all. Then, bit by bit, the craft of metalsmithing began to emerge. The definition and aims of a custom metalsmith are entirely different from that of gunsmithing. Whereas a gunsmith is primarily concerned with repair, a custom metalsmith is interested exclusively in building or rebuilding the metalwork for a custom firearm. This includes not only fitting and chambering barrels but modifying the basic action and building sights, scope mounts, buttplates, gripcaps and trigger guard units.

One might ask what can be done to, say, a Mauser action other than perhaps turning down the bolt handle for scope use and drilling a few holes so scope bases can be fitted. The answer is, plenty. The process begins with truing all the surfaces by precision grinding, lapping locking lugs and going on to a dozen other details. If you have a top metalsmith rework your action,

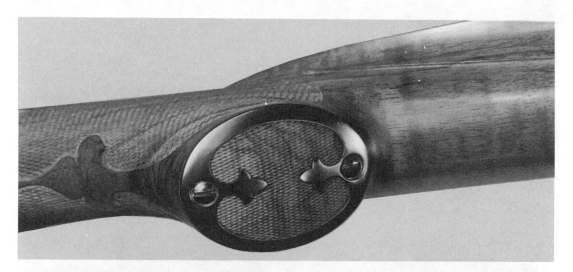

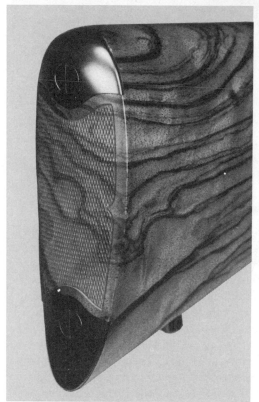

Here are three striking deviations from the usual metalwork on gripcaps and butts. One is a skeleton gripcap by Maurice Ottmar featuring twin fleur-de-lis. Another is a butt by Bob Emmons, who likes to checker this area and cap only the heel and toe. On this rifle, no one would want to hide any of the stunning grain of the walnut, which came from Roberts Wood Products. The third is a finely bordered, checkered steel buttplate by Clayton Nelson, with a felt-lined trapdoor compartment.

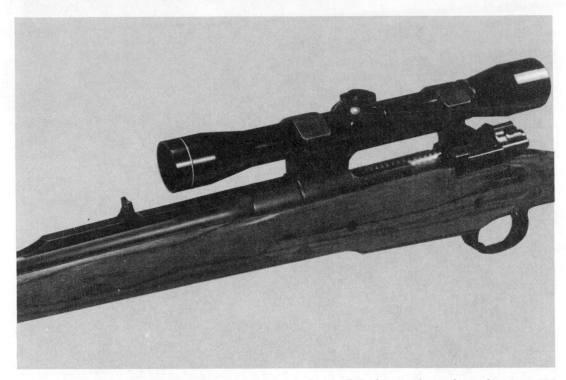

The David Miller Company of Tucson, as Carmichel says, does it all. In this case the work was done on a .338 Winchester Magnum built on a 1909 Argentine Mauser. This view shows an integral quarter-rib and Miller scope-mount assembly—incomparable metalwork.

you'll invest $1,000 or more in an action that originally cost you no more than $100. The idea of custom metalwork is to provide a mechanism that is not only worthy of the best stock work but to achieve an artistic balance of wood and metal. That's why a custom rifle firm such as the David Miller Company of Tucson, maker of what are generally considered the finest custom rifles in the world, may spend weeks rebuilding an action until it is as good as human talent and imagination can make it. Only then is it considered ready to be beautifully stocked with expensive wood and delivered to a discriminating collector.

The pity of good metalsmithing is that you get a lot more than you see. Here of late the names of metalsmiths have become better known to lovers of fine rifles, and in time may even rival the fame of top stockmakers and engravers. Already the names of Ted Blackburn, Tom Burgess, Ken Jantz, Ron Lampert, Dave Talley and Herman Waldron are famous in the industry. Of course, all of the great custom riflemaking houses such as David Miller, Pachmayr, Paul Jaeger, Champlin Arms and Griffin & Howe provide superb custom metalsmithing. And some multi-talented craftsmen such as Al Biesen and Pete Grisel provide great metalworking as well as stockmaking and richly deserve the title *Riflemaker.*

This is a close-up view of a 1909 Argentine Mauser in .30/06, built for the author by metalsmith Dave Talley and stockmaker Dale Goens, with scope bases fitted by David Miller. It is almost impossible to see where the bases are fitted to the receiver. Few craftsmen are capable of such perfection.

This .270 Ruger No. 1 blends Kevin Campbell's woodwork with Herman Waldron's metalwork. It has a gorgeous color case-hardened receiver and rich, brilliantly detailed walnut.

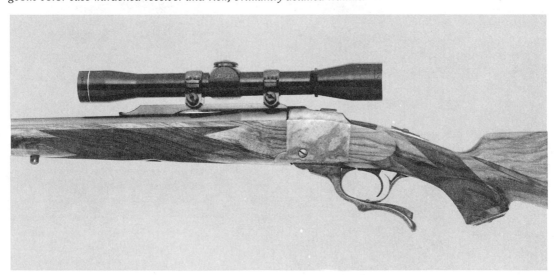

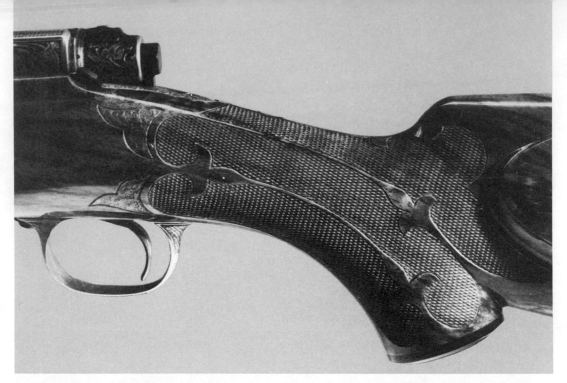

A restocked Sako, this rifle shows engraving and stockwork by Pachmayr and it represents just about the ultimate. Altogether, the patterns on forearm and grip include 13 fleurs-de-lis, and in this view of the grip you can see the delicate ribbons joining fore and aft fleurs-de-lis. This is extremely detailed and demanding craftsmanship.

Few stockmakers can equal the art of Dale Goens of New Mexico. Carmichel's .30/06 Model 1909 Argentine Mauser shows the grace, strong lines, and delicacy of Goens's contouring—as well as the perfection of his borderless checkering.

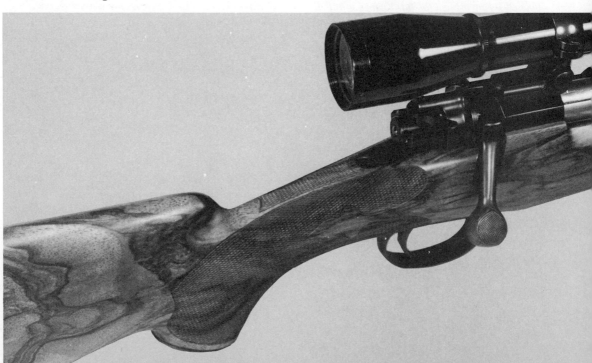

This detail of the author's 1909 Argentine Mauser shows another smooth blending of Goens-Talley workmanship. Goens has provided a delicate molding that seems almost a continuation of Talley's sling-swivel stud and escutcheon.

LINSEED OIL AND MIRACLE FINISHES

Traditions die hard, especially the ones we love most, so it's no wonder we still hear members of the shooting brethren speak in reverent tones of the beloved hand-rubbed oil finish for gunstocks. Anyone who has ever tried to hand-rub linseed oil on a stock probably has a less than holy opinion of the results. According to legend, and a certain amount of historical fact, the bagpipe was actually invented by the Irish, who passed it on to the Scots in one of the greatest hoaxes of all time. I think the legend of hand-rubbed linseed oil was dreamed up by someone with a similarly diabolical view of guns and shooters.

This is not a condemnation of commercial stock finishes such as Lin-Speed or Birchwood-Casey's Tru-Oil. Though they claim the hand-rubbed linseed connection they are more similar to a good varnish. Many gun owners like to rub a few drops of linseed oil on their stocks and get all aquiver at the rich glow that emanates from the wood's surface after a few seconds of rubbing. "Ah," they say to themselves, "Nothing makes a stock look better than hand-rubbed linseed oil." But the effect is only temporary and the same look can be achieved by hand-rubbing

The concept, design, and exquisite execution of this floorplate show why Winston Churchill is regarded as one of the world's greatest engravers.

Here you see another floorplate and gripcap by Churchill. At one time the Germans (famous for deep-relief sculpture) and the English (famous for delicate, light scrollwork) were considered the world's best. America has caught up.

Another American master of engraving is Frank Hendrix of San Antonio. This deeply cut floorplate is done primarily in a style once considered to be German or Austrian—but with English intricacy and the new American finesse.

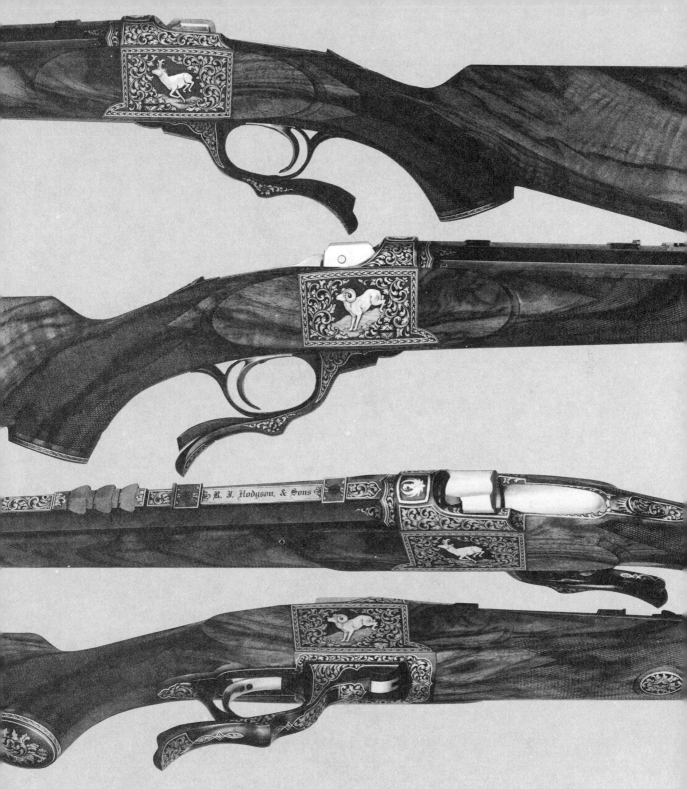

Here are four views — both sides, top, and bottom — of a Ruger No. 1 that has been turned into one of the most splendid custom rifles ever built. The stock and the metalwork are by Richard Hodgson, the engraving by Linton MacKenzie. A connoisseur has to question whether such a masterpiece belongs in a gun rack or an art museum.

a few drops of motor oil. The day after a stock has been rubbed with linseed oil the finish is somewhat dulled, the after-effect of the oil's scumming and oxidizing. As these layers of residual oil build up, the stock gradually darkens until the original beauty of the wood fades and is lost.

Books and articles on stock-finishing sometimes attempt to spell out the differences between "raw" and "boiled" linseed oil, warning in strict tones against the use of raw oil. Such advice is only the mindless copying of previous articles which in turn copied even earlier books and articles. The difference between raw and boiled linseed oil is that the boiled stuff has had some of the impurities and contaminants removed by chemical means. The difference is only a matter of degree, boiled oil simply being somewhat less harmful to your stock's finish. If you cannot resist the primal urge to rub linseed oil on your gunstocks (and I confess to a periodic weakening myself) rub it on in a thin layer, then buff away remaining traces with a soft cloth. Buff until the wood feels clean and dry and you'll discover that it not only has a rich glow but

Alaskan stockmaker Mike Conner hand-rubs the finish into one of his richly grained stocks. He may be using boiled linseed oil—but then again, he may have started with an epoxy compound to fill pores and toughen the surface, then switched to some modern miracle finish that is known to few amateurs.

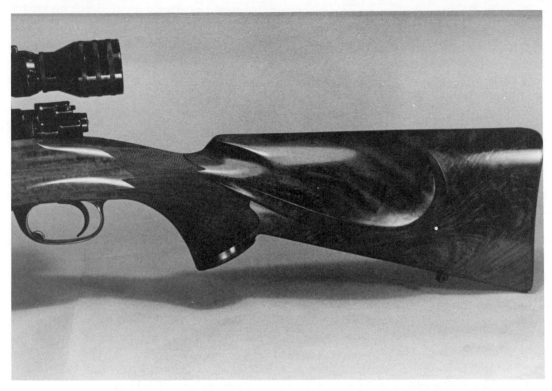

The author considers himself a stockmaking amateur—though he worked his way through college fashioning stocks. Here is a sample of his work: a Mauser Model 98 in .35 Whelen caliber, restocked in vibrant black walnut. Carmichel did all the woodwork—shaping, inletting, finishing, checkering—but the great Al Biesen contributed the fine metalwork, including a classy gripcap and buttplate.

looks good a lot longer than when you slop on some oil and leave it there. And for God's sake, don't heat the oil or the wood! That will cause the oil to penetrate into the wood, causing it to darken and dull long before its time.

I used to be a stockmaker of sorts and all-around jake-leg gunsmith. That's how I earned my way through college and even graduate school. I wasn't very good, but I sure as hell was fast, usually guaranteeing 48-hour delivery if not sooner, with prices seldom exceeding $25 for the whole job, including fancy checkering. I read all the available books on stockmaking, especially the parts on wood finishing, and was greatly confused and frustrated by the seemingly endless types of finishes that were described.

The only thing I knew for sure about the finishing processes of that time was that the finishes that looked the best took the longest and required the most work. Usually I opted for the quick procedures. There's no point in describing them here, because they are all utterly obsolete. Space-age chemistry has brought us the miracle finishes our founding gunmakers spent their lives in search of. Ironically, the "old-fashioned" deep-luster stock finishes that truly fill the wood's grain, honestly repel moisture, and best protect the beauty of a good piece of wood are the result of the modern laboratory.

Most custom stockmakers have developed their own combinations of stock finishes and finishing procedures. Some will tell you what they use and some won't, but it's a safe bet that they begin with an epoxy-type compound to fill and toughen the wood's surface, then finish with something similar to Flecto Plastic Oil. Some of today's miracle finishes even smell as good as linseed oil!

One has to wonder if there are any limits to what can be achieved in the world of custom riflemaking. Will today's trends reach a conclusion and go no further? Will excessive ornamentation find its own dead end? One thing that is becoming clear is that the term "custom" rifle no longer has the meaning it once had. The traditional proposition of making a rifle to fit the owner's physique and suit his whims is giving way to a concept wherein the total form of the rifle as an artistic package is more important than how it fits the shooter or performs in the field. This trend is obvious in the number of outrageously priced "speculation" rifles being built these days. Obviously, when a rifle is built before the buyer is known, the term "custom" doesn't apply. This trend is not a healthy one and will probably be short-lived. I have much more respect for a craftsman who can tell you what his work is worth than one who feels he has to bag a sucker to make a living.

The exceptions, of course, are rifles such as the SCI Big Five series which are specifically made to sell at auction to help finance conservation projects. When a rich bidder offers over $100,000 for a rifle, which has happened in recent times, he's making a heavy contribution to wildlife conservation. The rifle is only a symbol.

Fashions change, and I expect that by the year 2000 we will look back on this era of custom work and see it as a period of rapid artistic transition and achievement but certainly not as the ultimate development of the custom rifle.

Chapter 6

TRIGGERING A REVOLUTION

Until Word War II, the great watershed of modern gun design, shooters paid little attention to rifle and pistol triggers and even less to the triggers of shotguns. Gun books, magazines, and catalogs, especially those published before 1930 or thereabouts, are full of lavish testimonials to the workmanship, firepower, and accuracy of sundry guns, but there is scarce mention of trigger performance.

SPORTING, MILITARY, TARGET TRIGGERS

For reasons that I'll discuss later, I peg 1948 as the year the great revolution in triggers was triggered. Until that time, most triggers could be classified as being of the sporting, military, or target type.

Sport triggers were all about the same, and their makers weren't inclined to improve them. They were generally reliable, they were usually safe; and if they were diligently pulled, they would fire the gun. A good example of a pre-WW II sport trigger is to be found on the Model 1894 Winchester lever-action rifle. It represents no improvement over the trigger of the Model 1886 Winchester, which in turn was no better than the triggers of the model 1876, the 1873, or even the 1866 Winchester lever-action rifles. Trigger design and operation was not recognized as an area of competition between manufacturers. Thus a Winchester trigger felt about like a Savage trigger, which felt like a Marlin trigger, and on and on, make after make, and model after model.

When you pull a typical sport-type rifle trigger designed before, say, 1940, you'll notice certain characteristics. As pressure is applied, the trigger begins to move rearward. After sufficient pressure is applied, usually enough to lift a five- to 15-pound weight, the sear releases and the hammer or firing pin falls. At this instant, the trigger lurches rearward a few more fractions of an inch and comes to a stop.

The trigger of a Brown Bess musket used in our War of Independence feels exactly the same. The trigger pull is no worse than that of a typical bolt, lever, pump, or self-loading rifle of the mid-1900's. This is not necessarily a criticism, but it amply illustrates the point that despite a series of revolutionary advances in gun design and performance, trigger design was neglected.

Paradoxically, some improvement did occur in military triggers during the latter half of the 1800's. At least, some changes were made, which indicated that someone was giving thought — for the first time in centuries — to how a trigger ought to work. Notable among these were von Dreyse and Paul Mauser, giants of European armsmaking.

The new cartridge-firing, repeating rifles made by these and other manufacturers featured trigger mechanisms best identified by their two-stage pull, a development of considerable importance. When you put a little pressure on a military two-stage trigger, it moves rearward for about half an inch before coming to a definite stop. When additional pressure is applied, the trigger moves again, and after some travel, the sear is released and the rifle fires. Though the

The Model 98 German Mauser has the two-stage trigger pull characteristic of military rifles. In this photo the trigger is fully forward and the sear is at the maximum point of engagement.

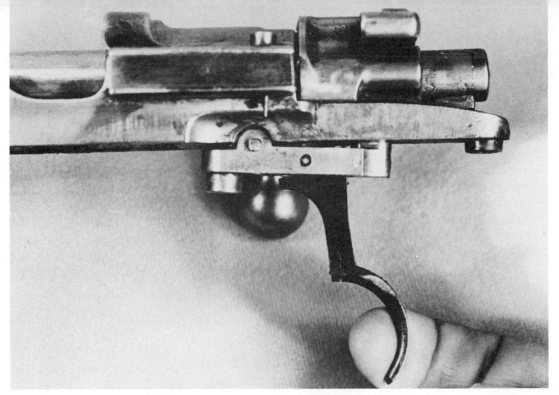

Here, the first stage of the Mauser's pull has been taken up, and the sear—located at the rear of the rocker arm—is somewhat withdrawn. However, the striker has not fallen. At this point the trigger pull hits a "bump," signaling that the pull is nearing its end.

When the two-stage trigger is fully to the rear, the sear has been released and the striker has fallen. Compare this with the first photo and you will note that trigger movement is exceptionally long.

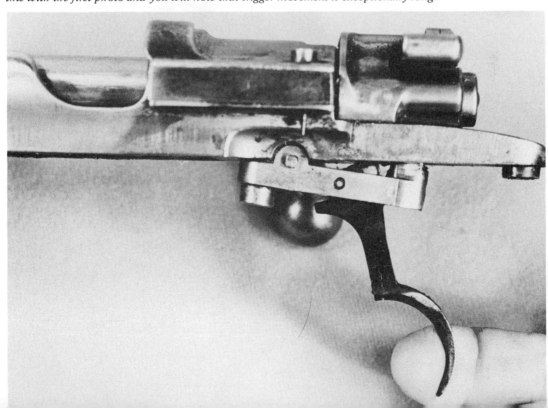

two-stage trigger originated in Europe, this is the kind of trigger used on all U.S. military rifles since the adoption of the U.S. Krag in 1892.

Though a two-stage trigger is hardly ideal for most sport shooting, the design has been a good one for military purposes. The long movement of the first stage, followed by the hard "bump" of the second stage, gives a soldier a definite feel of the trigger under battlefield conditions, even when the trigger finger is numb with cold or padded by a glove, so that he knows when the rifle will fire.

From the mechanical aspect, the two-stage military trigger is particularly safe because of the abundant sear engagement. When the first stage is taken up, the sear engagement is reduced considerably, thus permitting the shot to be fired with relatively little additional trigger movement. A similar mechanism, with equal sear engagement but without the two-stage feature,

In this gunshop modification of the Mauser two-stage trigger, an extension has been welded to the front of the trigger shank and an adjustment screw added. Adjusting this screw eliminates the first stage of the pull. This is just one way—a marginally satisfactory one—of sporterizing the military trigger.

would have a long pull and would give no signal to the shooter that the sear was near the release point.

The military and sport triggers were safe and reliable, and for the most part, they were suitable for the rifles of the late 19th and early 20th centuries. They were not, however, conducive to great marksmanship, a fact that becomes more than obvious when we agonize through the long gritty pull of an unaltered 98 Mauser, 03 Springfield, or some other military rifle.

Modern shooters accustomed to wonderfully crisp, smooth triggers may wonder why shooters of that era did not demand better triggers. Actually, shooters and manufacturers alike had been lulled into complacency because they thought they had all the bases covered so far as trigger mechanisms went.

Target shooters—the most demanding and vociferous of all riflemen—should have been the first to demand better triggers, but they were well satisfied with the hair- or set-trigger mechanisms of that era. These delicate mechanisms were standard on most target rifles, especially the graceful Schuetzen single-shot rifles used in offhand competition and some of the powerful Creedmoor-type rifles fired in ultra-long-range tournaments. Hair triggers were also available on sporting rifles such as Winchester's lever-action models as special-order items or they could be custom fitted by gunsmiths. Though hair triggers were not widely used by hunters, they were favored by some professional buffalo hunters, who knew the value of a fine trigger for long-range shooting.

SET TRIGGERS

The terms hair trigger and set trigger were used interchangeably to describe the same kind of mechanism. It was said that a hair trigger would fire at the touch of a hair. This was an exaggeration, of course, but it pretty well describes the feel of the trigger. Set trigger is a more correct term because the trigger device is set, or cocked, prior to firing. The mechanism is more or less independent of the rest of the rifle and is usually not an integral part of the rifle's sear or firing mechanism. It is a spring-powered device that supplies the energy to release the main sear. In effect, it is an automatic trigger-puller.

When a shooter touches off a set-trigger mechanism, he does not directly release the sear. Instead, he activates a mechanism that, in turn, does the heavy work of kicking the main sear free. The mechanism is powered by a rather stiff spring that must be cocked, or set, before each shot.

The most common type is easily identified because the rifle has two triggers, one in front of the other. One of these is pulled to set the mechanism. A slight click can be heard and felt when it sets. This cocking movement withdraws a spring-powered lever, or arm, which is held in a cocked position by a delicate sear arrangement connected to the firing, or hair, trigger. When the hair trigger is touched and moves slightly, the spring-powered arm snaps up and delivers a sharp kick to the rifle's main sear, causing it to disengage and fire the rifle. The operation of a set trigger can be aptly illustrated by imagining a mousetrap tied inside a rifle's trigger guard.

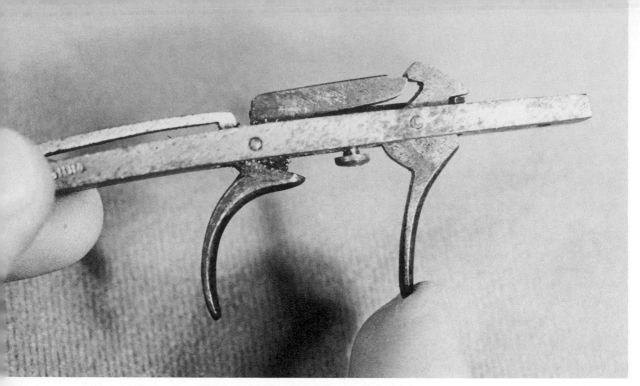

This antique mechanism illustrates the operation of a set trigger. When the rear trigger is pulled, it loads the spring located above and behind it, and it also engages a sear at the top of the front trigger.

Here is the same mechanism in the firing position. Light pressure on the front trigger has released the sear, allowing the spring to drive the arm of the rear trigger upward to "kick off" the main spring. Weight of pull is adjusted by the flat-headed screw between the triggers.

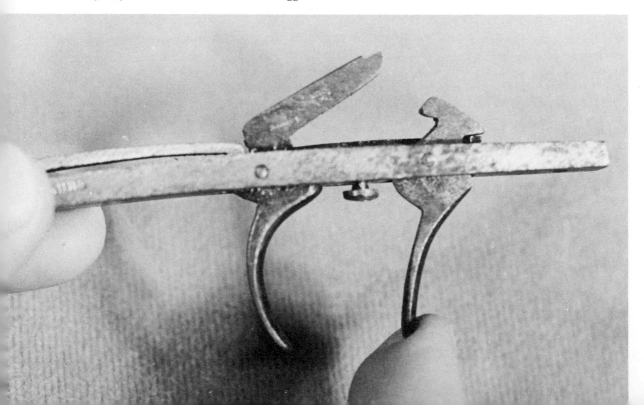

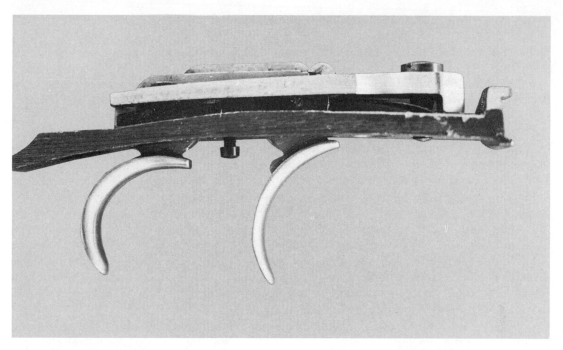

This modern double-set trigger operates in essentially the same manner as the antique double-set trigger shown in the previous photographs. It, too, employs a screw between the triggers to adjust the weight of pull.

Here you see the modern version of the double-set trigger in its firing position. The first trigger pull has engaged the second—that is, the hair trigger. A very light pull of the hair trigger has then allowed the "kicker" arm to be driven upward.

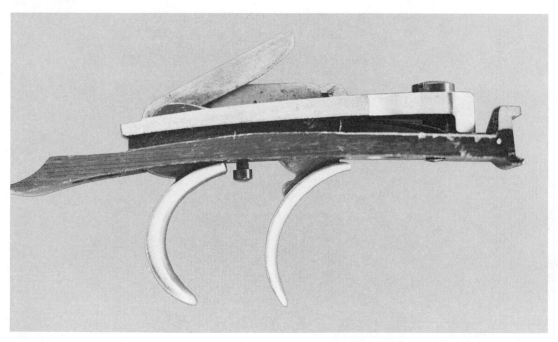

When the "cheese" is touched, the wire mouse whacker springs forward and slaps the trigger, releasing the sear.

Most double-set triggers are adjustable for weight of pull by means of an adjustment screw located between the two triggers. Turning the screw regulates the amount of sear engagement. The weight of pull can be set as heavy as two pounds or thereabouts and as light as mere fractions of an ounce.

Double-set triggers are usually arranged with the setting trigger at the rear and the hair trigger in front. This arrangement was and is popular among German and Austrian riflemakers, and is seen on many liberated rifles brought home by GI's following WW II. A more modern double-set arrangement places the setting trigger in front, where it is cocked by pushing it forward. This type was employed on some post-WW II target rifles, notably Anschutz and Schultz & Larsen products. It has the advantage of placing the firing trigger in a more convenient rearward position.

Double-set triggers are most often seen on German Mauser sporters and the Austrian Mannlichers, reflecting the love of Teutonic gunmakers for mechanical doodads. Custom gunsmiths also fitted double-set triggers to U.S. 03 Springfields, 1917 Enfields, and even such commercial rifles as Winchester's Model 70 bolt gun.

By now, you have no doubt realized that the double-set trigger mechanism is not all that different from the set triggers used on the famous Hawken rifles favored by the mountain men

Although double-set triggers are not as popular as they were before World War II, they're still seen on modern rifles such as this trim sporter made in Austria.

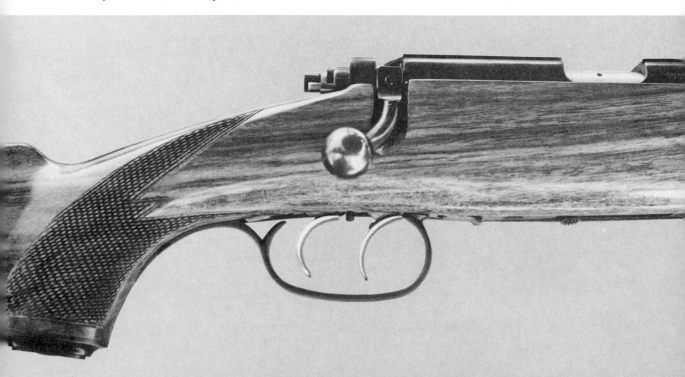

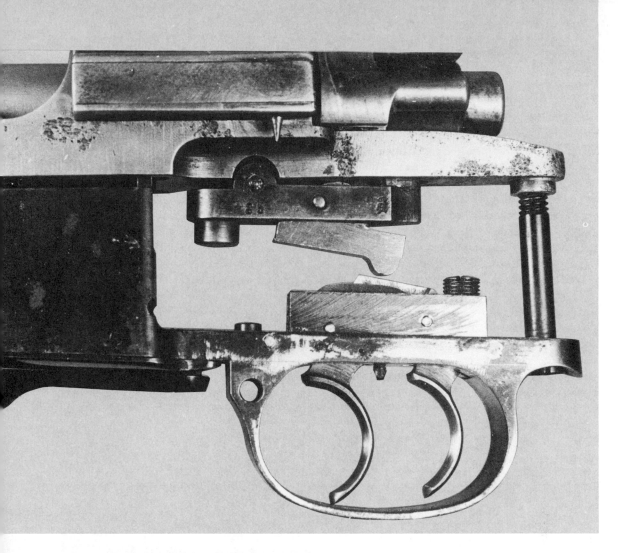

Here is a double-set mechanism installed in a Mauser. If you compare it closely with the first photograph in this chapter, you'll see that much of the original Mauser trigger mechanism is utilized. However, the shank has been replaced with a short lever. When bumped by the upward blow of the set trigger arm, this lever releases the sear.

and the beautiful "Kentucky" long rifles of Colonial days. That's exactly what I'm getting at. Even the best triggers made before World War II did not really improve a great deal on a design dating back some 300 years. The mechanism had simply been adapted to successive developments in rifle design, from the European Jaeger rifle of the 1600's right up through the Mausers and Springfields of the 1900's. Apparently gunmakers were not giving much thought to whether the old trigger design was suited to modern rifles or how it might affect performance.

They tended to keep pace with more modern, more accurate, and more sophisticated rifles by making finer, more delicate, and more complex set triggers without altering the basic design.

The one problem that seems to have been recognized was that using set triggers tended to increase lock time. Lock time is the interval between the instant the trigger breaks and the time when the firing pin strikes the cartridge primer. Even with guns that have the slowest lock time, this takes a fraction of a second. But guns that have a fast lock time have a significant accuracy advantage, because the gun has less time to move off target. Since a set trigger has considerable motion even before it kicks the main sear, it was recognized that these mechanisms might double a rifle's lock time. Even so, the advantages of the very light trigger pull were believed to outweigh the disadvantages. The revolution was yet to come.

During the last half of the last century, variations on the double-set mechanism and even a single-set trigger came into vogue. Actually, the single-set mechanism has a long history, probably dating back hundreds of years. It was widely used in dueling pistols during their Golden Age, from 1760 to 1830. The mechanism is set by pushing forward on the single trigger. Then it is touched to fire in normal fashion. Sometimes single-set triggers are made so as to conceal the fact that they can be set, though usually they can be identified by a tiny screw just behind the trigger, which is turned to adjust the release pressure.

Usually, single-set triggers are designed and installed so that they will also function like an ordinary trigger if they are not set. Aside from pistols and single-shot rifles, the most common use of single-set triggers on factory-made guns has been on European drillings (combination three-barreled guns with both shotgun and rifle barrels). Again, their use on these guns is a reflection of the Germanic love of complicated mechanisms, even when they aren't needed.

This is a Canjar single-set trigger mounted in a Ruger No. 1 Single-Shot rifle. Like other custom makers, Canjar supplies trigger mechanisms for a variety of commercial and military rifles. When not used as a set trigger, this single-set mechanism functions as a normal trigger, adjustable for weight of pull, creep, and backlash.

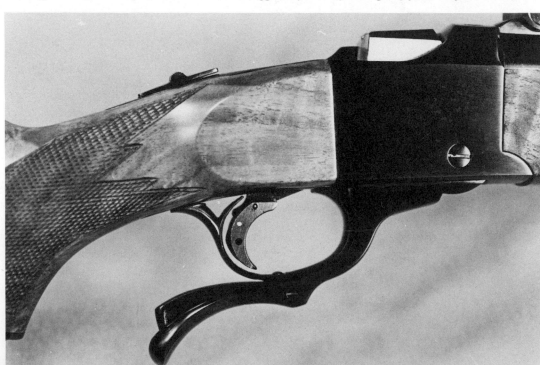

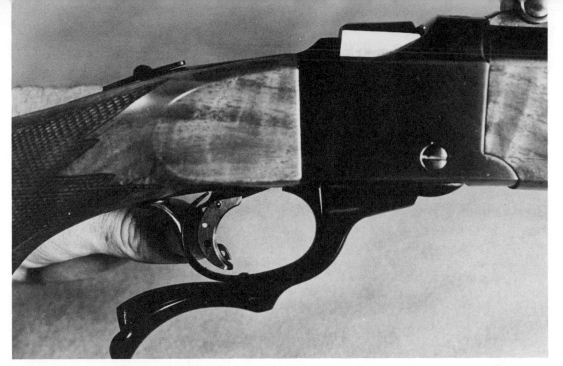

To activate the set feature of the Canjar trigger, the trigger shoe is pushed forward, as shown in this photograph. As it is moved forward, it cocks and a small tab protrudes from its lower face. This little tab is the set trigger — a light touch on the tab and the rifle fires.

These schematic drawings show the innards of two Canjar single-set triggers. The simpler mechanism at left is the one most often used. It operates as shown in the previous photos. At a touch of the tab, the shoe flies back to move the trigger lever and fire the rifle. The Canjar at right is a three-lever single-set trigger. The addition of an extra lever increases the mechanical advantage, further lightening the pressure needed to fire. Slight pressure releases the sear, which in turn releases the sear connector and permits the rifle to fire. It's more complex but provides an excellent pull.

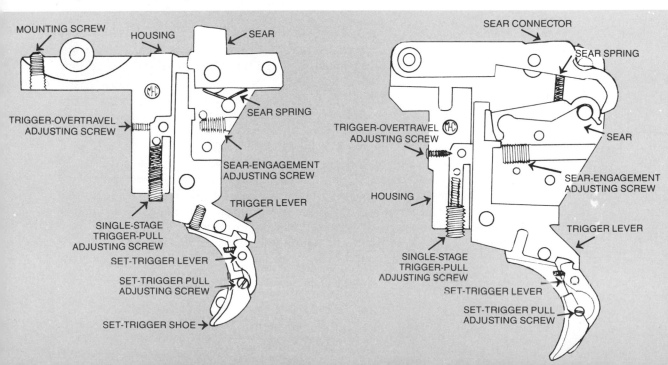

Another variation on the single-set theme is manufactured in the U.S. by Matt Canjar. The Canjar mechanism is contained within a rather large trigger shoe and is distinguished by a small tongue that extends from the face of the shoe when it is pushed forward and set. Touching the tongue trips a spring, which jolts the massive shoe. The vibration of the shoe, in turn, releases the sear.

The purpose of all this history of trigger mechanisms is to explain why shooters and gun-makers thought they had all the bases covered. The two-stage trigger was unsurpassed for military purposes, and target shooters were happy with their fancy set triggers. As rifles improved in performance and accuracy, the demand for better triggers was met simply by refining existing mechanisms. Some set triggers made between 1900 and 1940 were as precisely fitted as a fine watch and would fire by the trigger weight alone if the rifle's muzzle was tilted up.

Sport triggers, however, did not keep pace quite so well. This was true even of the "improved" sport triggers, found on fine British bolt rifles by Rigby or Holland & Holland and those made by Griffin & Howe in the U.S. These were only slicked-up versions of existing mechanisms. To paraphrase Gertrude Stein, a trigger was a trigger was a trigger. No one saw any need to improve the basic design.

IMPULSES TOWARD CHANGE

During the 1920's and '30's, a couple of interesting developments occurred that were to have considerable effect on trigger design in the U.S. Among these were growing interest in NRA-type big-bore (high power) and smallbore (.22 Long Rifle) target shooting. Unlike European-style target shooting and earlier forms of American rifle competition, the NRA rules called for a three-pound or 3½-pound minimum-weight trigger pull, depending on the course of fire and type of rifle. This ruled out the use of set triggers, which had been long favored by target shooters.

The standard big-bore target rifle of that time was the Model 1903 Springfield, either in its original military dress or in one of its specialized target forms. Either way, the 03 trigger was not much to get excited about, especially in target-shooting circles. All sorts of things were done to make the Springfield trigger lighter, smoother, and crisper, but the distinctly military-style trigger really couldn't be improved much. This caused target shooters to start thinking in terms of a sport-type trigger that, aside from a stiff three-pound pull, would have all the crispness of their beloved set triggers. It was revolutionary thinking.

Smallbore shooters were also having their problems. Recent improvements in .22 rifle accuracy, highlighted by the introduction of Winchester's wonderfully accurate Model 52, followed by Remington's equally accurate Model 37, pushed smallbore target performance well beyond pre-WW I levels. Better sights, more consistent ammo, and improved shooting techniques also played a large role in improving target performance. Shooters began wondering how to improve the triggers of their smallbore target rifles. In fact, trigger performance became such a focal point that within a few years of their introduction, both Winchester and Remington were forced to improve the design and performance of the triggers on their premier smallbore target rifles.

THE MODEL 70 TRIGGER

About that time, Winchester introduced a centerfire bolt-action rifle, the Model 70, which was to have a profound effect on trigger development. Though safe, sturdy, and one of the most reliable triggers ever put on a rifle—and vastly better than the Springfield trigger—the M-70 trigger was not the answer to a target shooter's prayer. What it did have, however, was a secondary sear arrangement which, by leverage, significantly reduced the pressure and friction generated on the primary sear by the mainspring. This takes some explaining.

With the simple sear arrangement employed by sporting triggers of that time, the trigger

This is a Winchester Model 70 trigger mechanism, one of the first to utilize a lever system to reduce the heavy pressure of the mainspring. The secondary sear seen here—at the end of the arm extending from the trigger shank—does not hold the main force of the spring, but rather supports the primary sear arm.

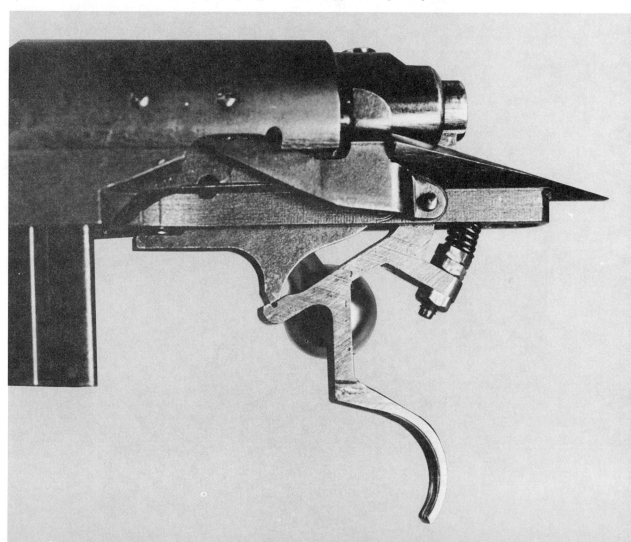

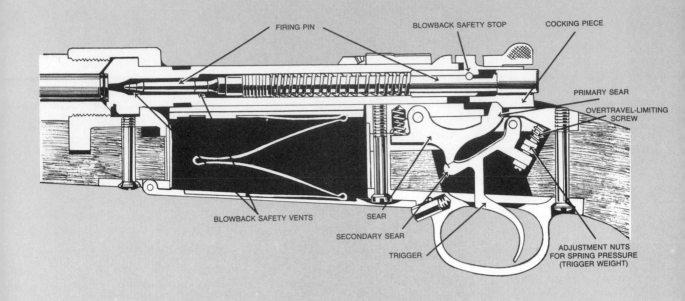

FIRING PIN

BLOWBACK SAFETY STOP

COCKING PIECE

PRIMARY SEAR

OVERTRAVEL-LIMITING SCREW

BLOWBACK SAFETY VENTS

SEAR

SECONDARY SEAR

TRIGGER

ADJUSTMENT NUTS FOR SPRING PRESSURE (TRIGGER WEIGHT)

In this photograph, the Model 70 trigger is in the release position. The sear extension is free of the sear, allowing the primary sear arm to drop down and forward, releasing the striker. The accompanying schematic drawing reveals the connection and relationship of the working parts.

itself was a simple toggle, acting as a ratchet dog. When the gun was cocked, the hammer or firing pin was drawn to the rear until the ratchet dog fell into a notch, called the sear, that held it in a cocked position. As the hammer or firing pin was drawn to the cocked position, the powerful mainspring was compressed. Thus the ratchet dog (trigger) was locked in the sear notch under considerable pressure. When the trigger was pulled, quite a bit of pressure was required to overcome the friction of the contacting sear surfaces. One way to reduce this friction, and thus the felt weight of the pull, was to reduce the amount of sear engagement. But without ample engagement, a sear is liable to slip, causing the gun to fire accidentally. This is why sport-type triggers of generations past had been characterized by excessive weight of pull and motion.

With the new Model 70 trigger, the principle of leverage had been put to work to hold some of the mainspring's pressure. This permitted less sear engagement and proportionally less trigger motion. The concept was mechanically sound and resulted in the best sport trigger of the pre-WW II era. Winchester's designers did not go as far with the idea as they might have, but they did set the stage for the coming revolution.

Just after World War II, this revolutionary trigger mechanism was introduced in Remington's Models 721 and 722. It is still used in Remington's best rifles, including the currently produced Model 700. The sear engagement surfaces can be seen through the small opening at the top of the trigger housing. Only slight engagement is necessary, because the sear is secondary rather than primary.

REVOLUTIONARY REMINGTON TRIGGERS

The revolution did not come with a great flurry of publicity releases or the clatter of gun writer's typewriters. For a while, no one seemed to realize what had happened. The event was Remington's introduction of their first post-war centerfire bolt-action rifles, the Models 721 and 722. At first look, these rifles were rather homely, with little evidence of pre-WW II Remington craftsmanship. They were designed to be produced fast and cheap, and that's the way they looked with their generous allotment of stamped and bent sheet-metal parts.

The trigger mechanism, in keeping with the rest of the rifle, looked like a sandwich of stamped sheet metal held together with pins and wire. The whole mechanism was so shoddy looking (by pre-war standards) that it was a while before serious shooters discovered what it had to offer. When they did, they were astonished. Here was a trigger that did it all. It was safe, reliable, and brought a new phrase—fully adjustable—to firearms advertising.

Like the earlier Model 70 Winchester trigger, Remington's mechanism featured a secondary sear arrangement. This secondary sear was located at the long end of a lever, so that the mainspring pressure was drastically reduced. With only marginal pressure on the secondary sear, it was possible to have only minimum sear contact and at the same time maintain a high degree of reliability. This was good, but the Remington designers had gone further. Small screws sticking out of the trigger housing, fore and aft, made it possible to adjust and limit the motion of virtually all the trigger's components. The weight of pull, creep, backlash, and even the depth of sear engagement could be adjusted to suit the owner. Virtually every new rifle of any consequence introduced since then has featured a trigger mechanism advertised as being adjustable. The Remington design is one of the best, and the same design, little changed, is used today on their Model 700 and even the super-accurate 40-X target rifles. It's *that* good. A special two-ounce version is available on special order.

I've given Remington all the credit here because Remington was the first major U.S.

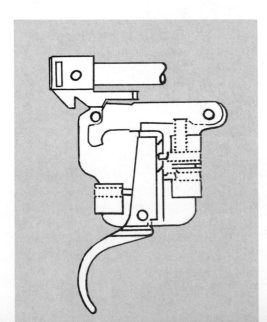

Operation of the Remington Model 700 trigger is clarified in this diagram. When the trigger is pulled, the surfaces of the secondary sear arrangement disengage, allowing the primary sear to drop clear of the striker. Also shown are the adjustments for weight of pull, creep, and backlash.

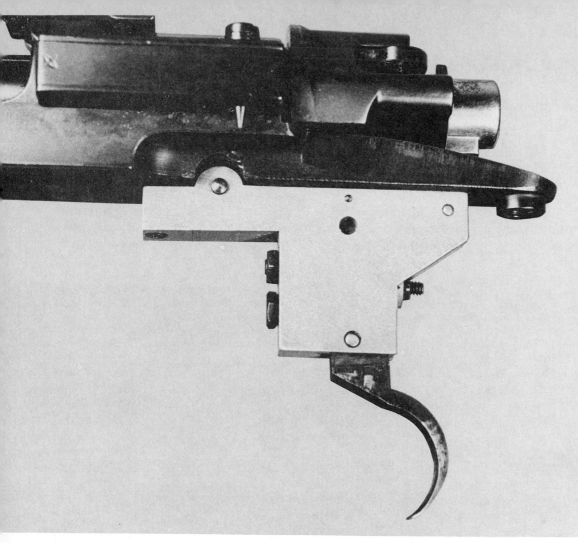

This is a Timney adjustable trigger fitted to a Mauser action. Adjustable triggers such as this can be easily installed and are available for a number of commercial and military rifles.

manufacturer to think in terms of providing a really good, fully adjustable trigger on a center-fire rifle. To be strictly fair, however, I must point out that the Remington trigger appeared at a time when small custom shops were manufacturing similarly adjustable triggers, which replaced the original triggers on Mausers, 03 Springfields, Arisakas, Enfields, and other surplus military rifles. These triggers, bearing such trade names as Dayton-Traister, Mashburn, and Jaeger, were a blessing to gunsmiths and do-it-yourself tinkerers at a time when converting surplus military rifles to sporters was all the rage.

About 1950, when do-it-yourself sporterizing of military rifles was in full bloom, I was a certifiable black-belt gun nut, but as teen-age farm lads tend to be, I was as penniless as a parson's pig. Occasionally, I picked up a few extra bucks with one of my woodshed rifle projects. A good 98 Mauser could be had then for about $15. Five or six dollars more bought a semi-finished stock of good walnut, and for my deluxe models I invested another six or seven dollars for one of the adjustable triggers then available. With a cash investment that seldom topped $30 plus a couple of days for inletting, scraping, and sanding, I was able to offer a genuine oil-finished big game rifle for $50 (or whatever I thought the market would bear). The workmanship wasn't very exciting, and I knew it, but I always made a point of adjusting the new trigger mechanism, usually a Mashburn or Dayton-Traister, so that it felt quick and crisp and let go with about a two-pound pull. That was what usually sold the rifle. Shooters had never felt such a wonderfully smooth and crisp trigger on an ordinary sporting rifle.

Matt Canjar, maker of the single-set trigger mentioned earlier, also offered a beautifully machined single-stage adjustable trigger for commercial bolt-action rifles (Winchester, Sako, etc.) as well as the military models. Thus, older rifles could be considerably upgraded by install-

Known as the Canjar 2 Oz., this trigger really is fired by a pressure of only two ounces — but it can also be adjusted up to several ounces. The trigger itself is just a curved piece of aluminum wire. This is to keep weight to an absolute minimum. If it were heavier, the trigger's inertia might cause accidental discharge. Shown fitted to a Remington Model 700 Silhouette rifle, this trigger is available for other makes and models and is popular among serious varmint shooters, silhouette shooters, and other target riflemen — especially benchresters.

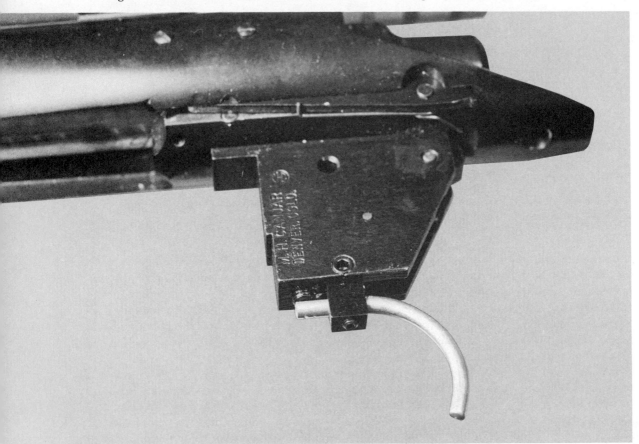

ing a better trigger. These improved triggers are still the mainstay of the Canjar firm, perhaps the most respected of all custom trigger makers. Their latest model is adjustable down to a two-ounce pull and uses a super-light aluminum trigger in order to avoid the accidental "bump-off" discharges that could result with a trigger made of steel or other heavy metal. When a trigger mechanism lets go as a result of trigger weight or momentum alone, say from a jolt or even the sheer weight of the trigger, it is called a "flywheel" effect.

I must confess that I wasn't all that quick to catch on to the trigger revolution, but I can claim the ignorance of youth. When I was 17 or so, my idea of the rifle to end all rifles was my wildcat .22/250 (Remington hadn't even thought of such a cartridge then) built on a choice Oberndorf Mauser action with an extra-heavy 28-inch barrel. I whittled the stock out of a walnut timber that had been the fireplace mantel in an abandoned log cabin near my home. The rig was topped off with a giant Unertl 12X Ultra Varmint scope—the first ever seen in my county. To make things even better, I fitted a double-set trigger pirated from an old German sporter.

I can't say how accurate that rifle was, because I never fired it for group size. (At something like $3 per hundred for bullets, plus powder and primers, I couldn't afford to trifle away my hard-earned handloaded ammo on targets.) Every available round was sent in the direction of a groundhog or crow. Naturally, when I lined up on a crow and caressed the set trigger, it was pure bliss. Nothing, I reckoned, could be finer than that big rifle with those fine set triggers.

BENCHREST INNOVATION

At about that time, quite a few fellows, real experts, felt pretty much the same way. They were tinkering with a new game called benchrest shooting. The idea was simple enough—put all the shots as close together as possible. The smallest group, measured between the centers of the two widest bulletholes, was the winner. The goal was pure accuracy—to shoot every bullet into the same hole—and to that end, elaborate rifles were constructed. Some weighed 50 pounds or more and had barrels as big as sewer pipes and stocks as thick as bridge timbers.

The shooting itself was not all that tough because just about everything possible was done to eliminate human error. The big rifles were rested on sandbags, which in turn were supported by stout benches. Naturally, high-magnification target scopes were used, and the shots were fired by caressing ultra-fine set triggers. Most of these rifles were built on surplus military actions, usually 98 Mausers, and the most common set triggers were the spring-action models built in Germany or Austria. As in generations past, set triggers were considered the only way to go. But not for long.

The shooting world had never seen anything like this new band of riflemen. Nothing was sacred to them; everything was suspect. Every part of a rifle came under critical scrutiny, and it wasn't long before set triggers were weeded out.

In addition to prolonging lock time, it seems that set triggers were committing an even more insidious crime. All that kicking and springing that went on when a set trigger was unleashed created vibrations unfavorable to accuracy. The effect of these vibrations is complex, but the basic result is easily described: When a rifle barrel is shooting well, it vibrates or "hums" in a certain way; but the whack of a set trigger mechanism makes it "hum" a different and inconsistent way. The result is a measurable loss of accuracy.

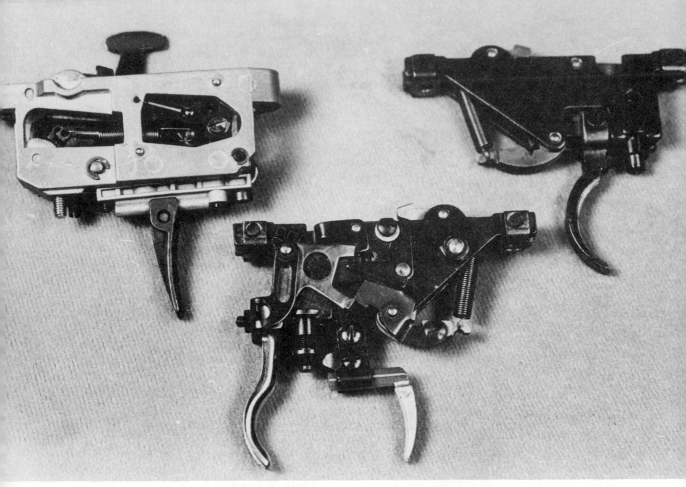

Here is a trio of triggers used in the magnificent Anschutz target rifles, which have an unsurpassed record in world competition. At upper left is the current (and best) Anschutz trigger. Weight of pull can be adjusted down to a few ounces, and type of pull can be set for two-stage operation or single pull. Some target shooters prefer a two-stage mode with extremely light triggers. The shank itself can also be adjusted for ideal finger position-ing. At upper right is an older Anschutz featuring a multilever sear arrangement. Below these is the double-set Anschutz, one of the best ever designed. The setting, or cocking, trigger (at left) is activated by pushing it forward. The firing trigger will then release at the slightest touch, yet it is now considered virtually obsolete because the single trigger at upper left can be set to such light letoff.

Within a few years, the two-hundred-year-old rule of set triggers as best for precision shooting came to a crashing end. The timing was perfect because, as you'll recall, beautifully adjustable single-stage triggers were just coming into flower. With the basic principles of multi-lever triggers now well understood and developed, it was a relatively simple matter to refine the new single-stage mechanisms until they could be adjusted to a weight of pull as light as that of the most delicate set triggers. It was a revolution.

Once it was realized that set triggers were no longer acceptable for target shooting, there was no end to the flood of truly wonderful new triggers. Today, the shooter can select a mechanism that will send his bullet on its way with only a loving touch on the trigger, no fuss or bother to set the trigger, and no loss of accuracy.

HOW THE TRIGGER AFFECTS YOUR SHOOTING

The way a trigger operates can have a drastic effect on a rifle's accuracy, and it can also have a drastic effect on the shooter. We hear a lot of trigger terminology—break, creep, backlash, weight of pull, stop, shoe, etc. Most shooters have a good idea of what the terms mean, but are vague about how these things influence performance.

When a trigger "breaks," it releases the sear, firing the gun. Some triggers are said to break "clean," or crisply, while others have a sluggish break. Why some break well, while others do not, depends on a number of mechanical factors.

The most discussed trigger characteristic is weight of pull: the pressure required to break the trigger, release the sear, and cause the rifle to fire. In the U.S. and some other English-speaking countries, the pressure required to break the trigger is expressed in pounds and ounces. People who use the metric system express trigger pulls in kilos, or grams in the case of sensitive triggers. The International (Olympic) shooting rules specify trigger-pull weights in grams, so some American target shooters are beginning to use metric units in describing their triggers. It is a convenient system when ultra-light triggers are used.

Though most shooters judge a trigger's weight of pull simply by squeezing it off and making a guess, the accurate way is to use scales designed for the purpose or to use a set of special weights that hook onto the trigger of a vertically held rifle to determine the minimum breaking weight. Since a trigger is really a lever, the weight of pull needed to break it is less at the lower tip, where leverage is greater, than at the upper part of the shank. Therefore, weight of pull is measured either at the trigger's midpoint or at the rearmost point of the curve.

I think the best weight of pull for an all-around hunting rifle is between three and four pounds. This is a lot lighter than it sounds, considering that the average weight of pull of off-the-shelf commercial rifles is well over five pounds and getting heavier. Once a shooter gets used to the three- to four-pound-pull, it can be managed quite well, even with cold fingers or when wearing gloves.

Some shooters, especially varmint hunters and some target shooters, like a much lighter pull, two pounds or even two ounces, but these take some getting used to. Shooters not accustomed to an extra-light pull tend to fire before they are ready, usually to their acute embarrassment. This is another reason I favor a three- to four-pound trigger for most shooters and hunters. It is the lightest pull they can manage while exercising some control over the exact timing of the shot.

A trigger is too heavy if the shooter is conscious of the pressure he is applying to break the shot. This annoys the shooter and takes his concentration away from aiming. Also, the muscular effort required to pull a heavy trigger introduces jerks and tremors, which make the aim less steady. Then, to make matters worse, there is abrupt relaxation of strong tension just after the trigger breaks, which interferes with a smooth follow-through. Of course, some shooters can manage a heavy pull better than others, but no one shoots a hard trigger really well.

A trigger in the three-pound range offers resistance enough to tell the shooter's *subconscious* mind that the trigger is being pressed and controlled, but does not intrude into his concentration before the shot breaks. In other words, the shooter presses the trigger at the right moment without thinking about it. On the other hand, if the pull is too light, the shooter will subconsciously pull the trigger before his conscious mind has perfected the aim and hold. Shooters can train themselves to use increasingly lighter triggers, even as light as a fraction of an ounce, but when the pull is much over five pounds, one only learns to cope as well as he can with a tough situation.

Despite the really excellent adjustable triggers which now come as standard equipment on many good rifles, the weight of pull, as set at the factory, is almost always too heavy. This is largely a result of today's consumerist trends in the courts. In order to protect themselves against unwarranted suits by reckless gun owners, the makers have to build in an extra margin of safety, even though it may result in reduced performance of the product.

Linked to *weight* of pull is *consistency* of pull. For various reasons, many triggers do not break at an identical pressure shot after shot. Bad triggers may vary as much as two or three pounds or even more. Even the better hunting-style triggers may vary a few ounces. A variation of a few ounces is not detectable with, say, a three-pound trigger, but it is quite noticeable with a one-pound target trigger. Perhaps the worst thing about an inconsistent trigger is the way it keeps the shooter guessing when the shot will break.

A few decades ago, little gadgets called trigger shoes came into vogue. They clamp over the original trigger of a rifle or pistol (or sometimes a shotgun) and enlarge the trigger's face, or front surface, three or four times. The purpose of the shoe is to distribute the weight over a larger area of the finger and thereby make the pull feel lighter. This is really a self-induced con game. These trigger shoes were popular for quite a few years, but nowadays they seem to be on the wane. The current fashion is to commit the pressure of the pull to a small area of the finger, thus increasing sensitivity and improving control.

The term creep describes the motion of the trigger before the break. Creep is seldom desirable because it annoys the shooter and adds an element of uncertainty as to when the shot will break. Triggers with excessive creep also tend to have a gritty feeling when pulled. This is caused by the friction of poorly finished parts in the trigger mechanism and rough sear surfaces. Ideally, a trigger should have no creep whatever, and it should break cleanly when sufficient pressure is applied. Mechanically, this is all but impossible because some movement is necessary to separate the sear surfaces. Some multi-lever target triggers, though, have so little creep that the movement is imperceptible.

Another problem is backlash, the movement of a trigger after the sear breaks. One might suppose that backlash is no problem because the bullet is on its way when the sear breaks. This is untrue. The problem is that backlash disturbs the gun while the bullet is still in the barrel. The momentum of the rearward moving and accelerating trigger finger is abruptly halted when the trigger comes to a hard stop at the end of its travel. This sudden start and stop is actually like hitting the rifle a swift lick with a small mallet. If the backlash is of sufficient length the entire rifle is buffeted somewhat, altering the direction of aim. Backlash is most damaging when combined with a heavy weight of pull because the trigger finger moves proportionally faster and harder.

From the foregoing information, one might judge that the perfect trigger is consistent from shot to shot and has absolutely no creep and no backlash. Does such a trigger exist? If not, how

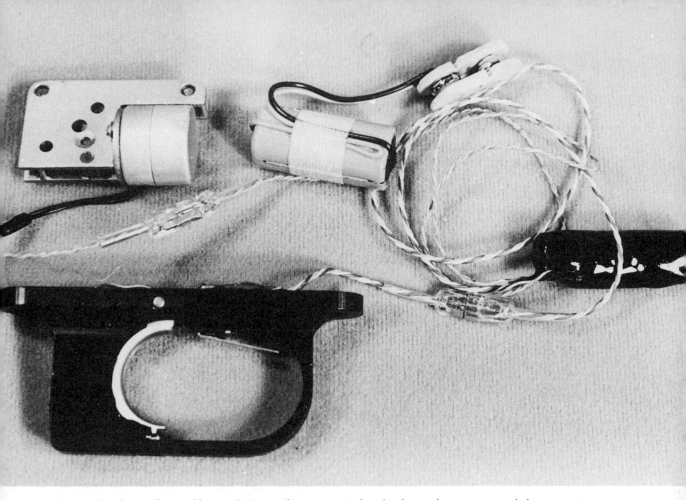

Designed and manufactured by Frank Green of Montrose, Colorado, this is a battery-powered electronic trigger. A solenoid releases the sear. The trigger itself is merely a switch that completes the circuit. It can be set to a release weight so light as to be nearly imperceptible — which takes a good bit of getting used to. Such triggers are chiefly used for varminting and target shooting — particularly silhouette shooting.

close are we? The present state of trigger technology is so high that even the target shooters have almost stopped squawking. That's saying a lot! The best triggers are highly consistent and there is so little motion and vibration that these factors are virtually imperceptible. These triggers are also complicated and expensive.

THE ELECTRIC TRIGGER

Is the revolution over? Not on your life. At last, shooters and gun designers are thinking about their triggers, and "good" will never be good enough. Already we have reached beyond the sear-release concept to electric triggers.

A clever fellow by the name of Frank Green in Montrose, Colorado, designed an ultra-sensitive, battery-powered solenoid mechanism, which replaces the trigger in some rifles and pistols. The weight of "pull" can be set so light as to be almost imperceptible. But even this approach will not be the final answer. When we slip the sear, all we're doing is turning loose a spring-powered hammer or firing pin. When you think about it, that whole concept is woefully outdated. Why are we making these beautiful triggers to fire rifles and cartridges that are pitifully overburdened with obsolete strikers, sears, mainsprings, and primers? The *next* revolution may get at the heart of the problem. If, for example, the vibrations of a set trigger mechanism reduce accuracy, just think of all the havoc when a powerful striker spring slams against the inside of a bolt.

Probably, the answer will be electric ignition—rifles fired by an electric current that activates a chemical propellant charge. There will be no mechanism to cause problems, no vibrations, and there will be instantaneous lock time. The ultimate trigger will be just a simple electric switch.

Chapter 7

. . . .

RIFLE AMMO,
PAST AND PRESENT

. . . .

Aside from some differences in bullet shape a .30/06 cartridge made, say, in 1910 is identical to a .30/06 made last week.

The new cartridge, however, incorporates chemical, metallurgical, and manufacturing innovations that give it a performance edge over its ancestor as great as that of a modern high-performance sports car over a 1910 roadster.

If you are a product of the post-World War II baby boom, you probably haven't been exposed to corrosive priming except through references in faded shooting journals. Those who pine for the "good old days" would just as soon forget corrosive priming.

About 1950 when I was a freckled farm lad of some 14 summers, my most cherished possession was a Model 1903 Springfield rifle of early and elegant vintage. This wonderful machine was my constant companion, devastating rats in the barn and groundhogs in the pasture. When I slept, it rested in a homemade cedar rack over my bed. Given my meager resources, ammunition was a sometime thing, so I thought I'd found the gold at the end of the rainbow when a well-meaning neighbor gave me a dusty shoebox full of wartime 06 ammunition. That day is still remembered as the blackest of my early shooting career.

With so much free ammo at hand, I was able to expand my shooting to include such frivolous exercises as discovering how many oak slabs the pointed bullets would penetrate and even kicking up dust around a rusty bucket positioned some 500 paces away on a plowed hillside.

Every evening, the beloved Springfield was lovingly wiped clean and oiled. Since I owned no cleaning rod, the bore was cleansed with a patch pulled through the barrel with a length of butcher's string. No gun ever had more care.

That summer we had two weeks of nearly non-stop rain, and the Springfield lay in the cedar rack unused and untended except for an occasional wistful glance. When the sun finally reappeared, I took out for a groundhog stalk and was horrified to discover what looked like red moss sprouting around the muzzle. That wasn't the worst. The once glistening bore was a wasteland of rust—not soft brown rust that could be wiped away with an oiled cloth. The bore looked as though it had been rinsed with acid. I scrubbed at it all day, even hitching a ride to town to buy a stiff cleaning rod and bore brush. But the bore was ruined. Even with the rust gone, the lands and grooves were so pitted and scarred that I was unconsolable for days.

I was a victim of corrosive priming and my rifle was only one among tens of thousands to suffer a similar fate. The cause was a priming mix containing potassium chlorate, a salt that attracts and holds water and thereby promotes rapid, corrosive rusting. Ignorant of this evil, I blissfully contaminated my beloved barrel with my windfall supply of old ammunition. At first, there had been no signs of rust because of the dry weather and my continual shooting, but during the rainy two-week layoff a layer of salt in the bore had sucked water from the humid air, and ruin was inevitable.

IMPROVED PRIMERS

As terrible as the corrosive primers were, they were once considered a wonderful innovation. An even earlier priming mix, dating to the introduction of self-contained cartridges, was composed largely of fulminate of mercury, an unstable compound that detonates when struck a sharp blow. The fulminate primers deposited mercury on the interior of the brass cases where it eventually altered the characteristics of the brass, causing the metal to become brittle and severely limiting the reloadable life of the cases. Mercuric primers contained corrosive salts as well, but at that time, the need for constant barrel cleaning was an accepted fact of life.

With the advent of non-mercuric primers, shooters felt they were the beneficiaries of a quantum leap in cartridge development. Barrel cleaning was as necessary as ever, but at least their brass cases lasted longer. Even through mercuric primers had been around as long as brass cases, they didn't cause any problems to speak of until the development of smokeless powder. Black powder, used previously, formed a crusty layer of fouling on the interior of the case that absorbed much of the mercury and thus protected the brass. Smokeless powder does not form a protective coating.

It is worth mentioning that the mercuric primers had bad habits even if they weren't fired. Apparently, the mercury tended to migrate from the priming compound and attack the brass during storage. This was especially likely to happen when ammo was stored in warm or damp climates and could occur within a year or two after manufacture. When the mercury migrated from the priming mix, the primer went dead and the ammo was unusable. Today we think nothing of using ammo that has been around for decades, but up until 1915 or thereabouts, ammunition could become useless in only a few months. So shooters in 1920 were happy with the non-mercuric chlorate primers that only rusted their barrels; at least the ammo was vastly more reliable.

Mercuric primers were a long time going to the grave. Despite their bad habits, they were long felt to have superb ignition characteristics, especially regarding accuracy. For this reason,

Loaded with smokeless powder, full metal case
boat tail Lubaloy bullets, and special mercuric,
corrosive primers for finest match accuracy.
Adapted to Winchester Model 70, and other arms
chambered for this cartridge.

Rifle should be cleaned, immediately after firing,
with Winchester Bore Solvent.

20

Western
SUPER ● MATCH
CENTER FIRE   CARTRIDGES
30-06 SPRINGFIELD
Match Ammunition
180 Grain Full Metal Case Boat Tail
Lubaloy Bullets—For Single Loading Only

Western
SUPER ● MATCH
30-06 SPRINGFIELD

Because mercuric primers were considered to offer superb ignition, they were used for special match ammo long after non-mercuric primers became standard. As late as the 1960's, corrosive primers were made for ammunition such as Western's Super-Match .30/06's. The labeling carried the message that this was for "finest match accuracy," but also warned that, with these loads, a rifle must be cleaned immediately after firing.

they were used in special lots of tournament-grade centerfire ammo long after World War II. I'm not sure exactly how long this practice continued, but it lasted into the 1960's. When I was on the Army Rifle Team in the late 1950's, we were issued .308 match ammo that had been "handloaded' by Winchester-Western. The labels on the boxes noted that the loads used "special mercuric, corrosive primers for finest match accuracy." Likewise, Western's Super-Match .30/06 load used mercuric primers. Fortunately, we are now done with mercuric primers for good, and judging by the performance of today's ammo, we can say that performance has never been more reliable nor accuracy better.

The development of cartridge priming did not proceed in orderly steps but in irregular leapfrog jerks. In 1901, the German ammo-making firm RWS was already manufacturing ammo with rust-free non-chlorate primers. This put the Germans a quarter of a century ahead of developments in the United States, not because we didn't have the brains but because American arms and ammo manufacturers are notoriously hidebound. Once a manufacturing procedure has been set in motion, they resist change almost to the grave. But to be fair, American shooters are equally conservative, so I suppose we deserve each other. When German-made .22 Rimfire ammo with *"rostfrei"* (rust-free) priming was for sale in the U.S. before World War I, American shooters took little notice and went on scrubbing their barrels—or letting them rust—as always.

The tide turned in 1927 when Remington first marketed ammunition that featured Klean-

Non-corrosive ammunition had been made in Germany for a quarter-century when Remington turned the American tide in 1927 by introducing Kleanbore priming—a non-chlorate priming mixture that left no salt deposits in a gun barrel. Although this cured some old problems, it revived others because Kleanbore contained fulminate of mercury.

bore priming. Essentially this was a non-chlorate priming that left no salt deposits in the barrel, but strangely, it did contain fulminate of mercury. This caused Remington's ammo to suffer from the old problems of short storage life and brass contamination even after U.S. government arsenals had decided that chlorate-corrosive priming was the lesser of two evils so long as mercury could be eliminated from the mix.

Fortunately, Remington improved the Kleanbore priming with a mix that had been patented by the German chemists Rathburg and Von Herz. This new compound featured an absence of both chlorates and mercury. At last, American shooters were treated to "no-fault" priming. The essential ingredients of this patented formula was and is lead tri-nitro-resorcinate, more commonly known in the trade as lead styphnate. Though Remington profited long and well from Kleanbore priming, the patents eventually ran out. Today, lead styphnate priming is the worldwide standard, though of course each primer manufacturer may use a somewhat different priming formula as well as varying manufacturing processes.

Predictably, the makers of military ammo dragged their feet and wallowed in indecision

U.S. arsenals used chlorates after all of the American commercial makers had switched to non-corrosive priming compounds. An exception was the .30 Carbine round (left), adopted in 1940, which had to be loaded with non-corrosive priming to protect the carbine's gas system. The .308 (center), introduced much later, did not use a corrosive mixture, but the switch to non-corrosive priming for GI .30/06 ammunition was not complete until about 1950.

about adopting non-corrosive primers for small-arms ammo. Even as late as 1940, after all commercial ammo makers had switched to non-corrosive priming, the government arsenals were still using chlorates in their priming compound. The exception was the little .30 caliber carbine round, which had to be loaded with non-corrosive priming in order to protect the carbine's gas system. From the time of its adoption in 1940, throughout World War II and thereafter, .30 carbine ammo featured safe priming. By contrast, .30 caliber rifle ammo (.30/06) fired in our M-1 Garand rifles was primed with a corrosive priming. The changeover was not completed until 1950.

As anyone who has served in any of the armed services knows, it takes a long time for the word to come down. When I was in the Army during the second half of the 1950's, our rifle manuals still specified the three-day clean and reclean bore-protection regimen that had been necessary during the days of corrosive priming. Even though we were firing "safe ammo," we had to scrub our rifles as long and hard as the Doughboys of the War to End Wars.

Even after conquering mercury and corrosion, the primer war is still being fought. There's always something that needs improvement, and primers have a way of staying in the spotlight. For instance, if you've spent any time with smallbore target shooters, you've undoubtedly heard repeated references to the British-made Eley Tenex match-grade .22 Rimfire ammo. For upwards of a quarter-century, the accuracy of this brand of ammo has so overwhelmed all

Among the various kinds of match-grade rimfire cartridges, the British-made Eley Tenex .22's have overwhelmed all challengers in competition. The reason seems to be the way in which the wet priming mix is put into the cartridges—and the procedure is a secret closely guarded by Eley.

challengers that it is axiomatic in target-shooting circles, especially in the ultra-precise prone game, that if you don't use Eley you can't win. Why?

Apparently it's the priming used by Eley, or more specifically, the way the priming compound is put into the case. Everything else about the Eley cartridge has been duplicated and even surpassed in terms of quality and uniformity, but there's something about the way they put the wet priming mix in the rimfire case that makes a big difference. Naturally, the folks at Eley aren't giving away their secret. I have heard that they happily show visitors how they make their ammo but always keep the doors of the priming room locked.

Precision handloaders, especially benchrest shooters and long-range rifle competitors, are very much aware of the role primers play in accuracy. This awareness of the individual effect of primers on accuracy created a demand for more uniform primers that culminated in the special benchrest-grade primers currently offered by some manufacturers. However, saying that some primers are better than others is simplifying the issue. The situation is really that certain makes of primers perform better under specific circumstances while others tend to give better results under other conditions. I routinely use four different brands of primers for specific handloading requirements, and my evidence shows that each is best for a particular job.

I've also noted, as have most benchrest shooters, that particular lots of primers by a given manufacturer tend to produce better accuracy than others. That's why competitive shooters tend to hoard certain batches of primers and reserve them for actual competition. This tells us that the manufacture of primers is still something of an art form, and that for unexplained reasons some batches are better than others, just as some batches of cookies taste better than others, even though the recipe and stove are identical.

A quality-control engineer of a major armsmaker once told me that primer-making problems are extremely difficult to diagnose and that attempts to utterly standardize the process

Precision handloaders—like this man using a Wilson seating tool in the course of loading .222's—are keenly aware that accuracy is affected by primers, as well as by such other factors as uniformity of cartridge cases, bullets, and powder charges.

Some lots of primers produce better accuracy than others supplied by the same manufacturer. Benchrest shooters tend to hoard the best batches for competition. They also do a good bit of on-the-spot handloading to achieve the greatest accuracy under prevailing conditions.

seem to end in frustration. It would seem, then, that future improvements in the accuracy of factory-loaded ammo may to some degree center around advanced primer-making technology. This will be especially true when and if the various armsmakers "balance" different loads with a particular primer that demonstrably yields better accuracy.

To some extent this is already happening, but the emphasis is on performance rather than accuracy. By way of background, let's step back a century or so to the era when ammunition was loaded with black powder. Since old-fashioned black powder is so easily ignited, the strength of primers wasn't all that important. As long as the priming compound in a metallic primer was able to emit a feeble spark, black powder would flash. But with the coming of smokeless powder the situation became somewhat critical. Because smokeless powder is harder to ignite, it was necessary or at least desirable to introduce more flash to the charge. As you would expect, the primers used in some ammo, especially the huge, British-made Nitro Express sporting cartridges, were increased in size so as to produce a thunderous ignition. In the U.S., no such problem existed. The days of buffalo hunting and the giant buffalo cartridges had come to an end by the beginning of the smokeless-powder era, so American sporting-ammo makers were not faced with the task of igniting huge volumes of powder. Instead, little hotshots like the .30/30 reflected the American hunter's needs. In time, to the everlasting credit of U.S. ammo makers, two primer sizes were standardized for use in all American sporting and military rifle ammo. These two sizes are used in all centerfires from the .22 Hornet to the .458 Winchester Magnum and are simply known as the Large Rifle (.210 inch diameter) and Small Rifle (.175) sizes. By contrast, the Berdan priming system, commonly used in Europe and other parts of the globe, employs a host of odd primer sizes.

THE MAGNUM PROBLEM

The American primer system worked just fine for a while, but in the late 1940's problems began to spring up in unexpected quarters. One problem was posed by a fellow in California who had the idea of burning tremendous quantities of powder behind relatively lightweight bullets to attain extraordinary velocity and energy levels in his rifles. His name was Roy Weatherby, and while the idea of big-case wildcats was nothing new, his zest and promotional talents were revolutionary.

The workability of the big Weatherby magnums depended on the availability of large-grain, slow-burning smokeless powders. The burning characteristics of these powders makes it feasible to achieve high velocities without generating excessive peak pressures. But propellants of this type also tend to be hard to ignite, especially when used in large volumes. On occasion, a cartridge would not fire. The primer would spark as it was supposed to, and perhaps a few grains of powder would ignite, but before the charge really got going the fire would simply go out.

At first thought, this seems like a simple problem to fix. Why not use more priming compound and get a bigger flash or just use a more highly explosive chemical mix? These solutions, as logical as they seem, wouldn't produce the desired effect without introducing a new set of problems with even more critical consequences. The trick to good ignition is getting a good fire started without unduly disturbing the propellant. If, for example, the primer is made more explosive, its detonation may shatter the kernels of powder. This would increase the surface area of a given volume of powder and make it burn faster. In turn, this would create higher peak pressures and possibly cause a dangerous situation. Clearly, a more powerful primer was not the answer. That's when Dick Speer, a clever shooting buff, and Dr. Victor Jasaitis, a chemical whiz, entered the picture.

During the early 1950's the Speer Cartridge Works, which employed Jasaitis, was involved in a military-sponsored research program aimed at improving cold-weather ignition of small-arms ammunition. As smokeless powder becomes cold it becomes increasingly difficult to ignite, and if it gets cold enough, ignition is unreliable. The armed services were interested in finding a solution. As Dick Speer and Dr. Jasaitis viewed the problem, it was something like holding a burning match to a log. If the match burns only for an instant, the log isn't ignited, but if the match burns long enough, the log will eventually catch fire. By their very nature, however, explosions don't last very long, so the problem facing the Speer team was to make a primer explosion last longer or burn hotter without making it significantly more violent.

Their history-making solution was to enrich the basic lead styphnate mix with boron and aluminum. The aluminum particles, having been heated by the initial explosion, retained the heat and thereby increased the duration of the ignition period. The formula's effectiveness was further enhanced by the hot particles penetrating the powder charge and getting more kernels ignited simultaneously.

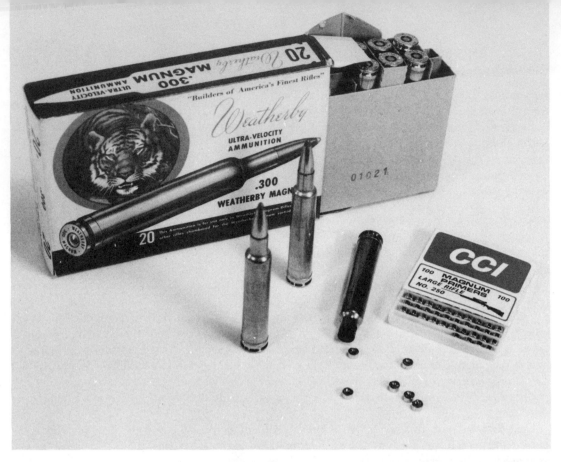

Dick Speer and Dr. Victor Jasaitis of the Speer Cartridge Works developed the revolutionary CCI Magnum primer in the early 1950's. It was this new type of primer — providing ideal ignition for large-grain, slow-burning, high-velocity powders — that made the big Weatherby Magnum cartridges a reliable proposition.

The concept was an overwhelming success, so successful in fact that it became an early mainstay of a new firm that Speer called Cascade Cartridge Industries. This is the famous component and ammo manufacturer we now know simply as CCI, and the name Speer gave his revolutionary product was, of course, the Magnum Primer.

Jasaitis's Magnum Primer could not have been better timed. It made Weatherby's big cartridges a reliably workable proposition and helped usher in the era of magnum cartridges.

TODAY'S CARTRIDGE CASE

If you were to ask a relatively uninitiated handloader why reloaded ammunition *can* be more accurate than factory-loaded ammo in the same caliber, he would probably say it's because the powder charges in handloads are more uniform. This explanation is almost wholly incorrect, but it does a good job of demonstrating the shooting public's rather casual attitude toward the causes of good or bad ammo accuracy.

Actually, the factors affecting accuracy are so many and so varied that it would require a rather large book to cover what we know about them and a much larger volume to discuss what we don't know. But little by little, and sometimes even by leaps and bounds, we are unlocking the secrets of rifle accuracy, and despite evidence to the contrary, this knowledge is making itself felt in the improved ammunition we buy off dealers' shelves. These improvements begin with the way the case is made.

Without going into details, cartridge cases are manufactured by a series of operations which draw and squeeze a brass disk into a cup and then into its finished form. Anyone who complains about the price of centerfire ammunition should visit the Olin-Winchester plant and study the process of stamping, drawing, annealing, drawing, turning, trimming, and final annealing that goes into the manufacture of a shell casing. He will then wonder why cartridges are so cheap.

He might also wonder how long some of the machinery has been used. Obviously, the case-forming machines at Olin and other ammo plants have been punching out cases for generations, and one wonders if more precisely uniform cases could be made if the machinery were more modern. The answer is perhaps, and a definite "not necessarily." One reason brass cases can be manufactured so inexpensively is that the machinery has long since been paid for. Also bear in mind that the cartridge cases used by a benchrest champion to cluster 10 shots inside a quarter-inch circle at 100 yards were made on the same machines that have knocked out millions of .30/30 rounds for decades past.

SAFETY FIRST

The foremost consideration of any manufacturer of ammunitioin is that the product be safe. The second is that it be reliable. Today's shooter, using a modern rifle and modern ammunition, seldom if ever gives any thought to the possibility that his rifle might blow up in his hands. And if a cartridge were to misfire, he'd be astonished. We have been spoiled by the consistent performance of today's ammo. The situation was not so favorable just five decades ago. At the time of World War I it was common for cartridges to rupture and spill a blinding wave of hot gases into the action. That's why rifles of that era, notably the Model 98 Mauser and its copies, featured so many escape routes and deflection baffles. The big forward face of a Mauser bolt sleeve is just such a gas baffle.

Principal reasons for these case failures were improper heat treatment of the brass, which caused them to be hard and brittle rather than tough and elastic, and occasional mercury contamination, which could make the brass shatter like cold plastic. And of course, there was the ever-present problem of primer failure, which could make any ammunition unshootable. Anyone who doubts this should read "Hatcher's Notebook," by General J.S. Hatcher. Among other notable achievements, he was once in charge of small-arms ammunition production at Frankfort Arsenal. Despite Frankfort's ranking as one of the world's best-equipped and scientifically advanced ballistic centers at that time, ammo failures were legion. According to Hatcher's account, as late as 1930 even the best Frankfort ammo was capable of developing erratic pressures high enough to devastate rifles or, at the other extreme, failing to fire.

With such problems, ammunition makers weren't all that concerned about hair-splitting

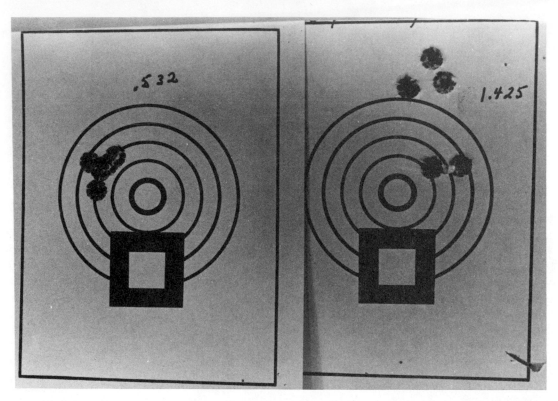

Ever since Lucian Cary and Warren Page publicized benchrest shooting in the 1950's, target riflemen have exerted an influence on ammunition design and manufacture. The difference this can make is graphically illustrated by these two targets.

accuracy. If a particular lot of ammo happened to be accurate, that was very nice indeed, but it was a whole lot nicer if all the cartridges fired and didn't wreck the rifles. Eventually, the art of making and heat-treating brass became a science, and as we have seen, primers reached a state of wonderful reliability. With these major problems conquered, the last remaining challenge would be the improvement of accuracy, so it would seem.

ACCURACY LAST

Incredible as it may appear to dedicated shooters, the pursuit of accuracy has not been popular among makers of sporting ammunition until recently. One reason was the lack of a definition of accuracy. If you think about it, we still have no accepted definition of accuracy. Misfires or ruptured cases leave no doubt that the ammunition was unsatisfactory, but accuracy of a batch of ammo is subject to considerable interpretation. Thus the management of ammo companies have traditionally preferred to avoid qualitative references to accuracy lest they get caught in their own trap. Their advertising literature makes repeated references to "good" accuracy, but where have the ads specifically stated just what that accuracy level is? By contrast, the maker of a fancy sports car may state that the car will exceed 120 mph, and the importer of a quartz watch will claim an accuracy of plus or minus two seconds per week. Ammo makers have steadfastly refused to describe the accuracy of their product, *even when fired from their own test barrels.*

This is largely because there is no clear knowledge of what constitutes good, bad, or average accuracy. Though it is nearly impossible for dedicated shooters such as you and me to comprehend, the truth is that for some people, making ammo is just a job. There are research engineers, ballistic technicians, production supervisors, and sales managers who have little or no *personal* interest in the ammunition they produce, and they actually play golf or tennis or watch football when they could be out shooting! Add to this the attitude of management that accuracy is a boat not to be rocked.

This began to change in the 1950's when benchrest shooting got started. There weren't and still aren't all that many dedicated bench shooters, but their early rifles with gatepost stocks and sewerpipe barrels titillated the shooting public and a rash of publicity followed. Two well-known writers of that era, Lucian Cary of *True* Magazine and Warren Page of *Field & Stream,* happened to be dedicated bench shooters and gave the budding sport nationwide publicity. In the process, they gave casual shooters an idea of what accuracy was all about. When an average rifleman read that some guys were putting 10 shots inside a one-inch circle at 100 yards, he had to see how Old Betsy stacked up. Old Betsy, it turned out, shot groups that measured about 3½ inches between the widest holes at 100 yards. So he called the makers of his rifle and ammo and generally raised hell about poor performance.

The manufacturers told him to return his rifle and ammo and they would see what was causing the trouble. Of course, they found that his rifle was no worse than any other rifle, and the ammo was just as good as the ammo they had been selling for years. Since no one except a few nuts and troublemakers had ever complained before, they put his complaint in the "Nut and Troublemaker" file, returned his rifle, and sent him a fresh box of shells. Their tersely worded letters assured him that his rifle and ammo fell within their accuracy "standards," but they carefully avoided mentioning what those standards happened to be. Actually, the manufacturers had only a slightly better idea of what constituted their in-house accuracy standards than the complaining rifleman had. Their standards were little more than the average accuracy performance of the past 50 years of production runs.

But soon there were more than a few nuts and troublemakers. Thousands of shooters were reading about benchrest shooting. For the first time, they had a definite idea of what accuracy was all about, and when lots of customers complain, management listens. Word filtered down that maybe somebody ought to investigate what all the complaining was about and see if there was any justification. Such investigations can take years, however, and even more years can pass before any results reach the consumer. In the meantime, manufacturers put up their traditional smokescreens. Ammo makers said that accuracy problems must be due to bum rifles; riflemakers claimed that poor accuracy had to be caused by rotten ammo.

Just about that time, another phenomenon was taking place that shifted the burden of proof to the makers of ammunition. That phenomenon, which continues in full glory, was the specialty barrelmaker. Specialty barrelmakers have existed ever since the first tube had its insides scratched with rifling, and their best efforts have been the source of shooting legend. The first half of this century was graced by Harry Pope, John Buhmiller, Bill Sukalle, and other great barrelmakers. But their barrels were made one at a time, and for the most part, were tenderly placed in the loving hands of an exclusive clientele of rich and/or famous target shooters.

After World War II, a host of barrelmakers arose who possessed not only the inclination to make superbly accurate barrels but also the technology and means to make *lots* of them. The high quality of this new genre was much publicized in articles about bench shooting. Yard-bird

Another phenomenon that influenced ammunition manufacturers was the highly publicized proliferation of specialty barrelmakers after World War II. Barrels like those being turned out in this shop have an accuracy potential that presents a challenge to ammo producers.

shooters who might otherwise never have heard of a custom barrel found themselves owning wonderfully accurate rifles. Back then, surplus Model 98 Mausers could be had for $10 or $15, and a barrel by Douglas cost another $25 or so. With a semi-finished stock from Fajen or Bishop for another $5 to $10, the shooter had a rifle capable of shooting inside the magic inch at 100 yards. And about that time, Remington introduced the amazingly accurate Model 722, which set new standards for off-the-shelf rifle accuracy.

HANDLOADING'S INFLUENCE

To complete the circle, that same era was the beginning of the big boom in handloading. As thousands of novice handloaders were quick to discover, even amateurishly assembled reloads more often than not surpassed the accuracy of factory loads. Naturally, thousands of shooters outfitted themselves with reloading tools, and at least one finely accurate custom-barreled rifle graced their gun racks. Never again could a manufacturer of rifles or ammunition dictate to the poor customer what he was to accept in the way of accuracy. Now it was the customer's turn, and when he told a manufacturer that ammo was no good, he could back it up. As a reloader, he didn't have to settle for junk. That got 'em where it hurt.

Then as now, there were a number of dedicated and experienced shooters working in the various ammo plants at all levels of management, research, and production. Many were handloading hobbyists and competitive shooters, and generally felt it was better not to make waves. After all, the official view of most ammo manufacturers about handloading was that it was a dirty word and should never be uttered on company time. Perhaps if they ignored handloading, it would go away.

But handloading didn't go away. In time, even the hard-nosed ammo-plant executives had to recognize that a properly assembled handload represented *the* prevailing standard of accuracy. When some fumble-fingered rifleman could drill five handloaded bullets inside a one-inch circle with his Douglas-barreled .257 Roberts, while groups shot with factory loads were twice as large, there really wasn't much doubt about what constituted accuracy.

I began reloading in 1952 at the tender age of 15 with a wonderful old Pacific press and assorted equipment made by various makers who have long since escaped the miseries of this world. Oh, how clever I thought I was, blasting crows and groundhogs with smug delight and never missing an opportunity to sneer at any poor soul so unfortunate as to be burdened by factory-loaded ammunition.

Thinking back on those days, I quake to think how many times I must have been within a whisker of blowing my head off with the loads I concocted. I've since come to suspect that angels look after fools and handloaders. At that time, along with thousands of fellow shooters, I figured that loading accurate ammo was simple, and that if any of the major ammo makers would give me a call I could easily set them straight in a few minutes. How innocent I was!

THE AMMO MAKER'S HEADACHES

The complicated fact is that a mass manufacturer of ammunition cannot think the way a handloader thinks. For example, the handloader assembles ammunition for a single rifle. Quite often, ammunition reloaded for a given rifle will not fire accurately in other rifles and may not even fire or function in another rifle of the same caliber. By contrast, commercial ammunition has to function safely and reliably in thousands of rifles. These rifles have so many variations in barrel, chamber, and headspace dimensions that the problem is something like making shoes in one size to fit everyone comfortably.

Whereas most handloaders use a single tool, thereby insuring a high degree of uniformity, the mass manufacturer may have a dozen or more loading machines running at once, each contributing cartridges to a common batch. Though this sounds like a road to poor accuracy, the big manufacturers carry it off pretty well. By contrast, imagine the accuracy debacle that would result if a dozen handloaders turned out their versions of a given cartridge and mixed them in a single batch.

The problems facing the big producer go far beyond working up a load, carefully weighing a powder charge, and assembling the loads. In fact, these are simple exercises for the manufacturer. Even on a scale of thousands of rounds per day these things are routinely handled with greater precision and uniformity than the typical handloader can achieve.

DOWN TO CASES

One obvious way the manufacturers could improve accuracy was, of course, to use better bullets. Bullet quality was and is the main reason that handloads improve accuracy. We'll talk more about what the various ammo makers have done about bullets a bit later in this chapter, but a better bullet isn't the only way to improve performance at the target. Accuracy begins with the primer and cartridge case. Until fairly recent times, the role played by the brass case in regard to accuracy was not very well understood or at least it was not considered especially important. If a case was properly hardened so it would not rupture on firing and it was sized to fit a rifle's chamber correctly, there wasn't much else to worry about. The function of a cartridge case is to act as an envelope for the powder charge and to hold primer, powder, and bullet together. What has that to do with how straight a bullet travels when it leaves the muzzle?

We get our first clue to the effect of the cartridge case on accuracy every time an armsmaker announces a new cartridge. Invariably, the new round is touted as not merely accurate but accurate in dazzling superlatives. And to back up what they say, the proud manufacturers send samples to gun writers so that they can witness this milestone in accuracy achievement for themselves. And, sure 'nuff, the test groups almost always are delightfully tiny. Funny thing, though, a year or two later, that same caliber isn't quite so exciting. For some strange reason, the factory ammo no longer wears the golden cloak of accuracy. From afar come rumblings of customer complaints about poor accuracy.

Mass producers cannot turn out ammo by the methods a handloader uses. A factory may have a dozen or more loading machines running at once. All the same, uniformity and quality control have improved immensely on the assembly lines. Here, the author looks over loads being assembled at a Winchester-Western (Olin) plant.

How can a particular batch of ammunition be wonderfully accurate while another batch made by the same firm on the same machines by the same technicians with identical bullets, powder, and powder charge weights is often measurably less accurate when fired from the same rifle? Again, the laymen's view centers around the powder charge, as does the hobby handloader's. The reason "bad" or inconsistent powder charges are easy to blame is that this is one of the few variables about which a handloader has some knowledge and over which he can exercise some control. Handloaders tend to view an ammo manufacturing plant as a giant reloading operation and tend to see poor accuracy as the result of working up a poor load. In reality, the variables in the manufacture of ammunition would boggle the mind of a typical handloader. For example, the variables that affect the making of the brass cartridge cases may have a drastic bearing on accuracy, dooming a batch of ammo to mediocrity, regardless of the quality of the bullets used, and even ordaining that subsequent handloads assembled with those cases will be below par. To explain how this can happen, let's attend the birth of a new cartridge.

When a cartridge is first manufactured, the early production runs are carefully supervised by a host of concerned personnel. In addition to the usual production technicians, the new round's progress is monitored by sales executives, research technicians, and ballistic engineers. With all of this attention being paid to production, it is only natural that the machine operators and set-up men give more than casual service to the drawing dies and related fixtures. Of course, the dies are all new, carefully aligned, and at the peak of performance. This means that the brass cases are cupped and drawn with particularly good uniformity and that the case heads are square to the lineal axis of the cases. No wonder those first sample lots of ammo sent to gun writers for testing are outstandingly accurate.

I'm sure you've already guessed what happens next. In time, interest in the new baby begins to wane. Sales managers go back to their desks, and the research engineers go back to their labs and computers to design even newer cartridges. The new baby is being pounded out on dies that are beginning to wear, and the machines are attended by production personnel whose only concern is that the machinery keeps running and that the resulting cases fall somewhere within tolerance specifications. Now the case walls aren't so uniform, neck thickness varies three or four thousandths from one side to the other, and the heads aren't as square as they once were. Accuracy deteriorates gradually in small steps that are almost impossible to identify and isolate.

Of course, accuracy is routinely tested at the plant in special test rifles. The personnel doing the testing aren't necessarily concerned with noting any loss of accuracy but only in determining that accuracy is within in-house standards for that particular caliber. One might say that the accuracy of the cartridge is not as good as it once was even though accuracy isn't bad.

ACCURATE FACTORY LOADS

But don't kid yourself that ammo makers don't know how to make exceedingly accurate cartridges. Among the most accurate ammo ever assembled by a major ammo maker was a special lot of .308 Winchester cartridges loaded by Winchester-Western for the 1976 Palma Match at Camp Perry. This lot was so accurate that 10-shot groups were measured in small fractions of an inch, and these loads vastly exceeded the performance of most handloads. These cartridges

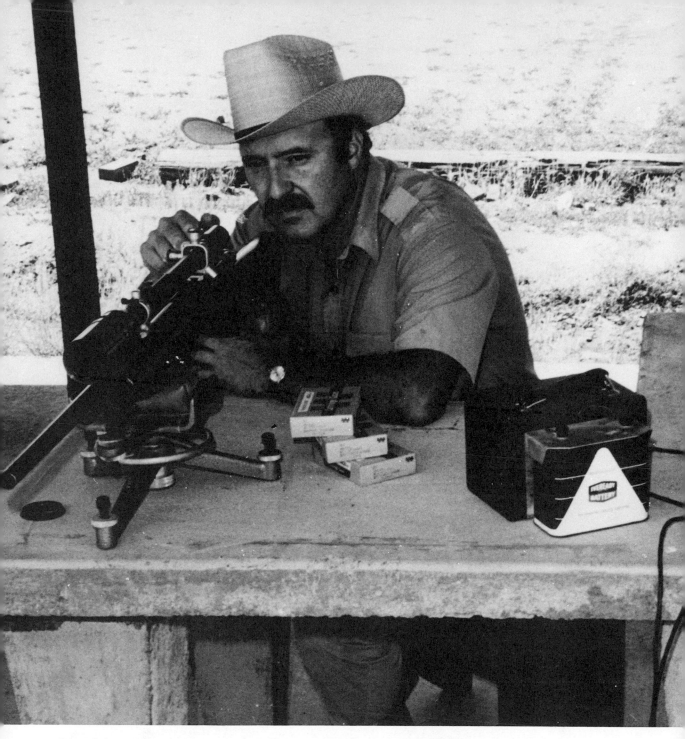

Carmichel is seen here testing new loads. Early production runs of a new cartridge are closely monitored by sales executives, research technicians, and ballistic engineers. The cases are cupped and drawn with particularly good uniformity, and the case heads are square to the lineal axis — which means that samples sent to gun writers are apt to be outstandingly accurate.

This shooter is using loads that are among the most accurate ever assembled by a major manufacturer — a special lot of .308's loaded by Winchester-Western for the 1976 Palma Match at Camp Perry. These loads were so good that 10-shot groups were measured in small fractions of an inch.

The finest accuracy demands careful checking of dimensions, tolerances, and straightness. This is relatively easy for a precision handloader but would send the price of mass-produced ammo sky-high.

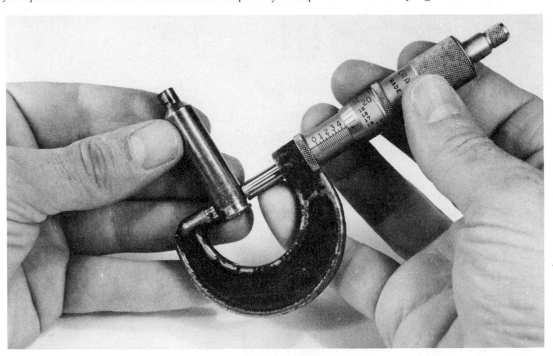

might not have been so accurate if the project director had not recognized a problem early in the manufacturing stage. Charged with making the most accurate ammunition possible, Herman Bockstruck, head ballistician for W-W and an experienced target shooter, checked the run of Palma match cases and found the head to be somewhat out of square with the axis. Knowing this would cause a loss of accuracy because uneven case heads cause erratic rifle flexing and barrel vibration, he ordered the entire lot of some 40,000 cases scrapped. This won him no friends on the production lines, but the next lot of cases measured up to his specifications and the resulting ammo was wonderfully accurate.

Why can't the ammo makers always maintain Herman Bockstruck's tolerance specifications? The answer is that they can, but few of us would be willing to pay what it would cost if every case were made to utterly precise standards. Even while holding the price line, most ammo makers are moving toward more accurate ammunition by eliminating the tiny variables that tend to enlarge group sizes.

Without meaning to defend ammo makers, I must say on their behalf that upgrading accuracy is not an easy task. I'm reminded of the dilemma of American auto makers during the early 1980's when they were being hard pressed by foreign importers. The principal area of buyer dissatisfaction was poor quality as compared to the imports. Homing in on this problem, some American manufacturers, especially General Motors, announced in a blast of advertising that the quality of their products was to be immediately upgraded. The folly was that they were and are so deeply entrenched in a specific manufacturing philosophy that not even Moses, bringing tablets from the Mount, could expect any basic changes in quality. If such changes are to be significant, they must be bought at tremendous expense, including new factories, new machinery, re-trained personnel, and a new executive cadre.

This is not meant to compare American or foreign-made ammo to U.S. automobiles. Our ammunition is vastly better than our cars. I only want to emphasize the basic difficulty of uprooting manufacturing philosophies that have been in effect for generations. Bit by bit, though, improvements do occur. When these improvements are dovetailed into the manufacturing process and become part of the maker's philosophy, we all benefit, even though some shooters don't know and possibly don't even care. There are also those who are so blinded by prejudice that they don't recognize a good thing when it smacks them between the eyes.

OUTSTANDING BULLETS

The bullets made and loaded by major ammo manufacturers provide a good example. Rank-and-file handloaders have long held that one of the main reasons reloaded ammo is so accurate is the use of beautifully made bullets offered by various component makers. These bullets by Speer, Nosler, Hornady, Sierra, and some others have served me so well that there was a time when I would have gagged at the prospect of loading bullets made by Winchester or Remington. So it is with many handloaders who operate under the impression that the poor accuracy of some factory loads is due to substandard bullets. That's why sales of factory bullets by the major ammunition makers as components have never been great. This leads to an interesting yarn.

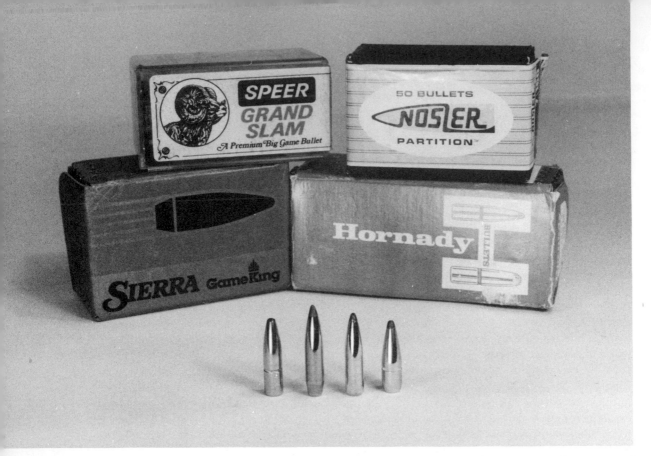

Bullets that have attained top reputations among handloaders include these, made by Speer, Nosler, Sierra, and Hornady. But the author contends that some of the bullets supplied by mass ammo manufacturers are as accurate as those made by the specialty component firms.

In an effort to offset the prevailing attitude of handloaders toward their bullets, Winchester launched a match bullet program in the early 1970's or thereabouts. In order to make sure their bullets would be ultra-accurate, they hired Ferris Pindell, a Benchrest Hall of Famer and a superb tool maker, to design their new bullets and make the forming dies. The bullets initially offered to the accuracy trade were .22 and 6mm hollow-points and .30-caliber slugs weighing 168 and 190 grains. Winchester was justly proud of these bullets and sent samples to the writing trade and a few select target shooters. And they were *accurate,* not just in the varmint-shooting sense but in terms of stacking bullets on top of one other. My test groups ran as small as two-*tenths* of an inch for five shots at 100 yards.

Did handloaders come screaming for these bullets? Sales were so poor that after a couple of years the match series was dropped. I bought up the remaining stock and now have thousands of the most accurate bullets ever made.

Why did handloaders refuse to buy these superb bullets? It could be because they were not promoted effectively. I can't remember a single ad that described their fine accuracy. Perhaps they represented such a small part of Winchester's operations that there was insufficient in-house interest. I really think, however, that handloaders had done such a good job of indoctrinating themselves against anything that came out of a major ammo plant that they were blind to those magnificent bullets. The final irony was that the management at Winchester also failed to recognize the potential of these bullets. At that time, I suggested to Winchester that they would be smart to load some of these great bullets in a few select calibers and offer the cartridges at a premium price as ultra-performance target and varmint loads. Their .22-caliber benchrest bullet loaded in .222 Remington or .22/250, for example, would have been more accurate than those produced by nine out of 10 handloaders. And the same bullet in a hot .220 Swift load would have found an eager market. Even if marketed on a break-even basis, a few calibers loaded with those beautiful bullets would have added tremendous prestige to the overall Winchester line and would have helped to promote bullet sales. Alas, the only Winchester "Super Bullets" loaded by the factory were used in the 1976 Palma Match cartridges described earlier.

A somewhat more successful component bullet-making adventure produced Remington's benchrest-grade .22 and 6mm masterpieces. These were made in a small facility far from the rest of Remington's ammo-making operations. In fact, it was part of the custom shop, only a few steps from where Remington's 40-X target rifles are made. The work was thus supervised by accuracy specialists. The whole idea of a bench-grade bullet was to duplicate the precision of hand-swaged bullets made in custom dies. Accordingly, Remington simply set up some custom swaging dies, just like the ones used by particular bench shooters, in a mechanized press and began popping out beautiful bullets.

These outstanding bullets might have been ignored by handloaders had it not been for Mike Walker and Jim Stekl. In addition to being involved in Remington's accuracy programs at the time, these two men were quality benchrest shooters. They went out and won benchrest tournaments with the new Remington bullets and set records in the process. Predictably, bench and varmint shooters rushed to buy the wonderful bullets. Even at premium prices, orders exceeded production.

But these bullets are no longer available. They were phased out when Remington stopped selling bullets as component items. During their brief life, like Winchester's, they served to demonstrate that the major ammunition manufacturers can produce some of the most accurate bullets known to shooters if they wish to do so.

What a maker of sporting ammunition is, and what shooters expect the manufacturer to be, are often very different. This situation is the result of our profound dedication to the shooting sports. Because of the intensity of our involvement, we tend to see the makers of guns and ammo as larger than life—Olympians. This is not overlooked by the gunmakers in their publicity campaigns. Think how often you've heard major arms and ammunition makers call themselves a "legend" or a "heritage."

The problem is that when a godlike figure fails, it creates bitter resentment among former followers. And once these followers are lost, they are exceedingly difficult to win back to the fold. Take, for example, my typical, if fictitious, old pal Marvin Misque. Marvin goes about his daily affairs in perfectly normal fashion except when the talk turns to his singular love in life, guns and shooting.

If Marvin buys some mustache wax that melts in the sun, he just throws it in the trash, or at worst, demands his money back. The wax and its maker are quickly forgotten. But if he buys a box of rifle ammo that doesn't shoot inside a one-inch circle, Marvin feels he's been *betrayed* by a firm in which he had limitless faith. Marvin writes to the manufacturer and he isn't just irate, he's unreasonable. He asks for his money back, but what he really wants is his faith restored.

TWO KINDS OF CUSTOMER

Consumers of sporting ammunition, as viewed by the armsmaking industry, can be divided into two main classes. The larger class is the traditional meat-and-potato hunter who takes his annual deer and does no other shooting except for an occasional plinking session and possibly some pre-season sighting-in and practice. His ammo consumption runs around two boxes of centerfire rifle shells per year. Likely as not, he's not overly influenced by guys like me, and if his choice in ammo got a deer last year, then it's good enough this year.

The other group is much smaller but their per-month expenditure of ammo is much greater, averaging perhaps 500 rounds or more per year. Even though Group Two is smaller, its total consumption of ammo is about the same as that of Group One. Group Two is dedicated and vocal. Its members tend to be influenced by what they read in gun publications, what they hear from other shooters, and what they experience. Members of Group Two are the ones who are likely to feel betrayed when a product made by their favorite manufacturer doesn't perform as expected.

Group Two includes almost all the handloaders. There is little doubt that with the reloading boom of the '60's and '70's, there also came a sense of betrayal because accurate handloads presented proof positive that the factory loads weren't as good as they could be. Thus, allegiance to an old favorite ammo maker was converted to hostility, and loyalty was pledged to a Sierra, a Speer, or a Hornady. These dedicated makers of component bullets capitalized on their new loyalists by offering them what they craved most—visual satisfaction in the form of shiny, beautiful, streamlined bullets that zipped through the air like skinny lightning and, best of all, put tiny groups on paper. This was and still is a beautiful relationship. While all this was taking place, the traditional mass-manufacturers of sporting ammo were, and still are, making progress very slowly. Not because they don't know how to make streamlined, accurate bullets because, as we've seen, they can make astonishingly accurate bullets with ease, but because they see their role to be that of making the best bullet as they perceive the requirements of a bullet to be.

A good case in point is Remington's Core-Lokt bullet, which is offered in several calibers and weights. It is one of the best hunting bullets ever offered by any ammo or bullet maker, large or small. Yet, if you were to use some Core-Lokt shells in your snazzy MOA target rifle, you'd probably be disappointed in their accuarcy. Not that accuracy would be poor, but five shots in a 1½-inch circle at 100 yards is close to typical. A razzle-dazzle handloader would condemn this as miserable accuracy and berate the folks at Remington. His opinion is based only on what he sees as holes in paper. What he can't see is the beautifully controlled expansion of a Core-Lokt bullet as it strikes an elk's chest cavity. He doesn't see the jacket, thin at the tip, split and peel back toward the base, exposing a mushroom of lead that radiates nerve-shattering jolts of energy throughout the elk's vital organs.

Our critical friend doesn't know that the way a Core-Lokt bullet is made introduces by-product characteristics that cause some loss of accuracy. Literally, it's a matter of having good performance on game or fine accuracy. Remington, without apologies, opted for terminal performance. The company deliberately caters to the vast number of once-a-year hunters who want to kill a deer with as little fuss as possible.

One has to ask why Remington feels the customers buy performance on game at the cost of accuracy. Indeed, there are executives and technicians at Remington who are asking the same

Introduced in the late 1970's, this Federal .30/06 Springfield loading has been a landmark innovation. It utilizes a 165-grain boat-tail spitzer bullet whose retained velocity equals that of the 150-grain bullet at 100 yards, outruns the lighter bullet at 300 yards—and at that distance yields more energy than the 180-grain bullet.

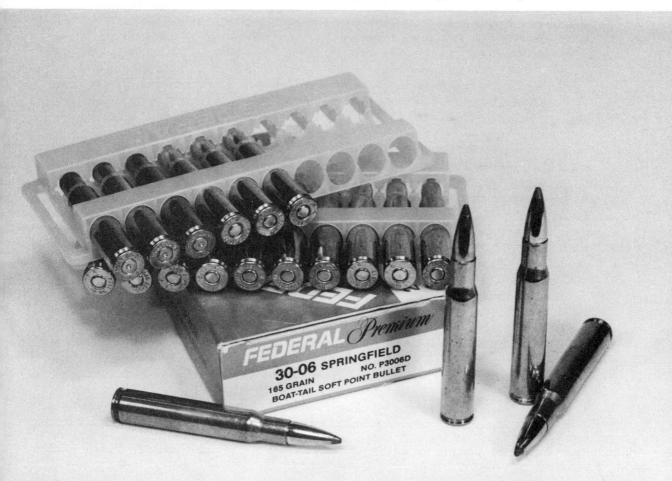

question. They want fine accuracy, too, but this can only come slowly by refining their manufacturing process bit by bit and always taking care not to sacrifice terminal performance. Remington's primary duty to the consumer, as that company and similar firms see it, is to continue and promote those features that have proven workable by the tests of time and experience.

This is a slow but sure route. Other routes are open to ammo makers. During the late 1970's, Federal introduced a .30/06 loading that created something of a sensation and in retrospect is possibly a landmark. The innovation was a 165-grain boat-tail spitzer bullet loading to a muzzle velocity of 2,800 fps. That isn't particularly exciting news seeing as how this bullet weight is about halfway between the popular 150-grain and 180-grain .30/06 bullet weights. But it starts getting interesting at the 100-yard flag where its remaining velocity of 2,610 fps is equal to that of the initially speedier 150-grain bullet. At 300 yards, it is outrunning the 150 by over 150 fps and yielding over 200 more foot-pounds of energy than the 180-grain bullet. That's why it was called the ".30/06 Magnum" load.

This work of ballistic wizardry was accomplished by observing basic laws of external ballistics. Federal's 165-grain bullet has a clean, streamlined shape, plus a boat-tail heel that permits it to slice through the air with minimal velocity loss. In short, the application of an air-slick bullet is so logical and so overwhelmingly obvious that one can't help wonder why major ammo makers haven't been doing it all along. To a certain extent they have, especially with their high-velocity varmint bullets, but the great middle class of bullets loaded by ammo makers tend to have a poor aerodynamic shape. This, of course, leads to an unnecessarily high rate of velocity loss. But here again we must remind ourselves that most of these bullets were designed for terminal performance. And ammo makers know that a large segment of their customers still cling to the mistaken notion that blunt-nosed bullets crash through brush more effectively than needle-like shapes.

Instead of resisting the widespread preference among savvy shooters for the types of bullets made by reloading-component makers, Federal has jumped on the bandwagon. Federal makes no secret that some of the bullets used in their high-performance loads, especially the Premium line, are produced by Sierra and Nosler. When their Premium line got rolling, I suggested to the Federal powers that be that they would be smart to offer some super-deluxe hunting cartridges using the Nosler Partition bullet. After some talk and looking into the sales possibilities, this is exactly what they did. The company also took my advice that their use of the highly respected Nosler bullet should not be kept secret, but should be publicized. In this way, they are able to take advantage of the reputation earned by Nosler and get free word-of-mouth advertising from handloaders. If you can't lick 'em, join 'em.

A few days before writing this, I tested a sample lot of a new .233 Remington loading offered by Federal. With their 55-grain hollow-point, boat-tail bullets, this lot averaged close to six-tenths of an inch extreme spread for five shots at 100 yards. Since that is as accurate as that particular rifle ever gets even with the best handloads, I assume that the Federal loads might be capable of grouping under half an inch—and that surpasses the accuracy of all but the very best handloads.

A while back, when Briarbank Ballistic Laboratory, OUTDOOR LIFE's research center, was doing initial development work with the .22 CHeetah (Carmichel-Huntington) we had difficulty finding bullets that would not disintegrate when launched at velocities over 4,300 fps.

The unique, ultra-high-velocity .22 CHeetah ("CH" for Carmichel and Huntington) is remarkably accurate at long range, as this target shows. Carmichel found that one particular bullet—a Remington Power-Lokt bullet—performed exceptionally well at sizzling velocities in this round. Ironically, Remington had to discontinue its component bullet line.

Almost by chance, we tried an old lot of Remington "Match" bullets made with their Power-Lokt process. These bullets held together and consistently grouped inside half an inch at 100 yards, even at our sizzling velocities. I wish these bullets were still made because they would be a revelation to doubters, but alas, they were discontinued along with the rest of Remington's component bullet line.

The mid-1960's saw the birth of a short-lived varmint cartridge called the .225 Winchester. For various reasons, it was one of the all-time great flops, but whenever the subject of rifle accuracy is raised, we should all stand and toast the woebegone .225 Winchester. The ammunition produced in this caliber was among the most consistently accurate ever produced. This may have been because so little of it was ever made, but back when MOA rifles and ammo were not all that common it was no trick for these factory loads to group around a half-inch at 100 yards.

My descriptions of particularly accurate factory loads may only be a backhanded way of pointing up the poor accuracy of the remaining 95 percent. That is not my intent. Today's factory-loaded centerfire ammunition, as well is most rimfire, needs no apologies. When a bad lot gets out, the manufacturer invariably makes every effort to find out what went wrong and insure that it doesn't happen again. Characteristic of this growing concern are the occasional recalls of ammo suspected of developing high pressure or other unsafe conditions. Such recalls were unheard of a generation ago, not because the ammo made then was better, but, because testing procedures were not nearly so refined and because concern for quality wasn't as strong as it is now.

Accuracy is the layman's guide to ammunition performance because it is one of few factors he can recognize and judge. Using this guide as our only yardstick to performance, we perceive very little improvement in factory-loaded ammo on a year-to-year or even decade-to-decade basis. If, however, we had at our disposal laboratories equipped with data-gathering and statistical-compilation instrumentation (the same sort of equipment used by any ammo manufacturer) we would be revising our opinions of factory-loaded cartridges on a regular basis. The improvements are so regular and so significant that when we talk about today's product and the ammunition made only a generation ago, we're talking about two different things.

Chapter 8

UNDERSTANDING BALLISTICS

The average shooter knows less about ballistics than about any other aspect of firearms. Those who claim to be experts can tell you practically anything you want to know about a gun: where and when it was made, how many brothers and sisters it has, and all sorts of obscure production data. For good measure, they'll provide enough handloading poop to make your ears ring. But ask a simple question about what a bullet does from the time it leaves the muzzle until it arrives on target, and nearly everyone becomes a mental basket case.

Our ballistic ignorance stems mostly from the fact that bullets travel so fast that we can't see them in flight. Since we can't follow the bullet's path as we can that of a football, we tend to imagine what happens, and imagination plays tricks. To make matters worse, the language of shooting often is misleading. You might hear someone say that a bullet from a 7mm Remington does not fall as fast as a slug from a .30/30 carbine. Though we generally understand what is meant by this statement, it is incorrect in the strict sense, as we shall see before this chapter is out.

As Shooting Editor of OUTDOOR LIFE, I get stacks of mail from readers who never cease to amaze me with the variety of their questions. One constantly recurring question, despite my best efforts to publicize the answer, is, "Does a bullet rise when it leaves a gun barrel, even if the gun is held perfectly level?" The answer to this is, of course, no, but there is so much ballistic confusion that the question never stays answered.

I must admit that it's easy to understand why so little is understood about ballistics. Ballistic scientists and engineers speak to each other in a bizarre language I call "ballistese." It is beautifully precise, if you understand all the symbols and equations. But if you don't happen to speak the lingo, a 15-minute conversation with a ballistician leaves your head reeling. That's why so many shooters avoid the science of ballistics, preferring sublime ignorance to exposing their innocence of ballistic mathematics.

Actually, the beautiful science of ballistics can be clearly explained with scarcely a whisper of mathematics or the hint of an equation. All you have to understand is one basic fact, and it is something you already know.

THE EFFECT OF GRAVITY

The single most important ballistic fact is something you learned when you were learning to walk—*things fall!* Let a brick or a feather or a bullet drop, and the effect of gravity is instantly apparent. Everything about practical ballistics is based on that one basic fact. Gravity makes bullets fall. No matter how fast or slow the bullet is moving, streamlined as a needle or blunt as a pancake, every bullet is a slave to gravity.

Though we can't see a bullet in flight, there is something we can see that goes a long way toward explaining ballistics. Hold two bullets as different in size and weight as you can find at shoulder height and let them drop together. You may be amazed to discover that the lighter bullet falls as fast as the heavier one, just as Galileo's audience was amazed when two iron balls of different size and weight hit the ground at *nearly* the same instant when dropped from the Tower of Pisa. Don't take my word for it, drop two bullets yourself. Once you've demonstrated this to yourself, you will have leaped the highest hurdle in understanding ballistics.

You may logically conclude that a bullet fired from a rifle falls at the same rate as one dropped from your hand. In the strict sense of classical physics, this is exactly the case. But to demonstrate the validity of the concept, you would have to do the shooting in a vacuum in order to avoid aerodynamic drag. If it were possible to conduct shooting experiments in a huge vacuum chamber, we could demonstrate some very interesting ideas. One such demonstration would be to fire two rifles locked in a vise so that they were perfectly horizontal, positioned, say, three feet above a level plain. One rifle fires an ordinary .22 Long Rifle Rimfire cartridge with a muzzle velocity of 1,200 fps. The other rifle is a .220 Swift centerfire with a muzzle velocity of some 4,100 fps.

Now let's say that you are also holding a bullet, any bullet, in your hand, also three feet above ground level. By means of a precise timing arrangement, we fire both rifles and drop the bullet from your hand at exactly the same instant.

The bullet from your hand would, of course, fall at your feet; the bullets from the rifles would impact the level plain hundreds of yards downrange. All three would hit the ground at the same exact instant in our handy vacuum chamber.

At this point, you are surely wondering what the difference would be if we repeated the three-bullet experiment in the normal earth's atmosphere. This experiment would show two different results. First, rather than traveling many hundreds of yards before coming to earth, the .220 Swift bullet would travel only about 450 yards before impacting, and the rimfire .22 bullet would go only some 150 yards. Second, the bullet dropped from your hand would reach the ground first; the .220 Swift bullet would hit last. The time differences would be so slight as to be almost imperceptible, but they would exist.

These differences in range and time of fall would be caused by aerodynamic factors acting on the speeding bullets. The total effect of these aerodynamics, as we shall see later, is considerable.

TIME

The next important concept to master is *time;* not just the time it takes a bullet to reach the target, but the time intervals along its route.

The path of a bullet is called its trajectory. By looking at a schematic drawing of a typical trajectory, we see that a bullet's long-range line of movement is curved and that as the range increases, the curve becomes more pronounced. This is not because gravity has more pull at longer ranges. The pull of gravity is constant. To get a clearer understanding of trajectory, let's consider it from the time-interval viewpoint.

When a bullet exits a barrel or is dropped from your hand, it begins to fall immediately, though at first it falls rather slowly. This initial drop velocity is sluggish because gravity must overcome the inertia of the bullet. Even though the bullet may be moving forward at high velocity, the downward gravitation effect is the same as if the bullet were stationary.

An object dropped in a vacuum will reach a speed of 32.17 feet per second during the first second of fall and increase its speed of fall by 32.17 feet per second every second thereafter. An object such as a bullet dropped in the normal earth's atmosphere falls at about this same rate at first but, because of air resistance, will not continue to accelerate indefinitely. However, since a bullet does not fall very far before coming to earth when fired from a level barrel, we can use our high-school physics figure of 32.17 feet per second to calculate speed of bullet drop. Since I promised not to speak in equations, here is a table showing how long it takes a bullet to fall a foot in the earth's atmosphere, inch by inch:

Inches	Seconds
0	0
1	.0719
2	.1017
3	.1246
4	.1439
5	.1609
6	.1762
7	.1903
8	.2035
9	.2158
10	.2275
11	.2386
12	.2492

This table shows that a bullet's rate of fall is some .0106 seconds per inch (.2492 − .2386 = .0106) by the time it has fallen 12 inches. This is more than 6½ times faster than its rate of fall for the *first* inch. Obviously, this difference is in the rate of drop accounts in part for the fact that a trajectory is relatively straight at first and then becomes increasingly curved. Let's look at it another way.

Going back into our wonderful vacuum chamber, let's fire a rifle bullet at a muzzle velocity of 3,000 feet per second. In a vacuum, there is no air drag on the bullet, so it will maintain a constant velocity of 3,000 fps. This is handy for our purposes because we are only interested in time intervals. As we see by the time-of-fall table, it takes .0719 seconds for the bullet to fall one inch. With a forward velocity of 3,000 fps, the bullet will have traveled some 216 feet during the .0719 seconds it took to fall one inch. As the bullet continues to fall, the effect of gravity causes an acceleration of the rate of fall so that it requires only .0298 seconds to fall from one inch to two inches. During this shorter interval of time, the bullet travels only 90 additional feet horizontally. Still accelerating downward, the bullet requires only .0229 seconds to fall another inch, allowing only 69 feet of horizontal travel. The additional drop interval from three inches to four inches is .0193 seconds, and from four inches to five inches is .0170 seconds. The respective forward travel distances are 58 and 51 feet. Thus, in a time span of .1609-second, during which the bullet fell five inches, it had a forward travel of 483 feet. A corresponding trajectory diagram would look like this:

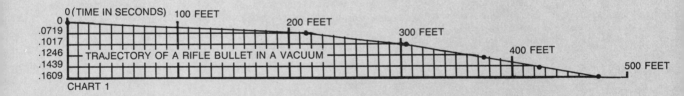

In this graph, the bullet is traveling at a constant speed of 3,000 feet per second because there is no air resistance in a vacuum. Each square in the grid represents 10 feet horizontally and one inch of drop.

THE ATMOSPHERE

With this bit of knowledge tucked away, let's move out of the vacuum chamber and into the real world. It is here that a speeding bullet gets its second biggest shock. The force that most affects a bullet's flight is atmospheric resistance, or drag. Strolling around on foot, we scarcely feel the air as we move through it, but put your arm out the window of a car traveling 60 miles an hour and the atmospheric drag is quite obvious. Imagine the atmospheric drag a bullet "feels" when it comes whistling out of a rifle barrel at 2,045 miles per hour (3,000 fps). It's like diving into a pool of molasses from a great height, and the immediate loss of velocity is astounding.

This table, showing the short-range velocities of a 55-grain bullet from a .22/250 Remington cartridge, gives an idea of the immediate velocity loss.

Range (yards)	Velocity (fps)	Range (yards)	Velocity (fps)
0	3,730		
1	3,724	20	3,618
2	3,719	30	3,563
3	3,713	40	3,508
4	3,708	50	3,454
5	3,702	60	3,400
6	3,696	70	3,347
7	3,691	80	3,294
8	3,685	90	3,242
9	3,680	100	3,190
10	3,674		

This table shows that the *rate* of velocity loss diminishes as velocity drops. This tells us that building high velocity into a bullet is severely subject to the law of diminishing returns.

Let's say you are handloading .300 Winchester Magnum ammo with 150-grain round-nose bullets. You figure a muzzle velocity of 3,000 fps will be good for long shots at mule deer, but just to make sure, you check the ballistic tables in your loading manual. The remaining velocities for this load, you discover, are:

Yards	FPS
0	3,000
100	2,649
200	2,324
300	2,022
400	1,745
500	1,498

Clearly the 150-grain bullet is losing a lot of velocity in a hurry and won't have as much punch at long range as you would like. Out of curiosity, you check the reloading tables to see what the remaining velocity would be for the same 150-grain .30 caliber bullet if you loaded to only a muzzle velocity of, say, 2,600 fps. This is what you discover:

Yards	FPS
0	2,600
100	2,278
200	1,980
300	1,707
400	1,465
500	1,264

"Now hold on a minute," you say. "Something ain't right. How come a 400-fps velocity difference at the muzzle becomes only a 234 fps difference at 500 yards?"

That is what I mean by the law of diminishing returns. This sorry state of affairs is caused by air resistance. Few of us got through high-school physics without coming to grips with Isaac Newton (1642-1727), the British mathematician and physicist. By comparison to him, many of history's geniuses are functional morons. I don't know if Newton was a shooter, but his heart was certainly in the right place, because he was fascinated by projectiles and air resistance.

One of his experiments involved dropping glass bulbs from the top of St. Paul's Cathedral, the highest enclosed place he could find. Filling the globes with mercury, air, or water, he compared their actual rate of fall with their theoretical rate of fall and came up with some interesting conclusions. Air resistance, he calculated, is proportional to the square of the velocity. In other words, when you double the velocity of a bullet, you *quadruple* the air resistance. To give an example, let's say that a bullet traveling 2,000 fps encounters air resistance equal to one pound of weight pushing against its tip. If the velocity is doubled, the air resistance becomes four pounds! But wait, there's more to it.

It seems that Newton erred somewhat. His observations were accurate, but he had no way of observing or measuring high-speed projectiles. If means had been available, he might have discovered that air resistance at higher velocities is even *greater* than he postulated. Which means that the bullet going 4,000 fps encounters even more resistance than our hypothetical four pounds.

Considering the unrelenting force of gravity and the atmospheric barriers encountered by a fast-moving projectile, it may seem a wonder that a bullet goes anywhere or hits anything. Happily, as we shall now see, we have some loopholes in the laws of air resistance, and we can even make gravity work *for* us.

Going back to Galileo's experiment, we noted that the two iron balls dropped from the Tower of Pisa struck the ground at *nearly* the same instant. This seems odd; why didn't they hit at *exactly* the same instant? The larger and heavier ball will hit an instant sooner because of the difference in air resistance acting on the two balls. But, you say, wouldn't the smaller ball, having less cross-sectional area, encounter less atmospheric resistance? In truth, there's more to it than surface area. In order to explain what is involved let's go back to our round-nose bullet in the .300 Winchester Magnum. This time we use a round-nose bullet weighing 180 grains and again we compare the remaining velocities out to 500 yards.

150-Grain Bullet		180-Grain Bullet	
Range (yards)	Velocity (fps)	Range (yards)	Velocity (fps)
0	3,000	0	3,000
100	2,649	100	2,682
200	2,324	200	2,386
300	2,022	300	2,109
400	1,745	400	1,851
500	1,498	500	1,616

Right away we see some interesting changes. First of all, the remaining velocities are notably higher with the 180-grain bullet than with the 150-grain slug.

There are different ways of explaining this. First we might discuss it·in terms of energy transfer. We know that it takes more energy to push a 180-grain bullet to 3,000 fps than to achieve the same velocity with a 150-grain bullet. So, speaking simplistically, we can say that if we put more energy into the bullet when it is fired, we get more energy back in the form of velocity out at 500 yards. But what makes the heavier bullet able to efficiently utilize this expenditure of energy?

SECTIONAL DENSITY

It is *momentum*. All moving objects have momentum, but for our purposes right now, let's talk about the two round-nose bullets in terms of *sectional density*. Many shooters love sectional density, even when they don't know what it means.

Essentially, sectional density describes the weight of a bullet in relation to its diameter. Bullets that are relatively long in relation to their diameter have a high sectional density whereas short, squat bullets have lower sectional densities. A good example of a bullet with a high sectional density is the 162-grain bullet once loaded in the Italian 6.5x52 Carcano service cartridge. An example of low sectional density is the short, squat 240-grain bullet loaded in the .444 Marlin cartridge. Though the .444 bullet is actually heavier than the 6.5 Carcano, it has a lower S.D. because it is so light in relation to its diameter. The S.D. of the .444 bullet works out to .186 while that of the 6.5x52 Carcano is a whopping .334. (In case you're wondering, the formula for sectional density is bullet weight ÷ 7,000 ÷ bullet diameter squared, but forget I mentioned it.)

Now, going back to our two .30-caliber bullets, the 150-grain bullet has a sectional density of .226, and the S.D. of the 180-grain bullet is .270. (Take my word for it.) This still doesn't explain why the heavier bullet is going faster at 500 yards, but we're getting closer to the answer. One thing we have discovered is that if two bullets of the same caliber and nose shape, but of different weight, start off at the same muzzle velocity, the heavier bullet will lose its velocity less rapidly.

If you've done much reading about hunting-cartridge performance, you've probably run across some mention of the excellent performance of various European 6.5mm cartridges, which seems to be all out of proportion to their modest bullet diameter (.264-inch). The big reason for the excellent performance is the long, pencil-like bullet, which tends to bulldoze through brush and penetrate deep into the target. This is an example of high sectional density.

Sectional density alone is just a number, and it remains the same whether the bullet is traveling 3,000 fps or just lying in your hand. For sectional density to do its stuff, we must add velocity, and this is what yields *momentum*.

Let's say you have a ping-pong ball and a lead ball of the same diameter. You're going to throw these balls at a gallon bucket of water balanced on a fence post. Standing very close to the bucket, you take a big windup and throw the ping-pong ball at the bucket as hard as you can. It hits the bucket at a velocity of 100 miles per hour but simply bounces back. Now you wind up and let fly with the lead ball, which also hits the bucket at 100 miles per hour. Instead of bouncing back, the lead ball crashes into the bucket and sends it tumbling in a shower of water. This is because of its greater momentum. If you throw each of the balls as hard as you can, you'll also see that the lead ball goes many times farther than the lighter one, even though each is launched at the same speed. Again, this is because of greater momentum.

Now you may be wondering if momentum is the same as bullet energy. Believe me, it is not. I'll give you a comparison of the two which may help clarify momentum. Shooters who compete at silhouette shooting by knocking over metallic cut-outs of animals know that a hit with a 100-grain .243 Winchester bullet will not always knock over the ram at 500 meters, but you can bet that a hit from a lumbering 400-grain bullet from the venerable .45/70 will topple it. Let's compare the two. Beginning with a muzzle velocity of 2,960 fps, the .243 bullet has slowed to about 1,698 fps at 500 meters (547 yards). This computes to an evergy level of 640 foot-pounds. The 400-grain .45/70 bullet, launched at 1,330 fps has remaining velocity and energy of 780 fps and 540 foot-pounds at 500 meters.

Even though the .243 bullet has higher calculated energy, its momentum is only .75 pounds/second at 500 meters, compared to the .45/70's momentum of 1.39 p/s. That's why the .45/70 bullet more easily topples the iron ram. You might think of momentum as the tendency to keep moving, thus toppling the target.

By now you've probably decided that this momentum business is pretty hot stuff. Clearly, you say, the road to retaining velocity at long range is to use long, slender bullets having high sectional density. Sadly, it's not that easy. Since we cannot safely load ammunition beyond a certain pressure level, we must face the fact that heavier bullets with a high sectional density cannot be loaded to as high a velocity as lighter bullets. Consulting our handloading manuals, we find that the top safe velocity for our 180-grain bullet in the .300 Winchester Magnum is about 3,000 fps. With the lighter 150-grain bullet, however, safe velocities may be as high as 3,300 fps. Even though bullets with a high S.D. still have something of an advantage at long range, the real difference is not all that great. Don't be disappointed, we still have an ace up our sleeve.

THE WONDROUS BALLISTIC COEFFICIENT

Until now I've been using a pair of round-nose bullets to illustrate various ballistic phenomena. Now let's try our experiment again, but this time we'll change the shape of the bullet's nose. Everything else is the same. It is still a .30-caliber slug weighing 150 grains, and we'll launch it at 3,000 fps. Instead of a round nose, however, we'll give the bullet a long, streamlined point. The following table shows the remaining velocities. So you won't have to turn back a few pages, I've again listed the figures for the round-nose. The comparison, as you see, is remarkable.

	.30 CALIBER 150-GRAIN BULLETS	
Range (yards)	Pointed Nose Velocity (fps)	Round Nose Velocity (fps)
0	3,000	3,000
100	2,768	2,649
200	2,548	2,324
300	2,339	2,022
400	2,139	1,745
500	1,950	1,498

What? Can merely changing the shape of the bullet's nose yield a 452-fps velocity difference at 500 yards? No kidding, the shape of a projectile plays a tremendous role in the way it flies through the earth's atmosphere. As I said earlier, when a bullet slams into the atmosphere, the effect is like diving into molasses. Ask yourself which cuts through molasses more easily, a knife or a spoon? Its the same when we penetrate the air at high velocity with a bullet. The sharper the point, the easier the penetration. Look at a jet fighter. Why is it like a dart instead of a boxcar? The streamlined shape lets it pierce the air with less expenditure of energy.

The energy in a powder charge is transferred to the bullet in the form of kinetic energy. The bullet uses this energy in its struggle through the atmosphere. If the bullet has a blunt shape, it has to spend more energy fighting the air, and the velocity continually drops in proportion to its remaining energy. In this sense, velocity is just another way of expressing energy, and is an indicator of the energy remaining in the bullet.

To make sure we're grasping all this, let's go back to our vacuum chamber and fire both the round-nose and pointed bullets. How would their ballistics compare? If you say they would have identical velocities at all ranges, you are exactly right. But just for the fun of it, let's make a more practical observation. We can't very well shoot our rifles in a vacuum, but we can do the next best thing by finding thinner air. Gravity works on air the way it pulls bullets to earth, and its effect causes air to be thicker at sea level. Most ballistic tables and charts show the flight of a bullet at sea level where the air is thickest. But let's go up to 15,000 feet, where the air is thinner. Once again, firing the round-nose 150-grain bullet and measuring the velocity, the ballistics look like this:

Range (yards)	Velocity (fps)
0	3,000
100	2,772
200	2,554
300	2,348
400	2,153
500	1,971

The round-nose bullet at 15,000 feet of elevation loses 473 fps less velocity at 500 yards than at sea level. Did you ever read about the great "Paris Gun" used by the Germans to shell Paris during World War I? This huge cannon (actually there were three of them) launched an 8½-inch-diameter shell weighing 330 pounds at a muzzle velocity of 5,000 fps. These guns bombarded the French capital from a distance of some *70 miles*. To do this, the barrel was elevated to an angle of 54° so that it would throw the projectile 25 miles high! The idea was to get the shell into the stratosphere, where air resistance would be minimal, thereby conserving velocity and adding to the gun's range.

This is the principle employed by jet airliners that cruise at over 30,00 feet. By climbing into the thinner atmosphere, these aircraft are able to cruise at high speed with a lower expenditure of fuel (energy).

Target shooters take adventage of this knowledge by using highly streamlined bullets for long-range shooting. A typical bullet used in 600- and 1,000-yard competition is relatively heavy for its diameter (high sectional density) and has a long, streamlined point and a tapering

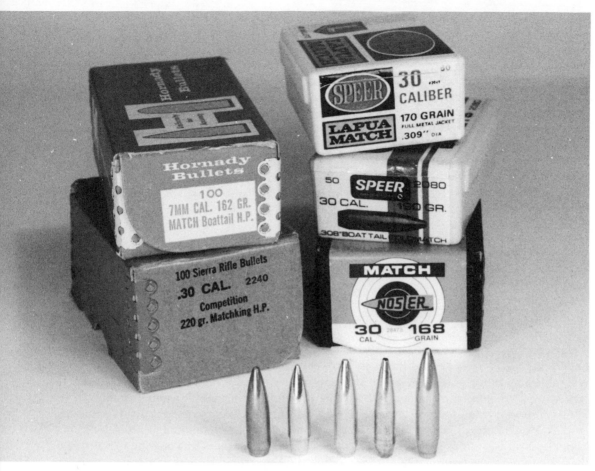

Here's a line-up of long-range target bullets (from left): a 168-grain Nosler, 170-grain Speer Lapua, 162-grain Hornady, 190-grain Speer, and 220-grain Sierra. The Hornady is a 7mm; all of the others are .30 caliber.

boat-tail base. This streamlined shape gives it flight characteristics that are appreciated by long-range shooters. Since it retains downrange velocity better, the bullet arrives on target with greater momentum and energy. The higher velocity also means a flatter trajectory. And the higher retained velocity means the bullet is less affected by wind. (We'll talk more about windage in Chapters 9 and 10).

THE FORM FACTOR

The relative ability of a bullet to slip through the atmosphere is expressed as the form factor. Bullets with higher form factors are more streamlined than those with a lower form factor.

Though the meaning of form factor is easy to explain, the mathematics that go into determining the form factor of a given bullet are quite complex. In fact, the pencil-and-paper drudgery of calculating the form factor of a bullet is so complex and fraught with so many variables, that it really isn't worth the bother. That's why handloading manuals and bullet maker's specification sheets of a decade ago made scant mention of bullet form. With the advent of today's in-house computers, it is relatively quick and easy to calculate the ballistic form of anything from a speeding bullet to a falling piano. The computer I use to arrive at the tables given in this chapter is smaller than an average typewriter, but a 1965 computer capable of the same functions would have filled a two-car garage.

Now that we have a surface idea of the meaning of ballistic coefficient, let's take the cover off and look at the nuts and bolts. (Don't worry, I'm not going to break my promise. There will be no fancy arithmetic or equations).

MEASURING VELOCITY

As mentioned earlier, Newton did important pioneering work in ballistics, especially in calculating the effect of gravity, and he gained considerable insight into the effect of atmospheric resistance. He did not, however, have the means to measure the effect of air on a bullet's flight. If he had, he would surely have been astonished. The first instrument to give a workable clue to the real effect of the atmosphere around us was the ballistic pendulum. Invented by an Englishman named Robins, the principle seems simple enough today; in the 1740's, it was revolutionary. The working of a ballistic pendulum is simple. As its name suggests, it is only a weight attached to a hinged support. When the pendulum is struck by a moving object—a fist, a rock, or a bullet—it swings a certain distance. By knowing the weight of the pendulum and measuring the distance it moved when struck, Robins was able to calculate interesting things about the object that struck it. Using principles handed down by Newton, Robins calculated the velocity of the projectile by a sort of reverse arithmetic. Newton's formula told him that a projectile of a given weight, traveling at a given speed, would impart a specific level of energy to whatever its struck. Knowing that his pendulum was moved a specific distance by a specific energy level, all Robins had to do was figure in the weight of the bullet to arrive at the velocity of the bullet when it hit. What Robins discovered astonished himself and just about everyone.

Measuring the impact force of a British musket ball, Robins correctly calculated a muzzle velocity of about 1,500 fps. When he measured the speed of an identical musket ball, fired with the same weight of powder, at 100 yards, the velocity worked out to only about two-thirds of the muzzle velocity. Could it be? Was the effect of atmospheric drag so great that a musket ball lost nearly 500 fps, a third of its velocity, in only 100 yards? The army's ordnance specialists didn't believe it and subjected Robins to considerable ridicule. After all, even the great Newton hadn't anticipated anything that drastic.

Now we know that Robins was right, and since his time ballisticians and ammo makers have been preoccupied with air resistance.

During the next hundred years or so, scientists put in a lot of head-scratching hours trying to devise a formula by which they could calculate the remaining velocity of a projectile at any given range. What they were looking for was a comprehensive, universal formula of the kind that Newton had been so good at devising. Every time a mathematician thought he had it figured out, he subjected his mathematical predictions to measurements with a pendulum, which had become accepted. The figures didn't mesh.

In the 1740's an Englishman named Robins invented a ballistic pendulum with which to calculate bullet velocity. He then discovered a surprising loss of velocity at 100 yards because of atmospheric drag. Long before shooters had chronographing setups like this one, scientists pondered air resistance and tried to devise a formula by which to calculate remaining velocity at any given range.

Until about 1825, the universal projectile had been a round lead ball, but by 1850 the pointed, cylindrical bullet as we know it today had evolved. Experiments with the ballistic pendulum showed that bullets of this type retained a higher portion of their velocity downrange, and observers deduced that it was because of improved aerodynamics. Since no one had come up with a precise, universal formula for calculating remaining velocities, some clever fellows decided to approach the problem from another angle. Why not design a stream-lined artillery shell and fire it at many different muzzle velocities? Then, by measuring the remaining velocities at different ranges, a formula could be constructed for calculating its velocity at any range based on any given muzzle velocity. This would be the *standard* ballistic form. Then the performance of other bullets could be compared to the ballistics of the standard bullet. In other words, the flight of the standard bullet became a mathematical model to which the flight of other bullets are compared. Roughly, here's how it works with small arms:

Let's say that we fire the standard bullet at 3,000 fps, at sea level. The remaining velocities read like this:

Range (yards)	Velocity (fps)
0	3,000
100	2,901
200	2,804
300	2,709
400	2,616
500	2,524

Arbitrarily, we give the standard bullet a ballistic coefficient of 1. Then we fire another bullet, say our 150-grain round-nose bullet at the same muzzle velocity and measure the re-maining velocity at some point downrange. The round-nose bullet has considerably more drag, and by mathematically comparing the two sets of velocities a *relative* drag value can be assigned to the round-nose bullet. In this case the "C" value, or ballistic coefficient, of the 150-grain round-nose bullet is .266, meaning it is only .266 that of the standard bullet. In case you're wondering, the B.C. of our 180-grain round-nose bullet is .304 and that of the pointed 150-grain bullet is .409. (This does not mean that all 150-grain, pointed .30 caliber bullets have a B.C. of .409—just that particular one.)

This is not a really precise system of comparison. A few little variables creep in to muddy the arithmetic somewhat, but not enough to make any important differences.

One problem of considerable bother was that most countries (meaning the artillery branch of that country's military) had their own standard bullet. This meant that mathematical com-parisons were confusing. To set things right, the French government commissioned a select committee to analyze the various standard bullets and devise conversion tables. What this study group, known as the Gavre Commission, wound up doing was to formulate a com-

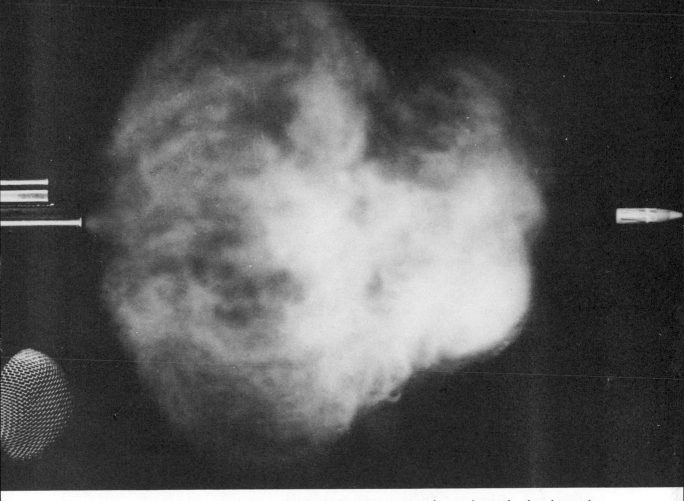

This high-velocity bullet is traveling much too fast for the human eye to see it, but modern technology has made it possible to see such a bullet's flight — by means of astonishing high-speed photography, as well as indirectly, by electronic chronography.

prehensive set of ballistic tables. While the Gavre Commission was in session (1873-1898), the huge Krupp cannon works in Germany was busy with tests of their own, developing a standard bullet that was to become the model for virtually all sporting arms. Basing his calculations on Krupp's findings, a brilliant Russian artillery officer, Mayevski, came up with a mathematical model for predicting the atmospheric drag on a given small-arms bullet. Mayevski's model, in turn, provided the basis for a comprehensive set of ballistic tables worked out by Colonel James Ingalls of the U.S. Army. These tables, published in 1917, were the standard source of ballistic information on small-arms ammunition until computers became available.

The failing of the Ingalls tables, so far as the average shooter is concerned, is that the tabulations require the bullet's ballistic coefficient or the velocity at two different points along its path. If both are unknown, the tables are of little value. During the 1930's, the Dupont Company tried to solve this problem by publishing charts that contained a series of gradually altered bullet profiles. To use it, you simply placed your bullet on the chart and found the profile that most nearly matched. Then, using other tables, the ballistic coefficient or coefficient of form (as engineers Wallace Coxe and Edgar Beugless called it) was determined. Properly used, the Dupont tables came reasonably close to predicting downrange performance, but the system was cumbersome and tedious.

At any rate, shooters did not bother themselves with this sort of information until recent years. Even makers of sporting ammunition were content to let things rock along with no significant ballistic research. The viewpoint of both shooters and sporting ammo makers was that if one hit the target and killed the game, there was not much else to worry about. From 1900 until about 1945, the only significant ballistic investigations conducted in the U.S. were carried out by or for the military, principally at Frankfort Arsenal. The most complete small-arms ballistic tables available, until about 1948 or possibly even later, were compiled for the various .30-caliber bullets loaded at government arsenals. That's why nearly all of the ballistic writing done since World War I focuses on just a few GI-type bullets, usually the 150-grain flat-base service bullet or the 173-grain boat-tail.

MODERN AWARENESS

By the mid-1950's, this complacent situation began to change dramatically. This was due to increased shooter awareness of ballistics which, in turn, was due to the handloading boom and the growing numbers of high-velocity magnum cartridges. The effect snowballed as new high-performance cartridges begot more high-speed cartridges, with ammo makers and shooters alike seeking ways of hitting targets and killing game faster, farther, and surer.

As muzzle velocities jumped, there was a corresponding need to improve downrange ballistics. For the past two decades there has been a steady move toward more streamlined bullet shapes. If you compare any illustrated 1960 bullet maker's catalog with a current catalog, you will be struck by the improved ballistic shape of today's designs.

In 1960, for example, the Sierra bullet catalog listed some 30 bullets, only eight of which were spitzer-type boat-tails, and three of these were target types. Hornady, Nosler, and Speer did not make boat-tail bullets. Today, all bullet makers offer a full line of boat-tails, and the streamlining of bullet points is noticeably improved as well. Such improvement raises the ballistic coefficient of bullets and provides higher downrange velocities.

Please note, however, that ballistic performance can be described in a number of ways. Hunters, for example, are much concerned with terminal ballistics—the way a bullet performs when it hits a game animal. A bullet may have a wonderful ballistic form and yet perform poorly on game. Right now, when we talk about good or bad ballistics we're concerned only with the bullet's *flight*.

THE BOAT-TAIL BULLET

The boat-tail design mentioned above is a good example of attempts to improve ballistic performance, so let's discuss it. The boat-tail bullet is not new. It dates back to the turn of the

Boat-tail bullets date back to the turn of the century—and probably earlier. Here are several modern versions that deliver high performance at long range by reducing aerodynamic drag.

century and probably earlier. During World War I, the U.S. Army discovered that the standard .30-caliber cartridge (.30/06) used in their Browning machine guns was not as effective at long range as some of the European small-arms cartridges. Accordingly, tests were conducted, which in 1925 resulted in the adoption of a ballistically superior bullet loaded in the 1906 cartridge case. This new bullet, called the M-1, weighed 173 grains. By comparing its sectional density with the earlier 150-grain service bullet, we could predict that long-range performance would be better. In practice, it is. Another factor that made an important contribution to the M-1 bullet's excellent velocity-retaining characteristic was the tapered shape of its base. Commonly called a taper-heel or boat-tail shape, this configuration cuts aerodynamic drag by reducing the area affected by the vacuum created behind a speeding bullet. It's as simple as that. But to get a clearer idea of the actual advantage, let's compare the downrange performances of two otherwise identical bullets. One has a boat-tail base and the other has an ordinary flat base. Again we'll use 150-grain pointed bullets with a muzzle velocity of 3,000 fps.

Range (yards)	Flat Base Velocity (fps)	Boattail Velocity (fps)
0	3,000	3,000
100	2,768	2,789
200	2,548	2,587
300	2,339	2,394
400	2,139	2,209
500	1,950	2,033

This remaining velocity difference of 83 fps at 500 yards is probably not important in most hunting situations, but it does dramatically point up the effect of aerodynamic drag on a bullet's flight.

Until recently, it was widely held that the streamlining advantages of the boat-tail design were apparent only at velocities below the speed of sound (1,087 fps at sea level) and thus were of no use at normal sporting-rifle velocities and ranges. Now we know that the boat-tail shape offers a retained velocity advantage at all sporting-rifle velocities, with a corresponding improvement in trajectory curve and wind resistance.

SOME HEADSCRATCHING

Digging deeper into the mysteries of bullet shape and its effect on ballistic performance, we make some startling discoveries. The reason I say startling is because just about the time we think we have this ballistic-form business figured out, something pops up to muddy the water. Most of the anomalies are of minor importance, but a couple are cause for considerable headscratching.

One of the lesser problems is that bullets don't always behave in predicted fashion. We can do a precise time-of-flight study of a given bullet at a given muzzle velocity and calculate a ballistic coefficient which *should* make it possible to predict its drag characteristics at other velocities. But what the tables and computers predict may not be what actually happens. Therefore, we must assume that the ballistic coefficient of a bullet is somewhat different at different velocities.

It has also been discovered that a bullet does some peculiar things when it travels near the speed of sound. Thus ballisticians must take into account whether the bullet is traveling at subsonic, transonic, or supersonic speed. When a bullet is traveling at a transonic velocity it tends to lose velocity at a somewhat higher rate than one might predict. As we shall see in the next chapter, this is why high-velocity .22 Rimfire ammo is more affected by crosswinds than standard-velocity loads.

The temperature of the air, like the altitude, has a measurable effect on a bullet's progress. A 150-grain bullet from a 7mm Remington Magnum, traveling at sea level in normal atmosphere, will lose about 55 fps more velocity at 20° (F.) than at 70° by the time it has gone 200 yards. This starts getting messy when you add in the fact that the speed of sound also changes with altitude and temperature. I'm not trying to make the problems of ballistic arithmetic sound more complicated than they really are. I'm just pointing out some of the variables with which ballisticians must contend. Some of these variables are so slight as to have no use other than to titillate a foxy computer. Some variables, though, pack a pretty good punch.

Carmichel is shown praticing for competition — and simultaneously making notes on the performance of various .30-caliber and 7mm bullets. Tests by Sierra showed the 7mm Match King bullet to have a higher ballistic coefficient than was calculated mathematically, whereas test firing showed .30-caliber bullets to have a lower B.C. than calculated.

One of the most impressive is described in the Sierra Reloading Manual (Hayden, Hull, Almgren, and McDonald). Prior to a series of comprehensive ballistic tests and computer analyses of Sierra bullets, it had been estimated that the ballistic coefficient of their 168-grain, 7mm Match King bullet was .594. This was based on physical and mathematical comparisons to a standard bullet. Yet, for some unexplained reason, test firing showed the B.C. to be .628. At the same time, test performances of .30-caliber bullets resulted in a lower B.C. than previously calculated. For some reason, the 7mm bullets are ballistically superior.

PUTTING IT ALL TOGETHER

Feeding all the foregoing grist into the mills of your logic and imagination, you've probably, by now, arrived at some solid deductions. I'm sure you've concluded that if two bullets of different caliber and weight but with an identical ballistic coefficient are launched at the same velocity, they will lose velocity at identical rates and have the same time of flight. On the other hand, if weight, caliber, and muzzle velocity are identical but the B.C.'s are different, the bullet with the higher B.C. will have a higher remaining velocity at any range. True.

You may also have begun to wonder if perhaps bullets with higher ballistic coefficients are more accurate. This is a fascinating question, and while there may be some evidence that streamlined bullets are indeed more accurate, it cannot be proved one way or the other until we perfect rifles and bullets capable of "pure" accuracy. In the practical sense, we know that highly streamlined bullets, being less affected by crosswinds, produce smaller groups at long range, all other factors being equal.

Until this point, despite my efforts to illustrate science with practical examples, we've been dogpaddling in a pool of theory. Now it's time to put on our boots and climb the hills of ballistic reality.

Nearly all ballistic tables show remaining velocities at fixed points along a bullet's path, usually in 50-yard or 100-yard increments. This is a simple way of providing useful information, because we normally think of ballistic performance in terms of range intervals. This system, however, has the unfortunate effect of causing shooters to think that a bullet has slowed a given amount or dropped a definite number of inches only because it has traveled a specified distance. This is why the language of shooters says that a bullet from a .30/30 falls faster than one from a 7mm Magnum. By reading the ranges in a ballistic table, that's the impression we get. Consider these two drop tables, and you'll see what I mean:

.30/30 W.C.F.		170-grain bullet with a M.V. of 2,200 fps		
Range (yards)	0	100	200	300
Drop (inches)	0	−3.47	−16.73	−46.20
7mm Rem. Mag.		175-grain bullet with a M.V. of 2,860 fps		
Range (yards)	0	100	200	300
Drop (inches)	0	−2.12	−9.14	−21.60

The problem is that this approach programs our thinking in terms of distance rather than time. In order to truly "think like a bullet," we must consider its flight in terms of *time*. That's why an early section in this chapter was about time intervals. Gravity makes bullets fall, and time tells us how far they fall. Take another look at the chart on page 188. The trajectory curve shows the theoretical path of a bullet in terms of time only, without regard for atmospheric drag. Since then, we've found that the air around us has a tremendous effect on a bullet's speed. So let's look at another time-interval chart.

The time intervals here show the relative distances traveled by the 150-grain round-nose bullet and the 150-grain pointed bullet. The muzzle velocity for both is 3,000 fps. For further comparison, the curve of a bullet traveling 3,000 fps in a vacuum is shown too.

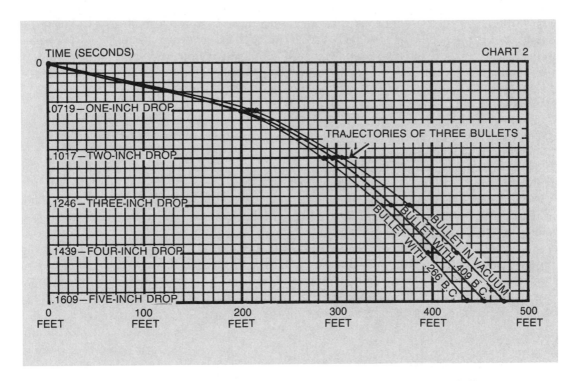

In this graph, each grid square represents 10 feet horizontally and 0.2-inch vertically. The bullets are a 150-grain round-nose with a ballistic coefficient of .266; a pointed 150-grain bullet with a ballistic coefficient of .409; and a third bullet—any bullet—fired in a vacuum at a muzzle velocity of 3,000 fps.

By comparing the time intervals of the three bullets, we see that each falls the same amount in a given time. Yet the pointed bullet has dropped less at a given distance than its round-nosed brother. This tells us is that when a bullet appears to have "dropped" more at a given range, the reason is simply that *it took longer to get there.*

If you compare the drop figures in this chart with the drop tables published in various handloading manuals, you'll note a slight difference. The chart, which is based on precise gravitational acceleration computations, indicates that the pointed bullet falls two inches slightly before it has traveled 100 yards. Yet most published drop tables say that the bullet will have fallen only about 1.92 inches by the time it reaches the 100-yard line. Why the difference? Obviously, a tiny tenth of an inch or so isn't going to make much difference when we level down on a whitetail buck, but if we're going to call ballistics a science everything has to fit nicely.

You'll recall that at the beginning of this chapter I said that bullets dropped from the hand and fired from a horizontal rifle would hit the ground simultaneously in a vacuum. Then I went on to say that in a normal atmosphere, the bullet fired from a rifle would take slightly longer to fall.

Without going into a mathematical explanation, this is because the bullet fired from a rifle gets a bit of aerodynamic lift. As the bullet's point angles downward, it meets with a certain amount of air pressure resisting the downward pitch. Thus the bullet gets a little help, almost like floating on a cushion of air, which ever so slightly retards its rate of fall. And this is where we get that tenth of an inch or so of difference in the 100-yard trajectory curve of our 150-grain pointed bullet.

Now everything fits beautifully. Looking back on this chapter, we see that we have accumulated some useful information. Gravity, for a fact, causes bullets to fall, and even when accounting for the minor vagaries of aerodynamic lift we can say that all bullets, regardless of caliber, weight, and forward velocity, fall at the same rate. Thus we have come to understand that bullet drop is a function of *time,* not distance. This, in turn, leads to the understanding that in order for a bullet to have a flat trajectory in relation to horizontal distance, it must make efficient use of the time interval gravity has allotted. But we have also learned that high muzzle velocity alone is not the answer. If a bullet is to make efficient use of its uniformly prescribed time intervals, it must *retain* its velocity. In our discussions of retaining velocity, we have unraveled the mysteries of momentum, sectional density, and ballistic coefficient. We have learned to "think" like a bullet and to understand some of the things it does after it leaves the muzzle. In the following chapter, we'll use this ballistic wizardry in discussions of trajectory, wind drift, and the curious effects of shooting uphill or down.

Chapter 9

LESSONS IN TRAJECTORY

As we learned in the preceding chapter on external ballistics, a bullet fired from a horizontal barrel begins to fall the instant it leaves the muzzle. We can, however, play a trick or two on gravity which, if we are really clever, causes it to work for rather than against us. To play such tricks, we need to have a clear understanding of trajectory.

As you'll recall from the previous chapter, there is a widespread belief among shooters that a bullet actually rises when it leaves the gun barrel. There is no logical reason for anyone to arrive at the conclusion that bullets rise, so how did the notion become so widespread. Alas, I fear this tidbit of misinformation comes down to us from our founding gun writers. They certainly knew better, but they weren't altogether clear in imparting information to their readers.

Here is a diagram adapted from an old and once widely read book on shooting. Over the years, it has been copied, recopied, and redrawn in so many hundreds of books, magazine articles, and arms catalogs that almost everyone who has been exposed to gun literature has at least glanced at it. Look familiar?

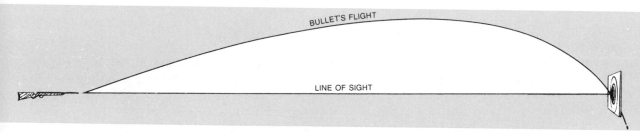

This is an adaptation of an old diagram that has been misleading or confusing shooters for many years. The rifle in this drawing is positioned horizontally, along the line of sight. For the bullet to rise—as it appears to— would be impossible.

They say a picture is worth a thousand words, but in this case, I'm not so sure. Hundreds of thousands of shooters have looked at this drawing without bothering to read the fine print. Clearly, this drawing gives the impression that the bullet rises after leaving the muzzle of a horizontal barrel. In fact, the only way to make a bullet rise on exit from the barrel is to elevate the muzzle above horizontal. That's a big difference.

From now on, we're going to talk about bullet flight in respect to *bore line*. The bore line is an imaginary line running through the center of the bore and continuing, dead straight, into space. It can be diagrammed as shown here, and I do so with the hope that future generations of gun writers will choose this drawing to illustrate their prose.

In this corrected version of the old trajectory diagram, the rifle is tilted up—which is the only way to make a bullet rise. The bullet exits along the bore line, and its flight curves downward to the target as gravity pulls it earthward.

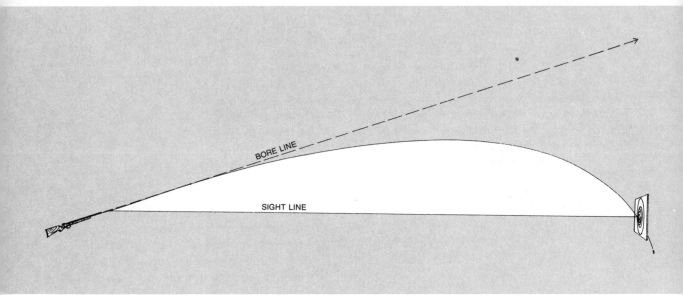

MANIPULATING THE TRAJECTORY

If a bullet traveled in a perfectly straight line, it would be both wonderful and disastrous. There would be no need to calculate trajectory or guess "Tennessee elevation." To hit a woodchuck at 800 yards, you'd just aim dead on target. But the world would be full of whizzing bullets that would never come to rest, and we'd have to live in armored houses.

Trajectory can be described in terms of pure, or absolute, drop, that is in relation to the bore line, or in terms of corrected trajectory, which is the relationship between the bullet's path and the line of sight. Sport shooters are mainly concerned with corrected trajectory, because it is a corrected trajectory that makes a bullet hit where we aim. The study of absolute trajectories is useful, too, especially when comparing the trajectories of different cartridges and bullets. The following drawing shows what appears to be two different trajectories. Actually, they are identical. Trajectory A shows the bullet's absolute drop in relation to a horizontal bore line. Trajectory B is corrected or elevated somewhat so that it is in reasonably close proximity to the line of sight. Remember, the line of sight and the bore line are *not* the same.

Compare trajectories A and B. At first glance they appear to differ, but they are the same—except that B has been elevated so that it will intersect the line of sight.

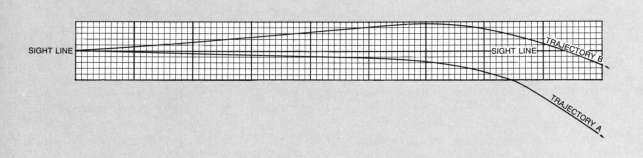

When we sight-in a rifle, we are coming to terms with a bullet's curving flight path. Since a line of sight is perfectly straight while a bullet's path is a continuous curve, there is no possible way the two can be joined except for two brief interludes along their respective routes. When we say we have sighted-in, or "zeroed," a rifle at a particular distance, we have caused the line of sight and the bullet's path to intersect at a specific point. We can control this point of intersection simply by turning the sight adjustment knobs or screws. Therefore, we are also able to manipulate the bullet's path in relation to line of sight so that it best serves our needs.

Let's say you are going on a back-country elk hunt and will be using your new 7mm Remington Magnum rifle. The outfitter advises that most elk are killed at about 100 yards. Accordingly, you sight-in your rifle to hit "dead on" (to hit exactly where you aim) at 100 yards.

As often happens, though, the best bull you see is out at about 350 yards, grazing around a stand of quakies on the other side of a creek wash. You belly down, put the crosshairs on his chest, and pull the trigger. What happens? The elk jerks his head up, takes a quick look around, and hightails it into the quakies.

You missed, and you're mighty disappointed. Also, you're more than a little confused. The 7mm Magnum is supposed to be a flat-shooting wonder that easily drops elk out to 400 yards and beyond. What went wrong? What happened is that the 175-grain bullet hit nearly 20 inches below point of aim at 350 yards and passed under the animal's chest line. Though the 7mm Remington Magnum does have a much flatter trajectory than many other big game cartridges, the disturbing fact of the matter is that the bullet still falls at a fast rate.

You really missed, though, because you failed to *manipulate* the 7mm Magnum's trajectory to make it work for you most efficiently. You could have used a trick or two to change the bullet's path in respect to your line of sight, thus putting the bullet right in the old bull's boiler room. The most vital trick in dealing with trajectory is sighting-in the rifle so that the bullet's path is close to the line of sight for as great a distance as possible. By "close" I mean close enough to effectively hit the intended target even if the bullet doesn't hit the exact point of aim. For instance, a varmint rifle that is sighted-in so that the bullet hits within two inches above or two inches below point of aim will still hit and kill a woodchuck with certainty. In the case of your big bull elk, you had considerably more margin, several inches more.

Let's say you had zeroed your rifle to hit point of aim at 250 yards. Using 175-grain Remington bullets loaded at a muzzle velocity of 2,860 fps, this sight setting would put the impact 2.9 inches high at 100 yards, plenty close enough to point of aim to mean good shot placement. At 200 yards, the bullet would be 2.4 inches high and then dead on at 250 yards. At 300 yards, the point of impact would be 3.95 inches low, and at 350 yards, some 9.6 inches below point of aim. With this zero, you would be close enough to point of aim to kill a deep-chested elk anywhere from zero range out to 350 yards. This is what I mean by making efficient use of a rifle's trajectory.

Remember, though, the actual trajectory hasn't been changed. That can't be done without changing the characteristics of the cartridge. You've simply altered the trajectory's relationship to the line of sight. To give you another perspective, here is a table showing the relative points of impact for the two different zero settings.

7mm Rem. Mag, 175-Grain Factory Load at 2,860 fps (with 100-yard zero)						
YARDS: 100	150	200	250	300	350	400
0″	− 1.06″	− 3.45″	− 7.29″	− 12.69″	− 19.79″	− 28.75″
(with 250-yard zero)						
YARDS: 100	150	200	250	300	350	400
+ 2.91″	+ 3.31″	+ 2.38″	0″	− 3.95″	− 9.59″	− 17.09″

Of course, not many cartridges offer as much range within acceptable hit margins as the 7mm Magnum. To take an example from the other extreme, let's consider the .30/30 with a 170-grain bullet, factory-loaded to a muzzle velocity of 2,200 fps. This caliber is used mostly for whitetail deer, so we have to assume that we have, at most, an allowable margin of about four inches above or below point of aim. Since most whitetail are shot at a range of no more than 50 yards, we first consider zeroing the .30/30 at that range, and when we test the point of impact at greater distances the trajectory looks like this:

YARDS:	50	100	150	200
	0″	− .72″	− 4.19″	− 11.09″

With a 50-yard zero setting we get outside our allowable margin of drop at 150 yards, so let's try a 100-yard zero and see what it looks like.

YARDS:	50	100	150	200
	− .14″	0″	− 2.61″	− 8.65″

This is better, but can we do better still? Let's try a 175-yard zero. It works out like this:

YARDS:	50	100	150	175	200
	+ 2.05″	+ 3.37″	+ 1.95″	0″	− 2.90″

Clearly, this is the best setting if we anticipate shots at any range up to 200 yards, because it keeps the bullet within acceptable margins while permitting a point-blank aim all the way out to 200 yards. By simply adjusting the sight setting, we've manipulated or "corrected" the rifle's trajectory so that it works for us most effectively.

RANGE AND TRAJECTORY

You've noted in the above tables and illustrations that a bullet's trajectory is not a perfect rainbow-curve but rather an ellipse that curves more and more sharply downward as the range increases. Though we cannot see a bullet in flight, we can see larger, slower projectiles such as a hard-hit or thrown baseball, the flight of which clearly shows us the elliptical path characteristic of a bullet's flight. Come to think of it, a well-hit golf ball is a very good example. As it flies away from the tee, it seems to be going almost string-straight, but as it loses velocity, the downward curve becomes steeper and steeper.

This rapidly increasing curvature of the bullet's path is the single most difficult problem hunters must deal with when taking shots at long range. The trajectory problem is more complex than the problems of simple marksmanship for a number of reasons. Let's say that an experienced rifleman, firing an accurate rifle from a solid rest, is able to place his bullets inside a two-inch circle at 100 yards. This means he should be able to hit within a four-inch circle at 200 yards, inside six inches at 300 yards, eight inches at 400 yards, and 10 inches at 500 yards. It would seem that he could easily kill a whitetail deer at 500 yards, not to mention a big mule deer or an elk. Yet we all know it is extremely difficult to hit a deer at ranges beyond 300 yards, even with the most accurate rifles, and more bullets miss elk at 400 yards than hit.

The problem is that at the longer ranges, even a fairly small miscalculation of the range can cause a clean miss. As a specific example, let's suppose you're hunting antelope with your favorite .30/06. You know you'll need a flat trajectory, so you select 150-grain bullets that leave the muzzle at 2,910 fps. Sighted-in dead on at 200 yards, the bullet is two inches above point of aim at 100 yards and only some 8.5 inches low at 300 yards. That's plenty close enough to hit the chest cavity at 300 yards, if you use a few inches of "Tennessee elevation" and hold a bit high. The ammo maker's ballistic table also tells you that the bullet is 25 inches low at 400 yards and 52 inches low at 500. "No problem," you tell yourself. If he's out at 400 yards the thing to do is hold two feet high—and about four feet high if you have to go for a really long shot at the 500-yard mark. "So what's hard about long range shooting? Just remember how much the bullet drops and hold over accordingly." Right?

So you're on the plains of Wyoming, and you see a fine buck. He looks like he's about 400 yards out, but your guide says he's closer to 500, and your hunting pal says the range can't be more than 300 or 350. Suddenly your carefully memorized trajectory figures aren't much help. The real problem is that you don't know the distance to the target.

We can all judge a 50-yard distance within a few feet, and anyone who has ever watched a football game knows what 100 yards looks like. Guessing quite accurately at 200 yards and fractions thereof can be mastered with a bit of practice. But beyond that, it is exceedingly difficult to differentiate distance units of as great as 50 or even 100 yards, especially on unfamiliar terrain. What makes this so perplexing is that it's at the longer ranges that we need to be most precise in our range estimation.

At 250 yards, you don't even have to think about the range because the trajectory of your 150-grain .30/06 bullet is so flat you just aim where you want to hit. If the antelope is at 450 yards, however, a range-estimating error of only 50 yards either way will cause the bullet to go over his back or under his belly. That's why game is so often missed at ranges beyond 300 yards. We're likely to miss *not* because we're poor marksmen but because we don't estimate the range accurately.

The solution, it would seem, is simply to develop rifles and cartridges with trajectories so flat that variations in range won't make any difference. That's what gunmakers have been striving to accomplish for the past century. The 250-yard point-blank range I just discussed so casually was unthinkable at the turn of the century. But rifles as they exist today have their own limitations. In order to have significantly flatter trajectories, we will need a lot more velocity. Since velocity is mainly a product of gas pressure, we will need a major overhaul in gun and cartridge design before we can make any major advances into the realms of higher pressure.

Even so, bit by bit, gun makers offer improvements. Improved cartridges such as the 7mm Remington Magnum have increased practical hunting range a great deal.

ZEROING AT SHORT RANGE

"I just bought a new .30/06 rifle and will be fitting it with a 4X scope. I plan to hunt antelope this fall and want to have the scope set so that the rifle is zeroed at 250 yards. Our local gun club only has a 25-yard pistol range, so I must zero my rifle at that distance. Where do I want the bullets to strike at 25 yards, in respect to point of aim, so that my rifle will be dead on at 250 yards?"

And so go hundreds of letters from readers who must sight in at short range. Other shooters simply like the idea of sighting at close range because the target is easier to hit or because less walking is involved.

Several years ago, a famous firearms writer, who has since wandered off to that Big Rifle Range in the Sky, wrote an article glorifying the advantages of sighting-in a hunting rifle at close range. Since then, there has been widespread belief that the short-range technique works like a charm. The melancholy truth, though, is that short-distance sight setting has serious shortcomings that are seldom noticed until it's too late.

To understand the principles of short-distance zeroing, let's take an example and see how it works. Let's say we are working with a very accurate scope-sighted .30/06. Using 150-grain bullets factory-loaded by Remington and firing at 250 yards, we adjust the sights so that the bullets hit exactly where we aim.

With this accomplished, we move the target up to 25 yards, and without making any sight changes, we fire a trio of shots. The three shots form a nice little cloverleaf pattern, the center of which is a tenth of an inch above point of aim. Eureka! We've discovered the key, haven't we? From now on, all we need to do to achieve a 250 zero with any .30/06 and the same ammunition is shoot at 25 yards and set the sights so that the point of impact is a tenth of an inch high. Wonderfully simple, ain't it? Or is it?

It so happens the scope mounts we used on our test rifle positioned the scope so that it was centered 1.5 inches above the center of the bore line. As luck would have it, the next time we try this, we happen to be using see-through scope mounts that position the scope 2.5 inches above the bore line. Sublimely confident in our data, we sight-in to hit the prescribed .1 inch above point of aim at 25 yards and then take off on a pronghorn hunt in Wyoming.

The first morning of the hunt, we spot a fine buck out at about 250 yards. What luck! All we have to do is aim where we want to hit and the trophy buck is ours, isn't he? Probably not, because the one-inch-higher scope position will cause the bullet to hit some nine inches higher than expected at 250 yards.

If the initial data had been for longer yardage, the difference would have been more extreme. For example, had we originally sighted our rifle in at, say, 350 yards, the 25-yard point of impact, with scope 1.5 inches above bore line, would have been .93-inch high. Using this data for a scope mounted 2.5 inches above the bore, the actual difference in where the bullet hits at 350 yards is nearly 13 inches higher.

This is for a one-inch difference in scope height. Smaller differences will cause proportionately less variation in point of impact and, of course, larger differences will have a greater effect on impact variations. Taking into account that there is a possibility of upwards of three inches' difference between the lowest and highest extremes in sight height above bore line, we can conclude very quickly that using short-range zeroing data can cause problems. These problems become all the more complex when compounded with variations in bullet shape and muzzle velocities.

Had we used 50 rather than 25 yards in these examples of error, the difference at 250 yards would be over four inches. With a 350-yard zero, the error would have been some six inches. Therefore, I consider any general table of short-distance zeroing for long-range shooting essentially unreliable. That's why rifles should be sighted-in over a distance of at least 100 yards if you plan on doing some long-range shooting.

Carmichel utilizes short-range zero checking to provide himself with a comparison target which he packs with his hunting gear. Upon arrival in camp, he rechecks his zero using the same target at the same distance. The shots should group right in with the original group fired at the range. If they don't, the zero has slipped.

This does not mean that short-range zeroing is useless. There is at least one way it can be used very effectively. Before going on a hunt where I anticipate some long-range shooting, I sight-in my rifle to hit point of aim somewhere between 200 and 300 yards (depending on caliber and game to be hunted). With the rifle perfectly zeroed at long range, I then set up a target at 50 yards and fire a couple of shots for group. I pack this short-range target along with the rest of my hunting gear, and upon arrival in camp, I recheck my zero using this same target. If my shots group right in with the original group, I know the rifle is still sighted-in perfectly. It's a convenient way to check your rifle in hunting camps, where it is often difficult to find sufficient yardage for a full-range zero check. Remember, though, this technique works only for one particular rifle and one particular kind of ammunition. If someone else should try to test his rifle's sights on your target, he may be seriously misled. Also keep in mind that correct target spacing is critical at the shorter distances. If, for example, you fire your short-range test target at exactly 50 yards back home but check your zero at a roughly paced "50 yards" in camp, the distance may be a few yards off. You will then run into some confusing differences in relative bullet impact. To make sure you are duplicating ranges exactly, carry a length of string that has been cut to the exact yardage.

SCOPE HEIGHT VS. TRAJECTORY CURVE

As you read the preceding account of how a scope mounted an inch higher than another can make a bullet hit several inches higher at long range, it may have occurred to you that all we need do to flatten a rifle's trajectory is to mount the scope as high as possible. In a sense, this is true, as varmint shooters have long known.

Many, many years ago, my shooting buddies and I spent just about every winter weekend shooting crows. Our technique was to drive along farm lanes and fields, shooting from special rests built onto our cars' windows. Back then, shooting from a car window was not only legal, it was accepted as the only efficient way to hunt crows with a rifle. The procedure was simply to find a sizable flock of crows and follow them about the countryside. Every time they'd land in a safe shooting area, we maneuvered as close as possible and fired a shot or two.

During this era I went through at least two dozen varmint rifles, in all sorts of calibers. Two of my favorites were a pair of .22/250's. That was years before Remington "legitimized" the .22/250. Cases were made by necking .250 Savage hulls down to .22-caliber neck diameter. The .22/250 was by far the most popular wildcat of that era. It combined fine accuracy with high velocity, and every serious varmint shooter sooner or later had to have one built.

One of my .22/250's was a fairly lightweight model (as varmint rifles go) built on a Model 70 Winchester action with a Fajen semi-finished stock I'd fitted myself, and topped off with a Weaver K-10X scope. It was a wicked rig for those days, but my other .22/250 was even deadlier. Built on a beautiful old original Oberndorf Mauser action, the rifle had a heavy barrel, double-set triggers, a target-style stock, and it was fitted with a 12X Unertl Ultra Varmint scope. Back then, the Ultra Varmint scope was the absolute final word in varmint-shooting optics.

With its two-inch objective lens, and target-style mounts on top of a heavyweight barrel, the Unertl scope was about 2.5 inches above the bore line of my heavy .22/250. The 10X

These rifles—one equipped with a target scope and one with an aperture sight—show the wide variation that may occur between the sight line and the bore line. With a high-mounted scope, the sight line may be a full three inches above the bore. This is one reason why generalized zeroing data—such as a table of short-distance zeroing for long-range shooting—can be very unreliable.

Weaver on my light .22/250 was no more than 1.5 inches above the bore line. Using identical handloads, it was my custom to zero both rifles so that they grouped one inch above point of aim at 100 yards. The light rifle was used for fast, close shots out to about 200 yards; the bigger rifle was used for shots beyond 200 yards. It may seem that I was using two rifles to do a job that could be handled by one, especially in that they were the same caliber and zeroed the same. In fact, the one-inch increase in scope height caused the heavier rifle to be sighted-in for considerably longer ranges than the lighter rifle. This created the illusion that bullets from the heavier rifle had a flatter trajectory. Actually, of course, absolute trajectory was absolutely the same.

The light rifle, sighted-in to hit an inch high at 100 yards, was almost dead on at 200 yards and nearly two inches low at 250 yards. The heavier rifle with the higher scope, also sighted in the same way at 100 yards, was dead on at *250 yards*. How does mounting a scope an inch higher than normal add 50 yards to the dead-on zero?

The answer is found simply by comparing the bore lines and lines of sight of the two rigs. Since the line of sight is a constant factor, we should not think of the sight as being *over* the barrel. Instead, think of the barrel as being *under* the sight. This sounds like doubletalk, but thinking in these terms makes understanding the principle a lot easier. Since the barrel is under the line of sight, the bullet's path must climb in order to intersect with the sight line. Obviously, the higher the sight line is in respect to the bore line, the steeper the angle the bullet must rise in order to intersect with the line of sight at a given distance. In order to be sighted-in an inch above point of aim at 100 yards, the bullet's path angled more steeply upward with my heavy rifle than with the lighter one with the lower scope. Since the bullet's line of departure was at a steeper angle, it naturally follows that the entire trajectory curve was angled upward more, resulting in a higher point of impact at longer ranges. You must keep in mind, though, that the trajectory *curves* of the two rifles were identical; the differences in scope height simply had the effect of changing their positions on a horizontal scale as illustrated by this diagram.

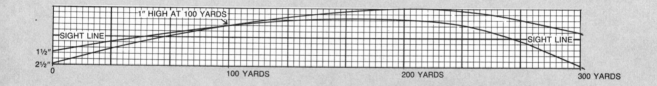

These two trajectories both put the bullet an inch high at 100 yards, but the one that begins farthest below the line of sight—that is, fired from a rifle with a high-mounted scope—is at a steeper angle and therefore crosses the line of sight for the second time at longer range.

Since a high-mounted scope has the effect of making a rifle's trajectory perform as though it were flatter, one might naturally assume that it is smart to mount all scopes as high as possible. This is not the case. All things considered, I still prefer to mount a scope as *low* as possible. The stock dimensions of most rifles make aiming awkward if the scope is too high, and this has a bad effect on marksmanship. Also, a high-mounted scope sticks out like a sore thumb and is subject to all sorts of snags and bumps. And, too, a rifle with a high scope is noticeably harder to hold steady and aim in a stout crosswind. Again, we found a trick that seemed to offer some positive advantages, but the price we have to pay is too high except in special situations.

UPHILL AND DOWNHILL

When you shoot uphill, you aim over the target, and if the target is downhill, you hold low. Or is it the other way around? Or does it make any difference? Shooters love to argue this, but seldom do we hear a convincing argument or explanation. The answer is easy once you understand the principle. Before getting into reasons why, let me promise you that the point of bullet impact in respect to point of aim does indeed change if you shoot at a target either above or below you. Also, as the uphill or downhill angle increases, so does on-target bullet displacement.

Let's say you're going after a mountain goat with your new rifle in .270 Winchester caliber. You adjust the riflescope so that the bullet hits dead center at 200 yards. This means the point of impact is 1.5 inches high at 100 yards, about 6.5 inches low at 300 yards, and 19.5 inches low at 400 yards. In the mountains, you get a shot at a big billy at what you and your guide estimate to be close to 400 yards. It's a longish shot, but you roll your down vest into a rifle cushion and, taking a solid rest, settle the crosshairs a few inches over the goat's back. Allowing for the 19.5-inch drop at 400 yards, you hold high and figure the bullet's trajectory will curve right into the goat's boiler room. But you have forgotten something.

The goat is 45° above you. What difference will that make in the bullet's flight in respect to the line of sight? Do you need to aim higher perhaps? Or lower? Think about it before reading on.

If you aimed at the goat the same way you would over level ground, the old billy would live to see another winter because the bullet would zip harmlessly over his back. At an upward angle of 45°, the bullet would only fall 8.5 inches in respect to line of sight, less than half as much as it would drop when shooting horizontally. Exactly the same is true if you shoot *downhill* at a *45° angle.*

The reason this peculiar situation is so difficult to understand is the lack of available visual demonstrations. We can get good idea of what a trajectory curve looks like by watching the flight of a hard-hit golf ball, but how do we demonstrate the peculiar curve of a bullet going uphill?

There are a couple of ways. One is imaginary, requiring some logic, and the other is a perfectly simple visual demonstration, which we'll use to support our logic.

By now we're very much aware that gravity causes the path of a bullet to curve downward. But let's put gravity to work another way. Imagine, if you will, a rifle held perfectly perpendicular so that when it is fired the bullet goes straight up. If there were no wind or other variables to disturb the bullet's flight, the projectile would go straight up until it ran out of momentum. Then gravity would pull it straight back down again, base first. The most important thing about the path of this bullet, for our present purpose, is that it is totally without curve—the bullet moves along a perfectly straight line, up as well as back down.

Here's where you need to use your imagination. This time we'll tilt the rifle slightly, say one degree off plumb. This time, the bullet's flight is almost straight, *but not quite.* As it nears the apex of its trip, it begins to curve ever so slightly. So let's keep shooting (and using our imagination). Each time we fire, we tilt the muzzle another degree from the vertical and the bullet path of each succeeding shot is progressively more curved. At last, we come to 90° *(horizontal), and the bullet follows its normal curved trajectory.*

Let's not stop there. Let's keep shooting, now angling the muzzle *below* the horizontal until, at last, the muzzle is pointed straight down. Just as it did when the muzzle was pointed straight up, the bullet travels in a straight line.

By now I'm sure you're getting the picture. We know our logic is sound, but it must be demonstrated. How? With an ordinary fly rod, the one you take trout fishing! Assuming the rod is not warped, set the butt on the ground and hold it vertically. It remains perfectly straight. Now, holding it by the grip, extend it horizontally. See how it curves downward? (If it is too stiff to bend very much, attach a weight to the tip). Now, slowly angling the rod from the vertical to dead level, note how gravity causes the curve to increase as the angle nears the horizontal. It's a beautiful demonstration.

As we have seen, the bullet follows a less curved trajectory when we fire up or down. That's why you shot over the trophy mountain goat that was above you at 45°.

Now let's get down to basics. Realizing that shooting up- or downhill causes the bullet to strike higher than on the horizontal, in respect to point of aim, how can we judge where to aim? The easiest way is to use a cartridge with a flat trajectory. Obviously, if a bullet has relatively little curve in its trajectory, that curve will be less affected by variations in shooting angle. For example, let's compare two cartridges with widely different trajectories. One is a 7mm Magnum with a 145-grain pointed bullet loaded to 3,100 fps. The other is a .30/30 Winchester with a 150-grain flat-nose slug loaded to 2,100 fps. Both rifles are scope-sighted with the scope 1.5 inches above the bore center, and both are sighted-in at 200 yards. Changing the angle from horizontal to 45° but still shooting at 200 yards, the 7mm Magnum hits 2.32 inches above point of aim and the .30/30 is all of 5.65 inches high. Now you see why a rifle with a flat trajectory eliminates some of the guesswork when shooting up- or downhill.

Another way of "guesstimating" where to hold on angle shots is my rule of thumb. For lo these many years, I've reasoned that a bullet fired at an upward or downward angle will hit very close to where it would hit if fired over the horizontal leg of the angle—the horizontal distance to a vertical line running through the target as shown in the illustration on the following page.

As you can see, a triangle is formed by the three lines in the illustration: the horizontal line, the steep (angled) line from rifle to target, and the vertical line from the horizontal distance up to the target. In any such triangle, the horizontal line is *shorter* than the uphill (or downhill) line. Gravity affects the bullet's flight only for as long as the projectile is in the air—that is, along the shorter, horizontal line.

Until the day this was written, I had never subjected my hypothesis to a computer. Just for the hell of it, let's do a little rough calculation and see if the computer approves.

Suppose we're shooting at a wary old rockchuck sitting up on a ledge at a range of 300 yards. He's 45° above us. Making a quick calculation, we find that the *horizontal* distance is only about 250 yards. The rifle, a .243 Winchester, is sighted-in at 300 yards with a scope centered 1.5 inches above the bore line. This means the bullet is about 2.4 inches above point of aim at 250 yards. Using my patented Indian remedy and holding 2.4 inches below the chuck's nose, will we make a hit? Let's punch a few computer keys and find out. Hmmm—according to the computer, the bullet will hit 4.82 inches high, which means either my old Indian remedy or my computer is off by nearly 2.5 inches, and obviously, the computer is more accurate than Indian remedies.

However, my guesstimate was still close enough to score a hit on a rockchuck, so we can be sure it works well enough for good hits on mountain game at any practical range.

In this drawing, the distance uphill to the target is 350 yards, but gravity is exerted along the horizontal— 250-yard—distance, so the bullet fired along Line A drops no more at target distance than it would if fired along Line B.

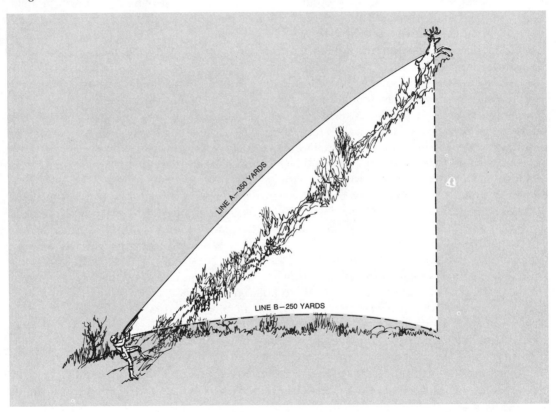

Chapter 10

WIND, THE SHOOTER'S CHALLENGE

It's the last hour of a gut-busting 10 days of elk hunting. You're digging your heels into your one-speed nag, hoping to get into camp before the full fury of the season's first storm hits you.

The wind speed has doubled in half an hour, and sheets of icy snow are swirling along the canyon floor. You've just turned your coat collar up when your guide reins hard and slides off his mount, motioning you to grab your rifle and follow. Then you see it—the biggest bull elk you ever hoped to lay eyes on. He's just below the tree line on the the opposite side of the valley, and the head is even bigger than the one in Lucy's Bar and Grill back in Cody. The bull isn't spooked. He's just standing there, head on, trying to figure out what your horses are through the gloom.

In the poor light and blowing snow, the bull looks a long way off, but you've been through the valley twice a day every day and know the range is at most 300 yards—an easy shot with your .300 Winchester Magnum and 180-grain loads. Snuggling down in a solid sitting position, you pull the sling tight under your arm, and the crosshairs vibrate lightly on the big bull's chest. The greatest trophy of your life is only a trigger pull away.

But wait! What about the wind? You're shooting across the canyon and the wind is blowing along it. You're dealing with a right-angle crosswind gusting to 30 mph. How much will the bullet be affected? A couple of inches? Enough to cause a miss? Surely not—the 180-grain bullet leaves the muzzle at 2,960 fps with 3,500 foot-pounds of energy. Surely a bit of wind won't affect a bullet going fast and hard enough to kill an elk. Just to make sure, though, you hold six inches into the wind and press the trigger. What happens?

Depending on the shape of that particular bullet, it would be driven off course somewhere between two and three *feet!* In order to hit the elk solidly with the animal facing you, it would have been necessary to hold the crosshairs well *off* his body. Wind can be hell!

To most shooters, wind is an abstraction, a ghost that works its mischief on a bullet with unpredictable suddenness. Since we can see neither the wind nor a bullet in flight, it is difficult to perceive the interaction of the two, but the effect of wind is as precisely predictable as other ballistic phenomena, at least in theory. If the wind were to blow at a steady rate in a constant direction for only a few minutes, it would be possible to make a few calculations that would tell us exactly how far any bullet, traveling at any velocity, would be pushed off course at any range. But the wind never blows at the same speed or in precisely the same direction for more than scant seconds. That's why our best riflemen, those who excell at long-range high-power tournaments or the frustrating smallbore prone game, are expert not only at reading the wind but at *predicting* what it will do next. As an astute benchrest shooting pal of mine once remarked, "What the wind is doing when you pull the trigger will be history when the bullet leaves the muzzle."

CONFLICTING THEORIES

Since wind is such an everyday factor in our lives, one might suppose that puzzles about how wind affects the flight of a bullet would have long since been unraveled. In truth, these riddles are still largely unsolved. Of course, we've worked out ways of accurately predicting the effect of wind on bullets, and our computers can tell within fractions of an inch how much any given bullet will be displaced from its route by wind of any given strength from any angle. Even so, many experts are reluctant to agree on what actually takes place when a bullet is in the grip of a passing breeze. This is apparent in different terminology used to discuss the wind's effect. Some experts refer to the wind's effect as *drift*. Others say *deflection,* while still others call it *displacement.*

The deflectionists hold that upon exiting the muzzle, a bullet is *deflected* by crosswind in much the same way a bullet deflects, or glances off, an angled surface. Thereafter, the bullet continues to be deflected in an infinite repetition of the process, each deflection adding to the magnitude of what is ultimately the bullet displacement in relation to point-of-aim on the target. Obviously, the greater the force of the wind, the greater the deflection.

To understand the implications of the deflection hypothesis, let's build an imaginary 200-yard rifle range. On this wonderfully instructive range, the wind blows across the first 100 yards, and there is a dead calm over the second half. Let's fire a bullet over this course in a wind that is strong enough to deflect the bullet one inch at 100 yards. In what direction does the bullet continue for the windless 100 yards?

If the bullet is truly deflected, its direction, including its axis of rotation, is no longer parallel to the axis of the rifle barrel. Just as a bullet that has been deflected by impact on an angled surface, it has been given an entirely new direction of flight. Thus a displacement from the original direction of one inch at 100 yards will become two inches at 200 yards and so on *ad infinitum.*

Now if we turn the same wind on over the second half of the course, the bullet would be deflected another inch (actually more, but let's keep it simple). So, it addition to the original two-inch displacement at 200 yards, we add another inch. When plotted over several hundred yards, the path of the bullet would be a continuously increasing curve. Actual experiments do indeed show that the bullet responds to the wind by following a path of ever-increasing lateral curvature.

Proponents of the drift hypothesis state that a bullet rides or is carried by the wind just the way a boat crossing a river is caused to drift somewhat downstream by the current. A comparable situation would occur if you set out across the river at full power and then cut the engine and let the boat continue toward the opposite shore. At first, the drift is only minimal, but as the boat loses speed (just as a bullet slows in flight), the apparent sideward drift would become greater in proportion to the boat's forward progress. Thus the route of the boat would be an ever-increasing downstream curve.

Though the boat analogy seems perfectly logical, it leaves many questions unanswered, as I discovered the hard way when I was a student at a laboratory school for gifted kids. We all thought we were pretty smart and were always on the lookout for ways to demonstrate our dazzling brainpower. Fortunately, our teachers were way ahead of us and came up with some neat ways to bring us down to earth. One of the best at this was a physics teacher who delighted in throwning mental curve balls our way when we got too uppity. He was a shooter and gun nut of considerable knowledge so, to my everlasting appreciation, he often asked brain teasers involving ballistics. The best one he ever laid on me was an apparently simple question about calculating the effect of wind on a bullet's path.

"O.K., Carmichel, show us how smart you are," he said. "How much will a 10-mile-an-hour wind, blowing at right angles to a bullet's path, blow it off course at 100 yards? Come up to the blackboard and show us your calculation."

Figuring this was right up my alley, I swaggered up to the board, took up a piece of chalk, and smirked at my eager peers. Thinking I would handle this little exercise in a flash, they smirked at the teacher. He kept a straight face.

"It's all a matter of time and inches," I began. "Since our ballistic thoughts are expressed in seconds, feet, and inches, let's begin by converting a 10-mile-per-hour wind to inches per second." Hastily I scribbled on the board. "There are 5,280 feet in a mile. If we multiply this by 12, we find that there are 63,360 inches in a mile."

"Good," said the teacher.

I continued, barely able to contain my brilliance. "Since one mile per hour equals 63,360 inches per hour, we divide this figure by 60 to get inches per minute. Then we divide by 60 again to get inches per second." The chalk dust flew as I came up with the figure of 17.6. "So," I went on, "a 10-mile-per-hour crossing wind will have a velocity of 176 inches per second."

"Now," I announced, we come to the second part of the question—the bullet's time of flight. I don't know just offhand the 100-yard time-of-flight of any bullet, but if I did, I'd just multiply it by 176, and we'd know exactly how much the 10-mph wind would blow the bullet off course. Bullets at different velocities would be blown off course by varying amounts, depending on velocity."

By then I had become condescending toward the teacher, and my classmates were positively worshipful. I basked in the warm glow of their admiration.

"Wait a minute," said the teacher. "I've got some time-of-flight tables in my office. I'll be right back." As he left the room, I knew my final victory was at hand. He scurried back with a frayed manual and flipped to a page of ballistic tables.

"It says here," he remarked, showing me the page, "that a 180-grain bullet fired at 2,700 fps takes .1150 seconds to travel 100 yards. How about working that into your formula?"

Again, I scrawled on the blackboard. I found that .1150 × 176 equals 20.24—over 20 inches! I'd been suckered. I'd done enough rifle shooting to know a bullet isn't blown off course that much in 100 yards, but my math and logic were so clear that I couldn't see how I had gone wrong.

"That's a lot of Kentucky windage, don't you think, Mr. Carmichel? You can take your seat now." The teacher was cool in his victory, and I was devastated.

Where I'd gone wrong, of course, was to ignore the tremendous momentum of a speeding bullet. Had I stopped to think, I would have remembered Newton's law that explains how a body in motion tends to resist forces (such as wind) that try to veer it from its path. A bullet is driven by hundreds or thousands of pounds of energy. Also, a spinning bullet is a gyroscope and, in the manner of all gyroscopes, it resists being pushed around.

These forces work for us. If wind did move a bullet as severely as my schoolboy calculations indicated, we could hardly hit anything with the wind blowing. Long-range varmint shooting and many forms of target shooting would be pointless. Even so, crosswinds can cause considerable frustration. The elk-hunting situation I described is a case in point, and at the longer ranges the effect of wind is often difficult to believe.

Once when I was competing in the famed 1,000-yard Wimbledon match at Camp Perry, a wind blew up off Lake Erie that had me aiming at the target next to mine in order to get inside my frame. The following table gives some idea of how much wind affects a bullet's flight.

BULLET DRIFT (INCHES) IN A 20-MPH CROSSWIND			
Range (yards)	.22/250 Remington 55-grain bullet 3,730 fps	.30/30 Winchester 170-grain bullet 2,200 fps	7mm Remington Magnum 150-grain bullet 3,110 fps
100	1.7	5.6	1.4
200	7.2	23.7	6.6
300	17.4	59.6	16.0
400	33.5	108.5	30.1
500	56.5	170.0	49.8
600	88.2	242.2	76.1
800	180.8	418.4	149.0
1000	316.4	648.4	254.9

Since bullet drift is proportional to wind velocity, you can calculate drift for the above cartridges at other wind speeds by dividing or multiplying. A 10-mph breeze would result in half the drift shown in the table.

Wind does not affect all bullets equally, and we see from the table that the faster bullets appear to be less disturbed. That's why the rifles used in 1000-yard target competitions are usually of magnum persuasion. They are capable of getting their bullets to the target more quickly.

TIME OF FLIGHT

These observations indicate that a bullet's wind drift is related to time of flight: the time interval during which the bullet is subjected to the wind's pressure. We would naturally conclude that if Bullet A takes twice as long to go 500 yards as Bullet B, it would be blown off course twice as far. Alas, it's not that simple.

Let's say we are shooting a .22-caliber bullet at 2,000 fps muzzle velocity in a 10-mph crosswind. The time of flight over the 100-yard range is .1619 seconds, and the bullet is blown off course 2.1 inches. My computer tells me that the same bullet will have almost exactly half this time of flight if it launched at a muzzle velocity of 3,950 fps. But the wind deflection at this higher velocity is only .9 inches over the same 100 yards. If the time of flight is cut in half, why isn't the wind drift also cut in half? This takes some explaining, and the answer isn't easy to accept.

Many modern ballisticians and shooting hobbyists subscribe to what is commonly, though incorrectly, known as the *delay theory,* a method of calculating wind drift by comparing a bullet's time of flight in a vacuum to the time it takes to travel the same distance in a normal atmosphere. As we already know, atmospheric resistance delays a bullet's progress, so the difference between the real and the theoretical flight time in a vacuum is called the delay.

Without going into the formulas, let's put the delay theory to work. Since varmint shooters are always concerned about wind, let's consider the .22/250 Remington handloaded to 3,700 fps with a 55-grain bullet having a ballistic coefficient of .260.

Fired in a vacuum, where the bullet encounters no air resistance, the velocity remains a steady 3,700 fps throughout its flight. The time of flight for the 100-yard distance therefore works out to .0810 seconds. At normal sea-level atmospheric air pressure, though, the time of flight is .0863 seconds. The difference, or *delay,* is .0052 seconds. The delay factor is then multiplied by the wind velocity as expressed in inches per second to find total drift away from point of aim. Since a 10-mph wind equals 176 inches per second, we multiply 176 by our delay factor of .0052 and come up with .9152, which rounds off to a .9-inch drift at 100 yards in a 10-mph wind.

If this little trick seems too good to be true, rest assured that it is. The rub comes when we start trying to figure out the times of flight. Without the aid of a computer, this can be a matter of tiresome arithmetic. In fact, the reason I subjected you to the foregoing explanation of the delay theory was to sum up the general uselessness of the various wind-deflection formulas. Even if you could carry around a computer, by the time you keyed in all the necessary factors your trophy buck would have bounded away.

BULLET SHAPE AND WIND

Does this mean we are completely at the mercy of the wind? Not at all. As I see it, the wind is just another tool to help me win a rifle match (assuming I'm better at judging wind than my competition), or at its worst, a relentless but fascinating opponent.

There are some quite workable ways of getting around the wind problem. If you were paying close attention to my explanation of the delay theory, you probably discovered that it really isn't a theory at all but only a happy accident of mathematics. The delay factor itself—the difference in flight times when fired in a vacuum and in a normal atmosphere—is just another way of describing a bullet's coefficient of form, something we learned a lot about in another chapter. Bullets that have a shorter delay do so because they are more streamlined and less affected by atmospheric drag. We discover then that bullets which lose velocity at the lowest rate and therefore have the flattest trajectories are also the ones that are least affected by wind. Ain't it wonderful? We have again discovered the superiority of streamlined bullets!

When I was young and foolish and inclined to judge my personal happiness by the number of guns in my cabinet, I spent every spare evening and weekend in my workshop carving and cobbling away at a new acquisition for my collection. Looking back on these efforts, I can see that they weren't all that hot, but at the time I thought they were wonderful. One of my favorites was a .35 Whelen I'd built on a salvaged Mauser action. The .35 Whelen was once a popular wildcat, made simply by opening up the neck of a .30/06 case to hold a .35 caliber bullet. I used mine to bust a black bear or two and put a few elk and deer in the freezer.

All in all, it was a pretty effective cartridge out to a couple of hundred yards or so, but after that the steep trajectory made hits a bit iffy, and the Arizona winds tended to blow the bullets around like a weather balloon. The problem centered on the big 250-grain round-nose .35-caliber bullet Hornady was making at that time. To be sure, they expanded beautifully and when one smacked a bull elk in the pump room his time had come. But with a ballistic coefficient of .296, that bullet had a pretty dippy trajectory, and it took a beating in the wind. Loaded to 2,500 fps, this is how much it was blown off course in a 20-mph crosswind.

Range (yards)	Wind Displacement (inches)
100	2.6
200	11.6
300	28
400	53.2
500	88.6

Yielding to cries from the wilderness, Hornady redesigned the bullet somewhat and gave the nose a more streamlined shape. With weight and muzzle velocity the same, here's how the new nose "shaped up" in the same 20-mph crosswind.

Range (yards)	Wind Displacement (inches)
100	2
200	8.6
300	20.2
400	38
500	61.6

Obviously, streamlined bullets, (those with a higher ballistic coefficient) are less affected by wind than blunter ones, all other things being equal. As we have also seen, the faster a bullet is traveling, the less it is bothered by wind. So, the best way to fool that 'ol debbil wind is to use the pointiest bullets we can find and launch them as fast as possible. That's why those wonderful 1,000-yard target rifles are usually chambered for fast-stepping magnum rounds and the ammo is loaded with needle-nose bullets that slither through the air with the least possible wind deflection.

But wait. There are always exceptions, and bullets in wind don't always follow the rules.

Outdoor smallbore (.22 Rimfire) target shooting is largely a matter of wind "doping." The tournament winners are almost always those who have been most expert—or lucky—at compensating for the passing breezes. Several years ago it was common for shooters to use high-velocity Long Rifle ammo on days when the wind was kicking up. Then, as now, it was commonly known that high-velocity .22's are less accurate than standard-velocity loads (especially standard-velocity match-grade loads), but it was felt that the added wind resistance of the faster bullets more than made up for the accuracy difference.

This sounded pretty good, but after a while many shooters noticed that the high-speed .22's weren't winning any matches on windy days. If anything, scores made with them were even worse on windy days than those made with slow-moving stuff. Why?

The answer turned out to be a peculiar set of ballistic circumstances that occur at about the velocity of sound, and it can be explained by our old friend the delay theory. Again avoiding mathematics, let's simply say that a .22 Rimfire standard-velocity round with a muzzle velocity of 1,145 fps or thereabouts, suffers considerably less *delay* than a .22 high-speed round with a muzzle velocity of some 1,350 fps. Of course, it takes some figuring to come up with the differences, but the delay factor of the high-speed bullet is about a third greater than that of the slower bullet. This means the slower bullet will be blown off course a third less than the faster one! That's why today's target .22 ammunition is always loaded to the lower velocity. But when velocities are significantly above the speed of sound, say 1,600 fps or more, we can combat the wind with speed.

We have been dealing with a crossing wind. What about a wind blowing directly at your face or back? These winds are not as troublesome as a crosswind, thought they can make some difference in vertical displacement. If you fire a bullet in a 20-mph tailwind, you are, in effect, boosting its velocity by 20 mph or some 30 fps. And if you shoot *into* a 20-mph wind, it will have the effect of lowering the muzzle velocity by that amount. This small velocity difference won't make much change in the bullet's point of impact at normal ranges, so don't worry about it.

Sometimes, though, the wind doesn't blow horizontally, and there are some peculiar directions of drift. Several years ago when I was shooting in a smallbore tournament, I was puzzled by a tendency of my shots to go high when the wind was in my face. This seemed completely at odds with logic. What was happening was that the wind was pouring over the 10-foot backstop and sweeping down its near side. When the wind hit the ground, it billowed almost straight up. The updraft was catching my bullets. At the end of the day's shooting, I walked out to the backstop and tossed handfuls of dust into the air so that I could see the strong updraft at work. An old-time club member saw what I was doing and gave me a wink. "Now you're on to what goes on out there," he said.

So far we've been talking mostly about the theories. All the theories in the world aren't worth a snuffbox full of wet gunpowder unless we can come to grips with wind in practical ways. We have to learn how sensitive our favorite hunting or target bullet is to wind, either through consulting wind tables or by actual testing. A shot that is blown two inches wide of the bull's-eye, for example, is a very good object lesson in wind doping, and a target shooter quickly learns that he must make a two-inch allowance for the wind if he wants to win a match. Likewise, a varmint shooter who tries to bust a prairie dog in a stiff breeze will probably see his windblown bullet kick up dust anywhere from a few inches to a foot or more to the downwind side of his intended target. After a few such misses, he gets the hang of what the wind is doing to his bullets and starts allowing for it. With experience, target and varmint shooters become so expert at anticipating how their bullets will be affected by wind that they can put the first shot right on target.

WIND TABLES

Most shooters, especially once- or twice-a-year big game hunters, have neither the time nor the inclination to develop this sort of expertise and must rely on other methods. The best help is a wind table that tells how much a given bullet will be driven off course at various ranges by winds of different speeds.

Though various ammo makers' catalogs usually include ballistic tables that show trajectory, remaining velocity, and energy levels at different ranges for each load offered, they haven't yet bothered to include wind-drift data. This is too bad. Perhaps future catalogs will offer this data. For the present, we have to look elsewhere for workable wind-drift information.

Handloaders who tailor their own rifle and handgun ammo know (I hope) that some of the currently available handloading manuals include comprehensive ballistic information, including wind tables. These tables are computed only for a particular manufacturer's line of bullets, but with a little interpolating the data can be made to apply to other makes of bullets as well. One thing you must understand at the beginning, though, is that bullets of different sizes, weights, and shapes are affected by wind in varying degrees. Therefore, we can never make a general statement like: "A .30-caliber bullet traveling at 2,000 fps will be blown off course three inches by a 20-mph crosswind." When talking about crosswind effect, we have to be reasonably specific about our bullets and their velocities.

Benchresters aren't the only competitors concerned about the effects of wind. Look closely at this firing line and you'll see that the shooters are equipped with little windmills that look much like a child's pinwheel toy. These devices help in judging wind force and direction. In smallbore competitions, riflemen sometimes use up most of their time limit in order to fire for record when the breeze is right or when it stops blowing.

Let's say your favorite big game rifle is a .30/06 and you use 180-grain Remington Bronze Points. Consulting a Remington Arms catalog (which your dealer will give you or you can request directly from Remington), you see that the muzzle velocity is 2,700 fps, with remaining velocities of 2,485, 2,280, and 2,084 fps at 100, 200, and 300 yards. Then you buy or borrow, say, a Sierra reloading manual. Looking through Sierra's bullet descriptions, you find one that is the same diameter and weight as your Bronze Point and appears to have the most similar shape. In this case, Sierra's .30-caliber 180-grain spitzer flat-base bullet closely resembles your Bronze Point. You now flip to the ballistic tables in the back of the book and find the data for the 180-grain spitzer flat-base. Under the listing for that bullet at a muzzle velocity of 2,700 fps, you see that a 20-mph crosswind will blow it off course 1.25, 5.17, and 12.02 inches at 100, 200, and 300 yards, respectively.

Now you have in hand some very useful and perhaps surprising information. Chances are you never suspected your .30/06 could be blown around that much. As a double check, you compare your catalog data to the Sierra ballistic table and find that the Sierra spitzer is not losing velocity quite as fast as your Bronze Point. At 300 yards, the Sierra spitzer is traveling 2,144 fps compared to the Remington's 2,084. This tells you that the Sierra bullet has a slightly better ballistic form and is therefore less affected by the wind. This difference is so slight as to be insignificant, so there's no need to worry about it. The wind-drift difference at 300 yards works out to only about an inch and would be hidden by normal aiming and rifle accuracy errors at that range. To find out how drift affects a factory-loaded bullet, just match the bullet as closely as you can.

If you had consulted a Hornady rather than a Sierra manual, you would have found that the ballistics for the Hornady 180-grain spire point are almost a perfect match with the Remington Bronze Point's published catalog data. This matching game wouldn't be necessary if the major ammo makers published their ballistic coefficient numbers as do the makers of component bullets for handloaders. With the correct ballistic coefficient, you could get perfect or near-perfect wind-drift data from existing handloading tables. But the ammo makers like to keep ballistic coefficients secret so as to avoid direct comparisons, I suppose. In case you're so far out in the boondocks that reloading manuals and even ammo makers' catalogs are scarce, we've got a nice surprise for you at the end of this chapter.

HOW HARD IS IT BLOWING?

The next question when dealing with the wind is more elusive. How hard is the wind blowing? How can you judge it accurately?

First-time visitors to major benchrest matches are often dazzled by the colorful assortment of wind-gauging equipment used by competitors. In addition to flags, there are complex and ingenious geometric forms. I recall one fellow who used a series of electronic wind sensors. When you consider that bench tournaments can be won or lost by a tenth of an inch, the need for accurate wind doping is apparent.

Actually, benchrest competitors and most other target shooters aren't all that concerned about how hard the wind blows because their rifles are as accurate (discounting some

Here's a close-up view of the windmill device used by many smallbore competitors. The soft, whining sound of its whirring blades tells an experienced shooter when the breeze accelerates or subsides. Note that it has a rudderlike vane on a horizontal arm so that it can turn to indicate shifts in the wind's angle.

theoretical exceptions) in a strong wind as they are in a dead calm. If there were such a thing as a perfectly constant 20-mph crosswind, group sizes would be as small as they are when fired in a calm. The shooter could make a perfect and constant allowance for the wind. What really terrifies target shooters is a changing wind—one that blows the first bullet half an inch off course, and then slackens or changes direction sufficiently to carry the next bullet only a quarter of an inch off course, or perhaps allows it to strike half an inch in the opposite direction.

When time allows, many competitive shooters prefer to wait out the wind, hoping to fire all shots under identical wind conditions. That's why you may see a benchrest shooter fidgeting on his stool right up until the last few seconds of his allotted relay time. He is hoping for the return of "his" wind condition.

Outdoor smallbore-rifle competitions, as fired in the U.S., allow a time limit of 20 minutes for the firing of 20 recorded shots. A well-trained and conditioned marksman can usually rip off these 20 shots in somewhere between five and 10 minutes. Yet, competitors often use nearly all of their time limit if there is a feisty breeze. Some are waiting for the periodic return of their pet wind condition, while others sample the strength and direction of the wind by routinely firing non-scored shots at a special sighting bull on their target sheet. On tough days, some competitors fire two or three shots at the sighter for every shot fired for

Wind and mirage compensation can make a big difference to a competitor who is trying for a group like the one in the uppermost target.

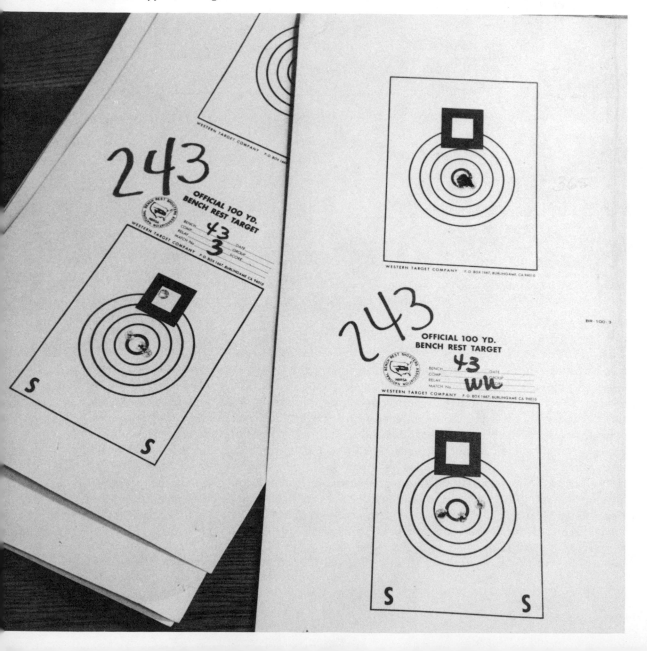

record. They check the effect of every detected wind shift before committing a shot for score.

A common wind-detecting tool used by smallbore shooters is a little windmill that spins and responds to every shift in wind force and direction. The windmills make a soft whining sound as they spin, and as the rpm's change, the pitch of the whirring changes. With a little practice, competitors get "tuned in" on their windmills and note the slightest change in pitch.

Though we learn a lot about the effects of wind in benchrest and smallbore target shooting, such luxuries as sighting shots and waiting for the ideal wind condition can seldom be afforded in the hunting field. A big buck deer or wary pronghorn isn't going to stand around while we test the wind, and sighting shots "off the record" will scare the game into the next county.

The target-shooting games which most closely resemble actual hunting conditions are silhouette and big-bore (high-power) long-range competitions. Once a silhouette match begins, you don't get any "free" sighting shots. You have to make up your mind and aim accordingly.

Big-bore competitions fired at 200, 300, 600, and 1000 yards, are about the same. You get a couple of sighting shots at the beginning of the 600-yard stage, and a few more at 1,000 yards, but after that every shot is for keeps, and trying to get 20 consecutive shots in that 12-inch circle at 600 yards (firing prone, no artificial rest, iron sights) is mainly an exercise in concentrated wind doping. I guess that's why long-range target shooters tend to share a distinctive personality trait. Smallbore target shooters approach each record shot with the timidity of a mouse stealing cheese from a lion; big-bore shooters must have the bold decisiveness required for every shot.

Having competed in scores of big-bore matches from Camp Perry, Ohio, to Black Canyon, Arizona, for over a quarter of a century, I have to say that the lessons I've learned on the long-distance target range are the ones that have proven most helpful when shooting at game.

With experience, shooters become subconsciously aware of the wind. It never leaves the thoughts of serious target shooters or expert varmint hunters, and when I line up on a big game trophy animal, I run through a mental checklist that includes a quick appraisal of the wind. A good big game guide will usually note the wind as well, and perhaps make a suggestion about how to deal with it if he thinks it will be a factor. An experienced guide knows that a last-instant wind check can mean the difference between meat and a miss.

My mental check runs something like this: Is there any wind blowing, and does it have enough force to significantly affect the flight of my bullet? What I call significant wind drift simply boils down to asking myself if the wind could cause me to miss. This depends on a number of factors.

For example, if I'm at the 300-yard stage of a high-power rifle tournament, a wind strong enough to drift my bullet three inches at that range is significant because three inches is enough to drift the shot into the next lower scoring ring, and I'll lose a valuable point. The same would apply if I were shooting at a prairie dog because they are about three inches wide when they stand up. But if you or I were aiming at the chest cavity of a bull elk or even a pronghorn, a three-inch drift from point of aim would not be significant because we'd still hit in the vital area.

Significant or insignificant wind involves calibers as well because of their varying wind sensitivity. Even in a 20 mph crosswind, you can hold dead center on a woodchuck with, say, a 6mm loaded with 85-grain bullets at 100 yards and figure on hitting within about an inch and a half of where you aim—certainly well centered enough for an instant kill. But try that with your favorite old .22 Hornet, and you'll be about four inches wide of your mark, enough to miss a woodchuck clean or only clip a patch of hair.

Most of today's high-intensity centerfire cartridges combine high velocity with well-shaped bullets, so the wind is seldom a significant factor at ranges under 200 yards. A typical cartridge of this class, the .280 Remington loaded with 140-grain bullets, suffers about 5½ inches of drift in a 20-mph crosswind. With animals the size of mule deer and larger, we can absorb that much drift, if necessary, without making a correction for the wind and still count on a solid hit in the chest area (assuming the shot is well aimed at the center of the chest area). Try to get away with the same thing using your .30/30 and you'll miss by two feet.

In case you're wondering, no sporting cartridge gives you any real measure of wind protection at ranges much beyond 200 or 250 yards. The exalted .300 Weatherby Magnum, for example, whistling a 180-grain sharp-pointed, boat-tail bullet out of muzzle at 3,100 fps is a terrific wind bucker, but even so, at 300 yards a 20-mph wind carries the slug off course by nearly 10 inches. That's much too much displacement, even when shooting at the largest North American game, particularly when you add in another 10 or so inches of inevitable aiming and holding error at that range.

Naturally, significant wind drift becomes less so as the range shortens. A 30-mph gale that blows a .30/30 bullet off course by some three feet at 200 yards will cause only two inches of drift at 50 yards. At the short ranges typical of woods hunting, a wind that isn't strong enough to blow you off your feet will not cause enough bullet drift to be significant.

WIND DOPING AFIELD

The second step in our mental checklist then is either to dismiss the wind as insignificant and aim normally, or recognize that the wind force and direction is significant and do something about it. As mentioned earlier headwinds and tailwinds aren't much bother. Way out at 300 yards, a 30-mph headwind or tailwind won't cause even the pokey .30/30 to hit more than a couple of inches high or low. Faster cartridges are proportionally less affected. The wind that most affects a bullet's flight comes from either side at a 90° angle or close to it. A wind coming from a lesser angle has less effect. So, in addition to estimating the velocity of the wind, you must consider the angle.

This sounds complicated, but with a bit of experience a shooter learns to make needed corrections in an instant. There comes a time when you don't think about wind velocity in terms of miles per hour. The computations are bypassed, and you simply know, "When the wind feels like this on my neck, I have to hold on the edge of a deer's chest, or just behind his back rib."

Long-range target shooters use a verbal shorthand for wind effect in which the wind strength is expressed in minutes of angle—the same minutes of angle we use to describe rifle accuracy and sight adjustments. A shooter may consider the range flags and decide the wind is worth three minutes of angle, meaning that he has to readjust his sights by three MOA to compensate for wind drift. All this is done without bothering to estimate the actual mph speed of the wind. Hunters, of course, don't have time to click their sights. They "hold off" to compensate.

It is hard for many experienced target or big game shooters to convey their wind-doping knowledge to beginners. A beginner may say, "Gee, Mr. Smith, that's a pretty stiff breeze. Would you say it's 15 or 20 miles an hour?" Mr. Smith is stumped because he doesn't consider wind in terms of miles per hour. All he knows is how far a wind that "feels" like that will drift his bullet. When it comes to beating the wind, there's no substitute for experience.

Even so, I think there are a few shortcuts in teaching wind doping that work well enough for a hunter to make that third and most crucial decision that comes up on his mental checklist when he aims at his trophy of a lifetime. Assuming he recognizes that both the direction and velocity of the wind are significant enough to carry the bullet off target, he must rapidly decide how much. To do that, he needs reliable ways to gauge the wind.

HOW TO USE MIRAGE

My favorite wind gauge is mirage, more commonly known as heat waves—those dancing streaks of air that we see rising from an asphalt highway on a summer's day or wiggling over a burning desert. With the unaided eye, we tend to notice mirage only during extreme heat, but it exists on all but the coldest, most overcast days. Any time there is sunlight, or even good light, you can see mirage. It's particularly noticeable over snow on a bright day, regardless of temperature. My friend Herb Hollister, the smallbore target-shooting wizard, calls mirage "wind you can see."

The great thing about using mirage as a wind indicator is that it is instantly responsive to the wind, always reliable, and tells you how hard the wind is blowing at any place along your bullet's path. It is also self-compensating for wind direction, a phenomenon I'll discuss a bit later.

We're not talking about the phenomena that make us see water in the desert or ocean liners on top of mountains. Mirage, in shooting, consists of waves or columns of rising air. The air rises because the air closest to the ground has been warmed by sunlight that is partially absorbed by the surface as heat and partially reflected. The air closest to the ground is therefore warmer than the air above it and tends to rise. This warmed air may not be warm at all, but it's warmer than the air above. This rising air seems to shimmer, making itself visible to us, because it rises in waves or columns of unequal density, causing the light passing through to be refracted or bent. You can see a very good example of mirage by turning on the kitchen stove and observing the rising heat waves. Then have someone stand to the side and gently blow or fan a breeze across the heat element. You'll see the heat waves bend with the breeze.

In the hunting field, you won't be able to see mirage as easily as in your kitchen unless you use some magnification such as a riflescope, spotting telescope, binoculars, or even a camera lens with a long focal length. The higher the magnification, the more apparent the mirage.

That's why some riflemen shy away from high-magnification telescopic sights. The mirage seems to make the target dance so much that aiming is difficult. If you have ever fired a rifle until the barrel became too hot to touch, you probably saw heat dancing off the barrel and may have had trouble shooting because the target seemed to jump about.

Sometimes, especially on cloudy or cool days, mirage is hard to find, so you have to know where to look. Mirage is easier to see against a dark background and is most apparent close to the ground. The trick to seeing mirage is to focus your telescope not on the target but at some closer point. That way, you are focused on the mirage itself at some point along your bullet's route.

If you watch a rifle tournament progress, you'll notice that the competitors spend a lot of time peering through their spotting scopes. They're not always looking at their targets. Rather, they are studying the mirage and trying to detect wind patterns. By patterns, I mean systematic changes in wind direction that switch or fishtail in a predictable sequence. Usually, a smallbore competitor firing the 100-yard stage of the match will focus his spotting scope at about 70 yards, so that the bullet holes, though indistinct, can still be seen and he can also keep a sharp eye on the midrange mirage. Long-range target shooters frequently change the focus of their spotting scopes so as to see what the wind, as indicated by mirage, is doing at several different points between the rifle and target. A 1,000-yard shooter, for example, may find that a brisk breeze on the firing line will be swirling at 400 yards, will change direction at 700, and then disappear—not blowing at all at 1,000 yards. The competitors tend to aim and fire rather quickly after checking the mirage through their scopes, because they want to get the shot downrange before the wind changes. Yet you'll hear lots of alibis about getting caught by a wind change.

One might suppose that the best time to shoot is when the wind is momentarily still and the heat waves are rising straight up. Target shooters call this a "boil," and most experienced shooters agree that it is unwise to shoot then. One reason is that a sudden stillness is usually followed by a sudden unpredictable shift. They feel more secure when shooting in a constant, known breeze.

When studying mirage, note that it appears as wavy lines, which either ascend straight up or lean with the wind. A 10-mph wind makes the mirage lines lean at an angle of about 45°. If the lines run horizontally, you can figure the wind force is 20 mph or greater.

Earlier, I mentioned that one of the things that make mirage a very good wind indicator is that it is self-compensating. For example, if the wind is blowing straight into your face or from straight behind you, the mirage lines appear to be vertical. For all practical hunting purposes, the bullet will not be significantly deflected. But suppose the wind is blowing 10 mph and quartering toward you at a 45° angle to your line of fire. Looking downrange through your scope, the mirage will not appear to be bent at a 45° angle as it is in a 90°, 10-mph crosswind. The mirage will look more vertical. This can be interpreted in terms of wind effect on your bullet's flight the same as a gentler wind coming directly across the range at 90°. In other words, you can forget the wind's direction and interpret the angle of the mirage wave as if a 90° crosswind were always blowing. What you see is what you get in terms of wind drift.

When shooting at game in the field, I usually use my binoculars to check mirage. I move the focus ring back and forth and look for the most apparent heat waves. Shooting in prairie-dog towns, woodchuck pastures, or typical pronghorn country where the terrain is usually flat to gently rolling, there is almost always plenty of mirage, sometimes more than you want. In hilly country where your shot may be from one hillside to the next, there's not much chance that you'll see much usable mirage, except perhaps quite close to or around the animal itself. In these situations, I forget about mirage and rely on more ordinary means of detecting wind.

You can practice gauging wind strength by watching a fluff of cotton hung on a string. However, no two shooters are likely to "read" a cottonball wind gauge the same way. It's just a rough guide for making a subjective judgment.

OTHER CLUES TO WIND SPEED

Leaves, grass, smoke, and dust tell which way the wind is blowing, but there's a trick to using the right indicator. If you were in the military service, you probably recall the red range flags that waved at the corners of rifle ranges. Their purpose was to warn that firing was in progress and the area should not be entered. Lots of shooters use range flags as wind indicators, but I'm not sure that's smart. If you fire on the same range all the time and always use the same flags, you may get pretty good at judging wind strength at that range. But flags elsewhere may be stiff, thicker, and heavy with dirt. These flags don't respond so well to gentle nudges of the wind; other flags may be light as a feather and inclined to ripple too much in a five-knot breeze.

The same can be true when judging wind under hunting conditions. I try to feel the wind in my face and, by experience, make an estimate of its force and direction. But I also want to know how the wind is blowing at the target. At ranges beyond 200 yards, this becomes increasingly important because wind tends to blow in narrow gusts or waves. I therefore study the foliage around the animal itself, to find out if it is blowing about the same there as where I am. More than half the time, it does so on reasonably level ground. On the other hand, if you're on the side of a mountain and the target is much higher or lower, wind velocity in the respective positions may be very different.

A few years back, I was freezing my tail off on the crest of a ridge in Wyoming while watching a herd of elk feed out of the woods and into an open meadow about 400 yards below me. As the sun sank lower, the air grew colder and it seemed that the arctic blasts were gusting at 40 mph or more. Then an old six-pointer eased into the clearing. When I laid the crosshairs on his chest, I noticed that the long, soft mane of hair on his neck and chest was hanging limp and straight. Clearly the meadow was protected from the wind I was feeling, and the elk were in a calm. Accordingly, I aimed at the big fellow as if I were shooting in no wind—and collected a beautiful trophy. If the wind is flattening the grass where you are, take a close look through your scope or binoculars and see if the grass is being similarly ruffled near your target. If necessary and you have the time, check several spots in between. Sometimes, beating the wind boils down to a matter of splitting the differences.

THE CHICKEN SYSTEM

Now that I've gone this far I might as well go all the way and let you in on my secret technique. I call it my "chicken system" for shooting in the wind, but for the sake of posterity maybe we should call it "Carmichel's No Fault Wind Insurance." Here's how you can make it work for you.

Let's say you've been stalking a prize pronghorn antelope. Toward sundown, he has you stymied. It's now or never and your only chance is to fire at 300 yards or more, with the wind blowing like the breath of hell. You figure it's blowing somewhere between 15 and 30 mph, enough to carry the 130-grain bullet from your .270 Winchester some 10 to 20 inches off

The closest device to a universal wind gauge is the plastic meter sold at boating-supply stores. An air current flowing over an opening at the top creates a low-pressure area inside the tube. This lifts a small plastic ball inside the tube, and it rises along a calibrated scale.

course. The wind is coming out of the west, and the buck is facing into it. You have to hold the crosshairs completely off the animal and aim at a spot somewhere out in space in order to get the bullet to drift into the target. But because of your uncertainty about the wind speed, you don't like the idea of holding off somewhere and depending on a force you can't even see to bend your bullet's path into the buck's boiler room. Holding off can call for more guts than most of us have.

That's when my chicken system comes to the rescue. I don't actually hold off the animal. In this case, I'd hold on the front edge of the antelope's chest, knowing with certainty that the wind would blow the bullet somewhere into his chest area. The beauty of the system is that when I'm not sure of the wind force or even the range, I have the entire width of the animal's chest cavity to provide a margin for error.

I use the same technique for varmints. When in doubt, I hold the vertical crosswire on the windward side of the animal and let the wind drift the bullet where it will, usually into a solid hit.

Over the years, I've tried all sorts of ways of gauging wind strength. For example, I've tried holding my hand out of a car window at different speeds, but all I learned was that it's almost impossible for me to tell the difference between a 10- and 12-mph wind. I did learn, however, that a cold wind feels a lot stronger than a warm one. I also experimented with a small lead fishing sinker and a fluff of cotton on a length of string. After a while, I pretty well learned how to use this rig for judging wind speed, but it doesn't work as a universal reference because one shooter's cottonball wind gauge may be heavier, denser, and wetter than the next man's. A cotton fluff blown out at a 45° angle could be read quite differently by different shooters.

The closest thing to a workable and universal wind gauge is a little hand-held plastic affair, usually available at boating-supply stores. It is essentially a tube, partly open at the top, with a cork or lightweight plastic ball inside. You hold the instrument vertically in the wind, and the current flowing over the open end creates a low-pressure area inside the tube. This causes the ball to rise, and the faster the air current, the higher the ball is lifted. A calibrated scale is then read at the ball's level, and you have a pretty good idea of wind force in miles per hour.

These little tools, costing only a few dollars, are compact and can be carried to the rifle range or even on a hunting trip. They are accurate enough so that wind velocity can be read and correlated with wind-drift tables to a reasonably accurate degree.

However, these wind gauges only tell you the wind velocity at one place. What it's doing 200 yards downrange may be an entirely different matter. In the final analysis, the chief value of a wind gauge is a teaching device. Carry one around and note how its readings compare with how the wind moves grass and leaves. Pretty soon, you'll find you're making a fairly accurate estimate of wind velocity not only where you are standing but hundreds of yards away.

Judging how far wind will blow a bullet off course is an acquired skill. Like all such skills, it is subject to considerable error. That's why we have to use every tool available; mirage, dust, flags, grass, and autumn leaves. As haphazard as all these things may seem, the degree of accuracy you can acquire is remarkable. I've seen good wind dopers group all their shots in an inch-wide cluster in a changing wind that was blowing the shots of others all over the targets. I'm convinced that wind drift can be dealt with, and that you can be a winner. But as with so many things in life, there are no shortcuts to that one element that makes a rifleman a master of the wind—experience.

The following table includes same basic information on how your favorite caliber performs in a crosswind.

	DRIFT OF COMMON RIFLE CALIBERS IN 10-MPH CROSSWIND		
Caliber	Bullet Weight (Grains)	100 yards (Inches)	200 yards (Inches)
.22 Hornet	45	2.9	14.7
.218 Bee	45	2.8	14.3
.222 Rem.	50	1.4	6.8
.223 Rem.	55	1.2	5.3
.22/250 Rem.	55	1.1	4.6
.220 Swift	55	1	4.1
.243 Win.	80	1.2	4.4
.243 Win.	100	.8	3.5
6mm Rem.	80	1.2	4.3
6mm Rem.	100	.8	3.2
.250 Savage	100	1.2	5.1
.257 Roberts	117	1.3	6.6
.25/06 Rem.	120	.7	3.3
.264 Win. Mag.	140	.8	3.1
.270 Win.	100	1.1	4.1
.270 Win.	130	.7	3.0
.270 Win.	150	.8	3.6
.270 Weatherby	130	.5	2.5
.284 Win.	150	.7	3.6
7mm Weatherby	160	.5	2.2
7mm Mauser	175	1.3	6.6
7mm/08 Rem.	140	.6	3.1
7mm Rem. Express	150	.8	3.5
7mm Rem. Mag.	125	.9	3.5
7mm Rem. Mag.	150	.8	3.3
7mm Rem. Mag.	175	.6	2.9
.30 Carbine	110	3.9	17.5
.30/30 Win.	150	2.3	10.7
.30/30 Win.	170	2.8	12.3
.300 Savage	150	1.2	4.8
.308 Win.	125	1.2	4.8
.308 Win.	150	1	4.4

| *DRIFT OF COMMON RIFLE CALIBERS IN 10-MPH CROSSWIND* | | | |
Caliber	Bullet Weight (Grains)	100 yards (Inches)	200 yards (Inches)
.308 Win.	180	.8	3.9
.30/06	110	1.5	5.9
.30/06	125	.8	4.2
.30/06	150	1.2	4.2
.30/06	180	.7	3.5
.30/06	220	1.2	6.1
.30/40 Krag	180	1.1	4.9
.300 Win. Mag.	150	1	4.2
.300 Win. Mag.	180	.7	3.3
.300 H&H	180	.8	3.3
.300 Weatherby Mag.	150	.6	2.7
.300 Weatherby Mag.	180	.5	2.5
.303 British	180	1.5	7.2
.32 Winchester Special	170	2.0	8.9
8mm Mauser	170	2.2	10.2
8mm Rem. Mag.	220	.8	3.6
.338 Win. Mag.	250	1.1	4.2
.348 Win.	200	1.2	6.1
.35 Rem.	200	2	8.5
.358 Win.	200	1.3	6.7
.358 Win.	250	1.5	6.7
.375 H&H	300	1.4	5.8
.378 Weatherby Mag.	300	1.1	4.8
.444 Marlin	240	3.3	15.4
.45/70	405	4.4	15.8
.458 Win. Mag.	500	1.7	6.9
.460 Weatherby Mag.	500	1.2	5.0

The wind-drift calculations in this table were computed from ballistic tables published by major manufacturers of sporting ammunition. The process involved computer analysis of the published muzzle velocity and downrange velocities, from which a probable ballistic form for each bullet was composed. Again using manufacturers' published velocities, the wind-drift data was compiled.

There are, of course, considerable differences in the ballistic forms of bullets of different makes, even though they are the same weight and caliber. The less streamlined of the two is more affected by wind. Generally, the bullets represented in the above table were the best ballistic performers in the given caliber and weight range. The data for the .270 Winchester, for example, with 130-grain bullet, is for the Remington Bronze Point bullet, which performs slightly better in the wind than does the Remington pointed Core-Lokt bullet.

Seeming contradictions in the table are explained by varying initial velocities and widely different bullet shapes.

Chapter 11

BULLET PERFORMANCE ON GAME

The way bullets behave when they hit game is a truly wonderful topic for hunting-camp debates because factual information is virtually impossible to come by. Every opinion is right and wrong, depending on how you look at it. Let me explain this contradiction.

The purpose of a hunting bullet is to kill game, be it as small as a squirrel or as big as a moose. If the animal is killed, there is little argument about the fact that the bullet did its job. But if the game does not go down and is lost, we cannot conclusively state that the bullet failed. If the animal is not recovered, the hunter can't always be sure the animal was hit, much less know *where* it was hit.

In recent times a new term, *terminal ballistics,* has crept into the language of shooters. This is the study of the way bullets behave upon striking flesh, bones, or any other impact medium. I'm not sure the terminal performance of bullets should be called ballistics. Ballistics is a science, and predicting what bullets will do when they hit an animal is something of a guessing game. Certain military and police agencies now use computers to predict the relative lethality of different types of bullets striking different areas of the human torso. But whereas a computer can determine the flight path of a given bullet to within one one-hundredth of an inch, or remaining velocity to within a fractional part of one foot per second, computer programs can only make generalized predictions about terminal bullet performance. Therefore I'm not going to pester you with a discussion of theoretical terminal ballistics that wouldn't really tell us what we want to know. Instead, let's talk about hunting bullets and what we want them to do.

HOW GAME IS KILLED

Game is killed or rendered immobile by bullets in a number of ways or combinations of ways. The most basic way is simply to interrupt vital life processes. For example, a bullet hole in the heart halts or impairs the organ's function of supplying blood. With no circulation or inadequate circulation, the animal dies rapidly. A bullet hole in the lungs creates violent bleeding that floods the vital air passages, causing the animal to die of oxygen starvation. A bullet in the brain can cause instantaneous cessation of all vital functions, and a bullet that severs the spinal column will cause instant stoppage of all bodily functions that take place aft of the hit. This, too, can cause quick death. Even a hit in the spinal column that is quite far to the rear will paralyze the hind legs and immobilize the animal. The speed of death depends on the severity of the wound. A deer that has suffered massive or explosive damage to the heart or lungs, or both, usually dies more quickly than one in which these organs are cleanly pierced or only nicked.

Game animals can also be killed, often quickly, by damaging secondary vital organs. These include the liver and kidneys, which are richly supplied with blood vessels. Rupture of these organs brings about massive blood loss that leads to death in minutes or even seconds. Another, though seldom mentioned, secondary vital organ is the diaphragm. This muscular tissue is the driving force of the lungs, and when its operation is halted, suffocation follows.

Animals are also rendered immobile and killed with what seems to be instantaneous swiftness by something vaguely known as shock effect, or hydrostatic shock. This phenomenon is what oldtimers commonly call "knockdown power." Actually, bullets don't knock animals down, at least not in the way a cow standing on a railroad track is knocked over by a speeding locomotive. It sometimes *appears,* however, that a deer is knocked down or has the earth jerked out from under its feet because of the way the animal may fall at the crack of the rifle. This instant paralysis is apparently caused by massive shock to the nervous system that transmits commands from the brain, both voluntary and involuntary, to the limbs and organs. For instance, a shot high in the shoulder can make the lights go out in the heart and lungs and turn a deer's front legs to instant rubber.

The mechanics of this phenomenon are based on the fact that an animal's body is composed largely of water. Water is an excellent conductor of shock waves. To illustrate, drop a penny in a calm swimming pool, and the waves travel many feet. The transfer of shock from a high-energy bullet can have an almost explosive effect on surrounding tissue, especially the nervous system. According to Webster, "hydrostatic" means "of or relating to liquids at rest or the pressures they transmit." The last part of this definition applies to what we're talking about, but I'm inclined to believe that "hydrodynamic" comes a lot closer to describing what happens when bullet shock is transmitted. Hydrodynamics is the branch of hydromechanics that describes how shock waves, transmitted via fluids, affect solid materials submerged therein.

Anyone who shoots prairie dogs with a high-velocity varmint rifle is abundantly aware of the way the small animals are sometimes blown in half or even into smaller fragments by the impact of the bullet. This explosive effect is a graphic illustration of hydrostatic shock in action. We do not observe this so clearly in larger animals because the bullet and its shock effect are proportionally so much smaller.

Another way of describing shock is *transfer of energy*. When gunpowder burns, it releases a tremendous quantity of energy that is transferred to the bullet in the form of kinetic energy. Some of this energy is used up as the bullet plows its way through the atmosphere, but at normal hunting ranges the bullet still arrives on target as an impressive package of energy.

When the bullet strikes a game animal or fleshlike impact medium, its velocity is quickly arrested, which means that the energy is rapidly transmitted from the bullet to the surrounding flesh. This is the source of hydrostatic shock. From this deliberately oversimplified description of energy transfer, one might logically conclude that in order to achieve the most devastating shock effect, we would simply use a high-energy cartridge for hunting. Following this logic a step further, we would conclude that the most efficient way to get energy from the gun into the target is in the form of high velocity. As we already know, if we double a bullet's weight, we only double its energy, but if we double its velocity, we *quadruple* its energy. This is one of the major reasons that 20th-century sporting-cartridge development has been primarily directed toward higher bullet velocities. As we shall see, however, there is a lot more to killing efficiency than bullet energy. This leads us to the problem of how to transfer kinetic energy from the bullet to the animal in the form of hydrostatic shock. This is where bullet expansion comes into the picture.

BULLET EXPANSION

When a well-designed and properly made bullet strikes a mass of animal tissue at an effective velocity, the front section collapses and peels backward. More specifically, the front portion of the copper jacket ruptures, exposing the soft lead core, which flattens and expands outward much as if it were being pounded by a hammer. In fact, one can usually get a graphic, slow-motion demonstration of bullet expansion by putting a bullet (not the entire cartridge) in a large vise and slowly tightening the jaws. Usually, the nose will rupture and peel back in the classic mushroom shape. That's why bullet expansion is frequently called *mushrooming*. We can make a bullet mushroom by firing it into water. This is how bullet makers usually test the expansion characteristics of their products. How does a mushroomed bullet benefit the hunter? It is widely assumed that a beautifully mushroomed bullet has a deadly effect on game because it makes a larger hole in the animal's body. To a certain extent, this is beneficial, but it's not nearly so important as the drag or "parachute" effect that occurs as the bullet expands.

You can give yourself a first-hand example of this parachute effect and how it aids energy transfer. The next time you are in a swimming pool, slap the water hard with your open hand, palm down. Then hit the water again with the same force but with the edge of your hand. The edge of your hand cleaves the water rather cleanly and penetrates well below the surface. When you hit with your palm, the larger frontal area causes a much bigger splash and more waves. The impact stings your hand more, and your hand doesn't penetrate so deeply.

The comparatively large volume of water adjacent to and below your open palm, as compared to the comparatively small volume below your hand's edge, can't accelerate fast enough to get out of the way. The kinetic energy of your open hand is therefore transferred to the water and manifests itself in the form of shock, which we see as waves. Applying this observation to bullet performance, we can easily visualize the comparative effects of expanding and non-expanding bullets.

Several years ago when I was an impressionable lad with buckets of water behind each ear, a representative of a then-fledgling archery manufacturer came to our gun-club meeting. Bowhunting was just getting started then, and the salesman was eager to demonstrate to our group the lethality of a sharp hunting arrow. Adjourning to the club range, he set up a sandbag which was about a foot thick and proceeded to have at it with a .30/30 rifle at about 15 paces. Everyone had a close look and noted that while there was an entrance hole in the bag, the bullet clearly had not exited.

Next he nocked a broadhead-tipped hunting arrow in a powerful bow and, again from 15 paces, proceeded to drive the arrow almost completely through the bag of sand. The head protruded several inches. Of course, all who witnessed the demonstration were tremendously impressed by what appeared to be the obvious superiority of the bow over the bullet. One doubting club member was so convinced that the salesman was using reduced .30/30 loads that he bid us wait while he went home to fetch his .30/06 and "real" ammo. We were happy to oblige, and I fully expected the archery salesman to be exposed as a faker. But when the club hero let fly with his 06, the sandbag ballooned and dust puffed from the fabric, but alas, there was no exit hole. To make his victory complete, the salesman emptied the sandbag and showed us the remains of our fallen hero's battered and expanded .30/06 bullet. That demonstration was a tremendous boost to local archery sales.

To be fair to the salesman, he may not have been aware that he was giving us a demonstration of energy transfer and was actually offering proof of the bullet's superior lethality. Had we wished to carry his demostration to its logical conclusion, the next step would have been to glue a bullet to the arrow point foremost. When launched from a bow the penetration of the bullet would have been about the same as the broadheads. Even more revealing, one of us could have simply pushed the bullet-tipped arrow through the sandbag by hand. Why, then, didn't the .30/06 bullet penetrate the sandbag when fired at a velocity of some 2,800 feet per second?

It did not for the same reason that the motion of your open palm is quickly arrested when you slap the surface of a swimming pool. The arrow, traveling at a relatively low velocity, easily pushes the grains of sand apart and cleaves its way through. Likewise, we can push a bullet-tipped arrow through the same volume of sand by hand. But when that same bullet is traveling at high velocity, the particles of sand simply can't accelerate fast enough to get out of the way. Of course, a small volume of sand would be blown apart, but a larger volume contacted by the bullet can't move fast enough to get out of the bullet's way because it is backed up by more grains of sand that, in turn, can't accelerate out of the way fast enough. As its velocity is thus violently slowed, the bullet nose ruptures and expands, which again increases the number of sand particles it is pushing against.

Though this sandbag demonstration gives us a graphic picture of energy transfer, an even more dramatic example is provided by a plastic jug filled with water. Again, a bullet attached to a shaft can be pushed through the jug by hand. The result is a couple of round holes through which the water leaks out. Next, the same bullet-tipped arrow is shot through the jug at a velocity of a few hundred feet per second with a bow. Again, the shaft penetrates cleanly. Finally the same bullet is fired into the jug at a velocity of over 2,000 fps with a rifle. The effect is

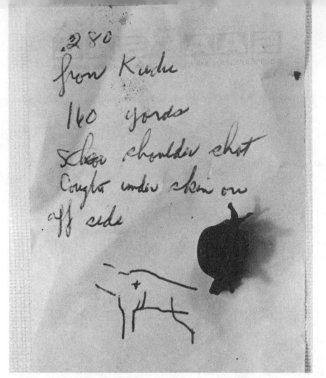

.280
from Kudu
160 yards
schee shoulder shot
Cought under skin on
off side

One of Carmichel's notes, made on an African safari, records the performance of a .280 bullet with which he took a kudu at 160 yards. The mushroomed bullet, which went through the animal's shoulder and stopped under the hide on the far side, is shown on the note paper. The second photo shows two bullets that expanded quite differently but retained most of their weight, and a piece of another that fragmented. The third picture shows four solids retrieved from elephants and buffalo. All four retained their original shape and, except for the marks of the rifling, show hardly a sign of having been fired.

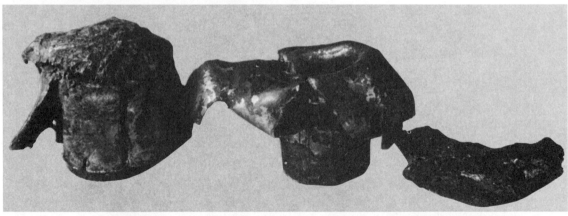

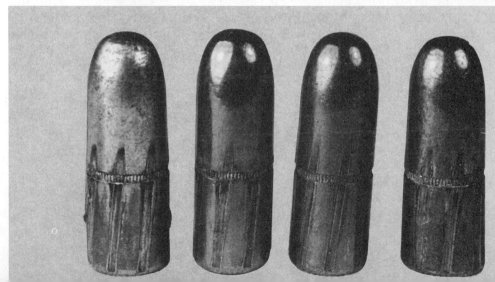

spectacular. The jug explodes in a shower of water. We are seeing hydrostatic, or rather, hydrodynamic shock. The bullet's energy is rapidly transferred to the water and the resulting shock wave wrecks the jug. This is quite similar to the shock effect a high-velocity bullet has on animal tissue, and we readily see how and why the animal's nervous system is grossly disrupted.

The foregoing examples of bullet expansion and the dynamics of energy transfer are only part of the story. The reason I go into such detail is to provide background that will help us understand why some bullets are constructed as they are, why other bullets should not be constructed as they are, and why it is best that some bullets do not expand at all.

THE THICK AND THIN OF BULLET JACKETS

Clearly, if all bullets behaved as they should by mushrooming in a well-mannered way, it would be a very good thing. But, something always comes along to complicate matters and interfere with orderly progress. In the case of bullet performance on game, we have abundant complications. The crux of the problem is to match the bullet to the velocity at which it will hit game. To give you an example of the varieties of problems that can occur with bullet construction, let's use an imaginary cartridge which we'll name the .270 Super Sabre Magnum Express. On paper, the .270 SSME looks great, whistling a 100-grain bullet out the tube at 3,600 fps for a computed muzzle energy of 2,326 foot-pounds. Obviously, this is more than enough energy to dispatch a deer in his tracks, but for some queer reason we keep getting reports of deer that were well hit with the .270 SSME but got away. This doesn't make sense because a bullet going that fast must deliver a terrific hydrostatic shock, and as we've already learned, nothing jerks out the rug like shock.

One day, you succumb to the lure of the .270 SSME, and the very first time you take it afield, you get a shot at a nice eight-pointer at a distance of about 60 yards. Naturally, at that short range, you expect a hit from the magic .270 SSME to spell instant lights out. To your utter amazement, the big buck takes a few steps before keeling over. Inspecting the freshly killed deer, you note that there's a fist-sized exit hole in the right side of the chest. This is understandable, because a bullet going as fast as the .270 SSME is expected to cause a big exit wound. But wait a minute! That buck was traveling left to right when you shot. That means the bullet *hit* the right side of the animal. Still not believing what your logic tells you, you roll the deer over, and sure enough, there's no hole on the left side. That means the crater-sized hole is where the bullet hit. What's going on?

Dressing out the carcass, you note that there is not much blood in the chest cavity and that neither the heart nor the lungs have been punctured. Instead, the lungs are the deep-red color characteristic of a massive bruise. Further inspection of the chest wall shows similar hematomata, and there is no clearcut sign of a bullet hole. But this is difficult to say for sure because the inside of the right chest wall (the pleural lining) is liberally spiked with fragments from a shattered rib.

Gradually the pieces fit together, and you conclude that the bullet actually exploded upon hitting the deer's rib on the near side. In other words, the bullet explosively shed its energy after penetrating only an inch or less. This accounts for the craterlike wound and the shattered rib.

Probably, if the bullet had not hit the rib, it would have penetrated deeper, but as it was, the deer was killed by lung damage resulting from shock and a scattering of bone fragments.

Thinking back on the reports of deer getting away after being hit with the .270 SSME, you realize that much the same could have happened in your case. You write a letter to the makers of .270 SSME ammo, complaining about poor bullet construction and suggesting that they use a thicker bullet jacket that won't fragment on impact and thereby give better penetration.

As it happens, the makers of the .270 SSME have been receiving scores of complaints like yours and realize the need to toughen their bullet jackets. Accordingly, the next lot of bullets is made a lot thicker in the jacket, and the company announces that the premature expansion problem is solved. Next season, you're on a mule deer hunt in Utah and see a fine buck in a stand of aspen out at about 350 yards. This is just the sort of shot your .270 SSME was made for, so you turn the magnification on your variable-power scope up to full horsepower. Taking a solid rest on a log, you center the crosshairs on the big buck's chest.

At the crack of the rifle, the buck stops feeding, raises his head, and casually looks around. Apparently, the shot was a clean miss, and you're so amazed that you forget to crank another round into the chamber. The buck walks into a draw, and in a few steps is out of sight.

Hoping for another shot, you race to the top of a ridge where you will have a view of the draw where the buck disappeared. With luck, you might get another shot. When you cross the ridge, you spot the buck and drop into position for another shot. But you're breathing so hard from the climb that the crosshairs won't stay on the buck's chest, so you make yourself hold off for a moment. After all, the buck is standing quietly. As you watch through the riflescope, the buck begins acting strangely. First he wobbles on his feet, standing wide-footed to remain upright. Then he lies down, and his head sags. You realize the big buck is dead. What happened?

Dressing out the deer, you find that the bullet cleanly entered the chest cavity, penetrated the lungs, and made a tiny exit hole. Obviously, the bullet did not expand at all, and therefore shed little energy in the buck's vital area. Judging by the condition of the lungs, there was very little shock effect, and the cause of death was that the animal literally drowned in the blood that leaked into his lungs. Apparently, the bullet passed through his body so easily that the deer scarcely realized he had been hit.

Piecing the evidence together, you conclude that the problem this time was a bullet jacket too thick and tough to expand at reduced velocities. The thin-jacketed bullet you used a year before had been too fragile for impact velocities in the 3,500 fps range; the thicker jacket you used on mule deer failed to expand at the 350 yard range where velocity had dropped to about 2,400 fps.

Of course, you're all steamed up about your two near disasters with the .270 SSME and vow to write another hot letter to the management when you get home. But that night, shoving chili down your neck by the campfire, you begin to understand the frustrations of a bullet maker. It occurs to you that the thick-jacketed bullet would have been great last year when you had a close shot and a thin-jacketed bullet might have expanded beautifully in the mule deer at long range.

How can ammunition manufacturers and makers of bullets for reloaders determine the velocity at which a bullet will arrive on target? Of course, they learn a lot from practical ex-

Before and after—a plastic milk container filled with water is used here to demonstrate hydrodynamics and the parachute effect of an expanding bullet. An animal's body is composed largely of water, and it is this violent displacement—a transfer of energy—that knocks down game efficiently.

perience, and reports from the field play a major role in bullet evolution. Still, bullet making often boils down to wise compomise. Sometimes the results are wonderful, and sometimes, inevitably, the hunter is not so well equipped as he supposes.

BRUSH BUSTERS DON'T BUST BRUSH

A very good example of this is provided by the so-called "brush busting" cartridges. A good example is the .444 Marlin with its muzzle velocity of 2,350 fps with the 240-grain bullet and a 100-yard remaining velocity of 1,815. The thumb-sized slug with its blunt ice-cream-cone nose looks like a brush hunter's dream, but let's take a critical look at the real situation. Since the velocity is low, it is necessary to use a thin jacket in order to insure reliable mushrooming. This is all well and good, and the bullet maker's burden is eased somewhat by the knowledge that hunting shots with the .444 Marlin will seldom exceed 100 yards.

The lizard in the stew, however, is that the .444 will most often be used in dense cover where there is some likelihood that the bullet will run into twigs and limbs on its way to the target. In fact, it is precisely for this purpose that the .444 is usually selected. But damn it, thin bullet jackets and brush don't go together, especially when the bullet features a full-moon nose with lots of exposed lead core. When the bullet hits a finger-thick twig, the exposed lead snags, or grabs for an instant. The jacket tears and the bullet becomes misshapen. This is followed by loss of direction and a rapid decay of stability. With some thin-jacketed bullets, it is common for the copper jacket to be ripped off the lead core entirely. In any event, a well-aimed shot often becomes a miss.

The bullet maker's dilemma is that if he uses a heavier jacket, the bullet won't mushroom properly, and letters of protest will rain down upon him. What then is the solution?

Bullets with thicker jackets are more likely to penetrate brush successfully, especially if a minimum of lead is exposed at the tip. Therefore the best brush buckers are fast-stepping cartridges loaded with pointed bullets. As a practical matter, however, we're only kidding ourselves with the notion that we can shoot through brush with impunity if we're equipped with anything less formidable than a .450 No. 2 Nitro Express loaded with 480-grain solids. Perhaps surprisingly, the cartridges that have continually demonstrated the best performance in woods hunting are those that offer a combination of flat trajectory and "shootability," meaning those that are easy to shoot accurately through holes in the brush. A prime example is the .250 Savage.

SINGLE-PACKAGE DELIVERY

Energy that is intended to kill game is most efficient when delivered in a single package. You could demonstrate this to yourself by throwing a brick through a plate-glass window. If you ground the brick into dust, you could throw the handful of particles at the window as hard as possible, but the glass wouldn't break. Even though the combined energy of the thrown brick particles is equal to that of the one-piece brick, their combined *effect* is far less impressive. So it

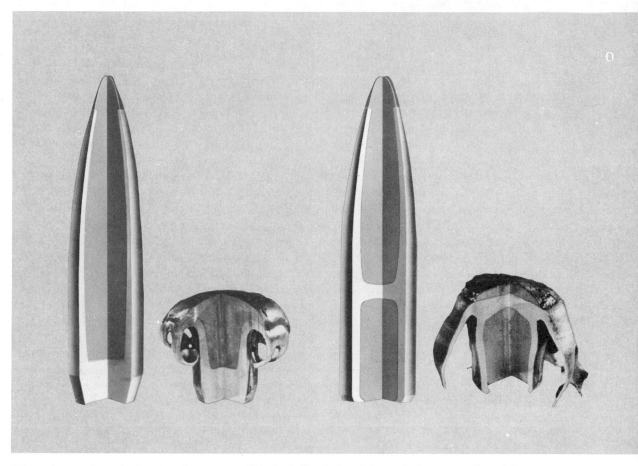

These pictures show the interior of two types of Nosler bullets before firing and after penetration and expansion in game. The Solid Base style is at left, the Partition bullet at right. The mushroomed bullets have been cut away to show the inner core after impact.

is with bullets. That's why bullets that remain in one piece are more effective on game than bullets that fragment. If, for example, a bullet breaks in half, the two pieces will not penetrate nearly so deeply nor cause so much internal damage as will one larger piece. Though one might be lured into assuming that two holes are better than one hole, it doesn't work that way, as we shall investigate when we get to the topic of momentum.

The desirability of keeping a bullet in one piece presents another problem to bullet makers. When a bullet mushrooms it is, in effect, coming apart, or beginning to do so, and therein lies a dilemma. One way of coming to grips (or at least compromising) with the problem is represented by the Nosler Partition bullet. This bullet is made up of two separate lead cores, fore and aft, divided by a solid partition which is integral with the jacket. The idea of the partition bullet is that even if the front part expands violently and even fragments, the rear section will remain intact and continue to penetrate. I've used the Nosler Partition bullet on a variety of game, from pronghorns to Kodiak bear to Cape buffalo, and the bullets I've recovered have almost always peeled back to the partition, shedding most or all of the lead in the front section. Invariably, the rear section has remained intact and penetrated satisfactorily.

In the late 1970's when I was hunting lion in a country then known as the Central African Empire, I ran across an especially large and particularly nasty lion. While he was in the act of charging from a distance of some 40 yards, I pumped three 250-grain Noslers into his hide with a .338 Winchester Magnum

By the time he was within a few paces, he was pretty much out of the mood to bite anyone and did a nosedive. All three Noslers did a fine job, and two of them exited, but I was especially impressed with one that hit the point of his left shoulder, transversed his body, and semi-exited on the left flank. The reason I say "semi-exited" was because while it was transversing the lion's body, the bullet got turned around and traveled base first. When it turned around, the peeled-back fingers of the jacket became grab hooks. These fingers hooked into the tough hide, which stopped the bullet.

That brings up the bullets we occasionally find just under the offside skin of a well-shot game animal. This is generally applauded because it is said that the bullet penetrated perfectly and yet imparted its last final ounce of energy within the animal. But it ain't necessarily so.

Animal skin is an amazingly tough and efficient bullet catcher. I got my first inkling of this many years ago when I was hunting groundhogs with my old pal Buck Fleenor in the hills of East Tennessee. Buck was on one ridge, and I was on another. A chuck below us was eating his way through some poor hillbilly's turnip patch. From where I was, I could see the offside of the chuck, and when Buck's .243 bullet struck, I was amazed to see the hide stretch out a foot or so and then snap back. Sure 'nuff, a large fragment of the thin-jacketed varmint bullet was found just under the hide. Years later, I was situated pretty much the same way on an elk hunt and was again amazed to see the offside hide of a bull stretch out well over a foot in a tentlike configuration when a heavy bullet hit. All this happens in a split second, and you have to be looking right at it with binoculars to see it. Since then, I've asked a number of professional guides if they've ever seen the same thing, and several said they had. Some insist that the skin extends as much as two feet.

The elastic skin gives when the bullet hits it from the inside and gradually arrests the projectile's momentum. The effect is about like trying to hurl a rock through a trampoline, and merely stretching a patch of skin does no real damage. I expect that properly expanded bullets traveling at several hundred fps are thus caught just under the skin.

A major cause of bullets coming apart on impact is separation of the jacket from the core. Once the two are separated, efficiency decays rapidly. One reason is that the copper jacket by itself is so light in weight that its velocity is quickly arrested. The soft lead core without the strong copper corset to hold it together is torn apart by its own energy. Obviously, penetration is thereby reduced dramatically.

CORE BONDING

A number of ways have been devised to bond cores to jackets and thereby keep fragmentation or "weight shedding" to a minimum while at the same time allowing for adequate mushrooming.

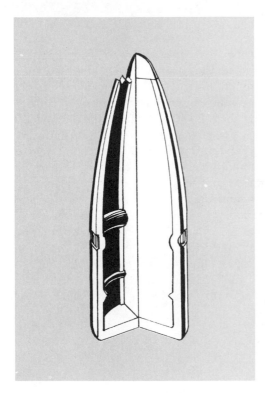

This cut-away drawing shows the interior of Hornady's Interlock bullet construction. A flange inside the lower part of the jacket interlocks with the core—gripping and keeping it in place to minimize fragmentation as the bullet mushrooms.

Perhaps the best known of these is Speer's Hot Cor process, in which bullets are made by pouring molten lead into the jacket cup to insure an extremely close core-to-jacket union. Another bonding technique is to glue the core into the jacket by means of epoxy or modern super glue. The Bitterroot bullet, which has an enviable reputation for minimal weight shedding, is apparently core-bonded by some sort of super glue.

A fellow by the name of Williams who operated in Texas once made some remarkable core-bonded .17-caliber bullets. I never used any of his tiny bullets for big game, but I expect these were the pills used by Vern O'Brien in taking Alaskan brown bears with his hot little .17 Mach IV rifles, a stunt I hope no one ever tries to repeat.

Another approach to the problem is represented by the Speer Grand Slam bullets which are almost two bullets in one. The jacket is made in varying thicknesses. The base half is relatively thick and becomes thinner toward the point. The core is made in two pieces. The base core is made of a hard lead alloy, and the nose core is made of softer lead. The soft lead nose held by a relatively thin jacket insures ready expansion, but mushrooming is progressively slowed as the bullet peels back toward the tougher base half.

Hornady gets at the problem with the Interlock bullet. There is a flange inside the lower part of the jacket which grips, or interlocks, with the core and keeps it in place.

A somewhat different approach to the problem which falls somewhere between the partition and Speer dual-core concepts is the bullet-within-a-bullet. The only bullets of this type with which I have any experience are made by Californian Ken Clark for his ultra-hotshot .224 Clark. Though of standard .224 caliber, this wildcat uses extra-heavy bullets in the 80-grain range. Figuring, correctly, that an open-pointed varmint bullet would fragment on deer-size game, Clark devised a cylindrical, fully jacketed unit which is tightly fitted inside a conventional pointed jacket. On impact at high velocity (and the .224 Clark *is* fast), the outer jacket presumably ruptures and strips away, leaving the inner bullet to go on its way. Though this inner bullet may be considered of full-patch non-expanding configuration, I expect that it becomes highly unstable when the outer jacket is lost and the core begins tumbling. The result of this internal performance would be about the same as that of a well-mushroomed slug.

Being a profoundly inventive breed, gun and ammo makers have long sought ways to achieve the perfect mushroom, and their efforts are too varied and sometimes too bizarre to detail here. Europeans have come up with all sorts of fancy ways to control expansion, and these are pretty much in step with the best results achieved in North America. The famed H-Mantel bullet loaded in Germany's RWS rifle ammo, for example, is quite similar in design and performance to the Nosler Partition bullet. The H-Mantel jacket is folded so that a deep inner flange is formed which pretty much partitions the core into two halves. The bullet's cross-

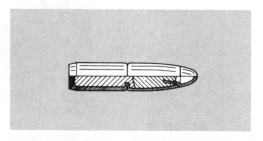

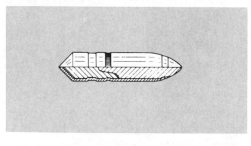

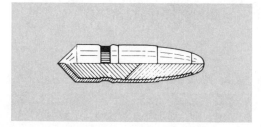

Control of expansion is achieved in several different ways by the bullets loaded in Germany's RWS ammunition. The famous H-Mantel bullet (top) is much like the Nosler Partition. Its jacket is folded to form a deep inner flange—an H-shape that divides the core into two halves. Another RWS bullet, the Brenneke-designed TIG (Torpedo Ideal) is shown at center. It has a hardened rear core with a funnel-shaped recess into which the front portion fits like a plug. At bottom is the Brenneke TUG (Torpedo Universal) whose hard rear core projects into a recess in the front lead portion.

section looks like the letter H, hence the name. Also well known and much respected in European shooting circles are the Brenneke-designed TIG (Torpedo Ideal) and TUG (Torpedo Universal) bullets. Each of these features a two-piece core with the rear part being of a harder alloy. Likewise, each has the jacket crimped near the base with a resulting internal flange that holds the core in place. Considering the years of success these bullets have enjoyed, it doesn't take much imagination to see where Speer and Hornady got the inspiration for their Grand Slam and Interlock features.

LOSS OF WEIGHT

We assume that a good hunting bullet is one that mushrooms reliably, and further assume that it is the nature of bullets to shed particles of core and jacket as they mushroom. The question that begs to be answered is how much weight can a bullet lose and still do its work effectively? Of course, this is open to all sorts of variables, not the least important of which are the initial weight of the bullet and the relative size of the game animal. For example, a 300-grain bullet from a .375 H&H Magnum can lose half its weight and still have more than sufficient mass to wreck a whitetail deer. But by the same measure, if this bullet loses half its weight in a Cape buffalo, the hunter might find himself needing to make some quick apologies.

Since most of our game is shot with more or less "matching class" cartridges, we can make some fairly reasonable determinations about what constitutes acceptable bullet weight. Whenever I kill big game, I make every effort to recover the slug from the carcass. Sometimes this has meant an hour of poking through elk plumbing during a blizzard, and sometimes it has been as simple as offering African skinners a cigarette for every recovered bullet. What I've learned has surely been worth the effort and the cigarettes. Before retiring a sweet-handling bolt-action .280 custom rifle by Clayton Nelson, I used it to take some 200 assorted head of the world's big game. Ranging in size from the African impala up through elk, most were killed with 140-grain 7mm Noslers. Almost all of the recovered bullets have a remaining weight of some 70 or 75 grains. On the surface, this sounds pretty scary because it represents 50 percent loss of mass.

However, since the bullets in question always gave exactly the results I wanted, I have to conclude that a 50 percent loss of weight in a bullet is acceptable, *provided* the bullet is of adequate weight initially. If, say, these bullets had weighed only 75 grains to begin with and had then shed half their weight, my experiences might not have been so favorable. Occasionally, hunters and bullet makers write me about recovered slugs that have lost as little as 20 or even 10 percent of their original weight. This is cause for rejoicing. The bonded-core Bitterroot bullets in particular have a reputation for minimal weight loss. Recovered specimens I've examined sometimes even have chunks of lead adhering to the fingers of peeled-back jacket material. This is remarkable when you consider that the two metals remained stuck together under forces that ripped the front of the bullet apart. No doubt the glue is mighty strong, and the performance justifies the expense of using these hand-built bullets.

In most cases, however, individual results aren't sufficient cause to rejoice or condemn the product. We need several samples to form a valid opinion. Several years ago while on safari in a fledgling African republic, I found myself in territory that was richly inhabited by both lion and Cape buffalo. I was mainly interested in hunting lion. Accordingly, I kept my .458 Magnum loaded with 500-grain soft-point expanding bullets that generate a terrific shock effect and make a lion go "all loose." Since buffalo were scattered through the tall grass where I was hunting, I began to wonder how well off I'd be if one acted ugly and I had to shoot it with a soft rather than the bone-busting solids that are preferred for buffalo.

I had a chance to find out after downing a particularly tough old bull with a prescribed dose of solid medicine. I had my trackers prop the bull up on his brisket in a more or less erect position. Then I backed off a few paces and let fly at his shoulder with a couple of soft-nose .458 loads. The reason for firing two shots was to double the chances of finding the bullets in the massive carcass, and as luck would have it, both were recovered.

One was beautifully mushroomed and had a very gratifying remaining weight of 421 grains out of the original 500. Based on the performance of that bullet, I would have felt snug and secure in buff country even when loaded with softs. But the other bullet was a total failure. The twisted remainder of the core was completely separated from the jacket, and their combined weight was considerably less than half the original. Thereafter, whenever my rifle was loaded with softs, a handful of solids was never farther away than my pants pocket.

I am equally disinclined to base bullet performance judgments on the pretty samples distributed by ammo and component makers. This is certainly not because they would knowingly misrepresent their products but simply because they unwittingly make the boy fit the shoes rather than vice versa. Many ammo makers test the expansion characteristics of their bullets by firing them into tanks of water at differing velocities. Since flesh is largely water, the assumption is that bullets will mushroom about the same in one as in the other. Water, however, is wonderfully uniform and free of hide, hair, and bones. Bullets fired into water tend to expand with beautiful symmetry. Since water is the usual test medium, I suspect that bullet makers sometimes get caught up in the innocent trap of designing bullets that perform best in water rather than in game. That's why bullet makers don't really know a new bullet has the right stuff until field reports begin filtering in.

Occasionally, I get letters from hunters, especially those who anticipate shots at very long range, asking if it would be a good idea to use the ultra-streamlined, superbly accurate match bullets made by the top component makers. At first thought this sounds like a thundering good idea, because the match-grade bullets made by Hornady, Sierra, Speer, et al, are beautifully accurate and so streamlined in shape that remaining velocities at long range are sometimes significantly higher than the remaining velocities of ordinary hunting bullets of similar weight. Therefore, they have the additional advantages of a flatter trajectory and less sensitivity to wind. What's more, almost all of the match-grade bullets are of hollow-point construction, which would seemingly mean they would expand well. Right here is where we discover the difference between hollow-points and hollow points.

HOLLOW-POINTS AND HOLLOW POINTS

As any barefoot boy who has shot a squirrel with a .22 rifle knows, hollow-points expand readily because the cavity in the bullet's nose collapses outward. That's why hollow-point bullets are

Hollow-points expand readily because the bullet's nose cavity collapses outward. This is especially desirable at low to medium velocities where soft-point bullets may have insufficient energy to expand adequately. Uninformed shooters are sometimes confused by hollow-pointed target bullets which are not designed for expansion. These have very small cavities whose only purpose is to accommodate an ejection rod that removes them from a die during manufacture. On impact, the nose of such a bullet tends to close rather than open. In this picture, it's easy to tell the target bullets from the true hollow-points by the size of the nose cavity.

especially desirable at low to medium velocities where an ordinary soft-point bullet may not expand adequately. Hollow-point bullets are also desirable where explosive expansion is preferable to deep penetration. That's why hollow-point bullets are now often used in police work.

Now let's talk about the other kind of hollow-point bullet, those we see loaded in cartridges for target shooting. Since all we want is accuracy, we don't care if a target bullet expands or not. The hollow point of most target bullets is the result of a manufacturing process that makes wonderfully accurate bullets but, by necessity, forms them with hollow points. I'm not sure that all manufacturers of match bullets use the same process, so I can't speak for all of them. Be that as it may, the process utilizes a single forming die to shape the bullets rather than the multi-part dies used to mass-produce hunting bullets. The advantage of bullet-forming dies with a two-piece outer body is that the bullet is easily removed by opening the die. The problem with a one-piece die is getting the bullet out after it has been shaped. This is done by a slender ejection rod that pushes against the bullet's point. Obviously, if the bullet had a soft lead point, it would be deformed by the ejection rod. Because the bullet has a hollow point, however, the rod engages the almost-closed lips of the jacket and pushes the bullet free of the die without deformation. It's as simple as that.

Naturally, in order for match bullets to be as streamlined as possible, the opening at the point is quite small, and this is why match bullets aren't great for hunting. On impact, the point tends to squeeze together rather than open.

THE SOLID CONCEPT

As concerned as North American hunters are with maximum bullet expansion, it's downright hard for us to believe that on this very globe there are hunters who wouldn't give two pins for an expanding bullet. I've mainly encountered these chaps in Africa, especially South Africa, and I refer to their kind as hole punchers because in their view the best bullets are those that punch the longest hole, preferably out the far side.

Naturally, their preferences in bullets run to solids, meaning non-expanding bullets with a fully cased nose that prevents mushrooming and keeps bullet deformation to a minimum. Let me make it clear that I'm not talking about the solids used in heavy rifles for dangerous game. Here, I'm talking about full-patch bullets in everyday calibers such as .243, .270, .30/06, etc. Using non-expanding bullets in these calibers insures maximum penetration, just what the hole punchers want, but it does not yield nearly as much energy transfer and shock effect as one gets with a mushrooming bullet.

It would be easy to dismiss these fellows as ignorant amateurs, but they tend to be vastly experienced. Some of them shoot more game in a year than many experienced American hunters shoot in a lifetime. So there's no point in arguing with them, and I never try. In fact, I find room for agreement. For instance, I'd much rather have a bullet that doesn't expand than one that fragments or opens up prematurely.

I'm inclined to believe that the preference of the "hole punchers" for non-expanding bullets is largely a matter of philosophy. The African sport hunter is usually attended by a skilled tracker. He himself, more likely than not, is probably a good tracker. Really good trackers can follow a mouse across a concrete parking lot. Therefore, the hunter is not so much concerned about where an animal goes down as about the certainty that it *will* go down. A hole punched through both sides of a game animal's chest represents a certainty that it will fall. By contrast, North American big game hunters prefer instant knockdown, because if an animal is not seen to fall there is a fair chance that it will be lost. It could be true, as the hole punchers claim, that our predilection for mushrooming bullets may be a compromise with American hunting conditions.

About the only experiences American and European hunters usually have with non-expanding bullets occur in the military or in Africa. By international agreement, the bullets loaded in military small arms ammunition are of full-patch, non-expanding construction. This is a humane gesture based on the assumption that such bullets create less nasty wounds.

On the Dark Continent full-patch bullets are pretty much mandatory for the three biggest of the dangerous big five—elephant, rhino, and Cape buffalo. (Please, they are *not* water buffalo!) The full-patch bullet is needed to penetrate an elephant's honeycomb skull or wreck a buffalo without fragmenting and losing its punch. The construction of these thumb-size boulder-busters is variously described as full-patch or full-jacketed, but just say "solid" and everyone will know what you mean, especially in African hunting circles. In African hunting lingo, if a bullet isn't a solid, it's a "soft."

Actually, the construction of solids isn't much different from expanding bullets except that the mouth of the jacket cup is at the nose on expanding bullets. With solids, it's the other way around. The closed end of the cup goes over the nose. I've even heard of emergency solids being made simply by reversing the bullet in the case. As you might expect, however, the jacket of solids is usually much thicker than that of softs and may be made of steel, copper-coated steel, and sometimes even of a copper jacket over a steel lining. Some solids also have a double thickness of copper or steel at the nose to further resist deformation. Yet, despite these precautions, one often hears yarns around safari campfires about how old Ian So And So got done in on elephant control because his solids turned to mush on an elephant's skull.

I've shot a fair number of big stuff with solids, mostly 500-grain Hornadys handloaded in .458 Winchester Magnum cases and the results have invariably been spectacular. The worst that has happened has been a minimal flattening on the sides, probably caused by slapping bone. Some of my bullets recovered from elephant skulls are in amazingly good condition. A few remained so perfectly round and unblemished, except for rifling marks, that one of my pet ambitions is to load them again. Think of it—two elephants with one bullet!

One of the most distinctive characteristics of big-bore, full-patch bullets is the blunted, semi-hemispherical nose. One might suppose that if the deepest possible penetration is the goal of a good solid, then it should do better with a pointed nose. This is true in theory, but there are more important practical considerations. The first is the difficulty of drawing a jacket cup into a streamlined nose shape during manufacture. The extreme drawing required to achieve a sharp nose would very likely result in a thin spot where thickness is most desired. This could allow the jacket to rupture on impact and let the core escape with disastrous results. Also, the blunt nose probably yields a greater shock effect than would a pointed shape.

There are, by the way, full-patch expanding bullets. One of the best known examples is the British .425 Westley Richards Magnum. A hunting pal who once ran a large ranch in Rhodesia used a rifle in this caliber with expanding solids for controlling "vermin" (lions) that got into his cattle. I used his rifle on a couple of hunts and was much impressed by the way it made lion go "all loose" as my guide described it. Back home, I cut one of the .425 bullets open and found a soft outer jacket over a more or less soft-nose bullet. On impact, the soft but full-patch outer shell collapses back and outward in a classic mushroom shape, but at the same time, it prevents any shedding of the core. Thus, retained weight remains 100 percent, and this provides optimum penetration. This is a very workable approach, but making bullets this way is probably expensive.

The large, strange object the author is propping up in one of these photographs is a section of elephant skull—which vividly illustrates why full-patch bullets are needed in Africa. The second picture shows such a bullet, which has retained its shape after penetrating a like mass of bone, and a mushroomed soft-point bullet that was retrieved from plains game. The third picture shows the author with a magnificent Cape buffalo—note the size of the animal's boss, or frontal horn structure, and the spread of the horns. Full-patch bullets are generally used for elephant, buffalo, and rhino.

ENERGY VS. MOMENTUM

If this chapter were to end right here, one would be inclined to sift through the accumulated evidence and arrive at a few broad conclusions. For instance, we know, or at least we think we know, that an effective hunting cartridge is one that delivers an intense package of energy to the target. And since the most efficient way to deliver energy is with velocity, one might further conclude that a relatively light, high-velocity bullet is a more effective energy package and therefore more deadly than a heavier but slower bullet. Theoretically, the best possible combination of both worlds would be a heavy bullet traveling at high velocity, but the practical limit to this sort of thing is how much punishment our shoulders can absorb. Given a limit on allowable recoil, we have to choose between velocity and bullet weight within reasonable tolerances. It's another compromise.

As we already know, when bullet weight is doubled, there is a corresponding doubling of energy, provided velocity remains the same. But if we double the velocity of the same bullet, the energy level is quadrupled. Naturally, high energy figures look mighty impressive in ballistic tables, so it's no wonder that cartridge development during the past several decades has rushed pell-mell toward ever-increased velocities.

When I was a lad, with a dog-eared copy of the *Shooter's Bible* hidden out in the woodshed, the world's most powerful sporting cartridge was the awesome .600 Nitro Express. Perched on the chopping block, I spent hours devouring the *Shooter's Bible* treasure trove of ballistic tables and invariably became giddy about the .600's 900-grain bullet churning up a muzzle energy of 7,600 foot-pounds. Of course, I has no real idea of how much power that represented but I imagined it was enough to blow a haystack apart.

Years later, no doubt weary of references to the giant .600 Nitro, Roy Weatherby achieved the horsepower crown of 8,095 foot-pounds with his .460 Magnum by the simple expedient of shoving a 500-grain bullet out of the muzzle at 2,700 fps. Here we have clear example of using increased velocity to generate more energy, and there is no doubting the incredible deadliness of the .460. But let's take this logic to its extreme conclusion and compare a BB to a .30/06 as a killer of moose. With its 180-grain bullet at a muzzle velocity of 2,700 and muzzle energy of 2,913, the .30/06 is a known performer in the North Woods. But why not simply take a 5-grain .117 caliber air-rifle shot and pack in enough powder to give it a velocity of 16,250 fps? By using the standard energy formula, this would give us an energy level of 2,932 foot-pounds. Surely that's as good as a .30/06. Or is it? Which would you prefer for moose hunting?

Though the spectacle of a BB traveling 16,250 fps is fascinating to contemplate, our reasoning and experience tell us that a 180-grain bullet lumbering along at 2,700 fps is going to be more effective on moose. Buy why? What's the difference? The difference is a matter of *momentum,* the stepchild of ballistic study. The reason momentum is seldom the topic of learned ballistic discourse is that it just ain't as impressive as foot-pounds of energy. For example, if you exclaim to your audience that the .458 Winchester Magnum has a muzzle energy of 4,620 foot-pounds, you'll be rewarded by nods of appreciation. But tell them that it yields a muzzle momentum of 4½ pound-seconds, and you'll receive blank stares. Yet it's momentum that does the work. When we talk about bullet penentration, to a large extent we're talking about momentum. Momentum is the force of a moving object that makes it want to keep pushing ahead, even when something is pushing it back. That's why momentum is expressed in pound-seconds. This figure tells how hard a bullet hits something and also gives us an idea of how *long* it keeps pushing.

To illustrate, let's compare golf balls and ping-pong balls. They are nearly identical in size, but if you roll them across a shag carpet at the same initial speed, the golf ball will continue rolling long after the ping-pong ball has stopped. Though this comparison gets our thinking on the right track, it is unfair because the golf ball is heavier and therefore has more energy. To equalize the test, we give the ping-pong ball a lot more velocity so that the respective launch energies are

Two very dissimilar cartridges with small but important differences in momentum are the .25/06 Remington and the old .300 Savage. At 50 yards, the 100-grain .25/06 will be traveling much faster and will deliver more foot-pounds of energy than the 180-grain .300 Savage—yet the big, slow .300 will penetrate a deer's body more effectively at that range by virtue of its greater momentum.

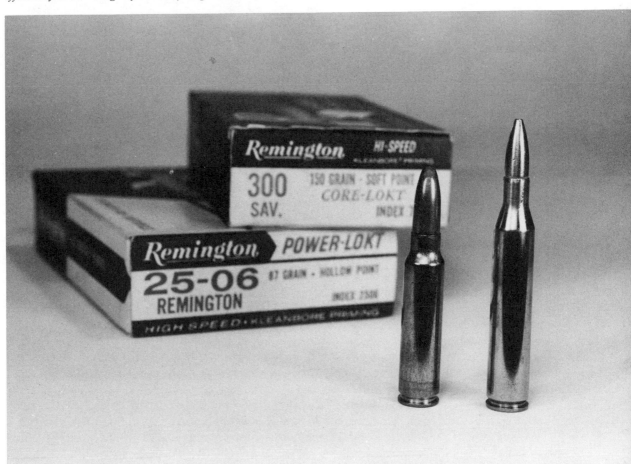

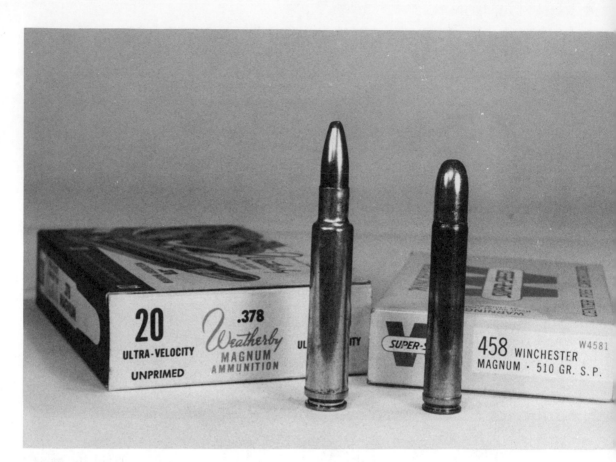

Another interesting comparison involves the speedy, high-energy 300-grain .378 Weatherby Magnum and the seemingly more prosaic 510-grain .458 Winchester. Because the .378 has a muzzle momentum of 3.9 pound-seconds while that of the heavier bullet is 4.53 pound-seconds, the .458 will penetrate an elephant's skull some 20 percent more deeply.

equal. But the golf ball *still* rolls farther through the shag. That's when we realize that the golf ball has something more than just the force of its velocity, that there's something in its weight that makes it want to forge ahead. Looking at it another way, we can simply view momentum as the handmaiden of weight. It may take more energy to get a heavy bullet started, but it requires more effort to stop it. This equals penetration.

Another way of illustrating momentum is to compare two very different cartridges that happen to have similar momentum. Two that come to mind are the speedy .25/06 Remington and the ponderous, almost forgotten, .300 Savage. Assuming we get a shot at a deer at 50 yards, the 100-grain .25/06 bullet will arrive on target at a velocity of 2,877 fps and deliver 2,206 foot-pounds of energy. The .300 Savage, with its 180-grain bullet, gets there at 2,242 fps with 2,008 foot-pounds of energy. Yet the .300 Savage bullet penetrates deeper and more effectively by virtue of its 1.79 pound-seconds of momentum compared to the .25/06 with 1.53 pound-seconds.

A similar comparison should delight hunters of dangerous game. The .378 Weatherby Magnum with a 300-grain bullet has muzzle-velocity and energy figures of 2,925 fps and 5,698 foot-pounds. The more prosaic .458 Winchester starts out with a velocity of 2,040 fps and 4,620 foot-pounds of energy. According to these figures, the poor old .458 isn't in the same league with the .378. But let's see what happens when the bullets run into an elephant's skull. That's where the .458's bullet momentum of 4.53 pound-seconds (at the muzzle) makes it penetrate some 20 percent deeper than the .378 with a momentum of 3.9 pound-seconds.

When one considers momentum, one realizes that perhaps the "old school" of ballistic thought has more to offer than today's high-velocity extremists would have us believe. To a certain extent, this is certainly the case, but don't put all your eggs in the momentum basket. Energy and momentum are easily formulated and we can use either one to prove just about any point we want to make.

The unknown quantity in the performance equation is bullet construction. Until we can predict with certainty how a bullet will behave when it strikes a game animal, all our tables of ballistics, shock effect, and knockdown values still lead to question marks. That's why what we really know about bullet perfomance has been learned in the game fields.

Chapter 12

. . . .

VARMINT RIFLES—THE SUPER-ACCURATE HUNTERS

. . . .

When I was just getting started in this writing business, one of the favorite topics of outdoor magazines was varmint shooting. Hardly an issue hit the newsstands without some sort of article on calling and decoying crows, busting woodchucks with zippy rifles, or sniping at sundry other varmints. I always enjoyed these articles because they represented genuine hard core shooting.

An elk hunt may be a once-in-a-lifetime adventure, and deer season comes only once a year, but varmint shooting is always available: chucks in summer, crows in winter, and other opportunities for thousands of challenging shots.

During the 1950's, authors and editors were burdened by a compulsion to justify the sport. Crows were evil birds that ate duck eggs in Manitoba, and woodchucks dug great holes in the earth in which stupid cows broke their legs and into which farmers on tractors were liable to disappear.

By the 1970's, these excuses were felt to have worn thin and New York's new breed of outdoor editor turned ashen-faced at the thought of murdering these quaint creatures. Articles on varmint shooting all but disappeared from the pages of the major outdoor magazines. The anti-hunters had triumphed again. The wishes of hundreds of thousands of readers who enjoyed varmint hunting were ignored just to appease a handful of anti-hunters, who didn't buy the magazine anyway. I never could figure it out.

Despite a dearth of magazine articles on the subject, varmint hunting is alive and thriving.

Varmint hunting accounts for more expended rifle ammo than all other forms of rifle hunting combined! Varmint shooting has become so important that the varmint rifle now reigns supreme as king of American firearms.

THE BEGINNING

The roots of varmint shooting go back to the late 1800's when an elite band of New England gun tinkerers and target shooters got to messing around with small-caliber cartridges and rifles that they called "pest" guns. Self-contained cartridges and breechloading rifles were still pretty new and most bore sizes were .40 caliber or larger, a big-bore tradition handed down from the

The author in a favorite chuck pasture. He's using a Ruger No. 1 Single-Shot rifle in .220 Swift with a Lyman scope. Earmuffs protect his hearing and a portable rifle rest enhances the long-range accuracy that is the essence of this demanding sport.

Some ideas retain their popularity among varmint shooters for generation after generation. At right, the late Larry Koller, an eminent firearms writer, is shown in the early 1960's with a heavy-barreled rifle that performed well on a wide variety of varmint species, from chucks in summer to foxes in winter. Below, Carmichel is at the bench with another heavy-barreled rifle. Both guns have custom thumbhole stocks that display a striking similarity in comb design and contour.

muzzleloading past. Any bore size less than .32 was small indeed, and .25 caliber was considered impractically tiny, certainly too small for shooting big game or any other worthwhile target. But this was one of the things about the pest guns that some shooters found so appealing. After a generation of earth-shattering buffalo cartridges, thumb-sized musket bullets, and thunderous long-range target loads, it was nice to plink with a mild little outfit that was, well, good for nothing.

The guys who tinkered with these mini-calibers were, for the most part, target shooters. As target shooters are inclined to do, they delighted in seeing how far they could hit small targets such as crows and woodchucks. Their problem was that the little bullets ran out of pep pretty quickly, and beyond a hundred yards or so they went into a steep dive. Even though the early experimenters were pretty advanced for their day they apparently had little idea of how velocity

The antique and the modern in varmint cartridges. At left is a .25/25 Stevens. Cartridges of this type were widely used by target shooters in the late 19th century, and the same loads provided early groundhog ammunition. At right is a 6mm Remington, one of the best of today's varmint rounds.

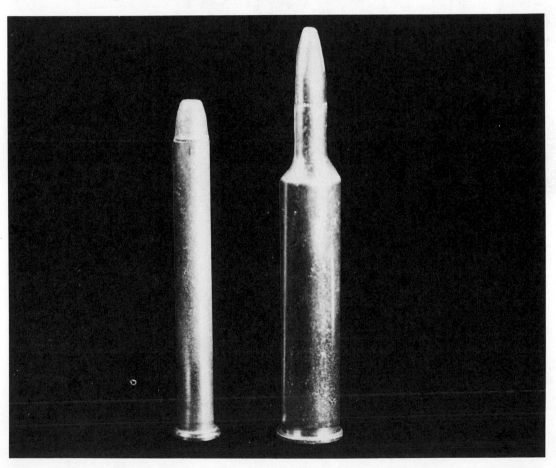

and trajectory are affected by bullet shape because the bullets were of a semi-conical, flat-nose design with poor ballistic efficiency. The overall ballistic performance was something on the order of today's .22 Winchester Rimfire Magnum.

They were well aware, however, that if they were going to hit groundhogs at 200 yards or beyond, they would have to boost velocities above the 1,300-1,500 fps levels. This called for more powder, so the tubelike rimmed cases were made longer in order to increase powder capacity. The only propellent was black powder, which at best generates only moderate velocities, but by burning enough of it behind the light bullets, velocities were increased to about 2,000 fps. Considering the propellents and greased lead bullets of those days, this was a considerable achievement, but accuracy tended to decline as velocity increased and burning all that black powder in a small bore led to heavy fouling after only a few shots. The seeds, however, had been sown in a new garden of ballistic discovery.

THE EARLY SMOKELESS ROUNDS

Though the varmint-shooting landslide did not really begin until the last half of the 1920's, when the .22 Hornet arrived on the scene, there were earlier attempts to produce and popularize small-caliber pest cartridges. The most potent was the .22 Savage High-Power, introduced in 1912. It was based on the old .25/35 Winchester case necked down to an odd (.228) caliber. It had a muzzle velocity of 2,800 fps with a 70-grain bullet. The .22 High-Power was no slouch, even by today's standards. Back then it was a real whizbang, yet it did not herald shooters into the age of varmint shooting because the .22 Savage never had a chance to prove itself. The problem was that the folks at Savage could never decide exactly what to do with their hot round. It would have been a great pest round, but in those conservative days a hunter who wasted his ammo on non-edible creatures was looked upon as a radical spendthrift, and folks suspected him of bizarre political views. Gunmakers who catered to such exotic whims were viewed with similar suspicion.

So Savage offered this remarkable cartridge in the Model 99 lever-action rifle, and they called the combination a hunting rig. It was an odd couple because the cartridge did not do justice to the rifle for big game, nor did the rifle do justice to the cartridge as a fast-stepping, long-range varmint round. As a result, the .22 Savage High-Power has never been taken seriously as a varmint round. Ironically, the Europeans had a clearer idea of what the .22 Savage was all about and by 1920 were making some great rifles in this caliber.

Another fast-stepping cartridge that had considerable varmint-shooting potential was the 6mm Lee Navy round. Designed for the 1895 Lee Rifle, and used for a short time by the U.S. Navy, the 6mm Lee had a muzzle velocity of 2,560 fps with a 112-grain bullet. Loaded with a lighter bullet, say, 75 grains, the velocity could have been pushed over the 3,000 fps barrier but, again, hunters weren't thinking in terms of varmint shooting in those days, and the promise of the 6mm Lee was overlooked. This is especially ironic in light of the fact that the 6mm Lee cartridge would eventually spawn two of the three most significant developments in the history of varmint shooting. The original Lee Navy case, with virtually no changes other than sizing the neck down to .22 caliber, became the great .220 Swift. Also, the Lee's odd 6mm (.243) caliber was eventually to gain lasting glory in the form of the .243 Winchester and 6mm Remington cartridges.

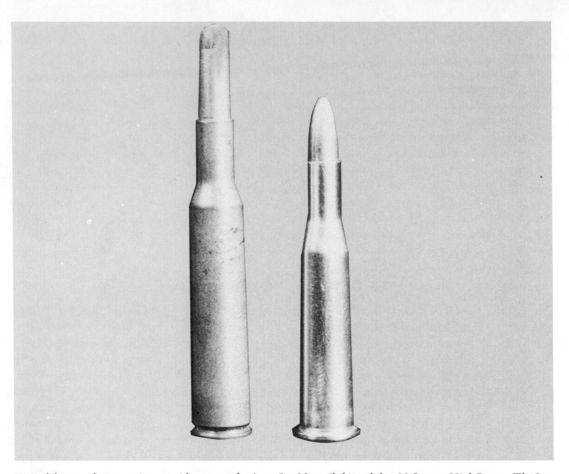

Two of the very first varmint cartridges were the 6mm Lee Navy (left) and the .22 Savage High Power. The Lee Navy wasn't used extensively for varmint shooting, but its case was to gain fame when it was necked down to become the .220 Swift. The Savage, a small-caliber, high-velocity cartridge, was years ahead of its time.

Going back even further, to 1885, we find a tiny .22 centerfire round known then as the .22 WCF (Winchester Center Fire). It was loaded with black powder. With a velocity of only 1,550 fps for its 45-grain lead bullet, it had hardly enough energy to kill a large rat. As you might imagine, the trajectory curved like the backside of a watermelon but it was pleasant to shoot and gained a fair measure of popularity as one of the earliest pest rounds.

With the coming of smokeless powder, the little .22 WCF was soon obsolete and would have become one more forgotten cartridge had not fate taken an unexpected turn. Under another guise and another name, the quaint .22 WCF was to become the granddaddy of modern varmint shooting.

THE HORNET

With the War to End All Wars a decade past and no new wars on the horizon, the boys at Springfield Arsenal, plus some civilian experimenters, began passing the time by tinkering with high-velocity cartridges. Notable among these experimenters were Army officers Townsend Whelen and G. L. Wotkyns. They were keen riflemen, dedicated handloaders, and varmint hunters. Not satisfied with existing fare, they experimented with wildcat cartridges in an effort to develop higher velocities and flatter trajectories. One case in particular caught their fancy — the obsolete .22 WCF. They found that by loading the .22 WCF with jacketed bullets and smokeless powder they could generate velocities close to 3,000 fps. The trajectory was flat enough for reasonably sure hits on woodchucks out to 200 yards or so. The light, high-velocity, jacketed bullets resulted in the massive tissue damage needed for instantaneous kills on small animals, and the cartridge was exceedingly pleasant to shoot. They liked their new cartridge so well that they even gave it a pet name — the .22 Hornet. The age of modern varmint shooting had begun.

The .22 Hornet was a phenomenon in shooting circles for a number of reasons, but mainly because it was the first round to be advertised as a varmint round and nothing else. Of course, there were a number of hunters who had to give it a try on deer and other big game, but except

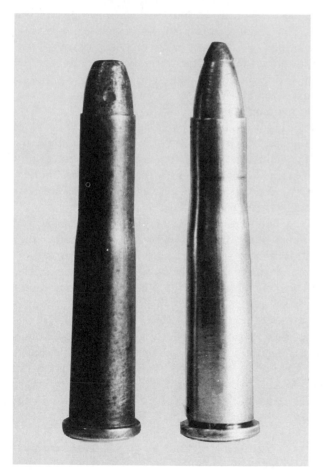

These might be called father and son cartridges. At left is the .22 WCF (Winchester Center Fire), a black-powder round introduced in the 19th century. At right is its direct descendant, the .22 Hornet. Note that there is hardly any difference in case shape.

for its obvious excellence as a turkey cartridge, the Hornet's promoters stuck mainly to the "varmints only" theme.

Another reason for the instant success of the .22 Hornet was the lavish praise given it in shooting and hunting journals. Its co-inventor, Townsend Whelen, was well regarded in shooting circles and as a contributing editor of OUTDOOR LIFE magazine he naturally wanted to promote his brainchild.

One more reason for the success of the Hornet was its timing. By the end of the 1920's, American hunters had to face up to the harsh realities of shortened hunting reasons and reduced bag limits for edible game. Varmint shooting became the only year-round hunting sport and this, more than any other factor, was what gave respectability to varmint rifles and the men who used them. Ever since that time, as hunting seasons have grown shorter and bag limits sparser, the popularity of varmint shooting has steadily increased. Since 1930, only two varmint cartridges have been commercial failures. All the many others, as we shall see, have been enthusiastically received. In fact, varmint cartridges and their rifles have the best commercial success record in the entire American arms business.

When you compare the performance of the .22 Hornet, with its 45-grain bullet puffing out the muzzle at 2,690 fps, to today's varmint cartridges, it certainly isn't impressive. Amateur rifle buffs and even some professional gun writers tend to assume that the modest performance of the Hornet represented the state of the ballistic art at the time of its development. This is not the case. The Hornet came nowhere near representing the ballistic know-how of the 1920's. The .22 Savage High-Power round, which predates the Hornet by almost two decades, was way ahead of the Hornet, especially in terms of long-range varmint shooting.

The .22 Savage had a poor reputation for accuracy, but that was simply because the rifles in which it was used weren't sufficiently accurate. Why then didn't someone simply make the .22 Savage, or some similar round such as the 6mm Lee, available in an accurate bolt-action or single-shot rifle? Well, dear reader, therein lies a story which provides not only the final explanation for the success of the Hornet, but also explains why the Hornet is not of the same .22 bullet diameter as other centerfire .22 varmint cartridges.

The experimenters at Springfield Arsenal had access to delightful little M-22 Springfield rifles. In case you've never seen one, they resemble the 1903 Springfield service rifle but they were made in .22 Rimfire caliber and used for marksmanship training. The M-22 Springfield was reasonably strong, quite accurate, and could easily be modified to fire centerfire cartridges. Best of all, the rifle was cheap and plentiful. Naturally this is the rifle Whelen and Wotkyns used most for their tinkering.

The M-22 had one major failing, and this failing led to the development of the Hornet rather than some larger, faster round. Unlike the 03 Springfield rifle, the lookalike M-22 had a rather short bolt movement. It was just long enough to function with the .22 Long Rifle rimfire cartridge, for which it had been designed. The bolt movement could be lengthened a bit, but such modifications were limited by the bolt-locking arrangement. Whelen and his pals had to devise a cartridge that would function within the length limitation of the M-22. This is why the .22 WCF was chosen for development and explains the ballistic limitations of the first modern varmint round.

If you reload for the .22 Hornet, you are accustomed to buying special Hornet bullets

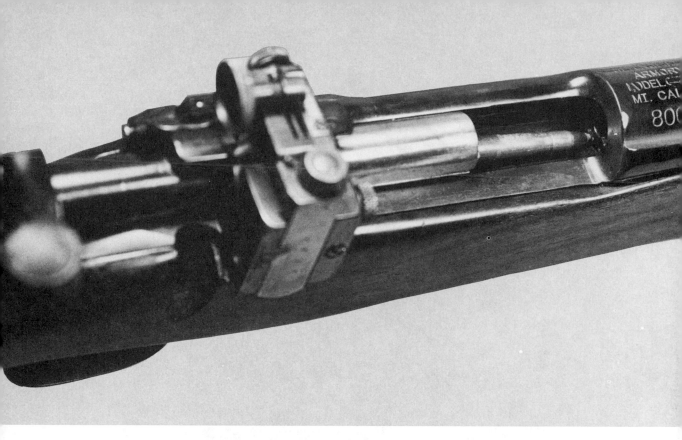

The short bolt motion of the Springfield M-22 (top), designed for .22 Rimfires, limited its adaptability to center-fire cartridges. This was why the .22 WCF—later to become the .22 Hornet—was chosen for it. Conversion to centerfire operation was easy. Below you see the two configurations: the bolt face of the original rimfire rifle and another M-22 bolt face after centerfire conversion.

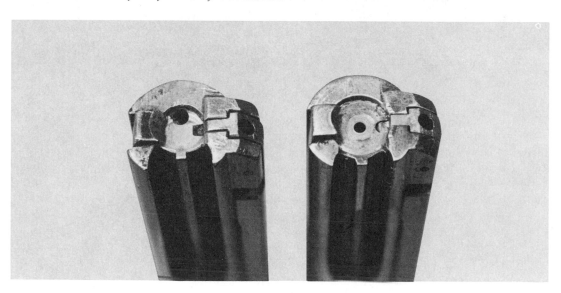

In striving for accuracy, varmint shooters are akin to benchresters. This hunter, using a bipod supported by a flat-topped boulder, looks as if he's shooting from a bench.

which have a diameter of .2225 (or .223) rather than the standard .224 bullets used in other .22 centerfire cartridges. The reason is that the barrels on the M-22 Springfields were originally made for the smaller rimfire bullets.

One more interesting tidbit is that though Winchester was producing Hornet ammo by 1930, it was not until a couple of years later that factory-made rifles in this chambering arrived on dealers' shelves. In the meantime, gunsmiths were doing a brisk business by converting M-22 Springfields and a host of other rifles to the exciting new Hornet caliber.

THE MAGNIFICIENT .220 SWIFT

The next episode in the saga of varmint rifles takes us to the great .220 Swift. Introduced in 1935, only five years after the commercial entry of the Hornet, the Swift was far ahead of its time in terms of performance. In fact, it was so advanced over anything else at that time that shooters couldn't decide what to make of it. Even today, there are plenty of varmint shooters who haven't managed to catch up with the Swift.

Unfortunately, the history of the Swift has been marred by controversy, jealousy, misunderstanding, and ignorance. Even in the supposedly enlightened era of the 1980's, you have to sift through a lot of nonsense to get at a few simple facts about the legendary .220 Swift.

The Swift controversy began with the success of the .22 Hornet. Correctly calculating that if a little bullet going 2,600 fps was good, then one going, say, 3,600 fps would be wonderful, an army of experimenters began concocting all sorts of high-velocity cartridges. Considering the powders and other components of that day, and the rifles they were prone to use in their experiments, the casualty rate was miraculously low. Then as now, there was very little monetary gain to be had for developing a hot new cartridge, but there was a stronger incentive in the form

The .220 Swift, introduced in 1935, is still a great cartridge. This chuck hunter is using a Ruger No. 1 in that chambering with a Lyman scope, a solid rest, and a shooting stool. With this setup, hits can be made at 400 yards or more.

These two great cartridges are the .22/250 Remington (left) and the .220 Swift. The .22/250 almost became the original Swift, but Winchester decided to use the 6mm Lee Navy case, a choice that made possible a muzzle velocity of 4,000 fps.

of fame and glory. To be recognized by one's peers as the inventor of a dazzling new cartridge and be immortalized in shooting journals was heady stuff indeed. Such ambitions also plant the seeds of jealousy.

Among the eager cartridge designers were G. L. Wotkyns of Hornet fame and other notables such as J. E. Gebby, J. B. Smith, and Harvey Donaldson, plus dozens of lesser lights. Each had more or less hit on the idea of necking down the .250 Savage case to .22 caliber, and there was considerable squabbling over who thought of it first. Apparently, this configuration was felt to be the next big success story and there was no shortage of volunteers willing to take credit.

By 1934 there was a brushfire of rumors that Winchester would soon announce a hot new .22 cartridge based on the .250 Savage case. An editor for the *American Rifleman* magazine, F. C. Ness, jumped the gun somewhat and more or less described Winchester's amazing new cartridge in the May '35 issue of his magazine. Actually, all he knew about the cartridge was what he had been told by independent experimenters, and though he knew Winchester would call their new round the .220 Swift, he thought he was talking about the necked-down .250 Savage wildcat.

When Winchester finally announced the new varmint cartridge, there was a storm of surprise and indignation. It was not the expected .250 Savage "Swift" at all but something entirely different, made by necking the 6mm Lee Navy case down to .22 caliber.

The development work had been quietly accomplished by Winchester's research team and

These groups, fired at 100, 200, and 300 yards, prove how amazingly flat is the .220 Swift trajectory. The rifle was sighted-in to hit 1-1/2 inches high at 100 yards; it's slightly above point of aim at 200 and only 2-1/2 inches low at 300 yards. Also note how small the groups are.

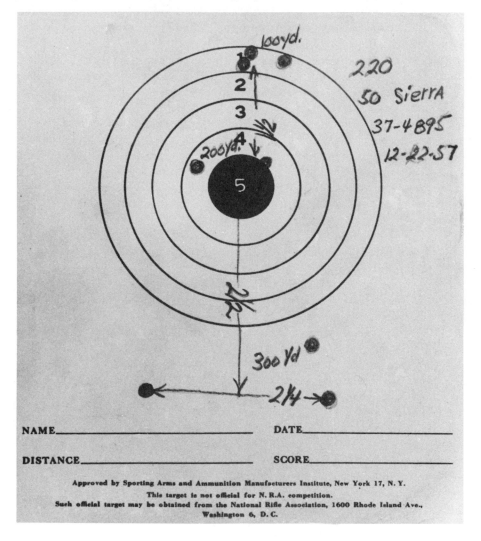

a California toolmaker by the name of Sweany. Of the perhaps half-dozen researchers who actually were involved in the development of Winchester's .220 Swift, I have been personally introduced to 30 or 40 and received correspondence from two or three dozen others. The competition to be the first with a great new varmint cartridge was so overpowering that some couldn't resist the temptation to grab for some of the glory even when it was totally undeserved. Others who had counted on Winchester to make their personal developments the new King Swift never forgave them the disappointment and, sadly, spent their years badmouthing the .220. This stupid gossip, inspired by jealousy, was the main cause of the controversy which surrounds the Swift to this day.

The research and development team at Winchester, we can be sure, took a long hard look at the .250 Savage cartridge case wildcatted to .22 caliber. They also looked at several other options, and for a while the Savage case *was* their first choice. However, getting so close to the 4,000 fps mark without quite making it was a frustration. The Savage case simply wouldn't do it, at least not with realistic pressures. The 6mm Lee case, as proposed by Sweany, had the necessary additional powder capacity and was also strong enough to hold the 55,000-odd pounds of pressure necessary for that kind of velocity. So the choice was clear to Winchester, and they made what they felt was the right decision, never expecting the storm of spiteful jealousy that would follow.

When Winchester unveiled the wonderful new round and announced a staggering muzzle velocity of over 4,100 fps, it didn't take the sword of spite long to fall. I've often suspected that much of the fury caused by the appearance of the .220 arose not just because it wasn't based on the Savage case but because it was so much *better* than that round. It piled insult on injury.

We get a clear idea of what was about to happen in the August '36 issue of the *American Rifleman*. J. Bushnell Smith, in one of the first articles on the Swift, wrote: "The chap who knows all the answers in reloading any other cartridge is just like a baby learning to walk when he tackles the Swift . . . it follows no accepted rule or traditions of reloading; the slightest irregularities in the load will jump pressure 5,000, 10,000, yes even 15,000 pounds without a word of warning."

Now this is mighty strong talk, especially for a respected shooting journal to print, but as anyone who reloads for the Swift knows, it is nonsense. Why Smith would have written something so technically incorrect is a mystery until you consider that he was one of the early supporters of the .250 Savage version of the Swift and no doubt a friend of other developers. But there's a lot more than what J. B. Smith had to say.

Harvey Donaldson once said that those who can shoot shoot, and those who can't write about it. Though I know three or four gun writers who fire more well-aimed shots in a decade than Donaldson fired in his lifetime, I also know there is more than a germ of truth in what he said. Some gun writers are inclined to copy other writers, especially when the subject is beyond their knowledge or is controversial or the deadline is drawing near. As a result, much shooting and ballistic nonsense is copied and re-copied, published and re-published in only slightly varying form. I'd say that about half the magazine articles written about the Swift between 1936 and 1963 were authored by persons who had never fired or reloaded a Swift cartridge or, at best, had only casual experience with the round.

The voices at Winchester also did their part in adding to the confusion. Still not willing to

The author at the shooting bench, checking velocities of .220 Swift handloads. He's using a Winchester Model 70 target rifle and an Oehler chronograph.

accept the notion that shooters would buy an expensive rifle for the sole purpose of busting varmints, Winchester spokesmen hinted broadly at the lightning-like effect their .220 Swift had on deer and even bigger game. When actually tried on big game, some animals did go down in their tracks as if hit by a locomotive. Sometimes, though, the tiny bullet exploded before penetrating to the animal's vitals. When this happened, the animal usually got away wounded. These unfortunate incidents heaped even more vocal and written abuse on the Swift.

If you shoot a bull elephant with a soft-point bullet from a .30/06 rifle, you might kill him in his tracks, but more likely the wounded beast will run. No one would think less of the .30/06, because after all, it isn't supposed to be an elephant-getter, is it? By the same token, the .220 Swift was, and is, a pure varmint cartridge. It isn't supposed to kill deer and other big game. Yet, when it didn't, the Swift became the point of very vocal criticism. When the .222 Remington was introduced years later, it was never criticized because it wasn't an effective deer cartridge. Likewise the .222 Magnum, the .22/250, and the .223 Remington were introduced as varmint cartridges, and no one was even vaguely concerned about whether or not they would kill deer. But even today, some well-meaning writers are compelled to advise the reader that the Swift isn't so hot on deer. I mention this to illustrate the long-lasting effect of the early criticisms of the Swift.

THE REAL SWIFT

How good is the .220 Swift? Is it really the ill-conceived concoction of a few bumbling ballisticians or is it the best varmint round you can buy? Is it hard to reload? Is barrel wear as bad as we hear? And how about accuracy? Whom can you believe?

Did you ever listen to a covey of gun cranks arguing about their favorite cartridges? If you have, I'm sure you have noticed that much of the talk is devoted not to promoting a favorite round but to putting down the opposition's favorite. A lot of people cannot be for something without being against something else. Remind you of politics? So it is with shooters.

I am not so inclined. My favorite rifle or caliber at any given time is simply the one I happen to have in my hands. Over the years I have probably owned and extensively fired some 20 to 25 Swifts. Right now I have quite a few around the gun room. Does this mean I favor the .220 to the exclusion of all others? Not at all. I own or have owned perhaps two dozen .22/250's, another dozen or two .22 Hornets and .222's, eight or 10 .223's, a half-dozen .222 Magnums, six or eight assorted .17's, enough mixed .243, .244, and 6mm rifles to stock a gun shop, two or three .225's, and another 20 or so wildcats of random varmint configurations. I have loved them all, especially the accurate ones. The point is that my conclusions are drawn from wide experience with a considerable sampling of varmint rifles and cartridges. I have no reason to arbitrarily favor one or another. It best suits my purposes, and the needs of my readers, to remain objective.

We judge any varmint cartridge by two fundamental criteria—accuracy and flatness of trajectory. The need for accuracy is self-evident, and a flat trajectory minimizes human error when shooting at unknown ranges. Let's say you're shooting prairie dogs with a .199 Super Swizzle Stick. You have the rig zeroed to hit dead on at 100 yards, but at 200 yards the downward curve causes the bullet to hit three inches below point of aim, nine inches low at 300 yards, and 22 inches low at 400 yards. A prairie dog is about five inches tall when he's squatting on his haunches. This means you have less than a five-inch margin for error. Suppose you see a prairie dog out at some distance which you guess to be about 300 yards. You hold the crosshairs about seven inches over his head, and hope for the best. But your range estimate is off and he's only a little over 200 yards out. The bullet goes over his head. Or, if the range is actually 350 yards, the bullet hits low.

But let's say you're shooting the .199 *Ultra* Swizzle Stick. Sighted to hit dead on at 100 yards, the bullet is half an inch low at 200 yards, two inches low at 300 yards, and only five inches low at 400 yards. Estimating the range is less critical because you know that by putting the crosshairs on top of the pup's head, you will make a solid hit be the range anywhere from 200 to 350 yards. Obviously, we want as flat a trajectory as possible.

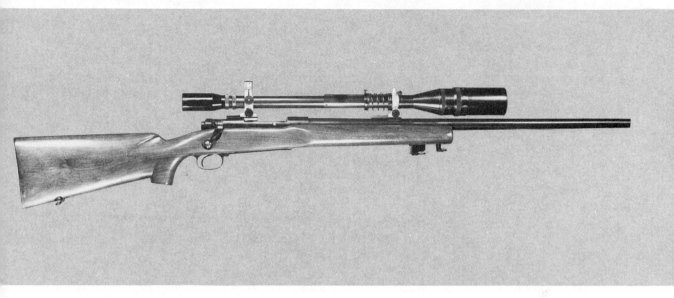

One of the all-time great varmint rigs is the Winchester Model 70 in its target version, chambered for the .220 Swift and topped with a Unertl 12X Ultra varmint scope.

All other factors such as bullet shape, weight, and diameter being equal, a bullet's trajectory is a function of its velocity. The higher the velocity, the flatter the trajectory. Also, as the velocity of a bullet is increased, it hits the target with greater force (energy) and is less affected by wind. There is, however, a practical limit to bullet velocity and a definite point of diminishing returns, discussed elsewhere in this book. Right now, let's return to the Swift and see how it stacks up in the velocity department.

Considered in terms of exterior ballistics (velocity and trajectory), the story of the Swift makes great reading. As currently loaded by Norma, the only major ammo maker commercially producing .220 Swift cartridges, the muzzle velocity with a 50-grain bullet is 4,110 fps. Remaining velocities are: 200 yards—3,133 fps; 300 yards—2,681. If sighted-in to hit dead on at 200 yards, this load hits .6-inch above point of aim at 100 yards, 4.1 low at 300 yards, and about 12 low at 400 yards. This assumes the scope is centered 1.5-inch above the center of the bore, as explained in Chapter 9.

As expected, the high muzzle velocity of the .220 Swift, which is the fastest factory-loaded sporting round ever produced, means that its trajectory is the flattest of any cartridge in its caliber and bullet-weight class. A surfeit of rumors will not erase this simple ballistic fact.

What is the cost of this performance? Do Swift barrels wear out as fast as they say? Since barrel wear is directly related to bullet velocity, we can logically assume that a .220 Swift rifle, other factors being equal, will have a shorter barrel life than other varmint calibers. But the real question is how many rounds can we expect from a Swift or any other caliber before the barrel is badly worn and accuracy is hopelessly lost?

It is hard to get solid information on this because very, very few shooters ever fire a rifle enough to wear out the barrel. As Shooting Editor of OUTDOOR LIFE I get scores of letters from readers telling me about a hot new hunting rifle and asking how long the barrel will last. There must be a notion that high-velocity rifles are only good for a couple boxes of shells before the barrels are ruined. My standard answer to these inquiries is that if the reader shoots every day of the year, year in and year out, he can start worrying about his barrel in about 20 years.

The only Swift I can honestly say I wore out was a Belgian FN rifle made during the 1950's. The barrel, in addition to being of mild steel, had wide lands which made the bore even more susceptible to erosion. I got upwards of 5,000 or so *accurate* rounds out of this rifle, even though I had to keep seating the bullets farther and farther out in the cases as the throat receded. I have other Swifts fitted with tough American barrels which have had upwards of 5,000 rounds through them with no loss of accuracy. Harvey Donaldson once told me he owned one of the very first Swifts produced by Winchester. After 10,000 rounds, it was nicely accurate. His secret, he said, was keeping the barrel clean.

I have bought three or four Swifts as "junkers" because their previous owners believed they were worn out. Indeed, their barrels showed the characteristic black streaking of bore erosion, but after a good scrubbing with diamond-grit bore-lapping paste they were ready for more years of accurate shooting.

It has often been said that the Swift's barrel life can be improved by reducing the velocity in handloaded ammo. This puzzles me no end, because I can't figure out why anyone with a Swift would want reduced velocities. If you want a watered-down Swift, why not buy something milder to start with? When you buy a racehorse, you want it to *run!*

What about accuracy? If you build an accurate rifle and fire good ammo, it will be accurate no matter what the caliber. So it is with the Swift. In good rifles, it is wonderfully accurate. If the rifles are no good, accuracy suffers. The Swift is one of the most accurate cartridges ever because it has never been offered in anything but the best rifles.

I have read and been told that in order to produce top accuracy, the Swift must be loaded to the maximum. With milder loads, accuracy is supposed to go all to hell. As I said above, I see no purpose in reduced loads, but for the record it is no more difficult to reduce velocities while retaining good accuracy with the Swift than it is with any other large-capacity varmint cartridge. Who cares?

A few years back, I bought a .220 Swift Ruger Model 77 that has a beautiful figured tiger-tail stock. I've been told that stocks with richly figured wood are liable to warp and cause poor accuracy, but this specimen is an amazing performer. With good bullets it is not uncommon for it to produce 100-yard five-shot groups as small as a quarter-inch across. It is so accurate that when I first tested it on a benchrest the thought crossed my mind that it would be fun to give it a try in a sanctioned benchrest tournament and give the boys something to think about.

Just this opportunity presented itself not long afterward. The tournament was scheduled for a spring weekend and the Arizona wind, sweeping across the southern deserts, was tumbling mobile homes and campers like matchboxes. If ever there was a day for the Swift, that was it. When I strode to the firing line with my out-of-the box Ruger Swift, eyebrows were raised, but there were also some knowing winks from a few oldtimers who knew the capabilities and advantages of a Swift when the wind is blowing. To make a long story short, I did not win that day, but I came in second in the grand aggregate. No one remembers who the winner was, but lots of the country's top shooters still talk about the day Carmichel got out his Swift.

Back when benchrest shooting was in its infancy, quite a few heavy target rifles were built in .22/250 caliber. This was before Remington legitimized the .22/250. Cases were made by necking .250/3000 Savage cases down to .22 caliber. Many of these rifles were wonderfully accurate, for that era, and the .22/250 earned a reputation for fine accuracy. It was natural, therefore, that the .22/250 was considered more accurate than the Swift. It was on this premise that the .22/250 gained such popularity after being introduced by Remington, while the Swift almost disappeared.

It is exceedingly difficult to conclusively prove one cartridge to be more accurate than another, especially if they are of the same caliber and have similar case capacities. One rifle may be more accurate than another, but almost always this is due to subtle mechanical and physical differences in the rifles rather than because of their respective calibers. If you compare a large sampling of, say, 100 or 1,000 or more rifles and statistically evaluate their accuracy, differences in the accuracy of the cartridges tend to diminish to insignificance. However, just such a large-scale comparison of the .22/250 and the .220 Swift was carried out, with astonishing results. The data come from the Sturm, Ruger plant in Newport, New Hampshire, where Model 77 bolt-action rifles are manufactured and tested. Every component in .22/250 and .220 Swift rifles — action, stock, and barrel — is identical. The only difference is the chambering. Each rifle is tested for accuracy, and group size is recorded. These records are plotted into graphs which show the relative accuracy of all calibers tested. The .220 Swift rifles are consistently and significantly more accurate than the .22/250's!

Why? Since the rifle components are identical, it would be reasonable to assume that accuracy would also be identical. Is it a difference in ammo quality? Very likely it is, but whatever the reason, in the only large-scale, impartial accuracy test between the .220 Swift and .22/250 ever conducted, involving thousands of rifles in each caliber, the Swift comes away the big winner. It looks like the guys at Winchester back in 1935 knew what they were doing, doesn't it?

RICOCHETS WITH VARMINT ROUNDS

There is one more thing I must say about the Swift and other high-velocity cartridges. According to popular myth, they are safe to shoot in settled areas because the tremendous speed of the bullet causes it to disintegrate on contact with just about anything, thereby eliminating the possibility of dangerous ricochets. Don't believe this nonsense. While it is true that the bullet may disintegrate upon impact, anyone who has had much experience with these cartridges will tell you it is common to hear the whine of a high-velocity bullet ricocheting across the countryside. This is especially noticeable in rolling prairie-dog country where a skipping bullet raises a long series of dust puffs like a flat rock skipping across water.

SOME VARMINT CARTRIDGE MISCUES

In 1938, Winchester demonstrated that they still were not attuned to varmint shooting when they introduced the .218 Bee. Though this was the fourth new varmint cartridge they offered in less than a decade, they still didn't seem to grasp the principles of the game. The parent rifle of the cute little Bee was their lever-action, the Model 65. The lesson learned by Savage Arms nearly a generation earlier, when they tried to sell Model 99 lever guns in .22 High Power, was apparently lost on Winchester. Or perhaps because they were the leaders in the field of lever-operated firearms they figured they could make the Model 65 Bee a success. It was discontinued in 1947, which means, if you deduct the five war years when none were produced, that the Model 65 had a lifespan of only five years. So few were sold that the Model 65 is one of the two rarest of modern Winchester lever rifles.

The other member of this rarest pair of Winchesters is the Model 64 "Zipper," introduced in 1937 and chambered for the zippy little .219 Zipper. The history of the Zipper is somewhat clouded, and the round is virtually unknown among today's army of varmint shooters. Designed for use in Model 64 lever rifles, the .219 Zipper was created by simply shortening and necking down .25/35 or .30/30 cases to .22 caliber. Since the Model 64 had a tubular magazine, which housed cartridges point-to-primer, .219 Zipper ammo was loaded with flat-tipped or round-nose bullets, as was the .218 Bee.

Though the .219, as factory-loaded, launched a 56-grain bullet at 3,110 fps and thereby offered plenty of varmint potential out to 300 yards, it was never a success. The Model 64 Zipper was dropped in 1947 along with the Model 65 Bee.

The problem with the lever-action concept in a varmint rifle was twofold. First, it was difficult to mount a telescopic sight on the Model 64. Second, rate of fire means nothing to a varmint shooter. Any hunter who fires more than three shots at a distant woodchuck will gladly trade firepower for accuracy. Buying increased rate of fire at the cost of accuracy, which is usually the case with lever guns, is unthinkable to a varmint shooter. That's why today's best varmint rifles are of the single-shot persuasion, even though they may be of bolt-action configuration. The perfect case in point is the single-shot bolt-action Remington Model 40X varmint rifle.

At any rate, Winchester learned their lesson so well that never again have they offered a lever-action centerfire rifle in a pure varmint caliber. Years later, in 1955, Marlin tried to sell their Model 336 lever-action in .219 Zipper caliber but buyers stayed away in droves. They gave up on the idea in '61, but not before having a try at selling their lever Model 57 (M) in .256 Winchester chambering. It was another quick failure.

Even though the Model 65 never hit the big time, Winchester still had hopes for the .218 Bee. In 1949, they introduced a trim little repeater, the Model 43. For the first time since the introduction of the Model 70, they were on the right track. Though rather plain, the Model 43 combined the essential virtues of an acceptable varmint rifle. It was a bolt-action, available in either .218 Bee or .22 Hornet (also .25/20 and .32/20 for a couple of years), and to the intense delight of younger shooters, it carried a 1949 price tag of only $66.95, compared to the burdensome $106 price of a Model 70 in .22 Hornet or .220 Swift.

Though the Model 43 had a pretty bad trigger and no convenient means of scope mounting, it put a functional varmint rifle in the hands of shooters who might otherwise never have tried the sport. After drilling and tapping for scope mounts and attaching a Weaver J or G scope in 4X or 6X magnification, the Model 43 was the terror of any woodchuck community.

Though the .218 Bee never achieved the standing of the .22 Hornet, it was in its own right an enthusiastic little performer that offered somewhat more punch than its older cousin. Winchester factory loads of that time were listed at a muzzle velocity of 2,860 fps with a 46-grain bullet, giving it a 210 fps edge over the Hornet. In practical terms this meant about a 50-yard range advantage over the Hornet.

Winchester's Model 43 — chambered in .218 Bee, .22 Hornet, and .25/20 — was a low-cost rifle that had to be drilled and tapped for scope mounts. However, it had the essential virtues of a functional varmint rifle and it introduced varminting to many shooters who might otherwise never have tried the sport.

Throughout the 1930's, while Winchester was forging ahead with four varmint rounds, Remington was content to sit back and watch the market develop, learning from the successes of competitors and no doubt benefiting from their failures. The .220 Swift, they recognized, represented the upper end of the ballistic spectrum and would be hard to beat in its own realm. In any event, the powers at Remington rightly figured they could do without the bad publicity that apparently went with a cartridge as radical as the Swift. On the other end of the scale was the .22 Hornet, which though popular had actually been obsolete even when it was being developed. Wouldn't the ideal velocity be somewhere between these extremes?

Another observation, surely not wasted on the Remington bosses, was that for some curious reason each of Winchester's four varmint cartridges had been on rimmed cases. Since rimmed cases had been more or less obsolete, especially for bolt-gun use, since 1888, wouldn't it be smarter to use a rimless case for a higher-performance varmint round?

THE TRIPLE DEUCE IS BORN

The boys in the back room at Remington thought about it, and in 1950 burst forth with their brainchild. They called it the .222. Unlike Winchester's clever names such as Bee, Zipper, and Swift, Remington used the simple designation .222 Remington. No one could speak ill of it. With a muzzle velocity of 3,200 fps it was comfortably in between, not too fast and not too slow. The modern rimless case was new and original, not a rehash of an older design. Best of all, the .222 was sensationally accurate and delightfully easy to shoot.

The little .222 Remington had a fine parent rifle going for it, Remington's Model 722, which had been introduced just a few years before. The 722 was plain, unexciting, and cheap looking, but it was also strong, had a wonderful trigger, and though no one realized it then, it utilized the most accurate receiver and bolt configuration yet devised by any gunmaker. Other makers, especially the Europeans, were quick to see the benefits of the .222 and lost little time offering rifles in this remarkable caliber.

One European firm in particular, a virtually unknown arms maker in the Finnish town of Riihimäki, made a beautiful little Mauser-type rifle that was exactly the right size for the .222 cartridge. Attempts to sell this rifle in .22 Hornet and .218 Bee chamberings met with only

These Remington centerfire .22's, all introduced since World War II, are (from left) the great .222 Remington, .223, and .222 Magnum. The .222 has forged a remarkable record for accuracy. The Magnum is also a superb varmint cartridge but has lost popularity to the .223, which is the current U.S. military cartridge.

limited success. In .222 Remington caliber it was a runaway best seller. It is hardly incorrect to say that this once-obscure firm owes its present-day worldwide renown to those first little rifles in .222 caliber. The name of the company, by the way, is Suajeluskuntain Ase-ja Konepoja Osakeyhtiö, better known by the less terrifying name of Sako!

While Sako, Krico, and other European makers were turning out .222's by the thousands, Remington and Savage (Model 340) were the only U.S. makers of rifles in this caliber for a good many years. Colt, Browning, and Marlin, plus some smaller firms, offered the caliber under their trade names but their .222 rifles were merely assembled around Sako actions.

Quite a few shooters liked the looks of the .222 but some were turned off by the homeliness of the Remington rifle. These riflemen opted to have the more elegant Model 70 Winchester converted to this caliber. Hundreds of Model 70's originally made in .22 Hornet caliber became .222 Remingtons. As a rule these conversions were not nearly as accurate as the Remington M-722, mainly because the .222 Remington cartridge fired a .224-diameter bullet whereas Model 70 Winchester Hornet rifles had barrels with a .223 groove diameter. Handloaders got the best performance out of the Model 70 .222 conversions by loading the smaller-diameter Hornet bullets in .222 cases.

Back in those lusty days the shooting editors of the two leading outdoor magazines had more or less aligned themselves with the two leading makers of sporting rifles. As the result of a hilariously improbable series of circumstances, Jack O'Connor, then the Shooting Editor of OUTDOOR LIFE wound up in the Winchester camp while Warren Page, his opposite number at *Field & Stream,* chose the Remington side of the fence. This peculiar set of circumstances aided the fortunes of the .222 for a number of reasons. Page, as an accuracy nut of the highest order and one of the guiding lights of benchrest shooting, felt compelled to extol the virtues of this wonderful Remington round. He eventually won a number of national benchrest championships and established a long list of accuracy records with the .222. Naturally, there was no limit to his praise for his pet cartridge, and this had a tremendous impact on sales.

One of the often repeated reasons for the success of the .222 is its mild muzzle blast, which in settled areas is less liable to rile local residents and landowners. I've never been much impressed by this reasoning, but I do know that the relatively mild report of the .222 as compared to, say, the .220 Swift, makes it easier to shoot. The .222 arrived in the dark ages of shooting when it was considered unmanly to wear any sort of ear protection. The rule was to grit your teeth and bear it even when your ears were ringing like steeple bells. The result was a marked tendency to flinch with each pull of the trigger. Of course, if you flinch, you also jerk the trigger, which leads to poor shooting. The soft report of the .222 reduced the tendency to flinch, and many shooters found they could shoot it better than any rifle they'd ever tried. Of course, no shooter believes he is ever guilty of flinching, so the cartridge itself was given all the credit for the fine performance.

Back in the early 1950's, I spent at least a day a week during the winter months patrolling the country's back roads and sniping at crows. There were plenty of crows and farmers wanted them shot, so it was not unusual to fire upwards of 100 rounds per outing and run up a good tally of hits. I drove a '52 Olds convertible, which I'd specially outfitted with rifle rests that made aiming at the predator birds almost as steady as if I were using a benchrest. My standard practice was to carry a heavy-barreled target rifle in either .22/250 or .220 Swift, which I used for all shots over about 250 yards, plus a sweet little .222 Sako, with full-length Mannlicher-type stock, which I used for the closer crows. My hit ratio with the heavier rifle was seldom more than 50 percent for the simple reason that I shot at every crow I saw, regardless of range, as long as the backstop was safe. On the other hand, I seldom missed with the .222 Sako. Most observers ignored the difference in range and concluded that the .222 was the deadlier rifle.

Such comparisons of cartridges tend to make the .222 look very good indeed. Its practical limit is about 275 yards, and within this range it is wonderfully accurate. If sighted-in dead on at 200 yards, the .222 hits about two inches high at 100 yards and four inches low at 250 yards. At 300 yards, though, the impact is 10 inches below point of aim, making hits rather iffy.

THE .222 REMINGTON MAGNUM

Sometime in the future, along about the year 2085, a firearms historian will attempt to analyze the cartridges of this century. He's going to draw some wrong conclusions about a short-lived little varmint number called the .222 Remington Magnum. Armed with a trunkful of musty old gun catalogs, he'll note that the .222 Magnum was introduced in 1958 and featured a velocity of 3,240 fps, which just happened to be a neat 100 fps faster than the earlier .222. "Aha," he'll shout, "those funny old guys were trying to add some pep to the tired .222, and all they could come up with was an extra 100 fps." This logical deduction is dead wrong.

If Remington's goal had been merely a faster varmint round, they could have, I promise you, done better than a piddling 100 fps. The real goal was to perfect a round which met certain military specifications. The Army wanted a small, high-velocity cartridge similar to Remington's .222 but with somewhat more velocity and loaded with a heavier bullet.

One of the cartridges that evolved from this development program was the .222 Remington Magnum. Though it was not, in this particular form, adopted by the military, Remington liked it and offered it in civilian dress to the varmint-shooting public. Magnums were all the rage and there was good reason to believe that a hotrodded .222 would be well received. The new "Magnum" was really nothing more than the original .222 case stretched by about an eighth of an inch to increase powder capacity. Actually, the ballistic improvement, as compared to the .222, was somewhat more substantial than indicated by velocities. Whereas the .222 was loaded with a 50-grain bullet, the new Magnum fired a 55-grain slug. This extended range and reduced wind effect somewhat more than the velocity difference alone would indicate. At any rate, the .222 Magnum comes very close to being a genuine 300-yard varmint round.

When announced by Remington, the .222 Magnum was chambered in the Model 722 rifle. Soon other makers such as Sako offered good rifles in this caliber, and the future of the new magnum seemed secure. Though a few benchrest rifles were chambered for the .222 Magnum, it never really caught on in accuracy circles in its original form. It was wonderfully accurate, but offered no accuracy advantage over the immensely popular .222 and theoretically—because of the longer case—might be less accurate.

Oddly, though, the benchrest shooters gave the .222 Remington Magnum what may be its most enduring claim to fame. At about the time when the .222 Magnum was earning a reputation the benchrest game was inaugurating a new competitive classification called the Sporter Class in which the rifles had to be of 6mm (.243) caliber or larger. The existing 6mm cartridges, such as the .243 Winchester, were deemed too large and hard-kicking for serious bench

At left is a .222 Remington Magnum. Next to it is the 6x47mm round, employing the same case necked up to 6mm. In this form the cartridge has become a benchrest favorite.

shooting, so it wasn't long before a number of 6mm wildcats were devised. Of these, the runaway success was a neat-looking little round made by expanding the neck of the .222 Magnum case to hold a 6mm bullet. Known as the 6X47 (because of the 47mm case length), this wildcat continues to be one of the favorite benchrest cartridges.

Ironically, the military research program that had been responsble for the birth of the .222 Remington Magnum was also the cause of its demise. It happened in 1964 when the Army adopted the 5.56mm round for use in the M-16 rifle. The .222 Magnum, as you may have guessed, was the cartridge originally intended for the new sub-caliber military weapons system, but it proved to be a trifle too long for satisfactory use in the Armalite AR-15, the prototype of the M-16 rifle. A slightly shorter cartridge case was devised, which yielded the same performance as the .222 Magnum. This latter version, which has a case length almost exactly halfway between that of the .222 and the .222 Magnum, became the 5.56 or, as it is known to varmint shooters, the .223 Remington.

Seldom, if ever, has an arms and ammo maker found itself in the dilemma of making rifles and ammunition in two different cartridge designations with identical ballistics. Clearly, only one could survive, and there was little doubt that it would be the .222 Remington, not the .222 Magnum. After all, the .223 was now an official U.S. service cartridge, and the prestige and popularity this brings is overwhelming. Quietly, Remington stopped making rifles in .222 Magnum caliber, as did other manufacturers, though the cartridges are still manufactured. The .222 Magnum, while it lasted, was a popular and commercially successful round. In fact, it was healthy right up until the day it died.

THE .223, CIVILIAN AND MILITARY

The .223 Remington is already one of the most successful cartridges of all time. At present, .223 ammo, in either civilian or 5.56 military dress, is being loaded by as many or more of the world's ammo makers than any other caliber. Some arsenals load *only* 5.56 ammo. You can have your pick of all sorts of models and types of rifles in this chambering. For the present, though, we'll forget all the military and police weapons and concentrate on the sporting rifles and loads.

As commercially loaded by Remington, Winchester, and Federal here in the U.S., the .223 Remington has a muzzle velocity of 3,240 fps with a 55-grain bullet. This means that as a varmint round the .223 offers the same performance as the .222 Magnum. Like the .222 Magnum, it has 300-yard varmint-shooting potential in terms of velocity and trajectory, but in theory the .223 may have an accuracy advantage because of its case configuration. The .223 has been moderately successful as an ultra-accurate benchrest cartridge, but along with the original .222 Remington, the .223 has lost ground in benchrest circles. I suspect that the .223's tidal wave of popularity may eventually drown even the .222, but it will take many years before it comes to pass. Already, rifle buyers who would otherwise have selected the eversweet .222 are opting for the .223. One of the inducements favoring the .223 is the opportunity to buy relatively inexpensive military-surplus 5.56mm ammo. Though the 5.56 and .223 are supposedly identical, there are some hazardous pressure problems when firing 5.56 military ball ammo in .223 sporting rifles. Apparently, this arises because of the full-jacketed bullets used in 5.56 military ammo and because of differences in the throat configurations of civilian bolt-action .223 sporting rifles and the military arm.

THE 6mm ROUNDS (.243 AND .244)

If this discussion of varmint rifles and calibers were arranged according to bore size, the various 6mm cartridges would be near the end of the chapter. But to bring proper perspective to the development of varmint shooting, the story must be told as it happened. Otherwise, the curious and often ironic twists of fate which so often determine the acceptance of rifles and cartridges would hold less fascination and suspense.

The most spectacular of these events was the introduction of the .243 Winchester and the .244 Remington calibers. Both appeared in 1955, and I can't recall any other new cartridge that received so much hullabaloo in the outdoor press. One of the reasons for all the excitement was that the 6mm caliber was completely new to American shooters. Only once before, in 1895, had a rifle of this bore size, the 6mm Lee Navy, been made in America. In Europe, a number of 6mm

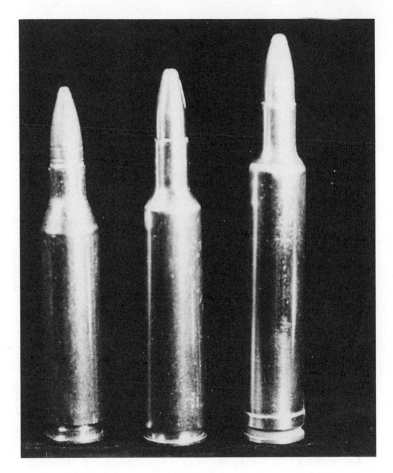

Here are the 6mm rounds (from left): the .243 Winchester, the .244 Remington—lately known as the 6mm Remington—and the .240 Weatherby Magnum.

cartridges had been developed, most notably the English .240 Nitro, but they were virtually unknown in North America.

The .243 Winchester was the brainchild, or so he is credited, of writer Warren Page and was originated simply by necking a .308 Winchester case down to hold a .243-diameter bullet. Six millimeters and .243-inch are the same and these designations are used interchangeably in describing bullet and bore diameters. When introduced, the .243 was loaded with 80-grain bullets at 3,500 fps or 100-grain bullets at 3,070 fps. The chambering was available in Winchester's Model 70 bolt-action rifle or Model 88 short-throw lever rifle. Naturally, it was the bolt rifle that interested varmint shooters, and it is in good bolt rifles that the .243 Winchester has made its reputation.

With a velocity of 3,500 fps, the .243 was second only to the .220 Swift, unless you also count the exotic .257 Weatherby Magnum, available only in Weatherby rifles. The .243 Winchester had instant appeal to varmint shooters.

Apparently, early .243 rifles were hard to come by because my first rifle in this caliber was custom-built on a 1917 Enfield action with a heavy Douglas barrel fitted by gunsmith Bob

Wallack. I was so eager to give the new rifle a try that I couldn't wait the week or so it would take to make a new stock, so I rebedded it in the original military Enfield stock. It was late on a winter's afternoon in 1955 when I leveled the crosshairs of a 12X Unertl Ultra Varmint scope on a crow and fired my first serious shot with a .243. The top half of the bird spiraled 20 feet into the air, and the rest was feathers and fumes. Like thousands of other shooters, I was enchanted.

The .244 Remington came into existence when Fred Huntington, then owner of the RCBS reloading-tool company, necked a .257 Roberts case down to 6mm and called it the .243 Rockchucker. The rockchuck is the symbol of his firm. As adopted by Remington and renamed the .244, it was factory-loaded with a 75-grain bullet at 3,500 fps and a 90-grain bullet at 3,200 fps. The Remington round actually has the same diameter as the Winchester, despite the .244 designation.

The "battle of the sixes" between Remington and Winchester was a closely matched affair with sharply divided adherents. On paper, the .243 had a tiny performance edge. No doubt the folks at Remington wished they had built in a few more feet per second. As handloaders were quick to point out, however, the somewhat greater case capacity of the .244 did permit greater velocity than was safely possible with the .243. For a while, however, it appeared that the .243 would win all the marbles, and it almost did.

Whereas Remington tended to view their .244 as being mainly a varmint round, Winchester proceeded from the beginning to sell the .243 as a combination varmint and big game cartridge. This is why they offered the 100-grain-bullet load. Accordingly, the Winchester rifle barrels were rifled with a rate of one turn in 10 inches. Remington, on the other hand, rifled their Model 722 rifles in .244 caliber with a one-in-12-inch twist, which is best suited to their lighter bullets. Much has made of this difference during the ensuing years. Just about all the magazine articles comparing the .243 and .244 have stated that the .244 Remington failed to achieve great popularity because the one-in-12 rifling wouldn't stabilize heavier bullets, and therefore the .244 was not liked by deer hunters. This explanation is only another case of writers copying other writers. It is not the sort of thing anyone would say who had actually handloaded heavier bullets in the .244. Good loads with 100-grain bullets work delightfully in the .244 despite the longer twist.

In reality, the .243 triumphed over the .244 for two other reasons. First, the factory loading of the .243 with the 100-grain bullet was attractive to customers who wanted the .243 as a deer rifle. Second, and this is probably the main reason, the Winchester Model 70 was the premier rifle of its day. Because it was stylish, beautifully made, and accurate, every hunter wanted to own a Model 70. Remington's Model 722 fared poorly by visual comparison. With its uncheckered stock and tin-can trigger guard, it *appeared* to be nowhere in the same league with the great Model 70. Thus, the decision between the .243 and .244 was mainly between two significantly different rifles.

While Winchester and Remington waged war at the gun counter, the two sixes were having profound effects on the varmint-shooting scene. Most significantly, a new army of hunters was encouraged to try their hands at crows, woodchucks, and other varmints. Many hunters, who might have spent their dollars for a strictly varmint-shooting rig, were attracted by the idea of a combination varmint and deer rifle. Thus thousands of fledgling varmint hunters roamed the meadows. Many became so fascinated that they bought other, more specialized, varminting outfits. These new aficionados focused more attention on the sport of varmint shooting and added to the demand for varmint rifles, cartridges, and scopes.

Another effect the .243 and .244 had on the shooting scene was to hasten the demise of other cartridges. One was the .257 Roberts. Though never a big-selling success, the .257 was a good dual-purpose round with a well-deserved reputation for excellence on long-range woodchucks as well as deer, antelope, and other medium game. When the .243 and .244 arrived, the days of the .257 were numbered, though cartridges and rifles are still made. The .250 Savage as a bolt-action rifle was doomed.

Another victim was the .220 Swift. Always controversial, the Swift had survived because of its unmatched velocity and flat trajectory. Faced with hot new rounds that offered excellent long-range potential, the Swift went into a decline. The powers at Winchester, tired of the Swift's bad press, were not unhappy to see it slide into oblivion. The .243 was a lot easier to sell and seemed to make everyone happy. In 1964, the Swift was quietly forgotten by Winchester. More about this later.

By 1960, five years after the introduction of their .244, the strategists at Remington knew they had been badly beaten by the .243. Knowing that the .244 was too good a round to forget, they pulled off a neat trick. In 1963, they reintroduced it under a new name and a whole new set of credentials. The new title was 6mm Remington, and the loads included a 100-grain bullet. Accordingly, rifles in this "new" caliber were barreled with a one-in-10-inch twist so that everyone would be content. The rifle itself, the Model 700, was essentially the old Model 722 but with a new set of clothes that made it a lot more appealing. The strategy worked. Today, the .244 — oops — I mean the 6mm Remington, is successful and competing very nicely with the .243. In fact, it is even proving itself to be what the folks at Remington suspected all along — somewhat superior to the .243, but you've got to be a handloader to find this out. One thing for sure, the .243 and .244 changed the varmint-shooting scene forever.

THE .22/250

Gunmakers are a conservative lot; perhaps hardheaded is a better term. Even so, they aren't nearly as hardheaded as they used to be, never admitting they could be wrong or that anyone else could be right even when they were sandbagged by evidence to the contrary. If you doubt this, just think how long it took anyone in the industry to adopt the .22/250. The astonishing thing is not that it took so long to legitimize the .22/250, but that it happened at all!

A wildcat cartridge is one that is not and never has been manufactured in a factory and is strictly a handloading proposition. Over the years, amateur cartridge designers have come up with thousands of such cartridges in just about every caliber imaginable. Few of these wildcats achieve any fame and most, if the truth were known, are inferior to existing factory-loaded rounds. Of the few wildcats that have deserved and achieved fame and widespread use, the runaway best seller is the .22/250. Dating back to 1930 and probably before, the .22/250 wildcat, as its name suggests, was made by squeezing the neck of a .250/3000 Savage case down to .22 caliber. Though there is no shortage of individuals credited with developing the .22/250, J. E. Gebby got a leg up on the others by naming this round the "Varminter" and

These cartridges are (from left) the .225 Winchester, .224 Weatherby Magnum, and .22/250 Remington. They're the medium-speed varmint rounds, with velocities ranging between 3,500 and 4,000 fps.

copyrighting the name. This no doubt made good business sense, because the cartridge was immensely popular. Gebby, I understand, intended to charge royalties for use of the Varminter name, and perhaps he intended to corner the .22/250 market. I don't know for sure, and it doesn't matter because scores of gunsmiths who rebarreled and chambered for the cartridge ignored Gebby's copyrighted "Varminter" and called it what they had always called it—the .22/250.

From the beginning, the .22/250 had a wonderful reputation for accuracy. This was mainly because all wildcat .22/250 ammunition was handloaded. In the '30's, '40's, and '50's handloaded ammo was much more accurate than factory loads, for several reasons. There were very few handloaders about in those days, but they were the shooting elite and tended to be quite skilled and knowlegeable. Factory-loaded ammo, regardless of caliber, was not nearly as accurate as it is today. So, if one compared carefully handloaded .22/250 ammunition to factory-loaded .220 Swifts or .22 Hornets, the wildcat did seem miraculously accurate. And many of those early .22/250 rifles were made by the best gunsmiths using the most accurate barrels available.

About 1955 or thereabouts, I came into possession of my first .22/250. In fact, I had a couple of them. One was built on a glass-slick Oberndorf Mauser action with double-set triggers, a heavy barrel, and a beautiful stock by Monty Kennedy. The other was a lightweight affair built on a Model 70 action in the original Winchester stock. The heavy rifle was dead accurate with a load of 36 grains of IMR 4320 behind a 55-grain bullet, and the number of crows it sent to the promised land was astonishing. I eventually traded it to a hunting pal, and as far as I know it is still blasting varmints.

One day in 1963 or '64, I walked into a country hardware store and there on the gun rack was a Browning bolt-action rifle with one of the most beautifully figured stocks I'd ever seen. After the first look I knew I was going to buy the rifle, regardless of caliber, but when I saw the marking—.22/250—I was even more delighted and more than a little puzzled. You see, the folks at Browning were committing the unheard-of act of selling rifles in a wildcat caliber. This was a year or so before Remington officially adopted the .22/250 and began making the ammo. For a conservative old firm such as Browning to recognize the excellence of the .22/250 wildcat, and horror of horrors, chamber rifles for it, was a historic event. When I left the hardware store I owned that Browning rifle, and it still graces my gun rack.

Since gunmakers are such a conservative lot, shooters were astonished when Remington made the .22/250 a legitimate factory cartridge in 1965. Everyone was surprised. If the big gunmakers had ignored this obviously superior cartridge for upwards of 40 years they were capable of ignoring it indefinitely. As I said, they seldom admit mistakes.

How could the "new" .22/250 Remington fail to be anything but a winner? With a muzzle velocity of 3,730 fps with a 55-grain bullet, it was second only to the Swift in speed and flatness of trajectory. It had proven its accuracy in the heat of benchrest competition and was preceded by 35 years of glowing publicity. Remington added to this by offering their new cartridge in the super-accurate 40-X target rifle as well as their Model 700, and from the beginning the company loaded superbly accurate .22/250 ammo.

There is little doubt that one of the reasons Remington offered .22/250 rifles and ammo in

This is a .225 Winchester Model 70 heavy-barreled varmint rifle mounted with a Redfield 3200 scope. The .225 was a fine varmint cartridge that failed commercially. The rifle and cartridge were a much better combination than shooters realized in 1964.

All the Winchester-designed varmint cartridges have been rimmed or semi-rimmed. Here (from left) are the .218 Bee, .225 Winchester, and .220 Swift. Another rimmed Winchester case was the .219 Zipper.

1965 was that only a year before Winchester had dropped the .220 Swift. This gave Remington the chance to pick up all the marbles and legitimately claim that they made the hottest factory varmint rifle you could buy. With their .222, .223, and .22/250 cartridges, Remington "own-ed" the .22 varmint-cartridge field.

During the early 1960's, the management at Winchester was making some decisions that still have shooters and Winchester dealers alike shaking their heads and wondering what the decision makers had been smoking. In 1964, when Winchester surprised the shooting world with a completely redesigned Model 70 rifle, they replaced the .220 Swift with a charming little .22 varmint cartridge which they elected to call the .225. I say it was charming with my tongue in cheek because the .225, like all previous Winchester varmint .22's, had a pronounced rim and evoked all sorts of nostalgia for the "good old" 1895 single-shot days. But the varmint shooters of 1964 weren't interested in nostalgia, and it wasn't long before the .225 Winchester joined the .219 Zipper as one of the only two commercial varmint rounds to be commercial failures.

In truth, the .225 was a damn good varmint cartridge. With a muzzle velocity of 3,570 fps with a 55-grain bullet, it was plenty quick and had the flatness of trajectory necessary to qualify it as an honest 300-yard cartridge with yardage to spare. But it certainly was not in the same league with the Swift, and one can't help wonder why the Winchester brass opted to trade their sweepstakes winner for an also-ran. The 1964 version of the Model 70 Winchester was ugly, so ugly that Model 70 fans of past years were disgusted and sales declined accordingly. Shooters who might otherwise have given the .225 a chance simply wouldn't buy the new Model 70 rifles.

Those who did try the .225 were delighted with the accuracy and performance of both the cartridge and the rifle. Some of the most accurate factory-loaded cartridges I've ever tested were those early .225 Winchester loads. But if the .225 wasn't doomed from the beginning, it was finished off a year later when Remington introduced the .22/250. Winchester quietly discontinued making rifles in .225 caliber, and it hasn't been heard from since, though you can still get cartridges. No other arms maker has seen fit to offer rifles in this caliber, and eventually Winchester will stop making .225 ammo. Interestingly, though, Ruger has been right successful at offering limited runs of odd calibers. The No. 1 and No. 3 Single-Shots, for example, have been chambered for such obsolete, rimmed shells as the .45/70, .30/40 Krag, and .22 Hornet. Since rimmed cases go with single-shot rifles like fringe goes with surreys, wouldn't a Ruger No. 1 Single-Shot be nice in .225 caliber? I understand a prototype was made, but . . . ?

THE WEATHERBY ENTRIES

An interesting little varmint round that deserves more attention than it gets is the .224 Weatherby Magnum. Though it has a belted case, as do all Weatherby cartridges, it can hardly be called a true Magnum. Actually, the .224 Weatherby is ballistically similar to the .22/250. Factory loads are available with 50- or 55-grain bullets with respective muzzle velocities of 3,800 and 3,600 fps. Of course, the reason the .224 Weatherby remains largely undiscovered is that Weatherby rifles are expensive. Those fortunate few who own .224 Weatherbys know they are delightfully accurate and capable of serious long-range performance. I've never owned a Weatherby rifle in .224 caliber, but I've tested three or four and each one was capable of better than minute-of-angle accuracy. For a while, I had a test rig in .224 Weatherby chambering which routinely turned in half-inch or smaller five-shot groups with factory loads, so I know for a fact that they are loading good stuff.

Another seldom-mentioned Weatherby varmint round is the .240 Magnum. Developed as a combination cartridge for deer-size game as well as varmints, the .240 is a true 6mm cartridge with the same bullet diameter as the .243 Winchester and 6mm Remington. With a muzzle velocity of 3,850 fps with a 70-grain bullet, the .240 WM is a very fast stepper, the fastest of the sixes. Other factory loads include a 90-grain bullet at 3,500 fps and a 100-grain slug traveling 3,395 fps.

The .240 Weatherby can almost be called a 6mm/06; the case is virtually the same length as .30/06 brass, and the rim diameter is the same. Like all Weatherby cartridges, the .240 case is belted, but if you are of a mind to do so you can make .240 cases, belt and all, by running .30/06 (or .270) cases into a .240 sizing die.

When the .240 was introduced in 1968, there was the usual spate of publicity, but curiously nothing much has been said since. I tested one of the first Weatherby rifles in this caliber and was not impressed by the accuracy I got with factory loads. Likewise, various handloads I tried weren't so hot either. I'd about decided the problem was the rifle when, on a whim, I tried swaging a belt on some .30/06 cases and sizing them to .240. Groups fired with these cases were much smaller than those fired with factory cases, but I don't know the reason. If I were giving some thought to an ultra long-range varmint rifle, I'd give the .240 Weatherby a lot of consideration.

SWEET SEVENTEENS

In 1971, Remington pulled a fast one when they unveiled a hot little number that whistled a tiny 25-grain .17-caliber bullet out of the barrel at 4,020 fps. Having been fascinated with the idea of .17-caliber varmint rifles for years, I, for one, was delighted, but I can't say that my enthusiasm was shared by the majority of my fellow gun writers. I recall one in particular who told all and sundry at the Remington Writers' Seminar that he saw no purpose for the .17 caliber and refused to shoot the test rifles that were available there. Seeing that he was so dead set, for whatever reasons, against the .17 Remington I was curious to know what the report to his

Here's a handful of .17-caliber bullets and BB's—which have the same diameter. The bullets weigh only 25 grains apiece. In the middle of the heap, for a comparison of size, is a standard .22 Rimfire cartridge.

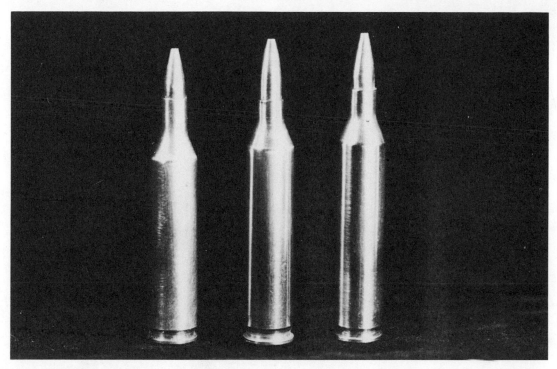

These .17-caliber rounds are (from left) the standard .17 Remington and two wildcats—the .17/223 and .17/222 Remington Magnum. The .17 is popular in Australia for a reason that may surprise many American shooters: the minimal pelt damage caused by the tiny bullet.

readers would be and bought the magazine in which his comments appeared. He did, as I suspected he would, go on at great length about the pitfalls of the .17 and wasted more space describing all the faults his "tests" had disclosed, though I knew for a fact that he had never fired a .17. I expect that in coming years other writers of similar stripe will rehash the fellow's nonsense and more innocent readers will be subject to his idiocy.

I was first bitten by the .17 bug back in the mid-1950's. I spent a lot of time shooting crows then, and the logic of an ultra-small, high-velocity bullet was inescapable. If you think about it, shooting a crow with a .22 caliber bullet is on the order of shooting a deer with a 20mm cannon. Even then, .17's were not all that new. Some experimental .17 rounds date back to pre-World War II days. Getting good bullets and, especially, good barrels, had been the big hang-up, and it was not until the now defunct A & M Rifle Company of Prescott, Arizona, began making really good .17 barrels that the sub-bore became practical. Their well publicized wildcat, the .17 Javelina, made by shortening, necking down, and blowing out .222 Remington cases, was the first truly successful .17 round. Other wildcats such as the .17 Bee and .17/222 also gained some recognition during the 1950's and '60's.

My first experience with the .17 was not all that pleasant and had I been so inclined I could have said some ugly things about the .17 tribe. The rifle was a pretty little thing, built on a Sako action with a fancy stock and chambered for the .17/222 wildcat, which is just the .222 Remington necked to .17 caliber with no other changes. It never shot worth a damn, either because of the three-groove barrel or because of the Sisk bullets, which were all I could locate, or both. I eventually gave up and got rid of it. This satisfied my .17 itch for a few years, but in the 1960's, when the Douglas Barrel Works announced that they were making .17 barrels, I was hot to try again.

This time I opted for a .17/222 Magnum, which is just a .222 Magnum case necked to .17. Fitted to a Sako action and stocked with Fajen classic stock, the Douglas barrel turned out to be

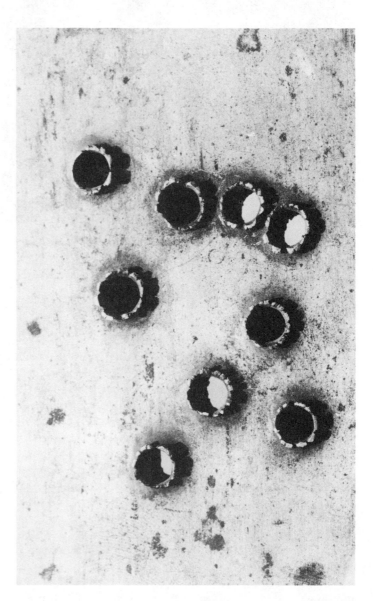

Never underestimate the might of high velocity. These holes were punched in a heavy steel plate by high-velocity .17 bullets.

a wonderful performer. A fellow by the name of Jim Williams of Cleveland, Texas, was making some excellent .17-caliber bullets then. They were probably the best ever made and it was common to get five-shot groups at 100 yards as small as three-quarters or even a half a minute of angle. This was the way I always figured a .17-caliber rifle should perform, given the right barrel and bullets. For a while, though, the care and feeding of my .17 was a frustrating task. All available powder funnels, for example, were too big, and it took months to find a tiny cleaning rod and bore brush. In the meantime, I was happy zapping scores of crows and groundhogs. The recoil of a .17 is so utterly mild that the crosshairs seldom bounce off the target when the trigger is pulled. You get to see all the action through the scope.

About the time I was messing with the .17/222 Magnum, a fellow who would soon become one of my best friends, and to whom this book is dedicated, Dave Wolfe, had the bright idea of necking down the new .223 Remington case to .17. The barrel work was done by Ed Shilen and produced another .17-caliber rifle capable of sub-MOA accuracy. Years later, I bought this first .17/223 from Wolfe and I still have it in my collection.

When I moved to Prescott, Arizona, in the late 1960's, I found myself in the thick of .17-caliber activity. Within walking distance of my house was the famed A & M Rifle works, home of the .17-Javelina and a source of prime .17 barrels. Paul Marquart, the "M" of the firm, was a keen prairie-dog shooter. He and I spent hundreds of hours and thousands of cartridges firing at prairie dogs in the huge dog towns near Prescott. Paul frequently used his original .17 Javelina, and he often fired several hundred rounds between barrel cleanings. A popular rumor of the time was that .17-caliber rifles had to be cleaned every 10 shots or so or the bore would become so badly fouled that accuracy would go all to hell. My personal experience and observations showed no such tendencies. I think such rumors got started early in the .17 era when barrels were rough and bullets weren't much better.

The .17 got another shot in the arm when a sharp operator by the name of Vern O'Brien, operating in Las Vegas, began making cute little rifles chambered for a round he called the .17 Mach IV. Made by necking down .221 Fireball cases, the .17 Mach IV was successfully used by O'Brien on all sorts of big game, including Alaskan brown bears. Eventually he sold his racy little rifle and stock design to Harrington & Richardson who for a while marketed it as the Model 317 Ultra Wildcat. They did not offer the .17 Mach IV chambering but instead used Dave Wolfe's .17/223, thus becoming one of the very few major arms makers ever to offer a rifle chambered for a wildcat cartridge. When Remington offered a legitimate .17-caliber cartridge H&R dropped the wildcat form. Indeed, all .17 wildcats became pretty much obsolete.

In my experience, the .17 Remington is about the best possible cartridge they could have devised in this caliber. Factory ammo is accurate, and with the present abundance of good-quality components, tools, and accessories made for the mini-bore, reloading is no more of a chore than for any other caliber. The future of the .17, however, is uncertain. Now that the novelty has worn off, few experimenters tinker with .17's. And, too, the .17 Remington never caught on with varmint shooters the way I would have wished. Perhaps it is just too exotic or perhaps performance really isn't that spectacular when compared to other varmint rounds. Even though it starts out mighty fast (4,040 fps), the light bullet loses velocity faster than a heavier .22-caliber bullet. The .17 is, however, a genuine 300-yard varmint cartridge with a tra-

The author's .17/222 Remington Magnum is a stylish-looking sporter built on a Sako action with a Douglas barrel and handsome Fajen classic-style stock.

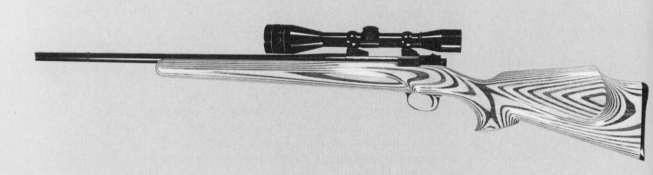

Designed by Dave Wolfe, this racy-looking varminter was the first .17/223. It has a Sako action, Shilen barrel, and laminated maple and walnut stock by Reinhart Fajen. Marvelously accurate, it can produce half-minute groups at 100 yards.

Vern O'Brien, who originated the .17 Mach IV, has been a successful promoter of .17-caliber rifles. This is an O'Brien rifle with a Sako action and a fancy stock complete with basketweave carving.

jectory almost identical to the .22/250's out to 400 yards. But the lighter bullet is more susceptible to crosswinds.

For a while I thought Remington might stop making .17-caliber rifles but suddenly it has proven to be enormously popular in Australia. The Aussies love the .17 because of the minimal pelt damage to furbearing varmints such as rabbits, and have thus assured the tiny cartridge a long life.

THE ACCELERATOR

In the mid-1970's, the inventive guys at Remington unveiled a super-fast .22 caliber-*cum*-.30/06 cartridge called the Accelerator, which represented a radically new approach to achieving high velocity in an ordinary sporting rifle. The first of what was to become a series was a standard .30/06 case loaded with a 55-grain .22-caliber jacketed bullet, the same bullet used in Remington's .22/250 cartridges. This is managed by fitting the bullet into a tough plastic sleeve called a sabot. (The word is pronounced sa-bow and means shoe.) The sabot, in turn, fits the .30/06 case and .30/06 barrels like a .30-caliber bullet. As they travel through the bore the sabot and bullet are spun by the rifling the same as an ordinary bullet. When the sabot exits the muzzle the centrifugal force caused by the fast rate of spin causes the fingers at the mouth of the sabot to open up and release the bullet, which goes on its way while the light sabot rapidly decelerates and falls to the ground within a few feet.

The sabot principle has been applied in several forms to ultra-velocity space research and to certain military uses. In fact, I understand that Remington's Accelerator cartridges are a spin-off of some military project with which the company was involved. The idea of applying the sabot principle to sporting use is a good one *if,* and this is a big if, accuracy is satisfactory. For example, shooters who own only a .30/06 deer rifle would, by using the Accelerator, also have a highly effective long-range varmint rifle. Carrying the idea a bit further, it could be adapted to .30/30 and .308 rifles, which is exactly what Remington has done, plus a host of other calibers.

The first time I tried the .30/06 Accelerator was at a Remington Writers' Seminar where a few of us had a chance to try sample runs of ammo. Firing from a benchrest with standard Model 700 rifles, we were able to produce a number of five-shot test groups that ranged around an inch or smaller. This, of course, is good accuracy and I suspected that it might be made even better by using specialized target rifles.

I put my theory into action a few months later when I received a supply of production-run Accelerator ammo. Taking some eight or 10 .30/06 rifles to the test range, I tried the new cartridges in every type of rifle from lightweight sporters to bull-barreled target jobs. The most significant thing I learned was that accuracy was just about the same, regardless of the rifle used. Apparently the accuracy factor of the Accelerator cartridge is almost entirely dependent on the ammo and not the rifle. Almost all groups measured around two inches for five shots with none coming close to the groups I'd fired with the earlier lot. When I discussed this with a Remington engineer, he told me that different lots of Accelerator ammo did tend to vary in accuracy, but he had no workable explanation.

Clearly, a varmint rifle that groups no better than two inches at 100 yards is going to do no

Above, you see the Remington .30/06 Accelerator cartridge, which employs a plastic sabot to guide its 55-grain .22-caliber bullet through the barrel of a standard .30/06 rifle. The two pictures, right, are high-speed photographs of an Accelerator bullet fired from a .30/06 rifle — one showing the bullet as it exits with a velocity of 4,080 fps and one showing how the sabot has been left behind when the bullet has traveled two feet from the muzzle. This cartridge bestows varminting capability on a big game rifle.

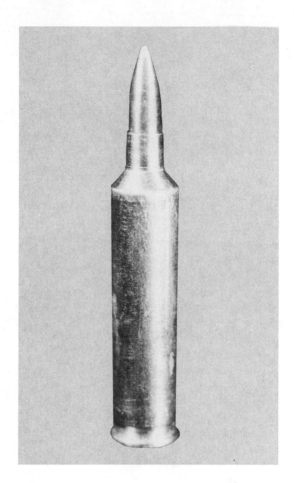

The .22 CHeetah, designed by Jim Carmichel and Fred Huntington, achieves a muzzle velocity of 4,300 fps with a 53-grain bullet, making it the fastest varmint cartridge around. Along with speed, it offers quarter-minute accuracy.

better than four or five inches at 200 yards, and that won't win many prizes or kill many chucks. If and when Accelerators are developed that reliably produce good accuracy they will probably be a success. For the present, though, the main advocates of the Accelerators are fox and coyote hunters, who like the idea of hunting these furbearers with their big game rifles.

THE FUTURE

Where do we go from here? Are the .220 Swift and .22/250 Remington the best varmint rounds we're likely to see, or is there something new and exciting down the road? The most promising of tomorrow's varmint cartridges appears to be a sophisticated wildcat called the .22 CHeetah. Designed by Carmichel and Huntington (hence the CH), the CHeetah combines advanced ballistic technology with state-of-the-art benchrest know-how. The CHeetah is not only the fastest varmint cartridge around, with a velocity of close to 4,300 fps with a 53-grain bullet, it also offers extremely fine accuracy. Two major arms and ammo makers have expressed interest

An ultra-high-performance varminting combination is this Remington Model 40X rifle fitted with a stainless-steel .22 CHeetah barrel under a Leupold 6.5X-20X variable scope.

in the CHeetah, and there is a fair chance that it may some day be a legitimate factory round. Now it is strictly a wildcat. Finished varmint rifles in .22 CHeetah chambering are being made by the Shilen Rifle Company and by Wichita Engineering, and some custom gunsmiths offer special barreling in this racy caliber. Reloading dies are available from Huntington Die specialties and others.

THE RIFLES

The varmint rifle has evolved from the single-shot pest guns of the 1890's to the rebuilt Springfields of the 1930's, to the ultra-accurate rifles of today. Varmint rifles are indeed the best of two worlds; they combine the best of both hunting and target-shooting equipment. As the varmint rifle evolved it constantly moved closer to the target-shooting end of the rifle spectrum. Since the name of the game is accuracy, natural selection, as practiced mainly by benchrest shooters, has eliminated the myriad factors that contributed to poor accuracy. That's why to-day's best varmint rifles are remarkably simple and free of the assorted gadgetry which infests most other types of rifles. As is often the case with good engineering, the final product is far less complicated than was originally anticipated.

I can best describe the development of today's varmint rifle in terms of my own experience. The .220 Swift and I were born only a year apart and more or less grew up together. And it was in 1950, the year the .222 Remington saw light, that I reloaded my first rifle case.

In those days, benchrest shooting was just getting cranked up and shooters were pretty innocent when it came to the subtle causes of poor accuracy. For centuries past, it had been assumed that rifles that shot accurately did so simply because they had good barrels with straight bores and well-cut shiny rifling. Of course, the importance of good bullets was also recognized, and shooters were pretty certain that having the right amount of gunpowder in the cartridge was of paramount importance as well. Mainly, though, when a rifle shot accurately, the barrel and the marksman shared the credit.

The prevalence of this attitude is obvious when you thumb through some shooting journals of the 1950's and consider the equipment used by benchrest shooters of that era. The reason I keep referring to benchrest shooting, by the way, is because virtually all of the useful information we now possess concerning accuracy and building of truly accurate rifles and ammunition was distilled in the heat of benchrest competition. The sophisticated varmint rifles we now enjoy would not exist if it had not been for the benchrest game.

The first benchrest rifles were made up by fitting a long, heavy barrel to whatever action was at hand, then inletting the works into a chunky stock. Most of the actions were from German Mauser rifles liberated during the two world wars. The reason so many Mausers were used was simply because they were cheap and plentiful and they were easy to rebarrel. Some 1903 Springfield and 1917 Enfield actions were used as well, plus a scattering of commercial rifles such as Model 70 Winchesters. It did not take the early bench competitors long to learn that the way an action and barrel were fitted into the stock played a tremendous role in a rifle's accuracy. For example, it was conclusively proven that if the stock did not touch the barrel, allowing it to vibrate freely, the rifle would be more accurate. Likewise, it was discovered that a rifle would not perform its accurate best if the action was bedded in the stock in such a way that it was bent or twisted by even a few thousandths of an inch. This was a significant bit of information, not just because it was another step along the long road to accuracy. It was also important because it began an era when shooters started to look critically at every part of their rifles and the interaction of the parts as well as just the barrel.

The Mauser action and a lot of its kin, the Springfields and M-70's, came under harsh examination. Not only was the Mauser action rather flimsy and easy to bend and twist, it was and is rather difficult to bed properly. And even when correctly bedded, the Mausers and Springfields could not support heavy, free-floated target barrels without some tendency to flex. Within less than a decade the Mauser and its cousins became obsolete in the benchrest accuracy game.

The giant Belgian gunmaking firm of Fabrique Nationale probably made the best Mauser-pattern rifles and actions during the post-World War II period. FN tried marketing a stiffer single-shot Mauser action, but it did not measure up in competition. Other problems in addition to flexing contributed to the demise of the Mauser action in accuracy circles. Even the technique of locking the action in a hard mixture of chemical resins and glass fibers, popularly known as glass bedding, couldn't solve the Mauser problems.

The reason I go into such detail is not to criticize the Mauser, but to clearly define that historic fork in the road where the pursuers of accuracy departed from traditional bolt-action rifle design and blazed new trails. Some of these trails lead to dead ends, and I'm sure the search for the perfect action is far from over, but we're already beginning to taste the delicious fruits of these labors.

THE BEST ACTIONS

The most accurate rifle actions you can buy these days have a number of factors in common. The lower half of the receiver is either a simple cylinder, seen in the Remington 40-XB, and the

Wichita rifles, or it is dead flat on the bottom as in the Shilen DGA. This simplicity of external contour guarantees the easiest and truest contact between action and stock. The best actions are also very symmetrical. The bolt alignment in the receiver is essentially a sleeve within a sleeve. The walls of the receiver are thick and stiff so they will resist flexing and twisting, and the firing-pin motion is extremely quick. The locking arrangement is simple, strong, and highly symmetrical, and the extractor is mounted within the bolt face. A Mauser-type external extractor requires a cut in the receiver wall which not only makes the receiver more prone to flex but also violates its symmetry. In order to retain as much mass and symmetry as possible, the loading/ejection port is as small as possible. The overall action length is also as short as possible. Naturally, such actions are of single-shot configuration because cutting a large hole in the bottom of the receiver for a magazine box significantly reduces the receiver's stiffness.

It is fascinating to note that a rifle action built along these guidelines is less difficult and less expensive to make than the older Mauser types or a 1903 Springfield or a Model 70 Winchester.

Back in the late 1940's when Remington was developing the Model 721 and Model 722, one of their chief goals was a basic action that would be simple and inexpensive to manufacture. Either by accident or intent, the resulting designs happened to have included nearly all of the accuracy features we've just discussed. The built-in accuracy of the Model 722 rifle was one of the reasons the .222 cartridge, for which the M-722 was chambered, gained such quick renown for accuracy. Curiously, it was to be a few years before more than a handful of benchrest shooters became aware of the built-in accuracy advantages of the 722 type of action, but once target shooters, benchresters, and varmint hunters caught on to these advantages it's been Katy bar the door. Virtually every Olympic-class 300-meter target rifle used by American medalists has utilized the basic 722 action or one of its descendants. Likewise, four out of five benchrest rifles utilize this type of action, and the same is true of top varmint rifles.

Today many makes, models, and calibers are available. Each varmint model possesses, or *seems* to possess certain features which make it irresistible. What are the really good ones and why?

THE REMINGTONS

Probably the most accurate varmint rifle you can buy over your dealer's counter is the 40-XB Remington. It comes in a variety of calibers from .222 up to .300 Magnum, but long-range varmint shooters are most concerned with the .22/250, 6mm Remington, and .243 Winchester. Originally, the 40-X was available with either a medium- or heavyweight barrel, and for a while you could get a barrel of blued chrome-moly or stainless steel. Now it is made exclusively with the heavy stainless tube, which is what you want anyway. The 40-XB comes either as a single-shot or a repeater, but the only real choice for a varmint hunter is the single-shot version because the action and stock are stiffer. For extra money, the 40-XB comes with a two-ounce (pull) trigger. That sounds great, but some shooters cannot manage it well. The standard trigger adjusts to two pounds or less, which is fine for varmint shooting. The 40-XB rifles are produced in Remington's custom shop where each rifle is more or less hand-built and tested. Each rifle is test fired for accuracy and test targets come with each rifle. Some of the groups are very small indeed.

Remington has never chambered a rifle in .220 Swift, and I doubt they ever will, seeing that gunmakers usually favor their own cartridge developments. If Remington ever offered the 40-XB in .220 Swift caliber it would be a great varmint rifle made even better. Some long-range varmint shooters buy 40-XB's in .22/250 caliber and have them converted to .220 Swift by the simple expedient of setting the barrel back a thread or two and rechambering. Likewise, experimental 40-XB rifles have been built in the .22 CHeetah caliber described earlier in this chapter. They are probably the best varmint-rifle/ammo combinations to date.

The stock profile and dimensions of the 40-XB are in pure target style. The comb is high and straight for scope use and there is a wide fore-end for a steady rest on the sandbags. The styling is beautiful only in the eyes of target and varmint shooters, but it does perform.

Remington's next best varmint rifle is the Model 700 Varmint Special, which is essentially a Model 700 Sporter. Both have the same stock, action, and trigger, but the varmint special has a heavy barrel. It comes in all the standard smallbore varmint calibers, except .17, and it is also made in .25/06, 7mm/08, and .308 Winchester. The M-700 and 40-XB Remington actions are virtually identical because they are direct descendants of the Model 722 with cosmetic changes. The M-700 is a repeater, which means there is a magazine cut in the bottom of the receiver. The stocking of the M-700 provides a standard assembly-line fit, and the barrels are not supposed to be as good as those of the 40-XB's. They do not get the hand treatment that goes into a 40-XB. Yet M-700 Varmint Specials tend to be outstandingly accurate. By way of comparison, a 40-XB may be capable of quarter-inch groups at 100 yards, whereas a really good 700 Varmint Special in the same caliber will get you half-inch groups or a bit larger. But the Varmint Special sells for about half the price of a 40-XB.

The standard sporter-weight Model 700's in either ADL or the fancier BDL grade come in all the varmint calibers (.17 in BDL only). They are not as desirable as the Varmint Special for varmint shooting because their lighter weight makes them rather more difficult to hold steady. Some individual specimens are exceptionally accurate but on the average they are about a quarter of an inch less accurate than the Varmint Specials.

THE WINCHESTERS

In 1950, the very best varmint rifle you could buy off a dealer's rack was a Winchester Model 70 Target Grade in .220 Swift. The second best was a standard-weight Model 70 in the same caliber. In 1956, Winchester added the varmint-grade rifle with a heavy target-type barrel in a plain sporter stock, and these three rifles continued to be the best available until 1963, when they were discontinued.

These were beautifully made rifles, American classics, and we may never again see that wonderful combination of style, class, and workmanship. I love them now as I loved them then, but logic and experience force me to recognize that if the old-style Model 70 in .220 Swift had been made until 1965 it would no longer have been the best available. That was the year the .22/250 Remington 40-XB appeared.

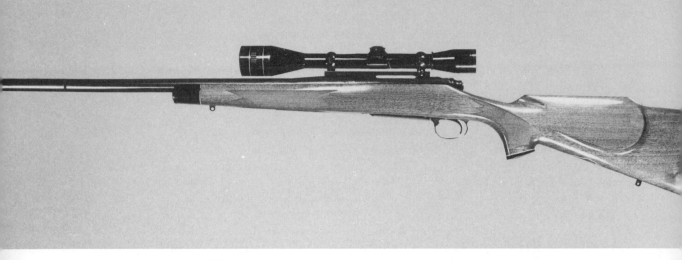

Here is a Remington Model 700 BDL varmint-weight rifle in .223 Remington caliber. The scope is a 12X Leupold.

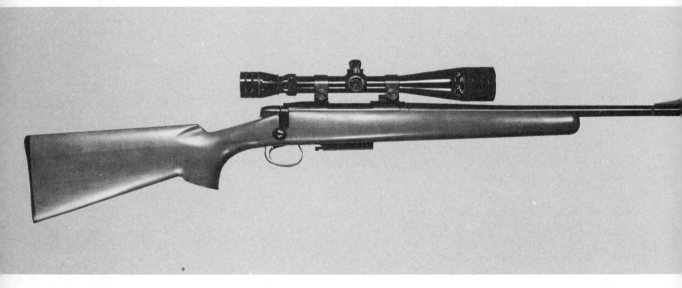

Bargain-priced, the Remington Model 788 is surprisingly accurate in varmint calibers. It's shown here with a Redfield 6X-18X variable scope.

The 40-XB action was basically more accurate than the pre-'64 Model 70, especially in the smallbore calibers. Also, Remington's custom-shop craftsmen, who produced the 40-XB, were obsessed by accuracy. Model 70's, even the premier Target Grades, were production-line items, not subjected to individual testing and tuning, but each 40-XB was tested and tuned until it was a tack driver. The reason for this comparison is to give you some perspective on the much maligned Model 70 as it has been made from 1964 until the present.

Though the Model 70 introduced in 1964 was not as beautifully finished as its predecessor it did incorporate more of the features essential to accuracy than the earlier Model 70's. If you examine the bolt of a modern Model 70 you will find that it is similar to the bolt of a Remington M-700 or 40-XB. In fact, the modern Model 70 bolt is closer to the Remington version than it is to a pre-'64 Model 70 Winchester bolt. The extractor is located in the recessed bolt face so there is no need for an extractor cut in the receiver. This contributes to a more symmetrical action.

Like most fanciers of the Model 70, I deplored the 1964 version, but it didn't take long for me to become aware of its fine accuracy. My first test rifle in the new configuration was a stiff-barreled varmint model in .225 Winchester chambering. With Winchester-Western factory loads this rig was capable of five-shot 100-yard groups as small as three-eighths of an inch, making it one of the five or six most accurate out-of-the-box rifles I've ever fired. That test also showed that the W-W factory loads were among the most accurate ever made.

Like most big-bore target shooters, I tended to favor the pre-1964 Model 70 Winchester action as the basis for the rifles I used in long-range competition. About 1970, however, when I began longing for a new "over-the-course" (rapid-fire and long-range) rifle in .308 caliber, I decided to try one of the new-style Model 70 actions. This was almost an act of heresy among big-bore target shooters. The resulting rifle, with heavy Douglas stainless-steel barrel and homemade stock, was and is the most accurate I've ever carried to the tournaments. With it, I've won dozens of trophies, and I even set a national long-range record. Five shot, 100-yard test groups *average* around three-tenths of an inch (.300), and one *10 shot* group fired at 200 yards measured a neat three-quarters of an inch! Since then, I've had two more long-range rifles built on the latest Model 70 actions and both have been winners.

The new M-70 ranks with the Remington 700 and Ruger 77 as one of the three most accurate production-grade rifles you can select from your dealer's shelves. The M-70 trigger is not so easily or precisely adjusted as the Remington or Ruger triggers and some other makes, but the barrels, made by the hammer-forge process, tend to be especially accurate and wear-resistant. In fact, I think the good barrels make up for other shortcomings in the Model 70 package. In any event, the new Model 70's, in either varmint or field weights, tend to be more accurate than their pre-1964 counterparts, and that's saying a lot.

THE RUGERS

The Ruger Model 77 varmint-weight rifle in .220 Swift with a 26-inch barrel comes very close to being the best varmint rifle made by any major manufacturer. Samples I have tested were exceedingly accurate, and I get the same report from other shooters. The Model 77 is not so unfailingly accurate as the Remington 40-XB but very nearly equal.

The Model 77 Swift comes with either a standard sporter-weight 24-inch barrel or a heavy 26-inch varmint-weight tube. For serious varmint shooting, the heavier, longer barrel is the only way to go, especially since the longer barrel nets you some 100 fps more muzzle velocity than the standard-length model. Ruger also offers the Model 77 in .22/250, .243, and 6mm Remington in the varmint-weight series, but each of these rifles comes with only a 24-inch barrel. When the Model 77 series was announced in 1968 (if memory serves me correctly), I bought a varmint-weight .22/250 and have shot varmints, mainly prairie dogs, with it every season since. It is a steady performer, reliably capable of three-quarter-inch groups with an occasional group going as small as half an inch. Also, I've used a couple more varmint-weight Ruger 77's which have been sub-MOA performers. None, however, have come close to equaling the accuracy of my two M-77 Swifts.

Taking a lesson from Remington, Ruger makes the Model 77 in two action lengths. The short-stroke version accommodates cartridges in the .308, .243, 6mm, .220 Swift, and .22/250 length range. This short, chunky action no doubt accounts for much of the accuracy delivered by these rifles, but in some ways the Ruger 77 is a phenomenon. For instance, the design incorporates the traditional external-leaf Mauser-style extractor. And the long tang-safety arrangement cannot contribute to accuracy, either. Probably the best thing the Model 77 action has going for it is a superb bedding system. The rearward-angled front action screw was much touted by Ruger as an aid to accuracy, and this is no doubt true. I am more inclined, however, to credit the large, flat surfaces on the receiver bottom and the very precise inletting of the Ruger stocks. In my opinion, based on experience with perhaps two dozen Model 77 rifles, the weak link in the accuracy chain of these rifles is the barrel.

Most Ruger barrels are excellent, but the incidence of bad barrels is considerably greater than it is with, say, Remington and Winchester rifles. Ruger does not make rifle barrels but buys them rifled and pre-turned from a supplier by the name of Wilson. I have a couple of Ruger rifles with barrels so rough that the irregularities in the rifling can be easily seen with the unaided eye. The bore surface is so rough that after 10 shots or so the accumulated jacket fouling ruins accuracy. Yet, for the first five shots the rifles group wonderfully well. Apparently, the stiff Ruger action and accurate stocking more or less overcome, at least temporarily, the ill effects of the occasional bum barrel. One Ruger Model 77 Swift in my collection ranks as one of the five

Carmichel has found the latest Winchester Model 70 actions to be excellent for varminting. This is one of his several Model 70's. However, one fault he finds with the Model 70 varmint rifles in current production is the continued use of full-length actions for short cartridges—the .222, .22/250, and .243.

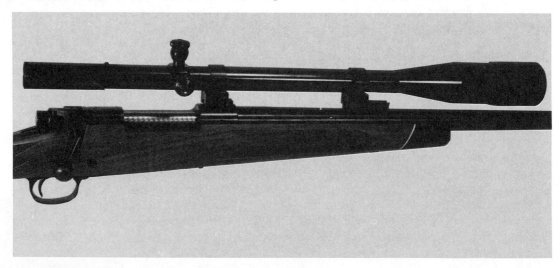

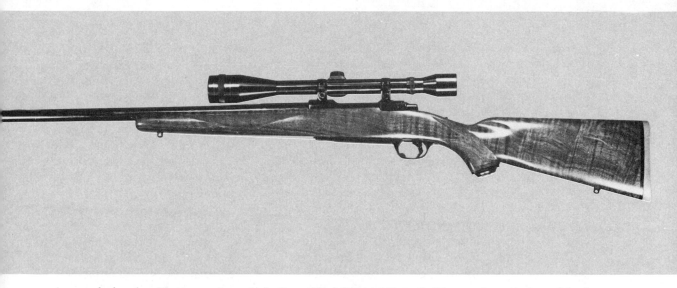

Among the best long-range varminters is the Ruger Model 77 in .220 Swift. The one shown is the standard-weight version with a 26-inch barrel (which the author prefers over the 24-inch varmint-weight). The scope on it is a 12X Weaver.

most accurate out-of-the-box rifles I've ever tested. And before you decide that the rifle was specially selected for me at the Ruger factory, let me add that I bought it at a local gun shop.

Another rifle that ranked temporarily as one of the five most accurate production-grade rifles I've ever tested was none other than a Ruger No. 1 Single-Shot in .220 Swift caliber. This is something of a paradox because of the No. 1's reputation for not always living up to accuracy expectations. A few years back when I was visiting Ruger's New Hampshire plant where the rifles are made, I learned of their plan to manufacture the single-shot in .220 Swift caliber and requested that a couple of the first ones be sent to me for testing. Both of the test rifles, as it turned out, were delightfully accurate. One of them from the very beginning turned in groups as small as three-eighths of an inch. Naturally, I immediately decided to buy this rifle and return the other one to the plant. Greed, however, raised its ugly head and caused me to outsmart myself. The rifle that shot so well had a rather plain butt and fore-end while the other had gorgeously figured stocks. The wood was so pretty that I couldn't resist exchanging the stocks. I was dreaming of a really beautiful tack driver. You've probably already guessed what happened. The next time I tried my beautiful and beautifully accurate No. 1 from the bench, after returning the plain Jane to the factory, it didn't group nearly as well as before. This story illustrates the endless variables to which the Ruger single-shot seems to be heir.

No one can deny that the Ruger No. 1 is a beautiful rifle. It is one of the most stylish rifles ever made in America and ranks with the world's classics. Some collectors, in fact, buy the No. 1's with no thought of ever shooting them. They simply enjoy them for their classic elegance. As varmint rifles they are especially appealing because of their close-coupled balance and target-like stock dimensions, which greatly aid scope use. There is something about single-shot rifles that seems just right for varmint shooting.

I admit to being a fan of the No. 1 and want to own every one I see. But they have frequently been heartbreakers. The biggest heartbreak of all was a varmint-weight .22/250 with the most stunning wood I've ever seen come out of an arms factory. How I would love to carry this rifle afield and show off the beautiful stocking, but alas, the saw-toothed gaps in the rifling foul after three or four shots and accuracy goes all to hell.

I suspect that if this same barrel had been fitted to a Model 77 action it would be performing better because of the 77's "accuracy-protecting" features. The single-shot has no such built-in protection and tends to be extremely vulnerable to vagaries in the way the barrel is fitted, the way the fore-end fits, and especially troubles with the barrel itself. The most inescapable proof of this, in my experience, is the number of previously inaccurate No. 1's which, after being fitted with a good barrel by a competent gunsmith, delivered first-rate accuracy.

These comments certainly do not imply that Ruger single-shots are inaccurate. As I said at the beginning, one of the most accurate rifles I've ever fired was a No. 1. Also, I must say there seems to have been a steady improvement in accuracy during recent years. The people at Ruger are aware of the criticisms and have tried to weed out the problems. At present the chances of getting a satisfactorily accurate No. 1 varmint rifle are pretty good but not as good as picking, at random, a tack-driving Ruger Model 77 or Remington M-700 or Winchester M-70.

One of the great attractions of the No. 1 as a varmint rifle, in addition to its good looks, is the wide choice of calibers: .223, .22/250, .220 Swift, .243 and 6mm Remington, in a remarkable selection of barrel weights and configurations. These range from the standard 22-inch light sporter through the medium 26-inch sporter to the heavy special varminter with 24-inch barrel. If I were selecting any varmint caliber except the Swift I would be inclined to go for this varmint model. The longer standard barrel is, I think, a better choice for the Swift because of the velocity you will gain by using it.

Ruger's lower-priced single-shot, the No. 3 carbine, comes in .22 Hornet and .223 chambering, in addition to others, but the stocking and general configuration pretty much rule this model out as a really serious varmint rifle. It is cute and fun to shoot but that's about all.

THE SAKOS

The Finnish-made line of Sako varmint rifles deserves thoughtful consideration because of their consistent effort to supply a full selection of varmint calibers in varmint-style rifles. In fact, the firm's reputation for accuracy and excellent workmanship was founded almost entirely on their early varmint rifles.

As of this writing, the line of Sako rifles as imported into the United States by Stoeger Arms includes rifles in .22 Hornet, .17 Remington, .222, .233, .22/250, .220 Swift, .243, and 6mm Remington. This selection is the widest available from any of the major riflemakers. Also, counting the Model 78 rifle which comes in .22 Hornet caliber, the Sako can be had in four action sizes, providing the largest selection of bolt-actions available from any maker. For serious shooting, however, only the short-action Model AI, standard on .17, .222, and .223 rifles, and the medium-length action, Model-AII on the .22/250, .220 Swift, and .243 Winchester rifles are of great interest to varmint hunters.

The "A" series of actions used on current-production Sako rifles are revamped successors to the earlier short and medium action lengths, known, respectively, as the Vixen and Forester.

Back in the late 1940's, when Sakos were first imported into the U.S., they made something of a splash because of the beautifully made little action which looked like a miniature Mauser, the superb stockwork which equaled the work of top custom craftsmen, and a very favorable price. The exchange rate for U.S. dollars at that time made it possible for Americans to buy superbly hand-crafted European guns for about the same money that we paid for production-grade U.S. arms. The Sakos were among the very best buys available but at first they did not enjoy any great reputation for accuracy simply because they were available only in uninspiring .22 Hornet and .218 Bee calibers. When Remington introduced the .222 cartridge in 1950 they unknowingly created a serious source of competition for their own rifles, because the .222 was perfectly suited to the little rifle from Finland.

The first Sako I ever saw was a trim little .222 with a Mannlicher stock that I ordered through the mail. You could do that then. It cost only $99. That was a fair piece of change then, especially for a teen-age farm lad, but I couldn't have been happier with the rifle's appearance and performance. Fitted with a 10X Lyman Wolverine scope, that Sako, light as it was, could put 10 shots inside an inch circle at 100 yards. I did it a number of times, to the utter astonishment of skeptical onlookers.

Hundreds, then thousands, of other shooters were discovering the same thing about the little Finnish rifle with the funny name, and before long it had an unmatched record for accuracy. During the later 1950's and into the '60's the name Sako seemed to be the password in shooting circles. Colt, Marlin, and H&R, plus a dozen lesser outfits offered even more rifles built on Sako actions, and the Sako star rose even higher.

But by the early 1970's, things started going sour. One of the best things Sako had going was the currency-exchange rate. In 1962, a Sako Vixen in .222 sold for $141.95. A Model 700 BDL Remington, which in no way stood up by comparison, sold for only $2 less. Ten years

The Finnish-made Sako rifles, available in a full array of varmint calibers, are accurate and are very popular among American shooters. The one shown here is a heavy-barreled varmint model with the short Vixen action in .222 Remington caliber.

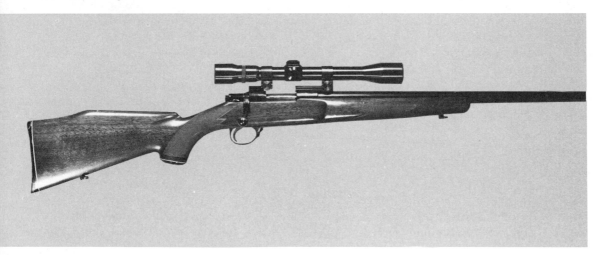

later, the price spread was $30, and in 1980, the spread came to a fantastic $207. This terrific pricing difference is enough to turn off even the most ardent Sako fan.

Worse though, today's Sako is not as good as those of a decade ago and certainly not equal to those of the 1950's. Caught in the price crunch, as was Winchester in 1964, Sako has made a series of modifications which have not always been for the better. American makers have managed to improve not only the appearance but the accuracy of their products; Sako has, at best, stood still. So the rifle that was once advertised as the world's most accurate is now an also-ran.

This is not to say that today's Sakos aren't accurate. Over the past couple of years, I've tested or observed the test-firing of six or eight Sakos in assorted varmint calibers. The best of these turned in a neat little group measuring scarcely more than half an inch. The worst could group no better than 2½ inches, though.

When the Sako landslide got rolling it was felt that the unique action was largely responsible for the sterling accuracy. Accordingly, a number of benchrest rifles were built on these actions and Sako even offered a special single-shot "benchrest" action. These rifles never performed with any notable success and the idea was abandoned. This demonstrated that the Sako action was no great contributor to accuracy. I believe the reason the early Sakos were so wonderfully accurate was because of extremely good, albeit soft, barrels and careful stockmaking. Reintroducing this sort of handwork to the Sako line would undoubtedly cause their price to become even more prohibitive.

WEATHERBY

Because Weatherby magnums are known as the bone-crushing playthings of rich Texans their little varmint rifles tend to get lost in the shuffle. Weatherby does, in fact, make a genuine varmint rifle complete with a stiff, 26-inch varmint-weight barrel in either .224 Weatherby or .22/250. It is a fine rifle, yet self-styled shooting sophisticates forget to include this model in their lists of top-rate shooting gear. If you take a Weatherby Mark V mechanism out of the stock and give it a close inspection you'll quickly discover that it is only a half step away from meeting the criteria of a really first-class target or benchrest varmint action. This is particularly true of the short varmint action. It is stiff, highly symmetrical, and locks like a vault. You may or may not like the stock shape, but the bedding is done with care. The rifles are individually tested for accuracy. This means the chances of getting a Weatherby varmint rifle that won't shoot in an inch or less are just about nil.

THE CREAM OF THE CROP

We've been talking about the best production-grade varmint rifles produced by the giant arms manufacturers. What about the smaller makers? Who are they and how good are their varmint

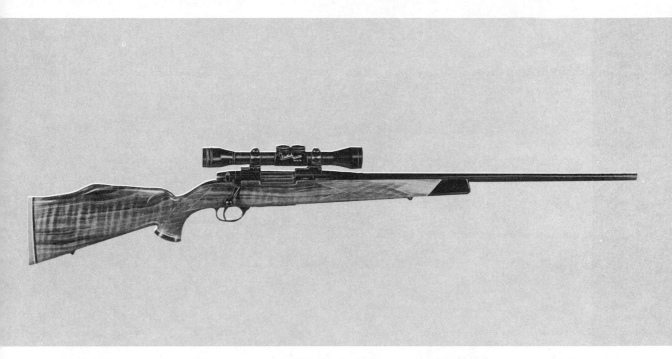

This is a Weatherby Mark V Varmintmaster in .224 Weatherby Magnum with a 26-inch varmint-weight barrel. Bedding in all the Weatherby models is done with care, and the rifles are individually tested for accuracy.

rifles? We could list dozens of fine custom shops that turn out superbly accurate varmint rifles, but almost all of them specialize in assembling top-grade components. Usually, a rifle from one of these shops will incorporate a barrel by Hart, Atkinson, Douglas, or Shilen, and a Remington action bedded in a target-grade fiberglass or laminated-wood stock.

There are, however, several relatively small specialty shops that manufacture the very best in varmint rifles from scratch. Probably the best known is the Shilen Rifle Company of Irving, Texas. Ed Shilen, the founder, is internationally famous as the maker of tournament-winning barrels. It was natural that his pursuit of accuracy led him into action designing. After marketing a few experimental benchrest-type actions over the years, Shilen developed his ultra-accurate DGA model. Originally conceived as the heart of a target rifle, the DGA has all the characteristics necessary for fine accuracy. It also happens to be an extremely handsome design that looks good in lightweight sporter dress. After a few years of making strictly benchrest rifles, Shilen expanded his line of finished rifles to include finished sporters and medium-weight varmint rifles. The stocks come close to achieving the perfect blend of classic sporter good looks and target performance, and the overall effect with the DGA action is wicked efficiency.

I bought one of the earliest Shilen varmint/sporters. It has a medium-weight 25-inch .220 Swift barrel and it is the deadliest, easiest-to-shoot varmint rifle I've ever owned. The most recent group fired with this rifle, after *exactly* 2,602 rounds through the barrel, measured .327 between the centers of the widest holes. There was a stiff crosswind blowing or the group would have been smaller. The barrel is not, by the way, made of stainless steel.

The small, dark spot at which the hunter at left is aiming—way out across the meadow—is the all-time star among varmints, the lowly woodchuck, the animal that has supplied the primary motivation for the development of great varmint cartridges, rifles, and scopes.

Varminting has many elements in common with target shooting, and particularly with benchrest shooting. This hunter is using carefully developed handloads, a heavy-barreled rifle with a finely tuned trigger mechanism, and an adjustable shooting rest. Other similarities involve technique rather than equipment, for the varminter must beat the problems of mirage and wind drift.

Carmichel at the bench, after testing a Shilen sporter-weight rifle in .22/250 caliber. He's discussing the results with Ed Shilen, who looks understandably pleased. Shilen's sporters and varminters — based on the same action used in his top benchrest rifles — are phenomenally accurate.

These rifles do not come cheap. They cost about half again what you would pay for a 40-XB Remington. But they are made in any caliber you specify and the performance is guaranteed to awe your shooting buddies.

Another super-performance varmint rifle miles ahead of any production-grade varmint model in the beauty department is the Wichita. Made by Wichita Engineering of Wichita, Kansas, the action, like the Shilen, began as an attempt to include in one mechanism all the basic building blocks of accuracy. Wichita succeeded very well indeed, as can be seen by the impressive list of benchrest wins and records set with Wichita rifles or rifles built on their actions.

These are very handsome actions, beautifully made, and the Wichita people go all out to make what is probably the best-looking varmint rifle ever offered. Their stock in trade is a barrel-fitting arrangement that forms one uninterrupted exterior profile from the rear of the action to the muzzle. Their more expensive Classic Model is basically the same but with the contour of both action and barrel milled to a striking octagonal cross section.

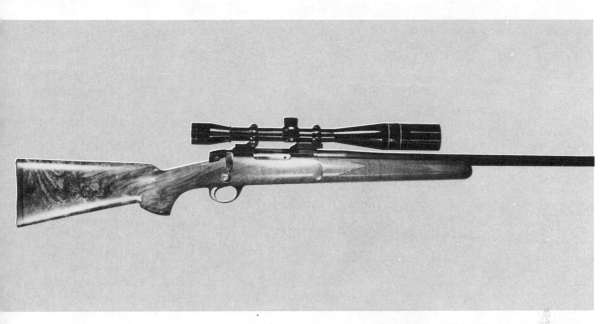

One of the best-performing varmint rifles in the author's collection is this Shilen DGA. The caliber is .220 Swift, the scope a Leupold 18X. Carmichel describes its long-range accuracy as astonishing.

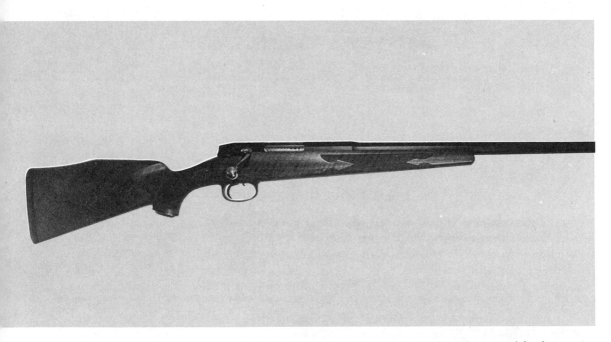

Another super-performance varmint rifle in the Carmichel collection is this Wichita Classic Model, whose action and barrel are milled to a striking octagonal cross-section. This sleek beauty proves that accuracy can be married to good looks.

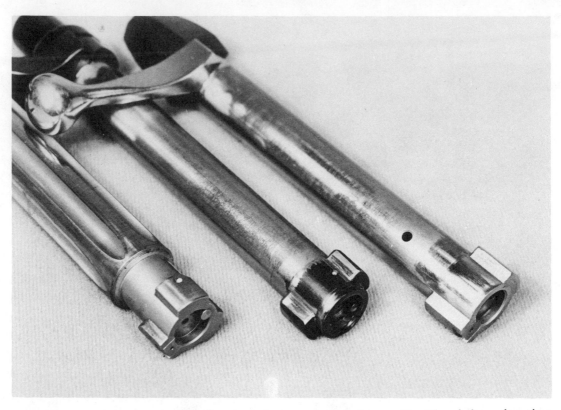

Stiff, highly symmetrical actions are characteristic of today's varmint and target rifles. These bolts are from three of the most accurate. At left is the Wichita, which has three-lug locking; at center is the Remington 40X; and at right is the Shilen DGA. Features shared in common are recessed bolt faces and simplicity of design.

Like Shilen, Wichita will make you a varmint rifle in any caliber from .17 on up, and if you feel really daring, the company will even chamber it for the blazing-fast .22 CHeetah.

WHAT PRICE ACCURACY?

As one contemplates today's wonderful assortment of varmint rifles and the wide array of cartridges, the question of dollar value arises. If price is no object, then it is easy to select a Shilen or Wichita or perhaps an exotic custom rig and enjoy the luxury of super accuracy. At what level of accuracy and at what price do we draw the line between necessary and unnecessary, reasonable and excessive? If your ambition is to pot standing woodchucks at no more than 200 yards, you can get by with very modest equipment. This sort of shooting can be managed nicely with a number of inexpensive rifles not previously described in this chapter. Several good-looking rifles are built on inexpensive imported Mauser-type actions in such varmint calibers as .22/250 and .243. They are capable of meeting the demands of all but the most sophisticated varmint shooters.

During a recent springtime prairie-dog hunt in west Kansas, I spent a couple of days firing a nicely finished Interarms Mark X .22/250 rifle. Built on a Yugoslavian-made Mauser 98-type action, it is quite accurate. Sophisticated varmint and benchrest shooters are likely to sneer at this kind of rig, yet it proved capable of smacking prairie dogs well beyond the 200-yard mark. These rifles are not expensive, and if you want to buy an Interarms Mark X barreled action or something similar and do your own stocking, the price is even lower.

On the other hand, let's say you shoot prairie dogs with a group of competitive target or benchrest shooters, the type that consider a prairie dog's head or even half a head a fair target at 300 yards. This is where exceedingly fine accuracy, not to mention marksmanship, is called for, and you can't get too much of it. This is where you need a rifle that groups under a half inch at 100 yards, or at worst groups no wider than an inch at 200 yards. This kind of performance costs extra; if you want to play, you have to pay.

With all the thousands of varmint rifles in use these days, and the millions of varmint cartridges that are fired each year, it is a wonder there are any varmints left to shoot at. In truth, varmint shooters scarcely dent the populations of crows, woodchucks, ground squirrels, and prairie dogs. Varmint populations will remain high for years to come, barring widespread habitat destruction. This is why varmint shooting will continue to increase in popularity.

Even so, shooting varmints at long range is, and always will be, only part of the fun. Most of the ammo fired in these remarkable rifles is not used afield. It is fired at rifle ranges where the quarry is a tiny hole in a piece of paper. That is the most elusive game of all.

Chapter 13

RIFLES FOR AFRICA'S DANGEROUS GAME

Facts and fantasy about rifles for African dangerous game are so intertwined that even gun experts are often misled. Storytelling doesn't shed much light on the matter. Authors such as Ruark and Hemingway were great storytellers, but when it came to firearms, they were bush-leaguers just like so many spinners of African yarns.

Even worse are writers who have the zinc-plated gall to write about and even recommend certain heavy-game rifles and cartridges without ever having looked a lion in the eye except in a zoo.

Even experienced African hunters sometimes get caught up in the excitement of the adventure, and I must confess that I have fallen into the pit. On my first African hunt several years ago, I found myself tracking lions on foot in northern Botswana. The technique was simple. We'd pick up fresh lion spoor early in the day and take out after it. The idea was that the lion or lions (there were usually two or more) had eaten a big meal during the night and would be looking for a place to sleep it off during the midday heat. The country was flat and sandy, and there were scattered patches of mopane scrub. If the tracks led into a stand of scrub, we'd send a pair of trackers around it to see if the trail came out the back side. If not, we could figure that the lions were still inside.

The next step was simple. Wade in, rifles ready, hoping to find them asleep or at least to see them before they saw us. Most lions do not make good trophies, so we hoped to catch them asleep in order to look them over. If a given lion didn't measure up as a trophy, we'd tiptoe away and leave him to his slumbers. That was the game plan, but things almost never worked out that way.

Usually the lions were awake and ran away before we got a good look, or they fussed and tore up the ground and scattered our crew. If the crew dispersed, the hunter and the guide were left at the edge of no return with a lion the hunter didn't want for a trophy. The lion usually wasn't willing to let me back off peacefully.

It was a foolhardy way to hunt lions or any other dangerous game, and not the way it is normally done. But I was younger then and overflowing with my own ability to pull my fat out of the fire if things got too hot. Added to that was the fact that I'd been working for OUTDOOR LIFE only a year or so and was still very much under the shadow of the great Jack O'Connor. I felt I had to prove my mettle and satisfy my readers by putting myself in harm's way. "Let old Jack try this one," I'd say to myself, snapping the safety off and wading into thorn bush full of lions, buffalo, and maybe a cobra or black mamba. My guide was a go-to-hell Rhodesian, who was generally as foolhardy as myself, so we managed to terrify ourselves almost daily.

My rifle was a .458 Winchester Magnum, custom-built on a Mauser action, which somehow looked smaller and smaller every time I thought about or looked at a lion. After about a week of staring down cross lions and outlasting false charges, I became convinced that my .458 wouldn't stop a charging lion and started to have fantasies about one that would. As I saw it, the ideal lion-stopper would shoot soft-nose 500-grain bullets at about 4,000 fps. It would literally blow up a lion the way a .220 Swift explodes a crow. Anything less, I reasoned, and a lion would surely get me, no matter how well I hit him.

When I finally got a shot at a big male from about 40 yards, he was down and out with such convincing certainty that I felt pretty foolish about my apprehensions. Since then, I've killed my share of lions, literally a trainload of Cape buffalo, and enough elephants to get the anti-hunters into a snit, and I've drawn a few conclusions about big guns and the people who use them.

THE BIG BATTERY

Time was when a sportsman on a leisurely ocean voyage to the Dark Continent could take a whole battery of rifles. In early, and some not so early, camp photographs, it's common to see anywhere from six to 20 assorted rifles and fowling pieces. It seemed as if a different rifle was required for each species of game. For the most part, I attribute this to overzealous salesmen at Abercrombie & Fitch and similar emporiums. I've never been able to figure out any other reason for taking such a big battery. Just keeping the ammo sorted out and stored must have been a formidable task.

The situation has changed. Modern jet travel, with its minimal baggage allowance, has engendered the one-suitcase, one-guncase African hunter. Foreign airlines, in particular, have the habit of weighing one's baggage and charging an exorbitant penalty for any excess. Many sportsmen have discovered that the excess-weight charges for a couple of extra rifles and the ammunition often exceeds their value. On the next safari, only one or, at most, two rifles make the trip. In my line of work, I get to Africa rather often, so I've beaten the weight rap by leaving a few rifles in assorted calibers with friends in several African cities.

The author with a big lion taken in Botswana. The rifle is a .458 Winchester Magnum that was custom-built on a Mauser action.

Others try to solve the problem in different ways. Rifles with interchangeable barrels, which had never achieved more than curiosity status in America, became sought after during the middle '70's. With the Mauser Model 66 system you can manage a variety of calibers. This proved modestly popular with African trippers, and there is irony in this because Mauser's popularity surge came not long after the parent company lost hope and discontinued their sales efforts in North America.

THE ALL-PURPOSE .375

The Holy Grail of American hunters is the all-purpose rifle. Predictably, more and more Americans headed for Africa with what they hoped was the gun for all seasons. The venerable .375 Holland & Holland was dusted off for another round. The reasoning behind using the .375 on a one-gun safari is that it isn't too big for smaller game such as Africa's myriad antelope and also delivers sufficient punch to drop Cape buffalo and elephant. This is a splendid thought, and it does sometimes seem that the .375 is good for everything. Or taking a different tack with the same logic, it often seems that the .375 is good for nothing. It is too big for small antelope, and it is too small for dangerous African game. Although I own a half dozen .375's which I never want to be without, I wholeheartedly subscribe to this latter logic. From my viewpoint, the .375 is an idea whose time should never have arrived in Africa.

In my wanderings I am continually beseiged by breathless hunters just back from Africa who paw my lapels and describe, wide-eyed, how many shots their buffalo soaked up before finally going down. "Don't tell me," I always reply, "you were using a .375, right?"

"How did you know?" they ask.

Hair-raising escapades with charging buffalo and rampaging elephants seem to go hand in hand with the .375. The only conclusion I can draw from this is that it doesn't get the job done. Several professional hunters have told me that they share this view. They like the .375 for plains game because of the way it overwhelms the smaller animals, provided the hunter scores a reasonably good hit. This eliminates long blood trails and long chases. But when it comes to the big, mean stuff, professional hunters tend to get more than a little antsy about a client who uses a .375.

"But," you say, "in the hands of a cool and deadly marksman, the .375 H&H is all anyone would ever need." I agree, but if we continue with this same logic, we have to agree that, in the hands of the same marksman, a .22 Hornet is sufficient for deer and elk. That may be true of exceptional hunters, but experience shows us that in the hands of the *average* hunter/marksman, a .22 Hornet is not adequate for elk or even deer, just as experience tells us that the .375 isn't what we want for buffalo and elephant.

THE .458

I've taken somewhere upwards of four score Cape buffalo. Most were killed unceremoniously on a couple of game-control shoots. The technique on these herd-control hunts is simple. I just got inside the herd and shot at everything, especially old bulls. Obviously, this is a dangerous sort of thing, especially after the first several shots when one loses track of how many are supposed to be down and buffalo are running in all directions. The next phase of the hunt is to take out after them on foot, crashing through brush and blasting away.

Despite these episodes and many sport hunts, I must confess that I have not one hair-raising buffalo tale to tell. The reason I cannot entertain you with how-I-escaped-the-wounded-buffalo stories is, I believe, because all save two were shot with a .458 Winchester Magnum rifle

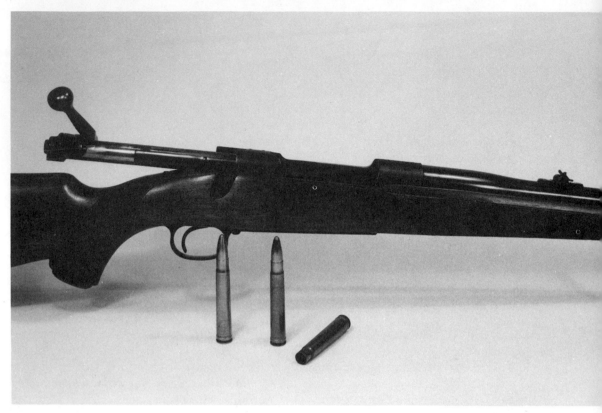

One of Carmichel's .375 H&H Magnums. This has sometimes been touted as the all-purpose caliber for Africa, but the author agrees with those professional hunters who like their clients to restrict its use to plains game.

using ammunition I handloaded with 500-grain Hornady solids. When a buffalo takes one of these, he seldom gets very mean. I remember one old bull I shot on a trophy hunt in Botswana. He was crossing me on the run at about 75 yards. I didn't lead quite far enough, so the bullet hit too far back in his ribs. "Uh, oh," I thought, now the bull is going to get into that tall grass, and I'll have one hell of a time." But he slowed and stopped after only a few steps and stood there wobbling. No thoughts of savage revenge—he just didn't have any more steam. He was dead before I pulled the trigger for the second shot.

When it comes to stopping dangerous game, I firmly believe in power, bone-smashing power, not just big, heavy bullets driven at turn-of-the-century velocities. I want big bullets driven at sufficient velocity to deliver overwhelming hydrostatic shock. As professional hunter Lew Games says, "I like to see them go all loose."

During the 1950's and 1960's, interest in rifle cartridges was mainly focused on high velocities and flat trajectories. By the 1970's there was renewed interest in the African super-bores. This renewed interest had a lot to do with boosting the prices of big-bore double rifles to unheard-of levels. Another reason has been the unprecedented interest in African hunting. "Get there before the game's all gone," is the cry. Another reason is the equally unprecedented number of professional hunters and booking agents who now offer special low-cost (comparatively speaking) "safaris." These and other factors have resurrected any number of old-time, near-obsolete big-bore rounds.

EXIT THE DOUBLE, ENTER THE BOLT

The professional hunter on one of my early safaris was a very proper type in the old Kenya tradition whose accent was as crisp as the tips of his mustache. His Land Rover was polished daily, and the creases in his hunting shorts were unfailingly starched to parade-ground sharpness. As you've probably guessed, his rifle was a beautiful Holland double. It was a .500/465, if I remember correctly, and it looked as new as the day it left London. Not once during our safari did he find it necessary to fire his rifle, which caused him great relief because of the high cost and scarcity of the ammo.

Another time I hunted with a tough little bandy-legged Angolan Portuguese who carried a cheap Spanish-made sidelock double in .450 Nitro. The sears must have been badly worn because every time he fired the right barrel, the left went off of its own accord. Despite my suggestions, he never caught on to shooting the left barrel first or loading only one round. He shot

Carmichel has participated in game-control shoots where Cape buffalo herds had to be thinned, and he has taken more than four score of the animals—all but one with .458 Winchester Magnum handloads using 500-grain Hornady solids. Shown here are an assembled load, two unfired bullets, and a retrieved bullet (note the rifling marks).

Very few professional African guides carry double rifles any more, but Carmichel used one in 1984—and took this fine buffalo with it.

this rifle at everything from Guinea fowl to elephants. *Ka-boomboom* it would go, and the little Portuguese would stagger backwards.

These two chaps constitute exceptions that prove the rule. They were the *only* professional African guides with whom I've hunted who actually carried double rifles, popular myth notwithstanding. Two other professionals, both Americans, carried much-altered bolt-action .460 Weatherbys. One of them had the barrel shortened to 20 inches, which was a real thrill to be near when the thing went off. Another professional carried a .375. All the rest of the professional hunters I have known carried .458 Winchester Magnum bolt-action rifles—Winchesters, Remingtons, Brnos, Mausers, etc.

The typical African dangerous-game rifle is a bolt-action .458. This may come as a bitter shock to readers of romantic hunting stories, who assume the African bush is full of gorgeous double rifles in all the proper British calibers, but I don't think it was ever that way, not even during the glorious days of Empire. Double rifles, like fine side-by-side double shotguns, are pretty things to write about. "Lord Percival, striding forth with his .577 Holland double," tells us something about the man, but "Lord Percival, striding forth with his bolt-action .458," is just another face in the crowd.

The unromantic fact is that from the turn of the century onwards, the bolt-action has been *the* African action by a factor of hundreds to one. Keep in mind that most African game, especially the dangerous species, was killed not by sport hunters, ivory poachers, or even game wardens, but by farmers. These practical men kept an inexpensive bolt rifle handy to knock off an occasional marauding elephant, lion, or leopard just the way North American farmers keep a rimfire rifle in the barn to snipe at rats and other vermin. The various African game departments also equipped their wardens and control shooters with relatively inexpensive bolt-action rifles.

Don't forget that the double rifle was confined mostly to English-dominated areas, most notably Kenya and Uganda. That's another reason English-language African adventure stories are so high on doubles. If you were to read German (from Tanzania) or Portuguese (Angola, Mozambique) hunting yarns, you'd find that double rifles are scarcely mentioned. The descendants of South Africa's Dutch settlers also prefer Mauser or Mauser-style bolt rifles.

Here's an array of popular African cartridges, antique and modern. From left, they are the .425 Westley Richards, .375 Holland & Holland, .378 Weatherby, .416 Rigby, .458 Winchester, .460 Weatherby, .577 Nitro Express, and the ubiquitous .30/06.

Most American sportsmen, and readers of African hunting stories, seldom if ever hear of many of the most popular cartridges for African dangerous game. Ask the typical American to name one British super-bore cartridge, and he'll probably mention the .600 Nitro. The .600 got much publicity because it was the world's most powerful sporting round (6,850 foot-pounds of energy at the muzzle) until the advent of the .460 Weatherby. Actually the .600 was never all that popular in Africa. More of them probably exist in the U.S. as curiosities than anywhere else. But who ever heard of the 10.75x73, 10.75x68 Mauser, 9.5x57 Mannlicher-Schoenauer, or the 12.7x70 Schuler? All of these are, or were, quite popular among African hunters, especially prior to World War II.

The effect of World War II on sporting arms design and production was nothing less than revolutionary. During and after the war, the great German and Austrian arms and ammo makers such as DWM, RWS, Mauser, the Steyr Werke, etc. produced nothing for the African hunter. Subsequently, stocks of existing European-made ammo dwindled and, in some cases, were exhausted. The same was true in considerable degree with British ammunition. Prior to the war, Eley and Kynoch had continued limited production of the various cartridges demanded by Africa's hunters. Orders for the more obscure English cartridges amounted to only a trickle, but if production was not profitable, at least it was not unprofitable, and the English firms did feel an obligation to fill the limited demands, and so did the Continental manufacturers. During the emergency retooling for World War II military production, virtually all of the existing tooling for sporting ammo was stripped out, scrapped, modified, or simply lost. At the end of hostilities the various firms were faced with the prospect of expensive retooling for sporting cartridges. In the case of many of the more obscure or obsolete calibers, the cost was not justified. This was regarded a blessing by the arms makers, who had been looking for a polite way to end production on the less popular rounds. So, the notice "not made after the war" was posted on quite a few calibers. As Continental sporting ammo production geared up after the war, the same easy route was followed.

That's how things stood in 1956. Ammunition for many African rifles was difficult or impossible to obtain, rendering many rifles useless. The supply of heavy-bore bolt rifles was a tiny trickle too, and they were expensive. You see, virtually all of the bolt-action rifles from England's great gunmakers were built on German-made Mauser actions. But these actions had become unavailable. What was the African hunter to do? Enter Winchester and the Model 70 bolt rifle in .458 Magnum. In the U.S., news of the new super-bore was greeted with, "Gee whiz, but what for?" In Africa, it was like rain after a long drought. African hunters had seen enough Model 70's in other calibers to know they were tough, accurate, reliable, and bargain-priced. Until 1956, however, the fattest M-70 had been made in .375 H&H. That cartridge is in the mid-bore category. But the .458 Model 70 is a solid bolt gun that pushes a 500-grain .45-caliber bullet out the muzzle at over 2,100 fps, generating a muzzle energy of over 5,000 foot-pounds. And the price was ridiculously low.

I've been told that the .458 was regarded with some suspicion at first. Aside from seeming too good and too cheap to be true, the .458 Winchester Magnum wasn't all that visually appealing to hunters who for generations had been judging cartridge power by sheer case size. Compared to some of the larger dangerous-game rounds, the .458 seemed almost a miniature.

But even though the .458 case is a full .35-inch shorter than even the .375 H&H case, the technicians at Winchester had developed a very powerful round. They wanted the cartridge to be no longer than a standard .30/06. This would permit the .458 to function through the magazine and action of the Model 70. (Model 70's chambered for the .300 and .375 H&H Magnum cartridges have special long magazine boxes and opened-up actions. The shorter .458 round would also adapt easily to other existing actions, notably the standard M-98 Mauser. Building so much power into the .458 case was no real trick using modern powders. Remember, some of the behemoth big game rounds of pre-World War II days were developed in the black-powder era, and even the newer ones were designed for stick-like cordite powder that required large-capacity cases.

In reality, the new .458 had more striking energy than many of its bigger brethren. For comparison, consider the following table of case lengths, bullet weights, muzzle velocities, and muzzle energies.

Caliber	Approx. Case Length (inches)	Bullet Weight (grains)	Muzzle Velocity (fps)	Muzzle Energy (foot-pounds)
.458 Winchester Magnum	2-1/2	510	2,040	4,712
.375 H&H	2-7/8	300	2,550	4,330
.350 Rigby	2-3/4	225	2,625	3,440
.369 Purdey Nitro	2-5/8	270	2,500	3,760
.450/.400 Nitro	3-1/4	400	2,150	4,110
.404 Jeffery	2-7/8	400	2,125	4,020
.416 Rigby	2-7/8	410	2,370	5,100
.500/.450 Nitro Express	3-1/4	480	2,175	5,080
.450 No. 2 Nitro Express	3-1/2	480	2,175	5,080
.470 Nitro Express	3-1/4	500	2,150	5,140
.475 No. 2 Nitro Express	3-1/2	500	2,150	5,140

So we see that the stubby .458 Winchester Magnum plows along with as much energy or more than traditional British cartridges that are as much as an inch longer and of greater diameter as well. When introduced, the .458 was listed as having a velocity of 2,130 fps and 5,140 foot-pounds of energy, which of course made it compare even more favorably.

The real proof of a cartridge is not numbers but field performance, and the .458 didn't take long to show what it could do. Elephant, Cape buffalo, and rhino went down as if pole-axed, and lions were blown loose at the hinges. In Africa, especially, a "heavy" cartridge and rifle acquire a reputation almost immediately. Professional hunters are a tight-knit bunch. They like to gossip about their experiences, and when someone has a bad time with a certain rifle or cartridge, the news gets around. Some perfectly fine cartridges were doomed from the start simply because of a lousy batch of ammo with cold primers or loose jackets. The .458 performed well from the beginning. As I recall, there were some problems with excess pressures in the tropical heat, and maybe even some bad bullets, but everything was quickly corrected, and the list of happy users continued to grow.

By 1970, only 15 years after its introduction, the .458 had become the overwhelming African favorite, and more and more manufacturers began to make rifles and ammo. Today, the .458 is the most popular dangerous-game cartridge.

MY FIRST .458

My first experiences with the .458 Magnum occurred when hunting in Africa was still only a dream. In the mid-1960's I was pecking out a living by writing articles for the various shooting and hunting magazines. One type of article that always sold well was the do-it-yourself piece, especially if it dealt with stock work. I wrote a dozen or more how-to-make-your-own-stock articles under nearly as many pen names. In order to get the needed step-by-step photographs for these articles, it was necessary to actually do the work I was describing. In time, I accumulated a fair collection of rifles and shotguns that I had stocked, restocked, or altered in some way. One article described a full-blown custom job, beginning with a surplus Mauser action and continuing through rebarreling, stocking, bluing, and mounting the scope. I decided on the .458 for this rig because I was also doing a series of articles on cast bullets, and I figured I could sell a piece on cast bullets for the .458.

The result was a Douglas barrel fitted to an F.N. Dutch Police Mauser, which I stocked with a Pachmayr semi-finished classic-style stock in Bastogne walnut. The rifle had the same kind of open-V express sights Winchester used on the early .458 Model 70's. The finished product was an elegant thing, or so I thought. I dearly loved using it to punch holes in hickory stumps and two-foot-thick oak blocks. "Some day," I promised myself, "I'll take this rifle to Africa and shoot big game," but the pledge was as unlikely of fulfillment then as a trip to the far side of Jupiter.

Five years later, my fortunes were so changed that I found myself deep in the African bush with that very do-it-yourself .458 Magnum and a hatful of ammo handloaded with Hornady soft-points (for lions) and their wonderful solid bullets for buffalo and elephant. I was hiding in some low scrub with my guide and three trackers. We were watching the approach of a very black, very ugly, and very big Cape buffalo. He was so old that large areas of his hide were bare of hair, and his horns swept majestically below his jaw before sweeping up into a rolled-over curl. He was alone, which probably meant he was too ornery to get along in a herd. Behind me, the trackers set up such an excited stream of whispering that the guide had to tell them to pipe down. Later I learned that their whispering was directed to me, imploring me not to shoot on the pretext that the buffalo was not a very good one and they knew where a much better one could be found.

The truth of the matter was that we were a long walk from the safari truck, and they desperately missed the security of its high, metal sides. This was only the second day of my hunt. To them, I was an unknown quantity as a marksman, and the "magic" of my rifle was still doubted. I understood none of this as the bull came within 40 yards, stopped, and snorted in our direction.

"Take him," was the whispered advice from my professional hunter. The crosshairs were on the vast, dusty shoulder, and I pressed the trigger of my home-built rifle. The 500-grain solid crashed through the shoulder bones and exited the far side. Before the big bull could take another breath, he was dead. My promise to myself was kept. Since then, I've re-kept my pledge nearly 100 times, and nothing—elephants, lions, nor buffalo—has escaped the deadly efficiency of that .458.

Of course, my explanation of the .458's unprecedented success is something of an over-simplification. In addition to the perfect timing of its introduction, and its sterling out-of-the-box performance, there are other reasons for the .458's sudden popularity. All the same, one incident pretty well sums up its universal acceptance. I was crossing the border from Botswana into what was then called Rhodesia, and the customs inspector wanted to look at my rifles and count my cartridges. As usual, there was a band of naked children frisking around the check station. When I uncased my rifle on the hood of the safari truck, they crowded around for a big-eyed look. One of the lads pointed a timid finger at my cartridges and uttered in understandable English "Four, five, eight." Those were the only English words he knew and would probably ever learn—"Four, five, eight."

WEATHERBY

When I was a teen-ager, I spent an hour or two daily poring over the wonderful shooting magazines to which I subscribed. My heroes were Pete Brown of *Sports Afield,* Jack O'Connor of OUTDOOR LIFE, and Warren Page of *Field & Stream.* After absorbing the breathtaking things they had to say each month, I'd spend long moments studying the pictures, devouring every detail and longing to touch the exquisite guns. Roy Weatherby was shifting into high gear about then, and by dint of his knack for publicity he managed to get a few pictures of his rifles published nearly every month. Hidden away as I was in the hills of East Tennessee, the likelihood of my seeing one of Weatherby's creations wasn't great. How I drooled over those pictures of the fantastic rifles and the stunning line of Weatherby Magnum cartridges! I could spout off Weatherby's ballistic tables the way most boys could reel off batting averages, and I still remember some of them.

Weatherby was mainly a custom house then. He built his rifles on whatever actions came to hand, mainly F.N. Mausers and a few 1914 and 1917 Enfields. The latter were especially desirable for long magnum rounds because of their greater length. He differed from other small shops, though, in that he did box and sell his own "Weatherby Magnum" cartridges. They were handloads at first. Then, as the operation grew, newly manufactured ammo was made bearing the Weatherby headstamp. Though he promoted his magnums by bagging a variety of dangerous African game with his smaller bores (rhino and elephant with the .300 W.M.), it was the .375 that most appealed to serious professional hunters.

The .375 was based on the .375 H&H belted case as were other Weatherby Magnums. By

Roy Weatherby made his own .375 belted Magnum obsolete by introducing the even more potent .378, whose case is extremely similar to the .416 Rigby—except for the belt. Here you see a .416 Rigby flanked by a diminutive-looking .30/06 cartridge and the belted .378 Weatherby Magnum.

blowing out the shoulder somewhat, powder capacity was increased, and velocity with a 300-grain bullet was upped to 3,800 fps, a 250-fps increase over the .375 H&H. As a killer of dangerous game, the .375 Weatherby gained some popularity during the 1950's, especially when the cartridges were loaded with thick-jacketed bullets. During that era, quite a few existing .375 H&H rifles, mainly Model 70 Winchesters, were converted to .375 Weatherbys by the simple expedient of rechambering. Nothing else had to be altered. In fact, some of the early .375 Weatherby rifles were only Model 70's with a recut chamber and the addition of one of Roy's spectacularly carved and inlaid stocks.

The .375 Weatherby is obsolete now because of Weatherby's desire to move on to bigger things. The limiting factor at the beginning of Weatherby's gunmaking career was the lack of a super-size rifle action. This problem was erased in 1958 with the appearance of the newly engineered, German-made Weatherby Mark V rifle. The door was open for Weatherby to make his cartridges as big and as powerful as he wished, and he did just that. During the early

1950's, Weatherby had begun experimenting with a .375 round that would deliver even more power than his first .375. Having pushed the powder capacity of the blown-out .375 Holland case to the limit, the only remaining option was to go to an even bigger case. There were bigger cases around, of course, such as the huge rimless Gibbs and the Jeffery, which would work in bolt-action rifles, but they were not belted, and Weatherby had become synonymous with the belted magnum case. The result was a wholly new case that looked something like a .416 Rigby with a belt added. In fact, you can make .416 Rigby cases by turning the belts off Weatherby .378 cases. The new cartridge was the .378 Weatherby Magnum. The bullet diameter was really .375, the same as his older magnum, but velocities were something else altogether: 3,380 fps with the 270-grain bullet, and 2,925 with the 300-grain slug. That hoisted muzzle energies almost to the three-ton level. The first Weatherby rifles in this caliber were built on a long version of the Danish-made, rear-locking Shultz and Larsen action, and the rifle was called, simply, the .378 Model. These rifles were discontinued in 1958 when, at last, Weatherby had his own actions.

I've never owned a .378, nor have I killed a single head of game with one, but I have shot them enough to know that the recoil is more than noticeable. In fact, it is absolutely wicked. According to my calculations, the recoil from a 9½-pound .378 Weatherby rifle firing 300-grain bullets works out to a cheerless 62 foot-pounds. By comparison, the recoil of a .375 H&H with the same bullet is about 42 foot-pounds.

Recoil is seldom perceived when you are firing at game, so I do not include the kick factor in my consideration of dangerous-game rifles. If I were going to make it my business to shoot a lot of hungry lions, I would, with only one reservation, probably choose the .378. I've had so many close calls with lions that they've made me somewhat skittish. The .378 would deliver enough shock to make them come all unglued, and that's what I like. The one reservation I have about the .378 is the same that I harbor about any cartridge that is longer than a .30/06. With these very long rounds, there is the distinct possiblity of "short-stroking" the bolt in a fast-shooting situation. Thereby you fail to feed a fresh round from the magazine. Interestingly, W.D.M. "Karamojo" Bell, the legendary elephant hunter, had the same fear. By his own account this is one of the reasons he chose the .275 Rimless Rigby (almost identical to the 7x57 Mauser) over more powerful, but longer, cartridges. If I were to use the .378 or even the .375 H&H in pursuit of ugly-tempered beasts, I'd spend a lot of time working the bolt to get the feel of the additional bolt travel.

Since velocity and its handmaiden energy had been Roy Weatherby's bag from the beginning, it was predictable that he would never rest until he garnered that final superlative—the world's most powerful cartridge. That came about in 1958, along with his new Mark V rifle. Called the .460 Weatherby Magnum, and based on the .378 W.M. case, Weatherby's super-bore launched a 500-grain bullet at 2,700 fps. That figures out to a muzzle energy of 8,095 foot-pounds. The appearance of the new round retired the .600 Nitro (7,600 foot-pounds) as the No. 1 stomper. Recoil works out to some 102 foot-pounds with an 11½-pound rifle, in case you're wondering. You're probably also wondering what any sane person would want with one of the things. The answer is neither elusive nor farfetched. The .460 is well accepted by the professional African hunting gentry. As mentioned earlier in this chapter, I know two professional guides who carry the .460 as their standard "heavy," and I expect there will be more.

The .460 Weatherby Magnum is well accepted by professional hunters in Africa, some of whom carry it as their standard "heavy." For a hunter who wants maximum knockdown power, Carmichel declares it's a logical choice.

For a hunter who feels he needs maximum knockdown power, the .460 is a logical choice because rifles and ammo are easily obtainable. There is seldom any waiting period before delivery. Double rifles often take years to reach the buyer. Compared to the cost of many other "heavy" rifles, the price of .460 rifles and ammo is negligible. The Weatherby rifles are also reliable, and the .460 really is in a class by itself. No other sporting cartridge has been quite able to do unto an elephant or Cape buffalo what it does. But why is this necessary? Are elephants harder to kill than they were a generation ago? In a way, yes, they are. The conditions under which big ivory must now be hunted very often call for more punch.

Time was when elephants were more or less plains animals. At least, that's where they were most comfortably and conveniently hunted. This type of African terrain is mostly covered by grass and scrub trees. A professional hunter and his client could spot elephants from a distance and plan a safe stalk. This allowed the gun to get within effective working distance while at the same time permitting ample leeway to back off if things took a bad turn. Much of this classic elephant-hunting territory has been turned into national game reserves where no shooting is allowed, or the land has been systematically stripped of its game by poachers. I hunted in terrain of this type a decade ago, notably in Northern Botswana and Rhodesia, but now I understand the bulls with big ivory have been pretty well shot out. This has caused hunters of really big ivory to penetrate the more inaccessible and difficult parts of Africa. Such places as the Southern Sudan and the Central African Republic (formerly French Equatorial Africa) still harbor big elephants, if you have the time, money, patience, and stamina to go after them. In these areas, the really powerful cartridges have become more necessary than ever.

A few years back when I was hunting bongo in the lower Sudan, I happened across the biggest set of ivory I've ever seen on a live elephant. The vegetation was so dense that I never really got a look at the bull's body or even much of his head. All I could see were two enormous columns of ivory curving out of the green gloom. As luck would have it, I didn't have an elephant license or even a heavy rifle, but the shooting would have been exceedingly tricky if I had been equipped. The range was short, only a few yards, but before shooting, it would have been necessary to tiptoe around to get a better line-up on the old bull's head. Judging from the sounds, there were at least two more nearby elephants that I couldn't see, and there might have been 15. If I had been a professional hunter taking a client into a situation like that, I would have been exceedingly apprehensive for a number of reasons.

SHOOTING AN ELEPHANT

Despite all the exciting yarns and endless advice on how to aim at an elephant's brain, the truth is that most elephants are now killed by heart and lung shots. Three out of five are probably brought down by an ordinary behind-the-shoulder shot just like the one you use on deer. This is because that target area is big and difficult to miss. The heart is about the size of a bushel basket. Guides want a successful client. Sometimes the animal falls right over, but more usually he runs a few hundred yards before going down. Guides like this, too, because other elephants in the herd usually run off with the injured member. This is vastly preferable to having them squealing and dashing everywhere.

The reason I mention all this is to further point up the difficulties faced by guide and client when shooting in thick vegetation. In this sort of situation, a heart shot is iffy because the elephant may very well run off and not be found. This is especially true if there are several animals in the herd, each making a separate trail and generally confusing your trackers. What professionals do, if necessary, is to have their clients shoot at whatever reasonable target they can see. If the target doesn't go down in its tracks, they start throwing heavy stuff themselves.

An elephant is vulnerable to a .460 Weatherby from all angles. Even if the beast is quartering away at a rear angle, a raking shot into the haunch will probably break some joints, run on through the guts, and then tear up some heart and lung. This is exactly the sort of insurance today's elephant guide needs.

A few years back, when the great gunsmithing firm of Griffin & Howe was still part of Abercrombie & Fitch, and their Madison Avenue store was only a block from OUTDOOR

Actions like this square-bridge Magnum Mauser are of the hefty sort appropriate to big-bore bolt rifles for Africa's dangerous game.

LIFE's editorial offices, I spent many a fascinating hour prowling through their musty storeroom shelves and long-unopened drawers. One happy day I ran across a Brevex Magnum action in the original factory wrapper. The bolt face was cut for a .586-inch case rim, meaning that it would work with really big cartridges such as the .416 Rigby or .460 Weatherby, so naturally I bought the action on the spot, intending some day to have it built into something special.

The action was put away and almost forgotten until recently when I received an invitation from a former Angolan professional to go with him on an exploration-hunt for elephant in the uncharted highlands of central Africa. He says he has word via the native grapevine that there are some tremendous bulls there but that the terrain is impossible. That means shooting at arm's length at patches of elephant. Nothing will do but a blockbuster rifle. So the Brevex is being made into an elephant rifle in the style of the beautiful pre-World War II British bolt guns—express sights and English-style engraving. The Douglas barrel is being fitted by Dave Talley, and it will be chambered for—you guessed it—the .460 Weatherby Magnum.

SUB-CALIBERS AND DANGEROUS GAME

Gun writers like to make mention of all the elephants W.D.M. Bell killed with the puny little 7mm cartridge. Their point is either that the 7x57 has some mystical powers or that elephants aren't all that hard to knock over. Since either perspective is misleading, let's talk a bit more about the effectiveness of "sub-calibers" on dangerous game.

First let me warn you against getting into discussions about Bell and his little .275 (7x57 Mauser) with African professional hunters. Many of them wax very hot on the subject. It seems that although Bell got off scot-free, his practices had some unpleasant aftereffects. It seems, or so I've heard from old-time ivory hunters, that Bell left a lot of wounded elephants in the bush that later took their anger out on innocent passers-by. Also, and I suspect this is the more accurate charge, a host of latter-day would-be ivory hunters, seeking to duplicate Bell's feats, discovered at the fatal moment that they couldn't pull off his 7mm trick.

In defense of Bell, let me say right off that he has been grossly misquoted. Anyone who bothers to actually read his journals will find that he used a number of different calibers for elephant and other big game. His use of the .275 Rigby, the British version of the 7x57

The famous elephant hunter W.D.M. Bell often used a .275 Rigby, the British version of the German 7x57mm Mauser cartridge — but Carmichel points out that he used it for reasons having nothing to do with its sometimes lamentable performance on elephants. This round was the same as the 7mm Full Patch cartridge shown here with its original 20-round box. The bullet weighed 175 grains.

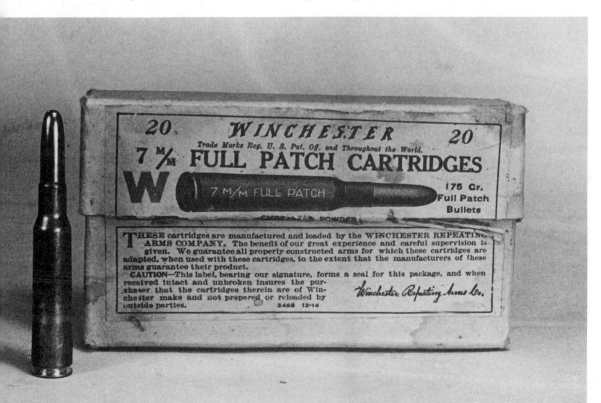

If "Karamojo" Bell were alive today, he would carry a lot more gun than a .275 Rigby. When going for big, tough, potentially dangerous animals like this elephant, Carmichel's caliber choices represent the repeatedly proven rule that one must carry enough gun for the game.

Mauser, was largely a matter of logistics. Since Bell's elephant-poaching expeditions were walking affairs, he was very much concerned about having his porters carry excess baggage. Poachers prefer to travel in small groups. Since .275 ammo was relatively small and light, it could be carried in greater quantity than traditional big-bore dangerous-game cartridges. He also made a habit of carrying his own rifle, a virtually unheard-of practice on the Dark Continent, and this, too, made him appreciate a light rifle.

A major factor in Bell's use of the 7mm was the general unreliability of ammunition in those days. In his *Wanderings of an Elephant Hunter,* he describes at some length the problems he experienced with misfires and bursting cartridges. (He refers to the cartridge as the .276, but that is only another designation for the .275 Rigby.) "The only one that never let me down was a .276 with German (D.W.M.) ammunition. I never had one single hangfire even—nor a stuck case, nor a split one, nor a blowback, nor a misfire. All of these I had with other rifles." Elsewhere he writes about the .276 with 200-grain bullets. "It seemed to show a remarkable aptitude for finding the brain of an elephant." So we might judge from his own words that had not that particular brand and bullet weight of .276 ammo been available, he might very well have used another rifle and caliber.

Bell was among the best marksmen who ever poached ivory. He made a fanatical study of the construction of an elephant's skull and placed his bullets from close range exactly where he meant them to go. Even so, a number of elephants he shot got away, a fact that he candidly admits in his books.

Though Bell is regarded the smallbore champion among elephant hunters, and has thus given much publicity to his pet .275 Rigby, the real fact is that two other smallbore rifles have accounted for vastly greater numbers of elephants. The first is the venerable .303 British service cartridge. Since it was the standard army round in a number of African countries—Kenya, Uganda, Sudan, Northern Rhodesia, Southern Rhodesia, etc.—ease of availability made it a favorite among low-budget poachers, especially native operators. We count Bell's take with the .275 at less than a thousand; the elephants that fell to the .303 must be counted in the tens of thousands.

The all-time great elephant killer, though, and the single round that threatens to wipe out Africa's population of these wonderful beasts, is the 7.62 NATO cartridge. That's right—the frail little .308 Winchester in military form.

Appealing to the World Bank, African despots beg money to equip their ragtag armies with guns, ammo, tanks, rockets, and aircraft, but it seldom occurs to them to buy food for their troops or pay them. Therefore, the army is turned loose on the land and the game population for sustenance and profit. The game, especially elephant, is being stripped from wide areas of Africa. The standard cartridge is the 7.62 NATO, otherwise known as the .308 Winchester, fired in a variety of full-automatic arms. The count *could* run into the hundreds of thousands, and it could wipe out all African elephants.

As pleasant as speculating on the worth of small-caliber rifles for dangerous game may be, the stark reality is that the casual days of African hunting are gone, gone in a brushfire of hungry humanity, gone in the treacherous wind of African politics, gone forever. The remaining hunting areas where dangerous game can be taken by sport hunters like you and me are jealously coveted by Africa's professional hunters, and they are guarded with watchdog efficiency by the various governments. An elephant is a national treasure, and a lion is worth its weight in money. So even if the game departments didn't spell out minimum bore sizes to be used for the Big Five, you'd want to use the surest rifle and cartridge combination you could lay hands on, not just to protect life and limb but because the shot you get might be the *only* shot you get.

If W.D.M. "Karamojo" Bell were alive today and trying to eke out a living guiding sport hunters, you can be sure he would carry a lot more gun than a .275 Rigby, and he would insist that his clients be equipped with artillery of similar persuasion.

Chapter 14

THE ALL-PURPOSE RIFLE—
HITS AND MYTHS

For the life of me, I can't understand what all the bickering is about. It seems that every other time I pick up a shooting magazine, there is an article about the mythical all-purpose hunting rifle. Some authors say the possibility does exist, at least in theory, while others claim that the whole concept is the product of an overworked imagination. I think I'm beginning to understand the purpose of the debate. It's a game, the rules of which prohibit the introduction of any logic or practical experience. This allows the debate to continue forever unresolved, thereby allowing scope for future articles on the same subject.

The simple fact is that all-purpose rifles are no myth. In fact, they're everywhere. Any gun shop with an inventory of five rifles will have a couple that will do wonderful service on whitetails in brush-choked river bottoms, black bears on timbered ridges, moose in the marsh, and caribou on the tundra.

THE DEFINITION

Before getting carried away with descriptions of workable all-purpose rifles and cartridges, let's define our subject. Many, if not most, big game hunters agree that an all-purpose rifle is one that can be used effectively to hunt deer, antelope, bears, goats, sheep, elk and moose. In short, most of the big game that can be legally hunted in the Lower 48 of the United States. I personally tend to be more demanding and insist that the rifle should be one that can be used in the *convenient* as well as successful hunting of *all* North American big game from mountain lion to musk ox. Note that I emphasize the word *convenient.* What I'm getting at is that, say, the .458 Winchester Magnum would certainly be effective on all North American big game, but it would hardly be convenient to carry through reed thickets, and it wouldn't be best for cross-canyon shots at bighorn sheep.

Also, using the all-purpose rifle shouldn't be a stunt. For example, I would willingly bet the ancestral farm that I can bag all species of North American game with the diminutive .22 Hornet. I'd even sweeten the bet to five grand per head of game that I'd need no more than two shots to kill each animal. But this would be a series of stunts, calling for fancy stalking, picking one's shots, and some calculating marksmanship. Obviously, the .22 Hornet is not an all-purpose caliber.

A true all-purpose rifle shouldn't handicap the hunter in terms of ease of shooting, range, knockdown efficiency, and portability. If the cartridge is a good one, the hunter doesn't have to mutter while watching a record-class bighorn ram stroll away: "If I had a Grand Slam Super Seven, I could get him." By the same measure, a whitetail hunter using the rifle in a Pennsylvania thicket wouldn't fail to get off a shot at a bounding buck because the rifle was too slow to get into action. With this in mind, we perceive that the all-purpose big game rifle is a blend of the right caliber and the right rifle. But how do we go about selecting the cartridge and the rifle?

One way is simply to do it by the numbers. Start with the largest game you'll be hunting, and match the cartridge to that game. Let's say your hunting needs are relatively modest. Your favorite game is whitetail, hunted in the second- and third-growth timber typical of an Eastern state. Since shots are almost always taken at ranges less than 100 yards, your choice of cartridge isn't all that critical. In fact, almost any legal caliber is fine. More important is a light, fast-handling, carbine-style rifle that helps you to get a bullet in the air in the quickest possible way.

But you also develop a fondness for stalking the pronghorn antelope and quickly discover that your woods rifle is no match for those fleet ghosts of the Western plains. Lumbering whitetail cartridges on the order of the .30/30 or .35 Remington are all right for woods hunting at short range, but they lack the sizzle and string-straight trajectories needed to tag a pronghorn where yards are counted by the hundreds. Likewise, the typical lever, pump and self-fed rifles that are great for snapping shots at bounding woods bucks suddenly aren't all that comforting when you snuggle into position and try to tickle off a long shot at a target that looks no bigger than a gaunt teddy bear.

The pronghorn then becomes the highest denominator because of the difficulty of long-range shooting. Even though whitetails and pronghorns demand very similar performance in terms of knockdown power, the means by which the bullet is delivered are at opposite ends of the spectrum. Happily, cartridges that are superb long-range performers also do great work in brush-country hunting conditions. So now it's simply a matter of choosing a good antelope cartridge. Popular choices range from the .243 Winchester and 6mm Remington up through the .250 Savage, .257 Roberts, .25/06 Remington, .270 Winchester, the various 7mm cartridges, and finally include the .308 Winchester and the .30/06. Obviously, the choice is wide.

However, a typical pronghorn rifle may very well be too long of barrel and too clumsy of shape for speedy work back in the whitetail woods. About half of the available rifles are therefore disqualified as you search for a *fast-handling* rifle that features accuracy, a good trigger pull, and chambering for long-range calibers. This means your eye probably comes to rest on one of the new breed of compact, lightweight bolt-action rifles such as the Alpha, Rem-

Despite the oft-repeated debates in magazine pages, there are plenty of good rifles that will serve well for hunting all kinds of North American medium and big game, from cougar to musk ox. For accuracy, good trigger pull, and long-range calibers, the light bolt rifles top Carmichel's list, but all-purpose rifles include levers, pumps, and autos, as well. Obvious contenders include (from top) Remington's Model 7 and Model 78, Winchester's Model 70, Ruger's Model 77, Savage's Model 99, Browning's BAR, and Remington's Models 760 and 742. There you have four bolts, a lever, two autos, and a pump—and there are others.

ington's Model 7, the stylish Model 70 Winchester Featherweight, or Ruger's trim Model 77 "International" (Continental-style) lightweight.

This doesn't mean you have to forsake other actions. Some lever rifles, notably the Browning BLR and Savage Model 99, are available in good long-range calibers, and Browning and Remington offer autoloaders and pumps in the right calibers. The problem with some of these fast feeders, however, is that their non-adjustable triggers are too heavy for pinpoint long-range shooting and quite often the buttstock configuration isn't much help in getting your eye aligned with the crosshairs when you need all the help you can get. Unless you're committed to a fast-feeding rifle by dint of long habit, you'll probably decide that a trim bolt rifle is just the ticket and happily discover that you've selected an all-purpose rifle that is just right for your kind of hunting. Obviously, though, selecting a good rifle for two similar game species isn't all that difficult to accomplish. So let's throw in a hatful of tricky variables.

Let's say a pal of ours wants to hunt *all* North American big game but is on a tight budget and can afford only one rifle. What's more, when his trophy room is lined with the New World species, he might use the same rifle in Asia and Africa. Now that's a mighty tall order for one rifle. Or is it? Let's look at the numbers.

Though the status of being the largest North American game animal is shared by the bison

Like the Savage Model 99, the Browning BLR is a lever-action rifle available in good long-range calibers. In firing tests, this BLR performed splendidly.

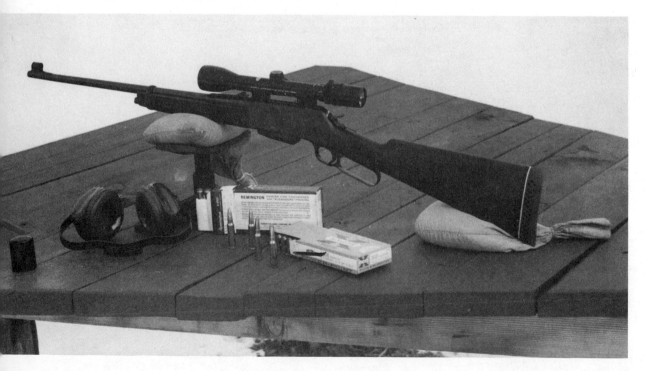

and the walrus (bulls of both species ranging up to a ton and a half), they are not so inclined to bite back as is the Alaskan brown bear and his smaller but equally ill-tempered brother the grizzly. Therefore, self-preservation dictates that our pal's highest common denominator is the enormous Alaskan brown bear, which includes the Kodiak. So right here we can eliminate every caliber below .270. At the same time, however, we can't skew our selection too far toward the heavier calibers, because the big magnums aren't very helpful when a hunter is trying to concentrate on a long shot at a bighorn sheep or snap off a shot at a running whitetail. So let's eliminate everything that calls itself a magnum and fires a bullet larger than .33 caliber (.338). This narrows our selection of all-purpose calibers to the .270 and 7mm Mauser (7x57) class on one end and the 8mm Remington Magnum and .340 Weatherby Magnum group at the other extreme. The .340 Weatherby bullet, by the way, is .338 in diameter. Those in the middle constitute most of the world's most popular hunting cartridges, so we have lots to choose from. Just about dead center in this range is the ever-popular .30/06. It easily meets the highest-common-denominator criterion. As a matter of record, the .30/06 has probably taken more big browns and grizzlies than any other caliber of this century. Further, the .30/06 cartridge has the exceptional advantage of being factory-loaded in a wide range of bullet styles and weights. Thus, in one rifle we have the choice of hard-punching heavyweight bullets and speedy, lightweight slugs for long shots at plains game. If he wishes, our pal can even use 55-grain "Accelerator" cartridges for long shots at woodchucks and other varmints.

Considering the .30/06 from the rifle viewpoint, one only has to thumb through an armload of gun catalogs to discover that it comes in the widest selection of styles, weights and mechanism types. No lever-action rifles in .30/06 caliber are being made at this writing (though they have been), but there are pumps, autoloaders, and more bolt-action models than I can count. Just to give one example, a Model 70 Winchester Featherweight in .30/06, topped off with a 2.5-7X scope, would give wonderful service in timber, on the rolling plains, from mountain to mountain, and for eyeballing big bears in elder thickets.

Obviously, we already have one highly qualified, indisputable all-purpose rifle for North American big game that can also do yeoman service on other continents. By investigating various gun racks we could find another dozen or so bolt rifles that would match our specifications so perfectly that the final model choice would be only a matter of personal taste. In the event that our ambitous hunting pal decides he'd prefer an autoloader, we can point to Browning's BAR, which rivals most bolt guns for accuracy and shootability, and the Remington Model 4 and Model 7400 self-loaders.

On the other hand, should our hero opt for a bit more range and horsepower, we can offer him the 7mm Remington Magnum, which has the dual advantages of excellent long-range ballistic performance and availability in a wide assortment of rifles from Remington's easy-handling Model 700 Classic to Browning's autoloading BAR. And if he wants a bigger bullet, essentially the same rifles, including the BAR, are available in .300 Winchester Magnum.

Actually, though, despite the temptation to move toward the bigger cartridges, there is no real need for any belted magnum to hunt any North American game. From the all-purpose standpoint, the disadvantages of the magnums outweigh their benefits. Not the least disadvantage is the simple truth that some hunters — make that lots of hunters — can't shoot magnums well. If we were searching for the genuine world-class all-purpose rifle, we could certainly take

Reliable workhorse cartridges, versatile enough for all kinds of American medium-sized and big game hunting, include (from left) the .270, 7x57mm, .280, 7mm Remington Magnum, .30/06, .300 Winchester Magnum, .300 Weatherby Magnum, and .338 Winchester Magnum. These and other suitable calibers are available in plenty of rifle models.

anything from pronghorn to pachyderms with the .300 Winchester, Weatherby, or H&H Magnum as well as the wonderfully flexible .338 Winchester Magnum, but so long as we hunt on native soil it's smarter to stay with less powerful calibers and take advantage of the wider selection of rifles chambered for the old favorites.

Without trying to crowd in a few additional calibers that might do in a pinch, here are the reliable workhorses that are made in the U.S.

North American	World
.270. Winchester	.270 Weatherby Magnum
7x57 Mauser	7mm Weatherby Magnum
.284 Winchester	.30/06
.280 Remington (7mm Remington Express)	.300 Winchester Magnum
7mm Remington Magnum	.300 H&H Magnum
.308 Winchester	.338 Winchester Magnum
.30/06	

A long while ago, in an OUTDOOR LIFE article on all-purpose rifles, I said something that seemed of no particular importance at the time. Since then, my words have been quoted often enough to give me a sense of paternal pride. With your forgiveness, I'll say it again: "There is no shortage of all-purpose rifles—where are the all-purpose hunters?"

Chapter 15

THE RIFLE SIGHT, PAST AND PRESENT

Whenever my wanderings take me to a new city, I invariably make a point of prowling its museums. The main reason is to study their collections of antique arms. I don't claim to be much of an authority on antique guns, and I don't find just any gun particularly intriguing because it happens to be older than I am by two or three centuries. I am, however, utterly fascinated by how they were made, who used them, and the circumstances under which they might have been used. Thus I may stand before a glass-cased specimen, recreating in my mind the tools and hands that fashioned the piece, then letting my imagination run wild with episodes of the gun's use in battle or on the chase.

Most fascinating of all is trying to evaluate how well these old guns performed. Were they reliable? How accurate could they have been? We have only sketchy accounts of the accuracy of man's earliest rifles so it is difficult to envision the ranges at which, say, a Bavarian nobleman might have toppled a stag with his pearl-and-ivory-encrusted wheellock rifle.

To estimate roughly how accurate those old rifles might have been I once developed a theory that one could draw conclusions simply by examining their sights. There seemed to be ample support for my theory because those smoothbore muskets that I knew to be woefully inaccurate had either no sights at all or only a primitive alignment system. Those I knew by reputation to be accurate, especially the "Kentucky" rifle of Colonial days and the German Jaeger style, tended to have fine, carefully crafted sights. So I figured I had a pretty solid handle on assessing the performance of firearms even as they reposed in museum showcases.

But as I began paying more attention to old sights, I found that they frequently didn't add up to what I knew to be typical accuracy. Some sights were so finely made that a rifle capable of delivering equal accuracy would easily group inside an inch circle at 100 paces. The rear sights on some ancient target and hunting rifles are precisely adjustable for windage and elevation, and the better front sights are hooded, as are modern target sights. Fairly often rear sights are of the "peep" variety similar to those used on today's target rifles. But peep sights were by no means confined to target rifles, often being found on well-made hunting rifles, indicating that some hunters were more adept at long-range shots at game than we might imagine. This is further borne out by the unusually broad range of elevation adjustment, indicating that the marksman could have made shots as long as 500 yards or more.

One particularly remarkable set of sights, found on a wheellock hunting rifle of the mid-16th century, included a globe aperture front sight of astonishing similarity to those used today in national and international rifle competitions. The peep-type rear sight was mounted on the rifle tang where it would have been close to the shooter's eye. Both windage and elevation were quickly and easily adjustable, and even the peep aperture was adjustable for size just like today's best target sights. Both front and rear sight could have been mounted on one of today's Olympic grade match rifles and used with as much confidence and accuracy as today's finest.

What this tells us is that rifle performance and the sophistication of sighting equipment did not evolve simultaneously. There is considerable evidence that the making of sights as a craft and as a science developed somewhat independently. It appears that there were periods when the art of sight-making exceeded that of gunmaking.

THREE CLASSIFICATIONS OF EARLY SIGHTS

Early gunsights can pretty well be lumped into three general classifications. The first classification is the rough and crude, meaning that they serve as an aiming device in the most basic way. The second is the ornamental. Such sights are found on highly ornamented guns and for the most part serve only as a vehicle of decoration. On occasion the scrolls, twists, inlaying, and coloring of these sights render them almost non-functional—but function obviously was not their primary purpose. The design and appearance invariably match the rest of the gun, and we can safely assume that these ornamental sights were made by the same hands that crafted the gun itself. This is also true of the rough and crude sights.

The third type is what I call the precision class. Such sights were made with accurate aiming and precise adjustment uppermost in mind. Sometimes these sights represent a fetish for precision and detail exceeding the realm of practicality. Thus, precision worksmanship becomes an end unto itself and virtually a form of ornamentation. Usually, sights of this sort are an attachment to the rifle and seldom reflect any effort of design continuity with the gun itself. No doubt this type of sight was made by the hand of a specialist, and I'm much inclined to believe they were made by clockmakers. Who else could have had the skill and equipment to craft the delicate adjustments of these marvelous mechanisms? The finely threaded and calibrated adjustment tracks, for example, could only have been turned on clockmakers' lathes.

This multiple exposure photograph of a wheellock gives some idea of the time lag between trigger pull and ignition—sparked by friction between the spinning wheel and a piece of iron pyrite clamped in the jaws of the doghead (the same principle that fires a flint-type cigarette lighter). During this interval the gun inevitably wavers, rendering aim uncertain at best. On the barrel forward of the doghead can be seen a serpentine rear sight—in this instance a device that might be classified somewhere between crude and ornamental. With such a gun, sighting was far from exact, yet some sporting wheellocks partly overcame their inherent aiming difficulty by use of precisely crafted sights mounted on adjustment tracks.

I also suspect that then, as now, the cost of a fine sighting instrument could come close to equaling that of the rifle.

One might assume the invention of telescopic sights to be a modern event. Even youngish middle-aged gentlemen like me have witnessed the blossoming of telescopic sights in our lifetimes, especially since World War II. As a matter of astonishing fact, however, the telescopic sight (or at least notions thereof) reaches back into the early days of the rifled barrel. In the early 1700's, for example, no less a person than Frederick the Great, King of Prussia, was using a telescopic sight for his target shooting.

Back in the 1950's, the American firm of Bausch & Lomb, a world leader in optical goods, introduced a line of riflescopes featuring "crosshairs" that were not crosshairs at all but lines delicately etched on glass. We'll talk more about this innovation later, but the point here is that an etched reticle was hailed as an innovative idea for rifle sights. So it seems until one blows the dust off a forbidding-looking tome entitled *Oculus Artificialis Telediaptricus,* a book in German by one Johannes Zahn. Herr Zahn describes a telescope with the usual lens plus a plain glass lens etched or engraved with an *aiming reticle!* The date of Zahn's book, by the way, was 1702.

We'll come back to telescopic sights, but in the meantime it's worth noting that the development of "iron" sights as we know them today did not precede telescopes but occurred more or less concurrently.

Drawing parallels between the development of rifles and their sights is sometimes confusing. In large measure, this is because during the first few hundred years of their development the philosophy of making and using military small arms differed from that applied to sporting arms. The thrust of sporting-rifle development was toward ever-increasing range and accuracy, but neither of these qualities was considered especially desirable in musketry. Despite a few isolated examples, such as rifled muskets used by Danish troops during the early 1600's, the smoothbore musket was the preferred small arm among European armies, a tradition favored by George Washington during the American Revolution. General Washington liked the smoothbore loaded with "buck and ball" that could be loaded speedily and generally wrought havoc among the opposing line of soldiers.

Military small arms tended to be devoid of sights during most of the 17th and 18th centuries. What is commonly supposed to be a front sight on many muskets of that era is a bayonet-retaining stud. Though it served as a rough aiming fixture, somewhat akin to a shotgun bead, it was of more importance as a bayonet holder.

ADJUSTABLE MILITARY SIGHTS

By the middle of the following century, however, the business of warfare had taken a new and nasty turn. By 1850, rifled muskets loaded with the deadly Minié bullet were used by the world's armies, and to make matters even more serious, notched rear sights were on every rifle. Furthermore, *adjustable* rear sights were in vogue, making it possible for a soldier to elevate the rear sight and thus deliver fairly accurate fire to the enemy at a distance of several hundred yards. By the 1870's, the British Lee-Metford had sights calibrated for shots out to 2,800 yards.

As early as the 1700's, telescopic sights had seen limited military use but their expense and delicacy made most applications impractical. They did show up from time to time, one of their strangest appearances being in naval warfare. According to literature of the period, some ships employed a sniper equipped with a scoped rifle. His job during sea battles was to snipe at enemy seamen as they climbed into the rigging to reset the sails. I imagine this had some psychological effect, possibly slowing the riggers' efficiency, but hitting a target on a rolling ship from the deck of another bounding ship must have involved as much luck as skill.

TARGET RIFLES AND SCOPES IN THE CIVIL WAR

Some deadly applications of shooting skill and precision sighting equipment occurred during the American Civil War. The coming of percussion ignition created a flurry of interest in ultra-accurate shooting just when the U.S. happened to produce a bumper crop of wonderfully skilled gunsmiths. These were not the rough and ready gunmakers of Colonial days who managed to piece together picturesque rifles from slag iron and slabs of curly maple, but polished craftsmen working in well-equipped shops. In quality, fit, and finish, their products equaled the world's best. From the standpoint of accuracy, they were in a class by themselves. They liked to make target-type rifles, and since shooting was the national pastime, there was a steady demand for their labors. The rosters of riflemakers included such legends as Billinghurst, Lewis, Gove, Perry, Wesson, and Morgan James. Their rifles commonly weighed in the 20-pound range, and at 40 rods (220 yards) could plunk 10 bullets inside a two-inch circle. To achieve this sort of accuracy their rifles were commonly equipped with telescopic sights made by the gunsmith himself or by optical specialists. Though usually as long as the barrel itself, and offering a limited field of view, these telescopic sights were good aiming instruments even by today's standards.

When the Civil War broke out, scope-sighted, heavy-caliber target rifles were applied to tactical assignments. Sharpshooter units were formed in both armies, the best known being Berdan's select squad of marksmen. Never before in the history of conflict had opposing armies been so expert in the use of small arms, nor had any been equipped with rifles capable of such awesome accuracy. Using scoped target rifles, snipers were able to make hits at previously unheard-of distances.

The decades following the Civil War were the heyday of firearms invention, with the Connecticut Valley literally swarming with inventors, manufacturers, and hucksters of guns of every conceivable configuration. Some succeeded and many failed, but most would have agreed with P. T. Barnum's sales philosophy: "There's a sucker born every minute." It was the nature of the times; America had passed its first great test as a Republic and now it was time to show the world how to do *everything*. Everyone wanted a piece of the action, the West was to be won, and any gun was good if it shot all day without reloading. Accuracy was an old-fashioned game,

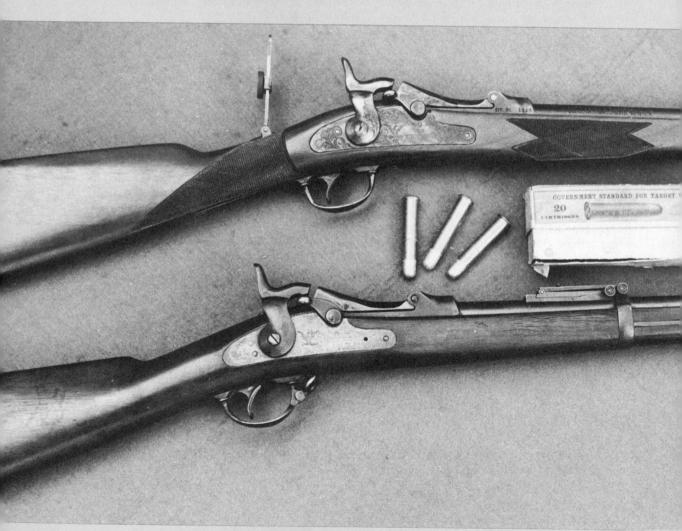

Here are some 19th-century military rifles with adjustable rear sights: an Enfield rifle with a calibrated ladder-type sight; a Spencer repeating carbine (being loaded from a Blakeslee cartridge box by a soldier) with a smiliar sight; and a couple of trapdoor Springfields, one with a tang-mounted aperture sight and one with a barrel-mounted ladder.

This front page from Harper's Weekly, *dated October 5, 1861, shows training procedures of a crack Union outfit, Berdan's Sharpshooters. They're using scoped target rifles at a distance of 35 rods—192-1/2 yards.*

as out of date as muzzleloaders. Why bother to aim when it was easier to fill the air with hot lead? Any reference to "improved" sighting equipment was usually a reflection of the hucksterism of the day, such as "Col. Wm. Markhom's magnetic sight that automatically and unfailingly draws the eye to perfect alignment." For nearly a half-century—while revolutionary firearms concepts spanned the gulf from single-shot percussion muzzleloaders to machine guns firing hundreds of rounds per minute and from sulfurous black powder to nitrated smokeless propellents—sighting equipment remained virtually unchanged.

Whatever concern remained for accuracy was retained by a small band of target shooters and makers of single-shot target-type rifles. For a brief span of history, the needs of a remarkable band of hunters were fused with long-range target-shooting know-how. But soon the great herds of bison were gone, and gone too were the thundering Sharps rifles and their vernier-scale peep sights that could arc an ounce of lead into a buffalo's shaggy hulk at 500 yards or more.

An interesting phenomenon, as much in evidence today as it was a century ago, is that both interest and developmental effort in rifle and handgun sighting equipment occurs in inverse proportion to firepower development. Conversely, arms with a low rate of fire tend to be equipped with the best sights available. Note that today our best sighting equipment is reserved for the slow shooters, while our autoloaders have the weakest sighting systems.

During that comparative ebb of sight development which occurred roughly from 1870 to 1910, a thin line of sighting excellence was maintained by a second generation of accuracy specialists. The Morgan Jameses became the Harry Popes, still making target rifles in limited numbers for a limited clientele of accuracy nuts. Even though the muzzleloaders had, by the 1880's, been replaced by breechloaders bearing names such as Ballard, Sharps, Winchester, and Stevens, their scopes (when used) were still the fragile instruments of two generations past.

Interestingly, the military attitude toward sighting equipment had done an about-face. At the beginning of the century, a musket's sights had been non-existent or, at best, vastly inferior to those on sporting rifles; by century's end, the situation was reversed, because musketry had become serious business, with the armies of the world racing to procure the most deadly cartridge shooters available. With smokeless powders boosting bullet velocities over 2,000 fps, it was possible for tacticians to think in terms of rifle fire at ranges of a half-mile or more. Accordingly, military sights were finely calibrated for long yardage. Sights of the Model 1892 U.S. service rifle (Krag), for example, were initially calibrated to 1,900 yards and later modified to 2,000 yards. In 1901, the Krag was fitted with the "Buffington"-style rear sight, which, in addition to an open V-notch, offered an aperture "peep" hole for precise aiming at long range. At that time, no off-the-shelf U.S. sporting rifle came with sights offering similar aiming precision. Instead, the trend in sporting rifles was toward gimmick sights that offered little if any aiming improvement over sights made two centuries earlier.

Typical of the gimmick sight was the "buckhorn" type that covered up most of what the shooter needed to see, especially at close range, and Beach's "combination" front sight. But perhaps that's just as well because by 1900 the death knell for open sights was being sounded. Though no one would have believed it at the time, those long, awkward, fragile telescopes were about to be revolutionized in design, shape, and utility, and within another brief span of shooting history the open sight would be a dinosaur.

TWO-PIECE SIGHTS—THEORY AND PRACTICE

The principle of the two-piece "open" sight was well known—and used—long before rifles were ever thought of. Ancient surveyors and builders used primitive sight-like transits to determine the straightness of a line from one point to another by aligning the eye with two index points. Among the index points used in these devices were narrow notches, peep holes, slender posts, and combinations of these, and they were set up to sight at a distant "target" marker. Very possibly such sighting instruments were used during the building of Egypt's Pyramids, the Parthenon of Athens, and most certainly in the digging of ancient canals and landscaping of biblical gardens.

Later, this two-point alignment principle was adapted to the crossbow in surprisingly sophisticated form. When firearms progressed to the stage where they could be expected to hit a given target with relative certainty, it was only natural for the ancient two-point alignment system to be adopted as an aiming device. Though some of the primitive two-part sights were simply a pair of sharp-pointed, conelike fixtures, the points of which were aligned on a target, open-V rear and bead-type front sights have been with us from the beginning. And since the time when bead and notch sights were first used on rifles, there has been astonishingly little improvement. There really isn't any way the system can be improved much because all theoretical improvements are stymied by one limiting factor of overwhelming magnitude: the shooter, or rather, the shooter's eye. Thus, aside from periodic improvements in the mechanical flexibility of the two-piece sight, virtually all efforts to improve the system have revolved around ways of improving our eyes' relationship with the sight. For example, differences in the shape, size, and color of front beads are all just ways of trying to accommodate the eye and deal with its limitations. (When I speak of the eye's limitations, I'm only speaking in relative terms. As we shall see later, the human eye possesses astonishing resolving power.)

Target-shooting rules, and target shooters themselves, refer to non-optical (telescopic) sights as "iron" sights. The layman's term is usually just "open" sights so we'll use that term. Most open sights supplied on today's rifles consist of a round front bead and a U-shaped rear notch. The bead is generally about 1/16- to 3/32-inch in diameter, though the "express"-type bead used on dangerous-game rifles may be as big as 1/8- or 3/16-inch across. Viewed from the rear, as when aiming, the bead should appear to be supported by a slender pedestal that is narrower than the bead itself. This bead pedestal or mounting should be as slender as possible so that a minimum area of the target will be covered and also so the bead will appear to "float" in the rear notch. Of course, the problem with making the support too thin is that it might be bent or broken off. The side profile of the front mount isn't a factor in aiming because all the shooter sees is the rear cross-section. The profile is, however, important to the strength of the sight and, of course, we want it to have an attractive "gunny" profile that won't snag on brush.

THE GREAT FRONT-SIGHT COLOR DEBATE

For centuries, shooters have argued over what material or color is best for front sights. Some claim that ivory is the best choice, others are just as determined to use gold, while still others

Here are a couple of fairly typical factory-installed rear sights — familiar to every shooter. Both examples are open notches mounted on ramps that permit some elevation adjustment. But even the obviously better of the two doesn't represent any improvement over sights made centuries ago.

preach the merits of dead black, fluorescent orange, and probably even seasick green. When I was a youngster, a local marksman of considerable repute confided to me that the secret of his unerring skill with a rifle was the use of a front sight made from a dog's tooth. To back up his claim, he showed me an assortment of rifles equipped with front sights that did, indeed, appear to be made of something like tooth enamel. Later on, an old gunsmith told me that "dog's-tooth" front sights had once been popular on muzzleloading squirrel rifles. I've seen a couple of samples, and it appears that a sliver of enamel was chipped from a long canine tooth, then ground and polished to a slender, bladelike sight. The coloring is a creamy alabaster white that seems to absorb light, making it more luminous than ivory.

What the old-time gunsmiths and squirrel hunters were trying to achieve was a front sight that could be seen in forest shade even at the end of a long barrel. That is precisely the key to selecting a front sight; it should contrast with the target and/or offer maximum visibility under a wide range of shooting conditions. We can make a front sight easily visible simply by making it big, but that isn't practical in most cases because a big bead obscures so much of the target. Let's consider an ordinary 1/16-inch bead. Assuming a distance of 30 inches from your eye to the bead, the target area covered by the bead will increase by a 1/16-inch for every 30 inches of range. At 100 yards the bead is covering 120 times 1/16-inch, which figures out to 7½ inches. Even at 50 feet, the bead is covering over three inches—enough to hide a squirrel's head and shoulder.

Thus, for most shooting purposes, we want the front sight to be as small as possible and still be visible. A dark front sight is most visible against a light background, and a white bead is best on a dark background. For example, a white bead would be next to impossible for potting a snowshoe hare on a field of snow. A gold bead is great for all-purpose work because it has a reflective glint that is easily seen and contrasts reasonably well with everything that occurs in nature. As you no doubt suspect, "gold" beads are brass or a gold-colored alloy except for a few custom sights using the real stuff. Likewise, "ivory" beads are more likely to be white plastic or painted metal.

An occasional problem with light-colored beads is a "flare" caused by strong sunlight coming from the side or from behind. This flare can glint strongly enough to make the target hard to see and also tends to cause some sight misalignment. This latter is due to centering the brightest side of the bead in the rear sight. Flare is especially common with front sights that have a rounded rear surface. The sighting surface should be dead flat.

Slight flare can be largely eliminated by using a front-sight hood that shades the bead and thereby reduces any chance of direct light being reflected to the shooter's eye. I recall Saturday-afternoon turkey and beef shoots in the Tennessee hills where the overall-clad contestants almost universally used sight hoods fashioned from Prince Albert tobacco cans. These keen-eyed marksmen made the hoods plenty big, usually an inch or more across and from top to bottom. I don't know if this was by design or chance, but they were doing it the right way. An undersized front-sight hood not only obscures the target but tends to darken and reduce the target by restricting light transmission. That's why the front-sight housing used by target shooters may be upwards of an inch in diameter.

I've never been able to work myself into a froth of excitement over odd-colored beads, especially the blaze-hued fluorescent colors. They are indeed quick to catch the eye but do so by intensely radiating an aura of color that is difficult for the eye to accept. The fluorescent colors are excellent for the front sights of handguns in certain shooting situations, but what's good for the goose isn't always so good for the gander.

Though gold and ivory sights have a certain glamour, there's nothing wrong with a bead that's dead black. So long as the black is non-reflective, it is accepted very well by the eye and tends to maintain a well defined edge, whereas some colors tend to create slightly fuzzy, out-of-focus outlines. Without exception, target shooters use dead-black front sights, regardless of configuration, because they are easy on the eye, because they contrast sharply with white target paper, and especially because a black edge can be more sharply defined by the eye than other colors. This is because black absorbs light. Other colors reflect certain light waves. (That's what gives them their characteristic color.) These radiations of reflected light tend to cause a slightly blurred effect that is especially pronounced at the edges of the object. So a black front sight is great except in low light or when aiming at a black target.

Speaking of shots in poor light, some rifles for dangerous or exotic game are fitted with special "night sights" that offer maximum visibility in poor to non-existent light. These are usually round ivory beads that may be as much as 3/16-inch in diameter. Of course, sights this big rule out pinpoint bullet placement but they were worth their weight in diamonds back when Maharajahs and British swells baited tigers and shot them by torchlight from elevated machans. Night sights are most usually found on big-bore double rifles, often mounted in a flip-up arrangement that offers a smaller daytime sight as well.

FRONT-SIGHT CONFIGURATIONS

There are all sorts of front-sight shapes, nearly all being variations of the basic bead, the straight-sided patridge type, a Mauser pyramid, or a globe aperture. The patridge-style sight is

Mounted on a ramped barrel band, this is a night sight—a large front bead that provides fast (though not very precise) aiming in poor light.

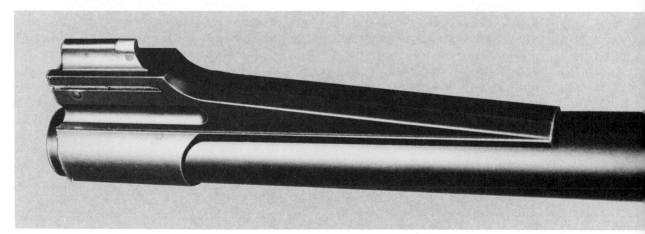

commonly used on handguns, especially those which have pretensions of accuracy, and on quite a few rifles. Essentially what a shooter sees when he aims a patridge sight is a flat-topped post of equal width from top to bottom, even though the rear face of the sight may be hooked to the rear or slanted forward.

The patridge sight is the best possible choice for most handgun use, especially target shooting, because the front-post outline, when fitted inside a square or rectangular rear notch, allows precise evaluation of sight alignment. Sight alignment is not nearly so critical with rifles as with handguns because of the longer sight radius (distance between sights) so any arguable advantage of a patridge sight as an aid to precise alignment is largely lost. The square-topped patridge post, when used with a square-notched rear sight, covers up more of the target than a round bead and requires some interpretation as to where the bullet will hit in relation to the sight picture. That's why patridge sights are usually adjusted to a "six-o'clock" hold with the bullet hitting above point of aim. Also, correctly aligning a patridge front with a square-notched rear sight requires a conscious effort to make sure the tops of both sights are in a level line and side spacing is equal. These several factors make the use of the patridge sight difficult for many shooters, and it does not seem as natural or fast as aligning a round bead inside a U-shaped rear notch.

When a patridge or post front sight is used with a peep rear, it becomes much more efficient because the target area normally blocked off by an open rear sight can be seen. This is also an exceedingly accurate sight combination for target shooting because the round bull's-eye can be precisely held in alignment with the classic pumpkin-on-a-post sight picture. The patridge-and-peep configuration has been the standard sighting arrangement on U.S. service rifles since prior to World War II and is an efficient combination for either target range or battlefield.

Another battlefield-type sight is what I call the Mauser pyramid. It is a rather squat front post tapering to a pointed tip and is usually used with a V-shaped rear notch. The resulting sight picture looks like two V's superimposed with one V upside down. This is the sight used on generations of Mauser military rifles and found on pre-war Mauser sporters as well. The thick, squat front sight is rugged and resistant to abuse, easy to see and use, and permits excellent bullet placement in normal light conditions. The tip of the front sight tends to fade in poor light, however, causing vertical error. Also, the broad base of the pyramid obstructs a lot of the target area, increasing the opportunity for aiming error. Generally, however, this is a faster, more accurate sight than a patridge front with square-notched rear.

Back when the world was young, which was a couple of years before I discovered, quite by accident, the fascinations of the female gender, I happened to own a Mossberg .22 Rimfire autoloader known as the Model 151M. The "M," I suppose, stood for Mannlicher because of its full-length stock which, in the manner of guns in those days, was of real walnut and nicely finished. I dearly loved that rifle and can't imagine why I ever sold it. Never was any rifle blessed with such a proliferation of sights. In addition to the usual U-notched rear sight, there was a receiver peep sight that pivoted out of the way—and above that, a Mossberg scope! What most intrigued me about the rig was the front sight, which was composed of four sighting elements that flipped up to offer a choice of ways to aim at a target. The most interesting of these was a round disc about a quarter-inch wide with a small hole in the center.

It seemed to me that this was a great idea for a front sight, because all one had to do was

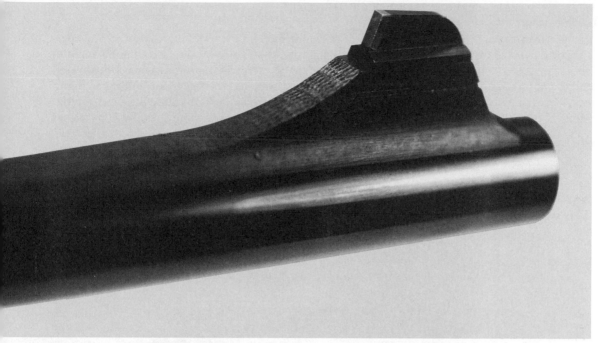

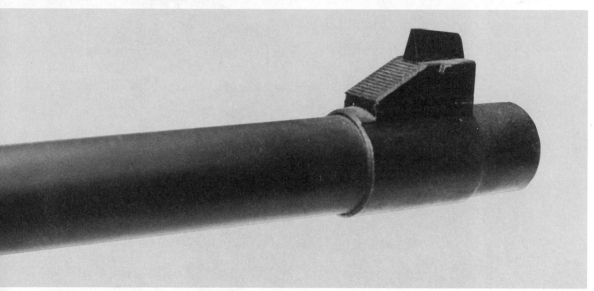

Here you see the straight-sided patridge type of front sight and the Mauser pyramid type. The patridge covers up more of the target than a round bead and is usually adjusted for a "six-o'clock" hold—with the bullet hitting above point of aim. It is more efficient with a peep than with an open rear sight. The Mauser pyramid works well with a V-notch rear sight in good light, but its tip tends to fade in poor light and its broad base obstructs a lot of target area.

center the target in the hole and a hit was certain. But it seldom worked out that way. The aperture ring blocked out so much of the target background that it was hard to see what I wanted to shoot at. So for a while I gave up on globe-aperture front sights. Later on, when I discovered target shooting, I found that the globe front aperture was just the ticket for aiming at round bull's-eyes. That's because the front sight completely encircles the bull, allowing precise judgment of vertical and horizontal alignment, while at the same time offering a totally unrestricted view of the target.

Target-type front sights come with an assortment of elements that offer the shooter a choice of posts in several widths plus a range of aperture sizes. At the beginning I made a mistake common among fledgling target shooters. I selected an aperture size that tightly encircled the bull, allowing little if any white to be seen between the bull and the sighting ring. This seems logical because, after all, if there is only a thin sliver of white seen between sight and target, any errors should be more easily detected than if there is a wide space. But as I was to

Here's a target-style globe aperture front sight with a bubble-type level and a slot to accommodate various post and aperture inserts.

learn, the bigger the hole, the better the shot. As the aperture diameter is increased, everything seen through the aperture appears proportionally larger—little hole, little target; big hole, big target. This is because what we see as a target is a column of light rays. If they pass through a small aperture they are restricted, causing the target to look darker and smaller. That was exactly why the globe-aperture front sight on my Mossberg rifle was such a disappointment. The small hole, combined with a thick ring, restricted light passage so badly that aiming was difficult and inaccurate.

When it comes to covering up a large area of the target, nothing outclasses the so-called "express" sights often mounted on dangerous-game rifles. These are generally used on the heavy-caliber British double rifles, though they are found on bolt guns as well. Whereas a front bead that hides the target is generally undesirable, in this instance it's a virtue. The idea of the express sight is to get on target as fast as possible. The presumption of the express sight is that the game will be big and close and very possibly charging in your direction. When the rifle is snapped to the hunter's shoulder, the oversized bead will instantly catch his eye, allowing a reasonably well-aimed split-second shot. Almost invariably, express sights are gold or ivory, the real stuff, and are frequently mounted in a flip-up arrangement that alternates the big express bead with a smaller bead for longer, carefully aimed shots.

Most express beads are around 1/8-inch in diameter, not quite so big as the night sights described earlier. To be truly fast, these kingsized beads must be used with an express rear sight, which is a wide, shallow V notch that permits a fast, almost unrestricted look at the front sight.

THE PROBLEM OF FOCUS

Before getting into the varieties of rear sights it's best that we have some understanding of how our eyes relate to sighting systems and the target. We've all heard old-time shooters say they're having trouble seeing the sights because, in their own words, "my eyes ain't what they used to be." We tend to reach a peak of visual acuity during the teen-age years, and from the age of 35 or thereabouts we suffer a gradual loss of sharpness. Assuming that the eyes are not damaged by disease or injury, what happens is that our eyes lose the ability to focus at certain distances and are unable to shift focus rapidly from one distance to another.

A youngster's eye can shift focus from the front sight to the rear sight and then to the target and back again so rapidly that the brain interprets the different images as a single clear picture. In time, when the teen-ager becomes middle-aged, the focusing muscles in his eye are working so slowly that he can see only the front sight *or* the target clearly, not both at once. When the front sight appears sharp, the target and rear sight are fuzzy or may not be seen at all. Normal aging usually results in farsightedness, a condition that makes reading or any similar close work impossible without reading glasses. It also makes it difficult to see the rear sight clearly.

With these creeping visual problems in mind, we easily recognize the aiming problems inherent in open sights. How can the problem be overcome? One way is to eliminate the open rear sight and replace it with a receiver- or tang-mounted peep sight. When properly using a peep sight, the shooter doesn't look at it but only *through* it, as if it weren't there. Thus the eye has only to focus on the front sight and target.

We can make the task of focusing somewhat easier for our aiming eye by positioning the rear sights as far forward as practical, usually some 10 to 14 inches from the eye. Oldtimers were well aware of the difficulties of switching focus from one sight to the other. That's why rear sights on muzzleloading rifles are a considerable distance from the eye. I've inspected a few old squirrel rifles that had a series of dovetail cuts on the barrel, indicating that as time wore on the owners were suffering progressive farsightedness and had to move the sight farther down the barrel.

How accurately can we expect to aim a rifle equipped only with an open or peep sight? Several years ago, during the salad days of my target-shooting career, I did a bit of research on the acuity of the human eye and found that experts tend to agree that a normal, healthy eye can resolve about one minute of arc. Now a minute of arc is what we shooters call a minute of angle which, as everyone knows, happens to be damn near an inch at 100 yards (1.047-inch). What I think they are saying is that the eye can make differentiations as small as an inch at 100 yards. This means we can see the difference between a one-inch dot and a two-inch dot but not between quarter- and half-inch dots.

This sounds like mighty good vision and indicates that a keen-eyed shooter should be able to aim a rifle to within an inch of error at 100 yards. Actual practice indicates that we can aim a rifle with an accuracy of a *half-inch* at 100 yards! I draw this conclusion from performances I've seen by smallbore target shooters at 100 yards. The standard 100-yard NRA target has an X-ring measuring one inch across. In theory, according to optical experts, the best a shooter can hope to do is hit that one-inch circle. Yet some 10-shot groups fired with iron sights are clustered well *inside* the X-ring, forming a group measuring between ¾-inch and ½-inch. Considering that these groups were fired from the unsupported prone position, and taking into account the accuracy limitations of rifle and ammunition, we can honestly conclude that the marksman's unaided eye was resolving alignment error of at least a half-inch at 100 yards.

Though you shouldn't expect to aim an open-sighted rifle with such precision, a key to accurate aiming is matching the rear sight to the front or vice versa. For example, a round-bead front sight combined with a deep, square rear notch will cause vertical error. Conversely, a square-post, patridge front is ill matched with a U-shaped notch. Sights have to work together if you are to shoot well.

If a bead front sight is used, the ideal rear sight is a U-shaped notch that surrounds the bead on three sides (bottom and sides) and matches the curvature. The proximity of the two sights, or their relative sizes, should be so that the bead floats in the rear notch with an open line between the two. If the bead is so large, or the notch so small, or the two positioned so close that the bead is too big for the notch, some aiming error will result. It is far better to have too much outline around the bead than not enough.

I favor a round bead and matching U notch over other open-sight combinations for most types of shooting, because they offer a good measure of both speed and accuracy. Alignment is speedy because the spacing between the sights is a continuous line. A quick, reflexive glance confirms both elevation and windage alignments. By contrast, alignment of square-post and square-notched rifle sights tends to require distinct judgments—one to determine that the windage alignment is correct and a second to make sure the top lines of both sights are on the same plane.

All sorts of schemes have been devised to draw the eye to the sights and thereby help you shoot faster and more effectively. Not many of these fancy sights work very well, and some are counterproductive. About all that can be done to draw the eye to the rear sight is to give the top of the sight leaf a slightly concave shape that gently curves down to the notch. If, however, the sides of the leaf curve up too sharply, you can figure that some of the target is being blocked out and this is what you *don't* want to happen. The old buckhorn is an example of this problem. It looked great and appealed to a shooter's natural love of gadgetry, but only got in the way.

Some rifle sights have been doctored by adding a white ring around the notch but, again, this can lead to loss of accuracy and efficiency because the object really isn't to see the rear sight but the space between the notch and bead.

For best aiming it is paramount that you focus on the front sight. Anything that attracts your focus toward the rear sight is a hindrance to good shooting. So about all we can really afford in the way of rear-sight aids is perhaps a white or gold line or pyramid just below the notch. This can help in poor light.

EXPRESS REAR SIGHTS AND FOLDING LEAVES

There seems to be some confusion over the definition and purpose of the so-called express sight. Some definitions hold that an express sight is a fancy affair characterized by two or more folding sight blades. Actually, this configuration should be described as a *folding-leaf* sight and may or may not fit the express definition. In simplest terms the express sight has a single, overwhelming purpose and that is for fast, instinctive aiming. Thus, express rear sights usually are a wide, shallow notch with the V extending from one side of the leaf to the other. Quite often a single gold bar is inlaid in the rear face of the sight, in the center of the notch, as an aid to speedy centering of the bead. Some extreme examples of express sights have no notch at all but are only a flat bar with the center marked by an inlay of gold wire. To aim, the big express bead is set atop the bar like a pumpkin on a wall. It is extremely fast. Clearly, the idea is not pinpoint bullet placement but rather, as African professionals say, to "aim for the brown and put a bullet in the bugger."

The most classic of express sights have but one leaf, which is low-profiled and rigidly mounted on the barrel(s). Purists feel that additional folding leaves adulterate the basic idea and are only something to get lost, broken, or in the way. Several years ago, when the late Pat Hepburn was guiding me on a safari in northern Botswana, he carried a bolt-action .458 that had the best example of an express sight I've ever seen. It was simply a hunk of steel milled to a wide, shallow V shape and anchored to the barrel by solder, pins, and screws. Even if the rifle were used as a jack handle, tent pole, or cricket bat (it looked as if it had served all three occupations), the sight remained in place and ready to stop a charging elephant. Which, as a matter of fact, is exactly what happened. Later on I tried to find a duplicate of Pat's rifle, but apparently only a few were made.

Most dangerous-game rifles that come equipped with express sights these days feature a combination rear sight that is composed of one rigid, open-V blade plus two or three folding leaves for longer ranges. Quite often the big front bead that is used with the wide, express rear sight folds out of the way so that a more delicate bead can be used for shots at ranges beyond 100 yards. Whenever you see your professional hunter lay down the distance-leaves and flip up

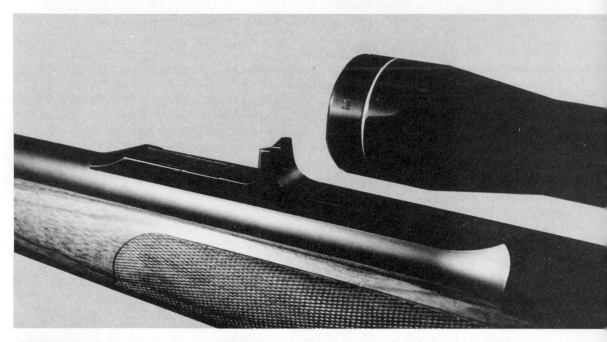

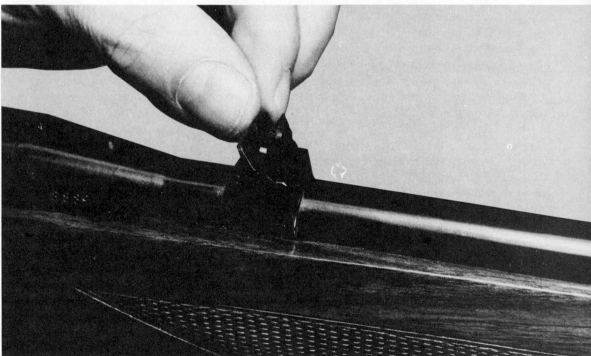

These pictures show an express rear sight and a folding-leaf rear. Contrary to a popular notion, the truly classic express has a single, low, rigidly mounted leaf with a wide, shallow V-notch for very fast aiming in emergencies.

the big express bead before heading into a thicket, you can figure he anticipates an encounter of the very close kind.

Some folding-leaf sights, by the way, may not be express sights at all. These are usually seen on small- or medium-bore rifles, and as often as not their main purpose is showing off the gunmaker's skills. They're pretty to look at and play with, but one leaf usually does all the work.

Any sight worth having can either be adjusted for windage and elevation or has already been carefully adjusted at the factory. Costly British doubles usually have a fixed rear sight, but you can bet your Rolls Royce that the bullets hit where you aim. With the more mundane rifles you can figure that if an adjustable sight isn't supplied, the manufacturer doesn't care if you hit anything or not. But even with adjustable sights, it often seems that the gunmakers leave the customer in the dark as to how to go about fine-tuning the sighting apparatus. There are manufacturers who zero the sights before shipping and some who don't, yet I don't know of any maker that lets the customer know if his new rifle is sighted-in or not. The unfortunate consequence of this is that too many shooters blithely assume the rifle will hit where it's aimed, when in fact it doesn't. To my mind, it behooves riflemakers to put a simple little tag on the trigger guard saying something like "The sights on this rifle have not been adjusted to coincide with point of impact. For best performance, follow these simple sighting-in instructions . . . ."

Makers of rifles and rifle sights also tend to let us down by not letting us know how much each increment of adjustment is worth. The notched or stepped slide ramp under the rear sight is the most common elevation adjustment ever offered, yet I have never seen a single bit of instruction telling a customer how much he should move the ramp if, say, the rifle is hitting four inches low at 50 yards. The effect of bullet placement on target that is caused by a given sight change is constant, regardless of caliber, the only variable being the distance between sights (radius). Using a pocket calculator or just a pencil and paper, any riflemaker could, in just a few minutes, work out the step or calibration value for any iron sight on any rifle and include the information with the instructions.

Today's open sights tend to be more easily adjustable than those offered a generation ago. I suppose today's shooters are more sophisticated and demand better sights, or it could be just because gunmakers have discovered that adjustable sights make good advertising copy. Even the greatest rifles of a generation ago, such as the Model 70 bolt gun made by Winchester prior to 1964, were almost invariably fitted with sights that were adjustable for elevation by means of a two-bit slide ramp and for windage by pounding the sight back and forth in its dovetail cut. That's about as good as they ever got, even when they were beauifully finished.

Today's sights, though not tending to be as well finished as the oldies, can usually be adjusted easily and precisely with a screwdriver. Sometimes, though, sightmakers seem to go too far to emphasize the adjustability of their product and end up with mechanisms that are ugly, oversized, and ill-suited to the rifle.

APERTURE REAR SIGHTS

Alas, the fastest and most accurate iron sight ever available to hunters has almost vanished from the scene. I'm talking about the peep, or aperture, sight which consists of a simple round hole and is aimed by looking *through* the hole at the front sight and target. Peep sights are, of course, widely used by target shooters in nearly all forms of competition. Target shooters call them receiver sights, and today's target-shooting models are vastly different from the hunting-type peeps of yore.

During my earliest shooting years I had good reason to become prejudiced against peep sights of any make or form. Not that I could claim any firsthand experience with the exotic aperture. Peep sights were as scarce in our farm community as princes of the blood royal; but the local experts who advised me about shooting and other manly matters simply said that peeps were only for sissified target shooters. The shooting expertise possessed by most of those folk scarcely extended beyond shooting rats in their barns or killing hogs on the first cold day of November. Yet guns were a part of rural life and youngsters were obliged to pay heed to their elders in such vital matters. And I did. Ex-GI's returning from the war further instilled my dislike of the peep sight by telling how hard it was to aim the M-1 service rifle because of its rear aperture.

And sure enough, the first time I tried a peep-sighted rifle I found out that everything they said was true! Later, though, I learned that on my first attempt I made the mistake of so many shooters—looking *at* the peep rather than *through* it. By looking at the peep, all one sees is a lot of funny-looking sight and very little of anything else. In time, when I had a chance to get accustomed to using good peep sights ("good" meaning the right peep for the rifle and caliber), I found that they were even faster than ordinary open sights, allowed me a much better look at the target and, best of all, offered significantly better accuracy than ever before possible without using a telescope.

Let me give you some idea of the speed and accuracy of a properly used aperture sight. Consider the big-bore target shooter who, during the National Match Course, fires 10 shots from the sitting position at a range of 200 yards with a total time limit of one minute, during which time he must pause and reload. A top marksman will group all 10 shots in the seven-inch 10-ring with more than half his bullets hitting the three-inch X-ring. The 300-yard stage is fired from the prone position and allows 10 more seconds, but the scoring rings are the same and again a large percentage of hits will be in the three-inch X-ring. This is *always* done with peep sights. Though the rules allow any non-telescopic sight, there is no way ordinary open sights could deliver this degree of speed or accuracy.

The peep sight as a hunting proposition was done in by the telescope. The type of hunter who once preferred the accuracy offered by the peep was quick to embrace the even greater advantages of the scope. Not that all that many peep sights were ever used anyway. Though aperture sights were popular on target rifles throughout the 19th century, they made little headway in hunting circles. Considering the limited range of most black-powder rifles, there really wasn't all that much use for a sight offering fine long-range accuracy. The notable exceptions were the buffalo hunters who, judging by surviving rifles, favored the aperture sight for their long-range style of hunting. The aperture sight used on many of the buffalo rifles was mounted on a calibrated frame or post which, in turn, was mounted on the rifle's tang behind the hammer. The tang-mounted sight pivoted flat for easy carrying and storage and it tilted forward somewhat with the recoil of heavy-caliber rifles, thus avoiding slapping the shooter in the eye. But the day of the buffalo hunter was only a flicker in history, with the great peep-sighted grasslands rifles surviving only as relics of a fascinating era.

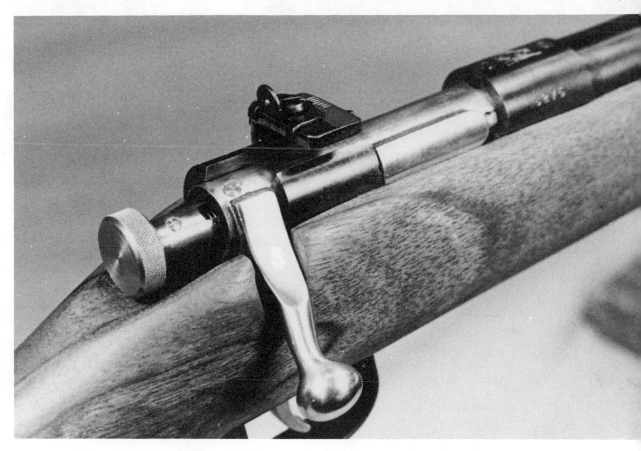

This is a simple but adjustable aperture sight, mounted on a Chipmunk .22 rimfire.

The arrival of smokeless powder was a reprieve for aperture sights because the zippy little nitrate-driven bullets offered more range than could be accommodated by old-fashioned open sights. Thus, the period from about 1895 to the end of World War II can be called the golden age of receiver sights. Shooting catalogs offered a rich assortment of peep sights for just about every rifle in existence, and rifle manufacturers themselves offered ready-mounted peep sights. Winchester, for instance, offered the Model 70 bolt rifle with a receiver sight, and Marlin even put a peep on the little M-80 rimfire.

One of the most interesting adaptations of the aperture sight was offered for Winchester's Model 71, .348-caliber lever rifle. This sight was attached directly to the bolt and rode back and forth as the lever was cycled. Actually, it was a quite good idea as the sight was compact and certainly well positioned for quick sighting, but the M-71 faded away back around 1957 or '58 as I recall. Winchester also offered peep sights as standard equipment, I believe, on the Model 65 in .218 Bee and Model 64 in .219 Zipper. The peep sight was a way of utilizing the extended range of these two varmint calibers. Until 1983, in fact, when Winchester introduced the scope-

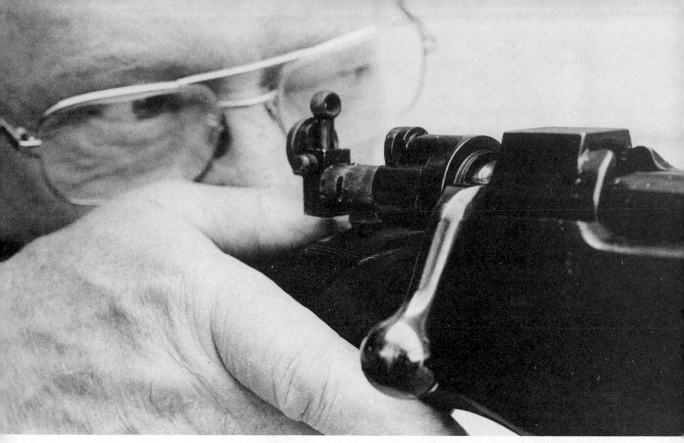

This is an adjustable peep sight mounted on the cocking piece of a bolt-action. Years ago, such sights were offered by several American makers and were also found on fine British rifles. However, the weight of the sight slowed lock-time by adding to the burden of the striker spring. This reduced accuracy, and by the 1950's cocking-piece sights were abandoned.

friendly angle-ejecting version of the Model 94, the receiver-mounted aperture sight was the best way to coax extra yards and accuracy from their lever-action rifles.

An ingenious way to mount a peep sight is on the cocking piece of a bolt-action rifle. Since the cocking piece is close to the eye anyway, some clever chap got the idea of attaching a small, adjustable aperture. The likelihood of getting poked in the eye by the sight on recoil is reduced, because when the trigger is pulled, releasing the sear, the cocking piece and sight jump forward. These sights were made by Lyman, Parker Hale, the old Pacific Gunsight Company, and small specialty gunshops for such diverse rifles as Mausers, 03 Springfields, Enfields, Russians, and the Mannlicher Schoenauer. Use of these sights reached a climax between the World Wars, and about the only survivors one sees today are on top-quality British rifles made during that elegant era. As you no doubt suspect, the cocking-piece sight, even the smallest and lightest models, added to the striker spring's burden and slowed lock-time. Accuracy could also suffer as the cocking-piece shoulder found different positions on the sear from shot to shot. The best-fitted specimens had an alignment notch cut in the sear to reduce this problem. Anyway, the idea never made much headway in the U.S., and by the 1950's cocking-piece sights had been written off by American makers.

A similar idea was the bolt-sleeve aperture sight made back in the 1930's by Marble and offered for Springfields, Enfields, and even the Winchester bolt guns. I've never seen one except in old catalogs, so apparently the idea never caught on. They probably were never very accurate because of the natural looseness of most bolt sleeves.

Back in the 1920's and '30's, when some of America's custom gun houses such as Griffin & Howe were in their heyday, the very finest rifles were routinely fitted with aperture sights, the most popular being the Lyman No. 48. Sportsmen who were wise enough to invest in high-quality rifles were also smart enough to realize the accuracy advantage of peep sights as opposed to ordinary open sights. Books and magazine articles dating from the pre-war years often picture hunters with peep-sighted rifles, especially those hunting sheep, antelope, goat, and other such long-shot game. Even after scopes became commonplace, it was not unusual for a good big game rifle to be fitted with a peep sight as a backup, in case the scope went sour. Some sights, notably the Lyman 48, had a quick-release feature that permitted the aperture slide and mount to be slipped out and stored in some safe, out-of-the-way place such as in a special trapdoor compartment under the buttplate. When needed, the peep could be put in use simply by dropping the slide in place. Pre-set stops insured that the setting automatically came back to zero.

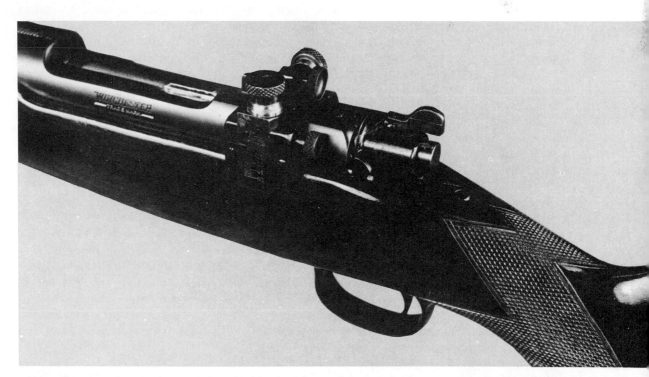

The excellent Lyman No. 48 peep sight had a quick-release feature for removal and storage of the aperture. When needed, the aperture slide was dropped back into place. Pre-set stops insured that the setting of the adjustable sight came back to zero.

In addition to the superior accuracy and aiming efficiency of the aperture sight, the better makes and models were, and are, calibrated for precise adjustments. The American standard sight adjustment is calibrated in minutes of angle, which is very nearly one inch at 100 yards, two inches at 200 yards, and so on. Good aperture sights for hunting rifles usually have index calibrations in four- or five-minute units, with clicks as fine as a quarter-minute. Thus a skilled marksman can make changes in his rifle's point of impact as precise as a quarter-inch at 100 yards. The adjustment system used on most of today's scopes is an adaptation of that used on peep sights. Obviously, one of the advantages of such fine adjustments is being able to reset the zero to put the bullet on target at different ranges, then precisely return to a previous setting. Another feature that knowledgeable riflemen can make use of is resetting the sight to allow for wind drift. The old aperture sights with these "micrometer" adjustments were not confined just to target shooting, though some models featured oversized adjustment knobs for fast, easy changing during tournament shooting. Special hunting versions were offered with rounded snag-proof knobs that could be locked in place.

A few years ago, I made up a lightweight, mountain-style rifle in 7X57 caliber that was a dream to carry and reliably grouped in a sheep's eye across a canyon. To keep the rig light, I forwent a scope in favor of a peep sight, thus eliminating another pound of weight.

It occurs to me that there's a generation of hunters who have never peered through an aperture sight at a bull elk and will never swing a peep and bead on a bounding buck. It's just as well, since scopes are better, but I still miss peep sights on hunting rifles because the sights themselves were often beautifully made examples of precision worksmanship. Lyman Gunsight Corporation once manufactured a terrific assortment of aperture sights and still offers a couple of micrometer-type peep sights, but Redfield, a company that began business as a maker of such sights, now offers only a specialized target model. Williams Gun Sight Company once offered a solid, dependable peep they called their Five Dollar Sight. It costs more than $5 now, so they call it the 5-D, but it's still a rugged hunting sight. When my sons first showed an interest in shooting, they were handed lightweight .22's equipped with peep sights. To my mind, the old-fashioned peep is not just a great way to learn to shoot but also a great way to learn *about* shooting.

TARGET-TYPE RECEIVER SIGHTS

Up until the 1950's, there wasn't much difference between peep sights used for hunting and those used for target shooting. However, as the performance of target rifles and ammunition — and especially shooters — continued to improve, it became increasingly evident that a weak link in the accuracy chain was inadequate sights. A target shooter's score will reflect the ruggedness and precision of his sighting equipment. During a day of tournament rifle shooting, a competitor will adjust, change, and rechange his sights anywhere from dozens to hundreds of times. Many of these sight changes will be only a quarter, a sixth, or even an eighth of a minute at a time, but splitting hairs is the nature of target shooting.

Some forms of competition, notably big-bore matches, do not allow non-recorded sighting shots once the event is under way. When a shooter has to make a sight adjustment in order to keep up with changes in wind, light, and myriad other complications, he must have faith that his sight will respond when he clicks the knobs. But as target shooters have learned, often the hard way, some sights don't always respond. This can be due to natural wear of the mechanism, too much "slop" in the fittings, abuse, or just poor design. The problem was especially bad in the "good old days." Savvy shooters dealt with backslash, a failure of the sight to respond to a change of direction, by a double shuffle of the knobs (five clicks left then three right in order to get an honest two clicks left), and others wrapped the fixtures with rubber bands to control slop. Eventually, the super sights used in today's competition evolved, and they are as different from the old Lyman No. 48 hunting and target sight as a computer is from a zither.

From the hunting standpoint, today's ultra-refined receiver sights (they aren't called peeps anymore) are grossly oversized and too complicated by knobs, scales, and price to be of much practical use. But to a feverish target shooter they are little less than works of art. Prices for the top sights by Anschutz, Redfield, or other specialty sightmakers start at over $100 and go on up to the price of a top telescopic sight, but to target shooters that's little enough to pay for peace of mind when the wind suddenly shifts and some well-considered changes must be cranked into the sight to get the bullets back on target.

What's more, really determined competitors will spend another bundle on a dial-indicator setup that checks the sight to make sure it is responding uniformly to clicks of the knobs and is promptly reversing course when the adjustments are clicked back and forth. Competitors fear nothing more than a sight that won't respond. I know a canny target shooter who once took a sight-testing instrument to tournaments and graciously offered it to all who wanted to check the accuracy and responsiveness of their sights. He knew from experience that at least half the sights on the line would have chronic irregularities and when these were revealed, the owner's concentration and confidence would be ruined for days.

SIGHT-MOUNTING FIXTURES

The manner in which open sights are attached to a rifle is a pretty good tip-off as to the rifle's quality and the usefulness of the sights. You've noticed that bottom-of-the-line economy rifles tend to have both front and rear sights simply dovetailed into the barrel, whereas the sights on better rifles are mounted on various ramp or base fixtures. Builders of high-class custom rifles make a big production of fitting banded front sights and delicately matted quarter-ribs that lend a stylish profile and, of course, soak their well-heeled customers an extra hundred dollars or so.

I own a long-barreled .32-caliber caplock rifle that has become my favorite tool for clipping squirrels out of tall hickories on crisp mountain mornings. Though of recent make, it was handcrafted along traditional lines and, as with long rifles of yore, its sights are a simple blade-and-notch affair mounted low on the barrel. After a couple of shots, the barrel warms up enough to create dancing waves of mirage that play merry hell with the sight picture, and I often wonder how the oldtimers aimed their long rifles in the heat of an Indian attack. The barrels on centerfire target rifles often get sizzling hot, boiling off heat waves like a tea kettle. Savvy shooters deal with the problem by mounting the iron sights to the side of the barrel, by stretching fabric mirage awnings between the sights, or at least by mounting the sights an inch or more above the barrel. Awnings and offset sights are obviously impractical on hunting rifles, but any well-made rifle has its sights well off the barrel.

Today's receiver apertures for target competition are a far cry from the old Lyman No. 48 — and from any other hunting peep, old or new. They aren't practical for hunting (too large, too expensive, and too encumbered by knobs and scales) but they are a marvel for match shooting. They permit adjustments as fine as 1/8-minute.

From the standpoint of strength, there can be no better way to mount a front sight than on a ramp that is itself an integral part of the barrel. But machining a ramp into the barrel bar stock calls for fancy and costly gunmaking. One of the few commercial examples of an integral forged sight ramp was on some Model 70 Winchesters. Most folks never realized the cost and effort involved.

Before rushing off to order a new barrel with an integral ramp, you'd better think twice. Another ramp style that is just about as rigid and has tremendous visual appeal is the banded type. With this type, the ramp is held by a band that tightly encircles the muzzle and is made fast by soldering. This is the type of front ramp used on top-quality British bolt rifles such as those made by Holland & Holland, as well as the better custom houses in the U.S. Some inexpensive rifles have been fitted with a cheap-looking plastic ramp that is feebly held on by a band but that's not the sort of stuff we're talking about. A good-looking, well-made banded front sight comes on the Ruger rifles.

The next best thing is a top-mounted ramp that is secured by brazing (silver solder) plus screws or pins. But since soldering and pinning gets a little complicated for some gunsmiths and gunmakers, the most common mounting technique today simply consists of a screw or two. For mass-produced rifles such as the Remington Model 700, this is a good idea because scope users can remove the iron sights entirely, putting plug screws in the empty holes for a streamlined profile.

The all-time classic mounting fixture for a leaf-type rear sight is the so-called quarter-rib, which begins at the front of the receiver and extends about a quarter of the way down the length of the barrel. Since a quarter-rib fits over the chamber contour of the barrel, it requires some fancy hand-fitting. That's why quarter-ribs are only found on the most expensive rifles. Some mid-European gunmakers offer barrels with full-length ribs, but the only result is additional weight plus a pronounced tendency for the barrel to warp as it gets warm. The more tasteful and sensible makers confine their rib-making to quarter-lengths or even less. Some gun-fitters show off their talents by machining the quarter-rib integrally with the barrel and, as you might suspect, this runs into serious money. But either fitted or integral, a quarter-rib provides a stylish and sturdy perch for a rear sight. Most ribs are fitted with multiple folding-leaf sights, but not always. One of the most used and utterly reliable hunting rifles in my cabinet is a .338 Magnum custom-built on a Mauser action by the David Miller Company. Though the rifle is fitted with Miller's earthquake-proof scope mount, it is further beautified by an integral quarter-rib on which is mounted a single express sight. It doesn't fold or move, and as far as I can determine, only an act of God could loosen it from its moorings. Which is exactly what I wanted.

Occasionally, the owner of a fine quarter-ribbed rifle discovers, to his unspeakable horror, that the rib comes loose when the barreled action is reblued by the modern caustic salt method. This happens when the rib and ramp were originally lead-soldered in place. The caustic bluing solution attacks the solder, and things tend to come somewhat apart, as do the barrels of shotguns that have been cold-soldered together. So when you have these beautiful rifles refinished, it's best to reblue by the old-fashioned cold-blue method, which looks better anyway.

A variation of the quarter-rib is an isolated, or "island," rib that is positioned farther down the barrel. In recent years, the soldered-in-place island rib has evolved into a simple ramp held

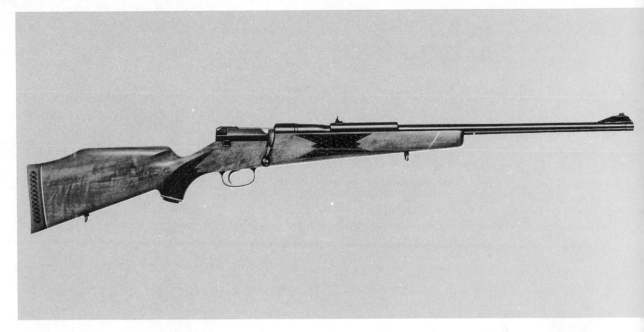

Rear sights are sometimes attached to the barrel by a simple screw-in ramp, sometimes mounted on a quarter-rib, and sometimes mounted on a band like the one on this Mauser Model 660.

on by a couple of screws. Like the screwed-on front ramps, the removable rear ramps offer the convenience of being easily detached so the rifle will have a streamlined scope-only look. Lots of shooters who never use their open sights, and would just as soon that they weren't there, don't realize that these sights can be easily removed with a screwdriver. The trick is just to remember to save the plug screws when the scope is mounted. These are transferred to the holes vacated by the open-sight screws so that the barrel will look neat.

Since the attachment of front-sight ramps by means of a barrel-encircling steel band is such a great idea, one could quickly get taken with the notion that a banded rear sight would be a good idea as well. It works all right and the applications have been abundant. One of the neatest looking, sturdiest, and best known of the band-mounted rear sights was used on the slick-working, slick-looking Mannlicher-Schoenauer sporters as they were made until the late 1960's. The way Mannlicher did it, the mounting was simple and strong, and that's about all anyone can ask. The best-known and certainly most common application of the banded rear sight is found on the old standby 03 Springfield and the M-98 Mauser, plus just about every other bolt action military rifle. But in these applications, the band is so long that it is more aptly called a sleeve. This is the sturdiest system of all, but it lacks the style and grace of an English-style quarter-rib. All the same, some British heavy-bore rifles have been fitted with sleeve mountings. Pre-World War II Mauser sporters were regularly fitted with sleeved sights that gave them a crossbred military-civilian look, no doubt causing the Teutonic heart to beat a little faster.

Chapter 16

. . . .

THE TELESCOPIC SIGHT

. . . .

The telescopic sight is not only the most accurate, efficient aiming instrument ever attached to a rifle, but also offers the invaluable service of making all shooters equal. Using a riflescope that is properly focused for his aiming eye even Great Grandpa sees the crosshairs and the target as clearly as a sharp-eyed teen-ager. That's because the crosshairs and the target appear on the same focal plane. Tired eye muscles don't have to shift focus from rear sight to front sight to target and back again; it's all there in one place.

From the standpoint of game utilization and conservation, the riflescope allows more precise bullet placement, thus reducing the ratio of wounded and lost animals. Scopes also promote selective hunting and have reduced the number of mistaken shots at females of the species. From the viewpoint of hunter safety, it would be impossible to estimate the number of accidental injuries and deaths that have been avoided because at the last instant a scope told the hunter he was aiming at a man rather than game.

A scope does not, however, reduce hunting to an unfair, lead-pipe cinch as has been claimed by anti-hunting groups and even some sportsmen. It in no way improves one's hunting skills, and until the crosshairs are on a target, a scope is only a useless piece of baggage. Nor does a scope made a good marksman out of a poor one. It is absurd to suppose that by using a scope one is guaranteed a hit and kill. Good marksmen use scopes very effectively; poor marksmen benefit little if at all, because a telescopic sight is only an extension of one's shooting skills. So even though a scope allows farsighted and nearsighted folks to see the target better, you still can't hit it unless you possess the basic skills of holding and squeezing.

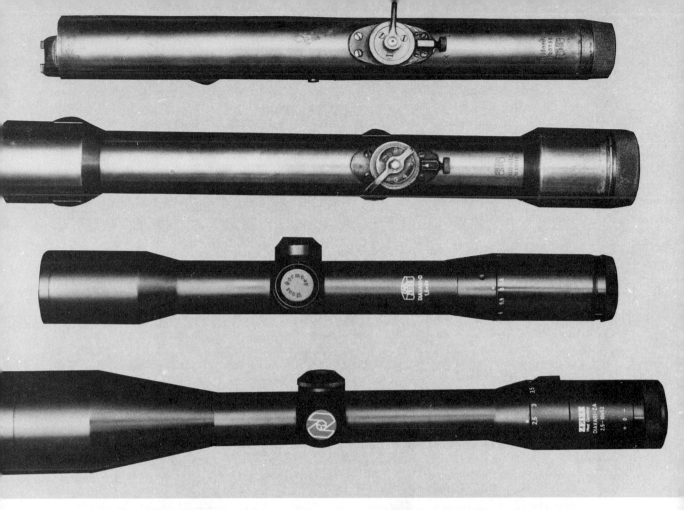

These four riflescopes were all made by Zeiss—the upper two in the 1930's, the lower pair half a century later. Perhaps surprisingly, the old as well as the new feature variable power. Magnifications (from top) are 1X-6X, 2X-7X, 1.5X-6X and 2.5X-10X. The principle is the same as that used in zoom camera lenses. The two older scopes have focusing rings on the eyepiece and turret dials to raise or lower magnification, but windage and elevation had to be adjusted externally—by means of the mounts.

The hunting riflescope as we know it today evolved around 1900. Scopes had been made in the U.S. for previous generations, but their use was confined almost exclusively to target and small-game shooting. The American makes were often of superb optical quality and offered aiming precision nearly equal to that of today's scopes, but they were clumsy affairs perched in delicate mountings and scarcely equal to the rigors of hunting.

Whereas American shooters, possessed by a passion for accuracy, saw the scope as a means of improving the precision of aim, Europeans viewed optical sights from an entirely different perspective. In much of Europe, big game hunting had become such a highly stylized sport that even the habits of the animals had evolved into a nocturnal regimen. With the practical shooting hours being faintest dawn and dusk, European big game hunters were obsessed with ways of aiming in poor to almost nonexistent light. Experience with telescopes and field glasses demonstrated that optical enhancement of an object has the desirable by-product of making it more visible in poor light, so it was natural that the principle be applied to rifle sights. When the first *hunting* riflescopes were made, their purpose was not as a better sight so much as a way to aim at night. This essential factor has characterized European scope design from its beginnings to the present. The passion for low-light hunting optics, most notable among Austrians and Germans, carried over into warfare, and German sniper manuals from both world wars cited the scope as an aid when sniping at dawn and dusk. When, in 1920, the famous German optical firm of Zeiss made their first big assault on the riflescope market, their most impressive model was the *Zielacht,* an 8-power job with a bucket-sized objective lens for scooping in big snootfuls of light.

Though the English and French have had their turn at making riflescopes, the only European makers of importance were and are in Austria and Germany. The Soviets make scopes, but apparently not for export, and the few samples I've seen were copies of outdated German military models.

The big names in hunting-style scopes during the first decade of the 1900's were Busch-Visar, Helios, Luxor, Schütz, and Voigtlander. If you were to compare most of the scopes of that time to scopes of today, you'd be surprised by their physical similarity. They weren't fogproof as are today's best, the lenses weren't coated, and they had only one or no internal adjustment. But the reticles were about the same as those of today, including plain crosshairs, dot, post, duplex, etc., with magnifications ranging from 2X to 5X.

Then as now, the German firm of Carl Zeiss was a powerful force in the optical industry, but their first effort at making a commercial riflescope was such a peculiar blend of gadgetry and binocular technology that even the Germans didn't go for it. The first Zeiss scope, which was of 2X magnification and introduced in 1904, was something of a prism periscope with the objective lens perched above the rifle like a thickly bandaged sore thumb. The unit was attached to a tube which extended over the rifle's action and was secured in more or less conventional mounts. By today's standards it was an awkward arrangement, especially one version that had a downward-angling eyepiece. The idea of the slanted eyepiece was to get it down close to the level of open sights, but in order to see through the scope one actually had to tilt one's head back and look at an upward angle. The concept was so poor that in 1920 Zeiss offered a whole new line of rifle optics designed along what by then had become the traditional form.

One of the oldest makers of hunting-style telescopic sights is the Austrian firm of Kahles. Founded in 1898, Kahles was by the 1920's exporting scopes to the U.S., and their Mignon line (sometimes thought to have been French-made) was carried by Stoeger Arms. In the 1925 *Shooter's Bible,* the Mignon scopes were priced at $17.50 for 2.5X, $21.50 for 4X, and $25 for 6X. Even at that time, those prices were pretty cheap for scopes of such good quality.

A fundamental weakness of the hunting-style scope of that era was its lack of internal adjustments or, at best, only a vertical adjustment. The scope had to be set in adjustable mounts or rigidly locked in a non-changeable position. The latter arrangment called for fancy gunsmithing not unlike the procedure used to get both barrels of a double rifle to shoot to the same point of aim.

With the unfailing brilliance of hindsight, we perceive the usefulness of having both windage and elevation adjustments built into a riflescope, but as recently as 1930 the concept was an elusive one. The convenience of simply turning a couple of dials to zero a rifle is due to a clever fellow by the name of Rudolph Noske. Only oldtimers will remember him, but before World War II the name Noske was on every shooter's lips.

He was a German-American instrument maker of impressive scientific credentials who, in the early 1920's, became interested in simplifying the problems of mounting a scope on a rifle. His first solution was a workable and reliable system which was mounted on the side of the rifle's receiver and featured lateral adjustment. We'll talk more about Noske's mount when we get into that subject more deeply, but the important thing about this inventor was that he saw his mount only as one way of dealing with the problem. Another solution he came up with, the one for which we are really grateful, was putting *both* reticle adjustments inside the scope. Nit-pickers will point out that dual-adjustment scopes had been made before Noske put the idea together, but these were generally one-of-a-kind affairs that were never offered to the public. Noske jumped in with both feet and by the mid-1930's was manufacturing 2¼X and 4X scopes that featured his dual-adjustment system and also happened to have superb optics.

One of the earliest of the Zeiss telescopic sight designs, this is a 2X instrument that operates as a periscope. The tube extending over the rifle's action is merely a rigid arm for securing mounts; it contains no lenses. The objective lens is housed in the bulky upper projection. The version in the photograph was a modification of the very first Zeiss, whose rear end tilted downward and thus made sighting awkward.

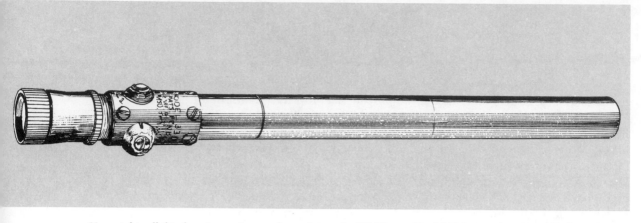

You might call this drawing a picture of nostalgia — the 3X Weaver Model 330, introduced in 1933 for only $19. Engineer Bill Weaver, who had begun building scopes as a hobby, altered shooting history by designing and marketing America's first popularly priced scope in a Depression year when few Americans could pay upwards of $100 for a German import.

In addition to being the first maker of dual-adjustment scopes, Noske can also be called the father of long eye relief. His later models featured a full seven-inch clearance between the ocular lens and the shooter's eye. This was twice as much eye relief as offered by any other scopemaker of the time, and it was developed for what would now be considered a trivial reason. Back then, the bolt handles of nearly all bolt-action rifles would hit a low-mounted scope. Thus, scopes had to be mounted up out of the way or else the bolt handle had to be altered to a lower sweep. Noske built in additional eye relief so that his scopes could be mounted well forward on the receiver and the bolt handle could come up behind the eyepiece.

By the end of the 1930's, the Noske scope and the Lyman Alaskan, one of the very few great American scopes of that era, compared quite well to Europe's best — the Hensoldt, Kahles, and Zeiss brands. While matching the great Austrian and German firms in quality and exceeding them in utility, Noske also matched them in price. And the price of a good scope in those days was in the neighborhood of that for a Browning Superposed shotgun or a Model 70 Winchester rifle.

That's why a mild-mannered fellow from El Paso was, in a very few years, able to become the king of riflescopes and to alter the course of rifle-shooting history. His name was Bill Weaver and the year was 1933. His scope was of 3X magnification and retailed for only $19! Today, whether you own a Leupold or Redfield or Weaver or Tasco or Zeiss, it was Bill Weaver who put that scope in your hand. Before Weaver stepped onto the shooting stage, scopes were the playthings of rich sportsmen and target shooters, hardly the stuff of typical American hunting. In his lifetime, the telescopic sight became an integral part of worldwide hunting, as common as scuffed boots.

Today, so many scopemakers and importers offer so many new models each year that any listing would be obsolete before publication. There are so many superb scopes on today's market that any shooting writer who attempts to proclaim which is best is entitled to a lifetime scholarship at the laughing academy. The best we can hope to do is divide scopes into general classifications and help the shooter decide which group is best for his particular needs.

OPTICAL TERMS DEMYSTIFIED

To the uninitiated, the terminology of scope optics can be mystifying, so let's take time out here to talk about what we're talking about. I'll start with the easy terms:

Tube. This is the main outer body of the scope. It may be made of steel or a lightweight aluminum alloy, and it houses much of the scope's optical as well as the reticle-adjusting system. It also serves to attach and support the objective and ocular bells, both of which are usually larger than the tube itself. American scopes and most imports have a standardized one-inch tube diameter. The exceptions are some 3/4-inch and 7/8-inch tubes characteristic of scopes made for rimfire rifles. Most European brands have 26mm or even 30mm tubes, but in recent years the Continental makers have offered models with one-inch tubes. Virtually all Japanese scopes, except for rimfire models, have the standard one-inch tubes.

Ocular lens. Also called the eyepiece, this is the lens closest to the eye. There's no standard size for ocular lenses in the U.S. or abroad. Lens diameters range around 1¼ inches, with the outside diameter of the lens housing averaging about 1½ inches. The ocular lens is usually round, but may have a rectangular TV-screen shape on certain wide-angle scopes. The ocular lens is adjusted by the shooter for a clear focus on the crosshairs.

Objective lens. This is the lens at the front of the scope and may be as small as the scope's tube or, in extremes, as large as 2½ inches or more. Scopes of high magnification generally have the

Appropriately perched on a typically fine Griffin & Howe rifle, this scope is the Lyman Alaskan — one of the great American scopes of a bygone era.

larger objective lenses, but there are plenty of exceptions. Objective-lens size is closely related to a scope's brightness, or light-gathering power, but again there are many exceptions. The objective lens may be fixed and focused parallax-free at 100 yards or closer, as with most scopes of 6X or less, or may be adjustable. Since focus becomes increasingly critical as magnification is increased, an objective lens that can be focused by the shooter is essential in a high-power scope. Focusing objective lenses are usually calibrated in yards and may be fast-setting (usually one turn or less) or slow-setting (requiring several turns of the focusing head or ring).

Eye relief. This is the clearance between the ocular lens and the shooter's eye. In extreme cases, the relief distance may be an inch or less or—with some specialized scopes, such as those designed for handguns—may be over a foot. The recoil of high-powered rifles makes a fairly long eye relief desirable, so most modern riflescopes offer a clearance of some three to 4½ inches. The eye relief of most scopes is not a precise distance, so a variation of an inch or so does not affect the field of view. However, if the eye is positioned too close or too far from the eyepiece, some of the field of view will be blocked out.

Along with eye relief, there is a limited amount of lateral leeway with the scope still offering a full field. If the lateral limit is exceeded, the field will begin to black out. Regardless of the eye's axial and lateral position in relation to the eyepiece, so long as the crosshairs and the target can be seen the crosshair position will continue to indicate the bullet's point of impact. An exception occurs if parallax exists in the focusing mechanism, in which case lateral eye motion will create an aiming error (see *Parallax*).

Reticle. Any aiming element in a riflescope—crosshairs, duplex, post, or dot—is the reticle. So

This diagram, from a Bausch & Lomb handbook, shows the basic parts of a telescopic sight, all housed in a trim cylindrical tube. The eyepiece is also called the ocular lens; eye distance is commonly called eye relief.

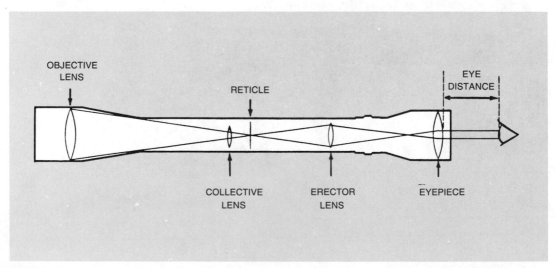

Carmichel is shown at the range, using a coin to turn the slotted elevation-adjusting knob atop a scope. The windage adjustment is on the side of the tube. Both knobs have scales calibrated in fractions of minutes of angle.

whenever we're discussing reticles, as we will be later on in this chapter, we're only talking about what we use to aim at the target.

Reticle-adjusting knobs. These may be pronounced knoblike fixtures or only slotted screws. They may be exposed or protected by screw-on caps, but they are easily accessible to the shooter and serve the purpose of moving the reticle so that point of aim coincides with bullet impact. Most modern scopes have two adjustments, one for elevation and the other for windage, but some models have only one or none at all. Some scopes have oversized knobs for convenient operation, a feature appreciated by target shooters, and some have removable knobs for conversion from target use to a low profile for field shooting. Virtually all adjustments have a graduated scale on or near the knobs, indicating how much a given unit will change the point of bullet impact on target. These graduations are calibrated in minute-of-angle units or fractions of MOA's. Some adjustment knobs give an audible "click" when turned, indicating units of movement, and some turn silently. Though clicking adjustments may be more convenient, they

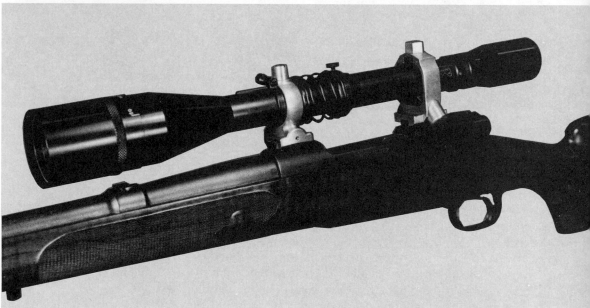

At top is one of the fine old Bausch & Lomb Balvar 8 scopes — an excellent instrument but without the internal adjustments of the hunting scopes now produced by B&L and all other makers. Some types of fine modern varmint and target scopes have no internal adjustments, either. The lower picture shows a Unertl varmint scope on a Winchester Model 70 in .220 Swift caliber, stocked by Al Biesen. It's mounted on a somewhat flexible suspension system that permits precise sight changes but is too delicate and bulky for most field use.

are not a sign of a superior adjustment mechanism. Silent adjustments are sometimes the result of a waterproof design.

Internal adjustments. An internal reticle-adjusting system is located entirely inside the scope, with the adjustment knobs on a turret on the tube. Though early scopes did not have internal adjustments, the system is almost universal today. Some hunting-style scopes, especially European models made prior to World War II, have an internal elevation adjustment only and rely on an external system for windage settings.

External adjustments. A few scopes, particularly some specialized target models made today, have no built-in reticle-adjusting system and rely on an articulating mounting system to move point of impact. The externally adjusted target-style scopes are mounted on a somewhat flexible suspension system that offers precise and convenient sight changes, but this system is not suitable for most hunting situations.

Though externally adjusted hunting-style scopes were fairly common until the 1950's, they have now disappeared. They were held in adjustable mounts that moved the entire scope rather than the reticle only.

Turret. This is the housing, usually located about midlength of the tube, that contains the reticle adjustment mechanism and adjusting knobs of scopes having internal adjustments.

Field of view. The field of view is the area that can be seen through the scope. Since the field of view is outward-angling and cone-shaped, it becomes wider as the distance increases. For the sake of comparison, the field of view at 100 yards—that is, the width of the area you see at 100 yards or 100 meters—is most often listed in a scope's specifications. The nature of telescopic sights (and most other telescopic instruments) causes the field of view to be comparatively wide when the magnification is low, more restricted for higher magnifications. A fairly typical field of view for a 4X scope is 28 feet. The field for a 12X model will be closer to 10 feet. With variable-power scopes, the field of view changes as the magnification is changed. A typical 3X-9X scope will have a field ranging from about 10 to 35 feet.

Variable power. A variable-power riflescope offers a change in magnification with the turn of a dial. The principle is no different from that used in "zoom" camera lenses. The advantage of a variable is its adaptability to a wide range of uses and shooting distances. Most hunting-style variables are in the 2X-7X or 3X-10X range, but variables have been offered with powers ranging from 6X to 24X.

Rangefinder. Determining distance with a telescopic sight can be done in a number of ways. It's easiest with scopes that have rangefinding features, including a calibrated distance scale. With any scope, distance can be determined on a subtention principle. Let's say your scope has a two-minute dot reticle. This means the dot covers, or subtends, a two-inch circle at 100 yards, four inches at 200 yards, etc. Now suppose your target is a tin can four inches wide. At 100 yards, your two-minute dot covers half of the can's width. But then someone moves the can to an

Here is the field of view—the area seen—through a telescopic sight. This area widens as distance to the viewed object increases. In this instance the field of view is small, with very little background showing around the chuck that has just been nailed, because the range is short and magnification high.

unknown distance. You look through the scope again and the dot covers the can from side to side. Since you know the dot covers a four-inch circle at 200 yards, the range must be 200 yards. If the dot appeared twice as wide as the can, you would quickly calculate the can to be 400 yards away. Intermediate distances are judged by gauging the relative sizes of the dot and the target. This basic principle can be applied even by using the width of crosshairs or the subtention length of the inner wires of duplex reticles.

Rangefinding scopes take the same principle further and make the procedure more accurate and convenient. The basis of their approach is to use *two* horizontal crosshairs, one of which is usually, but not always, the main aiming crosswire. Most usually, the activating mechanism is a variable-power scope. It works by turning the magnification ring one way or the other, enlarging or reducing the size of the animal until it fits, backbone to brisket, between the two horizontal wires. Many such rangefinding scopes assume the target will be a deer with the depth of the chest measuring 18 inches. The scope has a calibrated range scale which may be inside the field of view (Redfield), on the power-change dial (Tasco), or on the turret (Weaver). The scale interprets the range when the deer fits between the wires—showing you the distance

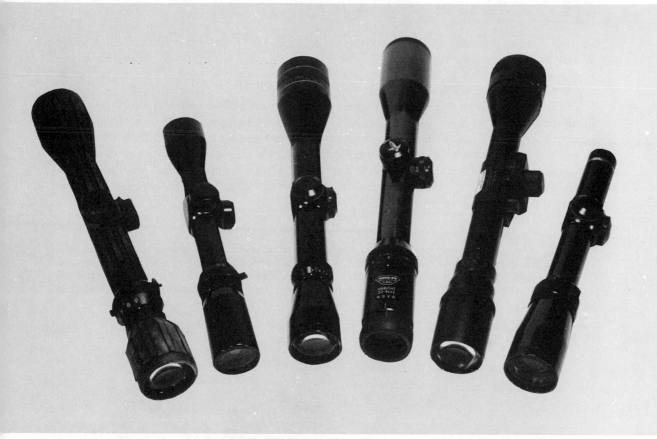

Here is a typical array of today's variable-power scopes. All employ a ring-type dial which is easily turned to raise or lower magnification instantly, and all have windage and elevation adjustments enclosed in capped turrets. The one at far left is sheathed in protective rubber, a currently popular trend in scopes, binoculars, and other optical instruments that get hard outdoor use.

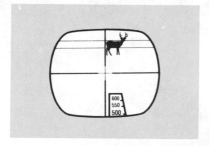

This diagram shows a Redfield rangefinding reticle, trade-named Accu-Trac, which is optionally featured on variable-power scopes. To operate it, the shooter turns the power ring, zooming in or out to fit the target snugly between the two upper wires. This moves a range indicator which can be read at the bottom of the reticle. (The deer in this diagram is just under 500 yards away.) The shooter then turns the calibrated elevation dial to that range and holds the crosshairs dead on target.

in yards. Some rangefinding scopes, notably those offered by Tasco, are calibrated for a wider variety of game, ranging from woodchuck to elk. The Weaver system is adaptable to a fixed-power scope and works by means of a movable stadia (crosswire). Thus it can be pre-set by the owner for a target of any size.

The weaknesses of rangefinding scopes are worth noting. The basic assumption—that a given animal will be of a specific size and will be viewed from the side—is the primary weakness. Also, the error factor becomes more pronounced at longer ranges where the downward-pitching bullet angle makes precise range knowledge most essential. A third negative aspect is that during the excitement of the hunt, especially in the presence of game, there is an increase in the chance of misuse or confusion. And the more complex a riflescope becomes, the greater is the likelihood of breakdown.

Bushnell's Rangemaster is another trajectory compensator. To use it, the shooter simply judges the range, turns the dial to that distance and holds dead on target. Since the dial controls the elevation adjustment, it compensates for drop. To be reliable, however, the adjustment must be calibrated to match the trajectory of a particular cartridge or a group of cartridges with similar characteristics. Scope manufacturers therefore offer several different dials, each compatible with a given cartridge category.

Trajectory compensator. This add-on feature is usually, though not always, part of a range-finding system. Theoretically, a trajectory compensator alters the scope's elevation adjustment so that it is instantly sighted-in at whatever yardage shows on the elevation dial. The kicker is the melancholy fact that every cartridge and bullet weight has a trajectory curve somewhat different from other calibers and bullets. An elevation change of, say, six clicks that would change a .270's point of impact from 100 yards to 200 yards would not work for a .35 Remington. Thus, trajectory-compensating scopes must be equipped with interchangeable elevation dials, each one calibrated for a specific cartridge. Since it would be impractical to offer a dial for every caliber, manufacturers of trajectory-compensating scopes have more or less grouped cartridges of similar trajectory characteristics together so that one dial will serve for several calibers, and three or four dials serve all calibers more or less well.

To use a trajectory-compensating scope, the hunter determines the distance to the target (either by estimating or by use of a rangefinder) and turns the elevation dial to the specified range. This alters the scope's reticle position so that the rifle is, in effect, sighted-in for that specific range. Rather than having to hold over the target for long shots, the hunter simply aims where he wants to hit.

Such mechanisms can be remarkably precise if everything is working correctly. However, the opportunities for error are several. One source of possible error is lack of precision in the adjustment systems of some scopes. Another is the grouping of several calibers in one dial. While the dial may be accurate for one caliber, it may not be so close for another. The wild card is the rifle itself. Because of different barrel lengths and other factors which affect bullet velocity, a given rifle may produce ballistics that vary from the standard by a considerable amount, so the actual trajectory curve can differ from the theoretical trajectory calibrated on the scope's dial.

Parallax. There is much confusion over parallax, probably because it sounds so threatening to accuracy. You can see a parallax condition simply by setting a riflescope on a fixed mount (such as sandbags) and aiming at small targets at different ranges. With the crosshairs on the target, slowly move your head from side to side. If parallax exists, the crosshair will appear to move on the target. Usually the apparent movement is negligible, only a fraction of an inch and certainly not enough to cause a miss at game. On occasion, though, it can be an inch or more and is then a serious problem to target shooters and varmint hunters.

Parallax can occur when the *primary image* of the target (the image that enters the objective lens) falls, or comes into focus, in front of or behind the reticle. To visualize how this works, consider a fat lady on a scale. When she looks straight at the dial, she weighs, say, 200 pounds. But when she looks at the dial somewhat from the side, the pointer appears displaced in relation to the dial so that she weighs a pound or two less. We get the same illusion by looking at clocks and auto speedometers from different angles. If the pointer lies flat against the dial, you will see no shifting of relative positions from different angles. The further the pointer is from the dial, the more displacement—parallax—will be apparent as you look from a side angle.

When the primary image is focused on the same plane as the scope's reticle, no parallax will be detected. The farther apart they happen to be, the greater is the parallax. You can see how this works by holding up a finger a few inches from your eye. Next hold up a finger from the other hand a foot away and align the two fingertips. As you shift your head from side to

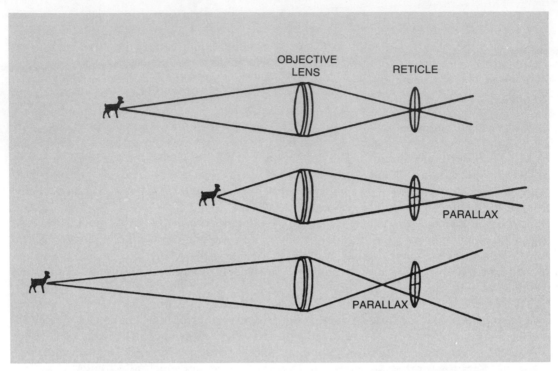

Have you ever noticed that an automobile's speedometer pointer seems to move on the dial—indicating higher or lower speed—when viewed at an angle? The farther the pointer is from the dial face, the more displacement you see. This is parallax, the same phenomenon that can make a scope's crosshairs seem to shift on target if you move your head. As illustrated in this drawing from a Bausch & Lomb handbook, parallax can occur when the target image comes into focus in front of the reticle or behind it rather than right against the reticle.

side, without moving your fingers, the two fingers will appear misaligned to one side and then the other. If you move the fingers closer together, the degree of parallax will diminish. It's the same way with the target image and the reticle.

Fortunately, parallax is usually of little or no consequence, and when it is, the problem can be easily corrected. Most big game scopes with non-focusing objective lenses are adjusted at the factory to be free of parallax at 100 yards. At shorter or longer ranges, some parallax can be detected but it is usually very slight, especially with low-magnification scopes. Scopes made for rimfire rifles are pre-focused at shorter ranges, usually 50 or 75 yards.

Since parallax becomes more critical as magnification increases, it's necessary, or at least desirable, for scopes of 10X or more to have a movable objective lens that can be focused at specific ranges by the shooter.

When a shooter focuses the objective lens, he is not only focusing the target image so it can be seen clearly but also bringing the primary image into focus on the same focal plane as the reticle. Sometimes this requires special care, especially with high-magnification target scopes. Even when the objective is adjusted so the image is sharp, some additional fine tuning may be necessary to remove all parallax. I do this by rotating the objective ring only a fraction of a turn at a time while constantly checking for parallax. Even though the objective focusing ring on a high-magnification scope is calibrated for range, the calibrations sometimes do not precisely indicate the ideal no-parallax position. Once this is determined by actual testing, all you have to do is make a small "witness" mark so you can come back to the same focus without additional testing.

Any time you're worried about parallax ruining a shot, just make sure your eye is well centered in the optical field and parallax won't be a problem. Parallax occurs only when your eye is off center and you are, in a manner of speaking, looking *around* the reticle at the image.

Coated lens. The "coating" of lenses is one of the great optical developments of the 20th century. Sometimes called anti-reflection coating, which is technically correct, or "hard coating," which is misleading, this lens treatment is of enormous benefit to shooters. The theory of coated lenses is rather complex, requiring an understanding of light waves of various lengths. But with a little explaining, the value of an anti-reflection coating becomes reasonably clear.

When you look into a store window, you not only see the display behind the glass but a

The problem of parallax has been somewhat exaggerated. Generally, it becomes critical only when magnification is high. For this reason, it's desirable for scopes of 10X or more to have a movable objective lens that can be focused at different ranges—bringing the image onto the same focal plane as the reticle. In this photo, Carmichel has turned the objective focusing ring to 100 yards.

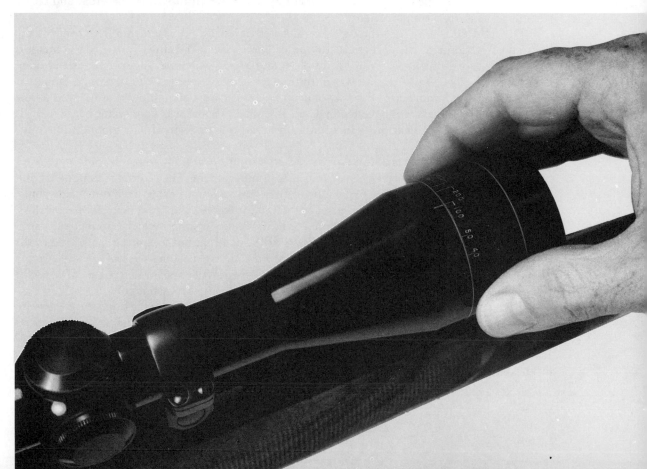

reflection of yourself, as well. The reflection consists of light rays that did not pass completely through the window but were reflected by both surfaces of the glass—and rebounded back out. Someone looking at you from the other side of the window would not get the full, glorious impact of your image because some light is being reflected back in the opposite direction.

Next let's say we set up a dozen panes of glass, one behind the other. Looking again, you'd see a dozen reflections of yourself, and a person looking from the other side would see only a dim image of you.

This is what happens in telescopes and binoculars employing a series of uncoated lenses through which an image must pass. With a scope having 10 glass-to-air surfaces, nearly half the entering light could be reflected back out before it could reach your eye. In most daylight shooting conditions, you have much more light than you need, but don't assume that coated lenses are worthwhile only in poor light.

When light is reflected inside a telescope, some of it can't find its way back out. If 100 units of light hit the objective lens of your uncoated riflescope, three units are reflected away by the outside surface, and since both surfaces are reflective, another three units are reflected by the inside surface (actually the compound lens is made up of a couple of elements). The remaining 94 units of light proceed to the next lens system, and six more units are reflected back. This time the light units must pass out through the objective lens, but part of these reflected light units are reflected *back again*. They are bounced back and forth like a ping-pong ball inside a length of closed pipe. These repeatedly reflected units of light become diffused, or scattered, and create something of a fog of random light.

The light units may pass through several series of lenses, all of which reflect some of the light and contribute to the random scattering of light waves. The effect is to give the image a ghostlike, washed-out look, with faded colors and reduced definition—sort of like looking through milky glass. That's how it was until the early 1930's, when one Professor A. Smakula, a German scientist, came up with a way of coating lenses with a compound that reduced reflection. Smakula's process was patented by Carl Zeiss in 1935 and was kept secret because of its obvious military applications—including famous World War II German "nighttime" binoculars.

The coating material is a thin layer of metallic fluoride (usually magnesium fluoride) applied to the lens surface by a process of molecular bombardment. The coating technique is complex and is carried out in a vacuum chamber. When you look at a coated lens from a side angle, the coating appears to be blue, violet, or sometimes gold. Actually, the material is colorless. What you see is a "complementary" colored light wave, the length of which happens to correspond, in complementary ratio, to the thickness of the coating, but let's not get involved in the physical characteristics of light waves or we'll be here all night. Some telescopes have coating only on the two outside lens surfaces so that the instrument will appear to be coated. This helps some, but the more surfaces that are coated, the better the light transmission.

The anti-reflection coating works by keeping light rays, and the image transported therein, headed in the same direction. When some of the light is reflected, or "bounced" off the front lens, it must pass back through the coating. The coating, in a manner of speaking, catches the rebounding light rays and shoves them back in the right direction. Inside the scope the process is repeated; light that would be scattered inside the tube is trapped and herded toward your eye.

Thus, over half of the light that would otherwise be lost by reflection is utilized. This saved light certainly brightens the image you see, but that is not the greatest value of coated lenses. Their greatest contribution is the reduction of internal glare which, in turn, results in vastly improved optical definition. In other words, the image you see through your scope is much sharper and clearer due to coated lenses.

Nowadays we are offered riflescopes and other optical goods having multiple lens coatings, sometimes a half-dozen or more layers of various metallic oxides. By varying the thickness of these layers, which run about *one-fourth* the wavelength of a given color (which is some .000016-inch to .000028-inch in length), a higher percentage of the total light can be transmitted, resulting in a total light transmission of over 90 percent. Light reflected and lost in an un-coated instrument can run as high as 40 percent.

Though lens coating is pretty tough, it can be scratched, so take care to clean your lens surfaces with a soft, clean cloth or lens tissue. If the coating does get a few scratches, it isn't ruined and will still be effective. But when as much as a quarter of the coating is rubbed away, its efficiency may be noticeably diminished.

Magnification. In optical terminology, one power (1X) means no magnification. You can think of the "X" as a times-sign in a multiplication table: $1 \times 1 = 1$ — no change. The unaided human eye has a magnification of one power, or 1X. A telescope that makes distant objects appear twice as big as with the unaided eye has a magnification of 2X, meaning twice as big as normal. Telescopes having magnifications of 10X or 25X make objects appear, respectively, 10 or 25 times larger than they appear to the naked eye. You might also say they appear to be that many times *closer,* though certain factors such as atmospheric pollution make the "closer" analogy misleading. An elk viewed from 600 yards on a misty morning through 10X binoculars might appear 10 times larger but certainly not 10 times closer. If it really appeared closer, it would be seen with much greater clarity.

Though the magnification of riflescopes is almost always expressed in whole or half values (6X or 2.5X) the optical characteristics of some models may actually determine that their power is some odd fraction in between whole and half values. This small difference is of no importance, but to be scrupulously honest some scopemakers publish the absolute powers of their scopes in their brochures. For everyone's convenience, though, if a particular model happens to check out at 5.7 magnification it's better to call it a 6X. A three-tenths-of-one-power difference isn't going to matter to you. Riflescopes are available in magnifications from 1X to 40X. A 1X scope "gathers light" but does not magnify.

Resolving power. This can be confused with magnification because each determines how well a target can be seen. Therefore, to explain resolving power I'll go outside the optical laboratory and use a common example. We've all read stories about the remarkable eyesight of the pronghorn antelope. Anyone who has tried to stalk these fleet ghosts of the prairie knows they can see you from incredible distances. Somewhat enthusiastic writers have described the vision of a pronghorn as being equal to a human using 8X binoculars. While this is a romantic exaggeration, there's no doubt that pronghorn have remarkable eyesight.

Their vision should not be described in terms of magnification, because they see objects as we do, in 1X, so that a mountain or a blade of grass appears no bigger to them than to us. Their advantage is acuity, or resolving power. Their eyes are capable of defining, or resolving, extremely fine detail. That's why they can see the top of your hat when you're crawling along a ridgeline hundreds of yards from the herd. They have this visual advantage simply because their eyes are superior optical mechanisms.

In a scope, the analogy to a pronghorn's vision is a lens system free of defects that reduce image quality. Optical defects blur the outlines of objects so that distinctions cannot be made from one object to the next. For example, a human may not be able to see another human sitting on a hillside a thousand yards away with the unaided eye, because the outline of the distant person cannot be *resolved* (defined) from the surrounding terrain. An antelope can resolve the outlines and make the distinction.

Though the resolving power of an optical instrument is most accurately evaluated in the laboratory, shooters can make some empirical judgments by comparing scopes. When comparing a high-quality 10X scope to a poor 10X scope, you will note that the edges of the target are crisply defined in the good scope. With the poorer scope, there is a fading of the edges. It doesn't exactly seem to be a blur, but you are aware that you're not seeing the target as well as you should be. The problem is caused by optical flaws that mess up the image and thereby reduce the scope's resolving power.

Since the topic of optical quality has come up, this is a good time to talk about flaws in lens and scope mechanisms. Technicians refer to optical flaws, errors, and problems as *aberrations*. For the next few paragraphs, I'll say "aberrations" when I'm speaking of something wrong with an optical system. There are six varieties of aberrations which will reduce the quality and performance of a telescope. Most of these you've heard or read about. Listed alphabetically, they are: (1) Astigmatism, (2) Chromatic aberration, (3) Coma, (4) Curvature of Field, (5) Distortion, and (6) Spherical aberration.

Astigmatism is a condition in a lens that impairs its ability to focus simultaneously on lines lying at different angles to each other. This is a fairly common failing in human eyesight. When a lens system is free of astigmatism it is said to be anastigmatic. Occasionally, a brochure describes a lens as being "anastigmatic," but so far as telescopic sights go it's no big deal.

Chromatic aberration is far more serious because it reduces the definition at the center of the field of view, which is the part mainly used. The problem is the failure of a lens to direct the various colors of light rays into focus at a single point. Since any image you are likely to see through a telescope is composed of a multitude of colors, you can realize the problem you'd have trying to look at an image that was at once both in and out of focus. Single lenses characteristically have chromatic aberrations, so the trick is to combine a pair or series of lenses that jockey certain colors until they all come into focus at a single point. Simply putting a couple of pieces of glass together won't work because the glasses must be different. When a pair or series of lens elements are united so the colors come into focus at a single point, the lens system is said to be color-corrected, or achromatic. Quite often you'll see these terms in optical brochures and catalogs. As you no doubt are thinking by now, each lens group within a telescopic sight must be color-corrected, because one bad lens can sour the whole system.

Spherical aberration is another serious problem because it will make it impossible for you to see a crisply defined image no matter how much you tinker with the focusing. This is because different areas of the picture will be out of focus. The eye tries to make up for these problems, but the result is sometimes a slightly seasick feeling in the pit of your stomach. Scopes that give the target a soft image that lacks contrast or definition probably suffer from spherical aberration.

Though this is a high-sounding phrase, it is easy to understand, especially if you've spent much time in a pool room. (Excuse me, I meant to say "billiards emporium.") Look at a telescope lens and you'll note that it has a curved surface. (In fact, the curvature is what makes it a lens.) This curved surface is its sphere, and if the curvature is not precisely as it should be, optical technicians say it suffers from spherical aberration, meaning curvature flaw. The key to the lens grinder's art is grinding and polishing lenses so that the sphere is as close to perfect as possible.

The reason the curvature must be perfect is because it bends light rays and redirects them toward a common point somewhere behind the lens. The angle at which the light rays are redirected depends on the angle of the lens at that point along its sphere and is as geometrically precise as a pool table. If you cue a billiard ball against the rail at a 20° angle, it will rebound at a geometrically precise 20°. But if the rail has a sag or bump that causes the ball to angle in some odd direction, we can say the rail has an *aberration*.

Actually, light doesn't rebound (except for what is reflected) but passes on through the lens on its new course. If the curvature (sphere) of the surface is correct, all the rays will coincide at a particular point and will be sharply in focus. If aberration exists, some of the rays will get where we want them but some will miss the "pocket" and cause parts of the image to be out of focus. This is what gives you a queasy feeling as your eye tries to figure out what's going on and correct a losing situation.

Sometimes a spherical aberration will result in a comet-shaped blur in the picture, caused by the light from a particular part of the image passing obliquely through the lens. This type of aberration is called coma. It isn't worth worrying about. When a lens system is properly designed and made so that no spherical aberration or coma exist, it is *aplanatic*. So the next time someone brags about having an aplanatic telescope, you can tell him what he's talking about.

A couple of riflescope terms that shooters tend to get confused are *distortion* and *curvature of field*. A common flaw in telescopic sights is a tendency for objects near the edge of the field of view to be bent out of shape. The lines of a brick wall, for instance, will appear somewhat curved. Since the field of view thus seems curved, it is natural for us to want to call this aberration curvature of field. But curvature is something else entirely. What manifests itself as curved lines is distortion.

Optical engineers will tell you that distortion occurs when magnification is not consistent across the entire field of view. This explains why the lines of a brick wall appear farther apart at the center of the field and closer together at the edges when distortion exists. Though it would also be possible to have a reversed form of distortion, with the image shrunk at the center of the field, we are not likely to see it in telescopic sights. What commonly results in distortion toward the edge of the field in some scopes is the result of an attempt to achieve the widest possible field of view. I've noticed that distortion is sometimes present in the finest brands of scopes, the manufacturers obviously having decided it is better to have the additional field even if it is somewhat distorted. Other makers, fearful of being charged with marketing distorted optical systems, block out the outer edges of the field in order to hide the distortion. If a scope has a particularly heavy black ring around the field of view, it may be there only to hide distortion.

Curvature of field exists when the image transmitted through the lens system is not focused on a flat plane. Imagine what it would be like to project a slide or a movie on a giant ball. With the center of the projected picture in focus, the outer surfaces would be progressively out of focus because of the increasing distance from lens to screen. If the outer edges of the picture were focused, the center would be out of focus. This is similar to the problem when a lens system has curvature of field, except that in this case the screen (your eye) is flat and the "projector" is sending out a curved image. If you focus the scope so that the center of the field is in focus, the rest of the field becomes increasingly out of focus toward the edges.

Minor aberrations of curvature aren't important in telescopic sights and are seldom noticed. If you're curious, you can check a scope by looking at a grid or brick wall at, say, 100 yards. If the focus is not sharp across the entire field you can figure there is some curvature aberration.

These six aberrations, either separately or in combination, detract from one specific goal in any optical device, that being *definition*. In simplest terms, if the definition of a scope is good, the colors are sharp and the myriad images that make up the field of view are crisply outlined and stand in stark contrast to each other. If definition is poor because of aberrations, there is a loss of image quality. Sometimes the deterioration of definition is so subtle that it can be detected only by an experienced technician who knows what to look for. For most of us, the definition of a scope must be poor indeed before it is realized. The layman's best way to detect faulty definition is by comparison with a truly good instrument.

Relative brightness. This term is obsolete. It is so grossly misleading as a way of describing a scope's usefulness that every time I hear someone flapping his yap about relative brightness, I have an urge to grab him by the neck and twist. But since the phrase is still a part of the shooting vocabulary, I'm going to give you the lowdown.

As discussed earlier, one of the primary reasons the hunting scope was developed was to extend the shootable hours further into dawn and dusk. Scopemakers, especially the European companies who were (and are) captivated by low-light performance, needed a means of comparing the "brightness" of their instruments.

A simple formula was devised for measuring relative brightness, and for generations the world's makers and users of telescopic sights made a big fuss about the importance of a scope having a high relative-brightness index. Sadly, some well-meaning souls even came to equate relative brightness with quality. It's sad because the relative-brightness index doesn't tell us a damn thing that's worth knowing about a telescope. In fact, it has had the effect of interfering with what we need to know by putting the emphasis on the wrong factors. You'll understand how this has happened when I explain how the relative brightness is calculated.

Basically, the RB is only the area of the exit pupil. You can see what an exit pupil is by holding a riflescope at arm's length and noting the circle of light at the center of the eyepiece lens. This is the exit pupil and is usually about a quarter to three-eighths of an inch in diameter. Even without looking at the exit pupil, you can determine its diameter by dividing the diameter of the objective lens by the scope's magnification. For example, a 4X scope having a 28mm objective lens will have a 7mm exit pupil (28 ÷ 4 = 7). The relative brightness is calculated by squaring the diameter of the exit pupil, so our 4X scope with a 7mm exit pupil works out to have an RB of 49.

You can easily understand how the concept has been so constantly abused. If that 4X scope were a 2X scope, still having a 28mm objective lens, the RB would be calculated thus: 28 ÷ 2 = 14^2—giving us a score of 196 as the RB index. On paper, we seem to have a truly wonderful scope, but in actual use it's not as good as the 4X version. Once the scope-buying population got homed in on relative brightness, they got what they deserved. To jack up the index figure, some scopes have been made with giant objective lenses that greatly exceed the limits of practicality. One of the most ridiculous that I recall was a German 4X scope with a 60mm objective, having an RB index of 225.

Sometimes the relative brightness is expressed as light-gathering power, which is another nonsense phrase because it suggests that the scope has some means of sucking in light like a vacuum cleaner sucking in dust. Another failing of the brightness index is that it has come to suggest optical quality when, in fact, a scope with a high RB could be so plagued with lens aberrations that you couldn't use it to spot an elephant on a tennis court.

The most serious crime of the relative-brightness index was the way it has misled shooters. Back in the 1970's, I wrote a book entitled *The Modern Rifle* in which I briefly described the comparative effectiveness of low- and high-magnification scopes when shooting in poor light. One reviewer, a writer whom I greatly admire, took me to task because I had dared challenge the sacred relative-brightness formula by suggesting that, all other factors being the same, an 8X scope is better in dim light than a 4X model.

My advice to you is the same I gave him: Forget outdated formulas and simply *see for yourself* what works best. Apparently, during a career of shooting and writing he'd never done one thing he should have—that being to set up a rack of scopes of different magnifications and lens sizes and see for himself which scopes let him see best in dim light.

Fortunately, scopemakers have about stopped publishing relative-brightness figures. Likewise, they have about given up telling us the size of the exit pupil. This is a good idea because, again, exit-pupil size can be misleading. The aperture in the human eye opens up to about 7mm maximum. If the column of light exiting the scope is bigger than 7mm what good can it do so far as making the image appear brighter? All the surplus light in the exit pupil spills over—like a six-inch column of water poured into a four-inch pipe.

Frankly, I'm not keen on any sort of formula that presumes to predict a scope's performance based on the physical specifications of the lens system. There are too many other factors that determine how good a scope is. However, one formula, the so-called twilight factor, gives us a reasonably realistic means of comparison and does correspond to actual "eyeball" comparison tests. The formula is simply the square root of the product you get when you multiply the scope's magnification by the objective lens diameter (in millimeters).

Our 4X scope with its 30mm objective lens works out to have a twilight factor of 10.95 ($\sqrt{4 \times 30}$ = 10.95). Clearly, the results of this formula favor scopes with higher magnifications, which is as it should be because high magnification, within certain practical limits, is a definite, easily perceived aid to aiming in poor light. You may have noted, by the way, that those great big European scopes with the giant lenses that are so favored for dim-light shooting just happen to have plenty of magnification, usually 8X. In other words, as indicated by both the twilight factor *and* actual tests, it's their magnification that makes them so effective in low light. The reason is simply because the added power lets us see detail better. You can demonstrate this to your satisfaction by looking through a variable-power scope in near-darkness. When the power is turned up to full force, the definition of images is much better.

This is not to say that oversized objective lenses serve no purpose whatever. A by-product of large lenses is somewhat improved image quality, all other factors being equal (though "other factors" are seldom equal). Image definition may be marginally better with a big-lensed scope, thus improving low-light performance. Given a choice, however, I'd say raw power is better than raw glass.

SELECTING RETICLES

The most common reticle is a simple crosshair, and that's as it should be. All things considered, the crosshair is the best way yet to aim at any target. Since about 1920, just about all of the world's scopemakers have jazzed up the crosshair concept with double- or even triple-thickness crosswires, variously called plex, duplex, triplex, 4-plex, etc. Whatever the maker has decided to call his version, the idea is a dual-thickness design—that is, crosshairs, or wires, that are relatively wide at the outer edges of the field and then step down to the narrower size at the center.

Scopemakers tell me that the duplex reticle (which is what Leupold calls their version) is the most popular type of reticle, outselling all others by a large factor. The duplex has a definite sales appeal besides having the practical advantage of catching the eye and directing it toward the center of the reticle. In my opinion, however, the duplex, as usually supplied, is not as good as it could be. This is because the outer arms of the crosswires are not as thick as they ought to be.

The whole idea of today's duplex reticle was inspired by a similar reticle that dates back to the turn of the century and features extremely wide outer arms that can be seen in low light. This bold reticle is still common in European scopes because so much of their hunting is done early and late in the day. The wide arms of the European design also come much closer to the center, so that even when the smaller center wires disappear in dim light the hunter can still aim with reasonable accuracy. This European reticle is also of considerable help when shooting at running game because less attention is needed to find the crosshair, thereby letting you concentrate on the target.

My criticism of the American version really isn't severe, because it is an excellent reticle and a worthwhile improvement over plain crosshairs. I anticipate, however, that as American hunters become more and more tuned in to early and late shooting, their demand for bolder duplex-type reticles will prompt U.S. makers to produce European-style crosshairs.

A pretty variation of the crosshair is the converging post, which is made up of four slender, tapering arms that come to a point at the center. The effect is about the same as with the duplex, directing the eye to the center—but so far as I'm concerned, it offers no other advantage and the duplex is a better choice.

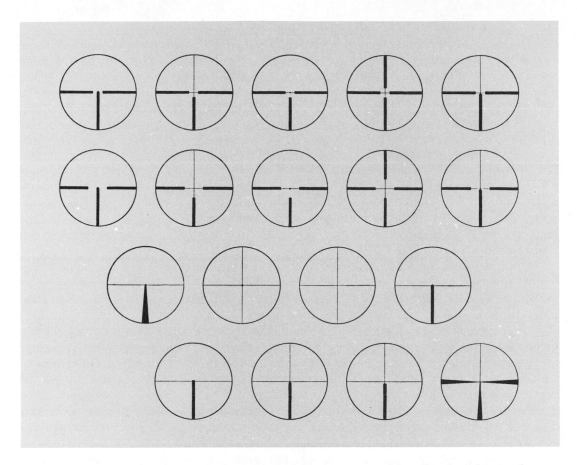

A wide selection of reticle styles and thicknesses is available, as you can see from this chart showing the types offered in the Kahles scopes imported from Austria. Most popular—and much older than most shooters realize— is the dual-thickness crosswire, several versions of which are among the types illustrated here. The thick outer segment of wire helps the shooter to get on target fast, while the fine central segment facilitates precise aiming. Some scopes present a sight picture that's widened somewhat at the sides instead of being circular—the idea being to offer a slightly wider field of view—but this has nothing to do with the wire, dot, post, or other aiming element that comprises the reticle.

I tend to run hot and cold on dot reticles. These days, they're just called dots, but old-timers like me can't help saying "Lee" dots because of T.K. "Tackhole" Lee, who installed so many of his dots on tiny, sometimes invisible, crosshairs. As a means of aiming at game, the dot isn't all that great. I've used a few dot reticles for hunting over the years, but the only one I ever liked was a big fat dot in an old 2.5X Lyman Alaskan. The size of the dot made it easily visible in poor light, so I mounted the scope on a .375 H&H for hunting big bears on the dark and drizzly Alaskan coast. For close encounters, this was great. But a dot that is big enough to be useful in marginal light tends to be too big for precise aiming at longer ranges. For most hunting situations—except possibly some varmint shooting—I prefer to forget dots.

When it comes to target shooting, and some specialized long-distance shooting, the dot is something else entirely—and is often the best choice of all reticle types. Target shooters who use a scope all day sometimes find that ordinary crosshairs cause eye fatigue. A fatter dot, being easier to see, reduces this tendency. Ironically, some target shooters go for dots that are too small to produce the desired result. I use a plump, one-minute dot for smallbore prone and big-bore shooting. The one-minute dot is easy to see and exactly covers the X-ring of both the 100-yard and 1,000-yard targets.

Here of late, I've also gone to using a dot for silhouette shooting. What with all the weaving, wobbling, and jiggling a rifle does when I try to fire offhand, the racing crosshairs are hard to keep up with. By using a one-minute dot, which is much easier to see, I don't have to concentrate on the reticle so much and I can give more attention to my hold on the target. And the larger dot has the appearance of not having so much tremor, which is right comforting when trying to shoot offhand with a 25X scope.

Benchrest shooters also tend to favor dot reticles—but extremely tiny ones. Some scope-makers who cater to the benchrest crowd have offered little-bitty one-eighth and one-tenth dots that can be aimed at a .22-caliber bullet hole at 100 yards. Of course, a tiny dot isn't much good unless the scope has at least 20X magnification or, preferably, a lot more.

Another application of dots involves a series of two or more dots, usually of different sizes, up and down the vertical crosswire. Dots of known subtentions can be used to estimate range (as described earlier in this chapter). By separating the dots by specific distances (subtentions), the scope on a rifle of given caliber will have a "hold-on" point of aim at various ranges. Of course, you can't walk into your local gunshop and pick up a scope with such specialized features. Custom dots are fitted by only a handful of specialists. As you might imagine, it takes a lot of head-scratching to figure out where to position the dots so they will coincide with the bullet path of a specific cartridge at particular points along its path.

The post reticle and variations of the post, be they pointed, flat-topped, or combined with crosswires, are pretty much out of vogue. I never much liked them, so I can't say I'm sorry to see them go. The basic idea of the post was to simplify the aiming process as much as possible and at the same time improve performance in poor light. A wide post does, indeed, show up well in bad light, but post reticles aren't all that easy to use. Whereas a crosshair or dot precisely indicates where your bullet is going to hit, the post is somewhat confusing and takes some getting used to.

The post is at its best in close-range shooting situations where an "approximate" point of aim is close enough to get the job done. At longer ranges, the coarseness of post aiming becomes a distinct liability, especially since the post covers so much of the target.

A variation of the post is a slender spire of a post that tapers to a point and actually forms only the bottom leg of the crosshairs. Supposedly, this combines the speed of a post with the precision of crosshairs, but actually it combines the worst features of both types because it reduces the precision of crosshair aiming by blacking out part of the target. At the same time, it isn't wide enough to work well as a post. Generally speaking, it's a good idea to be wary of non-symmetrical reticles, meaning those that are not the same on all four arms. They tend to create an illusion that affects your point of aim somewhat. If one arm is thicker than the others, there is a tendency to push the thicker arm deeper into the target. Thus, a shooter who uses the pointed post with crosshairs inadvertently tends to aim higher on a deer's shoulder.

All sorts of gadget reticles have been offered over the years, their main purpose being to entice buyers rather than to provide performance. One example is a simple crosshair arrangement tilted to a 45° angle to form an X rather than the traditional +. The saying that "X marks the spot" doesn't apply here. After all, the vertically positioned crosswire forms a reference that helps us avoid tilting a rifle to the side. When a rifle is canted one way or the other, a potentially serious loss of zero can occur.

Another gadget is the circle reticle, a doughnut-shaped ring suspended in the crosswires. This looks snazzy but in practice isn't very convenient because too much of the target is covered, and at longer ranges it is difficult to figure out where in the circle the bullet is supposed to hit. This makes the ring reticle slow to use.

Another general failure is the so-called flip-up post which is supposed to offer the best of all possible worlds at the flick of a switch. The only one of these I ever used apparently couldn't tolerate much recoil, because the jumping-jack post got loose on its hinge so that every time it popped up it was tilted out of alignment with the crosshairs.

During my long and sometimes bizarre shooting career, I've probably owned and used somewhere in the neighborhood of 300 riflescopes, which gives me more experience than the average scissors grinder. The scopes that have worked best and most reliably have been the simplest. The ones that have given disappointing results or failed outright have been those that were laden with gadgets or offered more features than a hunter can hope to use.

The rule for reticle selection is pretty basic: If a new type of reticle takes some getting used to, it isn't worth the bother. No one, not even a beginner, has to get used to a simple crosswire, it's automatic. If a hunter feels he needs a combination or "flip-up" type of reticle, he's only saying he hasn't selected the right reticle to begin with. A well chosen reticle does it all.

CHOICES IN VARIABLE MAGNIFICATION

Though the high popularity of variable-power riflescopes is a recent phenomenon, the idea of changeable magnification has been around for a long while. Some European makers offered scopes with a limited power span as early as the 1930's, probably even earlier; and just after World War II, Bill Weaver marketed a variable called the KV, which ranged from 2¾X to 5X. It was not a great success because the magnification span was minimal, and also because the power-change knob was located somewhat inconveniently on the turret.

During the 1950's and into the 1960's, a number of scopemakers, especially Europeans, offered a smattering of variable-power scopes that all suffered from one great failing. That failing was the plain mechanical fact that the size of the reticle changed along with the image as the magnification was changed. This might not sound like much of a problem, especially to youngsters who have been weaned on today's variables, but it was a bitch. When the power was turned down to the low end of the scale the crosshairs almost disappeared, and when power was on the high end the crosshairs were so fat-looking that pinpoint aiming was out of the question. This was particularly a problem with variable-power scopes having a significant magnification span, say 2.5X to 8X. Cautious makers such as Weaver, with his KV, sidestepped the problem by keeping the power range to a minimum.

In 1955 or thereabouts, the giant optical firm of Bausch & Lomb, who at that time made the most prestigious and probably the best scopes in America if not the world, sent the shooting world into a state of shock with the announcement of a variable scope ranging from 6X to an unheard-of 24X. It was called the Balvar 24 and, as I recall, sold for the staggering sum of $160—which, of course, left me out.

The big question was how could B&L offer so much change of power without having foot-wide crosshairs at the top power. Their solution was a reticle composed not of simple crosshairs but four slender, tapering arms that tapered to infinity at the center. No matter how much the power was changed, the center of the reticle tapered to almost nothing. This was a technical achievement of considerable importance because the reticle was finely etched on glass. The solution to the problem of the expanding reticle thus seemed to be solved in fine style, and so far as shooters were concerned scopes could not get much better. But someone is always thinking, especially in the riflescope business.

This time the thinker was a clever engineer named Don Burris, who has since made his mark as the founder of the Burris Scope Co., one of the top names in quality scopes. At that time he was an engineer for Redfield Gunsight Corp. Redfield had recently bought out the Stith "Bearcub" line of scopes and was getting established as a major scope producer. Burris developed an optical system for variable-power scopes in which the size of a crosshair, or any other kind of reticle, appears constant while the image grows or shrinks around it. Thus, a crosshair that covers (subtends) a half-minute with the power set on 3X will cover only a quarter-minute when the magnification is cranked up to 9X. Obviously, this is just dandy because the crosshairs are plump and easy to see when a scope is on its low-X setting, as it will be for timber hunting, but becomes fine enough to quarter a dime at 100 yards when the power is zoomed to the high end.

Predictably, zoom-power scopes offering such wonderful convenience were an instant hit. Within only a couple of years of Burris's development, variable-power scopes dominated the market, and continue to do so. But the road to variable-power perfection still had a few bumps.

My sainted predecessor at OUTDOOR LIFE, Jack O'Connor, was quick to discover a hard-core problem with variables and, in his distinctive manner, bellowed long and loud. So loud, in fact, that his echoes still haunt the variable-scope market somewhat. The problem was a tendency of some variable scopes to shift zero as the power was changed. A 3-9X variable with the power ring set on 9X might be sighted-in to hit dead on at 100 yards, but when the power was turned to another setting the rifle suddenly would be hitting wide by a few inches. This was the result of lateral movement of certain lenses during the magnification change. The lenses involved ride in an internal tube that is cammed to the front or rear when you turn the power-adjusting ring. Since this internal lens mounting must have enough free play to move, a by-product of looseness manifests itself by getting the lenses somewhat off axis as they are moved. This shifts the image in relation to the reticle so that the point of bullet impact is changed. And that, of course, is an ugly thing to have happen.

Some makes and models have been more guilty of this misdeed than others, but I've also noticed that some individual specimens of a particular model will be either more or less inclined to such error than other scopes out of the same batch. Some seem to have no error at all, while the next one will slap the image around so much that there will be several inches of displacement at 100 yards.

Even though criticism of variable-power scopes continues, especially from purists who rant against damn near everything, the fact is that today's best variables have precious little error. Leupold's 6.5-20X variable, for example, in addition to being a triumph of design and a truly superb scope (excellent even by fixed-power standards) has a run-out error of no more than a quarter MOA *at most!* Most specimens, in fact, have virtually no measurable error across the full range. Modern technology has pretty much eliminated the most serious objection to the variable-power scope (except for certain bargain-basement imports).

The most loudly proclaimed advantage of variable-power scopes is their "all-purpose" application. We're told that a 3-9X scope can be dialed down to the low end of its power range for snap shooting at whitetails in heavy cover, zoomed up to 6X for long shots at sheep or pronghorns, or cranked to full horsepower for blasting woodchucks across rolling meadows.

In practice, the application of variable-power scopes is seldom so all-encompassing. All too often, a hunter buys a variable when he will be using it for only one kind of hunting where a fixed-power scope would be preferable. Quite often I get mail from readers of OUTDOOR LIFE who are about to buy a varmint, deer, or bear rifle and plan to top off the dream rig with a variable of some persuasion. I'm astounded at the number of hunters who express their intention of buying a lever rifle in .30/30 or .35 Remington caliber and scoping it with a 3-9X variable. Similarly, there are varmint shooters who buy a .22/250 for blasting woodchucks and round out the outfit with a 3-9X or 4-12X variable. Apparently, there is a widespread notion that a variable-power scope is inherently a superior sighting instrument, or perhaps some shooters feel more secure if they have invested the maximum number of dollars in their scopes. In that regard, variable-power scopes do offer unique possibilities.

The best way to decide between variable and fixed power is to assess the uses to which the scope will be put. If the rig is to be used for a single type of hunting or shooting, you can be about 90 percent sure that a fixed-power scope will be the smarter choice. For instance, virtually any good varmint outfit will be all the better if the scope is of fixed power. If given the choice between a 12X and a 4-12X variable for my pet varmint rifle, I would rather have the fixed 12. It would offer superior optical quality (because of less glass in the system), simplicity, and the probability of greater precision throughout the instrument.

Likewise, if I were offered a 2-7X variable for a woods rifle, I'd be much inclined to turn it down for a fixed 2.5X or 4X scope. The fixed-power scope would add less weight to the outfit and offer a somewhat wider, clearer field of view than the variable with a matching magnification.

However, given all the types of hunting that I like to do, if I could own only one scope it would surely be a variable. I hasten to add that I'd mount it on a "variable" rifle, a caliber that would be versatile enough to reasonably hunt everything from groundhogs to elk. There's no point I can see in putting a multi-purpose glass on a single-purpose rifle, thus making the whole outfit as ungainly as a fish on a bicycle.

I also hasten to confess that I'm frequently guilty of using variables on single-purpose rifles—but for somewhat nontypical reasons. First of all, I tend to favor more magnification for a given job than most hunters. Just about all the medium-bores (.280, .270, .30/06, .300 magnum, etc.) that I regularly use are equipped with variables of 2.5-8X, 3-9X, or 3.5-10X magnification. While hunting, I invariably keep the magnification turned up to maximum and fully intend to do my shooting at the top power, because I like the improvement in aiming precision permitted by higher magnification. One of the reasons I use a variable at all is simply as a hedge in case I get into an arm's-length shooting situation where the lower power will be a necessity. As a matter of fact, it occurs to me that the only two magnifications of any variable scope I'll ever use are those on the extreme ends of the scale.

Another reason I find myself using so many variable-power scopes is because they are the best way to get the magnification I want in a relatively portable package. Since I routinely use 8X magnification where most hunters would be using a 4X or 6X scope, I like the relative compactness of today's variables. For example, Leupold's fixed 8X scope weighs 13 ounces and has a length of 12½ inches. Leupold's Vari-X III in 2.5-8X persuasion weighs two ounces less and is over an inch shorter. Lately I've started using variable-power mini-sized scopes such as the Burris 3-9X Mini and Leupold 3-9X Compact. This way I'm getting the magnification I want in the smallest possible package. If I could buy an 8X or 9X fixed-power scope that's as small as the variable compacts, I'd take it and run.

CLEARING AWAY THE FOG

I think it's fair to say that telescopic sights have, since World War II, progressed at a faster and more technically impressive rate than the rifles for which they are intended. The constantly centered reticle is commonplace in all makes and models; a scope that leaks or fogs is an exception to the rule; and the miscellaneous breakages that once tended to happen at the worst possible time have all but disappeared. Over the past few decades, I've used scoped rifles on more hunts than I can remember, from the Arctic to the Equator, and not once has scope failure caused the loss of a day's hunt or a head of game. When I was a youngster, the wise old hunters in my community (most of whom had never so much as seen a deer) assured me that "spy glasses" on a rifle were only toys and not at all suitable for serious he-man hunting. And they were almost right because hunting lore was rife with heartbreaking yarns about scopes that fogged with internal moisture and ruined the shot of a lifetime.

Today's hunters will probably never see a fogged scope, so for those of you who miss the opportunity let me promise that it's a hell of a thing to behold. What happens is that moisture trapped inside the scope forms droplets on the internal lens surfaces that can't be wiped dry. The droplets might be rather large but spaced far enough apart so that the scope could actually be used. On other occasions, though, the droplets were so fine and even that the lenses were entirely covered, rendering the scope useless. And then sometimes the lenses were clear. This happened when the atmosphere inside the scope was warm enough to evaporate the moisture. Of course, when the atmosphere cooled, moisture was again deposited on the internal surfaces. The most spectacular situation occurred when the scope got really cold, depositing a layer of water on the lenses which then froze into a pretty pattern of ice crystals like you see on your auto windshield in January. No wonder oldtimers said scopes would never catch on.

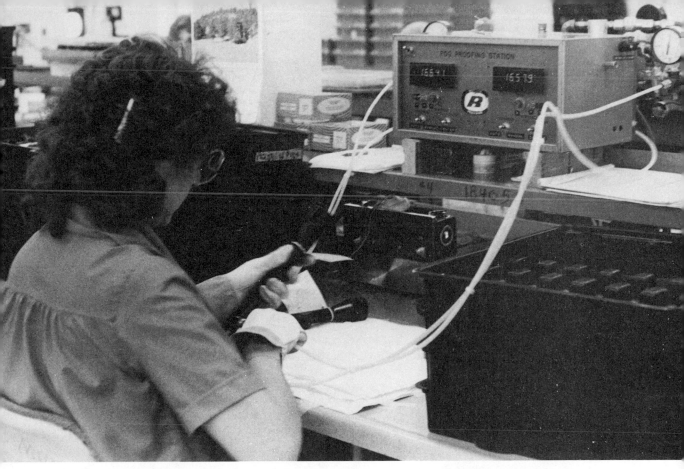

Today's scopes are effectively sealed against moisture. Some are assembled and sealed in a dry atmosphere; others have a dry gas pumped in and sealed after assembly. Here, a Redfield technician at a fog-proofing station pumps precisely metered dry gas into a scope.

Today's scopes are so effectively sealed that moisture leakage—and fogging—is virtually a thing of the past except for inexpensive bottom-of-the-line models and low-quality imports. Of course, if any scope is taken apart, it will be contaminated by moist air, so today's makers have developed tamper-proof seals that keep curious fingers from unscrewing the ocular bell to see what's inside. If your scope won't screw apart, don't force it.

Some scopes are assembled and sealed in a clean, dry atmosphere, while others have a dry gas pumped in after assembly. If you happen to notice a small, closed port in a scope tube or turret housing that doesn't seem to serve any purpose, this was used for gas-filling. Some makers like to talk about their scopes being filled with "dry" nitrogen, which is a redundant statement because nitrogen is always dry. It isn't better for filling scopes than any other of several gasses but it's easily available, inexpensive, and doesn't tend to combine chemically with a scope's internal components.

Every so often I get a letter from a reader who says the nitrogen must have leaked out of his scope because it's beginning to look foggy inside. He figures that if some fresh nitrogen is pumped in, the scope will be fine again. My advice is not to get new nitrogen but rather to get a better scope.

Today's truly waterproof scopes aren't necessarily filled with nitrogen or any other particular gas. In fact, a normal atmosphere is as good as any so long as it's dry and the scope is effectively sealed. Our best scopes are carefully checked at the factory for possible leaks. Leupold, for example, ruggedly tests every scope that comes off the assembly line. The scopes are placed in a tank of 120°F water which warms and thus expands the air inside the scope. This increased pressure forces the air out through any possible sources of leakage, causing a stream of telltale bubbles in the water. The test chamber is sealed and the internal air pressure lowered to further induce a failure of any possible leak points. This rigorous testing explains why a Leupold scope was found to be in perfect working order even after having spent several months on the bottom of a river.

Other makers use various methods which range from water immersion to filling the scope with "tracing" gasses that can be detected if they leak during tests. Most of today's scope bodies are assembled by threading or pressing the fore and aft tube sections into the turret housing. This system has worked well for decades, but lately a few scopemakers (Redfield, Simmons, and Zeiss at this writing) are offering models that feature a one-piece body in which the turret and tubes are turned from a single piece of metal. As far as the consumer is concerned, it doesn't make much difference, but there is a strength advantage and the added protection against leakage is obvious. I expect more scopemakers will adopt this manufacturing technique in the future if for no other reason than to keep up with the competition.

SILHOUETTE SCOPES

Back when the constantly centered reticle replaced the old "wandering" crosshairs, we figured our problems were laid to rest so far as scope adjustments were concerned, but such was not to be. The specter of scope adjustments returned during the early 1970's, when a band of Arizona riflemen journeyed south of the border and discovered a shooting game called *siluetas metalicas*. In only a few years, the game caught on big in the Southwest and spread elsewhere. The basic idea of this competition, as you know, was simply to knock over a series of metal profiles of animals situated at impossible distances. American shooters, carefully analyzing the elements of silhouette shooting, quickly determined that in addition to a very accurate rifle it was essential to have a precisely "repeatable" scope.

According to the rules of silhouette shooting, no sighting shots are to be allowed once the tournament starts. The competitors are therefore obliged to make "blind" changes in their scope's adjustments when going from one range to the next. This means a shooter must have faith that the adjustment changes he makes will be "answered" in the scope's mechanism so that the first shot will land on target at any of the four silhouette ranges. What's more, depending on the relay he draws, the competitor may begin the tournament at any of the four distances, thus pretty much ruling out the chance of getting started off with a pre-zeroed rifle.

What this boils down to is that the silhouette competitor has to know how to set his scope in order to be on target at each of the four stations. Many early competitors quickly discovered that when they clicked a scope's reticle-adjustment dial to a setting that had been on target previously, the bullets were not hitting where they were aimed. The problem was that some, indeed most, reticle-adjusting mechanisms did not answer the helm precisely and didn't want to come back to the same place time after time. In addition, some adjusting mechanisms were made of soft metal such as brass and couldn't stand the constant changing.

This came as a considerable shock to scopemakers because no previous group of consumers had voiced any complaints about a scope's repeatability. Of course, target shooters needed scopes with precisely repeatable adjustments, but they used only target-style scopes with highly refined adjustment systems. Silhouette shooters wanted hunting-style scopes but they needed precise adjustments.

Makers of scopes and other accessories are accustomed to dealing with shooting fads. They probably perceived the silhouette game as just another passing fancy that offered an opportunity to make a few extra sales. Accordingly, some scopemakers cataloged special silhouette scopes which, under examination, proved to be only cosmetically altered versions of their standard hunting models. At that time the Redfield people were the big guns in the target-scope business so it was only natural that they offered a specialized scope for the silhouette market. Accordingly, they dolled up one of their hunting scopes with fancy target-style adjusting knobs and a few other niceties and went forth to conquer the market. At that time a pal of mine by the name of Gaines Chesnut was the President of Redfield, and he made the mistake of going to a silhouette tournament to see how shooters were taking to his new scope. Instead of the accolades he expected, he was greeted by a hostile mob of ex-Redfield customers who told him in the clearest terms what he could do with his new scope.

I saw him a couple of days later, and he was shaken. "Why didn't you warn me about those guys?" he asked, "I've never been talked to like that." What he had discovered in such forceful fashion was that silhouette shooters were taking their game very seriously and would tolerate no inadequacies in equipment represented as being of silhouette quality.

This lesson was not lost on other scopemakers, who quietly scrapped whatever plans they had for "silhouette" scopes and scurried back to the drawing board. Weaver cashed in big in 1977 with a completely redesigned adjustment system they called the Micro-Trac. By using hardened steel components in the mechanism to reduce wear, and by refining the moving parts, the Micro-Trac did just about everything Weaver claimed it would, including winning lots of silhouette tournaments.

Only one shooter in a thousand cares about the silhouette game, but the technological fallout has carried over into hunting-scope making, the result being better reticle adjustments in virtually all the top brands. Over the coming years, I expect that these improved mechanisms will be adapted by all makers and utilized in just about every scope.

SCOPING THE FUTURE

As a rule, a scope is at its best when it's at its simplest. Various gadgets such as rangefinders and trajectory compensators have an obvious appeal to hunters who feel they need all the help they can get, but there's usually less to such add-ons than meets the eye. However, I'm willing to bet that within the next few years computer technology will find its way into the telescopic sight and yield some amazing innovations. Already we have hand-held calculators capable of

In silhouette matches, a competitor may be assigned to begin shooting at any of four distances, and afterward will have to switch distances without taking any sighting shots. A silhouette scope must therefore have fine adjustments that will return precisely and dependably to previous settings—so that a shooter can make "blind" adjustments for a given range. This has been accomplished by the use of hardened steel components and a refinement of moving parts. Here you see one such scope mounted on the Anshcutz Metallic Silhouette .22 rifle, and another model in use by a shooter. Silhouette scope technology has led to improved adjustments in hunting scopes.

sophisticated ballistic computations, so it's only natural that micro-chip technology will be adapted to scopes.

I foresee trajectory-compensating scopes so accurate that they will put any bullet precisely on target at any range (provided a means of exactly determining range is developed). Perhaps some day we'll have electronic rangefinders that work on a sonar principle, like today's self-focusing cameras. You'll just look through your scope and there in a small window will be a readout showing you the distance to the target, while at the same time the scope's micro-chip computer adjusts the crosshairs so that your bullet will unfailingly hit where it's aimed. I have no qualms about this sort of technological application as applied to hunting because the big hump in taking game is, and always will be, fundamental marksmanship. Unless a hunter can hold and squeeze, all the electronic gadgets in creation won't get his bullet on target during a fair-chase hunt.

One sort of electronic scope that does trouble me, however, is the so-called light-amplification device developed for military use during the Vietnam era. Though once costing in the tens and even hundreds of thousands of dollars, such devices are getting close to what poachers are willing to pay for a scope that can see deer in blackest night. They have no sporting purpose whatever, except for possible vermin control, and I think the day will soon be here when sportsmen are going to have to lead the fight to see that such optical devices are kept out of the hunting scene.

Today's telescopic sights are so wonderfully efficient and marvelously foolproof that it is hard to imagine how they could get much better. Yet I suspect that from now until the turn of the century there will be more dramatic improvements than occurred during the 35-year "rush" that followed the end of World War II. Optical design is one of those sciences that challenge the impossible. Over the past few decades, I've known of any number of technical "impossibilities" that have fallen to imagination and know-how. Today's compact scopes will spawn ever lighter and smaller scopes, which will offer such "impossible" improvements as increased accuracy, brighter, better-defined images, and wider fields of view. You wait and see . . . .

Chapter 17

HOW TO SIGHT-IN A RIFLE AND HAVE IT STAY THAT WAY

Ah, the mystery of sighting-in (zeroing) a rifle! It is a deed of black magic, performed during the dark of the moon while chanting incantations. My favorite is:

> *Tongue of toad,*
> *And blood of bat,*
> *Send my bullet*
> *where the crosshair's at.*

Is it really all that mysterious or are many shooters mired in confusing information? One of the most frustrated men I've ever known was an itinerant gun trader named Will, whose one desire in life was to own a rifle that would "shoot true." To his way of thinking, an accurate rifle would hit where he aimed, and to this end he bought, shot, and traded scores of rifles. Alas, none ever seemed to put the bullet just where the sights said it would, and that gave poor Will the fits. Between gun trades, Will picked on a five-string banjo, and the last I heard of him he'd gone to Nashville and made it big in a Country-Western band. I've often wondered if he ever found a rifle that "shot true." I hope so, because if anyone ever explains to him that getting a rifle to shoot true is only a matter of adjusting the sights, there's no telling what he might do to himself.

Despite all the troubles we're supposed to have getting our rifles correctly zeroed, there are only three conditions under which a rifle cannot be easily and accurately adjusted: 1. The rifle is inoperable or so basically inaccurate that no two shots hit in the same vicinity. 2. The sights, scope mounts, or both, are nonfunctional or incorrect for the rifle. 3. The shooter is such a poor marksman or the conditions at the rifle range are so unsuitable that well aimed shots are impossible.

Proper sight adjustment involves no guesswork and can be done without previous experience. Once the shooter has a clear understanding of the principles the rest is easy. When we see a shooter sight-in his rifle by the "try-and-see" method, we can be pretty sure he doesn't quite understand what he's about, even though he may eventually adjust his sights. Once you understand how it's done, you can zero a rifle dead-on every time and do it quickly, easily, and with a minimum of ammo expenditure. It's possible to zero a rifle with only *one* shot! We'll get to that later, but first let's talk about doing it more conventionally.

CHECKING THE RIFLE AND THE SIGHTS

The first step in sighting-in is a thorough inspection of the rifle, especially the screws that hold the barrel and action in the stock and the screws or pins that hold the sights in place. I'd say that at least 19 out of 20 new rifles are taken to the range for their first shooting session with loose action screws. With these screws loose, even if the scope screws are tight, the action will shift in the stock and cause an ongoing variation in the point of impact.

Let's say you have a new rifle which you intend to use with the factory-installed open sights. The first step is to run a patch through the barrel in order to remove the protective coating of grease or oil. Then wipe the action clean of any heavy grease that might interfere with the gun's operation. If the rifle is a bolt-action or an autoloader with a one-piece stock, take the action and barrel out of the stock. (Two-piece stocks may require special tools for removal, and in any event, they are almost always properly secured to the barrel and action at the factory). A one-piece stock can be removed by unscrewing one, two, or three screws located in the underside of the stock. They usually pass through the trigger guard. Use a screwdriver that fits the slots precisely so you won't mar the screws. Be careful not to let the action fall out of the stock when the screws are removed. Pull it out carefully.

It's best to remove the stock because the screws almost always need to be tightened anyway, and since you have your screwdriver handy, you can take care of another important job.

When you lift the action clear of the stock, check to see if the metal areas covered by the stock have a coating of protective grease. Unseen moisture is often trapped in the stock where it raises hell with the metal's finish, even getting into the working parts. If necessary, wipe on a pretty heavy coat of anti-rust grease such as RIG (Rust Inhibiting Grease). Also take a look at the inside surface of the stock. It should be coated with a water-resistant finish, but sometimes the wood is as bare and dry as a skeleton and eager to soak up any moisture that comes its way. Naturally, this calls for a coat or two of waterproofing varnish, stock oil, or even paint. If you're in a hurry to get on with your shooting, you can rub a heavy coat of paste-type floor wax into the inner surface of the action inletting and the barrel channel.

Waterproofing the innards of a rifle's stock may not seem to have anything to do with adjusting the sights, but it does, friend, it does. When you zero your rifle, you want it to stay that way. A changing point of impact (loss of zero) is often the result of the bends, twists, and warps

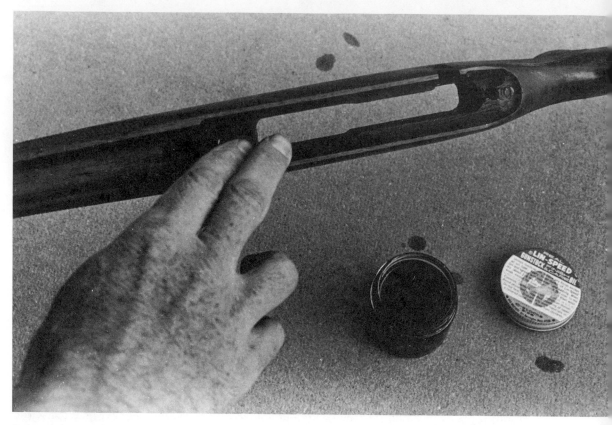

Before sighting-in, it's best to remove the stock to see if the inletting is coated with a water-resistant finish. If not, coat it yourself as shown here, and be sure the finish is completely dry before reassembling the rifle.

a stock goes through as it absorbs and expells atmospheric moisture. These changes alter the wood's pressure on the barrel and cause it to point in ever-changing directions. By reducing, or eliminating, this tendency to absorb water, you significantly reduce the likelihood of losing your zero.

The way you put the rifle back together is especially important to an unchanging zero. If the rifle is a .22 Rimfire model with only one stock screw, there isn't a lot to do except pull the receiver as far as possible to the rear (depending on the free play in the screw hole) in the stock before turning the screw up tight. If the action isn't in the rearmost position, it will work toward the rear by itself through recoil, and that may alter the stock's pressure on the barrel and cause a change in zero.

If the rifle is a centerfire model, it will have two or possibly three action screws. Regardless of the make or model, *tighten the front screw first* while holding the action to the rear. This is Carmichel's First Law of Sighting-In. The effect it has on accuracy is often astonishing.

Next tighten the rearmost screw, and if there is a middle screw, snug it up last, but do not force it tight. When I say tight about the front and rear screws, I mean really put some muscle into it, especially with that front screw. That's another reason why you need a screwdriver that fills the screw slots to full depth and width. If the screwdriver doesn't fit, you'll bugger up the screw slots, and you'll never get them tight.

THE ALL-IMPORTANT RIFLE REST

When you sight-in, use the steadiest rest available to support the rifle, and make yourself steady and comfortable. Nothing quite beats a benchrest with sandbags; but if such niceties aren't available fire from a comfortable prone position with the rifle resting over a lightly padded but firm support—four thicknesses of blanket over a block of wood, for example. If the support has too much built-in bounce, you introduce a variable that could cause trouble later.

Sandbags are easily made from cloth shot bags (shotshell reloaders have plenty of them) or by cutting sections from the legs of old pants (denim is best). Fill with *dry* sand, sew closed, and you're in business. Make a large sandbag to support the forearm and a smaller one for the butt section. You might want to make a "sissy bag" to hold between the buttplate and your shoulder if you are shooting a hard-kicking magnum.

THE TARGET

Achieving a correct zero depends largely on very careful aiming and shooting during the sighting-in phase, and good aiming with open sights calls for a target that can be seen clearly. If you are shooting at 50 feet, use a black aiming bull 1½ to two inches in diameter. Fifty yards calls for a four-inch bull when using open sights, and at 100 yards, you'll do best with an eight-inch bull. The idea is to have a round aiming point that appears somewhat larger than the front bead. When the target hides behind the bead, you can't see exactly where you're aiming. Let's say your rifle has a 24-inch barrel that puts the front bead 30 to 32 inches from your eye when you're aiming. If the bead is one-sixteenth of an inch in diameter (about typical), it will subtend, or cover, an area about seven inches in diameter at 100 yards. The formula for calculating this is: range (in inches) divided by distance from eye to front sight, also in inches, divided by fractional diameter of the front bead.

THE FIRST SHOTS

When you are satisfied that you have a solid rest and steady aim, fire a couple of shots and note the order as well as the location of each shot. As the rifle settles in the stock, there may be a tendency for the point of impact to change. Thus it may be a good idea to disregard the first few shots. Do not be surprised if the shots do not hit anywhere near the point of aim. Your first shots may even miss the target paper completely. Some manufacturers make an effort to sight-in their rifles, some only test-fire for an acceptably tight group, and some merely proof-fire for safety and proper functioning, making no effort to adjust the sights. This is why it is essential to check the sight adjustment of any new rifle.

If the first shots miss the target entirely, you have two options. You can use a large sheet of backing paper behind your target (newspaper will do) to catch the errant bullets, or you can shorten the range. If necessary, continue shortening the range until your shots land on the paper. Once you discover where the shots are going, the rest is easy.

ADJUSTING OPEN SIGHTS

The next step is only a matter of moving the sights, and thereby altering the direction of aim until the line of aim coincides with the path of the bullet. The Golden Rule of sight adjustment is simple: *Move the rear sight in the direction you want to move the bullet's point of impact.* For example, if the bullet hits to the left of where you aim, move the rear sight to the right. If the bullet hits low, raise the rear sight. Sometimes the design of open sights for rifles makes it more convenient to move the front sight. In that case, you move it in the *opposite* direction you want to move the bullet's strike.

How much do you move the rear sight to make a correction in bullet placement? Simple open sights usually are not calibrated in any way that makes precise adjustment possible. Ad-

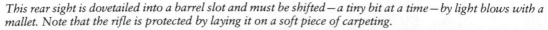

This rear sight is dovetailed into a barrel slot and must be shifted — a tiny bit at a time — by light blows with a mallet. Note that the rifle is protected by laying it on a soft piece of carpeting.

The most common elevation device for an open sight is an angled ramp or notched slide, which can be moved. Raising the rear sight elevates the point of impact.

justment is usually a trial-and-error process, meaning that you fire a few trial shots, move the sights a little, and repeat until you arrive at the exact setting you want. There is, however, a mathematical trick you can use to determine exactly how much sight movement is needed.

First, find the sight radius by measuring the distance between the front and rear sights. Divide this measurement into the range in inches at which you will be sighting-in. This gives you the "radius multiple." This handy figure, multiplied by the distance you move the rear sight, will tell you how much the point of bullet impact will be shifted. Alternatively, divide it into the existing impact displacement, and it tells you how much you need to move the rear sight to make the needed correction. Suppose your sight radius is 15 inches, and you are shooting at 50 yards. Dividing 15 inches into 1,800 inches (50 yards), we get a radius multiple of 120. That means that every movement of the rear sight will be multiplied—or magnified—120 times on the target. If the rear sight is moved, say, one-sixteenth of an inch, the bullet's impact will move 120 times that much, or 7½ inches. Or, working the other way, let's say the bullet is six inches to the right of point of aim. Just divide six by 120, and you get .05 inch. Move the rear sight .05 inch to the left and you'll be on target.

Simple open sights either fit into a dovetail slot in the barrel or are dovetailed into a base or ramp mounted on the barrel. Though these mounting systems look rather permanent, the front and rear sights can usually be moved sideways. This is best done by supporting the rifle on a padded surface and tapping the sight with a drift and a light hammer or mallet. Do not hit the sight with a steel hammer. That would mar the sight's finish and shape. Instead, use a short length of nylon, copper, or brass as a drift. Tap the drift lightly with your light hammer and carefully note the movement of the sight. Remember—a little goes a long way.

Most open rear sights have a device for adjusting elevation. This is usually a notched slide but may be an angled ramp. I've never known a gunmaker to provide any information on how much each notch or calibration of the elevation slide changes elevation. Probably they don't bother to find out themselves. You can figure it out by trial and error or by the radius-multiple formula described earlier.

Rifles in need of sighting-in usually are somewhat off the mark both in both windage and elevation. It is best to make one correction at a time. I generally make the windage adjustment first by bringing the bullet's impact into vertical alignment with point of aim before going on to correct the elevation.

ZEROING APERTURE SIGHTS

Aperture, or peep, sights are much easier to zero than ordinary open sights because they almost always give more precise shot placement and because most aperture sights are easily adjusted for windage and elevation. The adjustment mechanisms of some models are so precisely calibrated that they can be adjusted for range or crosswind on a shot-to-shot basis and then returned to zero.

When you first inspect a good brand of peep sight, you'll note the calibrated scales on the vertical and horizontal arms. Also, the adjusting knobs or screws may be indexed with notches and numbers. When you turn the adjusting knobs, you may also notice slight "bumps," or soft stops, which are called clicks. Some click audibly, hence the origin of the term. Target shooters are quite concerned with these scales and clicks, though hunters seldom give them enough thought to understand their purpose. Generally speaking, this is okay because once a hunting rifle with peep sights is sighted-in, it is seldom readjusted. Most hunters merely hold a bit high for long shots or hold off to left or right for windage since game may move before the hunter can adjust his sights. Just the same, it's important to learn to use these scales. In order to understand them, it is necessary to understand what we mean by *minute of angle.*

MINUTE OF ANGLE

Most of us know that a circle is divided into 360 degrees and that each degree is divided into 60 minutes. The widths of degrees and minutes of degree depend on the length of the radius. Being fan-shaped, minutes and degrees grow increasingly wider as the radius increases. By a fortunate coincidence of English measurement, the width of one minute of a degree at a radius of 100 yards is almost exactly one inch (1.0476-inch). Shooters often use the terms minute of angle and one inch interchangeably. For example, rifles that group their shots inside one inch at 100 yards are sometimes called 1-MOA rifles. Naturally, when the range is doubled, the width of the fan-shaped degree of angle is also doubled. One minute of angle at 200 yards is almost exactly two inches wide; it is three inches at 300 yards, and so-on. This system is very convenient because the angle of departure of bullets, in respect to line of aim, can be described in identical terms.

Let's say your rifle is hitting one inch to the right of point of aim at 100 yards. Theoretical-

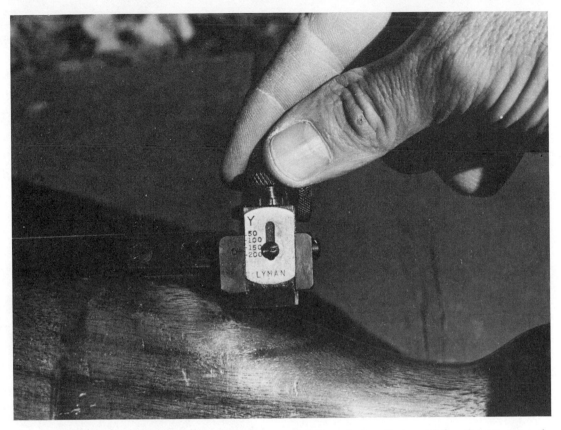

Peep sights are not only much better than the open type but far easier to adjust — and the adjustments are far more precise. Here the author turns the calibrated elevation knob to raise or lower the point of impact.

ly, this angle of departure will place the bullet two inches to the right at 200 yards, three inches at 300 yards and, incidentally, half an inch to the right at 50 yards. In other words, the error is one minute of angle at any range. It is simpler to think in terms of minute of angle than in terms of so many inches at various yardages. Once this system is grasped, you'll understand and use the adjustment scale on peep sights speedily and accurately.

Most American-made peep sights employ a click value of one-quarter of a minute of angle. In other words, one click or calibration of an adjusting knob shifts the point of impact one-quarter of one minute of angle. This is equal to one-eighth of an inch at 50 yards, half an inch at 200 yards, etc. Remember, though, that there's no need to think about all that. Just knowing the degree of angle tells us everything we need to know, regardless of the distance to target. Many American-made peep sights have 12 quarter-minute clicks built into one complete revolution of the adjustment knob. Thus, one complete turn equals three minutes of angle. Each calibration on the flat scales indicates one complete revolution of either the windage or elevation knob.

After the rifle is sighted-in, the adjustable indicators on the scales can be set on a reference calibration and locked in place, giving you not only a zeroed rifle but a highly flexible sighting system. You can sometimes make this work for you when you are hunting. If your rifle is sighted-in dead on at 100 yards, but you have a shot at a fine buck at 300 yards, you can simply turn the elevation knob up the number of clicks necessary to compensate for the drop of your bullet at that distance. This is possible only if you are sure the game isn't about to run. Or say you have a crosswind worth about two minutes of bullet drift. You just click in the correction and fire away. Later it's important to return the adjustments to your original zero-zero setting (zero windage-zero elevation) so that you can click for windage or elevation from zero adjustment whenever you want too.

Of course, not all peep sights work the same way. Some may have one-half, one-eighth, or even one-sixth minute clicks, and one complete turn of a knob may have a value of only one minute or as many as six minutes of angle or even more. Likewise, the reference scales may indicate three, four, five, or more minutes per calibration. With some sights, the calibrations may only be arbitrary references with no particular minute-of-angle value. In any event, once you learn to think in minutes of angle, you can use any sight with greater speed and efficiency.

One variable that can affect aperture sights involves the distance between the front and rear sights. Most manufacturers assume the sight radius will be about 30 inches and calibrate their sight adjustments accordingly. This is based on an average barrel length of 24 inches plus six inches of receiver (action) length. Obviously, there are considerable variations in action and barrel lengths, which causes the click value to vary when the same sight is installed on shorter or longer rifles. The shorter the radius, the greater the value. In other words, a sight that has one-quarter minute clicks with a 30-inch radius will have approximately one-third of a minute clicks when the radius is reduced to 24 inches.

ZEROING SCOPES

Sighting-in a scoped rifle is easier than zeroing either open or peep sights, because a scoped rifle can be aimed easily and very precisely and because the adjustments are so convenient. Just the same, you can come to grief if you don't pay attention to what you are doing.

Several years ago, my old shooting pal Buck Fleenor told me he had located a field full of woodchucks and asked if I'd like to pot a few. The idea was especially appealing because I'd just received a special-order rifle which I figured ought to be the be-all and end-all of varmint rifles. It was a Model 70 Winchester bolt gun in .243 Winchester caliber, made in the special heavy-barreled target style they offered back then. The problem was that I didn't have any ammo loaded as yet, nor had I mounted the snazzy new target scope I'd bought for the rig. I was determined to shoot it though, and prevailed on Buck to give me half an hour to get the scope mounted and handload some cartridges. All this was a mistake because none of these jobs should be hurried, but I was young, then, and had limitless faith in my abilities.

After the agreed-upon half-hour, all seemed ready and we were on our way to the ground-hog patch, where, according to my modest estimate, I would smite them at astronomical distances. The only further holdup was a brief stop at the shooting range where I would sight-in and establish a fiendishly precise zero.

The first couple of shots were on the target paper and grouped close enough to cover with a dime. "You ain't seen nothing yet," I grandly advised Buck, clicking the scope adjustments a few times to center the windage. The next shot wasn't where it was supposed to be, so I turned in a few more clicks and fired again. The bullet hole was again off my point of aim. "Damned odd," I thought, spinning the knobs again. This time the impact was right where I wanted it — dead center over the aiming square and about an inch high. "One more shot, Buck old boy," I said, "and we'll be on our way." The next shot was off four or five inches in another direction — and so was the next shot and the next and the next. That afternoon Buck busted all the chucks while I fulminated over my very expensive bum rig. "They'll hear from me," I promised myself.

That evening when temper had been replaced by reason, I took a closer look at the rifle and discovered at once that the front scopebase was as loose as a sailor with six months pay. It was a lesson never forgotten.

INSTALLING MOUNTS AND SCOPE

The first step in sighting-in a scoped rifle is to make sure the rig is *ready* to be zeroed. After following each of the steps in rifle preparation described at the beginning of this chapter, there is a check list for scope mounting. Most scope-mounting systems feature separate rings and bases. This means the bases must be securely attached to the rifle before giving any thought to the rings around the scope tube. Nearly all modern rifles come from the factory already drilled and tapped to take the screws that secure the scope bases. Scope-mount makers supply bases that are contoured for just about every make and model of rifle you can think of. The first step is making sure you have the right bases for your rifle. I'm not being simplistic; the names and makes and model numbers can be confusing and, often enough, clerks in gunshops, sporting-goods stores, and, especially, discount houses will inadvertently sell you, say, a set of M-70 bases when you ask for M-700's.

At least half of the scopes mounted at home are installed incorrectly. This is because household screwdrivers do not match the scope-mount screw slots and burr the screw heads, splay the slots, and fail to tighten the screws sufficiently. If you don't have the right screwdriver, hold everything until you get it. Some scope-mount makers supply socket-type screws and a hex wrench with their mounts. This is great because it helps to assure tight bases without buggered screw heads.

When fitting the bases to the rifle, wipe away any grease or excess oil from the mating surfaces. If there is too much oil, the mount will "float" slightly even when it seems perfectly tight. Eventually, the oil will seep out, leaving the mount rather loose. But if the surfaces are dry, moisture may get between the metal surfaces some rainy hunting day and cause rusting where you can't see it. Coat the surfaces with a very thin wipe of oil.

If you want to be extra-sure that the mounts never get loose, you might put a drop of Loc-tite on the screw threads. This pretty well holds the screws in place but does not freeze them so tight that they can't be removed later. A drop of varnish or shellac also works well. Occasionally iodine is used for the same purpose, but it has a rusting action and actually freezes the threads together, and if a screw is ever removed the threads are so corroded they can't be used again.

Household screwdrivers should not be used for mounting scopes. They seldom fit the screw slots properly, and can cause burring or looseness. Use a gunsmithing screwdriver, one of exactly the right width and blade thickness, as shown here.

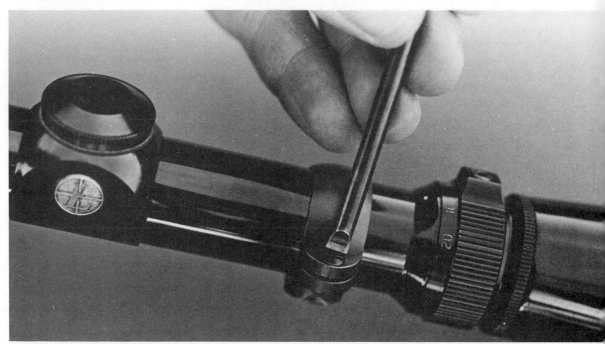

A fine idea, now coming into vogue, is the use of socket-head screws and Allen wrenches for scope rings and bases. This allows adequate tightening without the danger of damaging a screw head.

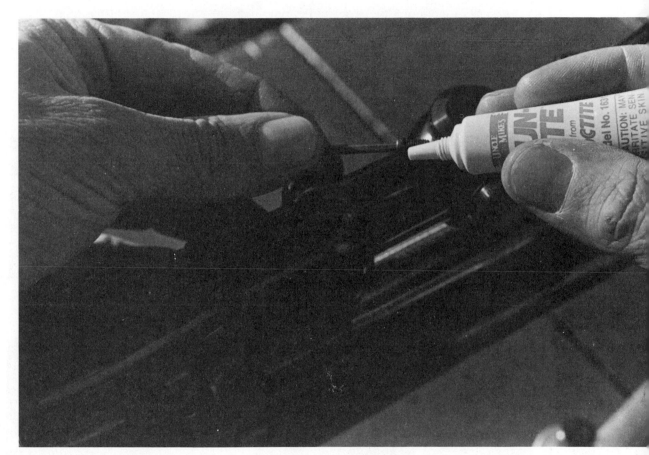

For insurance that your mounts will never work loose, you can apply a drop of Loctite or a similar "freezing" agent to the screw threads.

When securing the scope base or bases, I first turn all the screws snug to make sure the base is properly seated and aligned, and then I apply some real muscle. After pulling the screws as tight as possible, some gunsmiths whack the butt of the screwdriver with a mallet while maintaining turning pressure in order to seat them even tighter. Sometimes this yields another quarter of a turn.

The proper time to put the scope in the rings depends on the design of the rings. With Weaver rings, I remove the top strap completely and then clamp the lower half of the rings onto the bases. The scope is then positioned in the cradle-like ring bottoms, the top straps are slipped on, and the ring screws are tightened.

The rings made by Burris, Leupold, and Redfield require a different procedure because of the socket-type front ring attachment. The ring-to-base fit of the socket is necessarily snug, especially on the first try. Some misguided souls have come to anguish using the scope as a lever to pivot the tight coupling into alignment. Sometimes the strain is so great that it buckles the tube of the scope. Don't do it that way. Use a length of stout wood or a one-inch diameter piece of pipe. Fit it snugly into the front ring and use it as a lever during the first seating. When the ring is pulled into alignment with the base, take the top half of the ring off and then position the scope.

Socket-type front rings can be difficult to swivel into alignment. If you value your scope, never use it as a lever to turn the ring. Use a hardwood dowel or piece of one-inch pipe. Here, the author uses a mallet handle effectively.

When the scope and rings are in place, do not tighten the ring screws completely. Leave them loose enough so that the scope can be slid forward and back or rotated. This will give you a chance to hoist the rifle to your shoulder a few times to make sure the eye relief is correct for your particular shooting stance and the crosswires are not cocked at an angle.

When we merely look through a scopesight we tend to stand quite erect with our heads held farther back than is practical. Accordingly, shooters often tend to mount their scopes too far to the rear. When we are actually shooting a rifle, especially one that delivers a healthy kick, we lean into the stock with the head laid forward on the comb. This is the proper way to hold a rifle, but it can be painful and bloody if the scope is mounted too far to the rear. In such cases, recoil may drive the scope into your eye or eyebrow. When you position your scope in the rings, be sure to place it well forward. Usually, an inch or so farther forward than you think it should be is about right.

Also, when you position the scope axially be sure that both the rifle and the vertical crosshair are really vertical. Most of us do not hold a rifle perfectly vertical. We tend to introduce a slight tilt, or *cant*. When we think we have the scope held vertically, it may actually be at an angle to the vertical centerline of the rifle. This leads to bullet-placement problems at different ranges. (See the chapter on trajectory.) You'll find that it's difficult to judge when a rifle is truly vertical. Gunsmiths sometimes level a rifle by holding it in a padded vice or cradle and placing a small machinist's level on one of the few flat surfaces such as the top of the scope bases, the flats under the action (take the stock off to do this), or the side flats of autos, pumps, and lever-action guns. A few rifles do have flat-topped receivers, which is mighty convenient.

Once the rifle is truly vertical, it is no problem to align the vertical crosswire with some line or surface you know to be vertical such as the edge of a building. B-Square, a maker of gunsmithing tools, sells a clever little bent piece of clear plastic that slips into the receiver of bolt-action rifles and aligns on the bolt-way flats. The plastic device projects a vertical line just behind the scope's eyepiece that is aligned with the vertical crosswire.

After you have tightened the scope rings, it's a good idea to check the alignment one more time. Some rings, especially those made by Weaver, tend to twist the scope somewhat as the screws are being tightened, so you may have to readjust and tinker a bit in order to get them right. In the case of split rings, which are tightened with screws on either side, tighten the screws alternately, so that the small gap between the rings is equal on both sides. This is easier on the screws, looks better, and shows everyone you know what you're doing.

This sounds like a course in do-it-yourself gunsmithing, but these first few steps are vital to the long-term accuracy of your scoped rifle. If you do it right at the beginning, you'll probably never have to think about it again. Do it wrong and sooner or later it's going to cause problems — usually at the worst possible moment.

FOCUS FIRST

Before beginning your sighting-in session, make sure your scope is properly adjusted to your eye and, if the scope has a focusing objective lens, that it is focused at the range at which you will be firing. The eyepiece (rear lens) of most scopes is prefocused by the manufacturer so that the reticle will appear sharp and clear to shooters with normal (20/20) vision or properly corrected vision.

Many shooters who wear corrective lenses prefer not to wear them when hunting. This is particularly true of hunters who suffer only from common farsightedness. But time and time again, farsighted hunters have shouldered their rifles for a shot at a trophy buck only to discover that the crosshairs appeared fuzzy or almost invisible. This is easily avoided by focusing the eyepiece without glasses if you intend to hunt that way. (But, please, for safety's sake wear protective, non-corrective glasses when you're zeroing your rifle.)

The eyepiece focus is checked by simply looking through the scope at a neutral background such as the sky. If the crosshairs look sharp and black, the eyepiece is probably focused properly, especially if the scope is new and your vision is normal. In some cases, the crosshairs may appear crisp, but the muscles in your eye may feel "pulled" or you may experience a faint "queasy" feeling. This feeling results from the eye trying to adjust or accommodate itself to an out-of-focus condition. You may notice that the crosshairs appear out of focus momentarily but then sharpen as the eye compensates for the error. This is definitely a signal that focusing is needed. More usually, when the eyepiece is out of focus, the crosshairs appear fuzzy and poorly defined, or you may see a double image of one or both crosshairs. When this happens, there is no doubt that you need to refocus the eyepiece.

The standard procedure is to loosen the eyepiece lock ring and rotate the eyepiece a few turns to the left (counterclockwise). Take care not to screw the eyepiece off entirely. If you do, you'll impair the scope's fogproof qualities. If the crosshairs appear fuzzy, this backing off of the eyepiece will probably make them appear more so. If they appeared clear originally, just back off the eyepiece until they begin to look somewhat out of focus. Possibly, as you back off the eyepiece, the crosshairs will come into sharper focus, eliminating the eye-pulling sensation described earlier. If so, keep turning the eyepiece until the crosshairs are again out of focus. In other words, make sure the scope is completely out of focus first so that you can then focus it correctly.

Now look through the scope at the sky and turn the eyepiece slowly to the right (clockwise). As the focus improves, you will notice that the crosshairs look sharper and sharper. Pay particular attention to the edges or borders of the wires and to the junction where they cross. After every couple of turns, look away from the eyepiece and refocus your eye on some other object. This is necessary because your eye wants to accommodate to the image in the scope and make it appear in focus even when it really isn't. This tendency is corrected by occasionally refocusing your eye on other objects.

Stop turning the eyepiece when the crosshairs first appear sharp and black. If you continue turning it, the crosshairs will, for a while, continue to look sharp and in focus, but at some point your eye will again begin to accommodate and try to fool you. In other words, you can get too much of what looks like a good thing.

Once the eyepiece is focused for your eye, there should never be any reason to change it unless your eye changes. If you normally wear glasses, you'll probably notice a considerable difference in the appearance of the crosshairs when using the scope without them. Remember, the eyepiece focus is only a focus on the crosshairs and is not affected by different ranges. You should not try to correct an out-of-focus target image by adjusting the eyepiece.

If the scope has an adjustable objective (front) lens, be sure to focus it for the exact range at which you will be sighting-in. Later, when you are shooting at game at mixed ranges, you will

The scope's ocular lens must be focused for your eye. Look through the scope at the sky and turn the eyepiece slowly. When the crosshairs appear sharp and black, stop turning immediately. If the scope has an adjustable objective lens, it too must be focused in order to avoid parallax (see chapter on scopes). Focus the objective lens for the distance at which you will sight-in.

find that an exact focus is not necessary. A scope focused at 200 yards works fine even for relatively small targets such as woodchucks at ranges from 100 yards to 300 yards or even farther. To get a dead-accurate zero, however, you want an exact focus.

Focusing the objective lens accomplishes two things. First, it brings the image into optical focus so that you can see it very clearly. Second, it eliminates that mysterious goblin called parallax (see the chapter on telescopic sights), so that the crosshairs can't fool you about where they are actually aiming.

Most scopes with a focusing objective lens are calibrated for range, so you merely turn the focusing ring to the range at which you intend to sight-in. Some older scopes, however, such as the first-model Unertl Ultra-Varmint, are not calibrated and must be focused by trial and error, or rather, "turn and see." Other scopes of past decades were calibrated only with reference numbers. As the scope was adjusted to different ranges, the numbers were recorded for later use. On some scopes, notably the wonderful, early Weaver K-8 and K-10, the calibrated focusing ring freely turned on the threaded objective bell. If, by accident or carelessness, the ring was given more than a full turn, everything went out of focus and stayed that way until you "found" your way back.

Most of today's scopes with focusing objectives have either positive stops on the focusing ring or a reference line on the objective housing so you can't "misplace" your focus.

There may be other problems, however, and you must solve them too. For instance, sometimes the range scale is not exactly correct and requires some fine tuning. Let's say you're shooting at a range of 100 yards. Accordingly, you set the objective focusing dial at the 100-yard index. Almost certainly, the target appears sharp and crisp, and you figure you're ready to start shooting. But are you? With the rifle solidly resting on sandbags so that it remains pointed at the target without your touching it, look through the scope and move your head slowly from side to side and up and down several times. You are checking for parallax. If it exists, the crosshairs may appear to wander completely across the aiming square or perhaps an even wider area as you move your head. Or, if the parallax is slight, the movement may be scarcely more than the width of the crosshair itself. In any event, the degree of parallax you see indicates the degree of aiming error that may be introduced through no fault of your own. Fortunately, this is easily corrected.

Turn the focusing ring about an eighth of a turn in either direction. If the parallax appears to be reduced, turn the ring some more in the same direction. If it appears worse or there is no change, turn the ring the other way. Keep making fine adjustments until the parallax is completely removed and the crosshairs stay put when you move your head. On rare occasions, the shooter finds that when all the parallax is removed, the image is out of focus. This may be due to an internal problem with the scope, but more likely it is a sign that the eyepiece was improperly focused to begin with. This means it's time to start over by rechecking the eyepiece focus.

It's worth mentioning that a scope that doesn't focus exactly parallax-free at the exact calibrated yardage shouldn't be faulted unless the scale is way off. We're dealing with some very critical optics here, but in order for the focusing rings to turn, there has to be a bit of free play, or "slack." And then, we aren't always shooting at precisely measured ranges. Our "100-yard" benchrest may actually be anywhere from 85 to 120 yards from the target. One more thing. Even if your scope appears to be perfectly free of parallax, give the focusing ring a bit of a turn so that some parallax can be seen and then focus to eliminate it. Once you see parallax, you know what to look for next time and how to correct it.

SCOPE ADJUSTMENTS

Properly zeroing a telescopic sight calls for familiarity with the instrument's adjustments and operation. These tend to differ somewhat from maker to maker and even from model to model, but they are pretty well explained in the instruction booklet supplied by the maker. Sometimes, though, shooters who have owned three or four scopes don't bother to read the new instructions, and this leads to confusion at the sighting-in bench. The confusion stems from the different "click values" of various scopes. A "click" or turn of the adjustment knobs of different scopes may shift the bullet's point of impact by different amounts. This gets even more confusing with scopes whose adjustments do not "click" but turn silently, with only a calibrated scale as a reference.

If there is such a thing as a "standard" click or calibration, it has the value of a quarter of a minute of angle. As we saw earlier, this means that one click or calibration moves the bullet's point of impact a quarter of an inch at 100 yards. Nearly all target-type scopes have quarter-minute adjustments, as do most hunting scopes. However, some scopes have one-minute clicks, half-minute clicks, or even one-eighth clicks. As a rule of thumb, scopes with lower magnification have coarser adjustments. The Weaver "K" series of scopes, for example, have half-minute clicks in the 1.5X, 2.5X, and 3X magnifications, and quarter-minute clicks in the 4X and higher-power models. Leupold hunting scopes, on the other hand, do not have audible click adjustments at all; only silently turning screws with a graduated reference scale. The scale graduations equal a full minute on all fixed-power models up to 8X and half-minutes on the 10X and 12X models. The higher-powered (16X, 20X, 24X, and 36X) Leupold target and varmint scopes have audible clicks as well as calibrations in quarter-minute or finer values. Most scopes have no markings that indicate their click values, so you must remember what the instruction

The instructions or brochure packed with a scope will tell you the amount of change indicated by one click or calibration of the adjustment dials — but the scope itself is very seldom marked with this vital information. If you have several scopes with different "click values," don't trust to memory. Tape or glue a value notation inside one of the turret caps.

Here's an array of targets suitable for sighting-in with a scope. The author is pointing to his preference—the simple open square. For open or aperture sights, the traditional black bull's-eye is best.

booklet or sheet says. If you own several scopes, it may be hard to remember which scope has what click value, so make a note on a small piece of tape and glue it inside one of the turret caps that protect the knobs.

THE AIMING POINT

Unlike iron sights, which can be aimed most accurately at rather large, easily seen targets, scopes are sighted-in most precisely when the aiming point is quite small. If you try to center a scope's crosshairs in a large black circle, some shot-to-shot error will result simply because it is almost impossible to come back to the same exact spot on a large, featureless target bull. This is why target shooters do not aim at the center of the bull's-eye but rather pick out some smaller aiming point such as the numerals "X" or "10" or even a bullet hole. Benchrest shooters, the most particular shooters of all, use squares rather than circles as aiming points. A square can be precisely dissected into four exact quadrants by the crosshairs.

440   •

I prefer square aiming points above all other shapes and use them about 99 percent of the time when I'm sighting-in with a scope. Usually, I use the standard 100-yard benchrest type target, which is a one-inch black horizontal square with a half-inch white square in its center. With scopes of 6X or greater magnification, the white square can be clearly seen and used as an aiming point. With lower-magnification scopes, I use a two-inch aiming square. Some target-makers offer a sighting-in target with the aiming square positioned as a diamond, with one corner down and one up. This is not a very smart idea because the crosshairs obscure the corners, making it necessary to guess at the real center of the target. It's better to *see* the corners of the aiming square because they are your reference points.

Another idea that's not so hot is the blaze-orange target. There are several such targets on the market. At first stroke, the idea of blaze-orange or Day-Glo (safety) colors for targets seems great because they are so easily seen. The problem is the nature of these colors, which project their striking visual qualities because of a peculiar mix of wave lengths. Your eye doesn't want to accept the odd light waves because they are unnatural, and this is why they appear so vivid. When you look at a Day-Glo target for a while, you'll notice that the image seems to pulse as your eye grapples with the strange sensation. The edges, in particular, tend to go in and out of focus, making careful aiming difficult.

So, all in all, the best thing you can aim at is a simple, dead-black square or black box outline with a white center on a soft white or dull yellow background.

BORE-SIGHTING

Since there is no telling where a newly scoped rifle will be hitting, it's a good idea to make a few "guesstimated" adjustments at the beginning. Otherwise you may waste several shots before you even hit the target paper. The most common way to get a rough zero is bore-sighting. This works best with bolt-action or single-shot rifles because you must see through the barrel from the breech end. However, by using commercially available chamber-insert periscopes, you can bore-sight autoloaders, lever guns, and pumps. The technique is simple. With the rifle resting on sandbags or other steady supports, sight at the target through the barrel or the periscope. You are looking along the path of the bullet. When the target appears well centered in the barrel, carefully take your hands off the rifle and leave it so aimed in a dead rest. Now, without touching the rifle, take a look through the scope and see where the crosshairs are aiming. If they are on the aiming point, you're in luck, but probably they are several inches or even feet out of whack. Note how far each crosshair is off target and make your corrections. You can do this by counting minutes of angle and turning the adjustments accordingly, or you can do it the "automatic" way, as I do. Holding the rifle firmly in position on its rests with one hand so that the barrel-target alignment remains undisturbed, look through the scope and turn the adjustments until the crosswire is centered on the target. This is a fast, easy shortcut because you don't have to do any measuring or calculating.

Most bore-sighting is done at a round black target, simply because that's the target we're used to. I use a somewhat different procedure which I think is easier and more accurate. My way, however, does call for a rather large target frame with fairly heavy 2x4 lumber posts and cross members. I make the vertical and horizontal corrections one at a time by bore-sighting at

After all the preparations, the first step in actually zeroing a rifle is bore-sighting—assuming that it's a bolt-action or single-shot that allows you to look through the barrel. With the bolt removed, look through the bore, get it lined up on the target, and leave it that way, firmly supported, while you adjust the scope to get the same picture you see through the bore.

With the barrel bore-sighted and the reticle adjustments moved to match it, the crosshairs should be centered on the target, as shown here. But this is just an initial approximation of the zero and no substitute for actual firing.

the vertical and horizontal frame members. It helps if the posts are perfectly vertical and the cross members level. This method of bore-sighting will surprise you with its accuracy because it is easy to center straight lines in the circle of the bore. Try it and see.

If, after bore-sighting, your first shot lands on the target paper, all is well and good. But bore-sighting doesn't always work out, so don't be disappointed if your shot misses the target entirely. Sometimes a slightly crooked bore or stock pressure on the barrel will cause rifles to shoot in strange directions. If this happens, simply shorten the range until the target paper catches your bullet. For example, if you're shooting at 100 yards, bring the target in to 50 yards or even less, if necessary. Once you get the impact centered on a close target, you can move it back to 100 yards with assurance that you'll be close to the money.

During the past few years a handy little instrument called a bore sighter or optical collimator has come into fairly widespread use. Though they are a bit too expensive for most casual shooters, they are widely used in gunshops to put newly scoped rifles more or less on target. They work by locking a close-fitting rod, called a spud, in the barrel at the muzzle and attaching a device that houses a series of lenses and grids. When you look through the scope, you see—depending on the brand of collimator—either a simple crosshair or a detailed grid representing the theoretical place your bullet will hit on the target. You turn your scope's adjustments until the crosswires are centered, or *collimated* on the grid. Sometimes this puts the bullet's impact surprisingly close to the point of aim. At least, it almost always puts the bullet on the target paper. But it does not, as some users believe, give you a perfect zero. This can be done only by shooting the rifle and making precise adjustments. Some shops offer free scope mounting and sighting-in with the purchase of a new rifle and scope. Quite often, the sighting-in offered is only done in the shop with a bore-sighting device. Always double check the gunshop zero at the range.

THE SCOPE AT THE RANGE

At last, after all this preparation of the scoped rifle, we're ready for the fun part—real shooting. There are are all sorts of ways of doing the job, so we will discuss different techniques and you can take your pick. Different rifles sometimes require different zeroing techniques.

The technique I use most often is called the "one-shot" method. In actual practice, I always fire several shots, but in theory at least, only one shot is necessary.

With the rifle very firmly supported on sandbag rests, I carefully aim and fire a single shot at the target with the bore-sighted rifle. The next step is to locate the bullet hole in the target. Usually the bullet hole can be seen through the scope. In good light you should be able to spot a .30-caliber hole in white paper at 100 yards with a 4X scope. If not, I find it with a spotting scope or simply walk up to the target and mark the hole with a crayon or pencil. You must know

With a collimator inserted in the muzzle, as Carmichel demonstrates here, you can bore-sight without actually looking through the bore. With fixed-breech rifles this is a boon, and it eases the job even with bolt-actions.

Here's how a Bushnell collimator actually appears through a scope. The crosshairs in this instance are low and to the right of the theoretical point of impact indicated on the optical grid. The scope can be quickly adjusted to center on the grid before removing the collimator and proceeding with the target work.

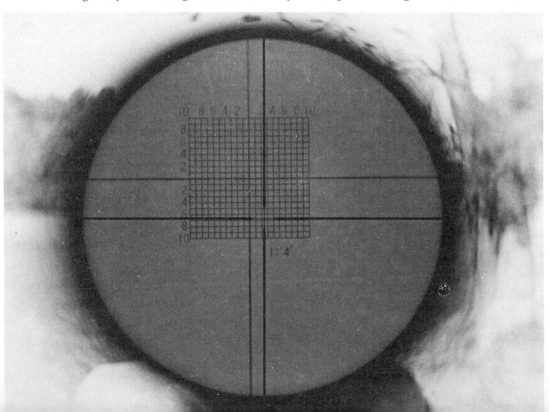

exactly where the bullet hit. The convenient thing about this method is that you don't have to measure how far the shot missed the point of aim or make any other calculations.

The third step is to carefully aim again and adjust the sandbag rests so that the crosshairs stay put on the target. It is important that the rifle be supported so that it rests steadily by itself or that it be held stationary by some other means. Now, with the rifle held so that it can't move, look through the scope and begin turning the windage adjustment. There is no need to count clicks or watch the adjustment scale. I simply turn the adjustment and watch the vertical crosshair march across the target paper toward the bullet hole. All I am doing is coinciding the crosshairs with the rifle's point of impact. When the vertical crosshair intersects the bullet hole, I move the horizontal crosswire the same way. If I want the bullet to hit, say, an inch above point of aim at 100 yards, I simply adjust the horizontal wire so that it is an inch below the bullet hole.

Obviously, if the rifle happens to move while you are making these adjustments, your point of reference is lost and you'll have to fire another round and begin again. In any event, I always fire additional shots to confirm that the zero is correct and to see how well the rifle and ammo are performing. Usually I make one or two final adjustments to get the group exactly where I want it, but if I actually had only one cartridge to fire, this technique would work well enough to get a rifle serviceably sighted-in for hunting.

The more traditional way of sighting-in a scoped rifle is not much different from adjusting open or peep-type iron sights. You fire a shot or a group of shots, measure the distance from

This is Carmichel's one-shot zeroing technique. After firing the first shot, he aligns the crosshairs again on the original aiming point and, holding the rifle motionless, turns the adjustments to move the crosshairs to the bullet hole. Theoretically, only the first shot is necessary, but he fires several for insurance of proper grouping.

Here's an efficient bench setup at the author's range. It's situated so that the sun is behind the shooter and on the targets. The target on the left is at 100 yards. The other one is in a movable frame at 50 yards. The rifle is supported on sandbags and a pedestal; a spotting scope and a pair of ear protectors are at hand.

where the bullet hits to where you want it to hit, and make the necessary adjustments. This calls for a bit more work and figuring than the one-shot system, but the results are the same.

As mentioned earlier, the only way you are likely to go wrong is by not knowing the click or graduation value of your scope's adjustments. As a rule, the adjusting mechanisms of telescopic sights are quite precise and respond correctly to specific adjustments. Occasionally, though, the clicks aren't what they are supposed to be, and the shift of impact is not what you expect. This calls for more shooting and checking.

Also, there is the possibility that the internal mechanism is frozen or sluggish and won't respond to your adjustments. This was especially common in scopes of a bygone era but still happens on occasion. The reticle is mounted in a ring or tube within the main scope tube and is more or less held in place by a flexible suspension system that moves when you turn the adjustments. These screws turn and contact the reticle tube and cause it to move. When they are turned clockwise they push directly and positively against the reticle housing, but when they are turned counterclockwise they move away from the reticle housing. The reticle mounting is returned by springs that are supposed to hold the housing firmly against the tips of the adjusting screws. Sometimes the springs can't do their work because the housing is mechanically stuck or, most often, held fast in gooey lubricant or sealant. Suppose you make an adjustment of eight clicks to the right. The point of impact should move two inches to the right, but when you shoot again, the bullet hits just where it did before you made the change. Puzzled, you crank in eight more clicks and shoot again. This time, the reticle breaks free, and moves 16 clicks. Now you're two inches too far to the right. Not too many years ago this was an everyday part of shooting life. Nowadays, it is only liable to happen with poor-quality discount-store scopes or some older models. If you watch an old hand sighting-in with a scope, you'll probably notice that he gives the tube or turret a good thump after each turn of the adjustments. He isn't trying to wreck his scope. He's making sure the reticle isn't sticking.

WHAT THE GROUP CAN TELL YOU

Much has been said about the importance of firing three-shot groups and then locating the group center so that you can make your sight changes accordingly. I'm not all that sold on the

Some shooters zero a rifle while resting it over a soft support such as this sleeping bag. Anything is better than nothing, but Carmichel disapproves of such soft supports because they allow too much rifle bounce.

The purpose of sighting-in is to make a rifle shoot where it's aimed, not to prove the shooter is a hero (or idiot). The author is shown sighting-in a hard-kicking .458 Winchester Magnum with the aid of a "sissy bag"—a 25-pound bag of shot held as a cushion between rifle butt and shoulder. This absorbs a lot of recoil and can improve accuracy by avoiding any tendency to flinch.

This is a comfortable, efficient position for sighting-in. Carmichel's left hand holds the sandbag under the butt-stock. By squeezing or relaxing his grip on the bag, he moves the butt up or down for slight adjustments in his hold on the target.

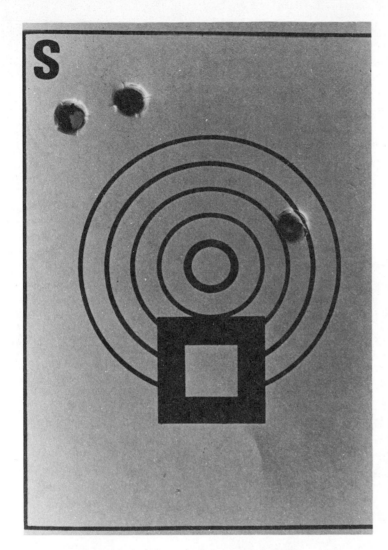

With a group like this, where is the actual point of impact? It's probably between the two closest holes, so Carmichel disregards the wide shot in a case like this. He also fires another shot or two in order to make sure.

idea. At best, it is becoming outdated. There was a time, not long past, when the accuracy of rifles and ammo wasn't much reason for hymns of praise. Since the successive shots tended to scatter, it was a good idea to fire a three-shot (or more) group in order to see where the rifle generally wanted to shoot. As a result, many shooters and gun writers, who should know better, still tend to follow and teach the old concept.

Let's say your first shot hits a foot wide. You don't need to fire two more shots into a group to know that you need to make some adjustment. If your rifle is reasonably accurate, one shot at a time will tell you enough so that you move the point of impact where you want it. After you have made the adjustments, it is then a good idea to shoot a three-shot group (five is better) to make sure.

If the three bullet holes form a neat little triangle, in the manner shown in most sighting-in guides, it is indeed simple to determine the center of the group, but there are so many variations that determining the center can get pretty owly. For example, if two of the shots are in a single overlapping hole and the third is two inches away, do you determine that the group center is somewhere in between? Not if you're smart. Probably the two overlapping holes indicated where the rifle is really shooting. Just forget the odd shot, but to make sure, fire one or two more.

SHIFTING IMPACT

Some rifles tend to shift point of impact as the barrel heats up and expands. This can result from different causes such as stock pressure on the barrel or unequal pressure on the sides of the

Here's a classic example of "walking" as a rifle barrel heats up and causes the point of impact to rise above the point of aim. When this happens, make no further scope adjustments—at least for the time being. Wait for the barrel to cool and start over.

barrel inletting. Some barrels just like to change directions as they get warm. With hunting rifles, this is no problem so long as you know it is happening. But if you don't know that your rifle has such bad habits, you can have a real problem.

The problem arises early in the sighting-in process. With the first few shots, you aren't likely to notice any tendency to shift point of impact. By the time you've gotten the point of aim where you want it, you've probably fired six or eight or even more shots in rapid order, and the barrel is sizzling hot. The group is nice and tight and everything looks grand, so you pack up your gear and happily head for home. But you may have real trouble later. As the rifle cools, the point of impact may shift. You believe your sights are adjusted to a gnat's hair, but when you level down on a buck or a groundhog, your bullet kicks up dirt. It happens all too often.

One of the most insidious things about this is that the point of impact usually moves just so far, and then the rifle begins shooting a stabilized group again. Of course, the group is not where you want it to be.

Here's what you do. After your rifle is sighted-in to your satisfaction, place it in the shade and let it cool completely. Then fire *one* shot, and see where it hits. Remember, you're not concerned with groups because game animals aren't inclined to idle about while we plaster them with neat little clusters of bullet holes. What you want to know is where that vitally important first shot out of a cold barrel wants to go. If the shot hits within the group area fired when the barrel was hot, you can figure you have a nicely stable rifle, hot or cold.

There is a good chance, however, that it may hit inches wide of the group fired when the barrel was hot, and the impact will probably be low. If so, don't change the sights yet. Just keep shooting until you get the barrel hot again. Plot each shot in order, and see if the bullet holes "walk" back to where the rifle grouped earlier when hot. Rifles that tend to walk, or change point of impact, usually do so consistently and walk the same distance after the same number of shots.

If your rifle tends to change impact as it heats up, don't get in a snit and yell at your dealer. I've had some great hunting rifles that were inclined to stroll as they warmed, but I used them effectively anyway because the first two or three shots were always on the money. The trick to sighting-in such rifles is to have a cold-barrel zero. That means adjusting the sights so that the first shot goes where you want it to in respect to point of aim. Usually the second and third shots, fired in fairly rapid order, go to the same spot, often in a tight little cluster. But after that, the barrel is hot and the shots walk. In order to convince yourself that the point of impact is consistent and reliable for the first few shots when the barrel is cool, you may want to check it three or four more times, letting the barrel cool completely before shooting each group.

The shape and size of a group can reveal some mighty important things about your rifle and ammo and even about yourself and your shooting technique, *if* you take the time to think about it. A few years back I built a fancy-looking target rifle barreled for the 7mm Remington Magnum round. I figured it would be a terror over the 1,000-yard target course. My first test groups, fired from the bench at 100 yards, further convinced me I had a winner. Some of the five-shot groups ran as small as half an inch between the centers of the widest shots. The first time I tried the rifle at a full 1,000 yards, however, the results were disastrous. The group strung vertically from the top to the bottom of the big target paper. "Why," I asked myself, "does the rifle perform so well at 100 yards but not at 1000?" When I dug out the 100-yard benchrest

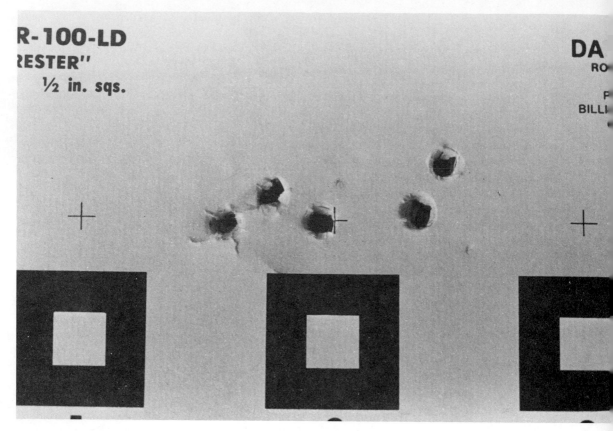

These shots look suspiciously like two distinct groups. This can occur if the ammunition isn't uniform or if the screws aren't tight in the scope rings or bases.

targets, the answer was apparent. Those half-inch groups I'd been so proud of were distinctly vertical. They were no wider than the width of the bullet holes. If I had taken more time to study the shape of the groups fired at close range, I could have predicted the long-range vertical stringing.

In case you're wondering, the problem was faulty ignition, which was easily corrected by just changing the load. The rifle did turn out to be a winner.

Sometimes a rifle seems to shoot two distinct or separate groups, with successive shots alternating from one to the other. The first thing to do about that is to make sure all your ammo is uniform. Different loads will definitely have different points of impact. The same weight of bullet by different makers can vary point of impact considerably. Even different numbered lots of cartridges made by the same manufacturer can vary considerably.

Two-grouping can also be a sign of loose screws in the scope rings or bases or even in the rifle itself. If screws are loose, the jolt of recoil bounces the sight to one side of the free play allowed by the loose parts. When you fire again it is jolted to the other extreme of the free play, causing two distinct groups. When this happens, it's time to go back to the beginning and start tightening screws.

THE RIGHT FIX

Right now I'm going to tell you something that you've never read, and probably never heard. It is so helpful that sometime during your shooting career it will save you several times the price of this book.

During the past couple of decades, glass-bedding a rifle's action in the stock or free-floating the barrel so that it does not touch the forearm, or both, have come to be regarded as cure-alls for all sorts of sighting-in and accuracy ills that afflict bolt-action, single-shot, and even some models of autoloading and lever-action rifles. Sometimes the treatment works wonders, but sometimes it doesn't. I get hundreds of letters from readers to the effect that glass-bedding and floating the barrel were no help.

I'm not surprised when a glass job or a free-floated barrel doesn't improve the accuracy of a rifle. I'm a doubter anyway. In my opinion, glass-bedding shouldn't be the first thing you try when a rifle misbehaves—it should be the *last!* Too many glass and floating jobs are done blind, meaning that they are done as trouble catchalls, when the real problem hasn't been analyzed and understood. If it works, great, but what if it doesn't? You've spent your money, devalued your rifle, and you are still no better off than before.

Glass-bedding a rifle's action is a touchy operation. On the average, only two out of three glass-bedding jobs are correctly done. If done correctly, a glass job holds the action firmly in the stock, thereby eliminating movement within the stock. It also cradles the action in a natural, un-warped, stress-free position. We know that when an action shifts, or is stressed, or tends to flex erratically on firing, there will be a bad effect on group size.

The reason a barrel is free-floated is to remove any uneven pressures against it and to allow it to vibrate freely and uniformly. Obviously, these two treatments can correct a multitude of sins. But what if the barrel is just naturally inaccurate, or improperly fitted in the receiver? The chamber may be incorrectly made, the lugs uneven, or the sights may be haywire in many different ways. I can think of five separate and distinct causes for vertical stringing and five more for horizontal stringing, and some of them have nothing to do with action or barrel bedding. So how can you be sure that glass-bedding or free-floating is the answer to accuracy problems?

Why not isolate the problem the way it would be done in the laboratory? This technique calls for artificially duplicating the projected changes to see how they would work, but how do you artificially duplicate glass-bedding and/or free-floating? Here's how.

Place a series of heavy shims under the action until it is substantially elevated, say, one-sixteenth or even one-eighth of an inch above its original position in the stock. With flat-bottomed actions such as Rugers, Mausers, Winchesters, Sakos, and so forth, I use stiff plastic shims cut from void credit cards. For round-bottomed actions such as Remingtons, I use thinner, more flexible plastic or heavy paper (not cardboard) shims. You must be careful to build up the layers evenly with full contact, so that the action is supported pretty much the way it was held by the wood alone. You can check for evenness by alternately loosening and tightening the guard screws. If the front or rear of the action tends to cock up more than a few thousandths when the other screw is loosened, it's a sign of uneven support under the action. So tinker with the shims until the action rests evenly and solidly on its bedding.

As the action is shimmed and raised above the original stock inletting, the barrel is also raised out of the channel, clear of the stock. In effect, the barrel is floating free of the wood. In other words, you have temporarily duplicated a precise action-bedding job plus a free-floated barrel. Now all you need to is test-fire the rifle.

Obviously, if your rifle is suddenly transformed into a hair-splitter, you're on the right track. Now you know that bedding problems were indeed the cause of poor accuracy and you can proceed accordingly, altering the original bedding, glassing and/or floating the barrel. If the shimmed rifle still shoots poorly, the problem has some other cause, and you have saved yourself the time and expense of a glass and barrel-floating job that wouldn't have worked anyway.

You still have a few options. First, experiment with some pressure under the barrel. Place shims under the barrel at the final inch or so of the forearm. Start off with a slight upward pressure and continue adding shims, if needed. You'll notice that the bullets print higher in respect to point of aim as you add more shims. The barrel is being bent slightly upward, but that is not important. What you're looking for is a tendency of the groups to get tighter. If you experiment with barrel shims while the action is still shimmed "up on blocks" as previously described, your results, or lack of results, will be more clearly defined because all other influences, such as side pressures, etc., are removed.

If none of these tests improves accuracy, you've made progress because about half of the possible causes of poor accuracy have been eliminated. Now you're ready to deal with other causes. Again, let me caution you about the obvious, but frequently overlooked, causes of accuracy problems. Are all the screws tight? Have you double checked your scope mounts and bases?

HOW ABOUT YOU?

Do you know the No. 1 cause of poor rifle accuracy? It's just plain poor shooting. In my OUTDOOR LIFE mail, I get all sorts of letters from readers describing poor accuracy. From the descriptions of their equipment, I know that many of the outfits should, and probably do, shoot very well indeed. In these cases, I must tell a loyal reader that his real problem is in his holding, aiming, and trigger work. Believe me, those one-inch and smaller groups you hear about aren't just the result of a super rig and fine ammo. It takes some mighty good shooting too, even when you are using a solid benchrest.

I once belonged to a rifle club that put on an annual sighting-in day a week or two before the opening of deer season. Dozens of hunters would come out with all sorts of rifles and sights. Presumably, most of these chaps were experienced hunters and competent field marksmen, but when they got down to gnat's-whisker shooting from the benchrest most of them were at a loss. When they complained that their rifles weren't grouping as well as they would like, one of the club's experienced benchrest shooters would give it a try. Nine times out of ten, group size would be cut in half, at least, revealing delightfully accurate rigs.

Firing a rifle for pure accuracy requires a finely honed technique. Like any other form of shooting, it takes practice and experience. Surprisingly perhaps, shooting from a bench is not nearly as easy as it looks. Some otherwise experienced marksmen claim that they shoot more accurately from the prone position than from a bench with sandbag rests. In any event, the greatest group tightener the beginner or expert shooter can have is a good set of ear protectors to minimize erratic flinching, but I guess I'm getting off the subject.

When a rifle refuses to shoot satisfactorily, and you've eliminated a number of possible causes by the procedures described above, it's time to look further. Unfortunately, many mechanical causes of poor accuracy are beyond the investigative ability and equipment of the average gun tinkerer. A bad barrel might be checked by forcing a soft lead slug through the bore

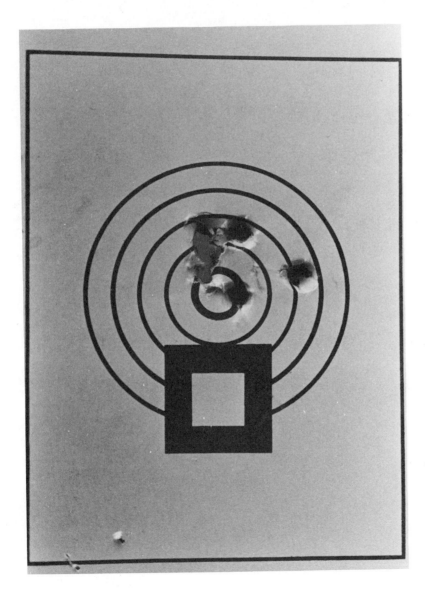

This is the kind of group you want. These five shots, fired from a 7mm Remington Express at 100 yards, are nestled just a little more than an inch above the point of aim. At 200 yards, shots will be almost dead on point of aim.

and measuring the slug with a micrometer, but even this calls for fairly specialized know-how. Likewise, checking for evenness of locking-lug contact, chamber disorders, faulty barrel fitting—all possible causes of poor accuracy—call for experienced technicians with specialized tools. This means that discovering and correcting the problem may call for fancy gunsmithing, usually the fitting of a new barrel.

Chapter 18

TEACHING YOURSELF TO BE A CRACK SHOT

I've been told that the Navy prefers non-swimmers for frogman training. The idea is that it is easier to teach them to swim from scratch than to correct existing faults. I know for a fact that the same thing is true of marksmanship.

Give me a teen-ager, preferably a girl who has never touched a gun and has no idea how they work. In six months or less, I will give you back a skilled competitor capable of busting 100 straight clay targets at trap or skeet with a shotgun or able to compete in top-level rifle competition.

Trying to coach an experienced shooter, on the other hand, can be an exercise in frustration. Part of the difficulty is trying to overcome bad shooting habits. Very few of us have had the good fortune to receive good coaching at the beginning of our shooting careers. As a result, some of our basic techniques and procedures are either totally incorrect or, at best, spotted with faults. More shooting experience only serves to reinforce the bad habits.

Another difficulty is a mysterious but widespread resistance to instruction. It seems that shooting is one of those macho endeavors at which men think they are naturally good. When a coach makes a critical comment or helpful suggestion, an experienced shooter often takes it as an insult to his manhood. This is one reason why women are easier to coach.

I think this mentality has been reinforced by all those articles we read about shooting 10 shots into a silver dollar at 200 yards with a deer rifle or busting geese at 80 yards. We've read so much of this stuff that it represents the sort of marksmanship expected of everyone. Is it? Let me tell you how the experts fare—the very guys who write the articles about fancy shooting.

Every year, the big arms and ammo makers put on what they call new-gun seminars. They invite the gun writers and editors, ply us with fine drink and rich food so we'll say nice things about their new guns, and take us on a fancy hunt or two. A few years back, when the use of the steel shot for waterfowl hunting in some areas first became mandatory, a gun seminar was held on the Eastern Shore of Maryland. No one was quite sure how the steel-shot loads were going to stack up against lead shot so a couple of agents from the Department of Fish and Wildlife came along to see how we experts would do on waterfowl with the new steel loads. From what the F&W agents had read about us and by us, they figured we were all deadly with shotguns and would give the steel shot a fair test. The plan called for half of us to shoot steel shot and the other half to use traditional lead shot so that a comparison could be made.

The test was a disaster. Out of some 30 hunters, only half a dozen were able to hit a duck or goose with any regularity, and only two were good enough to make any valid judgments on the relative efficiency of steel and lead shot. Remember, these were the same guys who wrote about how to hipshoot the heads off rattlers and shoot one-hole groups as far as the eye could see.

Another time—at the beginning of a big game hunt—one of our beloved gun writers had trouble zeroing his rifle. Either he didn't know how to adjust a scope or he just couldn't shoot well enough to hit the target. He was still hard at it when the beautiful Canadian sunset turned from red to purple to black.

Never let it be said that I am critical of our honored gun experts. The only reason I recount these cherished memories is to illustrate the fact that very few gun owners are good marksmen. Once it is realized that most shooters are in the same leaky boat, it may be easier to accept help.

Another problem is that quite a few shooters won't listen to good coaching because they sincerely believe they are good shots. Sometimes it is difficult to tell a gun owner that he is not so hot with his rifle, pistol, or shotgun because he thinks he is good. Rather than insult some-one late in the course, I believe it is better to get it over with up front.

Let's say that you qualified Expert with a rifle in the Army. Does this mean you're a good shot? Probably not. What it does indicate is that you've had sufficient experience with a rifle to make you difficult to train further. The quality of military small-arms instruction has been so poor in recent years that it is really worse than nothing. During the Vietnam war, soldiers in the field were found to be so incompetent with their weapons that special teams of instructors were sent to the front to give crash courses. Even soldiers good enough to make it to the regimental or post rifle teams are pretty lousy. Only those good enough to be ordered to the Advanced Marksmanship Units at Quantico or Fort Benning show real promise. Unless that happened to you, figure that you weren't so hot, no matter how many medals you won by shooting against the rest of the guys in your squad. In fact, military marksmanship training is so poor that vir-tually all the Army's top competitors are recruited from college varsity rifle teams.

If you have read this far, you've already had marksmanship lesson No. 1. I've been giving you a psychological test that you can grade yourself. If you got mad, you probably flunked. Anger at critical comments is a show of resistance, a sign of a tendency to defend your present level of skill. If you agreed with some of my comments, there is hope, and if you freely confessed that you didn't understand what I was talking about, there is real promise. Teaching marksman-ship is much the same as teaching any other sport. First, the coach has to break down the psychological resistance of the athlete. Then he must mold an attitude that discards bad habits on command and accepts new ideas without resistance.

YOUR NATURAL EQUIPMENT—THE EYES

How often have you heard someone say "I was a dead shot when I was younger, but now my eyes ain't what they used to be." Pathetic, isn't it? I'm not being sarcastic about deteriorating eyesight; I mean it's pathetic that the speaker thinks he could shoot well once upon a time. It's even sadder that the public's knowledge of shooting, and even our language, equates good marksmanship with ultra-keen vision. That's why we hear so much about sharp-eyed snipers or keen-eyed hunters or, worse yet, deadeyed gunslingers. What nonsense! I'm truly saddened when I think of all the visually handicapped youngsters who never tried shooting just because they had been brainwashed into thinking their eye problems ruled out success with a gun. I'm going to let you in on a secret; I'm so nearsighted that I can qualify as being legally blind, and I've been that way since I was in grade school. Yet, at last count, some 400 trophies and medals for trap and skeet, big-bore and smallbore rifle and pistol shooting line the walls of my office and den. As I've grown older, my vision has steadily grown worse, and yet I'm a better shot than ever. As far as I'm concerned, the keen-eyed sharp shooter of popular legend is just someone else I'm going to beat in a shooting match.

Anyone who has one eye in reasonably good working order, with vision corrected to normal or even somewhat subnormal by glasses or a contact lens can learn to shoot well. Among the ranks of shooting champions and consistent winners, I'd say that at least half wear corrective lenses.

The main thing is to protect the vision you have. Shooting glasses are an absolute must. If you won't wear eye protection when you shoot, then take up some other sport. Anyone who doesn't see the good sense of shooting glasses is too stupid to learn to shoot anyway.

Protective glasses aren't solely intended to protect you in case your gun blows up, which isn't at all likely, but also to guard against dozens of other hazards. Skeet shooters, in particular, are subject to all sorts of bombardment. On stations 1, 7, and 8 skeet shooters are frequently sprayed with sharp-edged chips of broken incoming birds, and several shooters have been blinded by shot pellets that bounced back after hitting clay targets. Dove hunters know how common it is to be sprayed with falling shot. Any centerfire gun—rifle, pistol, or shotgun—is subject to gas blowback because of a pierced primer and this is especially true when hot handloaded ammunition is used. Pistol shooters, in particular, have been plagued with gun blow-ups since the game of handgun silhouette shooting became popular. The extra pinch of powder some shooters feel they need in order to knock over the sheet-steel ram targets has caused lots of guns to come unglued. The lucky shooters in such cases were the ones who wore shooting glasses.

I shudder every time I think of anyone shooting a muzzleloading firearm without wearing eye protection. The spark and pan flash of a flintlock are only inches from the shooter's eye, and percussion caps frequently shatter into sharp-edged fragments. Then there are loose and leaky breech plugs, fragile drums or bolsters, and bursting barrels. I think shooting glasses should be mandatory at every black-powder shooting event. Some black-powder shooters who dress up in coonskin caps and buckskins and other period costumery say they don't like to wear shooting glasses because they are not "authentic." Carrying this reasoning to its logical conclusion, I say that shooting muzzleloaders without eye protection gives them the opportunity to be authentically blinded.

In addition to safety, shooting glasses can also provide an aid to marksmanship. Yellow-tinted glasses, for example, brighten up the sight picture and give clearer definition of the target, and this is especially helpful on dim, overcast days. Other lens tints, such as red, make green- or orange-colored clay targets appear brighter and easier to see. Gray is good on bright, sunny days, and smoky amber is good on sand or snow where there is a lot of glare and reflected light.

Most serious shooters who wear corrective lenses order prescription shooting glasses, sometimes in two or three different styles and shades. Any optician who makes prescription glasses can offer you a choice of styles in shooting glasses, or you can send your prescription to the leading makers of shooting glasses, and they'll make them for you. Here of late I've noticed that shooting glasses are in fashion, even among non-shooters, so wear your shooting glasses everywhere and be in style.

Every once in a while, I hear from a distraught father who says he's having trouble teaching his son or daughter to shoot because the child is unable to close one eye while aiming. "That's great," I tell him, "the kid will probably be a better shot for it."

I don't know how all this nonsense about shooting with one eye closed got started, but that's all it is—pure nonsense. It is actually better to shoot with both eyes open with a rifle, shotgun, or pistol. An optical phenomenon involving the way light is transferred from one eye to the other, via a nerve network called the optic chiasma, makes the target appear larger and brighter when both eyes are open. Some people can easily shoot with both eyes open, and they are lucky. Others, for various reasons, must keep one eye closed, but this is no great handicap. Some shooting champions shoot with two eyes, others with one eye. Obviously, either way works, so don't worry about it. But if keeping both eyes open comes naturally, do so by all means.

One of the most confusing eye-related shooting problems arises because of a mismatched master eye. The vast majority of human beings are right-handed or left-handed. Few are ambidextrous. A similar trait makes one eye dominant over the other. Just as we use our dominant hand to perform most tasks, our dominant or "master" eye is in overall visual command.

Fortunately, the dominant eye usually matches the dominant hand. If you are right-handed, your right eye is probably your master eye. There are exceptions, and they cause difficulty. When a right-handed shooter with a left master eye tries to aim a rifle or point a shotgun from his right shoulder, the left eye tries to do the sighting. Usually this causes double vision, and the gun appears to have two barrels. When the left eye is closed, the double-vision problem disappears, though it is usually difficult to keep the eye closed. The master eye still wants to take over. Shooters suffering from this problem, who have no shooting ambitions beyond becoming competent hunters and plinkers, can learn to close the dominant eye when shooting. Some try to learn to shoot from the other shoulder, but this may lead to other problems and usually isn't worth the trouble. Target shooters with a mismatched master eye often wear a patch over the eye so that it can be left open. This is generally easier than trying to keep it closed for long periods. Another way is to have special, custom-made crossover sights fitted on the gun.

A simple test for eye dominance is to form a circle with the forefinger and thumb, hold it at

To determine which is your dominant eye, form a circle with your thumb and forefinger and then look through it at a target or similar object. Without moving your hand, close one eye, then open it and close the other. One eye— your master eye—will maintain a centered view. The other eye will make the object seem to shift to one side.

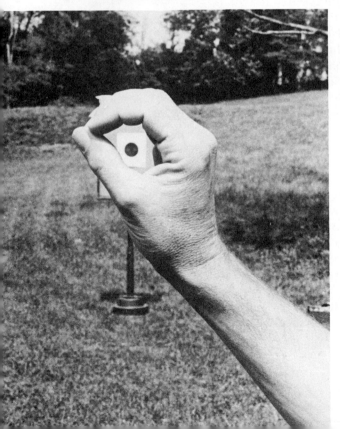

arm's length, and look at a nearby small object with both eyes open. Without moving the circle, alternately close your eyes. The eye that continues to hold the object within the circle is your master eye.

PROTECTING YOUR HEARING

The other MUST for any shooter, especially the beginner, is hearing protection. Back when I first started shooting, it seemed that almost no one used ear plugs or any other sort of ear protection. The practice was to grit your teeth and take it like a man, even if the blast of gunfire made your ears ring, your nerves jingle, and your head ache. Just about all the old-time shooters I know wear hearing aids now, or should. The simple fact of the matter is that the continued muzzle blast of a firearm will damage your hearing permanently. And if that doesn't make you want to use ear protection, perhaps this next bit of information will. You can't shoot your best without ear protection. The only exceptions to this rule are shooters who are already stone deaf.

How would you react if you had to shoot from a bench that had an electronic hot seat? Every time you pulled the trigger, you'd get a sharp shock, not enough to burn but enough to be uncomfortable. After a few shots, the continued discomfort would affect your shooting. You would start flinching and jerking the trigger because you would anticipate each shock. After a while, you would become conditioned, like Pavlov's dogs, to jump every time you pulled the trigger, even without the shock. Does this sound farfetched? It isn't. I'd say more than half of all shooters have been conditioned to jump or flinch every time they pull the trigger. The motivating force isn't electric shock; it is painful muzzle blast.

I frequently hear from shooters who say they are recoil-shy and ask for advice on buying recoil pads for their rifles or shotguns. My usual advice is that they may not need a recoil pad at all and that ear plugs or muffs could be the solution. One fellow wrote that his .243 was giving him fits and causing a serious flinching problem. He had read that the .243 had mild recoil and wanted to know why his kicked so hard. I advised him to try ear plugs. Sure 'nuff, his next letter read like one inscribed by a sinner who had been rescued from the fiery depths. His whole problem, he admitted, had really been a subconscious reaction to muzzle blast. With ear protection, the .243 doesn't kick much at all.

I see the same thing time and again in all areas of shooting. Four times out of five, when a shooter squeezes his eyes shut, hunches his shoulder, and jerks the trigger—and misses—he isn't flinching because of recoil but because of muzzle blast.

The "Mickey Mouse" muff-type ear protectors (I call 'em ear goggles) that have become popular in recent years are a blessing. Any number of makes and styles are available, and most of them are excellent. The manufacturers keep improving their designs, so the ear muffs sold today are lighter, cooler, more comfortable, and more effective than those made a decade ago.

Good muffs are more effective than ear plugs, and ear plugs are a thousand percent better than nothing at all. Folks used to stuff cotton, pencil erasers, and even cigarette filters into their ears, but real ear plugs are a lot more effective. The fancy valve-type plugs are not as good as the simple, solid type. The best are the molded variety that are custom fitted to the individual's ears. They are more expensive, of course, and must be fitted by an expert, but they are very comfortable and are almost as effective as good muffs. The funny little expanding plugs that you roll into a ball and stick in your ear are very good, too. They expand to fit the shape of your ear and are quite comfortable and effective.

If you are really smart, do as I do and wear plugs *and* muffs. The combination tames the blast of the wildest magnum. Muzzle blast, in addition to causing flinching and deafness, also has a fatiguing effect and tends to cause psychological problems, which usually take the form of irritability, inability to concentrate, and even disorientation. Hard-working gunnery instructors during World War II often collapsed into mindless jelly, sometimes weeping uncontrollably for no apparent cause. At first this was thought to be caused by the wartime pressures of training large numbers of recruits. Then someone thought of making the instructors use ear plugs and the problem vanished.

Whenever I go to the range or anyplace else where others will be shooting with me, I take a satchel full of ear muffs. I insist that everyone around me be fully protected, even if I have to furnish the protection.

Sometimes I'm asked which guns call for ear protection and which don't. As a rule, I do not wear ear plugs or muffs when I fire a .22 Rimfire *rifle* out of doors, but I'm not sure that even this is safe. I do wear muffs and plugs when shooting the hot .22 Rimfires such as the .22 Winchester Rimfire Magnum, Stingers, and Expediters outdoors, and I wear plugs and muffs when I'm shooting any .22 Rimfire pistol. I also use ear protection when firing any .22 Rimfire rifle indoors. Muffs and plugs are a must for me when firing any other caliber or type of gun.

LEARNING TO SHOOT A RIFLE

A few years ago the Army used a riflery training system called the "quick-kill" technique. It was an adaptation of the so-called "instinct-shooting" method. Using ordinary BB guns, GI's were trained to hit targets as small as cigarette butts when they were tossed into the air. It was an interesting approach to teaching marksmanship, and the needed skills could be mastered in surprisingly few sessions. Learning to bust aerial targets was also quite a morale builder. The training was, in part, a crash course in basic gun handling. The trainees were taught to handle their rifles naturally and with little conscious thought. Natural gun handling was the best thing the recruits got out of the quick-kill course.

Handling a rifle or shotgun is extremely awkward for some people. I cannot think of any sport that calls for a more totally coordinated effort of every part of the body, from the head right down to the toes. Recently I happened to be at a public shooting range where a fellow was attempting to teach an adult woman to shoot a rifle. With what I hope was sufficiently concealed disgust, I watched and listened as he explained sight alignment and trigger squeeze. When she tried to aim at the target, everything went wrong because her instructor had overlooked the first and most basic step—how to hold a rifle. It is easy to demonstrate, but it is hard to explain. Sometimes, natural gun handling is even harder to master, but once learned, it is never forgotten.

If time allows, I start a shooter by letting him or her simply mess around with a gun without ammunition. I do this for a while without coaching to let him get the feel of it, point it, snap the trigger as much as he likes, and generally get used to the idea of having a gun in his hands. It's a lot like learning to ride a horse or learning to swim. If you're not accustomed to horses or you are uneasy in the water, it's hard to make much progress. Once you get used to the idea, the rest comes pretty easily.

Confidence plays a big part in one's desire to continue. I've known any number of would-be shooters who bought a beautiful target pistol, a box of ammo, and a handful of targets and set forth to conquer the shooting world. After the first shooting session, though, confidence evaporated to such a degree that they couldn't get up enough courage to try again.

For this reason, I think beginners should start off with an easy rifle (a .22 Rimfire bolt gun is the best choice), and with an easy target at close range. Standard NRA-type paper targets with big black bull's-eyes are best because they let you see exactly where you are hitting. Shooting at such targets as tin cans is no good because they move when you hit them, and you therefore lose consciousness of the relationship between where you aim and where you hit—and also because misses cannot be accounted for since they do not punch holes in paper. With big paper targets, you can see where you miss and how far you miss the bull. It is vital that the beginner be aware of where each of his shots is hitting so that bad shots can be instantly related to a faulty hold, aim, or trigger pull. When a beginner can do this, he becomes largely self-coaching.

As soon as the target can be hit with some consistency, the range should be increased so that there is always a challenge. If shooting is too easy for too long, it stops being fun. Coaching, even self-coaching, is a psychological game.

The first phase of coaching a beginning shooter, even when it's self-coaching, is mainly a con game. Shooting looks very easy. A good shot with rifle, pistol, or shotgun appears to hit the target with practically no effort. For a beginner, however, shooting seems awkward and extremely difficult, and this causes him to be disappointed with his early performance. The coach has to be patient and offer encouragement even when it looks like the beginner will never learn. Sometimes the student can be conned into better performance simply by making him think he is a better shot than his performance indicates.

A "METHOD" COURSE

You've noticed that up to this point I have had nothing to say about the mechanics of shooting a rifle—such as positions, sight alignment, or trigger pull. This is because we're going through a "method" course of instruction. It is, I admit, a radical departure from most marksmanship-training methods, but it is highly effective. What's more, it's a lot more fun for the shooter because rather than having the elements of marksmanship drummed into his skull, he discovers them in logical sequence.

When Scott, my youngest son, was about 12, he expressed some interest in wingshooting and asked if I would teach him to shoot skeet. I was delighted, but I didn't make much fuss

In the Army's "quick-kill" training method, recruits shot at aerial targets with a BB gun. Just pointing a gun—any gun—moving it, handling it, snapping the trigger helps anyone get the feel of holding and aiming it smoothly, without awkwardness. It should become as easy—almost as instinctive—as pointing a finger.

about it. I wanted him to feel that learning to shoot a shotgun was a normal part of growing up. We'd get on with it in due time. I selected a gun for him without ceremony and didn't bother him with any details of why that particular gun was selected or overburden him with details on gauge, choke, or any of the dozen other details shooting coaches sometimes use to overwhelm their students. I made sure the stock was properly shortened but, again, without going into any detail about stock fit. The first time Scott stepped up to the No. 1 skeet station, he was totally innocent of the myriad theories of wingshooting. I simply handed him a box of shells and said, "Go at it." The only other coaching he had from me was in gun safety and skeet-field etiquette.

Naturally, he missed most of the targets in that first round of 25 shots. I told him to try again, and again. In fact, I let him go through this routine for three weeks, and he shot six or eight rounds of skeet. His scores got a little better, and I praised him for his improvement, but I made no suggestions on how he could make improvements. I did watch him very closely, noting his particular faults and making sure he wasn't getting into any really bad habits that might be hard to cure later.

The week before his fourth trip to the skeet field, I began to talk to him about the principles of wingshooting—lead, swing, and follow-through. It was like watering a thirsty flower. Every word sank in and stuck because he could relate what I told him to the experiences he had been having on the skeet field. Had I told him some things at the beginning, they would have had little meaning because they would not have related to anything in his experience. This was followed by a period of direct coaching on the finer points of wingshooting, and after a few more rounds he was hitting nearly every bird. Further experience with this coaching technique has convinced me that it is about the fastest and most pleasant way to teach shooting.

The method is especially effective for rifle instruction because such mysteries as trigger squeeze and sight alignment are not suddenly dumped on the completely innocent pupil. Instead, they are handed to the shooter when he is in a receptive frame of mind and able to see their importance for himself and register their effect on his performance. This kind of thing makes self-coaching especially productive.

THE MYTHICAL SQUEEZE

We've all heard time and time again that the proper way to activate a trigger is to squeeze, squeeze, and squeeze. Army marksmanship instructors made a fetish out of it. The idea behind squeezing the trigger is to steadily increase pressure until the rifle goes off at an undetermined instant. Why this is beneficial takes some explaining but Army instructors seldom explain the "whys" of squeezing the trigger.

The triggers of military rifles are, for the most part, designed to eliminate any possibility of good marksmanship. The long, creepy pull makes it difficult to anticipate just when the rifle will go off, so soldiers are taught to squeeze the trigger without trying to anticipate the letoff. This is thought to be better than jerking the trigger in order to make the rifle fire when the aim is at its best. When the trigger is jerked, the aim is spoiled, and a wild shot results. In other words, by squeezing, the shooter plays the odds. If he's lucky, the rifle fires when the sight picture is at its optimum, but it may fire when alignment is not so good. The total of all shots will average out better, it is assumed, than if the trigger is jerked. This system works out pretty well when it comes to mass-training Army recruits, who for the most part are more concerned about being kicked by the evil-tempered musket than they are about accurate shooting.

American shooters would be a lot better off if the squeeze technique had never been invented. Even the word itself is a cause of lasting confusion. Your trigger finger can't squeeze a trigger even if you want it to. It can hit the trigger, slap it, pull it, jerk it, push it, or press it, but it can't squeeze it. Thus millions of GI's have gotten the idea that squeezing the trigger means squeezing the grip of the stock with the whole hand with some of this squeezing effort drawing the trigger finger to the rear. It does work, but there is a much better way, so forget about squeezing. Let's say what we really mean: We want to pull, or press, the trigger. When this is done well, the trigger finger works independently of the rest of the hand, which should be busy controlling the whole rifle.

Many shooters cram their shooting finger into the trigger guard without giving any particular thought to where it lands on the trigger. The trigger is sometimes pulled with the tip of the finger, sometimes with the second joint, and sometimes with any place in between. This results in poor trigger control. If the finger is not positioned uniformly from shot to shot, the feel of the trigger and the way the shots are touched off will likewise vary.

When you watch a skilled competitive rifle, pistol, or shotgun shooter in action you are particularly impressed by the care with which he places his hand around the grip and positions his finger on the trigger. The exact way the finger is positioned may vary from shooter to shooter, but great competitors never stray from their individual styles.

Probably the most widely favored finger position, and the one I personally favor, is to center the trigger on the pad between the tip of the finger and the first joint. Some prefer to place the trigger in the crease of the first joint and others use the pad between the first and second joint. The latter position is not so widely used as the first two.

The advantage of pulling with the crease of the first joint is said to lie in the relatively thin and sensitive skin there. This greater sensitivity is said to provide a delicate touch and finer trigger control. This position is favored by many shotgunners.

I favor the center of the pad before the first joint because it offers more than one advantage. It is, from birth, our preferred touch sensor. When we want to feel the texture of any small surface, we do so with the tip of the index finger. It is the part of the finger most conditioned for jobs requiring delicate feel and control. It can detect variations of pressure in fractions of an ounce.

A second consideration has to do with the anatomy of the hand and is best demonstrated by making a soft fist with trigger finger extended. Now crook the finger until the pad between the tip and first joint is at right angles to a line formed by your forearm. This more or less duplicates the posture of your hand and arms when you grip a gun. By flexing the trigger finger, as if you were actually pulling a trigger, you will note that the first pad moves most nearly straight to the rear in line with the forearm. The pressure is directed more or less straight to the rear. If the second pad or the joint itself is used or the trigger is positioned even farther back on the finger, there is an increased tendency to push the trigger sideways, which can disturb the shooter's aim. This little demonstration also clearly shows that the physical operation of pulling a trigger is not a pull at all. Rather, we *push* it to the rear.

The third major advantage of using the first pad is that it causes the finger to crook to the side and out of contact with the stock. If the trigger finger touches any part of the gun or stock, it tends to disturb the aim just as the trigger is being pulled and some of the effort directed toward pushing the trigger to the rear is lost where the finger presses against the stock.

With practice and training, the trigger finger works unconsciously, as if it were electronically connected to the eye and activated when the sight picture is perfected. The last thing an

The first of these photos shows how your finger should be positioned for a good trigger squeeze. The first joint of the finger is bent to form a right angle with the hand and arm so that a contracting motion will pull the trigger directly to the rear. The second view, from underneath the rifle, shows that the finger touches neither stock nor trigger guard. For a straight rearward motion, it's best to press the trigger with the ball of the finger, not the crease of the joint.

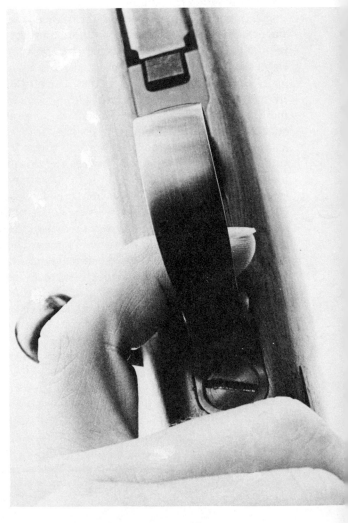

accomplished marksman wants is for the rifle to surprise him when it goes off as preached by the "squeeze" school of instruction. Top marksmen, be they hunters, varmint potters, or target shooters, want absolute control over the exact instant when the shot is fired. This is why gun designers have gone to such extraordinary lengths in recent years to produce precise, fast-acting triggers.

DRY FIRING

All really good shots, especially target shooters, spend hours upon hours simply dry firing, or snapping the firing pin on an empty chamber. This is possibly the single most instructive form of practice available to beginners and experts alike. It is certainly the best type of self-instruction.

The procedure is simply to align the peep, scope, or open sights on the target, aim as carefully as if you were firing live ammo, and pull the trigger with equal care. The "target" can be a speck on your living room wall. If you jerk the trigger, or have any sort of sympathetic muscle reaction, the movement is very apparent because there is no recoil. The reason this is often more effective practice than firing live ammo, especially for beginners, is because the recoil of a rifle, even the slight barrel bounce of a .22 Rimfire, tends to mask movement caused by jerking the trigger. Dry firing makes such faults easy to detect, analyze, and correct. With practice, you even learn to call the shot so that you can predict with great accuracy where the bullet would have hit.

No two triggers have exactly the same feel and that's true of identical trigger mechanisms installed in identical rifles. Dry firing helps you to get used to the trigger on your rifle, and you learn to anticipate exactly when it will fire. This is especially important when shooting at game, which is usually done from the standing or sitting positions or with an unsteady improvised rest. When the sights are wobbling all over the target you should be able to choose the exact split second when you send the bullet on its way.

Don't worry about dry firing harming your gun. With some old pistols and shotguns, especially those with firing pins integral (one piece) with the hammers, the firing pins are inclined to break or shatter, but almost all modern rifles and pistols can be dry fired till doomsday with no harm done.

FOLLOW-THROUGH

A frequently overlooked phase of firing a shot is follow-through. Many shooters aim long and carefully, holding their breath until tears come, pull the trigger, and instantly relax their hold on the rifle. This lack of follow-through should not, it seems, affect the shot. After all, the bullet is already on its way, or is it? Actually, the muscular effort required to look away from the sights or relax one's grip on the rifle is set in motion before the shot is fired or while the bullet is still in the barrel, and it definitely can cause a miss. A poor follow-through is therefore a signal to the shooter or coach that the concentration of delivering the shot was interrupted, albeit subconsciously.

Good follow-through with a rifle is a nothing. That's right—a nothing—it is a complete non-reaction to the shot, a continuance of holding the rifle still—or, in the case of a moving target, continuing to keep the gun moving. When you blink your eye or hunch your shoulder in anticipation of the recoil or muzzle blast, your follow-through is erased. Good smallbore target shooters have a finely developed follow-through. In this kind of shooting, the .22 rifleman can see his bullet in flight, especially when he is using telescopic sights. When the bullet in flight is not seen, it is usually a tip-off that the shooter is committing some sort of procedural error and needs to go back to the basics. Here again, dry firing is the quickest way to a diagnosis and cure. Quite often, the sickness turns out to be inadequate follow-through.

AIMING WITH OPEN SIGHTS

Aiming a rifle is a catchall phrase, widely used to describe just about every phase of firing a shot. That's why we say a fellow "had a bad aim" when he misses a shot. When considered by itself, though, aiming a rifle is one of the easiest elements of firing a gun. It just seems complicated because it is the only part of getting off a shot we are consciously involved with. Since we see the aim, we tend to give it more attention than, say, holding the rifle steady and pressing the trigger. When the sights bob about on the target, it's not because we have a bad aim. It happens because our muscles won't hold the rifle steady.

How we go about aiming a rifle depends on the sights. Since most rifles come equipped with open sights, let's discuss this type first. The front sight may be a round bead, mounted on a slender support and colored gold, white, red, or orange. Or the sight may have a simple, post-shaped cross-section. There are several other front-sight configurations, but let's keep the present discussion simple.

The rear sight is a blade, mounted across the barrel so that it is square to the shooter's eye. The top surface of this blade is cut with a notch that is either square or shaped more or less like a U or a V. If the front and rear sights are properly matched, the front bead or post will appear to fit quite comfortably inside the rear notch when the rifle is brought to the shoulder and the sights aligned. The fit should not be exact. There should be a little space or light showing on both sides when the front sight is centered in the rear sight. The amount of light seen cannot be prescribed, but it should be wide enough to make comparison easy. If the light band is too wide, it is difficult to judge the comparative widths, left and right, and this makes it harder to tell when the front sight is exactly centered in the rear notch. Of course, if the sight is properly centered, the widths should be equal.

The importance of centering the front bead or post in the rear notch, known as slight alignment, can best be illustrated by a bit of easy mathematics. Let's say the rear notch is one-tenth of an inch wide, expressed as a decimal in hundred-thousandths of an inch (.100). The front bead fills half, or fifty-thousandths (.050) of the notch, leaving a total light gap of .050. This, of course, is divided in two on either side of the bead or post if the sights are exactly aligned.

Let's say the front sight is not perfectly centered, and there is a .010-inch light gap on one side of the bead and .040-inch on the other side, an error of .015.

Now, to determine how much of an error this much misalignment will cause, divide the shooting distance by the sight radius (the distance between the sights), and multiply this by the amount of error. Say your rifle has a sight radius of 15 inches, and you are shooting at 100 yards. Dividing 100 yards (3,600 inches) by 15 inches, we find that the sight radius will go into it 240 times. Then multiplying 240 times the alignment error of .015, we see that the bullet will hit 3.6 inches wide of the mark.

No one makes such calculations every time he fires a shot, but understanding these relationships will make you a more competent and effective marksman. Fortunately, we usually don't have to worry about sighting errors of .015 or even .005 because the human eye is a marvelously accurate micrometer, capable of discerning alignment errors of only one or two-thousandths of an inch.

Naturally, the sights must be aligned vertically as well as horizontally or the shot will strike high or low. The vertical alignment may be somewhat more difficult because there are no light gaps above and below to compare. One common method is to nestle the round bead in the bottom of the U- or V-shaped notch. Another is to align the top surfaces of the front and rear sights. This latter technique is preferred when a square post or patridge-style front sight is used with a square-notch rear sight. The main thing is always to use the same technique.

In poor light, such as daybreak or dusk, there is a tendency to shoot high. This is because the front sight is harder to see and shooters unconsciously hold it somewhat higher than usual, in respect to the rear sight, so that it is easier to see.

With the sights properly aligned, the next element of aiming is aligning the sights on the target. Most shooters prefer to put a bead front sight on the target exactly where they want the bullet to hit. This works satisfactorily when the target is close or large, but if it is small or distant, the bead not only covers the spot where you want the bullet to hit, it covers a great deal of the surrounding area as well. If you are shooting at a groundhog 200 yards away, a one-sixteenth-inch bead will obscure the entire target.

This can be avoided by holding the bead just under the spot where you want to hit. This is known as the 6-o'clock hold. Naturally, the sights must be properly adjusted to compensate for different types of sight pictures. Since patridge (square post) sights form such a large bulk in the sight picture, they are almost always used with a 6-o'clock hold.

The alignment of the front and rear sights on the target is called the sight picture. Illustrations of sight pictures we have all seen show the front and rear sights neatly aligned and perfectly centered on the target. In actual practice, it never looks so neat because the sights and the target never appear so sharp and clear as they do on the printed page. The sad truth is that our eyes can't focus at three distances at once. Young eyes are flexible and can shift focus from one distance to another so rapidly that both the sights and the target all *seem* sharply in focus at once. As we grow older, this ability to shift focus is rapidly diminished, causing the blurring of the sights or the target. This has a disconcerting effect on the shooter and is the reason older shooters say, "My eyes ain't what they used to be."

It isn't much of a problem if you follow one simple, all-important rule: *focus only on the front sight!* If you concentrate on the front sight, you will be able to deliver a well-aimed shot

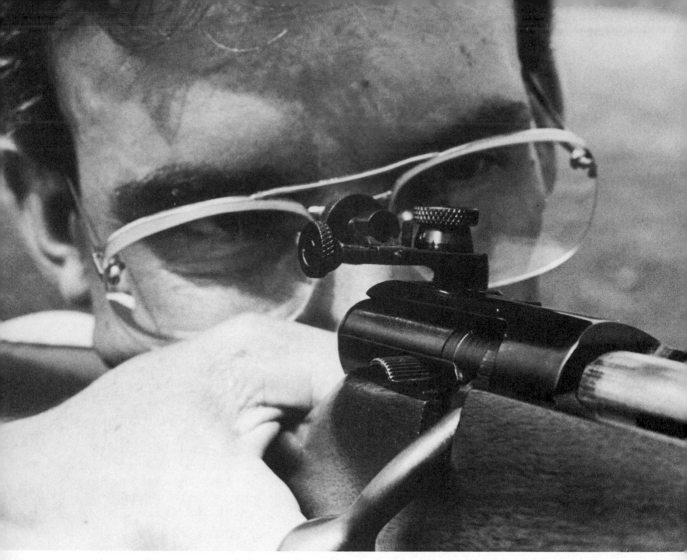

Shooters who are accustomed to open sights tend to use an aperture incorrectly. You must peep through a peep sight—getting your eye close and looking through rather than at it.

even when the rear sight and the target are blurred. The natural tendency, however, is to focus on the target, and that makes it impossible to see either of the sights well. Of course if you can't see either the front or rear sight, there is no way you can get them aligned.

AIMING WITH PEEP SIGHTS

The next step up the sighting scale is the aperture rear sight, known to target shooters simply as "iron sights" (as opposed to scope sights), and to most of us as "peep" sights because we peep through a little hole at the back. These sights, in the right combination, are truly wonderful

472   •

devices, allowing a precision of aim that comes close to that of telescopic sights. Target shooters, using otherwise identical rifles and shooting at the same targets at the same ranges, will score about the same with peep sights as with scopes.

Inexperienced shooters tend to look at—not through—an aperture rear sight. When you do that, about all you can see is the round face of the rear sight and that makes aiming difficult and tedious.

But when you get your eye up close to the aperture and look through the hole, you have a wide field of view and a clear look at the target. The advantages are threefold. First, the sights are brought into alignment almost automatically simply by looking through the rear sight at the front bead. Second, the target is not obscured or partially covered by the rear sight. Third, since alignment is automatic with peep sights, they make aiming faster. This is especially advantageous for shots at moving game. A simple peep rear sight combined with a bead front, properly adjusted, is light in weight, tough, and very efficient. In addition, most makes and models, even the simplest, least-expensive peeps, have convenient, built-in adjustments that permit the rifle to be accurately zeroed. (A more extensive description of different aperture sights is found in the chapter on sighting equipment).

Sadly, not many shooters have learned to use peep sights or are even aware of their advantages. As a result, these sights are not as widely used on hunting rifles as they were back in the 1930's. Most hunters who might have used peep sights now use scopes.

A sophisticated combination of sights is a peep rear and a globe or circular front sight. The globe is a simple ring or tube, available in different sizes, which surrounds the target. This kind of sight is almost universally used by target shooters because the round bull's-eye can be precisely centered in the circular globe front sight and then the front sight is centered in the circular rear sight. They are not particularly suitable for hunting, however, because it is difficult to center an irregularly shaped target inside the globe front sight. Also, the rather complicated front sight structure tends to obscure much of the area around any target, sometimes making it difficult to find the target in the sights.

So far we've had a pretty good course in two basic elements of marksmanship, pulling the trigger and aligning the sights. There is still a lot of ground to cover before you're a world-class marksman, but before going any further let's deal with a few difficulties before they have a chance to cause trouble.

CANTING

One problem is tilting, or canting, the rifle. All of us tend to do this to some degree, and it can lead to faulty shot placement, even when the sights appear to be perfectly aligned. This is because the line of sight and the bullet's path are on two different planes. When the rifle is truly vertical with the bore directly below the sights, the line of sight and the flight of the bullet are in vertical alignment or, expressed another way, on the same vertical plane. They are, however, on different horizontal planes, a complication made even more complex by the curving flight of the bullet. But by and large, we successfully deal with this by setting our sights so that we are actually pointing the bore slightly upward to compensate for the bullet's drop. When a rifle is canted to either side, the sights and bullet are not on the same vertical plane, and this causes the bullet to hit to one side of the target. What's more, the bullet doesn't just hit off center by a distance equal to the amount of cant. The problem becomes a matter of three-dimensional geometry in which the error of bullet impact may be several times the degree of cant. Right from the beginning, make a conscious effort to determine that the rifle is held as nearly vertical as you can manage. The crosswires in a telescopic sight are a considerable aid in judging if a rifle is held vertically, provided that the scope itself is properly mounted.

AIMING WITH THE TELESCOPIC SIGHT

I always choke and sputter when I hear someone say that telescopic sights are unsporting because they make it impossible to miss. True, they make up for some visual problems, but in no way do they make a rifle steadier or the trigger easier to pull. In fact, scopes introduce certain problems of their own. That's why I prefer that beginners start out using simple open sights. When shooting with them has been mastered to the point that holding, aiming, and pulling the trigger are second nature, then the shooter is ready to deal with the complexities of scope sights.

One of the problems with telescopic sights is the somewhat restricted field of view. This makes it difficult to find the target with the scope, especially when a beginner is having trouble enough trying to manage a rather shaky and awkward-feeling rifle. The problem is compounded by the rather critical eye placement needed to use a scope properly. When the eye is not positioned correctly, a common problem among beginners, the sight "blacks out," and it seems impossible to see through it. At times this becomes frustrating and can have a discouraging effect. So telescopic sights are best used only after the shooter gains some experience with open sights.

Telescopic sights magnify the target so that it is easier to see, and they put the target and aiming element on the same optical plane, so that both are seen very clearly in constant focus. Shooters who may have had difficulty in seeing a front and rear sight plus the target are able to aim as precisely as anyone when they graduate to a scope.

The beginner may, however, find the magnification feature something of a handicap because any amount of tremor in his hold is also magnified. This may create a tendency to jerk the trigger when the crosshairs are on or near the target. The answer to this problem is a steadier hold, and most shooters soon learn how to achieve it.

SHOOTING POSITIONS

During a shooter's career, especially if he is a hunter, he will find it necessary to fire from all sorts of positions. Some positions are extremely steady—for instance, sitting at a benchrest with the rifle supported by sandbags—but most positions will be much shakier.

The least steady position of all is the standing, or offhand, position followed, in order, by the kneeling, sitting, and prone positions. Any of these positions becomes more stable if the rifle can be steadied on or against a firm support such as a rock, limb, or log (padded in some manner, even if only by the left hand, to prevent bounce), but one can't always count on having such help available. When I take a beginner out for the first time, I insist that his first shots be

Ray Carter, who models the shooting positions shown on these pages, is internationally renowned both as a competitive rifleman and a coach of other champions. He has been a national champion and a member of several U.S. international rifle teams, and he has represented the United States in a number of World Championships, including Seoul, South Korea, in 1978 and 1979; Mexico City, 1977; Bisley, England, 1977; Finland, 1975, etc. His specialty is the difficult 300-meter free rifle. After a phenomenally successful term as coach of the top-ranked East Tennessee State University Varsity Rifle Team, he now serves as manager of the U.S. International Shooting Team and deputy administrative director of the International Shooting Development Fund.

If you're not an accomplished marksman, start at the beginning and don't make things hard for yourself. First practice shooting prone with the rifle rested over a solid but padded support—with your forward hand between the stock and the support. This eases the mastery of sight alignment and trigger pull, unhindered by the problems of muscle tremor and fatigue that occur with other shooting positions.

fired offhand. This is a psychological ploy which demonstrates that hitting a target can be difficult. Trying it puts him in a receptive frame of mind to learn easier ways to hit a target.

PRONE

The easiest shooting position for a beginner is prone with the forearm of the rifle resting on a semi-firm rest such as a small padded long, a sandbag or two, or even a tightly rolled blanket. If the support is very soft, such as a rolled-up, down-filled sleeping bag, the rifle will bounce too much and be hard to control. Do not use a rifle sling at first.

The elbows can be protected by a padded mat or a blanket doubled four or five times. When I was learning to shoot, it was "part of the game" to suffer on hard or gravelly ground at the firing line, but learning to shoot is a lot easier and more enjoyable if you are comfortable.

With the forward half of the rifle firmly supported, the shooter needs only to concentrate on holding the buttstock against his shoulder, aligning the sights on the target, and pressing the trigger. This is a fairly easy way to hit a target, even for beginners. After the shock and disappointment of a few shots fired offhand, the ease and success of shooting prone with a rest is pleasantly satisfying. I think that even experienced shooters who are giving themselves a refresher course in marksmanship would do well to go back to this basic position for a few shots. Since holding error is almost completely eliminated, any problems with sight alignment or trigger control are quickly revealed.

The best range for the beginning shooter is about 50 feet, and the standard 50-foot NRA target is plenty big enough to shoot at, even with open sights. No matter how much fun you are having, don't shoot too much. About 30 rounds is tops; more than 50 is way too much. Shooting is more physically and mentally demanding than most people realize. Beginners tend to become fatigued sooner than they realize, a condition that shows up in less-than-exact sight pictures and sloppy trigger control. This results in loss of accuracy and has a discouraging effect. I think the best time to stop is just when the shooter is showing some progress, say after making three or four bull's-eye hits in a row. This keeps him at a psychological peak and eager for the next lesson. This is no less important for those who are coaching themselves.

How long the forearm-rest/prone-position phase of instruction needs to be continued depends, of course, on the student's progress, but three to five sessions are usually necessary. I think it is a good idea to continue this part of the course until the student plunks his bullet into the target with a high degree of consistency. When he is able to hit the bull with relative ease, he will also be able to judge for himself when the sights need adjustment, and he should be able to zero his rifle as needed. This skill will become increasingly important as progress continues.

When the student (he's no longer a beginner) has mastered shooting prone from a rest, he's ready to try supporting the entire rifle by himself. This should be done from the prone position, firing at the same targets as before without a sling. The student does everything as before, except now he holds the forearm up too. Firing prone without a sling is not at all steady, even for experienced shooters, and the student will probably express some surprise at his difficulty in holding the rifle. In fact, the position is so difficult for most shooters that they may find themselves developing a tendency to jerk the trigger as the sights lurch across the target. Actually, there is seldom a good reason to fire from the prone position without a rest of some sort or

After considerable practice with a shooting rest, try it without a support or sling — though still from the prone position. The resulting waver will make anyone receptive to the benefits of using a sling.

without the aid of a sling. The purpose of the short lesson in shooting prone unaided is, again, a ploy that will demonstrate the value of a sling in a convincing manner. I definitely recommend this training procedure for rifle students who are teaching themselves to be crack shots.

THE SLING

When a shooter learns to use a sling speedily and efficiently, he has made a quantum jump toward becoming a truly expert marksman and game shot. Target shooters, who plunk their shots inside a six-inch circle at 600 yards or inside three inches, rapid-fire, from the sitting position at 200 yards are able to do so because they have mastered the use of a sling.

To shoot with the two-piece Whelen sling, give the sling a half-turn to the left (assuming you're right-handed) and thrust your left arm through the loop. Position the loop high on the arm, above the biceps, and secure it with the keepers. Then get into the prone position with your forward arm out and under, so that the sling forms a supportive triangle.

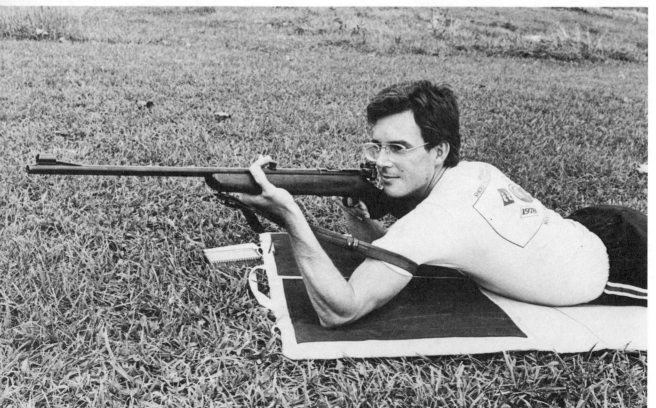

The first picture shows too loose a sling; the muzzle drops and the shooter loses support. The second shows the sling too tight, cramping the shooter and lifting the muzzle. The third shows it properly adjusted. With the sling doing the work, the shooter can relax and the rifle will stay pretty much in position even if he just rests it in the palm of his forward hand and drops the other hand.

For inexperienced shooters, I like the old-fashioned two-piece Whelen, or Army-type, sling because it is fully adjustable for all arm lengths. As a rifleman becomes more proficient at improvising a sling-supported position, he can make do with a simple one-piece strap-type sling.

To the beginner, a two-piece sling can look as complicated as a spider web. So, for early practice sessions, I remove the lower part—the length of leather strap that goes through the butt swivel. This makes the bracing portion much easier to adjust and use. A tight sling looped around the upper arm can get mighty uncomfortable after a few minutes. It constricts blood vessels and causes the arm and hand to go numb. This is one reason why target shooters wear those thickly padded shooting coats. The ordinary shooter is not likely to have a fancy shooting coat, but he can avoid discomfort by wearing a sweatshirt or two, or just padding the upper arm with a small towel. In any event, discomfort can be avoided by taking a break every five minutes or so.

This is a good prone position. The right arm adds some support, but the rifle is not tightly gripped because the right hand's primary function is to pull the trigger, not support the rifle. A poor position tends to pull the sights off target. With a good position, they remain on target without effort.

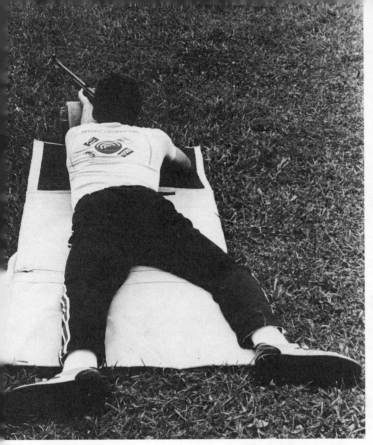

Regardless of what your grandfather may have learned in the Army, the legs must be comfortably positioned for accurate prone shooting — and comfort depends on individual build. Most shooters do well with the legs moderately spread and the toes turned out, as shown in one of these pictures. Many target shooters favor the "Estonian position"— shown in the other picture — with the right leg drawn up to shift the torso weight, lightening pressure on lungs and heart. Try both styles and suit yourself.

The reason a sling is so effective in helping you to hold a rifle steady is that it forms the third side of a bracing triangle. The other two sides are your forearm and your upper arm. The elbow is the pivot point at the bottom. In the illustrations, you'll see that when the sling is properly adjusted, the rifle is automatically hoisted to eye level and the butt is held on the shoulder with absolutely no muscular effort. In fact, the right hand does not even need to grip the stock in order to hold the rifle in position. This leaves the right hand free to operate the rifle's action, feed cartridges into the magazine, and make sight adjustments. New shooters have a tendency to grip the stock tightly at the fore-end, but this is not necessary with a properly used sling. Try to relax as much as possible.

When you are in a good prone position, the rifle will have a natural point of aim, with or without a sling. This natural direction can be determined simply by closing your eyes and relaxing the muscular tension in your arms, shoulders, and neck to let the rifle move at will. When you open your eyes, the direction of the rifle is the natural point. If it is not pointing directly at the target, don't try to muscle it around to where you want it. Instead, shift your whole body around until the rifle is naturally pointed at the target. In this way, you learn to take up the correct position in relation to the target when you first lie down.

As you get used to the sling, you'll want to experiment with different body positions that feel most comfortable to you personally. Some shooters lie with their bodies almost parallel to the rifle; others align themselves at about a 45° angle to the rifle. Some keep their legs together, and others spread them wide, still others draw up the right knee. You'll also notice that by adjusting the sling tension and shifting your hand forward or rearward, you can change the elevation of the rifle. Most target shooters fire from an extremely low position, with the butt almost touching the ground. This gives them a very low center of gravity. Military training, on the other hand, teaches a high prone position. I think the high position is best for plinking and

Note that if you lie prone so that your body is pointed directly toward the target, your bone structure and musculature will make you point the rifle off to the left (again assuming you're a right-handed shooter). Instead, your body should be lying at about a 45° angle to the target, which will make you point the rifle naturally toward where you're aiming. Experiment a bit with the angle to get it right for your own build. Then make vertical corrections by shifting the rifle's buttplate up or down against your shoulder, not by hunching your shoulder or raising the forward arm.

hunting because it puts the line of fire above grass, weeds, and other low obstructions. I have seen too many good shots using very different variations of the prone position to believe that one is better than another. The main thing is to practice until getting into the position becomes second nature and you do it consistently.

BREATH CONTROL

Take lots of time with the prone position. Certain fundamentals of shooting will be learned here that carry over to all other positions. Trigger control, for example, will be mastered in the prone position, as will the fine points of sighting and breath control. Most basic courses in marksmanship make a big thing out of taking a big breath, letting half of it out, and then holding your breath while you aim and fire. I think that proper breathing, like trigger control and sight alignment, should be learned in separate stages. Most usually, good breath control comes automatically as the shooter gains experience. In fact, proper breathing when performing an exacting task is a conditioned reflex in most people, even though they may never fire a gun. Watch your grandmother threading a needle. Just at the critical moment when the thread nears the eye of the needle, her breathing slows and comes to a stop. The same is true when we prepare to hit a baseball or swing a golf club. When we take a deep breath after completing a demanding task it is because we have been unconsciously holding our breath. We do exactly the same thing naturally when we perfect a sight picture and press the trigger.

The only serious breathing problem a shooter is likely to encounter is an occasional tendency to hold one's breath too long while trying to perfect the hold. When we do this, the heart lacks needed oxygen and beats harder and faster in order to increase the flow of blood. The diminished supply of oxygen to the eyes also creates temporary visual problems such as blurring and seeing spots. If you can't get the shot off within a maximum of eight seconds, relax for a few seconds, take a new breath, and start all over.

PRONE WITH SCOPE

When you feel you have pretty well mastered the prone position with a sling, you might try switching from open sights to a scope. If you use a scope of 4X magnification or higher, the first thing you'll notice when you get into position is that you aren't holding the rifle as steady as it appeared with open sights. Actually you are holding as steady as ever, but the scope magnifies tremors which were not noticeable with open sights. Some shooters say they can't use high-magnification scopes because it makes them shake too much, but that is a mistake. The trembling is the same.

When you are in a solid position, the most noticeable tremor is the rhythmic bounce caused by heartbeat. This can sometimes be reduced by altering your position somewhat or possibly by loosening the sling. When your position and sling are right, you should be able to

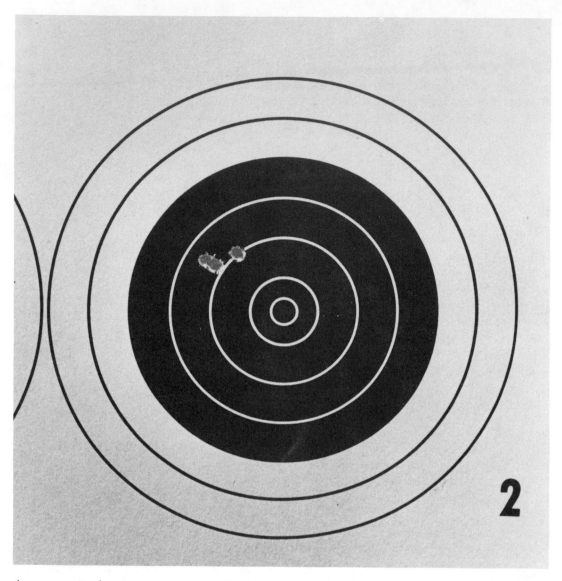

A common mistake is to interpret a group like this as meaning that the shooting position or trigger control is wrong — pulling the shots up and to one side. Actually, it's a fine, tight group and the shooting obviously has been good. The problem is not with position or technique but indicates only a need to adjust the sights.

keep the movement of the crosshairs within a quarter-inch circle at 50 feet. To give you something to strive for, bear in mind that an accomplished target shooter keeps the crosshairs inside half an inch or an even smaller circle at 100 yards. The tremor you see with a scope makes the need for proper trigger control even more obvious. With the sight bouncing all over the target there is a strong urge to jerk the trigger when the crosshairs are on the bull's-eye. This usually results in a bad shot. If your trigger finger is well trained, you'll soon be able to get the shot off between heartbeats.

THE SITTING POSITION

Learning to shoot sitting is only a variation of prone. Instead of resting the elbows on the ground, the upper arms are propped on the knees. The use of the sling, and the body angle, are pretty much identical.

The value of developing and practicing a stable sitting position cannot be overstated. It is an especially useful position for hunters because it is much more stable than offhand or kneeling, it can be quickly and easily assumed, and can be used on terrain where prone would be impractical or impossible. When combined with an impromptu rest, such as a rock or tree trunk, it is so steady that it is easily used to zap a woodchuck at 300 yards. More than any other position, it is the hunter's best bet for shots at over 100 yards.

Many target shooters cross their legs Indian style in the sitting position and brace their elbows in the pockets formed on the inside of the bent knee. This is an extremely steady position, almost as good as prone, but it is somewhat difficult if you are stiff of joint. There is a more serviceable all-round sitting style. Spread the thighs 60° to 90° and dig the heels into the ground support. Then lean forward until the upper arms lap over the knees somewhat and rest solidly on the shins just below the knee. This is a fairly stable shooting platform, even without a sling, but is much steadier with a snug sling.

The trick to getting into a good sitting position is positioning yourself at about a 45° angle to the target. If you face the target too squarely, the position is awkward, and you only have limited movement. If you sit at a good angle to the target, you can pivot at the waist quite freely. This movement is important when shooting at moving game.

THE KNEELING POSITION

The kneeling position is one of the required shooting positions in collegiate, NRA, and Olympic rifle competition. If it were not required, very few target shooters would bother to master this difficult position. Hunters and plinkers often drop into an impromptu kneeling position for shots that are too long or too difficult to try offhand. They do not realize that not much is gained in the way of rifle control and increased steadiness. In the kneeling position you have a high center of gravity. The position places bone (forearm) on top of bone (knee) with relatively little lateral bracing. Also, the shooter usually sits on his heel with his toes and ankle bent in an unnatural position. A few seconds of this torture is enough to make anyone uncomfortable and impatient.

From the hunting standpoint, the kneeling position has only a couple of advantages. It is a second or so faster to assume than the sitting position, and it is about a foot higher than sitting, which provides additional clearance over brush, grass and other obstructions.

When you first try the kneeling position, you'll probably notice that you can accurately align the sights on the target only briefly before you start to sway from side to side. This is a result of the absence of side support. It can be somewhat offset by turning the forward foot at a sharp angle to the direction of the shot. This provides a little lateral support. Also, don't place the point of the elbow directly on the ball of the knee. This is like trying to balance one ball on

The shooter's tilted head in the photo above is a giveaway. He has his legs and feet pointing directly toward the target, forcing him into an unnatural position and pulling the rifle sideward. As with the prone position, he should turn himself to put his body and legs at about a 45° angle to the target. A line drawn straight out from the rifle would then more or less cross his left ankle or shin, as you can see from the other photo.

A variation of the usual sit is the cross-legged position. Many target shooters favor this position as it adds stability. Every part of the body is braced, and the rifle is firmly supported. However, getting into this position is relatively slow and therefore inappropriate in most hunting situations.

top of another. Just above the elbow, there is a rather flat, almost concave area that forms a more stable support when placed over the knee.

Another aid to steadiness, if you have enough flex in your foot and ankle, is to turn the under foot sideways so the outside is flat on the ground and then sit on your instep. If you are wearing hunting boots your weight will rest mainly on the rigid sole and heel of the boot. This eliminates the wobbles inherent in trying to sit on the heel of a painfully bent upright foot.

Naturally, a sling looped under the arm, hunting-style, is of considerable aid to steadiness in the kneeling position. Experiment and you'll find that when kneeling, the sling is most effective when used low, closer to the elbow and below the bicep.

Unless you aspire to be an Olympic medalist, I think the time spent learning to shoot well from the kneeling position is better spent practicing offhand shooting. You should, however, be well enough acquainted with the position so that you can use it effectively if the occasion arises. And who knows, it may be your cup of tea.

A kneel puts the rifle higher than a sit, and a hunter may use it to shoot in brush or tall grass. However, it's more cramped and less steady. Shown here is a more or less typical kneeling position. The shooter would be better off with a sling, which has been removed to give an unimpeded view of the position.

The kneel is steadied somewhat if you lean forward slightly and lap the back of your upper arm over your knee. Resting an elbow directly on a knee creates a wobble. This position is also improved if you turn your forward foot inward. You'll find that the foot then forms a better lateral brace.

A less traditional but more stable kneeling position is almost a sit—with the rear foot turned on its side so that you can press your rump down on it, sitting on that foot rather than on your heel. Try this and you'll find it also lets you get your forward arm more solidly over your forward knee.

HOW TO HIT OFFHAND

Every shooting position we have discussed so far, every technique you have mastered is, in the final analysis, only a means of avoiding the frustrations of trying to hit a target from the off-hand (standing) position.

    The obvious problem with shooting from the standing position is that the rifle shakes all over the target, making it exceedingly difficult to get the bullet to go where you wish. The difficulty is brought on by natural and largely unavoidable muscle tremor. Even without a rifle in your hands, it is impossible to stand perfectly still.

For offhand shooting, you stand almost sideways to the target. If the front of your body is toward the target, you'll have to bend your torso, arms, and head unnaturally. The sideward stance is better balanced, far more relaxed, and puts the rifle closer to the body's center of gravity. With the legs spread moderately and comfortably, a line drawn across the toes of both feet would — and should — point almost directly at the target.

A popular target-shooting variation of the traditional offhand position has the shooter supporting the rifle with the extended fingers and thumb of his forward hand. This lets you rest your upper arm and elbow against your torso and the top of your hip. Note that you must lean back a little from the waist. This position, favored by most silhouette shooters, creates a brace for the rifle and tends to reduce tremors and jerks.

It's worth noting that women have physical characteristics that make them better natural offhand shots than men. These include their wider hip-to-shoulder ratio (which provides a lower center of gravity), shorter legs, and longer torso length. Some of our very best rifle shots are women, but let's not say too much about it.

Beginners can make the standing position more effective by adopting a good natural position. The natural tendency is to face the target. You'll find your hold is vastly improved if you stand almost at right angles to the target with the rifle angling across your chest. This is more comfortable, and it is noticeably steadier because it brings the rifle in closer to your vertical center line of balance. Some shooters stand at such a sharp angle to the target that the underside of the stock actually rests on the top of the chest.

Target shooters use several variations of the standing position, but most of them prop the left elbow on the tip of the hip bone and support the rifle with the outstretched tips of the fingers. This is a good position for shooting at a stationary target because the rifle is more or less propped on a continuous line of bones from the left foot to the fingers of the left hand. Most shooters find that it is slow to assume, however, and not suitable for most hunting conditions. The target shooter wants to exercise the least possible muscular control over his rifle. He depends on a well-developed shooting posture and the rifle's mass to provide a steady hold. The hunter, on the other hand, needs control in order to keep the sights on moving game.

This control comes from a proper stance and well-developed coordination of the arms and hands. Surprisingly, perhaps, most of this control should be provided by the same hand that pulls the trigger.

Years ago, when I was going through boot camp, rifle instructors had a fetish about hiking the elbow up to an elevation about level with the top of one's fatigue cap. I can hear 'em now: "Get that elbow up, soldier, or I'll break it off!" I don't know what purpose this was supposed to serve, and I'm sure they didn't either. It was just the Army way. Fortunately, the fad has passed. Except for a few old sergeants, we seldom see anyone holding a rifle as if he is hanging from a nail through his elbow.

For an easier, more-relaxed position, hold the trigger arm with the elbow about shoulder high. The arm is horizontal. Individual shooters may want to vary this somewhat, and they should. The shape of the pistol grip and the location of the trigger has a lot to do with how the arm is held, so experiment until the arm position feels natural. In any event, don't adopt a style that cramps the wrist (as did the old Army high elbow) or the hand. That causes problems with your trigger control.

The forward hand and arm only provide secondary control. Their main function is simply to heft the rifle and keep it balanced. If you find yourself gripping the forearm with your fingers, it is usually a tip-off that you're exercising too much control with that hand. You can cure this tendency by holding the forearm only in your slightly cupped palm, but don't do this with a hard-kicking magnum.

Target shooters who compete in high-power matches fire 20 shots offhand at 200 yards with iron sights. They fire at a black bull measuring 13 inches across and having a seven-inch 10-ring. The better shots put all their bullets into the black and miss the 10-ring fewer than five times. Good metallic silhouette shooters, firing a scoped rifle offhand at 220 yards, hit the steel cutout of a small chicken seven times out of 10. The reason I mention this is to give you some idea of what is expected of a really good offhand marksman. The target shooter, however, usually holds on the target until the natural wobble reaches a low point before pressing the trigger. Hunters can seldom afford such niceties. A shot at game must very often be fast as well as deliberate and controlled. Most of the time you have to put the crosshairs or bead where you want the bullet to go and press the trigger in a single calculated instant.

The first rule is trigger control, trigger control, and trigger control. We often hear shooters say, "I can hold a rifle on the target, but I can't pull the trigger well." That's a normal symptom, best corrected by lots of dry firing. When you practice the standing position, one of the things you'll discover is that your hold is shaky only when you try to hold the rifle motionless. When the rifle is in motion but guided by your hands, the movement is smooth and fluid. Hunters who use the offhand position most effectively have usually developed a technique of guiding the crosshairs onto the target, then pausing only for an instant before pressing the trigger. With good trigger control the rifle will fire just as the crosshairs stop on the target and before they start bobbing about. Some shooters say they press the trigger as "the target goes by" but this is an invitation to disaster. The proper sequence is move-pause-fire. If for any reason the shot doesn't seem right, start all over. Don't try to dwell on the target. That will only cause the hold to deteriorate.

Quite often I see and hear of wonderfully long shots made on moving or even running

The old ultra-high-elbow position, once taught in the Army because it was supposed to add steadiness, long ago went out of date. The other photo shows a much more natural stance, with the elbow dropped sufficiently to be comfortable. Remember that muscular discomfort induces tremors. Experiment until you find an elbow height that's comfortable, keeps you steady, and permits you to control your trigger finger with no interference.

game from the offhand stance. These shots are longer, in fact, than would have been likely if the target had been standing still. In such cases, it is the smooth motion of the rifle that makes a hit possible. It's really much the same technique I have just described for shooting at stationary targets.

To the inherent difficulties of offhand shooting, add the excitement we all feel when we see game, and firing a good shot seems impossible. Under those circumstances, the trigger-control technique just described is best.

Be all that as it may, I suspect that the reason many hunters shoot and often miss from the offhand position is simply and sadly because that is the only way they know. No matter how good you are, offhand shots at game are justified only when there is no other reasonable alternative or when the target is so close that it's difficult to miss. Another term for good shooting is smart shooting—knowing how to set up a shot and making the bullet go where you need it to go.

MORE TIPS ON USING A SLING

We all know it's nice to have a sling on a rifle so it can be carried easily, but a sling's greatest benefit is that it can make the difference between hitting and missing the trophy animal of a lifetime. Many hunters forget this primary purpose when they select and adjust the slings for their rifles. This is forgivable, I suppose, because some manufacturers of slings apparently have forgotten the basic purpose of their product. The market has been overrun with all sorts of weirdly embossed, pointed, widened, puffed up, and stiffened leather goods represented as rifle slings. That they should serve to steady the rifle when shooting is ruled out by their design and decoration. Ironically, their usefulness as shooting aids tends to diminish as the price increases.

The sling we are looking for is an inch wide and made of oil-tanned leather. If the leather appears dry with a rather smooth or glossy surface on one side, it probably won't last. You can check the leather for quality by bending it sharply, smooth side up, and pinching it between your fingers. If small cracks appear in the surface and start growing wider, it won't last. When you squeeze a good oil-tanned sling the same way, a little oil comes to the surface.

A currently popular sling design features a widened area where the sling fits over the shoulder. The idea is to distribute the rifle's weight over a wider area to make it feel lighter. The concept sounds good, but if the maker of these slings ever used one for hunting, they'd realize they've been barking up the wrong tree. These slings tend to be stiff and uncomfortable because the edges cut into your shoulder. Worse, they are inclined to slide off your shoulder and allow your rifle to fall. Some of these slings (really carrying straps) have anti-skid material on the underside in order to deep them from sliding. This is the maker's way of admitting the defect he has built into his product. Worst of all, these slings are almost impossible to use when it comes to firing from a sling-supported position, even when the hasty-sling method is used.

A soft, narrow, sling conforms to the shape of the shoulder and digs in slightly inside the shoulder joint. This holds the rifle fairly well even when both hands are busy climbing or glassing. For hunting, you only need a simple strap looped around the sling swivels and secured with

This is a natural offhand position, with the feet comfortably spaced and the rifle held as effortlessly as possible. Since offhand shooting is the most difficult, it demands the greatest attention to the development of a comfortable, steady, consistent position.

lacing, hooks, or a metal stud. Once it is properly adjusted, it need never be bothered with again. For many forms of target shooting and even for informal target practice, you need the two-piece Whelen-type sling with keepers so that you can put the loop around your arm and snug it down. Most hunting situations call for the so-called hasty sling which is simply pulled tight behind the upper arm. For that, a one-piece sling is fine. When the butt of the rifle is raised to the shoulder, it acts as a lever and pulls the hasty sling tight and steadies the hold. The trick is adjusting the sling so that it will pull tight enough when you get ready to shoot. This is a simple matter of trying it out and adjusting accordingly. I usually adjust the sling so that it is about right for the sitting position. Then it will work fine for prone and fairly well for offhand. You'll discover it also makes the sling just the right length for carrying the rifle over the shoulder. Now what could be nicer?

*Carmichel demonstrates the hasty sling, a steadying tech-
nique often used in hunting. He thrusts his forward arm
between sling and rifle, then brings the hand around so that
the forward end of the sling is under that hand and pressing
against it when he cradles the stock's forearm. With his hand
against the forward sling swivel, the sling—if the length is
properly adjusted—pulls tight to help brace the rifle.*

Chapter 19

· · · · · · · · · · · · ·

THE ACCURACY GAME

· · · · · · · · · · · · · ·

Once upon a time, when the air was clean and shooters were as innocent as babes, there prevailed a notion that bullets traveled through the air with the swift honesty of holy writ. Shooters were so sure that bullets flew straight and true that they even coined an idiom for our language: "As straight as a shot."

But alas, along with the curse of original sin and the loss of innocence it was discovered that bullets do not fly with unerring straightness. In fact, it is damn near impossible to get two consecutive shots to go in precisely the same direction even with the rifle locked in a vise.

The reasons haven't all been counted yet. For every puzzle solved, 10 more spring up. Probably the single greatest roadblock on the route to ultimate accuracy has been our inability to separate fact from myth. Firearms have always been surrounded by myth. Since a bullet's flight can't be seen, shooters have dreamed up all sorts of fantasies to explain what goes on in the invisible world of high velocity.

An example of these lingering myths is the notion that "perfect" rifle cartridges are those with absolutely identical powder charges. Many reloaders, in fact, set out to handload totally accurate ammunition by the simple expedient of weighing each powder charge to exact uniformity. Sadly, there are about 10 factors that are more critical to accuracy than exact uniformity of the powder charges. So it is with many notions about accuracy.

The quest for accuracy probably began about the time gunners grew weary of shooting in the general direction of their enemies and decided it would be fun to hit a specific target. This proved to be such a chore that witchcraft or similar devilment was blamed when a bullet didn't hit where intended. Before long, guns were marked with all sorts of hex signs guaranteed to improve performance. There is even some evidence that rifling was invented to make the bullet spin so fast that the devil couldn't sit on it and cause misses. Another theory had it that the devil *likes* to spin and will lead the ball straight to the target if he's given a dizzy ride.

EARLY EFFORTS

Despite the legend of the "Kentucky" rifle, it wasn't until about the middle of the 19th century that the pursuit of accuracy really got in gear in North America. The first great target rifles were muzzleloaders, but they had certain distinctive features in common with today's target rifles. Heavy barrels were common and telescopic sights were often used, as were super-light triggers and stocks designed for precision aiming.

Accuracy buffs of that day, as now, were primarily concerned with group sizes and used a scoring system called "string measure" to determine the size of their groups. Rather than measuring the distance between the two widest shots, as is done today, measuring with a string was done either by stretching a string around pegs driven into the bullet holes or by measuring the distance to each bullet hole in a group from a central position. Either way, whoever had the shortest string won.

Target rifles of the string-measure era saw some use in the Civil War by elite marksmen who managed to pull off some astonishingly long shots, even by today's standards. There were two problems—the great weight of the rifles, which ran up to 40 pounds or so, and the slowness of loading. But then, as now, the military application of long-range sniping was mainly psychological.

The next notable step in America's accuracy game was taken with the wonderful Creedmoor rifles, named after the famed firing range at Creedmoor, Long Island, in New York State. American riflemen got involved with this type of shooting by accident.

THE CREEDMOOR MATCH

A group of Irish crack shots, armed with superbly accurate rifles made by John Rigby of Dublin, himself a team member, had pretty well wiped the floor with the best marksmen England and Scotland had to offer, and were looking around for someone else to beat. Having heard of the exploits of Hiram Berdan and his corps of sharpshooters during the Civil War, they challenged the Americans to a rifle match to be fired at 800, 900 and 1,000 yards for the "Championship of the World." The newly formed Amateur Rifle Club of New York City immediately accepted the challenge and agreed that the tournament would begin in September of 1874 and be held at Creedmoor.

There was one problem of some consequence—the Americans didn't have any rifles! The Irish challenge called for the marksmen to fire from an unsupported position, meaning that no artificial rests such as logs, sandbags, or benchrests could be used. As contemporary prints of the great challenge match show, firing was done from all sorts of strange positions, including lying on one's back with the rifle held between crossed feet.

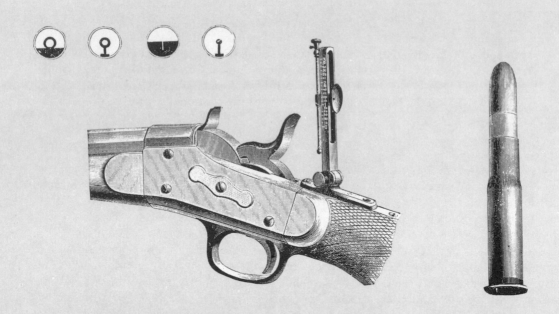

These engravings, from an 1876 issue of Harper's Weekly *and the 1877 Remington catalog, commemorate the historic Creedmoor match with depictions of the Remington-Hepburn rifle and cartridge, one of the medals, the wind-gauge sight discs, the firing line, and the peculiar positions favored for ultra-long-range marksmanship.*

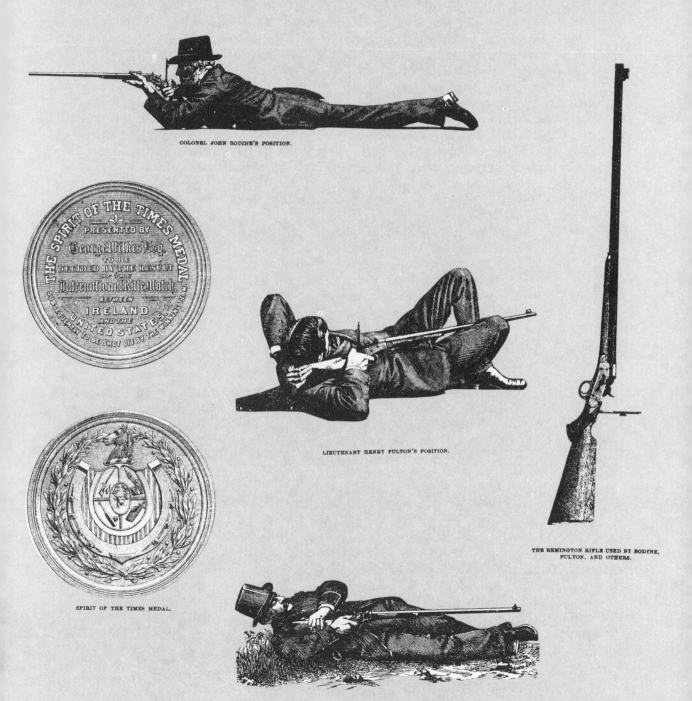

COLONEL JOHN BODINE'S POSITION.

THE SPIRIT OF THE TIMES MEDAL
PRESENTED BY
George Wilkes Esq.
TO BE
DECIDED BY THE RESULT
OF THE
International Rifle Match
BETWEEN
IRELAND
AND THE
UNITED STATES
SUBSEQUENT TO BE SHOT OFF BY THE WINNING TEAM

LIEUTENANT HENRY FULTON'S POSITION.

SPIRIT OF THE TIMES MEDAL.

THE REMINGTON RIFLE USED BY BODINE,
FULTON, AND OTHERS.

MR. G. W. YALE'S POSITION.

America's best target rifles of that era tended to be massive affairs with barrels nearly as thick as a man's wrist. They were fired from a rest, with the accent on accuracy rather than marksmanship. For the most part, these rifles were totally unsuitable for firing from an unsupported position. Another class of target rifle used by American marksmen of that day consisted of rather delicate affairs that were fired offhand at relatively short distances. These were by no means suitable for shooting at targets over half a mile away.

By contrast, the target rifles made by John Rigby for the Irish team were of moderate weight with long barrels and sights especially suited to long-range shooting and the peculiar firing positions used by the shooters. Some rear sights, for example, were mounted on the stock near the buttplate to be convenient for shooters reclining on their backs. And like all good target rifles up to that time, Rigby's guns were muzzleloaders. Even though breechloaders were widely used by then, it was universally understood that only muzzleloaders were accurate enough for serious target shooting, especially at the longer ranges. Clearly, if the Americans were to give a respectable account of themselves, they would need rifles as good as those used by the Irish, but where were they to be had?

Acting with speed and boldness, the Sharps and Remington companies offered to design and build suitable long-range target rifles in the short time allowed. Moreover, they would be *breechloaders!* From today's perspective, this seems like a perfectly logical plan, but at a time when muzzleloaders ruled the ranges it bordered on the ludicrous. It was thought that using breechloaders would give the Americans about as much hope of winning as there was of shooting a pebble to the moon with a slingshot. Hearing of the American rifles, the Irish were probably disappointed that they were not to encounter more serious competition. Well, at least they would enjoy the trip.

When the great day arrived, events took an unexpected turn. Contorting themselves into bizarre shooting positions and shoving mammoth cartridges into their breechloaders, the Americans took the 800-yard phase 326 to 317. "So be it," murmured Rigby and his team of powder-dusted Irishmen, "we'll prevail at the greater distances." And that's exactly what they did at 900 yards—by a slim two points. Clearly, the match wouldn't be over until the last shot was fired, and the crowd, one of the largest ever assembled at a sporting event, verged on hysteria. It was the World Soccer Cup, Super Bowl, Masters, and World Series all rolled into one. For weeks, a front-page story in every leading newspaper had covered events leading up to the match. The name of every team member was a household word—they were the heroes of their generation. And the shots they were about to fire at 1,000 yards would make banner headlines.

The Irish won again, by four points, but the total score of 934 to 931 gave the overall victory to America. Actually, the Irish would have won by a single point had not one of their shooters managed to fire at a wrong target. His shot centered the target but was scored a miss.

Though it would appear that a great new form of target shooting had come to America, long-range shooting didn't catch on in a big way. Then, as now, it was difficult to operate long-distance shooting ranges, especially near large cities. Even the wonderful Creedmoor rifles, as typified by the long-barreled Sharps rifles and Remington-Hepburns, enjoyed only brief popularity before being retired to the cabinets of collectors.

SCHUETZEN

By century's end, the predominant rifle-shooting games, other than military matches and informal turkey shoots, were gallery-type offhand tournaments. These were remarkable events, as notable for their social climate as for the shooting. Target shooting had long been a highly popular sport in parts of Europe, especially among the Germans, Swedes, Swiss, and Austrians. Naturally, immigrants from these countries brought their target rifles and love of shooting with them. By the late 1800's, a number of shooting clubs flourished in the Northeast and Midwest. These clubs were often formed along nationalistic lines, especially among the Germans, and a match, or *Schuetzenfest,* was something of a party attended by the whole family. There was singing, dancing, eating, and drinking as well as shooting. After each round of shots, the contestants would quaff down a flagon of beer, then totter off to load up for the next round. Naturally, as the tournament progressed scores got lower, but everyone had a good time and the winner was a hero. This status lasted until the next *Schuetzenfest,* an event that was held weekly in some areas.

The shooting was done from the standing, or offhand, position and the rifles were jewels of old-world workmanship. As might be expected, the target rifles made in the United States were mostly products of immigrant gunsmiths.

A similar but often more demanding competition was the outdoor match, usually fired at

The Schuetzen rifle was a marvel of Old World workmanship as well as late Victorian gingerbread ornamentation. It was also a very heavy piece of machinery, yet it was fired offhand and produced some targets that made heroes of the Schuetzenfest *winners.*

200 yards. Unlike the beerhall matches which were sometimes held at night on indoor ranges that made little demands on accuracy, the 200-yard matches called for the utmost in rifle and shooter performance. And thus came into being the superbly accurate Stevens, Ballard, and Winchester (to name only a few) which were essentially longer-range *Schuetzens*. The best of them sported custom barrels by Pope, Zischang, Schoyen, and other honored makers.

Since a rifle had to be accurate in order to win in this difficult form of competition, it was only natural that some riflemen became more fascinated by the pursuit of accuracy than personal marksmanship. This peculiarly American trait begot a game unto itself, and a good number of highly sophisticated riflemen contented themselves simply by firing their target rifles from a steady rest in the hopes of putting all their shots in a tight cluster. This type of shooting resulted in a degree of rifle accuracy that was not to be equaled for another half-century.

A bulwark of American target shooting, and the building of target rifles, had been the strongly nationalistic German-American shooting clubs. Since these clubs were the focal point of social life in the German-speaking communities, it was only natural that they became the center of political life as well. For a while, this was well and good, and politicians of all persuasions actively courted the German-American vote. A beer-swilling *Schuetzenfest* was a great place to make a campaign speech. But it was politics that did the *Schuetzenfest* in. As late as the beginning of World War I, before America got into the act, the gun clubs were hotbeds of political debate. But when America declared war on Germany, the gun clubs were attacked in the press and by non-German citizens. Accused of being covers for German propaganda and espionage, the clubs disbanded voluntarily or were outlawed. A colorful era of American target shooting came to a close.

BETWEEN THE WARS

The period between the two big wars was one of near extinction for target shooting in the United States. Guided by an overabundance of military influence, the National Rifle Association developed and promoted competitions for both smallbore and big-bore rifles that differed little, if at all, from purely military range exercises. The National Match Course for high-power rifles was designed for the 1903 Springfield service rifle, and even smallbore rules of that period specified a three-pound trigger pull. This was an effort to keep shooters "tuned" to the triggers of military rifles. Even the first editions of Winchester's great Model 52 smallbore target rifle (1919) and Remington's counterpart, the beautifully made Model 37 (1937), came with military-style stocks, complete with Springfield-like barrel bands.

Interestingly, while we were bogging down in our own military-type tournaments, Schuetzen shooting as we had known it in pre-World War I days not only flourished in Europe but evolved into what has become the International-style shooting featured in the Olympic games. This goes a long way toward explaining why, in 1950, we suddenly found ourselves about 20 years behind Europe, especially the Russians, in International shooting—in terms of both marksmanship and rifle development. Today we have the best shooters, but we haven't been able to overtake their lead in either smallbore rifles or smallbore ammunition accuracy.

VARMINT SHOOTING

Though between-the-wars target shooting in America represented technological doldrums that lasted over two decades, the games themselves were so entrenched that most competitions of that era continue today with little change. Those who preferred accuracy over form found themselves pretty well left out in the cold, but in time their fancies were captured by a new kind of rifle. The sport was called varmint shooting, and the targets were mainly woodchucks, but crows, prairie dogs, or Western digger squirrels also served. In fact, it didn't matter what the targets were so long as they were plentiful, legal; and hard to hit. It wasn't the target that mattered but the shot, and to this end new cartridges and rifles were developed. Typical of the strange new cartridges designed for varmint shooting were the .22 Hornet, .220 Swift, .218 Bee, and .219 Zipper. All were fast-stepping little numbers that covered ground in a hurry and were accurate enough to whiz through a buttonhole. The development of varmint cartridges and rifles is covered in an earlier chapter. What matters in this discussion is the motivation that went into their creation. It was the same love of rifle accuracy that went into the building of the Creedmoor rifles in the 1870's and the 200-yard Schuetzens of the 1890's. Here was the same impulse again in the 1920's and '30's, only this time the goal wasn't a bull's-eye but a common pest in a farmer's pasture.

The pursuit of inherent accuracy seems to be an American passion, or at least this was true until very recent times. One easily gets this impression by watching American shooters, but it becomes even more apparent if you observe the habits of shooters in other countries. Over the years my travels have led me to most European nations and to quite a few in Asia and Africa. Since I'm usually traveling on shooting or hunting business of one sort or another, I often visit the local shooting range. Only once have I seen a solid benchrest of the kind found on many U.S. ranges. The exception was in Australia, where they love American-style benchrest shooting.

Some time back, some pals of mine and I had occasion to sight-in some hunting rifles on a range near a large German city. Though the range was beautifully landscaped and equipped with all sorts of expensive target carriers and electronic scoring devices, nothing was available in the way of a benchrest, a benchrest pedestal, or even a simple sandbag. When my buddies and I explained to our German hosts the function of a benchrest and how it can be put to good use in testing the accuracy of rifles, they quickly got the idea and agreed it would be a great help. But even though our hosts were expert riflemen, it had never occurred to them to question the accuracy of their rifles as supplied by the makers—or that they *should* do so.

By contrast, an expert American rifleman can't wait to test the accuracy of a new rifle and will continue testing and improving its accuracy as long as it's in his possession. Typical of the American passion for accuracy was a fellow I knew a few years ago who decided to take up pistol shooting. Before getting into serious practice, he had a couple of handguns accurized by Jim Clark. Then he decided to work up the most accurate handload possible and spent several months tinkering with various bullets, powders, and crimping methods. Realizing his tests weren't proving anything, he bought himself a fancy machine rest and started all over with bullets, powders, crimps, and load combinations. Then he got into bullet casting and spent a bundle on molds and casting equipment and wound up designing his own bullets. Then he had more pistols accurized, and the whole process was repeated. That was years ago, and though he has yet to fire his first round in actual pistol competition, he has become a reknowned expert in the realm of handgun accuracy and handloading. Like many American shooters, he has found the pursuit of accuracy to be more fascinating and rewarding than personal marksmanship achievement.

BENCHREST

This passion took root and flowered in the late 1940's and early '50's when a handful of accuracy buffs started getting together and comparing the accuracy of their woodchuck rifles. Since the accent was on rifle performance, all shooting was done from solid benchrests with the rifles lying on firm sandbags to eliminate human error as much as possible. Virtually all holding error was eliminated, and to rule out mistakes in aiming and trigger pulling, high-magnification scopes and set triggers were generally used. Naturally, the name of the game was Benchrest, and from those founding shooters we have learned just about everything we know about modern rifle accuracy.

Those few beginning benchresters considered themselves to be quite expert on the subject of rifle accuracy. In fact, their pool of knowledge represented just about everything that was known on the subject at that time. However, their thinking was at first constricted by myths, half-truths, and outright ignorance that had been handed down in over 200 years of target shooting. Enormously fat barrels were the rule, and it was widely felt that the heavier the barrel, the more accurate the rifle. Likewise, massive stocks were favored, and before long some rifles became so gargantuan that they were hauled to the bench on carts.

Of course, nearly all the rifles used in these dawning matches of the Benchrest Era were custom-made affairs that had been assembled by their owners (many of whom were crack machinists) or by specialty gunsmiths. The basis of such a rifle was sometimes a commercial action such as the Model 70, but most were based on easily available and inexpensive Model 98 Mausers, 03 Springfields, or 1917 Enfields and the like. Mausers were the big favorites. After a few years of benchrest competitions, shooters began to realize that the actions being used were part of the accuracy problem. Accordingly, those who could afford them had special single-shot actions made that were as massive as a battleship's bilge-pump piston. Many of these were one-of-a-kind creations, and they were wonders of mechanical wizardry. Back then, I couldn't afford a six-pack of Pepsi, but I clearly recall drooling over pictures of the behemoths in shooting magazines. To my reckoning, these marvelous benchrest actions, ugly and massive as they were, represented the soul of accuracy, and I would have offered my soul to own one. Had I saved enough money to make the purchase, though, the rifle would now be little more than an oddity. That's because the founding fathers of the benchrest game took a long look down the road they were traveling and wisely decided on some alternate routes.

It was true that progress was being made. In 1948, the late Bob Wallack fired a 10-shot group at 200 yards measuring .521 inches, at last breaking the Rowland "world record" of .725 inches, which had stood since 1901. But it was equally true that heavy bench rifles were reaching the point of absurdity in terms of weight and configuration. Mass was becoming a crude substitute for finesse, and it became increasingly apparent that relatively few accuracy achievements could be incorporated in a rifle of traditional configuration.

Clearly, if accuracy know-how was to be useful, it had to apply to rifles of more or less traditional shape and weight. Thus benchrest shooting was divided into various classes which, along with the unrestricted-class behemoths, included the Heavy Varmint rifles, which could weigh no more than 13½ pounds scoped. The Light Varmint class had a 10½-pound limit. There was also the Hunting Class, which is of particular interest because the rifles can't weigh over 10 pounds, the maximum scope-power limit is 6X, and the bore size has to be 6mm or larger. This excludes the hotshot little .22's. One other class, the Sporter Rifle, is identical to Light Varmint rifles except that the caliber has to be 6mm or larger.

Here are three of the author's lighter benchrest rifles. Unlike the unrestricted-class behemoths, these must conform to the categories of sporter, light varmint, or heavy varmint, with maximum weights ranging from 10-1/2 to 13-1/2 pounds. Benchrest developments with such rifles have obvious applications to the improvement of other types of target rifles and to hunting rifles.

Developments in the unrestricted benchrest class may seem far removed from the needs of conventional riflemen, yet they can point the way toward mechanical improvements of anything from rifling to lock-time, and they can also encourage scope experimentation. To an even greater degree, they test and encourage advanced, often experimental concepts in ammunition development.

I was getting into benchrest shooting just about the time when the lighter rifle classes came into being, and I recall considerable grumbling among some "big rifle" shooters who claimed that lightweight rifles couldn't be made to shoot well and wouldn't provide the challenge of punching tiny groups. Other shooters, however, saw a whole new challenge in dealing with the finicky little rifles. What they learned and accomplished was and continues to be astonishing.

One of the reasons the lighter bench rifles have taught us so much about the myriad factors affecting accuracy is the way they pinpoint and even magnify specific problems. Whereas the massive action and barrel of an unrestricted rifle often tends to damp out and obscure, say, uneven locking-lug contact, the same problem with a light varminter is glaringly apparent. This is why the factors that cause accuracy problems have been so effectively isolated and identified. The result of this fine tuning and refinement is the development of lightweight rifles that not only seriously challenge the accuracy of today's massive "iron-monster" shooting machines but have rendered pitifully obsolete the giant bench rifles we regarded with such awe a few decades ago. For example, back in 1953 the world-record group for five shots at 200 yards measured .3896. Today a *light* varmint rifle must be capable of accuracy twice that good just to be a contender. In fact, you just might buy a rifle off a dealer's rack that, with a little tuning and some good handloads, could come close to equaling the world record of 1953. We have come that far.

In order to discuss accuracy and what we've learned about it, plus what we have yet to learn, let's consider an accurate rifle the way an expert benchrest shooter would regard it—each component separately. Then we'll put all the pieces together for a better understanding of why they work so well.

THE BARREL

Traditionally, the barrel has been regarded not only as the heart of a rifle but the soul and life's blood of accuracy. For centuries the barrel was thought to be the *only* part of a rifle that controlled accuracy. Until fairly recent times this viewpoint was essentially correct. The accuracy of muzzleloading rifles was almost entirely dependent on barrel quality because the lock was only semi-attached via the stock, and the stock itself merely hung from the barrel and provided little influence on accuracy one way or the other. Even with the coming of the beautiful single-shot rifles of the late 19th century the action provided only cartridge lock-up, a firing mechanism, and a means of holding everything together. The accurate rifles were those with good barrels, and a great target rifle was inextricably linked with the name of the barrelmaker.

Techniques used in barrelmaking, past and present, are pretty well covered in Chapter 1. What is, and has been, essential to barrel accuracy is exactness and uniformity of dimensions. No matter how bright and shiny a bore may appear, if the diameter is not correct and uniform, accuracy will suffer. Undersize or tight spots are especially damaging to accuracy because they squeeze the bullets to subnormal size. In addition to whatever harm this might do to the bullet itself, once the bullet is past the barrel's tight spot, it is thereafter undersize and does not fill the bore properly. In other words, the bullet is unevenly guided as it wobbles its way through the remainder of the bore. Barrels with oversize areas are especially destructive to accuracy if they happen to be at the muzzle.

Just as bore diameter must be uniform and correct, so must the lands. Over the centuries there has been a lot of experimentation with the number and shape of rifling lands. Even today, a variety of land configurations are offered by arms manufacturers and independent barrelmakers. High-sounding claims are made for various land shapes, and indeed there may be certain advantages to some of them, especially as regards barrel life, but it is exceedingly difficult to prove that one style is inherently more accurate than another. Most of today's ultra-accurate barrels have either six or eight lands and grooves, and most of these are of the old-fashioned, square-top and straight-sided Metford-Enfield type. Historically, when a particular style of rifling seemed to prove itself more accurate than other types, it eventually turned out that the real reason for better accuracy was the process by which the rifling was made rather than the actual shape. Harry Pope, the legendary king of barrelmakers, used a distinctive form of rifling which obviously resulted in brilliant (for its time) accuracy. However, considering the meticulous care Pope took as a craftsman, we can be pretty sure that his rifles would have been equally accurate had he used any one of several rifling configurations.

Naturally, surface smoothness of a rifle bore plays a vital role in accuracy. The nature of some, if not most, rifling processes can leave sawlike jagged edges on the upper corners of the lands. These imperfections rip chunks out of a bullet's jacket as it races by. Sometimes, even the groove bottoms of barrels are so rough that they tear away chunks of bullet metal.

By using a magnifying bore scope to peer inside a rifle barrel, I've often noted the way cop-

Carmichel uses a magnifying bore scope to peer inside a rifle barrel, noting—for example—the progressive build-up of copper fouling around a rough spot. Eventually, such fouling is a serious detriment to accuracy even though it may go unnoticed by the average gun owner.

per fouling progressively builds up around a rough spot until accuracy is destroyed. I do this by cleaning the barrel thoroughly and then using the bore scope to find a few rough spots, gaps, pits, or saw edges that snag and bite passing bullets. After a couple of shots, the suspected rough areas are clogged with chunks of copper bullet jacket, and with each subsequent shot or two, the clogged spot becomes noticeably larger until eventually the original flaw is so completely obscured by an irregular patch of copper scrapings that it will obviously interfere with a passing bullet, causing greater and greater inaccuracy.

I've fired a series of five-shot groups from the bench with such barrels and almost invariably, as the fouling buildup progresses, group sizes grow. A particularly notable rifle with this problem had an easily seen gap in the rifling about four inches from the muzzle. The first six or seven shots would go into a wonderfully tight little group of almost benchrest-tournament quality, but by the eighth or ninth shot, bullet holes would appear an inch or so out of the group. After a good scrubbing with a bronze brush, accuracy would return for a few shots and then the cycle would be repeated. I've tested scores of rifles with rough bores that exhibited good initial accuracy but had a similar pattern of group deterioration.

The question facing barrelmakers is how to remedy rough bores, or better yet, how to avoid them. The classic treatment is old-fashioned hand-lapping. This involves pouring a molten-lead lap in the bore (attached to a metal rod), doping the lap with fine abrasive flour and oil, and passing the lap back and forth through the bore until it is dead smooth or one's muscles give out. There was a time, I understand, when barrelmakers could be spotted in a crowd because of their muscular "lapping arms."

In addition to polishing away rough edges and slicking up the bore, lapping also improves the dimensional uniformity of a rifle barrel, but, obviously, hand-lapping rifle barrels is too slow for today's demands. Though most shooters aren't aware of it, shooting is also a lapping process of sorts, and this partially explains why most rifles shoot better after a hundred rounds or so have "slicked up" the bore.

Much of today's discussion of which rifling process produces the most accurate barrels boils down to the question of which turns out the smoothest, most uniform bores. With the traditional cut or "scrape" rifling process, there are many opportunities for jagged surfaces to occur, especially if the cutters are dull, improperly shaped, or incorrectly used. This is why the button process is so widely hailed. Supposedly, as the super-hard button presses its image into a rifle's bore, it irons the surface to ultra slickness and eliminates any possibility of dimensional error. But in actual fact, exceedingly rough barrels have been and are being made with button rifling. The process tends to break down when the steel is of poor quality, the boring is crooked, or the reaming rough and irregular. This occurs in mass-production plants that produce barrels on contract for gunmakers at the lowest possible price. Even with their production shortcomings, barrels mass-produced by the button process do, in my experience, tend to be more accurate on the average than barrels given a similar degree of attention and produced by the traditional cut-rifling system. But I'd better qualify this observation by adding that almost no mass-made barrels are currently being made by the cut process. Those I have tested were on older sporting rifles or were of World War II or earlier miltary vintage.

From the combined standpoints of high production and accuracy, the so-called hammer-forging process probably offers the best possibilities for the future. Production-grade, off-the-shelf rifles with hammer-forged barrels in my tests do tend to be quite stable and accurate, and some of the more expensive hammer-forged imports turn in exceptionally good accuracy in some calibers. I've used hammer-forged barrels on a couple of big-bore and some smallbore target rifles, and I found their accuracy to be superb. I have not, however, had one fitted to a full-blown benchrest rig because I suspect they have not yet reached gilt-edged perfection. A few years back, some long-range shooting pals of mine got hold of some hammer-forged barrel blanks made by Winchester and used them in 1,000-yard target rifles. Accuracy was excellent, and barrel life tended to be half again better than with standard barrels.

BARREL STEEL

Regardless of what process is used to rifle a barrel, much of the potential accuracy is determined by the kind of steel used and the drilling and reaming operations. From the standpoint of pure accuracy, the trick is to select barrel steel that offers a reasonable compromise between tough-

ness and machineability. It is possible to buy extremely hard, wear-resistant steel that might last thousands of shots longer than ordinary barrels, but it would drill and rifle so poorly that accuracy would be almost nonexistent. On the other side of the coin, I know of at least one barrel-maker who uses, or did use, extremely mild steel that was a dream to machine. His barrels are beautiful to peer into, and accuracy is superb. Alas, after comparatively few rounds, the barrel throat washes away, the lands flatten, and accuracy fades.

For several years now, the best target barrels have been made almost exclusively of stainless steel. In fact, the bright, unblued look has become synonymous with accuracy. It is widely held that the advantage of stainless steel is prolonged barrel life, but I'm not inclined to agree completely. There are all sorts of stainless-steel alloys, some of which are more erosion-resistant than others. Some stainless barrels I've used had a notably short accuracy life, considerably shorter than the chrome-moly barrels I've used in the same calibers.

I am convinced, however, as are most accuracy buffs, that properly selected stainless steel does have an advantage. This is not so much because the steel is stainless but because stainless is made to rigid quality standards with an absolute minimum of internal flaws such as carbon inclusions (pockets of unmixed carbon or impurities), voids, or folds that cause barrelmakers so much grief. As one top custom barrelsmith told me many years ago, "Stainless-steel barrels are good because the steel itself is good."

A fascinating problem that has long puzzled seekers of accuracy is why some barrels tend to be "naturally" accurate while a seemingly identical one doesn't perform as well. Top barrel-maker Bill Atkinson, who also does superior re-rifling, has often remarked that the foundation of accuracy or lack therof is in the bar of steel before it is cut. To back up this observation, Atkinson has recorded that barrels which were never especially accurate tend to continue to be poor performers while those that were once accurate tend to be finely accurate when rebored and re-rifled. A notable example was a heavy bench rifle in .222 Remington caliber that won an impressive string of tournaments during its life. When it became so worn that accuracy was declining, it was returned to Atkinson, who rebored and re-rifled the barrel to .30 caliber. In its new dress as a .308 Winchester, the barrel was again a winner and even set a new world record.

Though the hidden factors that seem to play a big role in determining the difference between a super-accurate tube and an also-ran remain largely mysterious, barrelmakers are gradually unraveling some of the secrets. The steel's homogeneity evidently is important, and of course the improvement in heat-treating methods is of vital concern. The stresses built up in the manufacture of a steel bar can be tremendous (enough to cause the bar to visibly kick and twist when heated), so finding ways of normalizing them before the first bullet squeezes down the bore is an ever-advancing art, but it apparently hasn't been improved enough to be called a science.

In the innocent days of barrelmaking, one important goal was simply to drill a straight hole through a bar of steel, the belief being that a bullet would fly true if guided by a perfectly straight hole. Nowadays, barrelmakers routinely drill deep holes so straight that any deviation from perfection is scarcely measurable. What we have learned is that some other factors are of even greater importance in the attainment of ultimate accuracy.

Regardless of the rifling process, a barrel's potential accuracy is largely determined by the kind of steel used and by the drilling and reaming operations. Most of the best target barrels are now made of stainless steel. Carmichel is seen here during a test of a long-range target rifle employing a stainless barrel.

LONG AND SHORT

Another holdover from the virginal era of riflery is the notion that long barrels are more accurate. Back in the muzzleloading days, a long barrel had particular accuracy advantages, but with the coming of breechloaders and smokeless powder, most of those reasons vanished. One reason long barrels, even on today's rifles, *seem* to be more accurate is because the increased weight makes for a steadier hold. Another reason is that on rifles equipped with iron sights, the long barrel offers a longer sight radius that makes for more precise aiming. Neither factor has any effect on *pure* accuracy, but just the same, many seekers of accuracy have long felt compelled to equip their rifles with barrels that sometimes reach ungainly lengths.

The big turn-around in barrel length and accuracy came about with the development of Light Varmint benchrest rifles. Since the total allowable weight is 10½ pounds, and the weight and general conformation of scope, stock, and action is more or less fixed, the one great unexplored avenue of possible improvement was barrel configuration. If, for example, a barrel can weigh no more than four pounds, will it be more accurate if the configuration is long and slender or short and fat? Naturally, the traditional viewpoint favored a long tube, but eventually it was pretty well concluded that fat, stiff barrels were more accurate, and inches were sacrificed in favor of greater diameter. Thus, ultra-accurate rifles with stubby 18-inch barrels are now common in Light Varmint class benchrest shooting. This does not mean that 18 inches has been found to be the optimum length for accuracy. Makers of bench rifles have stopped at this length because of the Federal law prohibiting short barrels (called the "sawed-off shotgun law") on rifles and shotguns. Who knows? Without this regulation, super-accurate rifle barrels might turn out to be even shorter.

Several years ago when barrelmaker Bill Atkinson was cutting a wide swath as a tournament smallbore shooter, he made up a special .22 Rimfire rifle with a fairly short barrel. Noting that accuracy was good, Bill got curious and started lopping off additional inches. His scores remained as good as ever, even when the barrel was so short that fellow competitors complained about the excessive muzzle blast. To cure this, Bill attached a sleeve to the muzzle that enclosed the blast, turning the sound into a peculiar *BONKK,* but accuracy remained as good as ever.

Of course, seekers of rifle accuracy aren't going to make a rush for the hacksaw to shorten their barrels. For most uses, longer barrels serve other important functions. In addition to the beneficial added weight and longer sight radius, a long centerfire barrel in most cases tends to increase velocity. Varmint hunters and long-range target shooters, who need all the velocity they can get, will still want all the barrel they can carry.

CONTOUR

Apparently there is still something—or lots of things—to be learned about barrel contour. Our most accurate rifles—the benchresters, specialized target models, and varminters—almost unfailingly have either a straight taper or no taper at all. The principal reason for this unimaginative contouring is, of course, that it's the easiest to turn on a lathe. Since rifles tend to shoot so well with this barrel shape, there has been no reason to change, and as for appearance, there is a very efficient, businesslike look about a straight taper.

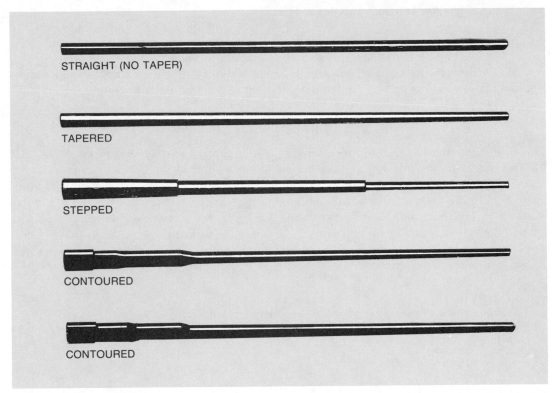

Barrel contour definitely affects accuracy. It is agreed that a straight taper is best suited to heavy barrels, but experiments — and heated debates — continue with regard to the best configuration for accuracy in a lighter, slender barrel. These drawings show some of the types currently made.

But the straight taper is best suited to heavy barrels, leaving us with the question of which contour is most accurate in slender, lightweight barrels — assuming that one particular contour really is most accurate. Rifle builders have been searching for this holy grail of accuracy for some time. The Germans, who always love such projects, have long experimented with accuracy contour but without any notable success. Most of their efforts can be identified by a barrel turned in a series of steps. Likewise, you may recall that the Browning rifles produced in Europe from the late 1950's until the early '70's featured unusually stepped barrels. The manufacturer had taken a page out of the German book and tried to make use of some alleged advantages of a stepped barrel, but I'm not convinced they were on the right track. The Browning rifles of that period tended to be about as accurate as other good-quality rifles, but no better.

More recently, an American firm went to a good deal of fuss and expense trying to come up with the most accurate barrel contour for their pet rifle, but nothing conclusive was proven. The problems of proving one contour to be better than another are rooted both in the testing methodology and the available equipment. The biggest problem is that two barrel blanks seldom perform identically, even though they appear identical. Thus, when a barrel of a specific contour performs better than one of some other contour, how are we to know the barrel isn't more accurate for some other reason? Also, currently made rifles having a variety of contours have reached such a high degree of accuracy that any further improvements will be a matter of small fractions of an inch. At any rate, shooters love to talk about such things when we really know nothing for sure, so I expect barrel contour will keep us busy for years to come.

ACCURACY IN ACTIONS

One of the ongoing tragedies of modern man is his discovery, one day after the wedding, that his sexy new wife hasn't the faintest idea of how to mix a batch of sourdough biscuits and can't fry an egg. A comparable heartbreak is discovering that your racy new rifle, the one that gleamed so beautifully on the dealer's rack and has the gun writers twittering like starlings, won't stack all the bullets in one hole at 700 yards and won't get more accurate no matter what you do.

Sometimes it seems impossible to get everything we want in one package, and when it comes to accuracy, rifle actions are no exception. I've had a love affair with trim, finely machined, slick-working, bolt-action rifles for longer than I can remember. Succumbing to my yearn-

Carmichel goes to work with a National Match "over-the-course" rifle built on a Winchester Model 70 action with a stainless barrel. This action and others of the same general class are well suited to a variety of competition demands involving slow and rapid fire.

ings, I've spent a good portion of the family fortune buying fine old Mauser actions and pre-1964 Winchester Model 70's and having them reworked. Yet, even though these beautiful actions offer me just about everything I can ask for in the way of reliability, ease of operation, strength, and pride of ownership, I would never consider one of them as the basis for a super-accurate tournament-class bench rifle. Nor would anyone else who is serious about accuracy.

I'm not saying the Model 70's, Mausers, and actions of this general class (1917 Enfields, 1903 Springfields, etc.) aren't capable of impressive accuracy, for they are. Even today, if I were contemplating the building of a National Match "over-the-course" rifle, I would almost certainly build it around either a new or old-style Model 70 Winchester action. Those actions are well suited to the variety of demands—one round at a time or rapid fire—of this type of competition. All of the National Match-style rifles I own that are built on Model 70 actions are reliably capable of well under one-inch groups at 100 yards, and an occasional group snuggles down under half an inch. Likewise, some of the best-performing rifles currently used in prone 1,000 yard matches are based on the faithful Model 70 action. Some delightfully accurate varmint rifles have been built on ordinary old 98 Mauser actions. In fact, these actions served as the basis for many if not most of the early bench rifles just after World War II. This includes those that set the initial records.

But as fine as they are, some of the characteristics that have made these mechanisms so good for their intended sporting or military purposes are liabilities from the standpoint of pure accuracy. Much of the reason is evident if you hold the front ring of a Mauser 98 action in a heavy vise and give the tang extension a gentle tweak with thumb and forefinger. The action flexes visibly with only moderate pressure. Imagine how much it flexes when it supports a barrel, and further imagine the flexing that must take place when a cartridge is fired. The action not only flexes easily but, because the right side rail is so thin, it flexes unevenly, assuming a somewhat twisted condition. Since the two action screws are at the extreme ends of the receiver, the middle portion of the action is somewhat free to bend. Of course, this condition exists to a greater or lesser degree with all actions, but the faithful old Mauser is a classic example of the problem, as is the 1903 Springfield. The Model 70 Winchester, because of its deeper side rails and its three action screws, does not suffer as seriously.

Considering the same problem in another light, look at the underside of a Mauser or Springfield action, the areas that bed against the wood. Or better yet, look at the action inletting cuts of a Mauser or Springfield stock. You'll note that the bottom contact areas are not only skimpy but are of a complex and irregular shape. Putting all these factors together, you inevitably come up with the observation that there's no way such actions can support a barrel, especially a heavy target-style barrel, without being in a state of constant tension. Under the stress of firing, the action is subjected to additional flexing and there's no guarantee the metal will "land" on the same place in the inletting where it rested before the shot.

Again, these are certainly not criticisms of the overall performance of Mausers, Springfields, Model 70's, and their like, for they have long since earned a reputation that can never be tarnished. It is, however, necessary to give clear examples of certain stumbling blocks to inherent accuracy in order to understand what we are looking for and what we are trying to eliminate.

Ideally, the most accurate action would be no action at all if we take the view that at best the mechanism that holds the barrel, locks the cartridge in place, and delivers a blow to the primer is a necessary evil. For the time being, at least, we have to make do with some sort of mechanism, and the next best thing to nothing, logically, is the simplest possible action. In fact, utter simplicity is the prevailing characteristic of today's most accurate rifle actions.

When, back in the late 1940's and early '50's, accuracy buffs began to catch on to the idea that a rifle's action was far more important to accuracy than had been formerly realized, there was a backlash effect in action design. Traditional mechanisms were abandoned in favor of giant receivers that were often more a tribute to the machinist's skill and imagination than any real benefit to accuracy. To be sure, simply adding mass to a rifle, especially in the action area, is one way of improving accuracy. However, the improvement can best be described as treating the symptoms rather than the disease. For example, we know that an action that bends reduces accuracy. Therefore, an action that doesn't bend should be more accurate. The simple solution, seemingly, is to build actions of such massive size that they won't bend. But this only leads to bigger and bigger actions. Obviously, this is not the answer because eventually we would end up with rifles too heavy and too big to carry. The solution therefore has to be the development of

One of the most efficient and easy ways of stiffening a rifle action is simply to add an outer sleeve, as seen here. The sleeve adds minimal weight and significantly improves accuracy.

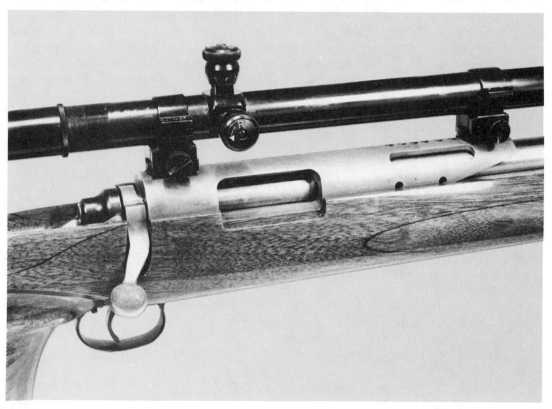

actions that offer sufficient rigidity *without* being oversize and overweight.

Developments in this direction have been expedited by the rise of the weight-conscious Varmint Class bench rifles. Since weight is restricted, the logical course is to make existing steel contribute as much to strength as possible. The most successful commonly available action in terms of pure accuracy has been Remington's 40-X or 40-XBR (for benchrest), which is only a slightly refined version of the basic Model 700 sporter action. The 40-X has been so successful because there is relatively little about the receiver that is not directly involved in holding the bolt and barrel or lending stiffness. By omitting the magazine cut, for example, the bonus in stiffness far outweighs the slight weight gain, and the simple cylindrical shape of the receiver lends itself to very positive stock bedding.

Likewise, the 40-X bolt is utterly simple and almost perfectly symmetrical. It forms little more than a cylinder within the sleeve of the receiver. In the search for perfect symmetry and utmost simplicity, some action makers have omitted the ejection port entirely, opting for a loading sequence that requires complete removal of the bolt from the receiver and hand-fitting of the cartridge into the recessed bolt face. While this no doubt results in an action that offers the best possible weight-to-rigidity ratio, it also moves a step or two away from practicality and once again offers only treatment for a symptom, not a usable cure.

There is no question that the usual loading/ejection-port cut in the side of a receiver upsets its symmetry and inevitably leads to uneven flexing, but the port is so important to convenient function that it must be viewed as a challenge to be overcome rather than something to be eliminated.

One of the most efficient and convenient ways of stiffening an existing action is by the addition of an outer sleeve. The earliest sleeves I can recall were massive, pipelike affairs some 2½ inches in diameter that were turned from steel bar stock. After one was squeezed around a round receiver (usually a Remington M-722) and hot-soldered in place, the rig constituted a sort of "poor-boy" benchrest action back when custom-built actions were selling for a month's wages.

I don't see these much anymore except on a few "antique" bench rifles, but I do see a lot of somewhat similar sleeves made of aluminum and attached to receivers with epoxy glue. Adding only a scant few ounces in weight, these sleeves not only add significantly to the stiffness of a receiver but also add considerably to the action-to-stock contact surface, thus improving bedding. Some are left round, but as often as not the sleeve is machined to a dead-flat bottom surface, which further simplifies the bedding situation.

When Ed Shilen designed his famous DGA action, he decided to avoid the prevailing trend toward round receiver design in favor of a simple design that is essentially square in cross section. Though this shape is in theory less symmetrical than a round receiver, it offers the advantage of vertical sides which need not contact the stock at all, and a huge, dead-flat bottom area to provide the simplest and most generous stock contact. The geometry of the cross section of the Shilen action suggests that this configuration is especially resistant to twisting or the torquing action of a bullet accelerating through a barrel. And there is no doubt that a full-width, flat-bottomed action better transfers twisting pressures to the stock without wanting to turn in the stock as does a round-bottomed receiver.

Despite these more or less apparent advantages of a square- or flat-bottomed receiver, there

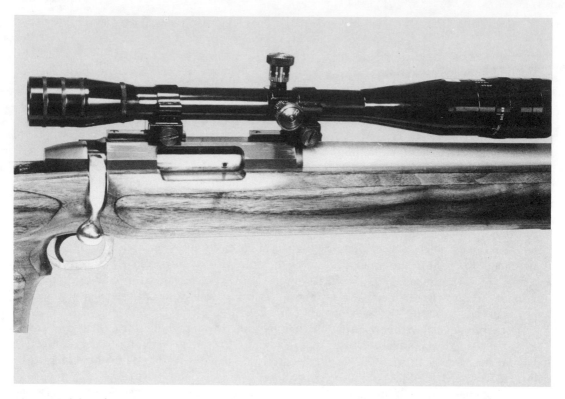

This is Ed Shilen's famous DGA action—a simple design that is essentially square in cross-section. It has vertical sides that do not need to contact the stock at all and a vast bottom area that provides generous stock contact. The DGA configuration resists twisting or the torquing action of a bullet accelerating through the barrel.

is criticism that the concept is flawed because of the difficulty of uniting two flat surfaces without stresses. This criticism is mainly based on the age-old machine-shop problem of creating a perfectly flat surface. It is easier and more accurate, say critics, to support a cylinder in V-ways. At any rate, the argument over which receiver can be more accurately bedded has been sidestepped in recent times by the simple expedient of gluing the barreled action into the stock.

Gluing an action into a stock by means of today's super-strong epoxy cements sounds rather permanent and perhaps a bit drastic, but the advantages are manifold. To understand why, it is best to have some experience in tightening action screws and, with a dial indicator or only by feeling with the fingertips, noting how the barrel shifts up and down in the stock as the screws are alternately tightened and loosened. The action or the stock—or both—bend, and it seems to happen no matter how meticulous the bedding job. The reasoning behind a glued-in action is to eliminate these stresses by eliminating their cause. When done properly, the action is pressed into the stock with the lightest possible pressure so that no flexing of either component occurs. When the glue dries, stock and action are welded into a single unit with neither having a bad influence on the other. In case you're wondering if the stock can ever be removed, yes, it can, either by heating or freezing.

By now you may be wondering if the pursuit of accuracy hasn't become so specialized that there is little carry-over to everyday hunting rifles. Actually, the carry-over has been and continues to be enormous. For example, one great help to builders of rifles is the benchrester's trick of lapping bolt lugs so that they contact uniformly on both sides. But first it must be understood that quite often bolt lugs do not contact evenly with the main portion of the cartridge thrust being held by only one lug (in the case of two-lug bolts). When this happens, the pressure is unequally transferred to the receiver, causing it to flex much more than it would if the lugs bore evenly. If only the bottom lug is contacting, it causes the receiver to bow upward on the ends, and if only the top lug contacts, the receiver tends to hump up in the middle. Either way, this makes the barrel do funny things, and the bedding takes quite a beating.

Despite what has been learned about the role of a rifle's action in accuracy, there are all sorts of opportunities for improvement. In fact, actions are still pretty much the weak link in the accuracy chain. For instance, the way we fit barrels to actions is still very much open to improvement. The old-fashioned way of screwing a barrel into place opens a Pandora's box of problems that we're just beginning to understand. No doubt, the future will see sleeved rather than threaded unions between barrel and receiver that will improve symmetry and vibration control.

IGNITION

Most of all, there is a vast amount of work to be done in the area of cartridge ignition. Fast lock-time is essential to accuracy. To this end, rifle designers strive for the quickest, shortest firing-pin fall. If you compare a Shilen or Remington bench rifle to a traditional Mauser-type rifle, you'll note that the striker travel of the target rifles is about twice as fast. But faster and faster lock-time really isn't the answer.

It has long been suspected that the very nature of today's mechanically fired cartridge introduces certain factors harmful to accuracy. For example, the initial impact of the firing pin against the primer jolts the rifle just as the bullet is being set in motion. Though the entire firing mechanism has been considered a necessary evil, the time is close at hand when it might not be so necessary after all. Electronic ignition offers a whole new area of research because all moving parts could be eliminated, and the lock-time would be literally the speed of an electron. Taking this idea a step further, we quickly see that the entire brass case could be eliminated. Then, joy of joys, we could forget actions altogether, at least as they now exist. Perhaps the ultimate "one-hole" rifle will be little more than a barrel and a stock.

STOCKS

Speaking of necessary evils, stocks have always been a very large bug in the honey pot of accuracy. A barrelmaker can tear out his hair trying to produce a perfect tube, and then the gunsmith can spend hours of tedious work to tune the action to the precision of a quartz clock, only to have accuracy go all to hell because of a queer kink in the stock.

The effect of a stock on a rifle's accuracy, the way it holds zero and its influence on shot-after-shot bullet direction can be astonishing. I have no reliable information or even a firm idea as to when gunmakers became aware of the role rifle stocks play in accuracy. Judging by the construction of muzzleloading rifles, I'd say their makers were scarcely aware, if at all, of what stocks can do to accuracy, and even makers of late 19th-century single-shot target rifles seemed

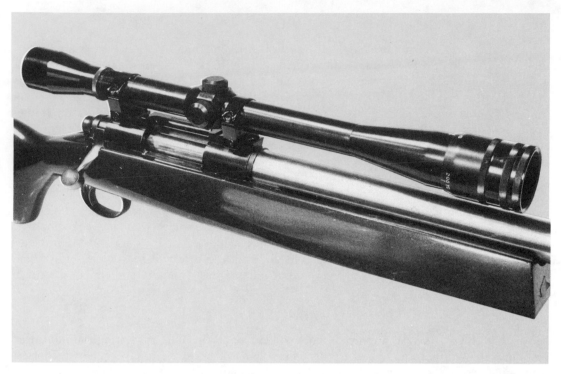

The great Al Linden, most famous stockmaker of the pre-World War II era, advocated stock pressure on the forearm. He did not know that his technique tended to bend the action as well as cause accuracy problems in the barrel. Today's accuracy buffs want a free-floating arrangement like this one, which lets the barrel vibrate without the impediment of stock pressure. When it is relieved of that pressure, the barrel vibrates, all right— but it vibrates consistently.

unconcerned about the role of stocking. Makers of bolt-action rifles, however, seem to have quickly grasped the idea that stocks exert considerable influence on accuracy. As early as 1890, Paul Mauser discovered that when his tapered barrels became hot, they expanded lengthwise and wedged tightly into the barrel groove of the stock. This caused the point of impact to shift. Accordingly, he ordered the Mauser barrels to be contoured in a series of steps, and the corresponding stock grooves to be cut with enough extra room to allow for lengthwise expansion.

Later, experimenters at Springfield Armory found that the accuracy of the 03 rifle could be improved by using stock tension to exert pressure on the barrel. By the 1930's, gun writers were humming like telegraph wires with the "discovery" that rifle barrels vibrated upon firing and that these vibrations were controlled or allowed to run amok, as the case might be, by proper or improper bedding of the barreled action in the wooden stock. No less a figure than the great Alvin Linden, our most famous stockmaker of the pre-war era, wrote articles and books on how to bed rifles for best accuracy by pressing the barrel upward with the forearm. His advice is still much followed—for better or worse—but I'll bet old Al never realized that his bedding technique was bending the action as well as exerting pressure on the barrel and thereby introducing additional problems. Today, accuracy buffs wouldn't dream of having a stock touch the barrel.

They prefer the free-floating system which allows the barrel to vibrate freely.

With the beginning of benchrest shooting as we know it today, the attitude toward stocks was either to use massive slabs of lumber or to have no stock at all. This latter concept is apparent in iron-monster rifles, which are simply barreled actions clamped to heavy I-beams or similar structures. Those who went with wood naturally suffered all the perils to which wood is heir, but at the same time had the satisfaction of using rifles that looked like rifles — almost.

Of course, the great failing of wooden stocks is their tendency to shrink and swell or twist and warp this way and that as they soak up or discharge moisture. In order to gain some protection from this accuracy-ruining tendency, target shooters and benchresters have used laminated wood that resists warping and even specially treated lumber that reduces moisture absorption.

A breakthrough of monumental proportions occurred around 1950 with the introduction of the glass-bedding technique. Accurate stock bedding had previously been a very exacting hand-fitting operation. The glass-bedding method only required that the stock inletting be hogged out roughly and then poured full of a semi-liquid epoxy compound laced with glass fibers. When the epoxy set hard, it formed a perfect casting of the barreled action which not only held the metal rigidly in place but was moisture-proof and resistant to any unwanted bends and twists from the wood.

The acceptance of glass bedding in accuracy circles was immediate and almost universal. Even today, virtually every wooden stock you see on the benchrest firing line is epoxy-bedded, or as they say, "glassed," even though the bonding filaments may be aluminum or steel. Realizing that fiberglass was a very good thing, a clever chap soon decided that if a little fiberglass was good a lot of fiberglass would be a lot better.

The fellow was Californian Chet Brown. To my recollection, he made the first all-fiberglass stock. The effect was stunning. A fiberglass stock is stronger and more stable than wood, and of supreme importance to makers and shooters of Varmint Class bench rifles, it is a lot *lighter* than

Californian Chet Brown was the pioneer of fiberglass stocking, turning out stocks like this one, which may lack the beauty of wood but are lighter, strong, more stable — and an undeniable asset to accuracy.

wood. The priceless ounces of weight that had previously been lost in stock wood could now be added to the barrel, making it stiffer and more accurate!

The only negative reaction to fiberglass (and other synthetic) stocks is that they lack the beauty of wood, which is certainly true. But to make up for it, benchresters have begun expressing their artistic whims in all sorts of dazzling color schemes. Today, just about every Varmint Class benchrest rifle you see has a brightly painted fiberglass stock, which makes the firing line look like a Mexican fiesta.

Here again, there has been considerable carry-over to hunting. Ultra-lightweight hunting-style stocks not only have taken pounds off sporter rifles but have added a degree of stability and zero reliability never before enjoyed. When a wooden stock gets water-soaked, it's a pretty safe bet that the point of impact will change, sometimes by enough inches to miss the trophy of a lifetime. Fiberglass stocks have gone a long way toward ending this problem and giving sheep hunters, in particular, some much-needed peace of mind.

Benchrest shooters have never numbered more than hundreds, but they have had an incalculable effect on rifle design, manufacture, and use. Benchrest shooting taught us most of what we know about accuracy, and it has also established the standards of accuracy that we commonly accept in our evaluations of sporting-rifle performance. Before 1940, shooters had only a vague idea of the differences between good, mediocre, and poor accuracy, and arms and ammo makers were only slightly better informed. Today, thanks to the benchrest game, we understand what to expect from a rifle, and some arms and ammo makers now realize that they have to measure up. All in all, it's been quite an accomplishment for a few woodchuck hunters who only wanted to know who had the best rifle.

Chapter 20

. . . .

IS HANDLOADING FOR YOU?

. . . .

A few years back, the National Rifle Association invited me to give a seminar on handloading rifle and pistol cartridges. The event was well publicized, and long before the appointed hour the hall began filling with hundreds of avid shooters, all eager to hear me extol the virtues of reloaded ammo. My opening sentence, however, outraged the throng.

"Ladies and gentlemen, friends and fellow NRA members," I said, "the simple truth is that you probably cannot reload ammunition that will be as good as new factory loads." I paused to let this sink in, and the silence was deafening. With one short phrase, I had bludgeoned the holiest of cattle and thumbed my nose at the most sacrosanct of shooting hobbies. Carmichel, at last, had spilt the last of his marbles.

For the next quarter of an hour, I explained in some depth why it is so difficult to load very good ammo. Then I spent the next hour and a half describing how, if a shooter really *worked* at it, he might be able to load shells that would shoot farther, faster, deadlier, and more accurately than any factory load. The crowd, thus reassured, happily left the hall in a state of tarnished innocence.

In the early '50's, when I first tried my hand at the black art of handloading, the practice was condemned by the great majority of the shooting public. "Reloaded shells might be okay for practice," most shooters said, "but I wouldn't use them for real hunting." Even stronger was the common remark, "Them things is liable to blow your head off."

I committed an occasional gun trade in those days, but when word got around that I was a handloader almost no one in my community wanted a gun I'd owned. The notion was that once a handloaded bullet passed through a rifle barrel it was ruined for all time. Most of those same folk were also convinced that the earth was flat, so I didn't grieve too much about their peculiar ideas on guns and shooting, especially when my handloads knocked over groundhogs at 300 yards or took first place at the Thanksgiving turkey shoot. What did bother me was the general nonavailability of reloading tools and components. The local sporting-goods dealer didn't stock them because, as he explained it, "If everybody got to reloading, it would ruin my regular ammo sales and I'd go broke." This notion was shared by the major ammo manufacturers. By refusing to actively promote sales of their bullets and primers, the large makers allowed aggressive young companies like Hornady, Speer, and Sierra to grab the biggest piece of the cake before the giants woke up to what was happening.

My handloading supplies and equipment were bought mail-order from what were then only a handful of suppliers. A box of 50-grain .22-caliber bullets sold for $2.50 then, and powder was under $2 per pound (salvage powder was four bits or less), but even so, I was usually so broke that I had to order bullets one box at a time. When I was about 16 or so and figured I knew all there was to know about guns and handloading, I ran an ad in the local newspaper offering "guaranteed" custom reloads at 10 for a dollar. I didn't get rich, or much more than manage to pay for my equipment, and my only regular customer insisted on watching me weigh every powder charge I put in his cases. That's how things went in those melancholy days.

REASONS FOR ACCEPTANCE

Gradually, but then at an ever-increasing rate, the pendulum of opinion began swinging in the opposite direction. Shooters who condemned handloads in 1950 were singing their praises with righteous certainty by the 1960's. There were, of course, hundreds of reasons for this mass conversion, but if I had to state the three most important causes, they would be: the total acceptance of the telescopic sight, the publicity given a small band of benchrest shooters and, certainly, the money to be saved through handloading.

As a rule of thumb, a handloaded cartridge costs about half the price of a factory load bought at retail. With a bit of judicious shopping, the savings are even more impressive. Shooters who cast their own bullets from scrap lead find the per-shot cost is something on the order of shooting .22 Rimfire factory ammo. This does not count the cost of one's time or the cost of loading tools. If included, these two items would make handloads far more expensive, but handloading is most of all a hobby in itself—a distinctly pleasant and fascinating part of shooting. Many handloaders don't handload so they can shoot, but shoot so they can handload!

Until World War II—that pivot point in worldwide firearms thinking—about the only Americans concerned with "pure" accuracy were a small, obscure group of select riflemen. They were target shooters, designers, and experimenters. The average shooter was concerned mainly with results. If the bullet hit more or less where it was aimed and the deer or elk or bear went down in a heap, both rifle and ammo were pronounced good. In fairness, this was about the only way most shooters had to judge the performance of their equipment. But after World War II, legions of ex-GI's, now vastly more sophisticated in their knowledge of arms and shooting techniques, viewed pre-war equipment with considerable skepticism.

A handloaded cartridge costs half the price of a factory load—and even less for shooters who cast their own bullets from scrap lead. This doesn't count the cost of tools or the shooter's time, but for those who burn up a lot of ammunition it's a big attraction. However, the chief concern of serious handloaders is performance, not money. A truly proficient handloader is striving for groups like those shown here.

The telescopic sight, which had been wavering toward acceptance in pre-war days caught on full-bore, giving thousands and then millions of shooters a more precise way of aiming their rifles. What they learned as a result was that a bullet does not necessarily go where it is aimed, even if it is aimed very carefully. Something, they reasoned, must therefore be wrong with the ammo, the rifles, or both.

About that time, benchrest shooting was gearing up. By the early 1950's, formal benchrest tournaments were being held. All told, well under a hundred shooters were involved in this "peculiar" type of shooting, but the publicity they garnered, and the resultant effect on shooting, was all out of proportion to their numbers. Two of these early benchresters, Warren Page and Lucian Cary, happened to be the shooting editors of two widely read magazines, *Field & Stream* and *True*. Writers are always looking for interesting subjects to write about, and whatever else they might have been, the huge early benchrest rifles certainly made fascinating reading. Page and Cary wrote scores of articles, and other gun authors wrote on the subject, too. One point that was continuously pounded into the minds of the readers was that the spectacular accuracy of the behemoth bench rifles was largely due to *handloaded* ammunition. Factory-loaded shells, they wrote, couldn't possibly deliver such razor-fine accuracy. This, of course, gave tremendous impetus to the handloading game. Newcomers found that even their first clumsy efforts did not blow up their guns or cause any other harm and discovered that handloads did kill game at least as dead as factory loads. They also discovered that handloads were noticeably more accurate and a hell of a lot cheaper. What could have been better than that?

Handloading also gained a certain snob appeal. Guys who did looked down their noses at guys who didn't. By the 1960's, the handloaded cartridge had become the aristocrat, and the factory load was a poor cousin. National rifle championships and Olympic medals were won with handloads, and no elitist varmint hunter would leave the house without a box of his carefully concocted handloads. But even as the art of handloading was coming into flower, other forces were at work. Factory loads were getting better, while the average quality of handloads was declining.

By then the major ammo manufacturers had been aroused from their stupor by a double thunderclap. The accuracy inadequacies of many of their products had been indisputably demonstrated and the brash new components makers were appropriating large chunks of their business. Something had to be done, and the first step was to upgrade the accuracy of their factory loads. Don't misunderstand—the ammo makers had never produced what could be called a deliberately inferior product. Their ammunition was, in fact, the very best they believed they could produce. It's just that their technology had improved at a tedious rate, and their channels of communications with the consumer had been pretty much a one-way street. They had thought they were making just what the customers wanted.

Perhaps the biggest stumbling block was that in the past there had been no clearly established standards for accuracy. Nearly all quality control had been concerned with reliability, pressure levels, and functioning in the firearm. If a particular lot of .30/06 ammo happened to produce five-inch groups, then that was the accuracy "standard" for that lot. This practice had seldom if ever been challenged, but now suddenly there was a definable accuracy standard—the performance of handloaded cartridges capable of grouping inside a one-inch circle or less at 100 yards when fired from a good rifle.

For many years, handloaders scoffed at factory ammo. They began to revise their thinking in the mid-1960's, first when the Army's Lake City Ammunition Plant shipped these tournament-winning .308 (7.62mm) cartridges and again when commercial loads in the new .225 caliber consistently delivered enviable groups.

Paradoxically, the expertise necessary to produce really accurate ammo existed in abundance at the various munitions factories. Most engineers and production technicians were themselves hobby handloaders and well knew the tricks of producing really accurate ammo. What they needed was "word from upstairs" to start upgrading the accuracy of the commercial product, and bit by bit, word did come down.

Though no official announcements of better accuracy were made, the improvements became evident in subtle ways. Most notable was the better accuracy of newly introduced cartridges. When the .300 Winchester Magnum, 7mm Remington, .280 Remington, etc., were first produced there was a definite effort to achieve a high accuracy level.

I was doing a lot of big-bore rifle shooting then, competing in as many tournaments as possible. Like most competitors, I kept a close watch on what was winning in the way of rifles, ammo, and related equipment. Handloaded ammo won just about every match, of course, especially at the longer ranges, and I felt pretty smug about the success of my own carefully developed loads. Then something happened that gave us all quite a turn. It was during the middle '60's, as I recall, when the Lake City Government Arsenal produced some National Match grade .308 (7.62mm) ammo that won just about everything.

"Impossible!" we said at first. We believed that a factory could not produce ammunition good enough to compete with a good handload. Then it began to sink in. I tested a lot of the Lake City loads in my heavy-barrel match rifle and found that it was every bit as good as my handloads. Other competitors didn't even try to match their handloads with the Lake City product and openly bartered with GI competitors for a supply of the wonderful cartridges. I imagine the arsenal technicians got quite a giggle out of the consternation they were causing us handloaders.

About that same time, I bought a Winchester Model 70 in the new .225 caliber and was even more confounded to discover that the new factory loads grouped close to half an inch at 100 yards. Clearly, the tables were turned. Handloaders found themselves struggling to keep up with the accuracy of factory loads. That was hard to admit after nearly two decades of howling, "I'm best." In fact, many handloaders refused to admit it for a good long while.

DECLINE OF THE AVERAGE HANDLOAD

The 1960's and early '70's were a period of tremendous growth for the reloading industry. Tiny garage-type operations became multi-million-dollar companies complete with corporate aircraft, computerized operations, and high-powered advertising. Everyone who owned a gun was considered a potential handloader, and they made it mighty easy to get started. Whereas the 1950's handloader had been a deeply committed shooter, knowledgeable about what he was doing and probably a perfectionist or at least damned particular, the typical beginning handloader of the 1970's was less dedicated. To him, handloading was just a way to kill time and save money until something better came along. With every loading tool sold, the quality of the *average* metallic handload sank a bit. That's why the typical handload of today is not as accurate as the average factory load, nor as reliable.

That's quite a mouthful of bad things to say about handloading, but it is true. What about the *better* handloads? And the best? How do they stack up?

THE BEST HANDLOADS

The most accurate ammunition is handloaded. Of that there is no doubt. I've used handloads exclusively on my worldwide sheep hunts, and every head of game I've taken in Africa has fallen to a handload. This includes Cape buffalo, lion, and elephant. Of the hundreds of thousands of rifle and pistol reloads I've fired, I can remember only two that failed, but I've had so many misfires with factory loads that I've long since lost count. If I couldn't shoot my reloads in rifle and pistol competition, I just wouldn't compete, and the benchrest game couldn't exist at its high level of excellence without handloading.

What, then, is the difference between good and bad handloads? It is *not* a matter of equipment, because exceedingly fine ammo can be loaded with any of the currently available handloading tools. And selection of components does not matter as much as is generally supposed. Today's cases, primers, and powders are superb. Bullets are so uniformly good that you'd need a heavy target rifle to sift the best from the worst. The crucial element in the quality of reloads is the attitude of the person doing the reloading. If a shooter is interested only in saving money, he probably lacks the commitment necessary to assemble really good loads. Though excellent rifle and pistol reloads are usually produced with what appears to be virtually no effort,

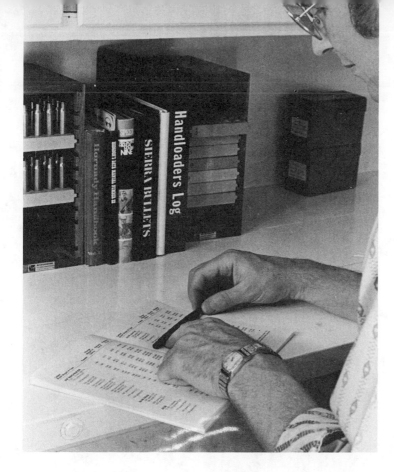

A conscientious study of the reloading manuals is mandatory if a shooter is to assemble even serviceable ammunition. For those who produce superlative loads, the hobby is not merely an adjunct to shooting but an activity undertaken for the sake of its own rewards.

the truth of the matter is that the guys who make it look so easy have carefully studied what they are doing.

I am continually amazed at the number of reloaders who attempt to assemble ammunition without so much as owning a single reloading manual. This is on the order of trying to fly an airplane without first taking flying instruction. It is also my observation that incompetent handloaders tend to learn from other incompetent loaders. The scenario goes something like this. A guy rushes into a discount store and looks for the best price on a reloading setup. The clerk, who knows absolutely nothing about guns, says "There it is—best buy in town. Everything you need." So the shooter takes the kit home, dumps everything on the kitchen table, and trys to figure out what the odd-looking things do. Finally he gives up and calls his buddy, who bought a reloading kit the previous week. "Hey, how about coming over and giving me a hand. We'll have a beer or two and you can show me how to use my reloader." So it goes.

If you are not a handloader but think you might like to give it a try, there are important things you should do. Buy a good handloading manual—Speer, Hornady, Nosler, Lyman, etc.—and spend a few evenings reading it and studying the instructions. This will help you decide if you want to get into the game. If you decide you really like the idea, your next step will be to look at an assortment of tools and related equipment at your local dealer's. Armed with the information provided by the manual, you'll be able to evaluate the various tools and select one that best suits your needs. After looking at the tools and perhaps asking a few questions, you might decide you prefer Brand A press, Brand B power scale, and Brand C powder measure.

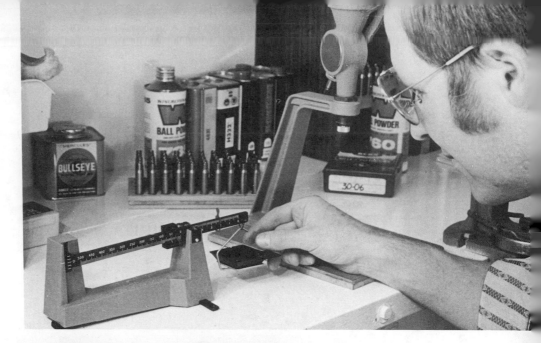

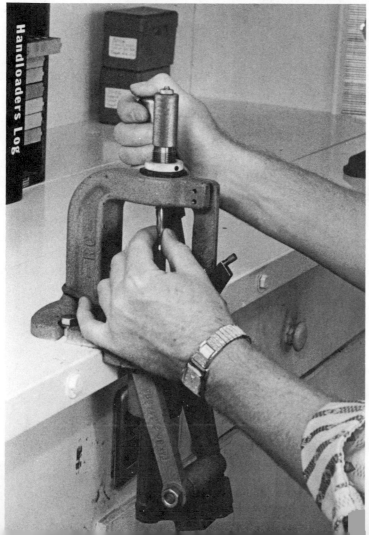

In every step of the loading process — from weighing and metering powder charges to seating bullets — the skillful handloader is extremely meticulous. This is a hobby best suited to perfectionists who have a passion for precision.

That's okay. It means you're thinking about what you are doing and beginning to make a *commitment* to the craft of handloading.

Don't run home and start throwing components together. Spend a few hours studying the tools. Learn where the adjustments are and what they do. Be sure you are completely familiar with the powder scale. Practice with it until you are confident and able to read it without error. Then, with your work area cleared of everything not essential to reloading, you're ready to load some cases.

Chapter 21

THE AGELESS .22 RIMFIRE

When Queen Victoria was a young woman, well-to-do ladies and gentlemen liked to pass a cozy evening sipping cognac and participating in a refined form of target shooting with air-powered rifles. Since the air-powered guns made little noise and practically no mess, they could be conveniently fired indoors, so the sport came to be known as "parlor shooting." If you were invited to someone's home for an evening of parlor shooting, you were expected to wear your best coat (or gown) and behave elegantly. This was a refined pastime. A manservant would change targets and pump air into the guns, tea would be served, and finally, the modest winner would be toasted and possibly even rewarded with a bottle of rare cognac, or with luck, a kiss from the host's charming daughter. It was a grand occasion.

Everyone would have loved to participate in such a fancy pastime, but the air guns of that time were hand-built by only a few craftsmen and exceedingly expensive. Reasoning that there would be a ready market for less expensive parlor guns, an enterprising young French gunsmith by the name of Louis Nicolas Flobert began experiments about 1845 with small-caliber, powder-burning rifles. Basically, he had the right idea, but even the smallest charges of black powder produced too much sooty smoke. After only a few shots, the parlor was as smoky as a pool room; particles of burned powder soiled the drapes and carpets and, worst of all, the ladies' gowns. Clearly, some other approach was called for.

Flobert got the idea of pressing a lead ball into the open end of a musket-size percussion cap. The force of the fulminate explosion, he reasoned, might propel the ball with enough velocity for indoor shooting. It worked like a charm. The next step was redesigning the musket

538 •

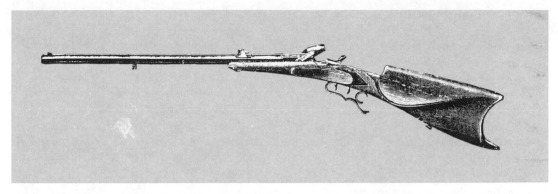

This .22 Rimfire appeared in the 1911 catalog of a Hamburg exporter. It was made in several grades. This one had a double-set trigger and was well enough crafted for target shooting, while cheaper versions were made for plinking—direct descendants of Flobert's parlor rifles and forerunners of today's plinking and small game .22's.

cap as a rimmed cartridge case and building a breechloading rifle to fire it. He quit his job and founded a gunmaking firm of his own, manufacturing not only parlor rifles but hundreds of thousands of inexpensive .22-caliber rimfire plinking rifles.

Why did Flobert settle on twenty-two one hundredths of an inch (.220 or .22/100) as the bore size for his little rimfire cartridge? Why not .20, say, or .23? This was just one of those accidents that make history. During his experiments, Flobert used round lead shot as bullets. The shot he liked and used was French size 3/0 shotgun shot, which just happened to measure (you guessed it) twenty-two one hundredths of an inch in diameter.

RIMFIRE AMMUNITION

Though rimfire cartridges were once a very common form of ignition, they have faded away one by one until only the .22 version remains popular. As the name suggests, the explosive priming mixture, which ignites the powder charge, is contained in the rim of the cartridge. Unlike centerfire cartridges, which are fired only when the firing pin strikes the primer more or less dead center, a rimfire shell fires when the firing pin hits the rim at any point around its circumference.

During the last century, the rimfire system was applied to some large-caliber cartridges, but these became obsolete even before the advent of smokeless powder. Though relatively easy and inexpensive to manufacture, rimfire cartridges have disadvantages. They are not reloadable, and they are not as strong as solid-head centerfire cases. Though rimfire ignition is ideal for the little .22, it is no longer practical for more powerful calibers.

Though the original Flobert .22 RF shell, known as the BB Cap, was loaded with a round lead ball propelled only by a priming charge, it was just a matter of time until gunmakers built in a little extra power. In America, for example, ammo makers added a pinch of powder and gave the bullet a conical shape. This added pep gave the BB Cap enough power to kill mice and rats out to several yards. American ammo makers no longer produce .22 BB Caps, though they are still made in Canada and Germany. Modern BB Caps have enough energy to shoot through an inch of soft pine. This is considerably more powerful than Flobert's parlor ammo.

A somewhat more powerful .22 Rimfire shell is the so-called .22 CB Cap. "CB" stands for the 29-grain Conical Bullet with which it is loaded. Early CB Caps were loaded with 1½ grains of black powder, but after about 1920 they were loaded with smokeless powder.

A cartridge more familiar to American shooters is the .22 Short. A seldom-noted fact is that the .22 Short has been in continuous production since 1857, longer than any other self-contained cartridge designed in America. Since it was first made for a Smith & Wesson revolver, there have been statements that the .22 Rimfire cartridge was an invention of that company. As we have seen, this was not the case.

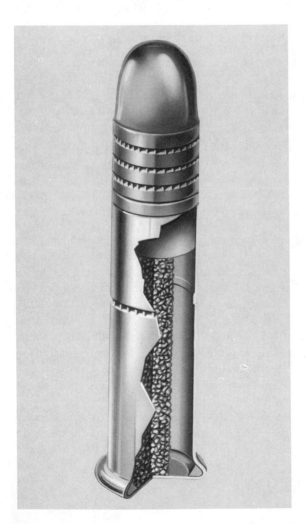

The basic principle of .22 Rimfire ammunition hasn't changed since the 19th century. This cutaway drawing of a Winchester Super-X .22 shows how the priming compound (a wet mix when inserted) is deposited around the rim.

From the time of its introduction until about 1920, the .22 Short was the most popular .22 shell. Dozens of makes and models of rifles and pistols were chambered for it, including highly accurate target rifles. Originally, it was loaded with a 29-grain conical bullet backed by four grains of finely granulated black powder. By the late 1880's, it was loaded with smokeless powder, making it one of the first cartridges to be loaded with the new propellent.

Because of the success of the .22 Short, it was only a matter of time until someone made a longer case which would hold five grains of powder and called it the .22 Long. This came to pass about 1870. Later, in 1887, a heavier 40-grain bullet was loaded in the .22 Long case. This was the cartridge we know today as the .22 Long Rifle, the most accurate, highly developed .22 of them all. But more of this later.

Actually, the .22 Long Rifle was preceded by a round known as the .22 Extra Long. It fired a 50-grain bullet in a case that held six grains of black powder, and was somewhat more powerful than the Long Rifle. It proved a bit too long to function in some repeating rifle mechanisms, however, and became obsolete by the 1930's.

When Winchester introduced their first autoloading .22 Rimfire rifle in 1903, the company had to deal with a perplexing problem. Rimfire ammo loaded with black powder was still being made, as well as the newer smokeless-powder ammo. It was essential that this new rifle be fired with smokeless ammo because black-powder residue would quickly foul the rifle's complex autoloading mechanism and render it inoperable. How could Winchester prevent the use of black-powder ammo in the new rifle?

The solution was a new cartridge called the .22 Winchester Automatic. This round had about the same ballistics as the .22 Long Rifle, but there was enough dimensional difference to prevent interchanging. Later, when black-powder loads were no longer available, Winchester dropped the 1903 Autoloader and replaced it with the Model 63 Autoloader, which fired conventional .22 Rimfire ammo. Remington took pretty much the same course when they introduced their Model 16 Autoloader in 1914. Their noninterchangeable version of the cartridge was called, naturally, the .22 Remington Automatic.

In the meantime, about 1890, Winchester had introduced a special higher-powered .22 Rimfire cartridge which was called the Winchester Rimfire or, for short, the .22 WRF. This round had a somewhat bigger bullet and longer case than standard .22's and considerably more killing power than the other .22's of its time. Remington followed suit with a similar cartridge which they called the .22 Remington Special. Though the .22 WRF and .22 Special were loaded somewhat differently, they could be used interchangeably.

Though these two rounds had pretty much faded away by the beginning of World War II, an almost identical cartridge was introduced in 1959. Called the .22 Winchester Magnum, this new version of the old .22 WRF has a muzzle velocity of nearly 2,000 fps with a 40-grain jacketed bullet. Since the .22 Mag generates much higher pressures than the old .22 WRF, the case was altered so that it could not be fired in old .22 WRF rifles built for lower pressure levels.

The latest chapter in the evolution of the .22 Rimfire has been the development of a new class of extra-high velocity loads known by such trade names as Stinger, Xpediter, and Yellow Jacket. Unlike the .22 Winchester Magnum, which is a dimensionally larger cartridge and can be fired only in specially chambered rifles, the new .22 hotshots fire and function in nearly every rifle and pistol chambered for the standard Long Rifle shell. The high velocities are obtained mainly by using lighter bullets, combined with more energetic powder charges.

.22 BULLETS

Since the time of Flobert's size 3/0 lead shot, .22 bullets have taken many forms. The four most commonly used bullet types today are: plain lead, plain lead with hollow point, copper-coated, and copper-coated with hollow point. The lead bullets are of swaged construction and are made of a lead alloy that has been hardened somewhat by the addition of antimony. Copper-coated .22 RF bullets are not made by pressing a lead core into a copper jacket as are centerfire bullets. Such a process would be too costly for rimfire production. Instead, swaged lead cores, either of solid or hollow-point shape, are plated with a layer of copper.

Lead bullets are coated with a waxlike lubricant that keeps the soft lead bullet from leaving strips and streaks of lead in the bore during its trip through the barrel. Bullets coated with copper and similar metals have a lower coefficient of friction and do not require lubrication. The characteristic knurled grooves on rimfire bullets, sometimes called "grease rings," are the "footprints" left by machinery that spins the bullet during the case-crimping operation.

Another useful rimfire bullet is the so-called splatterproof gallery slug. Also known as frangible, or "mossy lead," bullets, they are made by pressing lead particles together in a matrix. When they strike a reasonably solid object they shatter into harmless dustlike particles. This kind of bullet has long been loaded in .22 Short ammo used in commercial shooting galleries.

.22 RIMFIRE AUTOLOADERS—HOW THEY WORK

The low velocities and mild chamber pressures of the various .22 Rimfire cartridges make them readily adaptable to self-loading mechanisms. In fact, the mechanisms of rimfire autoloaders are so simple and inexpensive to manufacture that they can be priced competitively with other .22 action types. This is why .22 autoloaders sell in such great numbers.

Even .22 machine guns have been manufactured for specialized use. During World War II a .22 RF look-alike of the M-1917 Browning machine gun was used in gunnery training exercises. Likewise, a few .22 Thompson submachine guns have been made, and even miniature hand-cranked Gatling guns chambered for .22 Shorts.

Today's .22 autoloaders, both pistols and rifles, operate on the simple blowback principle. The rearward thrust of the expanding gases pushes the breechbolt to the full rearward, or open, position. This ejects the spent case, recocks the hammer, and compresses the bolt-return spring. As the spring-powered breechbolt returns to firing position, it picks up a fresh round from the feeding mechanism and thrusts it into the chamber. All this happens in a fraction of a second.

CHARACTERISTICS OF THE .22 RIMFIRE

Today's rimfire rifles and pistols have a nominal bore diameter of .217-inch and a groove diameter of .222-inch, and they may have four, six, eight, or more lands and grooves. The rate

Today's rimfire autoloaders all operate on the simple blowback principle, but display a wide variety of styling and purpose. Here (from top) are the Winchester Model 63 (a beautifully made rifle, unfortunately discontinued), the nylon-stocked Remington Model 66, the Ruger Model 10/22, and the Armalite Model AR/7.

of twist is usually one turn in 16 inches, except for guns chambered for the .22 Short only. These may have a twist of one turn in 24 inches. The modern rimfire bullet diameter is .2225.

(It should be noted that centerfire .22's, such as the .222 Remington, .220 Swift, etc., have groove and bullet diameters of .224. Exceptions are some older .22 Hornets, which have rimfire barrel dimensions.)

The .22 RF headspaces on the rim, with the allowable rim space between the faces of bolt and breech being .043 to .051. High-grade target rifles usually have minimum chamber and headspace tolerances and may not even accept standard sporting ammo.

The .22 Winchester Rimfire Magnum cartridge, in addition to being longer than the standard Long Rifle round, is dimensionally different in other ways. Bore and groove diameters of the .22 WRM are .219 and .224 respectively. Headspace allowance is .050 to .056. Rate of twist is one in 16.

RIMFIRE BALLISTIC TABLES (Rifle)						
	Bullet		Velocity (fps)		Energy (foot-pounds)	
Cartridge	Weight	Type	Muzzle	100 yd.	Muzzle	100 yd.
.22 CB Cap	29	L	715	—	33	—
.22 Short, Std. Velocity	29	L	1,045	872	70	49
.22 Short, High Velocity	29	J	1,095	903	77	52
.22 Short, High Velocity	27	HP	1,120	904	75	49
.22 Long, High Velocity	29	J	1,240	961	99	59
.22 Long Rifle, Std. Velocity	40	L	1,150	976	117	85
.22 Long Rifle, High Velocity	40	L or J	1,255	1,016	140	92
.22 Long Rifle, High Velocity	36	JHP	1,280	1,010	131	82
.22 Long Rifle, Match	40	L	—	—	—	—
.22 Win. Automatic	45	L	1,035	917	107	84
.22 Rem. Yellow Jacket	33	J	1,500	1,075	165	85
.22 CCI Stinger	32	J	1,687	1,158	202	95
.22 Win. Xpediter	29	J	1,680	1,079	182	75
.22 WRF	45	L	1,320	1,055	174	111
.22 WR Magnum	40	J	1,910	1,326	324	156
.22 WR Magnum	40	JHP	1,910	1,326	324	156
RIMFIRE BALLISTIC TABLES (Pistol, 6″ Barrel)						
.22 Short, Std. Velocity	29	L	865	—	48	—
.22 Short, High Velocity	29	J	1,010	—	66	—
.22 Long, High Velocity	29	J	1,095	—	77	—
.22 Long Rifle, Std. Velocity	40	L	950	—	80	—
.22 Long Rifle, High Velocity	40	J	1,060	—	100	—
.22 Long Rifle, Pistol Match	40	L	1,060	—	100	—
.22 WR Magnum	40	J	1,480	—	195	—

ACCURACY OF THE .22 RIMFIRE

Modern .22 Rimfire cartridges, and the rifles and pistols that are chambered for them, are capable of astonishingly fine accuracy or disappointingly poor performance. The spectrum of .22 accuracy is so broad that it must be divided into categories according to use.

The most demanding category, of course, is .22 Rimfire tournament shooting. The degree of accuracy needed for the various forms of target shooting is defined by the size of the target and the shooting distance. The competition that requires perhaps the highest degree of accuracy is American-style outdoor prone rifle shooting, which is fired at distances of 50 yards, 50 meters, and 100 yards. The 10-ring of the 100-yard target is two inches across, which theo-

Various kinds of rimfire matches, both national and international, have become enormously sophisticated and grueling competitions demanding the ultimate in sighting equipment, barrel, action, trigger, and match-grade ammunition. This photo was taken at the 42nd World Shooting Championships in Seoul, South Korea.

retically indicates that a rifle capable of firing 10 consecutive shots into a one-inch circle at 100 yards has sufficient accuracy to produce a perfect score. However, since a good marksman, using a good rifle and ammo, will usually put all his shots inside the two-inch 10-ring, there is a one-inch circle inside the 10-ring, which is used to break ties. The highest number of hits in this X-ring breaks the tie. Naturally, target shooters strive to get all their shots inside the X-ring. This means a good rifle has to be capable of at least one-inch accuracy, and the very best rifles are capable of 10-shot groups that average not much larger than a half inch between the widest shots. Such accuracy calls for the best sighting equipment, barrels, triggers, action, stocks, and very precisely made match-grade ammo. Though very few rifles are capable of such fine accuracy, we use this performance level as a standard by which to judge other guns and ammo.

The world's most accurate .22 RF rifles are the Remington Models 37 and 40-X, Win-

These are typical modern high-performance rimfire target rifles. At bottom is one of the last versions of Winchester's famous Model 52. The others are all made in Germany by Anschutz. The two upper rifles are both stocked for three-position shooting, the other two for prone position only.

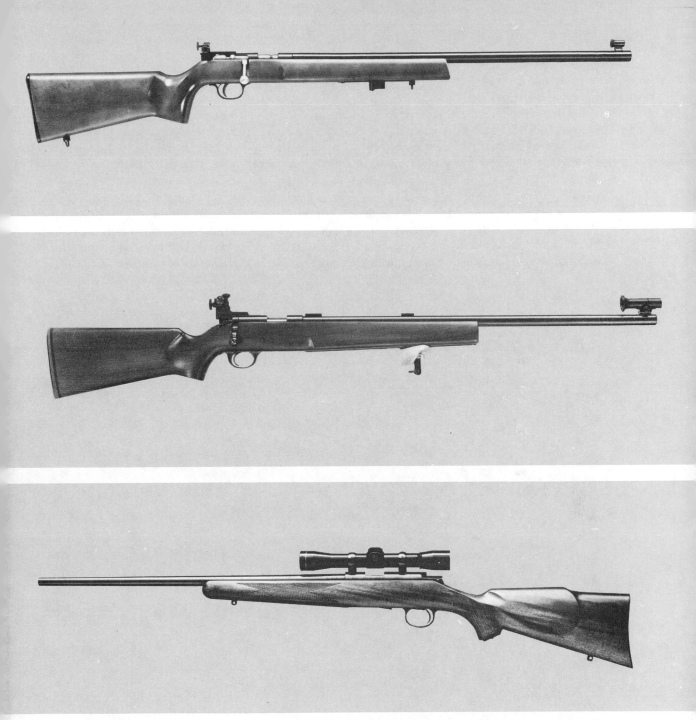

A step below the most accurate and sophisticated match .22 rifles — but still extremely accurate — are the lower-priced target rifles such as the Anschutz Mark 12 (top) and H&R Model 5200 (center) and the high-grade sporters such as the Kimber Model 82.

chester's M-52, the BSA of England, the Anschutz M-54 from Germany, the Swiss Hämmerli, and a handful of others. Even these are frequently improved by fitting special barrels, stocks, sights, and triggers.

One step below the best target rifles in accuracy are the lower-priced target rifles (Remington 540-XR, Savage/Anschutz MK-12, etc.) and the high-grade sporters such as the Anschutz M-54 Sporter, Remington 40-X sporter, Kimber M-82, and the old Winchester M-52 sporter. These fine rifles are, for the most part, target-grade actions fitted with lightweight barrels and sleek, hunting-style stocks. That's why they are called "Sporters." They are usually capable of grouping five shots inside an inch at 100 yards. Sometimes they do even better, but really good accuracy is *always* dependent on high-quality ammunition.

The third .22 Rimfire accuracy level includes those rifles (usually lightweight bolt-action models) that can group five shots inside a 1½ inch to two-inch circle at 100 yards. The fourth accuracy level is the classification into which most rimfire rifles fall. These are rifles that can-

Here are three excellent garden-variety .22 repeaters: (from top) the splendidly made but now discontinued pump-action Winchester Model 61; the Marlin Model 57 Levermatic, which has also been discontinued; and the Winchester Model 9422, the rimfire counterpart of the famous Model 94 lever-action.

not group inside two inches at 100 yards. Usually, they are tested at 50 yards rather than 100, because in reality, most .22 shooting is done at ranges inside 50 yards. A rifle that groups five shots inside one inch or 1½ inches at 50 yards is plenty accurate for most hunting, plinking, and informal target practice. After all, this is sufficient accuracy to hit a squirrel's head in the tallest tree.

.22 PISTOLS

Rimfire handguns, as might be expected, do not tend to be as accurate as rifles, though there are some notable exceptions. The accuracy of the best free-style pistols challenges the accuracy of the better rifles. In U.S.-style pistol shooting, however, the demand for accuracy is established by the NRA 50-yard, slow-fire pistol target, which has a 10-ring measuring 3.39 inches with a 1.695 X-ring. Most competetitors feel that a rimfire pistol that fires 10-shot 50-yard groups of an inch or less (from a machine rest) is sufficiently accurate to win these matches. Some target-type .22 pistols are capable of this degree of accuracy as they come from the box, while others require tuning in order to reach their full potential. Contrary to popular belief, autoloading .22 pistols tend to be more accurate than revolvers. This is because the chamber is more perfectly aligned with the bore in a rigid, one-piece unit.

Accuracy of rimfire ammo is dependent on a number of important factors. These include uniformity of the priming mixture, uniformity of bullet weight and shape, composition and uniformity of the lubricant, dimensional uniformity of the case, especially the rim, and the uniformity of the crimp. Surprisingly, exact uniformity of the powder charge is not as important to accuracy as some of the other factors listed here.

WIND AND THE .22 RIMFIRE

One of the most perplexing problems associated with shooting the .22 Rimfire is the effect wind has on the flight of the bullet. Since the typical .22 RF bullet is moving at a comparatively low velocity (as compared to most centerfire rifle bullets), the effect of wind can be considerable. Target shooters who compete on outdoor ranges must deal with the wind on a shot-to-shot basis and therefore go to considerable pains to calculate its effect. Hunters and sport shooters are no less affected. The following tables give an idea of the effects of a 90° crosswind on the standard-velocity Long Rifle cartridge.

AT 50 YARDS			AT 100 YARDS		
Wind Velocity MPH		Deflection (inches)	Wind Velocity MPH		Deflection (inches)
5	=	.40	5	=	1.80
10	=	.90	10	=	3.60
15	=	1.35	15	=	5.40
20	=	1.80	20	=	7.20

An interesting phenomenon peculiar to the .22 Rimfire is that, unlike high-velocity center-fire bullets, which suffer less wind effect as velocity is increased, standard-velocity .22 Rimfire bullets are less blown off course by the wind than are high-velocity loads. This unique trait is due to a sharp increase in air resistance which occurs at velocities near the speed of sound. A much-simplified explanation is that the 1,150 fps, or less, standard-velocity level is on the "safe" side of the barrier, while velocities in the 1,300-1,500 fps range are caught in the middle, so to speak. Thus, low-velocity loads are affected about a third less by the wind than high-velocity .22's. This is why .22 match-grade ammo is always loaded to low velocity levels.

.22 SHOTSHELLS

Though the .22 RF shot cartridge is useful for dealing with some pests, its effective range is severely limited by the tiny charge of small-diameter shot and random shape of the shot pat-

Some .22 shot loads employ a crimped case to hold in the pellets, while others have a plastic container of shot. The myth that shot loads will damage a rifled bore is untrue. Any lead deposits can be removed by a thorough brushing, and no permanent damage will be done.

tern. After passing through a rifled barrel the shot are severely distorted and tend to fly in unpredictable directions. Thus the effective range is seldom more than a few paces. Special smoothbore rimfire shotguns have been manufactured to improve rimfire shotshell performance and for miniature skeet games. Such games have not proven popular, however, and the smoothbore guns have been discontinued. In addition to controlling rats, sparrows, etc., perhaps the most practical application of .22 Rimfire shot cartridges is personal protection when one does not wish to fire lethal solid bullets, and as defense against poisonous snakes. Currently manufactured .22 shot loads, depending on manufacturer, are loaded with lead pellets measuring some .04-inch in diameter (known as "dust") or with No. 12 shot measuring .05. Rimfire shotshells loaded by Omark-CCI have the charge encased in a plastic capsule which protects the pellets from damage in the barrel. Omark-CCI also manufactures .22 Winchester Magnum shotshells loaded with No. 11 (.06) shot. Rimfire shotshells are loaded to a muzzle velocity of 900-1,000 fps.

A common shooting myth has it that firing shotshells in a rifle or pistol will damage the bore. While there may be some leading, no permanent damage will occur. A thorough brushing will remove any lead deposits from the bore.

HUNTING WITH THE .22

Hunting small game with the rimfire helps develop the hunting and shooting skills necessary for successful big game hunting with centerfire rifles, and it is in itself a very exciting and satisfying sport.

Probably the No. 1 quarry of rimfire hunters is the squirrel, followed by rabbits, tasty bullfrogs, foxes, coyotes, raccoons, crows, woodchucks, ground squirrels, rats, and the wild turkey (in states where rifles are legal for turkey hunting). Though a scope-sighted .22 Rimfire rifle is preferred by most squirrel hunters, more and more handgun marksmen are demonstrating that a well-aimed pistol is deadly medicine. While most pistol hunters use open sights, some equip their guns with special pistol scopes that have long eye-relief. These can be adapted to most revolvers and some autoloaders.

Opinions vary on the best type of rimfire ammo for small-game hunting. Most shooters make their choices according to the average range at which they will be firing and the size of the game. Squirrels are not hard to kill, and typical ranges are usually around 50 feet or less. A popular ammo choice is the .22 Short, especially the short hollow-point. The mild report of the .22 Short offers an advantage, and the expanding hollow point tends to provide some extra "push" for knocking squirrels off large tree limbs and out of forks.

Long-range shots at bigger game such as crows and ground squirrels call for higher-velocity cartridges that have a flatter trajectory. Here the high-speed Long Rifle or the super hotshots such as the Stinger, Xpediter, etc., serve best. The .22 Winchester Magnum is a sound performer on bigger-bodied game such as foxes, coyotes, and wild turkeys. The key to successful .22 hunting is a correctly sighted rifle and a thorough knowledge of the bullet's trajectory.

HOW FAR WILL A .22 SHOOT?

A 50-grain bullet fired from a .22 Long Rifle standard-velocity cartridge has an extreme range of approximately 4,500 feet. High-velocity Long Rifle .22's have slightly greater range. This is over four-fifths of a mile, so one is well advised to heed the warning on every box of .22 ammo. Magnum Rimfire .22 ammo has a range of *over* one mile.

CLEAN .22 RIFLES ARE MORE ACCURATE

Back when .22 shells were loaded with black powder it was necessary to thoroughly clean a rifle or pistol each time it was used. The black-powder residue formed a hard cake of fouling in the bore that not only caused loss of accuracy after a few shots but also caused rusting if left unattended. Even after smokeless powder was put to use in rimfire ammunition, salt deposits left by the priming mixture caused severe corrosion in the barrel unless thoroughly removed. About 1920 a new noncorrosive priming mixture was introduced that leaves no rust-causing deposits. This innovation was widely hailed and advertised as the end of gun cleaning, and within a short while the chore was all but forgotten.

Rimfire rifles and pistols do, however, function more reliably, last longer, and shoot more accurately if properly cleaned and cared for. Modern target shooters note a decline in accuracy after about 50 rounds have been fired. This is apparently due to a build-up of bullet lubricant and fouling in the barrel. This is easily removed with a nylon brush wetted with solvent and passed through the bore several times with a cleaning rod or pull-through cord. The wet brushing is followed by two or three clean patches.

The powder and grease residues that are deposited in the gun's mechanism tend to retard smooth functioning, and this is especially true of autoloaders. Sometimes this causes complete stoppages and also traps abrasive dust and other airborne particles that contribute to an excessive rate of wear. Even with steady use, it would be difficult to wear out a .22 in a lifetime of shooting, yet thousands of guns are ruined by neglect.

TRAJECTORY TABLES

The steeply curving trajectory of .22 RF ammo causes considerable differences in the point of bullet impact in respect to point of aim at different distances. This difficulty is compounded when the variables of sight height above bore line are added. All other factors being equal, the point-of-impact/line-of-sight relationship for a rifle with low-mounted open sights differs considerably from that of a rifle fitted with a telescopic sight mounted some 1½ inches above the centerline of the bore.

Hunting small game with a .22 is a satisfying sport, and one that helps develop the shooting skills needed for hunting larger game with a centerfire rifle. Squirrels and rabbits are probably the most popular quarry in America.

Here, published in a book for the first time, are trajectory tables for sights mounted at three different heights above the bore line. Table No. 1 shows the relative point of impact at various distances for open sights mounted ¾-inch above the centerline of the bore. Table No. 2 is for .22-type scopes (¾-inch tube) centered 1¼ inches above the bore line. Table No. 3 is for rifles equipped with full-size (one-inch diameter) scopes centered 1¾ inches above the bore line.

These tables are not based on computed predictions of bullet trajectories. They were developed in *actual* range tests of each of the loads listed. Though some variation from these tables will be encountered (because of the individual variations of different guns), these tables are very representative of rimfire rifle trajectories.

TABLE NO. 1: .22 RIMFIRE TRAJECTORIES					
Sights .750 (¾-inch) Above Bore Line					
	50 ft.	25 yd.	50 yd.	75 yd.	100 yd.
.22 Short, Std. Velocity	+ .33"	+ 1.50"	0	− 3.050"	− 13.750"
.22 Short, High Velocity	0	+ .50"	0	− 2.275"	− 8"
.22 LR, Std. Velocity	− .08"	+ .50"	0	− 2.130"	− 6.650"
.22 LR, High Velocity	− .190"	+ .40"	0	− 1.975"	− 6.380"
.22 Stinger	− .412"	+ .160"	0	− 1.40"	− 4.225"
.22 Xpediter	− .412"	+ .160"	0	− 1.40"	− 4.225"
.22 Yellow Jacket	− .412"	+ .165"	0	− 1.180"	− 4"

TABLE NO. 2: .22 RIMFIRE TRAJECTORIES					
Scope 1.250 (1¼ inch) Above Bore Line					
	50 ft.	25 yd.	50 yd.	75 yd.	100 yd.
.22 Short, Std. Velocity	+ .166"	+ 1.250"	0	− 2"	− 13.250"
.22 Short, High Velocity	− .134	+ .250"	0	− 2.80"	− 7.50"
.22 LR, Std. Velocity	− .034"	+ .250"	0	− 1.880"	− 6.150"
.22 LR, High Velocity	− .359"	+ .240"	0	− 1.725"	− 5.880"
.22 Stinger	− .58"	+ .09"	0	− 1.150"	− 3.725"
.22 Xpediter	− .58"	+ .09"	0	− 1.150"	− 3.725"
.22 Yellow Jacket	− .58"	+ .09"	0	− .930"	− 2.50"

TABLE NO. 3: .22 RIMFIRE TRAJECTORIES					
Scope 1.750 (1¾ inch) Above Bore Line					
	50 ft.	25 yd.	50 yd.	75 yd.	100 yd.
.22 Short, Std. Velocity	0	+ 1″	0	− 2.550″	− 12.750″
.22 Short, High Velocity	− .30	0	0	− 1.775″	− 7″
.22 LR, Std. Velocity	− .250″	0	0	− 1.630″	− 5.650″
.22 LR, High Velocity	− .525″	− .010″	0	− 1.475″	− 5.380″
.22 Stinger	− .745″	− .340″	0	− .90″	− 3.225″
.22 Xpediter	− .745″	− .340″	0	− .90″	− 3.225″
.22 Yellow Jacket	− .745″	− .345″	0	− .680″	− 3″

INDEX